Lecture Notes in Computer Science

Vol. 245: H.F. de Groote, Lectures on the Complexity of Bilinear Problems. V, 135 pages. 1987.

Vol. 246: Graph-Theoretic Concepts in Computer Science. Proceedings, 1986. Edited by G. Tinhofer and G. Schmidt. VII, 307 pages. 1987.

Vol. 247: STACS 87. Proceedings, 1987. Edited by F.J. Brandenburg, G. Vidal-Naquet and M. Wirsing. X, 484 pages. 1987.

Vol. 248: Networking in Open Systems. Proceedings, 1986. Edited by G. Müller and R.P. Blanc. VI, 441 pages. 1987.

Vol. 249: TAPSOFT '87. Volume 1. Proceedings, 1987. Edited by H. Ehrig, R. Kowalski, G. Levi and U. Montanari. XIV, 289 pages. 1987.

Vol. 250: TAPSOFT '87. Volume 2. Proceedings, 1987. Edited by H. Ehrig, R. Kowalski, G. Levi and U. Montanari. XIV, 336 pages. 1987.

Vol. 251: V. Akman, Unobstructed Shortest Paths in Polyhedral Environments. VII, 103 pages. 1987.

Vol. 252: VDM '87. VDM – A Formal Method at Work. Proceedings, 1987. Edited by D. Bjørner, C.B. Jones, M. Mac an Airchinnigh and E.J. Neuhold. IX, 422 pages. 1987.

Vol. 253: J.D. Becker, I. Eisele (Eds.), WOPPLOT 86. Parallel Processing: Logic, Organization, and Technology. Proceedings, 1986. V, 226 pages. 1987.

Vol. 254: Petri Nets: Central Models and Their Properties. Advances in Petri Nets 1986, Part I. Proceedings, 1986. Edited by W. Brauer, W. Reisig and G. Rozenberg. X, 480 pages. 1987.

Vol. 255: Petri Nets: Applications and Relationships to Other Models of Concurrency. Advances in Petri Nets 1986, Part II. Proceedings, 1986. Edited by W. Brauer, W. Reisig and G. Rozenberg. X, 516 pages. 1987.

Vol. 256: Rewriting Techniques and Applications. Proceedings, 1987. Edited by P. Lescanne. VI, 285 pages. 1987.

Vol. 257: Database Machine Performance: Modeling Methodologies and Evaluation Strategies. Edited by F. Cesarini and S. Salza. X, 250 pages. 1987.

Vol. 258: PARLE, Parallel Architectures and Languages Europe. Volume I. Proceedings, 1987. Edited by J.W. de Bakker, A.J. Nijman and P.C. Treleaven. XII, 480 pages. 1987.

Vol. 259: PARLE, Parallel Architectures and Languages Europe. Volume II. Proceedings, 1987. Edited by J.W. de Bakker, A.J. Nijman and P.C. Treleaven. XII, 464 pages. 1987.

Vol. 260: D.C. Luckham, F.W. von Henke, B. Krieg-Brückner, O. Owe, ANNA, A Language for Annotating Ada Programs. V, 143 pages. 1987.

Vol. 261: J. Ch. Freytag, Translating Relational Queries into Iterative Programs. XI, 131 pages. 1987.

Vol. 262: A. Burns, A.M. Lister, A.J. Wellings, A Review of Ada Tasking. VIII, 141 pages. 1987.

Vol. 263: A.M. Odlyzko (Ed.), Advances in Cryptology – CRYPTO '86. Proceedings. XI, 489 pages. 1987.

Vol. 264: E. Wada (Ed.), Logic Programming '86. Proceedings, 1986. VI, 179 pages. 1987.

Vol. 265: K.P. Jantke (Ed.), Analogical and Inductive Inference. Proceedings, 1986. VI, 227 pages. 1987.

Vol. 266: G. Rozenberg (Ed.), Advances in Petri Nets 1987. VI, 451 pages. 1987.

Vol. 267: Th. Ottmann (Ed.), Automata, Languages and Programming. Proceedings, 1987. X, 565 pages. 1987.

Vol. 268: P.M. Pardalos, J.B. Rosen, Constrained Global Optimization: Algorithms and Applications. VII, 143 pages. 1987.

Vol. 269: A. Albrecht, H. Jung, K. Mehlhorn (Eds.), Parallel Algorithms and Architectures. Proceedings, 1987. Approx. 205 pages. 1987.

Vol. 270: E. Börger (Ed.), Computation Theory and Logic. IX, 442 pages. 1987.

Vol. 271: D. Snyers, A. Thayse, From Logic Design to Logic Programming. IV, 125 pages. 1987.

Vol. 272: P. Treleaven, M. Vanneschi (Eds.), Future Parallel Computers. Proceedings, 1986. V, 492 pages. 1987.

Vol. 273: J.S. Royer, A Connotational Theory of Program Structure. V, 186 pages. 1987.

Vol. 274: G. Kahn (Ed.), Functional Programming Languages and Computer Architecture. Proceedings. VI, 470 pages. 1987.

Vol. 275: A.N. Habermann, U. Montanari (Eds.), System Development and Ada. Proceedings, 1986. V, 305 pages. 1987.

Vol. 276: J. Bézivin, J.-M. Hullot, P. Cointe, H. Lieberman (Eds.), ECOOP '87. European Conference on Object-Oriented Programming. Proceedings. VI, 273 pages. 1987.

Vol. 277: B. Benninghofen, S. Kemmerich, M.M. Richter, Systems of Reductions. X, 265 pages. 1987.

Vol. 278: L. Budach, R.G. Bukharajev, O.B. Lupanov (Eds.), Fundamentals of Computation Theory. Proceedings, 1987. XIV, 505 pages. 1987.

Vol. 279: J.H. Fasel, R.M. Keller (Eds.), Graph Reduction. Proceedings, 1986. XVI, 450 pages. 1987.

Vol. 280: M. Venturini Zilli (Ed.), Mathematical Models for the Semantics of Parallelism. Proceedings, 1986. V, 231 pages. 1987.

Vol. 281: A. Kelemenová, J. Kelemen (Eds.), Trends, Techniques, and Problems in Theoretical Computer Science. Proceedings, 1986. VI, 213 pages. 1987.

Vol. 282: P. Gorny, M.J. Tauber (Eds.), Visualization in Programming. Proceedings, 1986. VII, 210 pages. 1987.

Vol. 283: D.H. Pitt, A. Poigné, D.E. Rydeheard (Eds.), Category Theory and Computer Science. Proceedings, 1987. V, 300 pages. 1987.

Vol. 284: A. Kündig, R.E. Bührer, J. Dähler (Eds.), Embedded Systems. Proceedings, 1986. V, 207 pages. 1987.

Vol. 285: C. Delgado Kloos, Semantics of Digital Circuits. IX, 124 pages. 1987.

Vol. 286: B. Bouchon, R.R. Yager (Eds.), Uncertainty in Knowledge-Based Systems. Proceedings, 1986. VII, 405 pages. 1987.

Vol. 287: K.V. Nori (Ed.), Foundations of Software Technology and Theoretical Computer Science. Proceedings, 1987. IX, 540 pages. 1987.

Vol. 288: A. Blikle, MetaSoft Primer. XIII, 140 pages. 1987.

Vol. 289: H.K. Nichols, D. Simpson (Eds.), ESEC '87. 1st European Software Engineering Conference. Proceedings, 1987. XII, 404 pages. 1987.

Vol. 290: T.X. Bui, Co-oP A Group Decision Support System for Cooperative Multiple Criteria Group Decision Making. XIII, 250 pages. 1987.

Vol. 291: H. Ehrig, M. Nagl, G. Rozenberg, A. Rosenfeld (Eds.), Graph-Grammars and Their Application to Computer Science. VIII, 609 pages. 1987.

Vol. 292: The Munich Project CIP. Volume II: The Program Transformation System CIP-S. By the CIP System Group. VIII, 522 pages. 1987.

Vol. 293: C. Pomerance (Ed.), Advances in Cryptology — CRYPTO '87. Proceedings. X, 463 pages. 1988.

Vol. 294: R. Cori, M. Wirsing (Eds.), STACS 88. Proceedings, 1988. IX, 404 pages. 1988.

Vol. 295: R. Dierstein, D. Müller-Wichards, H.-M. Wacker (Eds.), Parallel Computing in Science and Engineering. Proceedings, 1987. V, 185 pages. 1988.

Lecture Notes in Computer Science

Edited by G. Goos and J. Hartmanis

328

R. Bloomfield L. Marshall
R. Jones (Eds.)

VDM '88
VDM – The Way Ahead

2nd VDM-Europe Symposium
Dublin, Ireland, September 11–16, 1988
Proceedings

Springer-Verlag

Berlin Heidelberg New York London Paris Tokyo

Editors

Robin E. Bloomfield
Adelard, 28 Rhondda Grove
London E3 5AP, UK

Lynn S. Marshall
Université Catholique de Louvain
Place Sainte-Barbe 2, 1348 Louvain-La-Neuve, Belgium

Roger B. Jones
ICL (UK), Eskdale Road, Winnersh
Wokingham, Berkshire RG11 5TT, UK

CR Subject Classification (1987): F.3.1, D.2.1, D.2.4

ISBN 3-540-50214-9 Springer-Verlag Berlin Heidelberg New York
ISBN 0-387-50214-9 Springer-Verlag New York Berlin Heidelberg

© Springer-Verlag Berlin Heidelberg 1988
Printed in Germany

Printing and binding: Druckhaus Beltz, Hemsbach/Bergstr.
2145/3140-543210

FOREWORD

VDM, the Vienna Development Method, is a formal method for software engineering. It is being applied to an increasing number of projects by companies throughout Europe and there is an active international research programme supporting this process. "*VDM: the way ahead*" is the second of a series of symposia sponsored by the *Commission of the European Communities* (CEC) and organised by VDM-Europe.

For those unfamiliar with "formal methods" it is perhaps useful to define what is meant by the term in this context. "Formal method" applies to a mathematically formal software specification and production method that has three components. It must contain a system of mathematically based notations that address the specification, design and development phases of software production. It must also contain a well-founded inference system in which formal proofs of correctness and other properties can be formulated and constructed. The third component is a methodological framework within which software may be developed from the specification in a formally verifiable manner.

Formal methods aim to increase the quality of software in two related ways: by improving the specification, and by making verification during the software production process more effective and easier to audit.

In VDM, sequential systems are modelled by a collection of operations defined in terms of pre- and post-conditions on an underlying state. Development is by a process of data reification and operation decomposition. The method includes a logical system containing the predicate calculus for the formulation of proofs, and each design step may require the designer to establish a number of proof obligations which show the correctness of the development.

Those readers requiring an introduction to VDM and an outline of its historical development should consult the proceedings of the first VDM symposium (VDM'87 LNCS 252).

The Technical Advisory Group, VDM-Europe, established by the Commission of the European Communities (CEC) meets regularly to discuss issues pertinent to VDM. These discussions focus around five main areas of interest:

–education and technology transfer

–experience and use of VDM

–tools and support environments

–method development and foundational work

–the standardisation of VDM

In addition VDM-Europe maintains a register of all VDM related activities in Europe. VDM-Europe is an open European group and anyone who is interested may attend and participate.

These five areas of interest are well represented in this symposium. The commitment to education and training and technology transfer is exemplified by the existence of the symposium and in particular by the two day tutorial to be given by D. Bjoerner and C.B. Jones (perhaps the two names most associated with VDM) as well as by the paper by Naftalin on "Correctness for Beginners".

The applications of VDM reported in this symposium are diverse, and they range from hardware test case selection through to the specification of Chinese characters as well as the more traditional use of VDM in compiler specification and development. There is also an increasing use of VDM in the definition and analysis of standards illustrated by the papers on ODA, GKS, Modula 2 and the deliberations of the BSI VDM-SL standardisation panel. In addition to the problem specific applications there are also generic issues such as the development towards a particular implementation language, Ada, as well as how to handle concurrency.

The availability of tools to support the use of VDM is essential for its successful industrialisation. The requirements for tools range from clerical support in editing and typesetting documents through type checkers and parsers to fully integrated support environments and theorem provers. The exhibition that runs in parallel with the symposium enables attendees to sample the latest developments. In these proceedings, tools are discussed in the papers on support for VDM specifications, the execution of programming language definitions, theorem proving assistants and project support environments.

The development of VDM and the definition or re-examination of its foundations are the subject of much research. Some of this, such as the structuring work for the BSI VDM-SL standard (Bear) involves extensions to VDM to assist in its application to large scale projects. The symposium also includes reports of research on logics and domain theory relevant to the theoretical foundations of VDM (Blikle; Tarlecki et al; Haxthausen).

The application and development of VDM must of course take into account work on other related formal methods. A comparison with FOREST is provided by the paper from Goldsack, while Abrial gives an invited talk on his development of B. Other work, such as the paper on the RAISE project (Nielsen, Havelund, Wagner, George), seeks to extend VDM to handle, among other things, concurrency. In addition there is the work on Metasoft, represented by the paper from Borzyszkowski et al.

Standardisation is the last of the five themes of the symposium and one of the most important. Widespread investment in VDM and associated tools requires a standard for the concrete and abstract syntax, a definition of the semantics and the associated inference system. It is imperative that the standard not only be technically adequate but also reflect the consensus of interested parties. Although some researchers may regard standardisation as merely a bureaucratic activity the BSI/VDM has had to grapple with considerable technical issues in its deliberations to date. A progress report is given by Andrews.

The title of the symposium is *"VDM: the way ahead"*. We hope that the proceedings do indeed show the way ahead both for those concerned with the application of VDM and those concerned with its development.

Brussels, July 1988

R. Bloomfield
L. Marshall
R. Jones

TABLE OF CONTENTS

APPLICATIONS AND TOOLS

FOUNDATIONS AND THEORY

DAY 3

Computing is a Physical Science

Donald I. Good

Computational Logic, Inc.
1717 West Sixth #290
Austin, Texas 78703

512-322-9951

Abstract

A digital computer is a physical object. To predict accurately the future, physical behavior of a digital computer, the approach of the physical sciences needs to be followed. Mathematical formulas that describe accurately the behavior of a digital computer need to be identified, and effective mathematical methods for applying these formulas need to be used.

These scientific foundations will enable digital system engineers to predict accurately how a computer system will behave before it is constructed and operated. This predictability is necessary to reduce the costs of system production and to produce trustworthy computing systems.

Structuring for the VDM Specification Language

Stephen Bear

Central Electricity Generating Board
20 Newgate Street, London, EC1 7AX.

Abstract

This paper describes a structuring scheme for the VDM Specification Language. A VDM *document* may be split into a number of *modules* which may be parameterised. Modules may *import* and *export* constructs. A parameterised module may be *instantiated* by another module. We define an abstract syntax and give a compositional denotational semantics. Context Conditions are discussed informally, but are not set out in any detail.

1 Introduction

Most existing descriptions of VDM Specification Languages just ignore the question of how a specification should be structured. Consequently large specifications, which have to be divided somehow, are handled by *ad hoc* methods.

However, structuring is no longer an unfamiliar subject. Structures are provided in various forms by other languages, for example the algebraic specification language CLEAR, the specification language Z, and of course certain programming languages. Experience of such methods provides some intuition of how to construct a *workable* scheme for the VDM specification language.

This paper describes a scheme of structuring for the VDM specification language. It is a conservative scheme using relatively well established concepts and it is not intended to be a radical reassessment of how a language should be structured. The work has been carried out as part of the BSI VDM standardisation exercise, and it will be one of the influences on the standard language.

2 Overview

A fundamental question in any discussion of structuring is, *what is the granularity of the structuring mechanism?* In this definition we follow the STC VDM Reference Language and adopt somewhat coarse *modules* as the basic specification unit. Here, a module is a high level construct which encapsulates a collection of related types, constants, functions and operations. Operations within a module may interact by updating a shared *'state'*. There are various reasons for this choice but the most important are that

- such modules correspond to the notion of abstract data types, as used in algebraic specification languages, so considerable experience of this style already exists;

- apart from names, such modules do not affect the way that the flat language is written, so the semantics of modularity may be treated separately from the semantics of the flat language.

The structuring facilities may be summarised as follows

- A module may *export* constructs. Exported constructs may be *imported* and then used by another module. If a construct is not exported it is 'hidden'; a hidden construct may not be referenced by any other module.

- A module may be *parameterised* by formal parameters. Within the parameterised module the formal parameters may be used like any other construct.

- A parameterised module may be *instantiated* by another module. The instantiating module provides actual parameters in the place of the formal parameters. Within the instantiating module the constructs defined by the newly instantiated module may be used like any other construct.

Part I

Syntax

In this part of the paper we define an abstract syntax for structuring and discuss other syntactic issues. We shall also give examples to illustrate the structuring facilities. The examples require the use of an *ad hoc* concrete syntax, which is not defined.

3 Syntax of Modules

A module consists of two parts: an *interface* and an optional *body*. The interface gives a syntactic description of types, constants, functions and operations which are provided by, or used by, the module. The body of a module is written in the 'flat' language, without using any of the structuring facilities.

```
Module ::  intf : Interface
           body : [Body]
```

If the body is missing then the constructs provided by the module are treated as *"not yet defined"*.

3.1 Export Clause

The interface contains the 'name' of the module and several clauses; we will begin by discussing the *export clause*. This gives a syntactic description of the constructs provided by the module.

```
Interface ::  id : Id
              ...
              exp : ModSig


ModSig    :: types : map Name to [Type]
             const : map Name to [Type]
               fns : map Name to [FnType]
              opns : map Name to [OpSig]


OpSig     :: state : Name
               dom : seq of Type
               rng : [Type]
```

Type and FnType are as defined in the abstract syntax of the 'flat language'. Notice that in the *abstract* syntax OpSig includes the type of the 'state' affected by the operation.

Often, a module exporting a type will only export the *name* of the type. In the abstract syntax this is represented by mapping the type name to **nil**. A module importing such a type cannot see the internal structure of the type. However, sometimes it will be useful for a module to expose the structure of the type being exported. In the abstract syntax this is represented by the type name mapping to the type definition.

An integer stack module might have the following interface

```
module INTEGER_STACK interface
...
export
  opn   POP () INTEGER,
        PUSH (INTEGER)
end interface.
```

We have said that in the abstract syntax the signature of an operation includes the type of the state that it affects. In our examples of concrete syntax we assume a convention that if an operation in a module M does not specify the state type explicitly then the name of the state type is also M, and that this type is implicitly exported. So in this example, the state type for the operations is called INTEGER_STACK and this type is implicitly exported by the module.

Notice that the abstract syntax allows the export clause to provide type information for the constructs which are exported. In the above example the operations POP and PUSH are given signatures.

This might be seen as an unnecessary repetition of information which must also be included in the body. However repeating type information in the interface allows the context conditions to 'type check' a group of modules *before* the module bodies are defined.

3.2 Import Clause

The *import* clause of the module interface gives a syntactic description of constructs which are provided by other modules.

```
Interface ::  id : Id
              ...
              imp : map Id to ModSig
              exp : ModSig
```

The *imp* component of the module interface maps the names of modules providing constructs to syntactic details of the imported constructs.

For example a module SYMBOL_TABLE might import constructs from the module INTEGER_STACK.

```
module SYMBOL_TABLE interface
...
import
  module   INTEGER_STACK
  opn      POP () INTEGER,
           PUSH (INTEGER)
...
end interface.
```

Notice that the abstract syntax allows the import clause to provide type information for the constructs which are imported.

3.3 Parameter Clause

The *parameter* clause of the module interface gives a syntactic description of constructs which parameterise the module.

```
Interface ::  id : Id
              par : ModSig
              imp : map Id to ModSig
              ...
              exp : ModSig
```

To simplify the abstract syntax the parameter clause is defined as a module signature. However, this must be restricted by context conditions. For example, a parameter must have a name with the same form as other 'local' names, and the structure of a type parameter must not be given.

Within a parameterised module the parameter types, constants, functions and operations may be used as undefined constructs. For example a module SORT might be parameterised by the type of the elements to be sorted and by a function which provides the ordering relation

```
module SORT interface
parameters
  type    ITEM
  fn      ARE_ORDERED( ITEM,ITEM ) Boolean
...
export
  fn      DO_SORT( seq of ITEM ) seq of ITEM
end interface.
```

3.4   Instantiation Clause

A parameterised module can not be imported. However, an instance of a parameterised module may be instantiated in the *instantiation* clause of the module interface.

```
Interface ::  id : Id
              par : ModSig
              imp : map Id to ModSig
              ins : map Id to Instance
              exp : ModSig


Instance  :: mod : Id
             view : map Id to Name
             sig : ModSig
```

The *instantiation* clause associates the name of the newly instantiated module with a description of the instantiation. The description consists of the name of the parameterised module, the names of the formal parameters and the corresponding actual parameters, and the signatures of the constructs provided by the instantiation. The signature is derived from the export clause of the parameterised module: formal parameters are replaced by actual parameters. The signature is not used by the semantics, but it is required for context conditions on an individual module.

For example a module MAILING_LIST might use an instantiation of the parameterised module SORT.

```
module MAILING_LIST interface

...

instantiation
  module INTEGER_SORT new SORT
    ( ITEM -> INTEGER, ARE_ORDERED -> ">=" )
    fn  DO_SORT( seq of INTEGER ) seq of INTEGER
export

  ...

end interface.
```

In this case the actual parameters are pre-defined constructs. Actual parameters may also be constructs provided by imported modules or by *another* instantiation of a parameterised module.

Notice that an instantiation is given a new name. It is not obvious that this is the best approach, but it does avoid the complexity of *'name expressions'* which would otherwise be necessary.

3.5 Names

It is essential that the specification language provides a way of managing the name space. Large specifications will be produced by groups of people and it must be possible for them to choose names without worrying about whether or not the name has been used before.

In this definition names reflect the structure provided by modules.

```
Name :: mod  : Id
        inst : [Id]
        loc  : Id


Id = NOT_DEFINED
```

A *full* name of a construct has three components, each of which is a simple identifier. The basic *local* name is provided by the component *loc*. This is qualified by the components *mod* and *inst* which indicate where the construct is defined.

A construct may be defined directly by a module, or it may be provided by an instantiation of a parameterised module. The *mod* component gives the name of the module which contains the definition or the instantiation of the parameterised module.

If the construct is provided by an instantiation of a parameterised module then the *inst* component provides the name of the instantiation, otherwise the *inst* component is **nil**.

Where there is no ambiguity, the concrete syntax should allow the prefix, (*mod* and *inst* components), to be omitted.

In the following example the module **INTEGER_STACK** exports the operation POP; it is imported by the module **SYMBOL_TABLE**. In *both* modules, the full name of the operation POP is **INTEGER_STACK.nil.POP**.

```
module INTEGER_STACK interface
...
export
  opn    POP () INTEGER,
         PUSH (INTEGER)
end interface.


module SYMBOL_TABLE interface
...
import
  module  INTEGER_STACK
  opn     POP () INTEGER,
          PUSH (INTEGER)
...
end interface.
```

In the following example the module MAILING_LIST instantiates the module INTEGER_SORT from the parameterised module SORT. The module INTEGER_SORT provides the function DO_SORT. The full name of DO_SORT is MAILING_LIST.INTEGER_SORT.DO_SORT

```
module MAILING_LIST interface
   ...
instantiation
  module INTEGER_SORT new SORT
    ( ITEM -> INTEGER, ARE_ORDERED -> ">=" )
    fn  DO_SORT( seq of INTEGER ) seq of INTEGER
export
   ...
end interface.
```

4   Syntax of Documents

A VDM Document is a collection of modules. For the purposes of this paper we define

```
Document = map of Id to Module
```

The module name, which is defined by the module, is repeated by the document. This repetition must be checked by the context conditions, but it makes other definitions and checks a little simpler.

The import relation may be cyclic, but the instantiation relationship must be *acyclic*.

We will not invent any concrete syntax for a document.

5   Summary of Abstract Syntax

```
Document    =  map of Id to Module


Module      ::  intf : Interface
                body : [Body]


Interface ::    id : Id
               par : ModSig
               imp : map Id to ModSig
               ins : map Id to Instance
               exp : ModSig


ModSig    :: types : map Name to [Type]
            const : map Name to [Type]
              fns : map Name to [FnType]
             opns : map Name to [OpSig]


OpSig     :: state : Name
               dom : seq of Type
               rng : [Type]


Instance  ::   mod : Id
              view : map Id to Name
               sig : ModSig


Name      ::   mod : Id
              inst : [Id]
               loc : Id
```

6   Examples

This section provides some slightly longer examples which show how the structuring facilities may be used.

6.1   Equivalence relations

In this example we provide interfaces for an example from [**Jones 80**].

```
module PARAMETERISED_FOREST interface
parameters
 type ELEMENT
export
 type FOREST_TYPE
 fn   IS_ROOT( ELEMENT, FOREST_TYPE ) Bool,
      ROOT( ELEMENT, FOREST_TYPE ) ELEMENT,
      COLLECT( FOREST_TYPE, ELEMENT ) set of ELEMENT
end interface.


module EQUIV_RELN_F interface
parameters
  type ELEMENT
instantiation
  module FOREST new PARAMETERISED_FOREST( ELEMENT )
    type FOREST_TYPE
    fn   IS_ROOT( ELEMENT, FOREST_TYPE ) Bool,
         ROOT( ELEMENT, FOREST_TYPE ) ELEMENT,
         COLLECT( FOREST_TYPE, ELEMENT ) set of ELEMENT
export
  opn  EQUATE( ELEMENT, ELEMENT )
       TEST( ELEMENT, ELEMENT ) Bool
end interface.
```

Notice that when PARAMETERISED_FOREST is instantiated the actual parameter has the same name as the formal parameter, *ELEMENT*. This has two effects. Firstly, we can use an abbreviated form of the concrete syntax, writing

```
module FOREST new PARAMETERISED_FOREST( ELEMENT )
```

instead of

```
module FOREST new PARAMETERISED_FOREST( ELEMENT -> ELEMENT)
```

Secondly, the signatures of the functions provided by the instantiation are identical to the signature of the functions exported by the parameterised module.

6.2   School Students

This example is a reworking of the interfaces to the *Students who do exercises* and *School* modules given in a BSI working document [BSI 40].

```
module STUDENTS interface
import
  module NAMES
  type   NAME
export
  type  NAME
  opn   ENROL( NAME ),
        COMPL( NAME ),
        RESULT() set of NAME
end interface.


module SCHOOL interface
import
  module STUDENTS
   type  NAMES.NAME
    opn  ENROL( NAME ),
         COMPL( NAME ),
         RESULT() set of NAME
export
  type  NAMES.NAME,
        CLASSID,
        STUDENTS
  opn   ENRS( CLASSID, NAME ),
        RESULTS( CLASSID ) set of NAME
  fn    CONT  : CLASSID -> SCHOOL -> STUDENTS,
        ASSIGN : CLASSID x STUDENTS -> SCHOOL -> SCHOOL
end interface.
```

Notice that the module STUDENTS explicitly *re-exports* the type NAMES.NAME. Also note that the state type is—by our convention—called STUDENTS and that it is implicitly exported by the module.

6.3   A Symbol Table

The following example gives the interface for a parameterised symbol table. The module is parameterised by the type of the data held by the table and by the type of the key used to access the data. It is also parameterised by a hashing function and the type of the values returned by the hashing function.

The module provides two operations, INSERT and EXTRACT. The operation INSERT takes an item of data and returns a value of type INSERT_RETURN. The structure of this type is visible, so we can see that in fact INSERT returns a pair of values: a Boolean flag which indicates whether or not the data was already in the symbol table, and a key value. The operation EXTRACT takes a key value and returns a Boolean flag which indicates whether or not the requested data was present, and a data value.

This example shows that sometimes it is useful to expose the structure of an exported type. The alternative would have been to provide additional functions.

```
module SYMBOL_TABLE interface
parameters
 type DATA, KEY, HASH_CODE
 fn  HASH( DATA ) HASH_CODE
export

 type  INSERT_RETURN    ::  kv   : KEY
                            dupl : Bool
 type  EXTRACT_RETURN   ::  val  : DATA
                            pres : Bool

 opn   INSERT( DATA ) INSERT_RETURN
       EXTRACT( KEY ) EXTRACT_RETURN
end interface.
```

Part II

Semantics

In this part of the paper we give a formal semantics for the structuring facilities described above.

7   Approach to the Semantics

In this definition of the semantics of structuring two main decisions have been taken:

- The module structure is flattened.

- The information hiding implied by the export clause is interpreted by the context conditions but is *ignored* by the semantic functions. Information hiding is viewed as a *pragmatic* concept which may be dealt with by imposing 'static' constraints.

These decisions may be controversial, but the approach has several significant advantages.

Firstly, the technical definitions are much simpler and shorter than the corresponding definitions in [**Monahan 85**] or [**Bear 87**][1] .

Secondly, the semantics are *compositional*. That is, the semantics of a document is given in terms of the semantics of its component modules, and the semantics of a module is given in terms of the semantics of its interface and the semantics of its body. For example, consider a document

$$\texttt{document} \triangleq [\ \texttt{n}_1 \rightarrow \texttt{module}_1, \ \texttt{n}_2 \rightarrow \texttt{module}_2, \ \dots]$$

for some function f, the semantics of the document is defined by

$$[\![\texttt{document}]\!] \triangleq f\Big([\ \texttt{n}_1 \rightarrow [\![\texttt{module}_1]\!], \texttt{n}_2 \rightarrow [\![\texttt{module}_2]\!], \dots] \Big)$$

Similarly, consider a module

$$\texttt{module} \triangleq \texttt{Mk-tag}(\ \texttt{'Module'},\ \texttt{interface},\ \texttt{body}\ )$$

for some function g, the semantics of the module is defined by

$$[\![\texttt{module}]\!] \triangleq g\Big([\![\texttt{interface}]\!],\ [\![\texttt{body}]\!] \Big)$$

The semantics of the module body, $[\![\texttt{body}]\!]$, is given by the semantics of the flat language which is discussed in the next section. To complete the definition we have to define the semantics of the interface and provide the functions f and g. Notice that the semantics of the structuring concepts are clearly separated from the semantics of the flat language. If the definition of semantics of the flat language is changed slightly, then there is a good chance that the semantics of structuring will still make sense, or that it will be easy to make the necessary changes.

Thirdly, we are able to allow modules which import constructs from each other. Cyclic import relations were explicitly prohibited in both [**Monahan 85**] and [**Bear 87**].

Lastly the semantics appears to provide a good basis for the proof theory. For example it should be possible to ensure that the import mechanism provides a *'conservative extension'*.

7.1   Notation and Auxiliary Functions

The general mathematical notation used in this paper is fairly standard, but it may be worth noting that $\oplus$ is the map overwrite operator and that $\cup$ is used for map union as well as set union. The following notation is less standard

- The set VAL is the universe of values provided by the type model for the language.

- The set Atom is some fixed countable set which is disjoint from VAL.

- For any sets X, Y $M(X,Y)$ is the set of finite maps from X to Y.

- For any set X $E(X)$ is $M(Atom,X)$.

---

[1]This paper described essentially the same facilities in a rather different style

- The function Mk-tag is a tagging function defined in [**Monahan 85**]. It corresponds to the
  `mk-` constructor functions in the VDM specification language.

We also assume two bijections

atom-id : Id $\longrightarrow$ Atom

atom-nm : Name $\longrightarrow$ Atom

and a related function

atom-map: $\mathbf{M}$(Id, Name) $\longrightarrow$ $\mathbf{E}$(Atom)

atom-map(map) $\triangleq$ [atom-id(i) $\rightarrow$ atom-nm(map(i)) | i $\in$ domain(map)]

8 The 'Flat' Language

The 'flat' language is the VDM specification language without any of the structuring concepts.
In the abstract syntax the flat language is represented by Body. The semantics of a specification
written in the flat language is given in terms of *models* which *satisfy* the specification.

For the purposes of this definition, a model is an element of the set

MODEL = $\mathbf{E}$(VAL)

where VAL is the universe of values provided by the type model for the language. In other words,
a model is a map which takes the name[2] of a construct to a denotation of the construct. Notice
that different models could provide different denotations. The notion of satisfaction is defined by
a relation

sat $\subseteq$ MODEL $\times$ **Body**

If the pair (model, **spec**) is in the relation **sat** then we write

model **sat spec**

and we say that the model *satisfies* the specification, or sometimes that the model *is* a model of
the specification.

8.1 Semantics

The semantics of a specification written in the flat language is defined to be the set of models which
satisfy the specification. It turns out that the semantics of a *document* is also a set of models, so
we define

DocDen = $\mathcal{P}$(MODEL)

---

[2]actually, an *atom* corresponding to the name

The fact that documents *are the same as* flat specifications is another pleasing aspect of the semantics.

The semantics of the flat language is defined by the following function.

$[\![.]\!] : \text{ Body} \longrightarrow \text{DocDen}$

$[\![\text{ body }]\!] \triangleq$

$\{ \text{ mod} \in \text{MODEL} \mid \text{mod } \textbf{sat body} \}$

□

8.2 Some Assumptions

We do not need to know the precise definition of the satisfaction relation, but we do need to make some assumptions about its properties.

Firstly we assume that a specification **spec** which has undefined constructs can still have models. Suppose that $\textbf{spec}_1$ and $\textbf{spec}_2$ are specifications written in the flat language and that they are identical, except that in $\textbf{spec}_1$ a certain construct is defined, and in $\textbf{spec}_2$ it is undefined, then

$$[\![\textbf{spec}_1]\!] \subseteq [\![\textbf{spec}_2]\!]$$

The additional models in $[\![\textbf{spec}_2]\!]$ provide alternative denotations for the undefined construct. Notice that undefined constructs are not represented by a special value in VAL, but are treated as being under-determined.

Secondly, we assume that adding 'junk' to a model of a specification does not stop it being a model of that specification. Suppose that at is some atom and v is some value in VAL, then

$$\text{model} \in [\![\textbf{spec}]\!] \wedge \text{at} \notin \text{domain(model)} \Longrightarrow \text{model} \cup [\text{ at} \rightarrow \text{v}] \in [\![\textbf{spec}]\!]$$

Recall that $[\![\textbf{spec}]\!]$ is the set of *all* models which satisfy **spec**, so there are models in $[\![\textbf{spec}]\!]$ which provide denotations for arbitrary 'junk'.

Notice that for any two specifications $\textbf{spec}_1$ and $\textbf{spec}_2$, if $[\![\textbf{spec}_1]\!]$ is non-empty then it contains models which provide denotations for the constructs defined or used by $\textbf{spec}_2$.

8.3 Definition

The flat language described above is essentially that defined in [**Monahan 85**]. Some details have been changed to simplify our technical presentation of the structuring concepts, but it would not be difficult to make the two definitions match precisely.

9 Introduction to the Formal Semantics

In this section we introduce the basic ideas behind the formal semantics by describing the semantics of simple modules which have import and export clauses, but do not have any notion of parameterisation.

For the moment we will leave aside the question of what the semantics domains for modules and documents should actually be. Whatever we choose as the denotation of a document it will, in some sense, *provide* denotations of the constructs defined or used within the document. Moreover, these denotations will be derived from the denotations provided by the models of (the bodies of) the modules which make up the document. It turns out that the choice of *how* to combine the models of (the bodies of) modules is strongly affected by the way in which we interpret the export clause.

9.1 A semantic export clause

There is a very natural way for the semantics to interpret the export clause. A model which satisfies a module body must provide denotations of all the constructs defined or used within the module body. Not all of these constructs are exported by the module—some are *hidden* by the module—so it is natural to use the export clause to *restrict* the model so that it only provides denotations of the *exported* constructs. Recall that a model of a module body is a map of Atom $\rightarrow$ VAL, so this is literally a matter of restricting the map to an appropriate domain. This approach has been taken in [**Monahan 85**] and [**Bear 87**].

Note that defining *"an appropriate domain"* is not entirely straightforward, because certain constructs may be exported *implicitly*. For example, if a record type is exported explicitly, then the associated constructor and selector functions are exported implicitly.

9.1.1 Modules

If we restrict the models associated with a module, so that the models only provide denotations of the exported constructs, then we must go to some effort to *re-introduce* denotations of constructs which are acquired from other modules.

For example in [**Monahan 85**] a module is essentially denoted by a function

$$\mathbf{E}(\mathcal{P}(\text{MODEL})) \longrightarrow \mathcal{P}(\text{MODEL})$$

which takes (sets of) denotations of constructs *imported* by the module and returns (sets of) denotations of constructs *exported* by the module.

The definition of this function quite complicated. Each of the imported modules may be undetermined, so each provides a *set* of models. These sets of models must be combined in a way which correctly reflects their joint underdeterminism.

In [**Bear 87**] it is possible to acquire constructs by instantiating a parameterised module, and the corresponding function is even more complicated.

9.2 A non-semantic export clause

If the export clause is used to remove denotations from models, then it is quite hard work to put them back. The alternative—which is taken in this definition—is for the semantics to ignore the export clause, so that denotations are not removed in the first place.

We should note that if export clauses are not interpreted semantically, they will not be ignored completely. The import and export clauses are intended to increase the amount of checking that can be performed by a reviewer or an automatic tool, so the context conditions should check that constructs imported by one module in a document are actually exported by another.

If the export clause is ignored by the semantics, then models associated with a module are not restricted. They provide denotations of all the constructs defined or used within the module body. Recall that we have assumed that adding 'junk' to a model does not stop it being a model, so 'many' models will also provide denotations for constructs not defined or used by the module body.

9.2.1 Modules

If we do not restrict the models associated with a module, then we do not have to re-introduce denotations of constructs which are acquired from other modules. The models *already* provide denotations for the acquired constructs.

Consider a module A which imports and uses a type T from another module. Let $[\![\text{Body(A)}]\!]$ be the set of all models of the (body of) module A. These models provide denotations for all the constructs defined or used by A. In particular they will provide denotations for the imported type T.

If A is an isolated module then we need do little more: we can define the (simple structuring) semantics of the module A to be $[\![\text{Body(A)}]\!]$. The models in $[\![\text{Body(A)}]\!]$ include all denotations of T which are consistent with the rest of the module A. The imported type is just treated as an *undefined* construct.

9.2.2 Documents

Now suppose that we have both a module A and a module B, and that we are going to combine the two modules into a single document.

All of the models in $[\![\text{Body(A)}]\!]$ provide denotations for the constructs defined or used by A. Recall that models of Body(A) may also provide denotations for undefined 'junk' and that it follows that there are models in $[\![\text{Body(A)}]\!]$ which contain arbitrary junk. It turns out that some of this junk is rather useful, in particular we can find models in $[\![\text{Body(A)}]\!]$ which provide denotations for all the constructs defined or used by *B*. The constructs defined by B are *undefined* by A, so in fact we can find models in $[\![\text{Body(A)}]\!]$ which provide *any* denotation for the constructs defined by B.

Conversely, we can find models in $[\![\text{Body(B)}]\!]$ which provide *any* denotation for the constructs defined by A.

The models in $\llbracket \texttt{Body(A)} \rrbracket$ satisfy Body(A) and the models in $\llbracket \texttt{Body(B)} \rrbracket$ satisfy Body(B), so models in the intersection $\llbracket \texttt{Body(A)} \rrbracket \cap \llbracket \texttt{Body(B)} \rrbracket$ satisfy both modules. We can define the (simple structuring) semantics of the document to be precisely this intersection.

10 The Semantics of a Module Interface

In the simple structuring described in the previous section we did not need to consider an interface at all. However in our full language, which includes the notion of instantiations of parameterised modules, we do have to take interfaces into account.

The interface clause of a module describes how the meaning of the module is dependent on its context. Consider a module which imports or instantiates certain constructs. If the module is isolated then the imported or instantiated constructs are essentially *undefined*. If the module is placed in a suitable context of other modules then the context will supply definitions for the imported or instantiated constructs. The interface of a module must define how the module might be affected by its context.

Notice that placing a parameterised module in a context does not provide any more information about the formal parameters. Parameters only become defined when the module is instantiated and formal parameters are replaced by actual parameters. Outside of an instantiation, parameters are always undefined.

Suppose that a module M is placed in a particular context. Semantically, the interface must provide information which makes it possible to relate models of (the body of) M to models of the context.[3] In more detail, it must provide the following information:

- the module name

- the names of the imported modules

and for each instantiation of a parameterised module

- the new 'local' name for the instantiation

- the name of the parameterised module

- the correspondence between formal parameters and actual parameters.

The interface does not deal with formal parameters, since these are always undefined; nor with exports, since these are not interpreted semantically. We represent the meaning of an interface by a value in the following domain

$$\text{InterfaceDen} = \text{Atom} \times \mathbf{E}(\text{ Atom} \times \mathbf{E}(\text{ Atom }))$$

---

[3]More precisely, models of (the bodies of) the modules in the context.

The semantic function is defined as follows

$\llbracket . \rrbracket$: Interface $\longrightarrow$ InterfaceDen

$\llbracket$ interface $\rrbracket$ $\triangleq$

     let interface $\triangleq$ Mk-tag('Interface', id, par, imp, ins, exp) **in**

     let imports $\triangleq$ $\big[$ atom-id(i) $\rightarrow$ (atom-id(i) , []) $|$ i $\in$ dom(imp) $\big]$ **in**

     let instances $\triangleq$ $\big[$ atom-id(i) $\rightarrow$ (atom-id(p) , atom-map(v)) $|$

                i $\in$ dom(ins) $\wedge$

                p $=$ mod(ins(i)) $\wedge$

                v $=$ view(ins(i)) $\big]$ **in**

   $\big($ atom-id(id), imports $\cup$ instances $\big)$

   $\square$

Notice that imports are represented by mapping the name of the imported module to itself and an empty map. Instantiations are represented by mapping the name of the newly instantiated module to the name of the parameterised module and a map which takes the names of the formal parameters to the names of the actual parameters.

11   The Semantics of a Module

The semantics of a module must combine the semantics of the module body and the semantics of the interface in a way that is convenient for the definition of the semantics of a document. We choose to define the semantics of a module in a very simple way—we just say that it is the pair consisting of the semantics of the interface and the semantics of the module body.

    The semantic domain for a module is

    ModuleDen $=$ InterfaceDen $\times$ DocDen

The semantics of a module is defined by the following function:

$\llbracket . \rrbracket$: **Module** $\longrightarrow$ ModuleDen

$\llbracket$module$\rrbracket$ $\triangleq$

let module $\triangleq$ Mk-tag('Module', interface, body) in

let bodysem $\triangleq$ **if** body = **nil then** MODEL **else** $[\![$body$]\!]$ in

($[\![$interface$]\!]$, bodysem)

$\square$

Notice that if the body of the module is not supplied then we use the collection of *all* models. If a model is a model of a given module body, then we will say that it is a model of the module.

12   Two Semantic Functions

Before we can define the semantics of a document we must define and discuss two functions **Acquire** and **InContext**.

12.1   The function Acquire

The function **Acquire** derives the set of models associated with an imported or instantiated module.

The main purpose of the function **Acquire** is to deal with instantiations of parameterised modules. It takes a set of models of a parameterised module and *derives* a set of models which define the denotations of the instantiated constructs. Strictly, we should not say that these are models *of* the instantiated module, because this would mean that the models *satisfied* some syntactic module body, and—of course—no such syntactic object exists.[4] However we will sometimes refer to these models as models *of* the instantiated module.

Before defining **Acquire** we define another function **Acquire1** which takes a single model of the parameterised module and derives a model which is closely related to the newly instantiated module. The signature of **Acquire1** is

Acquire1 : Atom $\times$ Atom $\times$ Atom $\times$ $\mathbf{E}$(Atom) $\times$ MODEL $\longrightarrow$ MODEL

Acquire1(mod, inst, pmod, view, model) $\triangleq \ldots$

The arguments of **Acquire1** should be interpreted as follows.

- *mod* is the name[5] of the instantiating module;

- *inst* is the name of the newly instantiated module;

- *pmod* is the name of the parameterised module;

---

[4]This indicates that this is not a *syntactic* definition!

[5]More precisely, the *atom* corresponding to the name.

- *view* is a mapping which takes the names of the formal parameters to the names of actual parameters;

- *model* is a model of the parameterised module.

The function is defined as follows:

Acquire1: Atom × Atom × Atom × $\mathbf{E}$(Atom) × MODEL $\longrightarrow$ MODEL

Acquire1 (mod, inst, pmod, view, model) $\triangleq$

    let mod-id $\overset{\triangle}{=}$ atom-id(mod) **in**
    let inst-id $\overset{\triangle}{=}$ atom-id(inst) **in**
    let pmod-id $\overset{\triangle}{=}$ atom-id(pmod) **in**
    [new-name $\rightarrow$ model(old-name) | $\exists$ x $\in$ Id .
      (new-name = atom-nm(Mk-tag('Name',mod-id,inst-id,x)) $\wedge$
      old-name = atom-nm(Mk-tag('Name',pmod-id,nil,x)) $\wedge$
      old-name $\in$ domain(model))]
    $\cup$
    [view(fpid) $\rightarrow$ model(atom-nm(Mk-tag('Name',pmod-id,nil,fpid))) |
      fpid $\in$ domain(view)]

    $\square$

If we look at this definition we can see that the function takes a single model of a parameterised module and then defines another model in two steps.

- For each construct defined by the parameterised module, there is a denotation for the corresponding construct defined by the newly instantiated module.

- For each formal parameter, there is a denotation for the corresponding actual parameter.

The derived model provides denotations for the actual parameters used to instantiate the parameterised module, and the instantiated constructs. It is important to notice that the relationship between the denotations of the actual parameters and the instantiated constructs in the derived model *is the same as* the relationship between the denotations of the formal parameters and the constructs provided by the parameterised module in the original model. So the derived model *'follows'* the model of the of the parameterised model.

We will now examine a number of candidates for the set of 'models of' an instantiated module. Consider an instantiation of a parameterised module defined by mod, inst, pmod, and view[6], and

---

[6]interpreted as before

let $[\![\text{pmodb}]\!]$ be the set of models of the parameterised module. The set

$$\left\{ \ \textbf{Acquire1}(\text{mod,inst,pmod,view,model}) \ \mid \text{model} \in [\![\text{pmodb}]\!] \ \right\}$$

is too restricted. There are not enough models to allow us to use the intersection technique when defining the *instantiating* module. The set

$$\left\{ \ \text{model} \oplus \textbf{Acquire1}(\text{mod,inst,pmod,view,model}) \ \mid \text{model} \in [\![\text{pmodb}]\!] \ \right\}$$

is also too restricted. In each model, the denotation of a construct defined by the parameterised model is *identical* to the denotation of the corresponding construct defined by the newly instantiated module; similarly the denotation of a formal parameter is *identical* to the corresponding actual parameter. This would prohibit a module instantiating a parameterised module more than once. However the set

$$\left\{ \ \text{model}_1 \oplus \textbf{Acquire1}(\text{mod,inst,pmod,view,model}_2) \ \mid \right.$$
$$\left. \text{model}_1 \in \text{MODEL} \wedge \text{model}_2 \in [\![\text{pmodb}]\!] \ \right\}$$

is too free. This set of models does not restrict, (and therefore does not define), any constructs which are acquired by the parameterised module and then re-exported. The most appropriate set of models appears to be

$$\left\{ \ \text{model}_1 \oplus \textbf{Acquire1}(\text{mod,inst,pmod,view,model}_2) \ \mid \ \text{model}_1, \text{model}_2 \in [\![\text{pmodb}]\!] \ \right\}$$

This set of models defines the instantiated constructs, *and* any constructs which are acquired by the parameterised module and then re-exported; it also contains enough 'junk' to allow us to apply our intersection techniques. Notice that by changing the definition of this set we could 'fine tune' the notion of instantiation.

The function **Acquire** is defined as follows:

Acquire: $\text{Atom} \times \text{Atom} \times \text{Atom} \times \mathbf{E}(\text{Atom}) \times \text{DocDen} \longrightarrow \text{DocDen}$

Acquire (mod, inst, pmod, view, models) $\triangleq$

    if view $= [\,]$ **then** models **else**
    $\left\{ \ \text{model}_1 \oplus \textbf{Acquire1}(\text{mod,inst,pmod,view,model}_2) \ \mid \ \text{model}_1, \text{model}_2 \in \text{models} \ \right\}$

    $\square$

If view is the empty mapping then this corresponds to an imported module, and the function just returns the set of models of the module.

If view is not the empty mapping then this corresponds to an instantiation of a parameterised module, and the function returns the set of models which define the instantiated module.

12.2   The function InContext

The function **InContext** *'evaluates'* a module *in a particular context*. That is, the function takes a module denotation and a context (of other module denotations) and returns the set of models of the module which are *consistent* with the module denotation and the context.

Notice that the function takes module denotations (which contain sets of models *and* information about interfaces) and return sets of models. The context dependencies described by the interfaces are eliminated by considering a *particular* context.

The function is defined as follows:

InContext: ModuleDen $\times$ **E**(ModuleDen) $\longrightarrow$ DocDen

InContext (module, others) $\triangleq$

      let (interface,models) $\triangleq$ module **in**
      let (id,views) $\triangleq$ interface **in**
      if views = [] **then** models **else**
      models $\cap$
      $\cap$ { **Acquire**(id, acquired, pmod, view, **InContext**(others(pmod), others)) |
                    acquired $\in$ domain(views) $\wedge$
                    (pmod,view) = views(acquired) }

      $\Box$

If views is the empty mapping then the module does not import or instantiate any modules, and the function just returns the set of models of the module. Otherwise, the function may be viewed as being in two steps

- The function **Acquire** is used to generate the sets of models corresponding to the imported or instantiated modules. Notice that an imported or instantiated module may itself import or instantiate modules, so the function **InContext** is used recursively.

- The function returns the intersection between the original set of models and the sets of models corresponding to the imported and instantiated modules. Each model in this intersection is a model of the module and a model of *all* of the imported and instantiated modules.

If a collection of modules import constructs from each other recursively, then this definition is not well founded, but it may be interpreted as defining a fixed point.

Note that, in a given context, if a module A imports a module B, and a module M instantiates a parameterised module P then

InContext($[\![A]\!]$, context) $\subseteq$ InContext($[\![B]\!]$, context)

InContext($[\![M]\!]$, context) $\subseteq$ InContext($[\![P]\!]$, context)

13   The Semantics of a Document

The definition of the semantics of a document is now very simple. For each module in the document we use the function **InContext** to *'evaluate'* the module in the context of the other modules in the document.

The semantics of the document is then defined to be the intersection of these sets of models. Each model in this intersection is a model of *all* the modules in the document.

The function is defined as follows:

$[\![.]\!]$: Document $\longrightarrow$ DocDen

$[\![\text{document}]\!]$ $\triangleq$

> let context $\triangleq$ [atom-id(i) $\rightarrow$ $[\![\text{document(i)}]\!]$ | i $\in$ domain(document)] in
>
> $\bigcap \big\{$ InContext($[\![\text{mod}]\!]$, context) | mod $\in$ range(document) $\big\}$
>
> □

---

14   Further Work

It appears that it would not be difficult to extend the semantics given in this definition to allow modules which place *requirements* on acquired constructs.

For example, consider a module which specifies a sort. This module could be parameterised by an ordering relation. In the extended language the module could *require* that any actual parameter was actually a partial order.

In conjunction with a suitable proof theory, such constraints would make it possible to prove properties of a document in a *modular* and *compositional* way.

The semantics of this extended language could be approached in the following way. Consider a syntactic function

> **i: Requirements $\longrightarrow$ Body**

which translated the 'requirements' into a very simple flat specification. Then $[\![\text{i(requirement)}]\!]$ is the set of all models which satisfy the requirement. We could define the semantics of a module to be

$$(\; [\![\texttt{interface}]\!] \; , \; [\![\texttt{body}]\!] \cap [\![\texttt{i(requirement)}]\!] \;)$$

Notice that if we allowed requirements on the constructs defined by the module *itself* then it would be possible to define modules in an 'axiomatic' or 'algebraic' style.

15 References

[Bear 87]   S P Bear, *Structuring for BSI VDM.*
                 BSI VDM Working Paper, BSI IST/5/50/53, 1987.

[BSI 40]   *VDM Specification Language Proto-Standard.*
                 BSI VDM Working Paper, BSI IST/5/50/40.

[Jones 80]   C B Jones, *Software Development — A Rigorous Approach.*
                 Prentice Hall International, 1980.

[Monahan 85]   B Q Monahan, *A Semantic Definition of the STC VDM Reference Language.*
                 Internal Report STL, Manchester University, 1985.
                 BSI VDM Working Paper, BSI IST/5/50/9.

Correctness for Beginners

Maurice Naftalin
Department of Computing Science
University of Stirling
Stirling FK9 4LA
Scotland

Abstract

Stepwise refinement can be formalised in a natural way by regarding specifications as unimplemented program components. We present a graphical notation for specifications and their refinement rules which supports this approach. The resulting development style is proposed as an appropriate model for introductory programming instruction.

1. Introduction

It is widely accepted that the poor technical education of software workers is the biggest barrier to the industrial adoption of formal methods. The great majority of software workers have been taught in the conventional manner, which can be characterised as encouraging students (or trainee programmers) to produce, as quickly as possible, large programs which they know will contain serious errors. Later they may be introduced to methods for precise reasoning about programs, but this topic is presented with such a wide separation in time, style of motivation and subject matter from the original introduction that it appears to be a quite separate subject. Clearly it would be much better to teach the logical foundations of programming together with its practical applications, from the very start.

Of the two main approaches to teaching formal methods in imperative programming, neither that following the tradition of [Dijkstra] nor that of constructive specification have so far achieved this integration. It will be argued in this paper (§6) that the approach of the former is inappropriate to elementary-level teaching. On the other hand, the pedagogic material presenting constructive specification methods (*e.g.* [Jones86], [Hayes]) reflects the primary purpose of these methods, that is their application to industrial software engineering problems. To make them suitable for elementary teaching, attention must be given to the choice of suitable refinement rules and to matters of presentation (such as an appropriate concrete syntax).

This paper addresses these issues. Its structure is as follows: §§2 and 3 present the syntax of the notation to be used in development, §§4 and 5 show briefly how it can be used in verifiable program construction, §§6 and 7 treat the notation formally, and §8 discusses the merits of the approach presented.

2. The Programming Language

We present a diagram notation (the "box notation") for depicting stepwise refinement, specifications (§3), and program correctness (§5). An algorithm is expressed in this notation by a structure of nested boxes. Each box contains either an informal description of a step of the algorithm or else a statement in a programming language. The language used here, a (slightly modified) subset of Pascal, has the following BNF grammar, in which the box is to be read as a terminal symbol:

Boxed_stmt = $\boxed{Stmt}$

Stmt = Simple_stmt | Structured_stmt

Simple_stmt = Assignment | Empty_stmt

Empty_stmt = **donothing**

Structured_stmt = Compound_stmt | Conditional_stmt | Repetitive_stmt

Compound_stmt = Boxed_stmt { ; Boxed_stmt }

Conditional_stmt = **if** Boolean_exp **then** Boxed_stmt

                                     else Boxed_stmt

Repetitive_stmt = **while** Boolean_exp **do** Boxed_stmt

The box notation allows algorithm refinement to be shown clearly by simply enlarging a box and revealing its detail. For example, suppose that we are demonstrating the development of a program to implement the informal specification "calculate the integer square root of the absolute value of a number" (henceforth referred to as "find square root of modulus"). Figure 1 could serve as a summary of the early parts of such a development (we assume the absence of built-in *abs* and *sqrt* functions).

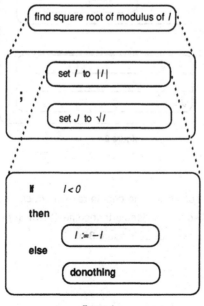

figure 1

3. Specifications

A key to the refinement method is the ability to regard specifications as unimplemented programs. This means that the same compositional operators (with the same meanings) must be provided for specifications as for programs. The syntax of the box notation is extended to include specifications as follows (boxes are again to be read as terminal symbols):

$Boxed\_stmt$ = $\boxed{Stmt}$ | $Specification$

$Specification$ =
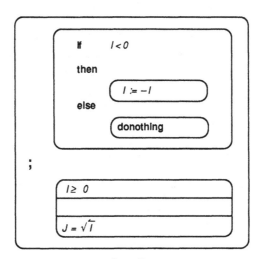

Figure 2 shows an example of a specification embedded in a program. The use of the decorated variable $\overleftarrow{I}$ is borrowed from VDM ([Jones]): $\overleftarrow{I}$ occurring in the post-condition of a specification S represents the value of the variable I in the initial state of S. In figure 2, for example, the symbol $\overleftarrow{I}$ refers to the value of I at the intermediate state between the execution of the two components.

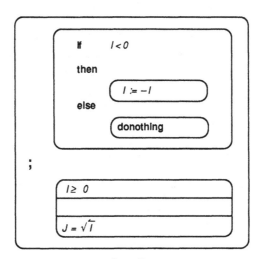

figure 2

It is straightforward to extend the box notation to denote refinement of a specification. Let the specification shown in figure 3(a) be called S. To denote that some Q (which may be either a program or a specification) refines S, we write Q inside S, as in figure 3(b).

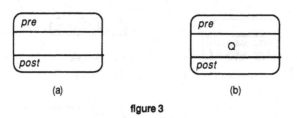

figure 3

For example, the assertion that the as-yet-unimplemented program "find square root of modulus of I" satisfies its specification could be written as in figure 4.

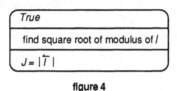

figure 4

The task of the developer is now to refine the algorithm "find square root of modulus of I" simultaneously with its specification in such a way that the truth of this assertion is preserved by each refinement step. The process is illustrated informally for the first step in §4.

4.   Justifying Program Development: the Refinement Process

In this section we demonstrate, by an informal treatment of a development of figure 4, how the process of verifiable construction can be explained using the box notation. The development chosen is based on the first-level algorithm refinement shown in figure 1. This refinement, and the corresponding specification refinement, are presented in figures 5(a) and 5(b) respectively. Both are in obvious modifications of their standard forms (as shown in figures 1 and figure 3(b) respectively) in order to emphasise the correspondence between them.

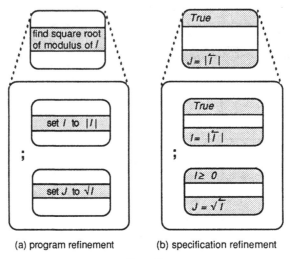

(a) program refinement   (b) specification refinement

figure 5

It is usually argued, with strong methodological justification, that specification should precede and motivate implementation. It may well be easier, however, for a developer with limited experience of formal reasoning to construct figure 5(a) first, using operational reasoning, and then derive figure 5(b) from it. A good method for this developer will be one which by accomodating a mixture of operational and formal reasoning permits such an approach without compromising the logical rigour of the development. Of course, some formal reasoning is essential: at the least, the specification refinement step must be proved correct as soon as it is complete.

Such a specification refinement proof has two parts. These are represented by arrows superimposed on the two parts of figure 6, which is figure 5(b) in standard form. First, the truth of the pre-condition of each component box must be a consequence of known facts about the state at the start of execution of the whole. These known facts are encapsulated in the overall pre-condition. So the truth of this, taken together with changes to the state made by other components, must be enough to ensure the truth of the component pre-conditions. This is shown in figure 6(a).

The second aspect of refinement correctness is that the effect of the component boxes, taken together, should be to guarantee the truth of the post-condition of the original specification. This is illustrated in figure 6(b)[1].

---

[1]Figure 6(b) actually shows a special case of the rule for refinement by sequence, which will be introduced in §5.

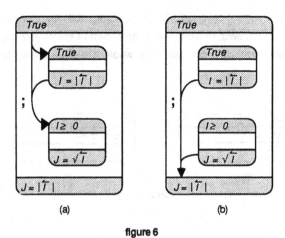

(a)   (b)

figure 6

Having argued the correctness of a single refinement step, we now show how to extend the argument to the entire refinement process. Consider figure 7, which is figure 5 relabelled. We want to prove that P satisfies S. First we refined the program P to its two components P1 and P2, and the specification S to its components S1 and S2. We then showed that the specification refinement was correct. To justify the program refinement, we now have to show that P1 satisfies S1 and that P2 satisfies S2.

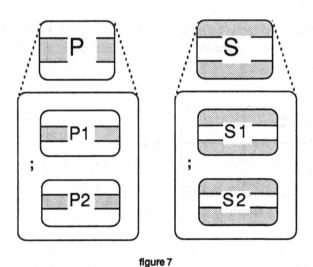

figure 7

Figure 8 shows the two boxes that need to be proved correct. Since neither P1 nor P2 is a single instruction, the boxes P1/S1 (figure 8(a)) and P2/S2 (figure 8(b)) must be further developed by the same method as was used for the original program. This procedure continues until the program has been refined into individual instructions each of which has been shown to satisfy its correctly derived specification. When this has been done, the program as a whole has been shown to satisfy the original specification.

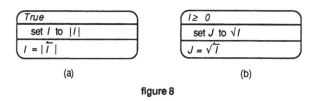

(a)   (b)

figure 8

5. Justifying Program Development: the Proof Rules

This section presents the rules for justifying refinement by the compositional operators. The rules are given in a diagrammatic form based on the box notation. (§7 shows how these rules, in their predicate calculus form, can be justified with respect to a relational semantics for the programming language). The use of each operator is illustrated by a step in the development of the square root program.

Refinement by Sequence

The starting point for the development is the specification shown in figure 9, from which the square root and modulus symbols have been eliminated. Clauses in the post-condition are "stacked" to denote conjunction.

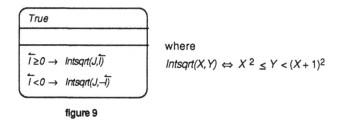

figure 9

Refinement of this specification by the first step shown earlier gives figure 10(a). The rule for proving the correctness of a refinement by sequence is shown schematically in figure 10(b). Clearly, to prove figure 10(a) correct it is necessary to invent a suitable predicate on the intermediate state. In other cases (*e.g.* in a refinement by repetition) this intermediate predicate may already be known; the requirement is then to invent a suitable specification for one of the sequence components.

The arrows on figure 10(b) represent implications according to the following conventions:

- a single unbranched arrow (from *source-pred* to *dest-pred*, say) represents the implication
  $$source\text{-}pred \Rightarrow dest\text{-}pred$$
- "fan-in" represents the conjunction of antecedents
- "fan-out" represents the conjunction of consequents

Proving the implications represented by the arrows on figure 10(b) establishes the correctness of the refinement.

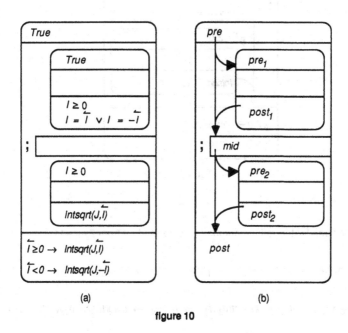

(a)　　　　　　　　　　　　(b)

figure 10

The hook notation cannot be used for the proof of a sequence refinement, as it provides no way of referring to the intermediate state. For the purpose of the proof, we therefore relabel each variable occurrence in the conditions. For each occurrence we use one of the subscripts 0,1, or 2 to signify that the occurrence refers to the value of the variable in the initial, intermediate, or final state respectively. For the intermediate condition we take the conjunction of the overall pre-condition and the post-condition of the first component. This gives figure 11.

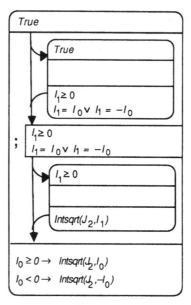

figure 11

The correctness conditions for the refinement may now be read off from figure 11. They are

$True \Rightarrow True$

$True \wedge l_1 \geq 0 \wedge (l_1 = l_0 \vee l_1 = -l_0) \Rightarrow l_1 \geq 0 \wedge (l_1 = l_0 \vee l_1 = -l_0)$

$l_0 \geq 0 \wedge (l_1 = l_0 \vee l_1 = -l_0) \Rightarrow l_1 \geq 0$

$l_0 \geq 0 \wedge (l_1 = l_0 \vee l_1 = -l_0) \wedge Intsqrt(J_2, l_1) \Rightarrow (l_1 \geq 0 \rightarrow Intsqrt(J_2, l_0)) \wedge (l_1 < 0 \rightarrow Intsqrt(J_2, -l_0))$

The proof of these is omitted.

Refinement by Selection

The component specification

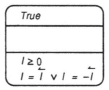

can now be refined by a step corresponding to the procedural refinement by selection shown in figures 1 and 2. If this procedural refinement is in fact carried out first, it will then be necessary to "reconstruct" the specification refinement. This is shown, together with an assertion of its correctness, in figure 12(a).

The rule for justifying such an assertion is shown in figure 12(b). ("~" inserted in an arrow signifies the negation of the corresponding predicate).

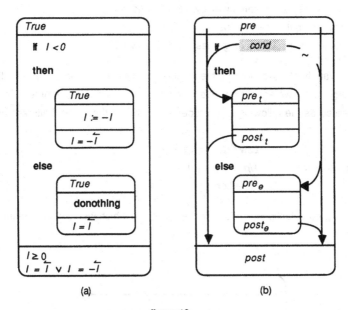

(a)   (b)

figure 12

The correctness conditions for the refinement of figure 12(a) are

$$True \wedge \overleftarrow{I} < 0 \Rightarrow True$$
$$True \wedge \overleftarrow{I} < 0 \wedge I = -\overleftarrow{I} \Rightarrow I \geq 0 \wedge (I = \overleftarrow{I} \vee I = -\overleftarrow{I})$$
$$True \wedge \sim\!\overleftarrow{I} < 0 \Rightarrow True$$
$$True \wedge \sim\!\overleftarrow{I} < 0 \wedge I = \overleftarrow{I} \Rightarrow I \geq 0 \wedge (I = \overleftarrow{I} \vee I = -\overleftarrow{I})$$

Proofs are again omitted. Note that the full details of a diagram like figure 12(a) (in particular the post-condition of the empty statement) might well be discovered only as a result of attempting to justify the refinement.

Refinement by Repetition

We turn to the refinement of the second component of the sequence, the specification of figure 13.

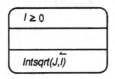

figure 13

We intend to use the method of successive approximations to find J. For the purpose of refining the specification, it is in principle necessary to know only the following facts about the algorithm:

- a range of values is to be searched for the desired value of J;
- this range is to be decreased in some way by each iteration;
- the repetition is to terminate when the range has length 1;
- at termination the lower limit of the range has the desired value.

One can envisage a variety of ways in which these facts could be established (not excluding the examination of a known algorithm): we are not however concerned with that question here. Once established, they may be formalised as the following loop properties (in which the range limits are called Low and Up):

Invariant:	$Low^2 \le I < Up^2$
Terminating condition:	$Up = Low + 1$
Variant:	$Up - Low$

The invariant must first be established. We omit the reasoning which would lead to refining figure 13 by sequence to figure 14.

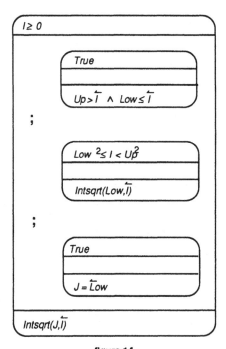

figure 14

Now the loop properties given above lead directly to figure 15(a) as a refinement by repetition of the second component of the sequence.

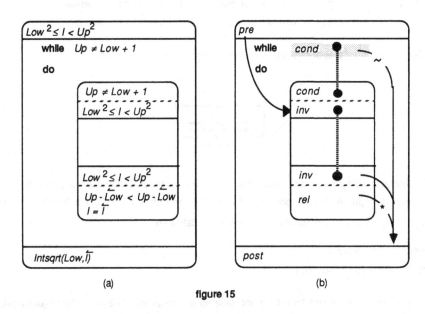

(a)   (b)

figure 15

Figure 15(b) shows the correctness conditions for a refinement by repetition. As this diagram is a direct translation of the rule given in [Jones] it is not explained in detail here. The identifiers *inv* and *rel* have been placed appropriately on the diagram to aid identification with the original rule. "*" inserted in an arrow signifies reflexive closure of the corresponding condition. The dotted lines connecting the different occurrences of the invariant and the loop condition signify syntactic identity.

The correctness conditions for figure 15(a) can now be read off from figure 15(b). They are:

$$Low^2 \le I < Up^2 \Rightarrow Low^2 \le I < Up^2$$
$$\sim(Up \ne Low + 1) \wedge Low^2 \le I < Up^2 \wedge Up - Low \le \overleftarrow{Up} - \overleftarrow{Low} \wedge I = \overleftarrow{I} \Rightarrow Intsqrt(Low, \overleftarrow{I})$$

and in addition it must be confirmed that the relation $Up - Low \le \overleftarrow{Up} - \overleftarrow{Low} \wedge I = \overleftarrow{I}$ is well-founded. The proofs of these conditions are omitted.

6. Formal Semantics of the Box Notation[2]

We represent both programs and specifications as relations on states. Informally, we can think of the meaning of a program as being given by the set of before-after state pairs that characterise its behaviour. This motivates the definitions of the program instructions:

---

[2]§6 and the first part of §7 are adapted from [Hoare].

1. $[\![\,\textbf{donothing}\,]\!]$ $\quad= I$

2. $[\![\,v := E\,]\!]$ $\qquad = \{s,t \mid t = s[v\backslash s(E)]\}$

I denotes the identity relation. For the sake of clarity, we have omitted the semantic function. In the second definition, s(E) denotes the result of evaluating the expression E in state s.

We now wish to represent a specification, for example figure 16, as a relation.

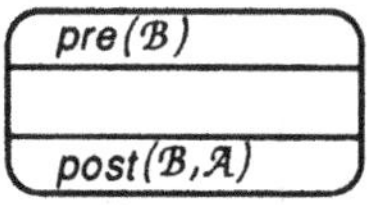

figure 16

We will sometimes write $pre(\mathcal{B})$ and $post(\mathcal{B},\mathcal{A})$ as in figure 16 in order to emphasise that the state variables $\mathcal{B}$ and $\mathcal{A}$ (representing, respectively, the before- and after-states) occur free in the predicates *pre* and *post*. The relations corresponding to these predicates are

$[\![pre(\mathcal{B})]\!] = \{s \mid pre(s)\}$
$[\![post(\mathcal{B},\mathcal{A})]\!] = \{s,t \mid post(s,t)\}$

From now on diagrams like figure 16 will be abbreviated to (*pre,post*). The meaning of (*pre,post*) can be thought of as being given by the set of before-after state pairs that the specification allows. This motivates the definition of a specification as a pair of relations, where the pairing operator for relations is defined as follows[3,4]:

3. $[\![(pre,post)]\!] = ([\![pre]\!],[\![post]\!]) = \overline{[\![pre]\!]} \triangleleft U \cup [\![post]\!]$

Note that the complement of the pre-condition is taken relative to a universe of states which includes $\perp$. Accordingly, every program is specified to be strict, and if its pre-condition is not satisfied it may do anything, even diverge, without failing to satisfy its specification.

Definition 3 leads immediately to the following useful lemma:

Lemma 1: If $P' \subseteq P$ and $R \subseteq \overline{P'} \triangleleft U \cup R'$ then $(P,R) \subseteq (P',R')$

Finally we give the definitions of the compositional operators for both programs and specifications:

4. $[\![Q_1 ; Q_2]\!] = [\![Q_1]\!] ; [\![Q_2]\!]$

---

[3]$P \triangleleft R = \{s,t \mid Ps \wedge sRt\}$
[4]U is used in this paper to denote both the universal relation (as here) and the universal set.

The semicolon on the LHS is an operator in the programming language, that on the RHS is the composition operator on relations.

5.　$[\![\text{If } B \text{ then } Q_t \text{ else } Q_e]\!] = [\![B]\!] \triangleleft U \cap [\![Q_t]\!] \ \cup \ \overline{[\![B]\!]} \triangleleft U \cap Q_e$

6.　$[\![\text{while } B \text{ do } Q]\!] = \bigcap_{n \geq 0} F^n (U)$　　　　where $F(X) = ([\![B]\!] \triangleleft U \cap ([\![Q]\!];X)) \cup \overline{[\![B]\!]} \triangleleft U \cap I$

(The last definition uses the greatest fixed point of a descending chain of relations in preference to the least fixed point of the ascending chain. This is because the least fixed point of a function on total relations is not necessarily total. Further details are in [Hoare]).

7.　Refinement

The relation of refinement denoted in the box notation as in figure 3 is defined to be $[\![Q]\!] \subseteq [\![S]\!]$. This relation has two possible meanings, depending on whether Q is a program or a specification:

Q is a program: $[\![Q]\!] \subseteq [\![S]\!]$ means that Q meets the specification S (because everything Q does satisfies S).

Q is a specification: $[\![Q]\!] \subseteq [\![S]\!]$ means that Q is at least as strong as S (that is, no less robust and no more underdetermined). Every program that satisfies Q also satisfies S, by the transitivity of $\subseteq$.

Compositionality

[Jones87] points out that the criterion of compositionality requires that each of the compositional operators should be monotone in the refinement relation. We now show that the definitions given satisfy this requirement.

The requirement for sequential composition is

$$\frac{[\![Q_i]\!] \subseteq [\![S_i]\!] \quad 1 \leq i \leq k}{[\![Q_1 ;...;Q_k]\!] \ \subseteq \ [\![S_1 ;...;S_k]\!]}$$

Proof:　Immediate, from the monotonicity of relational composition with respect to set inclusion.

□

The requirement for selection is

$$\frac{[\![Q_t]\!] \subseteq [\![S_t]\!] \quad [\![Q_e]\!] \subseteq [\![S_e]\!]}{[\![\text{If } B \text{ then } Q_t \text{ else } Q_e]\!] \ \subseteq \ [\![\text{If } B \text{ then } S_t \text{ else } S_e]\!]}$$

Proof:　$[\![\text{If } B \text{ then } Q_t \text{ else } Q_e]\!] = [\![B]\!] \triangleleft U \cap [\![Q_t]\!] \ \cup \ \overline{[\![B]\!]} \triangleleft U \cap [\![Q_e]\!]$

　　　　　　$\subseteq [\![B]\!] \triangleleft U \cap [\![S_t]\!] \ \cup \ \overline{[\![B]\!]} \triangleleft U \cap [\![S_e]\!]$　　　(by assumption)

$$= [\![\text{If B then } S_t \text{ else } S_e]\!]$$

□

The requirement for repetition is

$$\frac{[\![Q]\!] \subseteq [\![S]\!]}{[\![\textbf{while B do } Q]\!] \subseteq [\![\textbf{while B do } S]\!]}$$

Proof: Let $\quad F_Q(X) = (B \triangleleft U \cap ([\![Q]\!];X)) \cup \overline{B} \triangleleft U \cap I$

$\quad\quad\quad\quad F_S(X) = (B \triangleleft U \cap ([\![S]\!];X)) \cup \overline{B} \triangleleft U \cap I$

We show by fixpoint induction that $F_Q^i(U) \subseteq F_S^i(U)$ for $i \geq 0$, from which the desired result follows immediately.

Base: $\quad\quad F_Q^0(U) = U \subseteq U = F_S^0(U)$

Induction: $\quad F_Q^{i+1}(U) = B \triangleleft U \cap ([\![Q]\!];F_Q^i(U)) \cup \overline{B} \triangleleft U \cap I$

$\quad\quad\quad\quad\quad\quad\quad \subseteq B \triangleleft U \cap ([\![S]\!];F_S^i(U)) \cup \overline{B} \triangleleft U \cap I$

(by assumption and inductive hypothesis)

$\quad\quad\quad\quad\quad\quad = F_S^{i+1}(U)$

□

Rules for Refinement

The rules for program refinement, which have been presented so far in the box notation, can also be formulated in predicate calculus. In this form they can be justified with respect to the semantics of the notation given in §6. We now summarise the predicate calculus forms of the refinement rules, together with an indication for some of the constructs, of how a formal justification can be provided. We begin with the two simple statements:

1. Empty statement

Rule:

$$\frac{}{[\![\textbf{donothing }]\!] \subseteq [\![(\mathit{True}, \mathcal{A} = \mathcal{B})]\!]}$$

Proof: $\quad [\![\textbf{donothing }]\!] = I \subseteq \overline{U} \triangleleft U \cup I$

Box notation:

$$\boxed{\begin{array}{l} \mathit{True} \\ \hline \textbf{donothing} \\ \hline \mathcal{A} = \mathcal{B} \end{array}}$$

2. Assignment statement

Rule:

$$\frac{}{[\![x := E]\!] \subseteq [\![(\mathit{True}, \mathcal{A} = \mathcal{B}[x \backslash s(E)])]\!]}$$

Proof: Immediate, from the definition of assignment.

Box notation:

$$\boxed{\begin{array}{c} \textit{True} \\ \hline x := E \\ \hline \mathcal{A} \; = \; \mathcal{B}[x \backslash \mathcal{B}(E)] \end{array}}$$

Notes on the rules for statement correctness:

- The state variables $\mathcal{A}$ and $\mathcal{B}$ need not be used in actual practice once the nature of the pre- and post-conditions has been made clear. The hook notation, as used above, is much less clumsy.

- The pre-condition can be strengthened arbitrarily without affecting the correctness of a statement box. This can be useful if it is desired to make use of some stronger condition in achieving the desired post-condition. Since the pre-condition refers to the state only via free occurrences of the variable $\mathcal{B}$ its value is unaffected by execution of the statement and it can therefore appear in the post-condition box to be used in conjunction with the post-condition.

We now give proof rules for refinement into specifications and compositions of specifications. It will be noticed that the specifications required in the rule conclusions have been kept in as simple a form as possible. The resulting development style supports the integration of formal and operational reasoning proposed in §8. The rules have the added advantage that they can be represented very clearly in the box notation.

3. Specification

The rule that justifies refinement by a specification is

$$\frac{[\![pre_o]\!] \subseteq [\![pre_i]\!] \qquad [\![pre_o]\!] \lhd \cup \cap [\![post_i]\!] \subseteq [\![post_o]\!]}{[\![(pre_i, post_i)]\!] \; \subseteq \; [\![(pre_o, post_o)]\!]}$$

Proof: Immediate, from the hypotheses and Lemma 1.

The hypotheses correspond to the predicates

$$pre_o(\mathcal{B}) \Rightarrow pre_i(\mathcal{B})$$
$$pre_o(\mathcal{B}) \wedge post_i(\mathcal{B}, \mathcal{A}) \Rightarrow post_o(\mathcal{B}, \mathcal{A})$$

Figure 17 shows these proof obligations translated into the box notation.

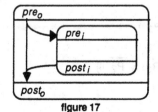

figure 17

4. Sequence

The rule that justifies refinement by sequence is

$$\frac{hyp(k)}{[\![(pre_1,post_1);...;(pre_k,post_k)]\!] \subseteq [\![(pre,post)]\!]}$$

where $hyp(k) \Leftrightarrow$

let $P = [\![pre]\!]$, $R = [\![post]\!]$, $P_i = [\![pre_i]\!]$, $R_i = [\![post_i]\!]$,

$T_0 = P$, $S_0 = P \lhd I$, $S_k = R$, $T_k = U$:

There exist $T_1, S_1, ..., T_{k-1}, S_{k-1}$ such that[5]

$\forall i \in \{1,..,k\}.(T_{i-1} \subseteq P_i \wedge S_{i-1};R_i \subseteq S_i \wedge T_{i-1} \uparrow R_i \subseteq T_i)$

Note that for the case $k = 1$ this rules simplifies to the specification refinement rule given above.

Proof: The rule is proved for the case $k = 2$; the rule for arbitrary k follows directly from the associativity of the composition operator.

$hyp(2) \quad \Leftrightarrow \quad \exists T_1, S_1.(P \subseteq P_1 \wedge (P \lhd I);R_1 \subseteq S_1 \wedge P \uparrow R_1 \subseteq T_1$

$\wedge \; T_1 \subseteq P_2 \wedge S_1;R_2 \subseteq R \wedge T_1 \uparrow R_2 \subseteq U)$

$\Leftrightarrow \quad P \subseteq P_1 \wedge \exists T,S.(P \lhd R_1 \subseteq S \wedge P \uparrow R_1 \subseteq T \subseteq P_2 \wedge S;R_2 \subseteq R)$

Hence the rule to be proved is

$$\frac{P \subseteq P_1 \quad, \; \exists T,S.(P \lhd R_1 \subseteq S \wedge P \uparrow R_1 \subseteq T \subseteq P_2 \wedge S;R_2 \subseteq R)}{(P_1,R_1) ; (P_2,R_2) \subseteq (P,R)}$$

Now by theorem A1 (for proof see appendix),

$(P_1,R_1) ; (P_2,R_2) = (P_1 \cap \overline{P_2 \uparrow \breve{R}_1} , R_1 ; R_2)$

so by Lemma 1 it is sufficient to prove

(1) $P \subseteq P_1 \cap \overline{P_2 \uparrow R_1}$

and (2) $R_1 ; R_2 \subseteq \overline{P \lhd U} \cup R$

Proof of (1): We show that $P \subseteq \overline{P_2 \uparrow \breve{R}_1}$, which together with the hypothesis $P \subseteq P_1$ gives

(1) immediately.

$P \uparrow R_1 \subseteq P_2$ \qquad\qquad\qquad (hypothesis)

$(\exists s.s \in P \wedge s R_1 t) \Rightarrow P_2 t$

$s \in P \quad \Rightarrow \forall t(\sim s R_1 t \vee P_2 t)$

$\Rightarrow \sim \exists t(s R_1 t \wedge \overline{P_2} \; t)$

$\Rightarrow s \in \{u \mid \sim \exists t (t \breve{R}_1 u \wedge \overline{P_2} \; t)\}$

---

[5] $P \uparrow R = \{ t \mid \exists s.Ps \wedge sRt\}$

hence $P \subseteq \overline{P_2 \mathbin{\raisebox{.5pt}{$\upharpoonright$}} \breve{R}_1}$

Proof of (2):

$S;R_2 \subseteq R$ (hypothesis)

$r\,S\,s \Rightarrow s\,\overline{R_2}\,t \lor r R t$

$P \triangleleft R_1 \subseteq S$ (hypothesis)

$P r \land r R_1 s \Rightarrow r\,S\,s \Rightarrow s\,\overline{R_2}\,t \lor r R t$

$\sim(\forall s.\, r\,\overline{R_1}\,s \lor s\,\overline{R_2}\,t) \Rightarrow \overline{P}\,r \lor r R t$

$R_1;R_2 \subseteq \overline{P \triangleleft U} \cup R$

$\square$

The hypotheses correspond to the predicates

$pre(\mathcal{B}) \Rightarrow pre_1(\mathcal{B})$

$\exists I.(\;\; pre(\mathcal{B}) \land post_1(\mathcal{B},I) \rightarrow mid(\mathcal{B},I)$

$mid(\mathcal{B},I) \rightarrow pre_2(I)$

$mid(\mathcal{B},I) \land post_2(I,\mathcal{A}) \rightarrow post(\mathcal{B},\mathcal{A})\;\;\;)$

Figure 10(b) shows these proof obligations translated into the box notation.

5. Selection

The rule that justifies refinement by selection is

$$[\![pre]\!] \cap [\![cond]\!] \subseteq [\![pre_t]\!] \quad [\![pre]\!] \cap \overline{[\![cond]\!]} \subseteq [\![pre_e]\!]$$

$$([\![pre]\!] \cap [\![cond]\!]) \triangleleft U \cap [\![post_t]\!] \subseteq [\![post]\!]$$

$$([\![pre]\!] \cap \overline{[\![cond]\!]}) \triangleleft U \cap [\![post_e]\!] \subseteq [\![post]\!]$$

$$[\![\text{If } cond \text{ then } (pre_t,post_t) \text{ else } (pre_e,post_e)]\!] \;\subseteq\; [\![(pre,post)]\!]$$

Proof: Let $P = [\![pre]\!]$, $R = [\![post]\!]$, $B = [\![cond]\!]$, $P_t = [\![pre_t]\!]$, $R_t = [\![post_t]\!]$, $P_e = [\![pre_e]\!]$, and $R_e = [\![post_e]\!]$.

From the definition of **If...then...else,**

$[\![\text{If } cond \text{ then } (pre_t,post_t) \text{ else } (pre_e,post_e)]\!] = (B \triangleleft U \cap (P_t,R_t)) \cup (\overline{B} \triangleleft U \cap (P_e,R_e))$

which by Theorem A2 (Appendix) is

$(((\overline{B} \cup P_t) \cap (B \cup P_e)), ((B \triangleleft U \cap R_t) \cup (\overline{B} \triangleleft U \cap R_e)))$

so by Lemma 1 it is sufficient to show that

(1) $P \subseteq (\overline{B} \cup P_t) \cap (B \cup P_e)$

and   (2) $(B \triangleleft U \cap R_t) \cup (\overline{B} \triangleleft U \cap R_e) \subseteq \overline{P \triangleleft U} \cup R$

Proof of (1):
$$P \subseteq (\overline{B} \cup P_t)$$ (hypothesis)

$$P \subseteq (B \cup P_e)$$ (hypothesis)

and (1) follows immediately.

Proof of (2): We show that $B \lhd U \cap R_t \subseteq \overline{P} \lhd U \cup R$. A similar argument shows that $\overline{B} \lhd U \cap R_e$ $\subseteq \overline{P} \lhd U \cup R$, and (2) follows immediately.

$$(P \cap B) \lhd U \cap R_t \subseteq R$$ (hypothesis)

$$B \lhd U \cap R_t \subseteq \overline{P \lhd U} \cup R$$

$$= \overline{P} \lhd U \cup R$$

□

The hypotheses of the selection rule correspond to the predicates

$$pre(\mathcal{B}) \;\wedge\; cond(\mathcal{B}) \;\Rightarrow\; pre_t(\mathcal{B})$$
$$pre(\mathcal{B}) \;\wedge\; {\sim}cond(\mathcal{B}) \;\Rightarrow\; pre_e(\mathcal{B})$$
$$pre(\mathcal{B}) \;\wedge\; cond(\mathcal{B}) \;\wedge\; post_t(\mathcal{B},\mathcal{A}) \;\Rightarrow\; post(\mathcal{B},\mathcal{A})$$
$$pre(\mathcal{B}) \;\wedge\; {\sim}cond(\mathcal{B}) \;\wedge\; post_e(\mathcal{B},\mathcal{A}) \;\Rightarrow\; post(\mathcal{B},\mathcal{A})$$

Figure 12(b) shows these proof obligations translated into the box notation.

6. Repetition

The rule that justifies refinement by repetition is[6]

$$\frac{[\![pre]\!] \subseteq [\![inv]\!] \qquad [\![rel^*]\!] \rhd (\,\overline{[\![cond]\!]} \cap [\![inv]\!]) \subseteq [\![post]\!] \qquad rel \text{ well-founded}}{[\![\text{while } cond \text{ do } (cond \wedge inv \,,\, inv \wedge rel)]\!] \subseteq [\![(pre,post)]\!]}$$

The proof of this rule is omitted.

The hypotheses correspond to the predicates

$$pre(\mathcal{B}) \;\Rightarrow\; inv(\mathcal{B})$$
$${\sim}cond(\mathcal{A}) \;\wedge\; inv(\mathcal{A}) \;\wedge\; rel^*(\mathcal{B},\mathcal{A}) \;\Rightarrow\; post(\mathcal{B},\mathcal{A})$$

Figure 14(b) shows these proof obligations translated into the box notation.

8.   Discussion

The development method outlined in this paper requires enhancement to make it suitable for a programming course. A minimum list of requirements includes facilities to handle non-numeric data types within the notation, a more expressive specification language than first-order logic, and not least a

---

[6] $R \rhd P = \{s,t \mid sRt \wedge Pt\}$

mechanical support system to make feasible the production of non-trivial specifications and programs in the box notation. In the following discussion, however, we neglect these issues in order to provide a justification of the technical basis of the method.

The approach described is motivated by the belief that the logical basis of imperative programming can be taught from the start. Constructive specification (specifically VDM) is proposed as the method of choice to complement procedural stepwise refinement. Used in this way, constructive specification can compensate for the main deficiency of conventional stepwise refinement, which is that while it is helpful in postulating solutions to programming problems, it gives no help in evaluating them. A formal method can provide such help, if it fulfils two requirements.

First, it should not force the programmer to use a refinement calculus. The essence of a refinement calculus is that refinement steps are formulated in the specification language. The disadvantage of this, especially at an elementary level, is that it makes no use of the programmer's operational intuition, which will usually be much better-developed than the corresponding formal skills. In such a case, it is better to permit the student to postulate a refinement from operational intuition and then to check it using a formal method. The proof rules and notation presented here are designed to accommodate this approach. Later, when the student has become more confident in using formal techniques, it will be possible to adopt a refinement calculus without changing notation. For example, the weakest prespecification calculus of [Hoare] fits in the same theoretical framework as the style proposed here.

The second requirement is that the formal method should place specifications and programs within the same semantic framework, and give the same meaning to the standard compositional operators (sequence, selection and repetition) when applied to either. This allows specifications, viewed as unimplemented programs, to be embedded in a program under development, and progressively replaced, initially by compositions of other specifications, and eventually by single program instructions. Provided that each replacement is provably correct with respect to an appropriately defined refinement relation, then the whole process cannot change the meaning from that of the original specification.

This requirement is fulfilled by systems[7] (like VDM) in which the triple {P}S{Q} is seen as an assertion that S is (in some sense) an implemention of the specification defined by P and Q. The difference in emphasis from the classical view leads to the style of program construction advocated here. This idea has been evolving within the framework of weakest precondition semantics for ten years. (A brief survey of its history is given in [Morgan]). It has also long been present in VDM ([Jones86], and more explicitly [Jones87]), but without adequate exploitation. It is hoped that the more accessible version presented here will bring it to the attention of a wider audience.

9.   Acknowledgements

Alan Hamilton and Lynn Marshall made helpful comments on earlier drafts of this paper, and Muffy

---

[7]"sat -based systems" ([de Roever])

Thomas gave useful advice on points of presentation. I am especially grateful to Simon Jones for discussions on §§6 and 7.

10. References

[de Roever] W.P.de Roever, *Different Styles of Compositional Proof Systems*, FACS-FACTS (Newsletter of the BCS Formal Aspects of Computing Science SIG), Vol. 9, No, 2 (July 1987), pp. 137 - 173.

[Dijkstra] E.W.Dijkstra, *A Discipline of Programming,* Prentice-Hall, Englewood Cliffs, N.J.(1976).

[Hayes] I.Hayes (ed), *Specification Case Studies*, Prentice-Hall (1987).

[Hoare] C.A.R.Hoare & He Jifeng, *The Weakest Prespecification*, Fundamenta Informaticae Vol. IX, No. 1 (1986) pp. 51-84 and Vol. IX, No. 2, (1986), pp. 217-252.

[Jones86] C.B.Jones, *Systematic Software Development using VDM,* Prentice-Hall (1986).

[Jones87] C.B.Jones, *VDM Proof Obligations and their Justification,* in *VDM '87. VDM - A Formal Method at Work*, Springer-Verlag Lecture Notes in Computer Science Vol. 252 (1987), pp. 260-286 .

[Morgan] C.Morgan & K.Robinson, *Specification Statements and Refinement* (1987).

Appendix

Theorem A1

$$(P_1,R_1) ; (P_2,R_2) = (P_1 \cap \overline{\overline{P_2} \, 1 \, \overset{\smile}{R_1}} \, , R_1 ; R_2)$$

Proof:

$$
\begin{aligned}
\text{LHS} \;=\;& (\,\overline{P_1}\,\sphericalangle U \cup R_1); (\,\overline{P_2}\,\sphericalangle U \cup R_2) \\
=\;& \overline{P_1}\,\sphericalangle U; (\,\overline{P_2}\,\sphericalangle U \cup R_2) \cup R_1; (\,\overline{P_2}\,\sphericalangle U) \cup R_1 ; R_2 \\
=\;& \overline{P_1}\,\sphericalangle U \cup R_1; (\,\overline{P_2}\,\sphericalangle U) \cup R_1 ; R_2 \\
& \qquad\qquad \text{(because } \overline{P_2}\,\sphericalangle U \text{ contains at least the pair } (\bot,U)) \\
=\;& \overline{P_1}\,\sphericalangle U \cup (\,\overline{P_2}\,1\overset{\smile}{R_1})\sphericalangle U \cup R_1 ; R_2 \\
=\;& (\,\overline{P_1} \cup \overline{P_2}\,1\overset{\smile}{R_1})\sphericalangle U \cup R_1 ; R \\
=\;& \text{RHS}
\end{aligned}
$$

$\square$

Theorem A2

$$B\sphericalangle U \cap (P_t,R_t) \cup \overline{B}\,\sphericalangle U \cap (P_e,R_e) = ((\,\overline{B}\,\cup P_t) \cap (B \cup P_e) \,, (B\sphericalangle U \cap R_t) \cup (\,\overline{B}\,\sphericalangle U \cap R_e))$$

Proof:

$$
\begin{aligned}
\text{LHS} \;=\;& (B\sphericalangle U \cap (\,\overline{P_t}\,\sphericalangle U \cup R_t)) \cup (\,\overline{B}\,\sphericalangle U (\,\overline{P_e}\,\sphericalangle U \cup R_e)) \\
=\;& (B \cap \overline{P_t}\,)\sphericalangle U \cup (B\sphericalangle U \cap R_t) \cup (\,\overline{B}\,\cap \overline{P_e}\,)\sphericalangle U \cup (\,\overline{B}\,\sphericalangle U \cap R_e)
\end{aligned}
$$

Understanding an informal description: Office Documents Architecture, an ISO standard

Andrzej Borzyszkowski
Stefan Sokołowski

Project MetaSoft[1]

Introduction

This report has come to being while we were reading the Draft ISO Standard 8613, Parts 1-6: *Office Documents Architecture and interchange format* [ODA]. The precise nature of that undertaking may be of no concern for the Reader but we think it is typical of many projects arising in an industrial environment, and as such it may serve to illustrate some ways of filling the gap between the VDM theory and the industrial practice. ODA is a large project seeking to fulfill conflicting demands of many partners. We believe many discussions and negotiations must have preceded setting up the final document. Without taking part in these activities [ODA] is rather difficult to understand. The authors of ODA apparently lacked means to communicate ideas: the description suffers from many ambiguities, loopholes, imprecise statements and unstructured presentation.

Some of these drawbacks could have been easily prevented or at least detected had they decided in the first place to use VDM in one or another available version. Although ODA is not a software project it may be conveniently viewed as a kind of a language, and VDM techniques may be applied where they seem unapplicable at first sight. We hope that using the well-established VDM methods in an unorthodox field may prove interesting to the VDM community.

We have tried to formalize ODA in the MetaSoft dialect of the VDM. The differences between MetaSoft and the other lines of VDM are not as far reaching as to require explanations for understanding this report, so just do not worry about them. In emergency respective references are [BJ] for VDM and [Bli] for MetaSoft. The notations appearing in this report are summarized in

---

[1]Polish Academy of Sciences, Institute of Computer Science, Group for the Mathematical Methods of Programming, c/o Gdańsk Division of the PAS, ul. Jaśkowa Dolina 31, P.O.Box 562, 80–252 Gdańsk, POLAND

$$= \quad \overline{((B \cap \overline{P_t}) \cup (B \cap \overline{P_e}), (B \triangleleft U \cap R_t) \cup (\overline{B} \triangleleft U \cap R_e))}$$

$$= \quad \text{RHS}$$

$\square$

Section 1. In our formalization attempt we have gone as far as could have been safely done on the basis of the existing written documentation of ODA.

Credits for this research are due to Andrzej Blikle, a coauthor of [BSB], upon which the current report is based, for his contribution and his encouragement.

1 Used notations

The main type constructors are:

- functions: $A \to B$ is the type of total functions from A to B; function application is denoted by the dot:

  $f.a$ f applied to a

- Cartesian product: $A_1 \times \ldots \times A_n$ is the type of Cartesian n-tuples $\langle a_1, \ldots, a_n \rangle$ where $a_i \in A_i$ for $i = 1, \ldots, n$; consistently, $\langle \rangle$ denotes the 0-tuple; tuples are treated as partial functions of integer arguments:

$$\langle a_1, \ldots, a_n \rangle.i = \begin{cases} a_i & \text{if } 1 \leq i \leq n \\ undefined \text{ otherwise} \end{cases}$$

- union: $A \mid B$ consists of all $a \in A$ and all $b \in B$;

- sequences: A^+ is the type of all non-empty sequences, i.e. Cartesian n-tuples for $n = 1, 2, \ldots$;

  $$A^+ = A \mid A \times A \mid A \times A \times A \mid \ldots$$

  every tuple has a length:

  $length : A^+ \to Nat$ (Nat – natural numbers)
  $length.\langle a_1, \ldots, a_n \rangle = n$

- powerset: A-SET is the type of all (finite or infinite) subsets of A;

- type comprehension: $\{a : A \mid F.a\}$ is the type of all a from A such that the predicate F is true of a;

- range: $k..\ell$, where k and ℓ are integer numbers, is the type of all integers between (inclusively) k and ℓ:

  $$k..\ell = \{n : Int \mid k \leq n \leq \ell\}$$

- finite type: $\{a_1, \ldots, a_n\}$ is the type that consists of precisely the named elements a_1 through a_n, for some $n \geq 0$.

When introducing a new type name Tn the following notations are used:

$tn : Tn = TypeExpr$

or

$tn : Tn :: TypeExpr$

The former means that the elements of the new type denoted by Tn are the elements of the type denoted by $TypeExpr$. The latter means that the elements of the type denoted by $TypeExpr$ are tagged with Tn to make elements of the type denoted by Tn:

$Tn = \{\text{"}Tn\text{"}\} \times TypeExpr$

The latter type definition implies the existence of the function

$out : Tn \rightarrow TypeExpr$

$out.\langle \text{"}Tn\text{"}, x \rangle = x$

that removes the tag.

Recursion and mutual recursion are permissible in type definitions. The "tn :" that precedes the new type name Tn is optional and names the variables ranging over Tn.

When defining a new function f the following is the basic notation:

$f : A \rightarrow B$

$f.a = expr$

It is sometimes used with a more complicated lhs, for instance:

$f : A_1 \times A_2 \rightarrow B \rightarrow C$

$f.\langle a_1, a_2 \rangle.b = expr$

but this should be self-explanatory in every single case.

Recursion and mutual recursion are permissible in function definitions. When an argument is declared to be coming from a union type it may be tested using the CASES construct:

$f : A_1 \mid \ldots \mid A_n \rightarrow B$

$f.a = \text{CASES}$

$\qquad a \in A_1 \implies expr_1$

$\qquad \ldots$

$\qquad a \in A_n \implies expr_n$

$\quad \text{END}$

which is equivalent to

$$f : A_1 \mid \ldots \mid A_n \to B$$

$$f.a = \text{IF } a \in A_1 \text{ THEN } expr_1$$

$$\text{ELSE} \ldots \text{IF } a \in A_n \text{ THEN } expr_n$$

$$\text{ELSE } undefined$$

2 What is ODA supposed to be ?

This question does not find a direct answer in [ODA]. The definition given in [ODA, 1:0] (this is our way of referring to fragments of [ODA]; this means Part 1 Sec.0) leaves it open whether the main concern is pieces of computer software, such as special purpose editors and word processors; or pieces of hardware, such as sheets of paper and diskettes; or maybe an arrangement of desks in an office. It only states that the purpose of the project is "to facilitate the interchange of office documents".

Most of the description is however devoted to defining a class of objects that deserve to be called "ODA documents" in terms of their logical structure and of their layout. For instance, [ODA, 2:6.1] characterizes documents as made of "chapters, appendices, headings, paragraphs, footnotes and figures" which is "the logical view" of a document; and also as made of "pages and areas within pages" which is "the layout view" of a document.

Although this is not stated explicitly in the description, ODA is therefore a definition of a language in which office documents may be written. ODA is neither a programming language nor a piece of software in any sense of the term, although a computer support to setting up and updating ODA documents is certainly feasible. The computer aspect of ODA is out of our concern at this stage.

In its final form, a *specific* ODA document, where "specific" is a technical term of ODA, is a sequence of pages, each page being a distribution of colored pixels in a rectangle of predefined dimensions. An ODA specific document is fully defined by its *logical* and *layout* structures, which are two different points of view on the same thing and must be compatible with each other. Both logical and layout structures are quite complex trees. Their definitions and their compatibility requirements are discussed in Sec. 4.

More interesting though are various unfinished forms of documents. For instance, one may deal with the logical structure of a document only, e.g. a book may be structured in chapters and sections but not yet in pages. Another unfinished form is a *generic* document which may be viewed as a blank form to be filled with a specific information. Specific and generic documents are interrelated by the relation of conformance of the former to the latter. In fact, a generic document also consists of logical and layout structures compatible with each other, thus the relation of conformance splits naturally in two relations. These issues are discussed in Sec. 5.

3 An outline of an algebraic model for ODA

ODA documents may be very complex objects. In order to describe them together with the rules for their creation and processing, the authors of [ODA] define auxiliary concepts such as specific document, generic document, specific logical structure, specific layout structure, generic logical structure and many others. We are going to describe these concepts in the "backwards" order: starting from the finished documents that leave the office, back to earlier stages of document preparation. This may be viewed as a sequence of algebras, each homomorphically mapped into a next one, until a final product is ready. This stratification of ODA's technical terms has been our first step towards understanding.

In the last resort ODA documents are simply printouts. They are called *specific documents* and are defined as non-empty sequences of pages, each page being an arrangements of pixels of different colors within a rectangle of predefined dimensions (see [ODA, 2:6.1]):

(1) $Spec\text{-}doc$ $=$ $Page^+$

(2) $Page$ $=$ $1..vertical \times 1..horizontal \rightarrow Color$

(3) $Color$ $=$ $\{White, \ldots, Black\}$

Producing and processing documents may be activities of people at different levels of hierarchies (not just different people). At some levels, instead of producing a specific document one may wish to produce a pattern (a type) of a document, thus defining a set of documents which satisfy this pattern. In ODA this corresponds to a *generic document* which is a set of specific documents (see [ODA, 2:6.3 and 2:7.4]):

(4) $Gen\text{-}doc = Spec\text{-}doc$ –SET

Actually, we doubt whether the authors of ODA have thought of generic documents as sets, the term "pattern" would probably better fit their taste. Anyway, they have not explicitly related specific to generic documents by set membership or, if you like, by conformance to a pattern:

(5) $doc\text{-}conf : Spec\text{-}doc \times Gen\text{-}doc \rightarrow Bool$

   $doc\text{-}conf.\langle sd, gd \rangle = (sd \in gd)$

The considerations of [ODA] focus on documents encoded by sequences of characters where among the usual symbols such as letters, digits, punctuation marks, etc. also occur special symbols denoting end-of-lines, end-of pages, font-changes etc. We understand this as the decision of the ODA's authors to introduce an auxiliary domain

(6) $Coded\text{-}form = Char^+$

along with a conversion function

(7)   *printer* : *Coded-form* → *Spec-doc*

that serves to visualize the documents encoded as sequences of characters. In the current paper we omit the discussion of printer's definition.

The specific and generic documents will be set up or processed using descriptions which are the main focus of ODA. We call them *specific structures*, i.e. the structures that describe specific documents, and *generic structures*, i.e. the structures that describe generic documents. Along with these domains,

ss : *Spec-str* = ...

gs : *Gen-str* = ...

which we define later, we have to define interpretation functions:

(8)   *spec-interp* : *Spec-str* → *Spec-doc*

(9)   *gen-interp* : *Gen-str* → *Gen-doc*

and a predicate of structural conformance:

(10)   *str-conf* : *Spec-str* × *Gen-str* → *Bool*

Now, the interpretation functions have also to "translate" conformance between *Spec-str* and *Gen-str* to conformance between *Spec-doc* and *Gen-doc*:

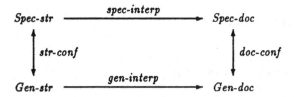

In other words, the following equality has to hold:

(11)   *doc-conf*.⟨*spec-interp.ss,gen-interp.gs*⟩ = *str-conf*.⟨*ss,gs*⟩

From the discussion on coded forms it follows also that there is a function which maps specific structures into coded forms:

(12)   *coder* : *Spec-str* → *Coded-form*

which has the property that if we first code and then print a specific structure, then the result is the same as if we perform the interpretation:

$$spec\text{-}interp.ss = printer.(coder.ss)$$

i.e. the following diagram commutes

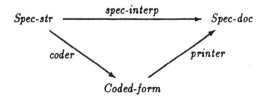

Hence the remaining task is to define *Spec-str*, *Gen-str* and functions *coder* (12), *gen-interp* (9) and *str-conf* (10) so that the property (11) could be proved. We do not claim we are prepared to give all these due definitions in this small report, we just show the way in the coming sections.

The small algebra from this section describes the end products the ODA processing is supposed to yield. We believe that beginning the description in this order contributes to clarity.

4   Specific ODA document as a pair of related trees

There is in [ODA] no definition of specific document. There is however a suggestive picture [ODA, Fig.4 in 2:9] that may reflect the intention of the design: a pair of trees with their "canopies" glued together; the trees correspond respectively to logical and layout structures which are two different ways of structuring the information in the leaves. Formally, this means:

(13) $Spec\text{-}str_0$ = $Spec\text{-}log\text{-}str \times Spec\text{-}layout\text{-}str$

(14) $wf\text{-}spec$: $Spec\text{-}str_0 \rightarrow Bool$

(15) $Spec\text{-}str$ = $\{\langle slg, slt \rangle \colon Spec\text{-}str_0 \mid wf\text{-}spec.\langle slg, slt \rangle\}$

What do these equations say? Equation (13) gives an upper estimate on *Spec-str*: it says that a specific structure is a pair of specific logical and specific layout structures. Equation (15) says that we will count among the specific structures only the pairs in which the two components match each other in the sense of the predicate *wf-spec* (well formed specific) introduced by (14).

By (15) the obligation to define *Spec-str* formulated in the end of Section 3 has been fulfilled, or rather replaced by the obligation to define *Spec-log-str*, *Spec-layout-str* and *wf-spec*, which is easier to do.

As the basis to define *Spec-log-str* we have taken [ODA, Fig. 12 in 2:11] (in general, while reading [ODA] we have learnt more from pictures than from accompanying text). We reprint the picture as Figure 1 and mechanically transcribe it to appropriate domain equations:

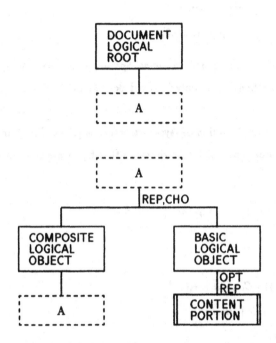

As explained in [ODA], REP means non-dummy repetition, CHO means choice, OPT means optional.

Figure 1: Document logical root

(16) $Spec\text{-}log\text{-}str$ :: A

    A $= (Comp\text{-}log\text{-}obj \mid Bas\text{-}log\text{-}obj)^+$

    $Comp\text{-}log\text{-}obj$ :: A

    $Bas\text{-}log\text{-}obj$ $= \{\langle\rangle\} \mid Content\text{-}portion^+$

    $Content\text{-}portion$ $= \ldots$ see [ODA, 2:9.3] $\ldots$

A content portion may be, for example, a piece of text or a picture.

Whoever likes meaningful names of domains and dislikes complex right-hand sides of equations, will certainly prefer the following equivalent set of equations (*A* is now *Log-obj-seq*, and there are two new domains: *Log-obj* and *Content*):

(17) $slg : Spec\text{-}log\text{-}str$ :: $Log\text{-}obj\text{-}seq$

    $los : Log\text{-}obj\text{-}seq$ $= Log\text{-}obj^+$

$$lo : Log\text{-}obj \quad = \quad Comp\text{-}log\text{-}obj \mid Bas\text{-}log\text{-}obj$$

$$Comp\text{-}log\text{-}obj \quad :: \quad Log\text{-}obj\text{-}seq$$

$$Bas\text{-}log\text{-}obj \quad = \quad \{\langle\rangle\} \mid Content$$

$$Content \quad = \quad Content\text{-}portion^+$$

$$Content\text{-}portion \quad = \quad \ldots \text{see [ODA, 2:9.3]} \ldots$$

With this we have fulfilled the obligation to define *Spec-log-str*, or rather replaced it by the obligation to define *Content-portion* — the only involved domain that has no equation of its own in (17).

The nearest [ODA] comes to a definition of layout structure is [ODA, Fig. 5 in 2:10] which we reprint as Figure 2. Domain equations which correspond to that figure are the following:

$$(18) \quad Spec\text{-}layout\text{-}str \quad :: \quad A$$

$$A \quad = \quad (Page\text{-}set \mid Comp\text{-}page \mid Bas\text{-}page)^+$$

$$Page\text{-}set \quad :: \quad A$$

$$Comp\text{-}page \quad :: \quad B$$

$$Bas\text{-}page \quad :: \quad \{\langle\rangle\} \mid Content\text{-}portion^+$$

$$B \quad = \quad (Frame \mid Block)^+$$

$$Frame \quad :: \quad B$$

$$Block \quad :: \quad \{\langle\rangle\} \mid Content\text{-}portion^+$$

$$Content\text{-}portion \quad = \quad \ldots \text{see [ODA, 2:9.3]} \ldots$$

It turns out, however, that the picture does not convey the whole truth about the specific layout structures. [ODA, 2:14.2.1] defines the *position* and the *dimension* attributes of frames and blocks and imposes the constraint that subordinate layout objects must be entirely within their superiors. To accommodate this, the definition (18) of *Spec-layout-str* has to be updated. We do it by first writing domain equations for *Spec-layout-str*$_0$, then defining the predicate *wf-slt* (well formed specific layout structure) and finally describing *Spec-layout-str* as the subset of *Spec-layout-str*$_0$ cut out by *wf-slt*. The domain equations are analogous to (18) with only a few alterations:

- the two attributes *Pos* and *Dim* have been added;

- we have taken the liberty to leave out *Bas-page* (basic page) which is redundant since every basic page is a block;

- we have introduced new domain names: *Bundle, Bundle-seq, Frame-block, Frame-block-seq*.

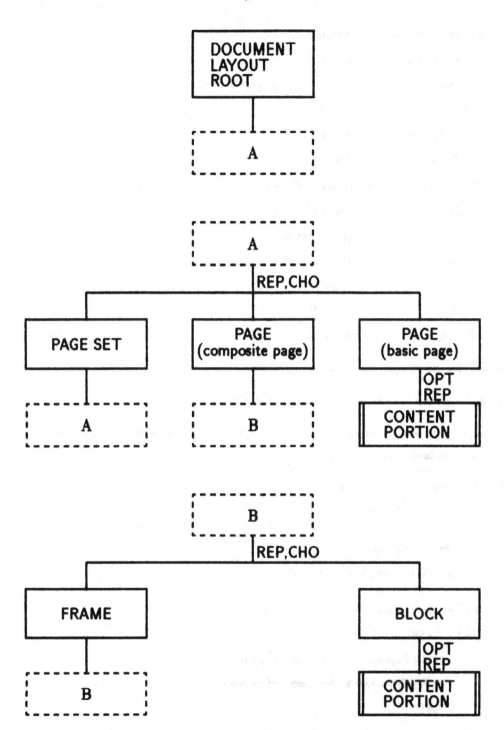

Figure 2: Document layout root

(19)　$slt : Spec\text{-}layout\text{-}str_0$　$::$　$Bundle\text{-}seq$

　　　$bs : Bundle\text{-}seq$　　$=$　$Bundle^+$

　　　　$b : Bundle$　　　$=$　$Page\text{-}set \mid (Comp\text{-}page \times Dim)$

　　$pgs : Page\text{-}set$　　　$::$　$Bundle\text{-}seq$

　　　$cp : Comp\text{-}page$　　$::$　$Frame\text{-}block\text{-}seq$

　$fbs : Frame\text{-}block\text{-}seq$　$=$　$Frame\text{-}block^+$

　　$fb : Frame\text{-}block$　　$=$　$(Frame \times Pos \times Dim) \mid (Block \times Pos \times Dim)$

　　　$fr : Frame$　　　$::$　$Frame\text{-}block\text{-}seq$

　　　$bl : Block$　　　　$::$　$\{\langle\rangle\} \mid Content$

　　　　　$Content$　　　$=$　$Content\text{-}portion^+$

　　　$Content\text{-}portion$　$=$　$\ldots$ see [ODA, 2:9.3] $\ldots$

　　　　$p : Pos$　　　$=$　$Nat \times Nat$

　　　　$d : Dim$　　　$=$　$Nat \times Nat$

Now we define the "proper" specific layout structure.

(20)　$Spec\text{-}layout\text{-}str = \{slt : Spec\text{-}layout\text{-}str_0 \mid wf\text{-}slt.slt\}$

And the predicate $wf\text{-}slt$ that cuts the domain $Spec\text{-}layout\text{-}str$ out of the bigger type $Spec\text{-}layout\text{-}str_0$ is recursively defined as follows:

(21)　$wf\text{-}slt : Spec\text{-}layout\text{-}str_0 \rightarrow Bool$

　　$wf\text{-}slt.slt = wf\text{-}bs.(out.slt)$

　　$wf\text{-}bs : Bundle\text{-}seq \rightarrow Bool$

　　$wf\text{-}bs.bs = (\forall i \in 1..length.bs)\ wf\text{-}b.(bs.i)$

　　$wf\text{-}b : Bundle \rightarrow Bool$

　　$wf\text{-}b.b = \text{CASES}$

　　　　　$b \in Page\text{-}set$　　　　$\implies$　$wf\text{-}pg\text{-}set.pc$

　　　　　$b \in Comp\text{-}page \times Dim$　$\implies$　$wf\text{-}cp\text{-}dim.pc$

　　　　END

　　$wf\text{-}pg\text{-}set : Page\text{-}set \rightarrow Bool$

　　$wf\text{-}pg\text{-}set.pgs = wf\text{-}bs.(out.pgs)$

$wf\text{-}cp\text{-}dim : Comp\text{-}page \times Dim \rightarrow Bool$

$wf\text{-}cp\text{-}dim.\langle cp, d \rangle = wf\text{-}fbs.\langle out.cp, d \rangle$

$wf\text{-}fbs : Frame\text{-}block\text{-}seq \times Dim \rightarrow Bool$

$wf\text{-}fbs.\langle fbs, d \rangle = (\forall i \in 1..length.fbs)\ wf\text{-}fb.\langle fbs.i, d \rangle$

$wf\text{-}fb : Frame\text{-}block \times Dim \rightarrow Bool$

$wf\text{-}fb.\langle fb, d \rangle = \text{CASES}$

$$fb \in Frame \times Pos \times Dim \implies wf\text{-}fm.\langle fb, d \rangle$$

$$fb \in Block \times Pos \times Dim \implies wf\text{-}bl.\langle fb, d \rangle$$

END

$wf\text{-}fm : (Frame \times Pos \times Dim) \times Dim \rightarrow Bool$

$wf\text{-}fm.\langle \langle f, p, d_1 \rangle, d_2 \rangle = (p + d_1 \leq d_2)\ \&\ wf\text{-}f.\langle f, d_1 \rangle$

$wf\text{-}bl : (Block \times Pos \times Dim) \times Dim \rightarrow Bool$

$wf\text{-}bl.\langle \langle bl, p, d_1 \rangle, d_2 \rangle = (p + d_1 \leq d_2)$

$wf\text{-}f : Frame \times Dim \rightarrow Bool$

$wf\text{-}f.\langle f, d \rangle = wf\text{-}fbs.\langle out.f, d \rangle$

Note that the $+$ and $\leq$ in the definition of $wf\text{-}fm$ and $wf\text{-}bl$ are respectively vector addition and component-wise vector comparison.

In this way we have fulfilled the obligation to define *Spec-layout-str*. The function $wf\text{-}spec$ announced in (14) is defined by

(22) $wf\text{-}spec.\langle slg, slt \rangle = (log\text{-}content.slg = layout\text{-}content.slt)$

where

$$log\text{-}content \quad : \quad Spec\text{-}log\text{-}str \quad \rightarrow \quad \{\langle\rangle\} \mid Content$$

$$layout\text{-}content \quad : \quad Spec\text{-}layout\text{-}str \quad \rightarrow \quad \{\langle\rangle\} \mid Content$$

are the functions that yield contents constituting the "canopies" of corresponding trees. We omit a precise formulation of the two definitions.

Remember that we have not yet satisfied the obligation from Section 3 to define

$$coder : Spec\text{-}str \rightarrow Coded\text{-}form$$

(see (12)) but we do not give the definition in this paper; we also have to define

$Gen\text{-}str$

$gen\text{-}interp : Gen\text{-}str \rightarrow Gen\text{-}doc$

$str\text{-}conf : Spec\text{-}str \times Gen\text{-}str \rightarrow Bool$

(cf. (10) and (9)) and to verify the equality (11).

5 Generic ODA document and conformance

According to what has been said in Section 3 a generic structure sets standards for a whole collection of specific documents.It may be viewed as a blank form with all its fields already decided upon but still not filled in.It is a decision of the authors of ODA that it too be split into logical and layout structures (see [ODA, 2:7.6]):

(23) $Gen\text{-}str = Gen\text{-}log\text{-}str \times Gen\text{-}layout\text{-}str$

For instance, if the document under consideration is driving licence, its generic logical structure consists of a field called "title" with the contents stating that the document is a driving licence; another field called "surname" with empty contents, another field called "bearer's photo" with empty contents, etc.; while its generic layout structure involves information on the exact placing of the photo in the document, etc.; but the fields are still empty since their contents belong to the specific rather than generic structure.

In the official presentation of ODA there seems to be no clear definition of $Gen\text{-}log\text{-}str$ even in a form of a picture, such as the ones that define $Spec\text{-}log\text{-}str$ (see Figure 1) and $Spec\text{-}layout\text{-}str$ (see Figure 2).The following equations that hopefully reconstitute the definition of $Gen\text{-}log\text{-}str$ are based on the considerations on document representation from [ODA, 2:A] and on the "Generator for subordinates" from [ODA, 2:14.1.2.1]:

(24) $glg : Gen\text{-}log\text{-}str = Bas\text{-}log\text{-}obj$

           | $Choice$

           | $Sequence$

           | $Repetition$

           | $Optional$

    $Bas\text{-}log\text{-}obj$ :: $\ldots$ see (17) $\ldots$

    $Choice$ :: $Gen\text{-}log\text{-}str^{+}$

    $Sequence$ :: $Gen\text{-}log\text{-}str^{+}$

$$Repetition \quad :: \quad Gen\text{-}log\text{-}str$$

$$Optional \quad :: \quad Gen\text{-}log\text{-}str$$

Definitions (23) and (24) fulfill our obligation from Section 3 to define *Gen-str*, modulo a definition of *Gen-layout-str* that is still missing. Now we are going to concentrate on the predicate

$$str\text{-}conform : Spec\text{-}str \times Gen\text{-}str \rightarrow Bool$$

introduced by (10) that checks whether a specific structure conforms with a generic one, for the definition of *Spec-str* see (15).

(25) $str\text{-}conform.(\langle slg, slt \rangle, \langle glg, glt \rangle) = log\text{-}str\text{-}conf.\langle slg, glg \rangle \, layout\text{-}str\text{-}conf.\langle slt, glt \rangle$

In this short report we are not going to give a definition of *Gen-layout-str* nor of the predicate

$$layout\text{-}str\text{-}conf : Spec\text{-}layout\text{-}str \times Gen\text{-}layout\text{-}str \rightarrow Bool$$

We are going however to define the predicate

$$log\text{-}str\text{-}conf : Spec\text{-}log\text{-}str \times Gen\text{-}log\text{-}str \rightarrow Bool$$

that checks the logical conformance of specific and generic structures. This definition has to reflect the equations defining *Spec-log-str* and *Gen-log-str* (see (17) and (24) resp.):

(26) $log\text{-}str\text{-}conf.\langle slg, glg \rangle = los\text{-}conf.\langle out.slg, glg \rangle$

(27) $los\text{-}conf : Log\text{-}obj\text{-}seq \times Gen\text{-}log\text{-}str \rightarrow Bool$

$los\text{-}conf.\langle los, glg \rangle =$

CASES

$glg \in Bas\text{-}log\text{-}obj \Longrightarrow$

$(length.los = 1) \, \& \, (los.1 \in Bas\text{-}log\text{-}obj) \, \& \, lo\text{-}conf.\langle los.1, glg \rangle$

$glg \in Choice \Longrightarrow$

$(length.los = 1) \, \& \, (\exists i \in 1.. \; length.(out.glg)) \; lo\text{-}conf.\langle los.1, (out.glg).i \rangle$

$glg \in Sequence \Longrightarrow$

$(length.los = length.(out.glg)) \, \& \, (\forall i \in 1..length.(out.glg)) \; lo\text{-}conf.\langle los.i, (out.glg).i \rangle$

$glg \in Repetition \Longrightarrow$

$(\forall i \in 1..length.los) \; lo\text{-}conf.\langle los.i, out.glg \rangle$

$glg \in Optional \Longrightarrow$

$(length.los = 1) \, \& \, ((los.1 = \langle \rangle) \vee lo\text{-}conf.\langle los.1, out.glg \rangle)$

END

(28) $lo\text{-}conf : Log\text{-}obj \times Gen\text{-}log\text{-}str \to Bool$

   $lo\text{-}conf.\langle lo, glg \rangle =$

   CASES

      $lo \in Comp\text{-}log\text{-}obj \implies los\text{-}conf.\langle out.lo, glg \rangle$

      $lo \in Bas\text{-}log\text{-}obj \implies (glg \in Bas\text{-}log\text{-}obj) \,\&\, ((glg = \langle \rangle) \vee (lo = glg))$

   END

Definitions (27) and (28) say that a generic *Choice* is matched by a specific structure that matches one of its options; *Sequence* is matched by a sequence of the same length with coordinatewise matching; and so on.

In (27) and (28) we have used the basic logical object made out of the empty tuple $\langle \rangle$ in two somewhat different ways. In (28) it stands for the empty sequence of content portions which means the generic structure does not require any specific information so that a given field may be filled with any specific counterpart (e.g. glueing any photo in); while in (27) the $\langle \rangle$ is a place holder to mark an option from the generic structure that has not been selected in the specific one. We do not like the use (27) of the empty tuple $\langle \rangle$ since it has the flavor of a coding trick: $\langle \rangle$ is around and for a moment not serving any other purpose, so let us use it to some aim that has nothing to do with tuples. It would be much nicer to have in the node an explicit information that an option has not been selected. To allow this the definition (17) of the specific logical structure would need an alteration:

   $Log\text{-}obj\text{-}seq = Log\text{-}obj^{+} \mid \{absent\}$

This would however amount to changes in the [ODA, Fig. 12 from 2:11]. The use of $\langle \rangle$ in (28) is fully justified. Note that (28) establishes the meaning of conformance on the level of basic logical objects: they conform if either the generic one is empty or both are equal (for instance if in a specific document it says "Driving licence" in the place where according to a generic document it should say "Driving licence").

For the Readers who may be familiar with ODA the following warning may be in order. Our approach is inconsistent with the idea that portions of information common to all specific documents of a certain class can be factored out to corresponding generic ones (see [ODA, 2:12.2 and 3:6.2.8]). We chose instead to be faithful to [ODA, Fig. 4 from 2:9] which suggests that the whole content has to be present in the specific structure.

6 Final remarks

We have ended the preceding Section with a warning about an inconsistency in the design. We have found many other trouble spots in [ODA]. The reason for most of them is the same: it is too informal.

Probably the largest single problem area in ODA is attributes. Some of them are redundant and should be simply discarded; some of them collide and should be thought over again; some others should be overtly incorporated in the definitions of document structures. Some other trouble areas are type checking which is missing and a too liberal attitude to errors.

The aim of this criticism is to draw the attention of the VDM community to problems faced by professionals from various fields that are out of the blue required to state their needs in view of an imminent computerization. It would be unreasonable to expect them to have enough sophistication to specify the nature of their job in a sufficiently formal way; or even to experience a necessity to do so. Here is where our participation may be an invaluable help.

References

[BJ] *The Vienna Development Method: The Meta-Language* (ed. D. Bjørner, C. Jones) LNCS, Vol.61, Springer Verlag, 1978

[Bli] Andrzej Blikle *MetaSoft Primer* LNCS, Vol.288, Springer Verlag, 1987

[BSB] Andrzej Borzyszkowski, Stefan Sokołowski, Andrzej Blikle *Towards a formal specification of ODA in VDM/MetaSoft* A Report for MetaSoft, May 1987

[ODA] *Information processing – Text and office systems – Office Document Architecture (ODA) and interchange format* parts 1-6, Draft International Standard ISO/DIS 8613/1-6

TOWARDS A FORMAL DEFINITION OF GKS
AND OTHER GRAPHICS STANDARDS

Clive Ruggles

Department of Computing Studies

University of Leicester, Leicester LE1 7RH, U.K.

Introduction

The Graphical Kernel System, GKS (ISO 7942) is one of a family of five international graphics standards and will be the first to come up for review in 1990. None of these standards is formally specified, despite the case for formal specification having been argued for some years. While there has been a good deal of recent work using formal notations, including META-IV, directed at clarifying the concepts underlying GKS, the case for expressing the standard itself in any form of formal notation once again needs to be argued from scratch.

Work in Leicester over the past eighteen months on the formal specification of GKS has aimed to complement work at the Rutherford Appleton Laboratories (RAL) in demonstrating to the graphics community the value of formal description languages in clarifying the specification of graphics standards in general and GKS in particular. It has also aimed to demonstrate how VDM-SL might be used to express a revised version of GKS. This work has contributed to the British position on the ISO GKS Review and its progress is reported upon in this paper.

There is an increasingly strong feeling amongst the international graphics community that the revision cycle of five graphics standards which are not all compatible should be broken and that effort should be directed to producing a Computer Graphics Reference Model to which the five existing standards, and any future standards, can be related and which acts as a framework against which new standards proposals can be evaluated. Recent collaborative work between Leicester and RAL has begun to explore this area; this work is also reported upon.

GKS

GKS is a functional standard providing an interface between an application program and a configuration of graphical input and output devices. It provides facilities for generating and manipulating pictures in two dimensions. GKS actually comprises nine separate standards, with varying levels of output capability (0 to 2) and input capability (*a* to *c*). A GKS Level 2*c* implementation has the full capability.

GKS is designed to be a kernel system, that is to provide an application program with a small but powerful set of 'functions' (actually operations upon the GKS state) upon which graphics application software can be built.

Central to GKS is the notion of a 'workstation' comprising zero or one abstract display spaces and zero or more abstract ('logical') input devices. Pictures are constructed in a 'world co-ordinate' (WC) space, then transformed in various ways, for example by co-ordinate transformations and by the addition of rendering attributes (see below), until they are ready for display on one or more workstations. The series of transformation processes involved is referred to as the 'viewing pipeline'.

In GKS, pictures are comprised of 'output primitives' such as *polymarker* (a set of points in WC space) and *polyline*. In order to display an output primitive, various rendering attributes must be 'bound' to it, such as (for a polyline) line type, line width and colour. One of the attractive features of GKS is that rendering attributes may be bound in a 'bundled' manner, meaning that instead of being directly assigned its rendering attributes an output primitive is assigned an 'index': different workstations map the index on to their own set of rendering attributes. Thus different lines might be distinguished by appearing in different colours on workstations supporting colour display or in different line styles if they were displayed on monochrome workstations.

GKS provides a level of structure between a picture and an output primitive, called a 'segment'. A segment is a set of output primitives which are manipulated as a unit. Certain rendering attributes such as visibility and highlighting are defined at the segment level. GKS segments are local to workstations and do not exist independently of them: the idea is that the segment manipulation operations are carried out by the device firmware in an efficient (although workstation-dependent) way. However application programs do sometimes wish to store segments in a workstation-independent manner. GKS's ingenious, if bizarrely self-contradictory, solution is the concept of 'workstation-independent segment storage' which is itself a type of workstation.

GKS logical input devices comprise a measure and a trigger. Depending upon the input mode (there are three possibilities—request, sample and event) the measure of the device is absorbed into the GKS state either when instructed by the application program or when the device is triggered by the external operator. GKS provides six classes of logical input device, such as *locator*, whose measure is a point in WC space.

The GKS standard itself comprises English definitions of 209 'functions' together with a model of the state. Language bindings which define the form in which the GKS functions are to be presented to an application program written in a particular language such as FORTRAN, Pascal or C are defined separately.

Formal specification of GKS

The acceptance of GKS as an international standard was preceded by a number of attempts to apply formal techniques to the general problem of defining standards for computer graphics (e.g. [Mal82;Car83;Gna83]). Almost all of the work specific to GKS has concentrated upon attempting to use formal techniques to clarify specific aspects of, or problems areas within, GKS and to demonstrate the value of a formal approach to the graphics community at large.

The earliest work in this area used VDM metalanguage. Duce *et al.* [Duc84; Duc86a] investigated the problem of implicit regeneration. The problem arises because on some workstations changes in a picture can only be achieved by 'regenerating' the whole picture (e.g. deleting a line from a plotter picture). Their paper includes a proof that, under defined circumstances, the same picture is obtained whether an existing picture is modified dynamically or by implicit regeneration. VDM notation was also used to specify formally the two mechanisms of individual and bundled rendering attributes [Duc85a]. Marshall [Mar84] dealt in detail with output workstations, giving a substantial VDM definition of the state and operations.

More recently, however, Duce and his collaborators have also used other formal techniques in their attempts to demonstrate the potential of formal techniques in clarifying the specification of GKS. Thus in one paper [Duc85b], the model-oriented approach of VDM is compared with the property-oriented approach of OBJ. It is concluded that one of the main benefits of OBJ is its modularity constructs. Another paper [Arn87] attempts to combine various strands from Duce *et al.*'s earlier work. The approach used here is to describe the data and control structures in the GKS viewing pipeline and to combine them using a 'piped-processes' approach. It is felt that Z is the most appropriate tool for expressing the concepts in this sort of approach. As a consequence, while VDM notation was used in an earlier paper which concentrated on definitions of the main types of output primitive in GKS [Duc86b], a more recent version, based on the approach of [Arn87], is expressed in Z [Duc87b].

Clarification through a top-down approach

Work in Leicester on the formal specification of GKS over the past eighteen months has aimed to complement the work described above both by aiming at different parts of GKS, namely (i) the overall structure of the GKS state and (ii) input, and by considering in some detail the types of deficiency in the current standard and how a revised standard might be expressed formally.

Any attempt to affect a straight 'translation' of an English specification into a formal specification language will, in general, soon encounter difficulties. Certainly this is the case with GKS. Because the formal approach forces a deeper understanding of the concepts involved, numerous deficiencies in the original standard are soon uncovered, many of which require policy decisions to be made (something which can not be done in an unambiguous way on the basis of the existing standard) before the formal description can proceed.

Thus as we proceeded to attempt to specify the GKS state in a top-down manner, concentrating on the overall concepts and upon input, we attempted to document the deficiencies uncovered and policy decisions made in order to overcome them. In [Rug87a] we give a step-by-step description of the deficiencies encountered in the very earliest stages of this process and our suggestions for their resolution with least disruption to the existing functional standard. In [Rug87b] we provide a full catalogue of the deficiencies encountered in these early stages.

The principal types of deficiency that are encountered in the existing standard may be categorised as follows.

(a)   *Lack of hierarchical structure.* The 'GKS state list' in the ISO GKS standard, which describes part of the GKS state model, consists of a list of approximately 80 attributes which are almost completely unstructured. Considerable clarification is achieved by adopting a hierarchically-structured abstract model of the state. Specifying this formally may introduce elements within the structure which are not present in the English original.

(b)   *Ambiguities.* The formal definition traps ambiguities and unintentional gaps in the English specification. In the case of ambiguities this forces a decision to be made about their meaning. If unintentional gaps are not filled in then the implementer is given a free hand if the situation in question arises, which is often highly undesirable. Additions must be made to the specification in order to prevent this.

An example within GKS is the following. GKS requires an error file to be provided where error messages are written if operation pre-conditions are not satisfied. The error file is identified through a 'unit number' which is provided by the application program when the operation *Open-GKS* is invoked. The standard specifies that there is no unit number attached to the error file until GKS is first opened. Yet errors can occur before this happens, most obviously by trying to close GKS before opening it. The error logging procedure is then invoked, but this requires the error file to have been specified. What happens?

(c)   *Confusing nomenclature.* This is by no means as trivial as it sounds. Confusing or misleading nomenclature can easily disguise the true abstract structure of a model. For example, in GKS the term 'list' is used (as in *State List*) to describe a set of attributes which is essentially unordered. The following table, which gives some examples of the names of concepts within the GKS state and proposed alternatives, also illustrates the inherent confusion:

GKS Name	Proposed Name
GKS State List	GKS
Workstation Identifier	Workstation ID
Workstation State List	Workstation
Segment Name	Segment ID
Segment State List	Segment
Workstation Type	Workstation Type ID
Workstation Description Table	Workstation Type
Workstation Identifier ×	
Device Class × Device Number	Input Device ID
(Entry in Workstation State List	
for a particular logical input	
device class and number)	Input Device
Device Class × Device Number	Input Device Type ID
(Entry in Workstation Description	
Table for a particular logical	
input device class and number)	Input Device Type
Device Number	Locator Device Type ID etc.
Polyline Index	Polyline Bundle ID
Polyline Bundle Table Entry	Polyline Bundle
Normalization Transformation Number	Normalization Transformation ID

(d)   *Insufficient abstraction.* The formal development helps identify features in the specification which are insufficiently abstract and, in particular, too oriented towards the implementation of the specification in a particular programming language (namely, in the case of the GKS standard, FORTRAN).

For example, in event mode input in GKS, when an input device is triggered its measure is enqueued onto the GKS 'input queue' ready for subsequent dequeuing by operations available to the application program. An input queue entry contains a 'last of group of simultaneous events' flag. The reason for this is that a single physical input device at a workstation may correspond to several logical input devices, and thus a single triggering may generate several measure values simultaneously. A cleaner abstract model would model an input queue entry as a set of event reports referring to simultaneous events [Duc87a]; however rather than specifying this, the standard specifies (and hence enforces upon every GKS implementation) a FORTRAN-like implementation of a set.

(e) *Superfluities*. Unless an abstract model is made significantly more understandable by their inclusion, it is strongly desirable to remove tautologous parts of the state (i.e. parts whose value can be deduced from that of other parts) in order to reduce the burden of invariant preservation proofs.

GKS, for example, has an 'operating state' whose value pervades virtually every operation precondition in the standard. Yet its value is always trivially deducable from the remainder of the GKS state [Rug87a: Section 3.2.5].

In order to develop a formal specification, general policy decisions need to be made in these instances, and documented in detail for discussion in the review process. A reversal of such a decision may lead to extensive changes, so it is desirable that the formal development does not proceed too far beyond the standards review process. On the other hand it dare not lag too far behind, lest crucial issues fail to be identified before it is too late to consider them in the review.

We suspect that the necessity for clarification will be more generally accepted in the case of deficiencies of, say, types (a) and (b) than with those of, say, type (e); and that policy decisions relating to them will generally be less contentious.

Doubtless if the review of graphics standards were purely an academic exercise we should end up very quickly by recommending that the existing non-formal GKS simply be abandoned and a new formal version be formulated from scratch. However, it isn't: instead it is highly desirable that, wherever possible, any suggested changes affect only the conceptual model underlying GKS. In other words the description of the GKS data structures could be rewritten, but the functional standard itself should remain unaltered. As soon as this ceases to be the case, the overheads may be considerable, since one must provide machinery for dealing with applications software which, although conforming to the old standard, does not necessarily conform to the new one.

Despite this it is clear (from a formal perspective at least) that some, and arguably many, changes affecting the functionality of GKS do seem strongly desirable.

Some Issues in the Possible Use of VDM-SL to Specify GKS

VDM-SL is clearly a strong candidate for any formal expression of the revised GKS standard, especially in view of a recent report from ISO JTC 1/SC 18 recommending that in future only standard FDTs or FDTs in the process of standardisation should be used in formal descriptions of standards.

If it is to be argued that any part of a revised GKS is to be expressed in VDM-SL then attention must be paid at this stage to any problems that would arise as a result. For example, S.T. Yee is currently attempting to provide a complete model of GKS input, including those parts (such as the interface between logical input devices in event mode and the input queue) which are beyond the scope of the GKS standard. CSP is being used to specify the concurrent aspects of the model, since VDM-SL is inadequate. How then should this part of the standard be expressed? In a different standard notation that *is* suitable, such as LOTOS?

Attention must also be paid to the possible presentation of the resulting standard. [Rug87a] and [Rug87b] both include a sample of the resulting formal specification as it might be presented to the world at large. It is extensively commented and cross-referenced, as the papers propose that any formal standard should be, and was constructed in order to promote discussion in the GKS Review.

Some associated general issues to do with the introduction of formal notations into the expression of standards, discussed in an accompanying report ('Formal methods in standards—A report from the BCS working group', see elsewhere in this volume), are relevant here.

Towards a Computer Graphics Reference Model

The four international graphics standards other than GKS are GKS-3D (ISO/DIS 8805); the Programmers' Hierarchical Interactive Graphics System, PHIGS (ISO/DIS 9592); the Computer Graphics Metafile, CGM (ISO 8632) and the Computer Graphics Interface (ISO/DP 9636). GKS-3D is, as the name suggests, simply an extension to GKS supporting three-dimensional pictures and primitives. PHIGS is an alternative functional standard for generating and manipulating three-dimensional pictures which can be defined in a more structured way than in GKS. At the heart of PHIGS is a database called the 'central structure store': pictures are generated by traversing it. CGM provides facilities for the storage and transfer of pictures. CGI is a standard device communications protocol concerned with the interface between an abstract workstation and specific physical devices. It provides facilities for the application program to inquire, and use as appropriate, the hardware capabilities of a device, thus removing the need for device-dependent code. Looming in the near future are suggested extensions to CGM and PHIGS as well as new areas for standardisation such as windowing and image processing.

Apart from GKS and GKS-3D, the latter of which includes the former, the five standards were not generally conceived within any unifying framework. Two examples of the sorts of problem that occur are (i) the ways of grouping primitives in GKS (segments) and PHIGS ('namesets') are incompatible; and (ii) a metafile produced by GKS is of a 'session capture' type, which leads to problems if one attempts to describe it as a CGM, which is of a 'state capture' type. A general feeling of confusion and disharmony is evident amongst the graphics community concerning the basic incompatibility of the existing standards and the lack of any framework against which they can be compared and new proposals evaluated.

It is scarcely surprising that there is an increasing interest in exploring ideas for a Computer Graphics Reference Model which would provide a general methodology for the description and comparison of graphics systems. Its terms of reference would need to be broad enough to encompass current systems and extensible so as to allow for future developments. It should not impose undue restrictions yet should enable different systems to be clearly distinguished. It should provide a basis for the evaluation of proposed standards.

Initial ideas emerging from collaborative work between Leicester and RAL, reported in more detail elsewhere [Rug88a; Rug88b], suggest a general way of describing a graphics system as a hierarchical framework of components which are defined to be abstract data types (ADTs) modelling objects within the system. Higher-level components are specified in terms of lower-level ones, down to atomic components or 'units' which are of four varieties—internal units, input units, output units and interaction units—and upon which basic operations are defined. These include standard operations for the type of unit concerned together with operations defining the interrelationships between different units (such as transformations between the objects they represent). Our conviction is that any graphics system, at whatever level of abstraction it is conceived, should be usefully describable in this way.

All systems are ultimately describable as a single interaction unit which exists alongside other ADTs available to an application program. The system at this level can be thought of both as a high-level input device, whose state can be manipulated by the external user, and a high-level output device, whose state can be observed by the external user. The application program has control over when this interaction can occur, but the detailed features of the interaction have all been abstracted out and are not under its control.

Any system may be developed by successive refinement steps from this starting point, down to the abstraction level required. A refinement step involves replacing an atomic component (unit) by a component whose state and operations are specified in terms of new atomic components. New operations may be added to the higher-level component at this stage. Different systems may be compared by deriving a set of units common to both.

It is hoped that this sort of approach may provide a more rigorous basis for models such as that of Arnold and his collaborators [Arn84; Rey86; Arn87] who have attempted to identify general classes of process and connectivity within a 'graphics processing pipeline' model of output in graphics systems (cf. mention above of the GKS viewing pipeline). It also provides a framework for describing input models such as that of GKS [Rug88a].

Our initial work in this area has used VDM notation in the development of ideas and examples (see [Rug88a; Rug88b]). However since ADTs form the basis of the approach it may be argued that ACT-ONE is a more appropriate standard notation for its eventual expression. For this reason it is also planned to develop a formulation of the ideas in ACT-ONE for comparison.

Conclusion

Clear indications are awaited from within the standards bodies before the most appropriate direction will emerge for the continuation of this work—i.e. whether it should be purely concerned with the GKS Review or with developing new graphics standards, possibly including a radically different successor to GKS, within the context of a Computer Graphics Reference Model. Either way (or both), there is a growing body of work which should aid the generally still slow progress towards the formal development and expression of future international graphics standards.

References

[Arn84]   D.B. Arnold, G. Hall & G.J. Reynolds. Proposals for configurable models of graphics systems. *Computer Graphics Forum*, 3(3), 1984, 200-208.

[Arn87]   D.B. Arnold, D.A. Duce & G.J. Reynolds. An approach to the formal specification of configurable models of graphics systems. In: G. Marechal (ed.), *Proceedings of Eurographics 87*, North-Holland, 1987.

[Car83]   G.S. Carson. The specification of computer graphics systems. *IEEE Computer Graphics and Applications*, 27-41, 1983.

[Duc84]   D.A. Duce, E.V.C. Fielding & L.S. Marshall. Formal specification and graphics software. Technical Report RAL-84-068, Rutherford Appleton Laboratory, Chilton, Didcot, Oxon. OX11 0QX, 1984.

[Duc85a]   D.A. Duce & E.V.C. Fielding. Better understanding through formal specification. *Computer Graphics Forum*, 4(4), 333-348, 1985.

[Duc85b]   D.A. Duce & E.V.C. Fielding. Formal specification—A comparison of two techniques. Technical Report RAL-85-051, Rutherford Appleton Laboratory, Chilton, Didcot, Oxon. OX11 0QX, 1985.

[Duc86a]   D.A. Duce & E.V.C. Fielding. Formal specification—A simple example. *ICL Technical Journal*, May 1986, 96-111.

[Duc86b]   D.A. Duce & E.V.C. Fielding. Towards a formal specification of the GKS output primitives. In: A.A.G. Requicha (ed.), *Proceedings of Eurographics 86*, North Holland, 1986, 307-323.

[Duc87a]   D.A. Duce, F.R.A. Hopgood, C.L.N. Ruggles & S.T. Yee. Input in GKS—A discussion paper. Technical Report RAL-87-057, Rutherford Appleton Laboratory, Chilton, Didcot, Oxon. OX11 0QX, 1987.

[Duc87b]   D.A. Duce & M.S. Parsons. A specification of the GKS Polyline, Polymarker and Fill Area Set primitives. In: *Proceedings of the GKS Review, a workshop held in September 1987, Disley U.K.* European Association for Computer Graphics, informal publication, 1987.

[Gna83]   R. Gnatz. An algebraic approach to the standardization and the certification of graphics software, *Computer Graphics Forum*, 2(2), 153-166, 1983.

[Mal82]   W.R. Mallgren. Formal specification of graphic data types. *ACM Transactions on Programming Languages and Systems*, 4(4), 687-710, 1982.

[Mar84]   L.S. Marshall. GKS Output Workstations: Formal Specification and proofs of correctness for specific devices. Transfer Report, University of Manchester, 1984.

[Rey86]   G.J. Reynolds. A token-based graphics system. *Computer Graphics Forum*, 5(2), 1986, 139-146.

[Rug87a]   C.L.N. Ruggles & S.T. Yee. Notes on attempting a top-down formal specification of GKS in META-IV. Technical Report no. 3, Computing Studies Department, University of Leicester, 1987.

[Rug87b]   C.L.N. Ruggles & S.T. Yee. Clarification through formal specification: some notes on attempting a top-down formal specification of GKS in META-IV. In: *Proceedings of the GKS Review, a workshop held in September 1987, Disley U.K.* European Association for Computer Graphics, informal publication, 1987.

[Rug88a]   C.L.N. Ruggles & M.S. Parsons. A Graphics Reference Model using Input, Output and Interaction Units, 1: The model. Technical Report no. 11, Computing Studies Department, University of Leicester. In press.

[Rug88b]   C.L.N. Ruggles & M.S. Parsons. A Graphics Reference Model using Input, Output and Interaction Units, 2: Types of refinement. Technical Report, Computing Studies Department, University of Leicester. In preparation.

Report from the BSI Panel for the Standardisation of VDM (IST/5/50)

1. Introduction

As has already been stated in a previous report of this panel [1], the introduction of VDM as an industrial software engineering tool has been made more difficult by the lack of a standard that defines both the method and its meta-language, VDM-SL (also known as Meta-IV). This lack of a standard, either de-facto or one supported by a standardisation body such as the BSI, has hindered the development of tools and led to a variety of dialects used both in Industry and in Universities, and by other Research Institutions.

In the early meetings of the Committee it was generally agreed that the BSI standard should be based on existing work wherever possible. However, it was recognised that there were shortcomings and problems with VDM as currently used. These were identified to be:

(i)   structuring of large specifications;

(ii)   the resolution of the different dialects of VDM currently in use; and

(iii)   polymorphism for functions and operations.

Decisions are still being made as to what form the extensions and/or changes should take to remove these problems. The main extensions to VDM are specifically designed to handle large specifications and are minimal to reduce the impact on the existing formal definition of the meta-language. The existing work on formally specifying VDM-SL was carried out by STC [2], and the documents donated to the standardisation effort by that company have been used as a starting point for the standard, together with the two existing VDM books [3,4].

Changes will be made to the STC documents to reflect the extensions and changes that are proposed by the Standards Committee. The lack of a standard for VDM is holding up the development of suitable tools and thus inhibiting the use of VDM in industry on large projects. The current plan is to provide a staged release of the standard, starting with the abstract and concrete syntax, continuing with the context conditions, the semantic mappings, and finally the proof rules. The semantics of VDM-SL are reasonably well understood, and the production of tools relies more on the definition of standard abstract and concrete syntaxs than any other part of the formal definition. Thus, there is a need to release the syntaxs as soon as they are in a form that reflects the wishes of the VDM panel. Because of this need, as soon as there is a version of a component of the standard that reflects the proposed VDM-SL, it is added to an existing

"Proto-standard" document and is under "change control" - full committee agreement is needed before any technical changes can be made.

2. Syntax

2.1 Abstract Syntax

This component of the standard is now under "change control"; this decision was taken when it was felt that the abstract syntax was fairly stable, and near the final version that would be released for comment to the (VDM) community at large.

The abstract syntax of VDM-SL has been developed from the STC version of the specification language, but with changes to make the BSI version closer to the original syntax of VDM-SL as developed by the Vienna Laboratory. One of the problems of the current versions of VDM-SL is the lack of facilities for structuring large specifications, and it has been decided to add some additional features to the meta language that allow for the structuring of large specifications. To this end modules with an interface language, not too dissimilar from the module concept of Modula-2, have been added to the meta-language to control the visibilities of types, operations, functions, and constants. These objects can now be exported from, and imported into, modules to provide a structuring mechanism with scope and hiding for objects.

Another aim of the abstract syntax is to capture as much structure as possible. This will reduce the complexity of the context conditions and thus to some extent will allow some simplification of the original context conditions in the STC specification of the language. An effort has also been made to resolve the major dialects of VDM-SL, that is, the original Vienna version, the current Danish dialect, and the English dialect which extended VDM-SL with pre- and post- conditions for implicit specification.

The unification has succeeded at the abstract level and there is work being done to continue this through to the concrete level where the differences are more obvious to the user. The resolution of the problems in the abstract syntax has focused attention on some other issues, most of which are not explicitly concerned with abstract syntax, but need to be resolved before the syntax can be finalised. These issues are listed below:

(i)   Side effects in expressions: should implicit changes to the state be allowed in expressions or should they be restricted to statements? The resolution of this problem will affect the proof rules which are to be derived later during the standardisation effort.

(ii)   Underspecification versus non-determinism: if a function or operation is incompletely specified so that more than one answer is possible, this could be interpreted as underspecification. This implies that a function is in mind but has not been completely specified yet. The alternative interpretation of an incompletely defined function or operation is non-deterministic; at this point in the specification more than one result is possible. This issue will have a fundamental effect on the semantic mappings and proof theory of the specification language.

(iii)   Polymorphism: though polymorphism has been identified as a possible area for extending VDM-SL, the decision to include this feature has yet to be made.

(iv)   Exception mechanisms: the panel has yet to decide the exact mechanism for dealing with exceptions. The "tixe" mechanism of the original meta-language is felt to be not powerful enough, but the exact form of the extensions that are required to provide the additional functionality has yet to be decided.

2.2   Concrete Syntax

There are two concrete syntaxs for VDM, one a mathematically based notation for production using tools such as $\mathcal{L}^AT_EX$, and the other a version based on the ASCII character set for use on "ASCII" terminals. It is the existence of an ASCII syntax which will allow non bit-mapped terminals to be used to enter and manipulate VDM specifications, since at present bit-mapped terminals and devices supporting multi-font output are not sufficiently available to ignore the provisions of an ASCII character-based syntax.

In the last quarter of 1987, when the abstract syntax of the VDM-SL had become relatively stable, the computer science department of Christian-Albrechts-University Kiel, in close cooperation with Norsk Data GmbH Germany, started work on a proposal for the ASCII concrete syntax. The aim was to integrate the two concrete syntaxs employed in the DDC Meta IV toolset and the definition of the STC VDM Reference Language with respect to the (informally given) existing notation as used in major VDM publications.

Two key features of the proposed concrete syntax are a close (nearly one-to-one) relation to the abstract syntax and the LR(1) property of the proposed grammar. The close relation leads to an easy concrete to abstract syntax transformation which is considered very important. A non-trivial transformation would be awkward for teaching the language and thus for language acceptance. An obvious transformation is also required because the VDM-SL semantic definition will be based on the abstract syntax. The LR(1) property enables easy generation and testing of prototype parsers using a YACC-like parser-generator system.

A draft version of the concrete syntax was first presented to the standardisation panel in December of 1987. It has subsequently been updated according to discussions at later meetings. Currently written comments and proposed changes from panel members are being collected together in preparation for the syntax to be added to the Proto-standard and thus be under change-control.

A mathematical version of the concrete syntax is also in preparation, based on the ASCII version, but with non-ASCII mathematical symbols to allow for publication using advanced output devices that can handle multiple fonts.

3. Semantics

3.1 Context Conditions

The context conditions will define the static semantics of VDM-SL. An initial study suggested that it might be possible to write the context conditions using attribute grammars. The style of attribute grammar used would be one suitable for translation into a form used by several of the structured editors that are currently available. These editors (e.g. Connell Synthesiser) can be configured with an attribute grammar to allow the semantic checking of the language which they have been syntactically set up to hold. Although re-writing the context conditions was feasible, it was felt that the work involved was both too difficult and too much of a change from those existing in the STC definition of VDM-SL. The current plan is to take the existing context conditions and modify them to take account of changes to language, especially the addition of modules, and also to cater for the possibility of translating them into an attribute grammar at a later date.

3.2 Semantic Mappings

The BSI version of VDM-SL will be given formal semantics; the standard will define semantic mappings which will map syntactic objects to corresponding semantic objects, and which will be based upon those defined in the STC document.

The Technical University of Denmark is currently analysing the semantics of the STC VDM-SL, and are proposing modifications to deal with the extensions and differences between the STC VDM-SL and that proposed for the BSI Standard.

4. Proof Theory

The objective of the proof theoretic work is to establish a set of proof rules which are sound and sufficient. Sufficient will not mean complete, since VDM, like Z, will need to be about as expressive as Zermelo set theory (or Church's type theory), and hence will have no complete proof system.

There are two possible approaches to the development of a proof theory. One is to develop proof rules for the VDM Specification Language as a whole, and then try to demonstrate their soundness against the semantics; this could be called a "top-down" approach. The alternative would be to work "bottom-up", starting with a formal axiomatisation of a suitable set theory, and working back through a number of languages adding to the syntactic richness, while retaining most of the mathematical expressiveness and proof theoretic strength of the original. The current thinking of the panel is to advocate the "bottom-up" approach. The current plan is:

(i)   Formal axiomatisation of first order set theory, in HOL. This gives a rich semantic base with a usable proof development system. This has been done, and a significant theory has been developed.

(ii)   Develop, by construction within the extended HOL system, the necessary theories to give an adequate formal account of a suitable intermediate language between set theory and VDM-SL. The intermediate language may be thought of as a syntactically meagre superset of (i.e. at least as expressive as) VDM-SL.

The semantics of the VDM Specification Language are then defined using the intermediate language and appropriate proof rules are derived in HOL. The final approach will very much depend on the decisions related to underspecification versus non-determinism; this decision will have an impact on the semantics and it is thus premature to make firms plans for the derivation of proof rules.

My thanks to the co-ordinators (S. Bear, T. Denvir, C.B. Jones, R. Jones, M. Haß, G. Parkin, B. Ritchie, and other members of the panel) responsible for the various components of the Proto-standard for providing me with the information to compile this report - the accuracy is theirs; any inaccuracies mine.

D. Andrews - Chairman IST/5/50

The Department of Computing Studies
University Road
Leicester
LE1 7RH

References

[1]   D. Sen: *Objectives of the British Standardisation of a languae to support the Vienna Development Method*, in Lecture Notes in Computer Science, Vol 252, Springer-Verlag 1987.

[2]   B. Monahan, A Walshe et al: *The STC VDM Reference Language*, STC plc 1986.

[3]   D. Bjørner & C.B. Jones: *The Vienna Development Method: The meta-Language*, Lecture Notes in Computer Science, Vol 61 1979, Springer-Verlag 1987.

[4]   D. Bjørner & C.B. Jones: *Formal Specifications & Software Development*, Prentice Hall International 1982

FORMAL METHODS IN STANDARDS—
A REPORT FROM THE BCS WORKING GROUP

Clive Ruggles
Department of Computing Studies
University of Leicester, Leicester LE1 7RH, U.K.

Introduction

The British Computer Society (BCS) has recently set up a Working Group on Formal Methods in Standards, of which the author of this report is Chairman. Its primary objective is to promote the practical application of formal description methods and techniques in improving the quality of standards used in computer systems and software.

At present the group comprises approximately twenty members, from academia and industry, actively involved in the application of formal methods in the development and review of standards. Their interests span areas such as communication protocols, the specification of programming languages, graphics standardisation, and document structure.

This paper reports upon the work programme of the group and its progress to date.

Objectives of the Working Group

With the primary objective in mind, the following list of secondary (enabling) objectives was drawn up:

a)   to identify where the use of formal description methods (FDMs) and techniques (FDTs) will improve the quality of standards in fitness for purpose, implementability and usability;

b)   to determine the current situation in respect of FDMs and FDTs and their practical application in the areas identified;

c)   to advise BCS members actively involved in standards of the findings of the above and to publish guidelines and recommendations regarding the application and use of FDMs and FDTs;

d)   to identify significant areas where further effort is required in the development, application and promotion of FDMs and FDTs;

e)   to identify and subsequently liaise with other bodies who are currently active, or can contribute towards, the Group's objectives in order that BCS views may be represented to these bodies;

f)   to propose a programme of work in the application of FDMs and FDTs as is considered to be beneficial in meeting the objectives; and

g)   to devise and undertake an educative programme, through publications, seminars and workshops, which will promote the effective use of FDMs and FDTs, by BCS members, in improving the quality of standards.

The work of the group

Following a series of meetings in which the aims and objectives of the group were decided upon and a framework for progression set up, a two-day workshop was held in April 1988 in order to establish a common knowledge base amongst the group and to prepare the ground for a first position document. The workshop papers aimed to provide a technical background and to offer case studies in the introduction of formal methods into standards in various areas.

One of the strengths of the group appears to be the breadth of the fields of interest of its members, where general reactions to the use, or attempted use, of formal techniques in standards development are often very different. In the field of communicating systems, for example, various semi-formal description techniques have been used for expressing specifications for open system interconnection (OSI) protocols, culminating in LOTOS—the Language of Temporal Ordering Specification (ISO/DIS 8807), which has fully formal semantics. The two main standards concerning document structures, SGML (ISO 8879) and ODA—Office Document Architecture (ISO/DIS 8613), are not formally expressed but a formal specification of ODA document structures, expressed as a single formula in first-order predicate logic, has been proposed as an addendum to the standard. No common terms of reference have emerged for the definition of programming languages with, for example, Modula-2 currently being defined formally using VDM specification language but the idea of a formal definition having been totally rejected in the case of C. None of the current graphics standards has a formal definition, despite the case in its favour having been argued for some years.

The group is attempting to build upon this breadth of experience in order to identify general issues which relate to the introduction of formal techniques into the development and expression of standards, and to offer general guidelines for those working to introduce formal techniques in different standards areas. Its concern is not simply to impart specialist knowledge of particular FDTs.

The output from the workshop, currently being collated, will form a draft Working Group document comprising the following.

a) A statement of principles: what is a standard; what is a formal description method/technique; the place of standards in the software development process; the process of standards development and review.

b) Descriptions of standards areas of interest: programming languages; graphics; communications; databases; office document architectures. Case studies in each area to include: motivation for the use of formal methods; problems encountered; assessment of success and failure.

c) Guidelines for the application of FDTs in standards: recommendations and the rationale for them.

d) A glossary of terms.

e) Bibliography.

A formal Position Document for outside circulation will be produced following a further internal workshop in October. Thereafter the work of the group will concentrate more on education in the form of seminars and courses. The first event will be a workshop primarily aimed at standards makers (rather than users): participation will be restricted to those—BCS members and others—involved in standards bodies, together with members of specialist groups involved in areas of potential use of formal standards. Subsequent events will be aimed more widely at standards users.

Some issues

It would be premature to attempt a full report of the issues raised and discussed by the group, as these discussions are far from complete, but hopefully the following summary will give a flavour.

General questions about the process of standards development immediately arose as a result of trying to define the scope of the group's interests. It is clear that this should not be restricted to the expression of standards in formal notations. While the quality of a standard is clearly improved if it can be expressed clearly, unambiguously and concisely, other considerations are also important such as whether or not the standard serves a useful function;

how easy it is to understand and to implement the standard; how easy it is to determine the conformance of implementations; and how easy the standard is to modify and enhance.

These considerations have led the group to an attempt to provide a model for standards development. Workshop contributions by Patrick Hall (Brunel University) and David Blyth (Incord Ltd.) sparked off a particularly stimulating discussion and are to form the basis of a paper to be published in the BCS Bulletin. Hall proposed that one can think of a 'standards development life-cycle' paralleling the well-known software development life-cycle comprising requirements analysis, specification, design, implementation, testing, use and maintenance. The requirements analysis in the standards development process arises through observing a range of existing systems and their use and identifying the scope of a new standard. The 'specification' stage consists of work items being raised in standards bodies, these comprising brief descriptions of what will be produced. There then in general follows a protracted production phase in which the standard is actually developed and written, followed generally by an even more protracted 'testing' phase in which it is argued towards acceptance through the various levels of standards bodies. 'Use' involves the development of implementations and conformance testing. Maintenance is synonymous with the standards review process.

Formal development techniques can clearly have a role throughout this standards development process, and one of the aims of the group is to provide guidelines for the application of FDTs at the various stages. In the development stages, for example, it is important to choose the most appropriate FDT for the expression and development of the conceptual model. In the acceptance process the important thing is to be able to argue the benefits of the FDT in the political context of the standards body concerned.

The formal expression of a standard, even when features such as lack of ambiguity are demonstrable, does not of course improve its quality if it is inaccessible to its users. Considerable attention has to be paid to their needs and abilities; format and style are crucially important. Also relevant is whether the 'users' in question are primarily conceived to be the suppliers of implementations or the end-users. While an arguable long-term solution is simply the education of the standard's potential users, it may be in the short term that the only acceptable solution is one of the following:

(i)   a formal standard with comprehensive annotation in natural language;

(ii)   a formal standard alongside one in (stylised) natural language; or

(iii)   formal annexes to a non-formal standard.

(i) has the advantage that the standard is still expressed formally, although conciseness will be lost. In the case of (ii) one must face the question of which standard takes precedence in the event of an inconsistency: the most acceptable solution seems to be that such a situation constitutes an error in the standard, but then one of the benefits of a formal approach, which is precisely to eliminate ambiguities and inconsistencies, has been compromised. (iii), while preserving the non-formal version as the definitive standard, allows that formal techniques could have been used to develop part or all of it. It also allows that annexes describing non-intersecting parts of the standard might be expressed in different notations.

In the stage where a standard is 'used', i.e. when implementations are developed and conformance-tested, it is clearly advantageous that the standard be expressed in a specification language, such as VDM-SL, which forms part of a development methodology. Indeed, if a proven implementation can be completely derived from the standard specification then the need for conformance testing is of course eliminated.

It is perhaps most tricky of all to suggest how FDTs may be applied to existing (non-formal) standards in the review stage, largely because the their use tends to reveal such lack of conceptual integrity and clarity that the only sensible recommendation is simply to restart from scratch.

A report of the ISO/TC97 Special Working Group on Formal Description Techniques has produced a set of criteria for the use and applicability of FDTs in the development of standards. Their guidelines are generally helpful and have been taken as the starting point for developing the BCS Working Group's position.

Some other points worthy of mention are the following.

It was generally agreed that there is a crucial need to develop tools alongside formal methods. Standards developers need the ability automatically to produce correct, production-quality specifications.

It is not clear whether proofs that the specified operations preserve the specified data type invariants should constitute part of a standard. Jones [Jon86:138] states that 'The more that can be done to postulate and prove theorems about a specification, the greater is the chance of discovering any undesirable properties. Thus the obligation to prove results about invariants can be seen as an opportunity to increase confidence in the consistency of a specification'. In the case of a standard, consistency must be guaranteed; however a series of invariant preservation proofs might be bulky and extremely offputting to those on standards bodies to whom one has to 'sell' the benefits of formal specification as well as to end users of the standard. An acceptable solution would seem to be to produce a separate annex document containing the proofs.

No position has yet been agreed amongst the group on prototyping and executable specifications.

The place of VDM

The ISO/TC97 SWG document referred to above contains the clear statement that 'In future, only standard FDTs or FDTs in the process of being standardized should be used in formal descriptions of standards'. Counter-arguments tend to centre round the fact that few standard FDTs will be available in the short term and that their enforced use is unduly restrictive. It is, however, likely that the BCS Group will strongly endorse the recommendation of the TC97 document.

The two formal specification languages currently progressing towards International Standard status are LOTOS (ISO/DIS 8807; [Tur87]) and VDM-SL [Sen87]. LOTOS is a formal specification language for OSI. Its behavioural semantics are based upon CCS and CSP; data types are described using ACT-ONE, a specification formalism for abstract data types. LOTOS is very suitable for producing implementation-independent specifications of OSI standards, allowing formal analysis of their syntactic and semantic correctness, and allowing specifications to be expressed in modular form. It is not, however, always the best tool if one wishes to describe a reference implementation [Tur87]. An Esprit-funded project is currently developing support tools for LOTOS.

Where VDM-SL has the edge over LOTOS is in being part of a development methodology, with the consequent implications for implementation development and conformance testing. As a consequence it is clearly set to be of considerable importance in the standards arena in the forseeable future.

Further Information

If you would like further information on the work of the BCS Formal Methods in Standards Working Group, are interested in participating, or would like copies of documents produced by the group, please contact either the Chairman

Clive Ruggles,
Department of Computing Studies,
University of Leicester,
LEICESTER LE1 7RH,
U.K.
+44 533 523409
rug@uk.ac.le.vax

or the group's Technical Co-ordinator

Tony Sale,
The British Computer Society,
13 Mansfield Street,
LONDON W1M 0BP,
U.K.
+44 1 637 0471

References

[Jon86]   C.B. Jones. *Systematic software development using VDM*. Prentice-Hall International, Englewood Cliffs NJ, 1986.

[Sen87]   D. Sen. Objectives of the British standardisation of a language to support the Vienna Development Method. In: D. Bjorner, C.B. Jones, M. Mac an Airchinnigh & E.J. Neuhold (eds.), *VDM '87: VDM—A formal method at work*, Lecture Notes in Computer Science, Vol. 252, Springer-Verlag, Berlin, 1987, pp. 321-323.

[Tur87]   K.J. Turner. LOTOS—A practical formal description technique for OSI. *Proc. Internat. Conf. on Open Systems*, London, 1987, pp. 265-280.

The B Tool

(Abstract)

J. R. Abrial

'B' is an interactive program whose function is to **assist** people in doing formal proofs.

The basic features of 'B' are the following:

- To **parse** formal texts according to a certain surface syntax that corresponds to the traditional structure of either mathematical formulae or program fragments.

- To recognize in formal texts the presence of **quantifiers** and of **variables**.

- To analyse the **non-freeness** of variable occurrences with respect to quantifiers.

- To perform (in a formula) the **multiple replacement** (substitution) of free occurrences of certain variables by some other formulae (provided this is safe from the point of view of variable capture).

- To recognize in formal texts the presence of certain **meta-variable** occurrences (each meta-variable stands for any formula).

- To **pattern match** a formula against another one containing such meta-variables. A successful pattern matching results in the construction of a **filter** assigning a formula to each meta-variable.

- To **instantiate** a formula by means of a filter (that is, to replace the meta-variables of the formula in question by the formulae assigned by the filter).

Built on these elementary features, 'B' also contains a simplistic inference engine allowing simple **goal-oriented proofs** to be conducted in an interactive mode.

During proofs, 'B' may dynamically generate some hypotheses.

The tool has a few built-in rules corresponding to a very limited knowledge of first-order predicate logic. These rules are the following:

Deduction: by which it destroys an **implicative goal** by constructing a hypothesis made of the left hand side of the implication (the new goal being the right hand side).

Conjunction: by which it splits a **conjunctive goal** into two separate goals.

Generalisation: by which it simplifies a **universally quantified goal** by removing the quantifier (provided the quantified variable is not free in the hypotheses).

Equality: by which it **removes** a goal of the form 'formula = same formula'.

Substitution: by which it **simplifies** a formula containing explicit substitutions.

Such built-in rules are tried systematically at each step of a proof. When none of them are applicable, the tool may try to apply some **user-defined rules**, which are stored in containers called 'theories'.

While performing a proof, the tools navigates through the theories according to the prescription of a so called **tactic**.

A tactic is either a theory or rule name, the sequenced usage of two or more tactics, or the iterative usage of two tactics. The user can change tactic in the middle of a proof, he can also **browse** manually through a tactic; when the 'tactic pointer' points to a theory, the user can ask for the applicable rules within that theory.

In fact, what one proves are just other rules. Of course, such rules might be used like the other built-in or user-defined ones.

Rules to be proved might also be stored in theories. Mores precisely, a tactic is always (dynamically) attached to a theory this means that all rules in a given theory are proved using the same tactic (at least, at the beginning of each proof).

In the middle of a proof, a goal can also be discharged by entering it as a **lemma** in a given theory (whose tactic might be distinct from the one used in the present proof). This possibility (of entering a goal as a lemma) can be 'programmed' in a rule, thus allowing us to **organize** large proofs as **layers** of lemmas all proved with their specific tactic.

SPECIFICATION OF AN OPERATING SYSTEM KERNEL
FOREST AND VDM COMPARED

S.J.Goldsack

Department of Computing, Imperial College of Science and Technology,

London SW7 2BZ

Abstract

The FOREST[1] project, supported under the Alvey initiative, addressed the problem of capture and specification of requirements of software systems. The specification technique is based on the use of a formal system built around a form of modal logic, which has come to be referred to as MAL, which permits both the effects of actions and the circumstances in which they are to be invoked to be defined. This paper uses the example of a real time operating system kernel to compare the specifications in VDM with those in MAL.

1. Introduction

In a tutorial introduction to VDM, Shaw [R. Shaw 1987] gave a VDM specification of the kernel operations of a simple real time operating system. This uses VDM notation to define formally the data structures maintained by the kernel, and the data structure manipulations which are required to keep record of the system state as the kernel operations are executed.

These definitions of the data structure manipulations fall short of specifying the system, since they do not define the circumstances in which the operations are executed. FOREST uses Modal Action Logic[2] (MAL) in which the deontic operators per and obl are used to construct logical formulae which hold when the execution of a particular operation is permitted or obliged to occur. Temporal extensions allow definitions of synchronisations and real time constraints. The following sections show how MAL may be used to give a more complete specification of system behaviour.

Section 2 of this paper first gives essentially the same specification as that given by Shaw, but using the style and notation of FOREST. Section 3 then extends the example to include deontic axioms, defining the circumstances in which each of the kernel operations must occur. Constraints of a temporal nature are then considered in section 4. In section 5 the extension of the specification to allow for time slicing is discussed.

---

[1]The FOREST project was conducted by GEC Marconi Research, GEC Avionics, Harwell Laboratory and Imperial College.

[2]A full account of the Logic may be found in the FOREST report R3 by T.S.E Maibaum [FOREST 1987]

2. The Basic Kernel Operations

The kernel of an operating system is responsible for organising the time sharing of the processor controlling its use by the processes executing on behalf of the users of the system. At any time at most one process, the current process, in the system is running the others being either blocked, unable to execute pending some external event (usually completion of an input or output operation) or ready to run, awaiting the opportunity to do so when the processor becomes available. It is therefore customary to consider them to be in one of three states, current, blocked or ready. The kernel software is responsible for switching the user processes between these states as appropriate to maximise the use of the processor, sharing its use between the processes, and simulating their concurrent execution. The actions of the kernel are a set of basic operations invoked whenever an event occurs which requires a change of state of one or more of the processes. The kernel operations are usually taken to be:

Dispatch   Starts a process in ready state executing.

Block   Transfers a process which is waiting for an external event, (awaiting i/o) into the blocked state.

Wakeup   Transfers a process from a blocked state to the ready state; it is invoked when the event for which it is waiting occurs.

Create   Introduces a new process into the active set normally bringing it from backing store.

Destroy   Removes a process from the active set, perhaps returning it to backing store. It will be invoked when the process completes its execution and becomes terminated.

As examples of the VDM notation adapted from Shaw, the definition of Dispatch, Block and Destroy may be given as follows

```
DISPATCH(pid : Process-id)
ext      wr current      : [Process-id]
         wr ready        : set of Process-id
pre      pid ∈ ready ∧ current = NIL
post     current = pid ∧ ready = ready' - {pid}


BLOCK (pid : Process-id)
ext.     wr current      : [Process-id]
         wr ready        : set of Process-id
         wr blocked      : set of Process-id
pre      pid ∈ {current} ∪ ready
post     (pid = current' ∧ current = NIL ∧ ready = ready' ∧ blocked = blocked' ∪ {pid})
                              ∨
         (pid ∈ ready' ∧ ready = ready' - {pid} ∧ blocked = (blocked' ∪ {pid}) ∧ current = current')
```

DESTROY(pid : Process-id)
ext.   wr current : [Process-id]
        wr ready : set of Process-id
        wr blocked : set of Process-id
pre   pid ∈ {current} ∪ ready ∪ blocked
post   (pid = current' ∧ current = NIL ∧ ready = ready' ∧ blocked = blocked')
                                ∨
        (pid ∈ ready' ∧ ready = ready' - {pid} ∧ blocked = blocked' ∧ current = current')
                                ∨
        (pid ∈ blocked' ∧ blocked = blocked' - {pid} ∧
                            current = current' ∧ ready = ready')

In this treatment, the ready list is treated as a **set** of ready processes; the operation Dispatch has a parameter to instruct the kernel which process from the set to dispatch. In fact, it is not clear how the appropriate process from the set would be selected by the caller. In the treatment given in the present paper, the set of ready processes is stored in the form of a FIFO list (a queue), and the Dispatch operation always selects the process currently at the front of the queue.

The following gives the corresponding definitions in FOREST style and notation. The specification begins with definitions of the data sorts, predicates and functions to be used, followed by the axioms which define the required properties of the system. At the present time the FOREST language has not been elaborated to provide pre-defined structured sorts, and any concepts such as sets and lists which are used should in principle be defined as part of the specification. Of course it is expected that in due course an interface language will be developed to simplify the process of specifying. The operations are considered to be actions performed by agents; the agent sorts and their possible actions are also declared. Here the only agent is the kernel.

Variables in MAL are implicitly universally quantified in all formulae: the scope of such a variable is therefore that of the formula itself. State variables in the VDM sense are defined as functions returning the values of the state; they may also be regarded as the non-rigid designators of modal logic.

Axioms of MAL may be formulae in predicate logic, but those relating to actions performed by agents take the general form:

pre $\Rightarrow$ [ag, ac] **post.**

This has the informal reading that if the conditions **pre** hold, and the agent **ag** performs the action ac then the result will be **post**. In the present section **pre** and **post** are written in first order predicate logic, and the difference from VDM is mainly syntactic.

To carry a value forward from the precondition to the postcondition, which is done in VDM using the convention of decorating the identifier in the postcondition, FOREST axioms use a quantified dummy variable. If x is a state variable (function) and n is a variable both of sort Natural, then

$x = n \Rightarrow$ [adder, incx] $x = n+1$

expresses the effect of adder performing incx. Informally, for all n, if initially $x = n$ and the adder performs incx then $x = n + 1$.

The following declarations establish the vocabulary for the specification.

data sorts:

        process-id
        current-process = process-id + nil -- a disjoint union
        process-queue = sequence of process-id

agent sorts

        kernel

agent constants

        kernel : kernel -- there is no ambiguity in 'overloading' the
                          -- names of the sort and the instance.

actions

  (of kernel)

dispatch	: process-id
block	: process-id
wake-up	: process-id
destroy	: process-id
create	: process-id

functions:

        -- functions returning values from the system state
        -- (non-rigid designators)

        blocked : $\longrightarrow$ process-queue
        ready   : $\longrightarrow$ process-queue
        current : $\longrightarrow$ current-process
        -- queue constructor functions

        <_>   : process-id $\longrightarrow$ process-queue

        _ :: _ : process-queue x process-queue $\longrightarrow$ process-queue
                            -- concatination of queues

        _ - _   : process-queue x process-id $\longrightarrow$ process-queue
                            -- deletes process from list

predicates:

        is-member : process-id x process-queue
                -- true if the process-id names a process in the process queue
        is-empty : process-queue
                -- true if the named queue is empty
        awaiting-io : process-id
                -- true if the named process is unable to execute pending completion of input or output
        terminated : process-id
                -- true if the named process has reached its termination
        known : process-id
                -- true the named process is known to (ie. already in) the system

variables:

        p,q   : process-id
        r, b, q : process-queue

axioms:

1. The following axioms define system invariants;

1a: no process is in more than one state list.

$\neg$ ((p = current $\wedge$ is-member(p, ready))

          $\vee$

(p = current $\wedge$ is-member(p, blocked))

          $\vee$

(is-member(p, ready) $\wedge$ is-member(p, blocked)))

1b. The ready list holds only ready processes

is-member(p, ready) $\Rightarrow$ $\neg$ awaiting-io(p) $\wedge$ $\neg$ terminated(p)

1c. The blocked list holds only processes waiting for I/O

    is-member(p, blocked) $\Rightarrow$ awaiting-io(p)

2. The predicate known is defined as follows:

    known(p) $\Leftrightarrow$ (p = current) $\vee$ is-member(p, blocked)
    $\vee$ is-member(p, ready)

3. The action Dispatch sets the process at front of ready queue to be the new current process. The dummy variable r is used to transfer the queue state forward as described above. The precondition implies that the queue is non empty.

    3a. (current = nil) $\wedge$ (ready = <p>::r) $\Rightarrow$ [kernel, dispatch(p)] (current = p $\wedge$ ready = r)

4. The action Block makes a current process which is waiting for I/O blocked or makes a ready process blocked:

    4a. (current = p) $\wedge$ awaiting-io(p) $\wedge$ (blocked = b) $\Rightarrow$ [kernel, block(p)]
    (current = nil) $\wedge$ (blocked = b::<p>)

    4b. is-member(p, ready) $\wedge$ (ready = r) $\wedge$ (blocked = b) $\Rightarrow$ [kernel, block(p)]
    ((ready = (r - p))$\wedge$ (blocked = b::<p>))

In the VDM specification of the same operation, the alternative pre-conditions are in fact given as postconditions which refer back to the initial state by using the convention of decorating the state variable.

Axiom 4b is not used here: it is included partly to correspond to the operation defined by Shaw, and partly to show how a complete action may be given as two or more definitions, defining the behaviour in cases with different preconditions. It is in fact not clear how the need for an operation to block a ready but non-executing process would arise.

5. The action Wake-up makes a blocked process ready:

    5a. blocked = b $\wedge$ ready = r $\wedge$ is-member(p, blocked) $\Rightarrow$ [kernel, wake-up(p)]
    (blocked = b - p $\wedge$ ready = r::<p>)

6. The action Create creates a new process, not previously in the system, and makes it ready to run:

    6a. $\neg$ known(p) $\wedge$ (ready = r) $\Rightarrow$ [kernel, create(p)] (ready = r::<p>)

7. The action Destroy removes a process from the system. There are three different cases, according to the initial state:

    7a. current = p $\Rightarrow$ [kernel, destroy(p)] current = nil

    7b. is-member(p, ready) $\wedge$ ready = r $\Rightarrow$ [kernel, destroy(p)] ready = r - p

    7c. is-member(p, blocked) $\wedge$ blocked = b $\Rightarrow$ [kernel, destroy(p)] blocked = b - p

At this level VDM and MAL are completely equivalent. However, in order to extend its expressive power, MAL treats each complete axiom as a formula in a Modal logic: the precondition holds true in an initial 'possible world', and so does the complete axiom. The post condition holds in the new 'possible world' reached by the agent's performing the action. The square brackets express a modality, stating the reachability of one world from the other. The pre and post conditions are also formulae in MAL so might contain further modalities. For example:

has-A-levels (John) ⇒ [university, make-offer(John)]
[John, accept-offer] is-student(John)

The post condition of the first action, tells us of an intermediate world in which the further modal formula:

[John, accept-offer] is-student(John)

holds.

In the absence of any assertion to the contrary the predicate has-A-levels(John) continues to hold in the post-condition. This is an example of a general frame rule which ensures that state values which are not explicitly mentioned are unchanged by the operation.

3. Deontic Elements

To give a complete specification of the kernel system, we must consider also the circumstances in which the above operations are invoked. Some are executed in response to requests by the operator of the system; others depend on the progress of the computations of the user processes. Thus, to discuss properly the behaviour of the complete system, we must describe the effects of operator commands, and of the execution of the user processes which are executed under the control of the kernel. Further declarations are therefore needed for the new agent sorts and instances, and for predicates relating to their behaviour. These are added in the appropriate places to those given above.

In principle we should distinguish carefully between a process-id and the corresponding process. A conversion function converting a process-id to the corresponding process could be used, so that a process with process-id p would be written process(p). However, in practice this is clumsy and unnecessary. In general we shall overload the notation and allow the reader to infer from the context which is the relevant interpretation for a variable symbol p or q. The definitions in section 2 are extended to include the following:

<u>agent sorts</u>
      process
      operator
<u>agent constants</u>
      operator : operator
<u>actions</u>
   (of process)
      execute
   (of operator)
      request-execution   : process-id
      request-kill   : process-id
<u>predicates:</u>
      terminated : process-id
      awaiting-io : process-id
      io-available: process-id
            -- note: this predicate corresponds to a flag set by an
            -- interrupt from the I/O system: the I/O handler should
            -- perhaps be another agent; for simplicity here the

```
-- setting of io-available is treated as a spontaneous
-- result of the arrival of I/O.
execution-requested : process-id
kill-requested : process-id
```

Next we add axioms describing the circumstances in which the actions by the system agents may or must be performed. These MAL formulae may contain terms which express that a certain agent has (or has not) permission to perform some action. Thus per(ag, ac) is an atomic formula which holds if the agent ag has permission to do the action ac. Equally if the the formula obl(ag, ac) holds, then the agent ag is obliged to perform ac as its next action.

There is, however a difficulty; the logic does not permit more than one obligation to be held by any agent at any time. The semantics of obligation state that if an agent holding an obligation ever does anything again the first must be the obliged action. It is not logical to have more than one obliged action. Careful study of the kernel system shows that multiple obligations can arise here only from the spontaneous arrival of I/O enabling the Wake-up operation, and from the operator requests enabling destroy and create. The solution adopted here is to assume that these are lower priority operations, performed at the discretion of the kernel when it has no obligation outstanding. They need therefore only to be given permission.[3]

Operators may always request process creation and subsequent execution of some process, and may also request the destruction of a process with a kill command; they may, however, only make one such request at a time. The permission to do so will probably be presented to the operator as a screen prompt, input being blocked until it appears. However, that is a design issue, not a concern of requirements at the system level. The axioms specifying this behaviour are:

8. The operator may request the execution of some process with request-execute and may request deletion of a process with a request-kill operation, provided he has no outstanding requests:

8a. per(operator, request-execution(p)) $\Leftrightarrow$ $\neg$ (execution-requested(q) $\vee$ kill-requested(q))

8b. per(operator, request-kill(p)) $\Leftrightarrow$ $\neg$ (execution-requested(q) $\vee$ kill-requested(q))

Operators cannot reasonably be obliged to perform any actions, so this is the complete deontic specification of the operator behaviour.

Circumstances may exist in which an agent's actions are obligatory whenever they are permitted at all; in other cases the circumstances in which they are obligatory may be a subset of those in which they are permitted, and in yet others only permission is required. In the case of the kernel operations there are examples of each form. The high priority kernel operations dispatch and block are obliged to perform their actions whenever they are permitted to do so. The same is true of the user processes: when a user process

---

[3]The effect of an 'eventual obligation' may be introduced by constructing an obligation sequence. This is an unnecessary complication for the purposes of the present paper.

is dispatched by the kernel, it is both permitted and obliged to execute. In the case of the destroy operation, it is obliged when it arises from the operation of the kernel itself, but only permitted when it is to be performed at the operator's request. In the following, the permissions are defined using the equivalence operator; this ensures that the action is not permitted if the conditions are false.

9. The kernel may create p if p is requested by an operator and is not already in the system:

9a. per(kernel, create(p)) $\Leftrightarrow$ execution-requested(p) $\land \neg$ known(p)

10. The kernel may destroy p if its destruction is requested by the operator and p is in the system; if p is the current process and is terminated, it is permitted and obliged to do so:

10a. per(kernel, destroy(p)) $\Leftrightarrow$ (kill-requested(p) $\land$ known(p) $\lor$ (p = current $\land$ terminated(p))

10b. (p = current $\land$ terminated(p)) $\Rightarrow$ obl(kernel, destroy(p))

11. The kernel may and must dispatch a new process if there is no current process and there is an eligible process in the ready list.

11a. per(kernel, dispatch) $\Leftrightarrow$ (current = nil) $\land \neg$ is-empty(ready)

11b. per(kernel, dispatch) $\Rightarrow$ obl(kernel, dispatch)

12. The kernel may and must block p if it is the current process and is awaiting I/O:

12a per(kernel, block(p)) $\Leftrightarrow$ (p = current) $\land$ (awaiting-io(p))

12b per(kernel, block(p)) $\Rightarrow$ obl(kernel, block(p))

13. The kernel may wake up a process if it is awaiting-io and io is available for it:

13a per(kernel, wake-up(p)) $\Leftrightarrow$ is-member(p, blocked) $\land$ io-available(p)

14. The current process may and must execute if it is not awaiting-io and not terminated:

14a per(p, execute) $\Leftrightarrow$ current = p $\land \neg$ awaiting-io(p) $\land \neg$ terminated(p)

14b per(p, execute) $\Rightarrow$ obl(p, execute)

15. The operator's request for execution of a process leads to its creation by the kernel through the predicate execution-requested (see axiom 9), unless the named process already exists. If the operator request is for an already existing process the effect is null. Creation cancels the request.

15a $\neg$ known(p) $\Rightarrow$ [operator, request(p)] execution-requested(p)

15b [(kernel, create(p)]($\neg$ execution-requested(p) $\land \neg$ terminated(p))

16. The operator request to kill a process leads to its destruction by the kernel through the predicate kill-requested, (see axiom 10) if the named process already exists. If the operator request is for an unknown process the effect is null. Destruction cancels the request.

16a known(p) $\Rightarrow$ [operator, request-kill(p)] kill-requested(p)

16b [(kernel, destroy(p))] $\neg$ kill-requested(p)

17. Since the actual effect of the user processes lie outside the kernel being specified, the effects of the execute operation cannot be given except insofar as they influence the kernel operations; execution stops when the process awaits I/O or terminates; it is not possible to say more.

17a [p, execute] awaiting-io(p) $\vee$ terminated(p)

4. Temporal considerations

These specifications determine for the most part the way in which the actions by the agents give rise to circumstances in which other actions must or may take place: however, to a large extent operations have been considered to be instantaneous. In fact operations take time, and care must be exercised to ensure that a specification does not give rise to situations in which resources shared by several agents may incorrectly be simultaneously accessed by them. Some constraints may be necessary to ensure synchronisation and mutual exclusion of the actions.

In general, it is usual in FOREST to consider that an agent can only perform one of its actions at a time; thus it may not be necessary to specify that the kernel operations are mutually exclusive. In any case, in a practical implementation, it is probable that all the actions will in fact 'run' on the same processor, so the mutual exclusion is in fact guaranteed. However, the latter concern is not part of the requirements. To permit considerations of this kind to be axiomatised, FOREST adds a temporal interval logic to the set of concepts used above. In particular, an interval of time during which some action ac is being performed by an agent ag is defined by a formula occurrence(ac, ag) which holds during the actual execution of the action, and not otherwise. Mutual exclusion of all the actions of the kernel may be specified by an axiom:

18. The kernel may not execute more than one action at a time.

18a $\neg$ (a = b) $\Rightarrow$ $\neg$ (occurrence(kernel, a) $\supset$ occurrence(kernel, b) $\vee$
occurrence(kernel, b) $\supset$ occurrence(kernel, a) $\vee$
occurrence(kernel, b)[occurrence(kernel, a)] $\vee$
occurrence(kernel, a)[occurrence(kernel, b)])

The terms in this formula specify that the occurrences are not contained within each other, nor overlap.

A possibly simpler version of this rule is:

18b happening(kernel, a) $\wedge$ happening(kernel, b) $\Rightarrow$ a = b

The predicate happening(ag, ac) may be observed to hold in any interval contained within the interval over which occurrence(a, ac) holds.

For the actions of the operator, mutual exclusion is sufficiently defined by the permission axioms, which give permission to request a process operation only if none of the outstanding requests is unfulfilled.

There is one circumstance in the above in which a kernel operation can change the state of a user process; as a result of the operator request to kill a process which happens to be the executing current process, the invocation of the destroy action of the kernel must pre-emptively stop the execution. Thus we need to add the axiom:

19. Destruction of the executing process stops its execution

occurrence(p, execute) $\Rightarrow$ [kernel, destroy(p)] $\neg$ occurrence(p, execute)

The following invariant applies to user processes:

20. Only the current process may be executing

occurrence(p, execute) $\Rightarrow$ (current = p)

5. Time slicing

The preceding specifications involve a cooperative scheduling policy; except for the pre-emptive kill operation discussed in the preceding paragraph, a user process will continue to execute once dispatched, until it reaches a natural break point, either waiting for I/O or terminating. This could mean a process running forever, eternally blocking other processes. The common way to handle this is to use time slicing, so that a process is deprived of its use of the processor if it has consumed its current time slice, being then moved to the ready list. To handle this we introduce a new kernel operation **suspend**. A first attempt at giving an axiom defining its effect is:

21. Suspension stops the current process and sets it to ready.

21a   occurrence(p, execute) $\wedge$ (ready = r) $\Rightarrow$ [kernel, suspend(p)]
           ($\neg$ occurrence(p, execute) $\wedge$ (ready = r::<p>) $\wedge$ current = nil)

Execution of the process is stopped and it is transferred to the back of the ready list, leaving the current process void.

The deontic parts of the specification must now define the circumstances in which the suspension takes place. The situation is non-deterministic, since when the process is launched, following a dispatch operation, the suspend operation must be invoked after a time slice, unless it has in the meantime become terminated or blocked as a consequence of its own behaviour. Let us define an interval start-of-next-slice forming a tolerance zone between adjacent time slices. In the spirit of the temporal interval logic such a named interval is a formula which holds during the interval in question; in this case it is to represent a time interval, perhaps of one clock tick, following a clocked interval defining the allowed time slice. We postpone precise definition of this interval. The following axioms should give the intended effect. First, suspension is permitted only during an interval in which the occurrence of the execution extends into the tolerance zone:

The kernel may suspend the execution of the current process if its execution extends into the tolerance zone.

21b   per(kernel, suspend(p)) ⇔ occurrence(p, execute) ∧ start-of-next-slice

In the event that the need for suspension arises, the kernel is obliged to perform it before the end of the tolerance interval. This is expressed using the timed obligation form, obl(ag, ac, α) which is read to mean that the agent ag must complete the action ac before the formula α ceases to hold. Thus:

21c   per(kernel, suspend(p)) ⇒ obl(kernel, suspend(p), start-of-next-slice))

22. The next axiom shows the non-deterministic nature of the system development following a dispatch operation.

22a.   [kernel, dispatch(p)] (occurrence(p, execute) < start-of-next-slice ∨
                                occurrence(p, execute)[start-of-next-slice])

As a consequence of the dispatch operation, some process becomes current; it may either complete its execution before the start of next slice, satisfying the first disjunct, or may overlap with the tolerance interval, in which case the kernel must suspend it before the end of the tolerance interval, as defined by axioms 21b and 21c.

The relationship between the various possible outcomes of dispatching a process are illustrated in figure 2.

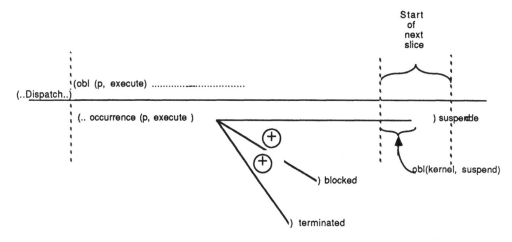

fig 2 The timing of operations Dispatch, Suspend and Execute with time slicing

Here is a possible definition of the start-of-next-slice:

22c   [kernel, dispatch] [clock, tick;tock^n] (start-of-next-slice = occurrence(clock, tick;tock))

If the kernel performs a dispatch operation, then if the clock tick;tocks n times, then start of next slice coincides with the next complete tick;tock of the clock.

There is a possible race condition present in the specification so far given. First note that after the obligation to suspend has been established, there may be a short delay before the kernel is actually able to obey it, and during that time the running process may become blocked or terminated. In view of the deontic rule for suspend, however, permission to suspend is cancelled, and with it the obligation. Nevertheless, if the suspend operation is actually started, it is still possible that the process could become blocked or terminated before the suspension has been able to take effect. In fact this would lead to a benign mal-function, since the process would be placed in the ready queue but in a state awaiting-io or terminated. The matter would automatically be corrected next time the process was scheduled. However, this is an untidy solution, and would violate axiom 1b. The correct handling of this may be left to the suspend operation, which should be redefined:

21b   occurrence(p, execute) ∧ (ready = r) ⇒ [kernel, suspend(p)]
            (¬ occurrence(p, execute) ∧
            (awaiting-io(p) ∨   terminated(p)) ⇒ current = p) ∧
            ¬(awaiting-io(p) ∨   terminated(p)) ⇒ ready = r::<p> ∧ current = nil))

The suspend operation must ensure that the execution of p is stopped, but will leave the process as current in the unlikely event that it finds it already stopped. The kernel will then invoke the block or destroy action as appropriate, according to axiom 10b or 12.

Finally, having introduced time slicing, there is one new concern which should be covered by the specification: so far it has been assumed that the effects of the execution of the user processes themselves could be ignored, but now the kernel is taking the liberty of interrupting an execution, so that the complete execution of a process is being spread out into a sequence of intervals during which occurrence(p, execute) holds. It is clearly a requirement that the net effect of the set of execution bursts should be equivalent to the single uninterrupted computation. A consequence of the suspend operation is the preservation of the current state of the process (actually its program counter, but that would be to talk too much in implementation terms)[4] . We introduce a new data sort **process-state** and for each process we define a new state function **state(p)**. There is also a function **current-state** returning the state of the currently executing process, and a variable **S** of sort state. We now add a new postcondition to the suspend operation:

22a   S = current-state ⟶ [kernel, suspend(p)] state(p) = S

The dispatch operation must restore the current state:

22b   state(p) = S ⟶ [kernel, dispatch(p)] ((current-state = S) ∧ (current-state = S)[occurrence(p, execute)])

The last axiom states that after the dispatch of p the current state is equal to state(p) and stays at that

---

[4]It is not possible to guarantee the integrity of any of the other variables in the context of a process, since in many cases the processes will be cooperating processes which share data; on restoration one cannot be certain that state data may not have been changed by other processes. In some systems there could even be privileged processes which are allowed to change the program counter, but we assume that that is not the case here.

value at least until the process starts computing. In the absence of any operation affecting state(p) during the idle periods of p, we have now ensured that it will resume where it left off.

For consistency, if the dispatch operation explicitly restores the state, then it would be better that, like the suspend, the block operation should explicitly save it. Thus we add also:

22c   current-state = S $\longrightarrow$ [kernel, block(p)] state(p) = S

6. Conclusions

The aspects of MAL as used in FOREST which concern the definition of agent operations seem to be entirely compatible with the basic VDM notations. However, the power of VDM as presently defined does not extend to the definition of system behaviour; MAL attempts to extend the range of use to include both causal and temporal aspects of system specification, and the extensions of the definition of the operating system kernel given here show that the technique is appropriate for real time systems. This may suggest a direction for development of VDM.

At the present time proof techniques for the more novel aspects of MAL are not well developed.

Acknowledgements

I am pleased to thank many of my colleagues in the FOREST project for helpful comments and suggestions in the preparation of this paper. Particularly, I must acknowledge the contribution of Tom Maibaum who was responsible for most of the development of the MAL logic.

References

R Shaw.   Tutorial introduction to VDM given at the VDM Europe Symposium, Brussels, 1987.

FOREST Report R3. T.S.E Maibaum. A Logic for the Formal Requirements Specification of Real-time Embedded Systems. 1987.

Compiler Prototyping with VDM and Standard ML

R.D. Arthan
ICL Defence Systems,
Eskdale Road,
Winnersh,
Berks. RG11 5TT

1 Introduction

This paper reports on experience gained and lessons learnt in the use of VDM, Standard ML and other software techniques and tools in the design and prototype implementation of a new programming language. The work arose as part of research into parallel processing architectures and techniques. The new language — DSL (DAP System Language) — is intended to support certain high-performance applications on hardware such as the AMT DAP (see [1,10]) range of SIMD processor array systems.

The particular set of language design objectives which came about from the intended applications and target architectures led to a proposal for a fairly simple imperative language with a rather large type system for defining the complex data representations which often arise in programming the target architectures and with a small, but essential collection of facilities which mostly serve to allow and encourage clarity of expression without compromising run-time efficiency.

This proposal took the form of an informal definition using a traditional mixture of BNF and English. In order to make the proposal rigorous it was decided to produce a formal semantics for the language along denotational lines using the VDM notation. This proved a most valuable exercise, highlighting a number of absurdities and redundancies in the original proposal and resulting in a language specification in whose self-consistency we could have a good degree of confidence.

It was observed along the way that a substantial part of the formal specification might be used as a basis for developing corresponding compiler components. This was particularly true of the large part of the specification which essentially deals with type-checking. After some research into methodologies and tools it was decided to begin implementation of a prototype compiler by first producing a type-checker based on the formal specification. (As we shall see later, the organisation of the formal specification meant that this type-checker has a more important role within the full compiler than might first be thought). This we would do by reifying the VDM specification, not into VDM, but into a suitable functional programming language, Standard ML being chosen for this purpose.

This first experience using VDM for specification and Standard ML as a prototype implementation language of sufficient expressive power to allow direct reification of the specifications proved quite successful. A team varying between three and four took about three months to produce a first cut type-checker comprising well over 10,000 lines of ML. After a small amount of work optimising and configuring this program, it has been possible both to release it to benign users and to use it ourselves as an effective checking tool for DSL programs. The decision was taken to use VDM for specifying the design of the remaining compiler components and to use Standard ML to implement them and this work is near completion.

2   The DSL Language

In order to give some idea of the issues which arise in its implementation we give here a brief overview of the DSL language and the motivation behind it. More detailed information may be found in [2] and [13].

The language is intended for implementation on SIMD processor arrays of the sort typified by the AMT DAP or the Connection Machine (see [9]). A number of high-level languages exist for such machines. Few, if any, of these are appropriate to the sort of signal and image processing applications for which these architectures are well suited. These applications areas will become particularly important now that VLSI technology has reduced volume and cost for AMT DAP, at least, to levels where embedded systems applications are attractive.

The sink of complexity in DSL is undoubtedly its type system. As well as supplying some high-level abstractions this has to deal with some rather low-level objects — this is in the nature of the applications. Depressing though the purist may find it, there are still some areas of programming left where assembly language programming reigns! The type system embraces:

(a) provision for specifying data of arbitrary run-time precision: this is particularly important on DSL's target architectures and applications areas such as signal processing where manipulation of say 4- or 5-bit data is natural; we can also form vectors and matrices of such data and these are processed in parallel by the target machines,

(b) provision for manipulating addresses within a type-checked framework: thus we have pointer and routine type constructors; we also have constructors for arrays, and C-like structures and unions; lists, trees and other recursive types may be built up with these constructors,

(c) mechanisms for obtaining a structured view of unstructured data and *vice versa*: thus in DSL a 32-bit IEEE floating point number is viewed as a specialisation (`real bit[32]`) of the type for a 32-bit object with no special interpretation (`bit[32]`); as an example, the exponent parts of such numbers might be extracted and used as 8-bit unsigned integers using casts (explicit type coercions) and ALGOL-68–like slicing constructs in statements such as:

```
exp_diff := :unsigned: x[1..9] - :unsigned: y[1..9];
```

Depending on the declarations of `exp_diff`, `x` and `y` this statement might result in a single subtraction or in a component by component operation on whole vectors or matrices.

(d) a mechanism — overloading — allowing different operations of the same name to coexist: this avoids having to write, say:

```
exp_diff := unsigned_minus(x[1..9], y[1..9]);
```

The complexity in the type system which arises here is that the resolution of a call of an overloaded name is settled on the basis of a measure of how well actual parameter types match the formal parameter types of the individual routines having that name.

(e) a mechanism for qualifying a type so as to steer the overload resolution algorithm: the token **real** above is a *derivation* — a qualifier for a type, rather like an adjective in natural language; derivations allow the user to choose between the structural type equivalence of say ALGOL-68 and the name type equivalence of Ada(R) or Pascal. Routines may be written which are generic with respect to derivations in the types of their parameters and results. The target architectures for DSL are uncommitted as to number representations — when dealing with the details of floating point arithmetic one might define a derivation **exponent** and use it thus:

```
exp_diff := :exponent: x[1..9] - :exponent: y[1..9];
```

to select automatically a user-written subtraction routine using the appropriate excess 127 arithmetic representation,

(f) a mechanism for passing precision information implicitly into called routines: routines can be defined which are generic as regards parameter and result precision with the choice of algorithm made either statically or at run-time; this saved an earlier example from actually having to look like:

```
exp_diff := unsigned_minus_8_8(x[1..9], y[1..9]);
```

or:

```
exp_diff := unsigned_minus_x_x(x[1..9], 8, y[1..9], 8);
```

The same mechanism supports dynamic length arrays. To handle this efficiently the language requires a powerful, and user-extensible system for static evaluation.

The language is built up from the type system in a fairly conventional imperative way. Expressions are built up from function and operator calls and some built-in forms (such as taking an address). Expressions live in statements which are assignments, procedure calls, the structured control constructs (which we stole from Ada(R) for their simplicity) and a special "**where**" statement — a parallel "**if**". Statements live in the bodies of routines (i.e. procedures or functions in our terminology). Routine and static variable declarations live in modules and libraries. Simple inter-module linkage features tie these together to form complete programs.

3 The Formal Specification

The formal specification of the language was produced between November 1986 and March 1987 by a team consisting of two experienced software designers and two recent graduate software engineers. All had considerable other commitments and were perhaps working on the specification for 60% of this time. None of the team had previous real-life experience of VDM although one of the software engineers had some experience with Z and other formal methods. The specification comprises some

150 pages of VDM (ignoring English commentary) and was prepared using a diverse range of word-processing systems. It was later ported onto UNIX filestore and some simple automatic processing (e.g. cross-referencing) was done using home-built tools.

Reference [3] was the basic reference used on the techniques of denotational semantics although it was found more convenient to use (an approximation to) the STC Reference Language notation for VDM as known to us from [14].

3.1   Factorisation of the Semantics

It is not appropriate here to go into the techniques of denotational semantics or our use of them in any detail. However a few key points are worth mentioning. In the ensuing discussion some of the names of VDM entities have been changed for reasons of clarity.

As we agonised over the syntax and value domains that the language required it became apparent that with the simple approach:

$$meaning : Program \twoheadrightarrow Input \twoheadrightarrow State \twoheadrightarrow (State \times Output)$$

$$meaning(prog) \quad \underline{\triangle}$$
$$\quad \text{if } is\_well\_formed(prog)$$
$$\quad \text{then } interpret(prog)$$
$$\quad \text{else } ERROR$$

the well-formedness function *is_well_formed* would be an object of considerable complexity which would not significantly ease the task of specifying the dynamic aspects in *interpret*. To handle issues such as overload resolution a complex naming environment would have to be built up in both functions. This reflected the fact that the language design complexity is mainly in the compile-time activity it requires (see appendix B below for some figures, and 2 above for some of the reasons). As a result of this the analysis of a program was factored as a composite:

$$meaning : Program \twoheadrightarrow Input \twoheadrightarrow State \twoheadrightarrow (State \times Output)$$

$$meaning(prog) \quad \underline{\triangle}$$
$$\quad interpret(resolve(prog))$$

where:

$$resolve : Program \twoheadrightarrow ResolvedProgram$$

$$resolve(prog) \quad \underline{\triangle}$$
$$\quad \vdots$$

$$interpret : ResolvedProgram \rightarrow Input \rightarrow State \rightarrow (State \times Output)$$

$$interpret(\,rprog\,) \quad \triangleq$$

$$\vdots$$

Here *ResolvedProgram* is the abstract syntax domain for a simplified form of the language in which names have been resolved to their defining instances, all implicit parameters are made explicit and the type system only reflects run-time storage requirements. The function *resolve* incorporates all the static well-formedness checks that would have been in *is_well_formed*. This factorisation better expresses the distribution of the semantics of the language between static and dynamic aspects and, not entirely fortuitously, enables the 100 or so pages of *resolve* to be used as the specification for the corresponding compiler components and interfaces. (It is the implementation of *resolve* which constitutes the bulk of our type-checker program). We were encouraged in this approach by [4] where a similar factorisation of the semantics is used for specifying Ada®.

3.2   Representation of the Type System

We have seen that the DSL language has quite a complex type system. As a result of an inherent difficulty with the type system as originally proposed, the representation of the type system in the static semantics was a problem for which our solution was not ideal. In order to represent the recursive types and define type equivalence and type coercions we used a representation based on labelled graphs. This representation let us draw appealing diagrams to illustrate our specification but some of the VDM formulæ manipulating the graphs were very involved.

Alarmed by the prospect of implementing this part of the specification we realised that the complexity could be decreased by removing some rather arcane features from the language. This permitted a neater way of representing the types which was more in line with the denotational approach. Unfortunately this had to be taken as an implementation decision. With hind-sight we should have realised much earlier on that the specification was becoming too complex.

It was fortunate that our factorisation of the specification did contain the problems within the static semantic analysis. The *ResolvedProgram* domains use a simple and workable representation for the type system which has been carried forward into the compiler specification without difficulty.

3.3   Follow Up

At the end of the formal specification exercise the specification as a whole was reviewed. This was a non-trivial task and took about six weeks of elapsed time (including necessary rework). This process would almost certainly have been shortened if we had had better tools than pen and eye for cross-referencing and type-checking the specification.

We were hampered by a lack of tools even for preparing VDM specification documents. More recently the use of the suite of LaTeX macros described in [17] has eased this problem and we have augmented them with an indexing mechanism. The reification into Standard ML has also proved valuable as a consistency checking mechanism.

The formal specification resulted in a number of rationalisations and simplifications of the original language proposal. These were subsequently included in a revised user-oriented definition of the language (reference [13]). In order to verify that the concrete syntax was satisfactory we constructed a parser for the language using the **lex** lexical analyser generator and the **yacc** parser generator (see [15]). This parser was subsequently mutated into a front end for the prototype compiler.

4 The Design Method

In the summer of 1987 it seemed likely that the opportunity would arise to produce a prototype implementation of the new language. It was intended that this prototype could be used, if desired, as the basis for a product implementation using a language such as Ada® but the choice of design method was not otherwise constrained.

Clearly our trump card was the formal specification but we did not at first know the best way to play it. A brief study strengthened a number of prejudices the author had formed and the rest of this section quotes heavily from that study.

4.1 VDM

The term VDM is widely used to describe two separate things:

(a) a formal specification language which can be used to give an abstract and precise mathematical model of the behaviour of a system,

(b) a design method which uses successively more detailed descriptions of a software solution using (a) until sufficient detail is attained for it to be possible to commit the solution to code in the programming language of one's choice, this process being known as *reification*.

The author felt strongly that while VDM *qua* specification language had manifold and proven advantages, the design method was perhaps inappropriate to a prototype development. We felt that the method in itself offers no guidelines or discipline which ensure that the implementation details added serve any useful purpose and that the review cycle required to monitor this would be too lengthy. In cases the author had heard of the method had often been supplemented by a more implementation oriented program design language.

We were aware of attempts to combine VDM with an implementation language such as Ada® fairly directly (see [8,11]). But felt that the linguistic gap between our VDM and Ada® was too wide to be spanned by a single bridge.

4.2 Our Approach

The design method we finally recommended was based on the text-book VDM method with two key differences:

(a) At each level of abstraction we would use conceptual or actual tools (VDM, functional programming languages, parser generators *etc.*) appropriate to the job in hand. Transformation between levels of abstraction is then the process of translating between the languages used at the different levels. Some flag-waving support for this idea was found in [12].

(b) We would derive from the top level VDM specification a design expressed in an implementable medium *viz.* a functional programming language. This would constitute a working model of the system being constructed and would enable early evaluation of the functionality of the system being implemented. This notion had some currency in ICL already (see [5,7]).

After some research the list of tools and techniques we arrived at included, VDM, `lex`, `yacc`, Standard ML and others. The bulk of the work would be in specifying those compiler components not directly covered by the formal semantics in VDM and in reifying all the resulting VDM into Standard ML. To prove the route we would first reify the static semantic analysis (the *resolve* function in 3.1 above). The resulting program could be used as a type-checker for the language.

4.3   Standard ML

We needed a functional programming language with sufficient expressive power to represent our VDM types and functions reasonably directly. Standard ML was chosen above what we felt was its main competitor — Miranda™ — chiefly because there were a number of compilers available for it and we felt this would reduce the risk of running against serious problems with a particular implementation. (Standard ML and Miranda™ are described in [6] and [16] respectively). In retrospect, I believe we would have found it hard going to work without using such dirty features as input/output by side-effect occasionally for diagnostic and other purposes and so feel the choice was a happy one.

Much of our specification was expressed in terms of sets and maps so one of the first tasks was to write a small library of generic functions to implement the set and map operations. A listing of the implementation of maps is given in appendix A below. Of necessity this library uses slow linear search algorithms. The approach followed was to use the generic functions initially resulting in a slow but functionally acceptable program. This can then be instrumented to locate the performance bottlenecks and faster algorithms can be used as appropriate.

It turned out that as far as sets and maps were concerned it was adequate just to implement better algorithms which implement the set and map operations corresponding to typical symbol table accesses efficiently and do their best for the other operations. It was possible to retrofit the use of the more efficient functions, where needed, without too much disturbance of the overall syntactic form of the Standard ML code which used them. This optimisation exercise would have been substantially easier if Standard ML supported overloading of user-defined functions since we would then not have needed to change the client code at all except to replace particularly inefficient constructs such as $x \in \text{dom} f$ by more efficient forms.

4.4 An Example

The following example may be of interest. It was used during our early investigations of Standard ML and Miranda™. It comprises a form of denotational semantics for a simple macro processor given in VDM and its reification as a Standard ML program.

Given a suitable concrete syntax and input/output functions the macro processor would be a usable program. Closest to the approach we adopted would be to use **lex** and **yacc** to create a C program which would map the concrete syntax into appropriate Standard ML value bindings for input and to use Standard ML's facilities for output. We do not show the input/output aspects here since in an example of this size they would swamp the VDM and Standard ML issues — in a real-life example they represent a minor part of the overall system.

4.4.1 The VDM Specification

The VDM specification of our simple macro processor starts with the abstract syntax domains:

$Macro\_text = Element$–list

$Element = Token \mid Set \mid Subs$

$Token$ :: text

Set :: $Name$
         $Macro\_text$

$Subs$ :: $Name$

$Name = $ text

Thus a macro processor input text is a list of items which are either $Tokens$ — simple text strings to be copied to the output, or Set commands — binding an arbitrary name to a piece of $Macro\_text$, or $Substitutions$ — causing the piece of $Macro\_text$ associated with a name to be inserted. We now give the value domain and an auxiliary syntactic domain for our semantics:

$Stream = text$–list

$Macro_env = $ text $\rightarrow Macro\_text$

Thus our macro processor output is like the input but with the macro processor commands removed and substitutions performed to leave just a stream of text items. Our auxiliary syntactic domain or static environment records the bindings resulting from Set commands. Given all this we can define our meaning function:

$m : Macro\_text \twoheadrightarrow Stream$

$m(T) \quad \triangleq \quad m\_aux(T, [\,])$

$$m\_aux : Macro\_text \times Macro\_env \rightarrow Stream$$

$$
\begin{aligned}
m\_aux(T, E) \quad &\triangleq \quad \text{if } T = <> \\
&\text{then } <> \\
&\text{else let } F = \text{hd } T \text{ in} \\
&\quad \text{let } L = \text{tl } T \text{ in} \\
&\quad \text{cases } F \text{ of} \\
&\quad mk\text{-}Token(X) \rightarrow X \frown m\_aux(L, E) \\
&\quad mk\text{-}Set(N, V) \rightarrow m\_aux(L, E \dagger [N \mapsto V]) \\
&\quad\quad mk\text{-}Subs(N) \rightarrow m\_aux(E(N) \frown L, E) \\
&\quad \text{end}
\end{aligned}
$$

4.4.2   The Standard ML Reification

A listing of the Standard ML reification of our simple macro processor follows. Note that the type systems of both VDM and Standard ML are asymmetric in their treatment of sum and product types but the asymmetries are dual — in VDM the product (or record) constructs a new type and the sum (or union) is just a type expression, in Standard ML it is the other way round. This is often reflected in VDM record types corresponding to ML type constructor names rather than type names as below. The strict rule of declaration-before-use in standard Standard ML forces us to reorder things. The transformation of type declarations is nonetheless straightforward and could doubtless be automated.

```
(* Abstract syntax domains *)

type text = string;

type name = text;

datatype element = Token of text
                 | Set   of name * element list
                 | Subs  of name

type macro_text = element list;

(* Value domain *)

type stream = text list;

(* Auxiliary syntactic domain *)

type macro_env = (text, macro_text) mapping;

(* Meaning function *)
```

```
fun m_aux (T : macro_text, E : macro_env ) : stream = (
    case T of
        nil => nil
    |   F :: L => (
            case F of
                Token X     => X :: m_aux(L, E)
            |   Set (N, V) => m_aux(L, E !+ N !-> V)
            |   Subs N      => m_aux((curry E N) @ L, E)
        )
);

fun m T = m_aux (T, empty_mapping);
```

4.4.3   Remarks

In our example we have given no well-formedness function, and indeed our specification is an under-specification in that it does not cover the case of *Subs*tituting an un*Set* name. Our Standard ML implementation of maps would actually raise an exception in **curry** as things stand. There are a number of interesting possibilities. The specification could legislate that un*Set* names *Subs*tituted to empty lists, or that a "run-time" error be raised, or that the macro processor functionality be slightly reduced allowing a well-formedness predicate to be specified to detect the condition. The whole problem could be considered as an implementation decision to be sorted out in the Standard ML code without cluttering the specification.

Another query about the specification concerns the value domain *Stream*. It could be argued that it retains too much structure in that typical macro processors produce a simple character stream or text file for their output. Moreover, it is clear that the **m_aux** function could produce its output directly by side-effect if that suited the context in which the program was to be used.

Situations analogous to these have often arisen in practice and there are no golden rules. It is clear however that having a reasonably rigorous specification and an implementation which is syntactically and semantically close to it gives a sound base for ironing out the details.

5   The Implementation

At the time of writing, the design and implementation of the prototype compiler for DSL is near to completion. The work has been carried out by a varied team of between three and five software designers and software engineers over a ten month period. Appendix B gives a few metrics we have gleaned over this period.

The design we have arrived at for our prototype compiler has seven main phases. Of these the VDM specification for all but the last phase have been completed and the specification for the last phase is well under way. Four of the phases have been implemented so far.

5.1 Technical Issues

Our specification and its implementation is organised with each phase as a separate function for ease of development. A more efficient implementation would doubtless merge some of these passes. It would be useful to have a way for describing this type of transformation at a higher level than simply rewriting the specification wholesale.

An important issue was the division of the implementation into modules (**structures** in Standard ML terminology). Our VDM specifications were usually informally partitioned into documents each dealing with a particular class of language construct (expression, statement, type *etc.*). Circumventing the restriction that Standard ML **structures** may not be mutually recursive required some ingenuity because of this, since mutually recursive language constructs are almost always analysed by mutually recursive functions.

As already mentioned, the input to the Standard ML part of the compiler is done via a parser which is a C program generated using **lex** and **yacc**. Essentially the parser translates the DSL input into a list of ML value bindings which when executed cause an abstract syntax tree to be built up. This mechanism is not very elegant but is surprisingly reliable. A parser generator producing parsers in Standard ML would be a cleaner solution.

5.2 Performance

The efficiency of our Standard ML programs was and remains a secondary concern. The initial type-checker using the linear search set and map algorithms throughout had a performance which quickly degraded to worse than one phrase/minute on inputs of more than forty or fifty phrases, where a phrase is roughly speaking a statement or a declaration. Its performance on small examples was acceptable for us to verify its functionality. The optimisation exercise mentioned in 4.3 above used binary tree representations for the important sets and maps to improve performance by a factor of more than 10 with a much more graceful performance degradation on large inputs. Further improvement is doubtless possible but has not proved necessary so far.

6 Conclusions

We have nearly completed development of a prototype compiler for a new programming language using a design method employing VDM for design specification and Standard ML as a way of rapidly implementing working models of the design. The method is pleasant and effective.

The VDM specifications give us an accurate language for discussing design issues. We view it as an *advantage* that these specifications are not executable programs since that would merely be a distraction.

Standard ML allows us to implement the designs straightforwardly adding necessary implementation details such as user-oriented error handling or the choice of a particular symbol table algorithm in ways which do not cloud the design. The implementations are sufficiently high-level for the design method to accomodate easily the changes which occur constantly in a prototyping development.

A   VDM Map Operations in Standard ML

The following simple abstract data type is used to implement VDM map operations in Standard ML. The functions elems, eps and less it uses are taken from an analogous datatype 'a set which implements the VDM set operations. (elems is as in VDM, eps (i.e. epsilon) is the set membership predicate, less is the set difference operator.) The infix directives allow us to preserve much of the syntactic appearance of the VDM.

```
abstype
    ('domain, 'range) mapping = mapping of ('domain * 'range) list
with
    exception curry ;

    infix   3      !->
    infix   2      !+
    infix   1      !! !\

    val empty_mapping = mapping nil;

    local

        fun     Apply(nil, v) = raise curry
        |       Apply((a, b)::tl, v) = if v=a then b
                                            else Apply(tl, v)

        fun     overwrite((v, w), nil) = (v, w)::nil
        |       overwrite((v, w), (a, b)::tl) =
                            if v=a then (v, w)::tl
                            else (a, b)::overwrite((v, w), tl)

        fun     restrict(s, nil) = nil
        |       restrict(s, (a, b)::tl) =
                        if a eps s then (a,b)::restrict(s, tl)
                        else restrict(s, tl)

    in

        fun     curry (mapping m) v = Apply (m, v)
                            (* curry lets us apply a mapping *)
        fun     (mapping f) !+ (mapping g) =
                        mapping (fold overwrite (g @ f) [])
                            (* mapping overwrite *)
        fun     a !-> b = mapping [(a, b)]
                            (* maplet former *)
        fun     (mapping m) !! s = mapping (restrict(s, m))
                            (* map restriction *)
        fun     dom (mapping m) = elems (map (fn (a, _) => a) m)
                            (* domain operator *)
```

```
fun      rng (mapping m) = elems (map (fn (_, b) => b) m)
                          (* range operator *)
fun      f !\ s = f !! ( (dom f) less s )
                          (* map subtraction *)
    end
end;
```

B Some Statistics

B.1 Language Complexity

It is interesting to attempt to use the size of a specification as a software complexity measure. As observed in [4] it is a trend in the design of programming languages for the complexity they demand in compilers to increase relative to the complexity of their run-time aspects. That DSL certainly follows this trend can be seen by including DSL in the table of "rough statistics" based on the size in pages of the specification of the static and dynamic semantics given in [4]:

	ALGOL 60	PL/1	CHILL	Ada[R]	DSL
Static Semantics	22%	26%	45%	55%	76%
Dynamic Semantics	78%	74%	55%	45%	24%
Relative Complexity	1	5	8	8	5

The "Relative Complexity" figures here are of debatable significance. Since I have not seen a definition of ALGOL-60 longer than 40 pages while the PL/1 standard is some 400 pages there is certainly a case for giving PL/1 a relative complexity of 10 or more as Ada[R] enthusiasts would doubtless agree.

B.2 Productivity

While there are clearly too many unmeasurable psychological unknowns to base a theory of "comparative software linguistics" on such crude measures as are given above, the economic implications of such statistics are perhaps of some relevance.

It is hard to give any useful statistics on the time it takes to produce a VDM specification in terms of the size of the resulting document since the dominant factor is the complexity of the problem not its solution. By and large, we have found that in cases where the problem is reasonably well-understood VDM specifications are produced and reviewed at a rate of about 10–20 pages per person/month.

The rate at which VDM specifications can be turned into Standard ML is much more predictable and, in our environment, is about 10 pages per person/week (to produce clean-compiled and desk-checked code). Unfortunate decisions on data representations in VDM have, in the past, forced us to produce implementations which are a lot further from the VDM than we would like. This definitely decreases productivity and is best avoided. Initially one should be prepared to throw some specifications away if their reification becomes problematic.

We have written some 500 pages of VDM specifications and some 20,000 lines of Standard ML. This has taken approximately 5 person/years. Some 14,000 lines of the Standard ML constitute the type-checker program which has been tested and used both within the project and by benign users. Approximately 35 errors have been detected in the type-checker by actual use so far (a few more have been detected by inspection). Maintenance and support activities have taken perhaps 1 person/month.

Acknowledgments

This work was jointly funded by the Royal Signals and Radar Establishment, Malvern and by International Computers Ltd.

Ada® is a registered trademark of the U.S. Government, Ada Joint Program Office.

Miranda™ is a trademark of Research Software Ltd.

UNIX™ is a trademark of AT&T Bell Laboratories.

References

[1] AMT DAP 500: FORTRAN-PLUS Language. Active Memory Technology Ltd., 65 Suttons Park Avenue, Reading, Berks. 1987.

[2] R.D. Arthan and T.W. Lake. DSL - a Language for SIMD Processors. To Appear. 1988.

[3] D. Bjørner and C.B. Jones. Formal Specification and Software Development. Prentice-Hall International. 1982.

[4] D. Bjørner and O.N. Oest. Towards a Formal Description of Ada. Springer-Verlag Lecture Notes in Computer Science vol. 98. 1980.

[5] P. Broughton et al. Designing System Software for Parallel Declarative Systems. ICL Technical Journal. May 1987.

[6] R. Harper, D. MacQueen and R. Milner. Standard ML. LFCS Report ECS-LFCS-86-2. University of Edinburgh. 1986.

[7] P. Henderson and C. Minkowitz. The me too Method of Software Design. ICL Technical Journal. May 1986.

[8] A.D. Hill. Asphodel - an Ada® Compatible Specification and Design Language. CEGB Internal Document.

[9] W.D. Hillis. The Connection Machine. MIT Press. 1985

[10] R.W. Hockney and C.R. Jesshope. Parallel Computers 2. Adam Hilger Ltd. 1988.

[11] M.I. Jackson. Developing Ada® Programs Using VDM. Software Practice and Experience. March 1985.

[12] M. Jackson. Articles in DataLink. March 9 and 16, 1987.

[13] T.W. Lake. DSL Reference Manual. ICL Internal Document. 1987.

[14] STC IDEC Ltd. A Perspective on VDM. (Course Documentation) 1985.

[15] A.T. Schreiner and H.G. Friedman Jr. Introduction to Compiler Construction with UNIX™. Prentice-Hall International. 1985.

[16] D.A. Turner. Miranda: A Non-strict Functional Language with Polymorphic Types. in Springer Lecture Notes in Computer Science vol. 201. 1985.

[17] M. Wolczko. Typesetting VDM with LaTeX. Dept. of Computer Science. Manchester University. March 1988.

VDM Development with Ada as the Target Language

David O'Neill

Generics Software Limited
7, Leopardstown Office Park
Foxrock, Dublin 18
Ireland.

Abstract

VDM development with Ada as the target language is examined. The aim is to study in detail the issues involved and to demonstrate the feasibility of providing semi-automatic tool support for VDM/Ada development, this support being based on a "rule set" for the process. Familiarity with VDM and Ada is assumed.

1. Introduction

VDM (The Vienna Development Method) is a rigorous software development method. VDM has been successfully applied to large-scale applications, and a considerable body of expertise in using the method has been accumulated in Europe [Bjørner 83]. VDM specifications are written using the wide-spectrum meta-language META-IV, which encompasses logic, functional, applicative and imperative styles. Since full META-IV is not executable, VDM is usually applied with a particular programming language as the target language. The built-in domains and domain constructors of META-IV (essentially data types and data type constructors) are central to VDM, and the more advanced features of Ada (including its typing, generic, information hiding and packaging facilities) make Ada a particularly suitable target language for VDM development.

The work reported here took place within the context of the development of a collection of tools called "AnimAID" [Chedgey 87a]. AnimAID is a graphical toolset supporting the rapid development of well-structured Ada software. At the heart of the toolset is a collection of data types and tools for the generation of new data types. These are called "Building Blocks". The Building Block types in fact correspond to the domains of META-IV. The AnimAID user constructs new application data types from the Building Blocks and implements the operations on the new types by calls to an extensive set of subprograms provided for the Building Block types. AnimAID includes tools to generate a graphical user interface to the application data types without further programming. Thus, separation of the user interface from an application program is achieved, i.e. the user interface may be created or modified without change to the application program. AnimAID provides the facility to "animate" a META-IV specification with a view to prototyping, testing and application development. A mixture of Object Oriented Design and VDM was successfully applied to specify AnimAID prior to its implementation [Chedgey 87b].

This paper examines VDM development with Ada as the target language. The aim is to study in detail the issues involved and to demonstrate the feasibility of providing semi-automatic tool support for VDM/Ada development, this support being based on a "rule set" for the process.

A set of generic Ada packages and package generators has been defined to implement the META-IV domains and domain constructors and their associated operations. Based on [Prehn 85], and on some experience in manually translating META-IV specifications into Ada, the translation of the various expression forms offered by META-IV (i.e. forms for object construction, conditional expressions, etc.) has been considered, and a small set of sample rules has been produced for the purposes of illustration.

2. From VDM to Ada

The possibilities for providing Ada equivalents for the domains and expression forms of META-IV are now examined in detail.

2.1 Domains

META-IV domains are intuitively seen as "data types": sets of objects and their associated operations. Domains are either predefined or composite (i.e. built by domain constructors). The predefined domains are BOOL, INTG, QUOT, TOKEN, N0, N1 and NUM (the domain of rational numbers).

The composite domains and their associated domain constructors are SET (-set), TUPLE (*, +), MAPPING (m→), UNION (|), TREE (::) and FUNCTION (→, ~→).

BOOL, INTG, QUOT, N0 and N1 can be represented by equivalent Ada types or subtypes.

BOOL, INTG, QUOT, TOKEN, N0, N1 and NUM can be represented by non-generic Ada packages (defining both the type and its applicable operations).

SET, TUPLE and MAPPING can be represented by generic Ada packages.

UNION and TREE can not be directly represented by generic Ada packages (as it is not possible in Ada to define packages with an arbitrary number of generic parameters); however, it is possible to write equivalent package generators.

Such a set of packages and package generators has been developed at Generics [Chedgey 87b].

META-IV functions may be specified in a number of different styles: implicitly (using pre- and post-condition axioms) or constructively (using expressions that will evaluate to the argument results, given the function values); applicatively or imperatively.

In general implicitly specified functions can not be directly translated into Ada. (Efficiency and executability will be discussed later.)

Executable VDM functions can be written as equivalent Ada functions. However, there are restrictions because there is no concept of a "function type" in Ada. In particular, functions may not be passed as parameters or returned as results by other functions (and so functions may not be "Curried"). The ability to define generic function parameters in Ada can alleviate these restrictions somewhat, as shown by the examples later.

Limited private types (as opposed to non-limited private types) should be used where possible to provide maximum encapsulation. It will in general be necessary to provide explicit copy and equality operations.

2.2 Translation of VDM Domain Equations into Ada

VDM specifications include a set of domain equations defining the syntactic and semantic domains of the application. These could be translated into equivalent Ada type or subtype declarations, WITH clauses (for non-generic packages) and package instantiations (for generic packages).

However, this approach will only work for sets of non-recursive domain equations (since Ada forbids recursive instantiation and directly recursive data types). Consider the following set of domain equations defining a simplified operating system (taken from [Bjørner 83]):

$$OS_0 :: DIR_0 \; FS$$
$$DIR_0 = Rnm \; m\rightarrow RES_0$$
$$RES_0 = Fnm \mid DIR_0$$
$$FS = Fnm \; m\rightarrow FILE$$

This can not be directly translated into a sequence of Ada generic package instantiations. It is necessary to refine ("reify") the domains thus:

$$OS_1 :: STG \; FS$$
$$STG :: Ptr \; (Ptr \; m\rightarrow DIR_1)$$
$$DIR_1 = Rnm \; m\rightarrow RES_1$$
$$RES_1 = Fnm \mid Ptr$$

... where in Ada the domain "Ptr" would be represented by an access type. The user must also transform the elaboration functions (system operations) accordingly before translation into Ada. An alternative would be either for a tool to automatically introduce the pointers necessary to remove recursion (or for the user to indicate where pointers should be inserted), and to semi-automatically translate the elaboration functions into Ada accordingly.

Every domain has an invariant (for semantic domains) or well-formedness condition (for syntactic domains) associated with it. (Where all possible elements of a domain are "valid", this is usually left implicit and taken to be "TRUE".) These (where executable) could be translated into Ada boolean functions, and used for example to generate automatic checks in the Ada definitions of the elaboration functions that the parameters are well-formed and the operations preserve the invariants.

This would be useful where the user had not (yet) formally proved the correctness of his specification, or where translation from VDM into Ada was only semi-automatic, or as an additional check where the proofs were "rigorous" rather than fully formal.

2.3 Expressions

The various expression forms offered by META-IV are now considered [Prehn 83].

Object Construction

The constants of the predefined domains may be represented by equivalent Ada constant (or 0-ary function) definitions.

Explicit enumeration of set, map and tuple objects (e.g. {e1, ... en}) may be supported by defining n overloaded Ada "make" functions taking from 1 to n parameters, where n is chosen to be some "reasonable" maximum. Alternatively, the values may be constructed by adding one element at a time.

Implicit enumeration (e.g. {f(e) | memb(s,e) AND predicate(e)}) can be supported provided the quantification is over a finite set: a generic "construct_set" function, with a predicate (boolean function) as a generic parameter, must be defined and instantiated appropriately.

Domain Associated Operators

These are the operators associated with the various META-IV domains listed above. They are defined as Ada functions and procedures in the package declaring the domain as a LIMITED PRIVATE type. Some functions (e.g. distributed set union and map composition) must be defined generically.

Conditional Expressions

The META-IV McCarthy conditional may be rendered by Ada's IF-THEN-ELSIF-ELSE statement. "Simple" META-IV "cases" expressions may be rendered by Ada CASE statements.

(See the section "Decomposition of Objects" below for when the "cases" expression includes object analysis in its branching conditions.)

Let Expressions

META-IV let expressions may be translated into Ada "DECLARE ... BEGIN ... END" blocks. Only constants need be declared where only functional constructs are involved.

Renaming of identifiers or the introduction of auxiliary declarations may be necessary.

Where the let expression defines a function, as in "let f(x) = e", f may be declared as an Ada function within the scope of the DECLARE block. The treatment of sets of mutually recursive function definitions involving least fixed point semantics has not been examined. (See the section "Decomposition of Objects" below for when the let expression includes object analysis.)

Quantified and Descriptor Expressions

Three forms of quantified expression are provided by META-IV: universal, existential and "exists unique". For each of these forms, an Ada generic boolean function, taking a SET as parameter and with a predicate (boolean function) as a generic parameter, could be defined in the SET package and appropriately instantiated as required (provided quantification was over a finite set).

Similar considerations apply to the descriptor expression "delta", which selects the unique element satisfying a predicate from a set. (Executability and efficiency are discussed later.)

Test for Domain Membership

These tests (e.g. the META-IV predicate "is-INTG") are implemented by Ada's typing rules, except for the UNION domain, where the corresponding Ada package generator generates an "is-T" function for every type T making up the union.

Exit Mechanism

The obvious counterpart of META-IV's exit mechanism is Ada's exception mechanism. However, META-IV is more general in that it allows values to be passed up by the exit and "trapped" at a higher level, whereas Ada only allows the user to define and handle named exceptions.

Where the number of possible values passed by a META-IV exit is small, this might be dealt with by defining a corresponding set of Ada exceptions.

Decomposition of Objects

The separation of a value into its constituent parts according to a prescribed template is allowed in META-IV constructs (such as "let" and "cases"). This is particularly useful for breaking a tuple into its head and tail, a tree into its constituent parts, and for distinguishing between the various possible types a value of a union could have. In Ada this would have to be performed using function calls to perform the decomposition explicitly.

2.4 Imperative Features

The imperative features of META-IV have direct counterparts in Ada. There is an implicit global state which corresponds to a set of global variables.

2.5 Structure

VDM does not predefine any means for structuring specifications (e.g. for grouping related operations and the definition of the domain(s) they work on into modules or ADTs, for making explicit the "imports" relationship between domains, for specifying which operations are visible to the user and which are hidden or auxiliary). A simple extension to META-IV has been defined at Generics to address this problem [Chedgey 87b]. A distinction is made between three kinds of entities: objects (variables of the global state), types (possibly generic ADTs defining a type and the operations available on it) and packages (a set of related operations not defining any new types). A corresponding Ada package structure would follow from a META-IV specification written according to these conventions.

3. Possibilities for Transformational Tool Support

Thus far the emphasis has been on semi-automatic transformation of META-IV specifications into Ada. This is not only because automatically generated Ada implementations would be unlikely to be efficient (although they might be acceptable as prototypes), but because full META-IV is non-executable. There are three transformational phases during which efficiency is increased and/or non-executable constructs are removed:

- META-IV → META-IV
- META-IV → Ada
- Ada → Ada

It would be useful to have transformational tool support in any of these phases (or even just a rule set to be applied manually). The results of the CIP transformation project are of relevance, in particular the work on transformation between different language levels (logic to functional to imperative) and recursion removal [Moeller 84].

META-IV → META-IV transformations are familiar to all VDM developers. Object and operation transformations are applied until an executable specification sufficiently concrete and efficient to be hand translated into the target language is obtained.

If a semi-automatic META-IV → Ada transformation tool and/or reusable Ada packages were available, the length of the META-IV → META-IV transformation phase could be reduced. Recursive domain equations might be handled by automatically introducing the pointers necessary to remove recursion (or by the user indicating where pointers should be inserted), and by semi-automatic translation of the operation definitions into Ada accordingly.

The number of levels of VDM object transformations (or "reification") necessary might be reduced by the presence of multiple Ada implementations for the built-in META-IV domains. Different representations would be used for the various domains (e.g. for SET there might be packages providing a linked list, array, binary tree or bit-map representation, depending on whether the set size was bounded and whether an ordering relation was available for the set elements), and the most efficient representation for the particular application would be chosen. Procedural implementations might also be made available where these would improve efficiency. Booch's taxonomy of reusable Ada components is clearly of relevance here [Booch 87]. In addition to the more sophisticated transformations mentioned above (which would probably be applied at the user's instigation), simpler operation transformations could be automatically applied by a META-IV → Ada transformation tool, having a significant impact on efficiency. For example a common expression appearing in META-IV specifications using mappings is "d ∈ **dom** m". Obviously, it would be more efficient in this case for the Ada MAPPING package to provide a function:

Is_Defined : (A m→ B) A → Boolean

... and to translate "d ∈ **dom** m" into "Is_Defined(m, d)", rather than computing the domain of m and then performing a set membership test for d. This kind of transformation is at the same level as compiler optimisation.

The nature of VDM developments make active management of a VDM project database possible (e.g. keeping track of the input and output documents of object and operation transformations, proof obligations, etc). For example, VDM database support is provided by the DDC META-IV Tool-set [DDC 86]. It should be possible to express the rules for managing such a database declaratively (as is done in SPRAC [Foisseau 84]).

Considerable knowledge on how to apply VDM within various application domains exists within the VDM community. For example, within the application domain of programming language definition and compiler construction, such knowledge would include how to construct an abstract syntax, how to model a machine store, how to deal with the particular problems given by looping or jumping constructs, how to handle scoping, etc.

4. Conclusions

It is feasible to semi-automatically translate META-IV specifications into Ada. An issue which remains to be addressed is where in the VDM Development Cycle a META-IV → Ada translation tool might be introduced (or at what stage this translation should be performed by hand).

It appears that semi-automatic META-IV → Ada translation could be introduced early in the development process (at least for prototyping purposes). Incomplete or "skeletal" translation, leaving the user to fill in the gaps, would be useful:

- Ada package specifications, i.e. type (META-IV domain) and function (META-IV elaboration function) declarations could be generated from the augmented "modular" META-IV notation mentioned above. (This would save a considerable amount of clerical effort.)

- Non-executable META-IV function specifications could be translated into Ada formal comments, with the user filling in the Ada function body. For example, implicit META-IV specifications using pre- and post-conditions could be translated into ANNA formal comments [Luckham 85].

- Recursive domain equations might be handled by introducing access types.

In the absence of any META-IV → Ada tool support, it would still be useful to develop a handbook of design rules for use by the VDM/Ada developer.

Example rules might be:

- Function definitions should not be "Curried".

- Recursive domain equations may be translated into Ada by introducing access types.

- Use LIMITED PRIVATE types where possible for maximum encapsulation.

Rules could also be introduced for selecting among the multiple Ada packages implementing the VDM domains. (Barstow has already developed a similar set of data structure selection rules for LISP programming [Barstow 79].)

Simple transformation rules from META-IV to Ada which express how to use the functions in the predefined Ada packages efficiently could also be given. Examples are given below (the reader should use his intuition):

(1)
dom m_1 ∩ **dom** m_2 = {}   (m_1 and m_2 are META-IV maps)
⇓
Is_Disjoint(m_1,m_2)

(2)
$[d \rightarrow f(m(d)) \mid d \in$ **dom** $m]$
⇓
function Apply_f_to_Map_Range **is new** Process_Map_Range(f);
....
Apply_f_to_Map_Range(m)

(3)
let $d \in$ **dom** m **be such that** p(d) **in** <body>
⇓
function Select_Domain_Element_Satisfying_p **is new**
    Select_Domain_Element_Satisfying_Predicate(p);
d : **constant** <domain type>:= Select_Domain_Element_Satisfying_p(m);
....
<body>

(4)
$f(t)$ = **cases** t:(<> → <>,
              <e> ^t1 → g(e) ^ f(t_1))
⇓
function f **is new** Apply_Unary_Op(g);
....
f(t)

Example (4) hints at a possible problem: the best Ada implementation of a VDM construct may not be "immediately obvious". For example (4), generics allow a concise and efficient implementation, whereas a VDM developer would tend to use recursion (particularly for tuples). It is really a question of knowing what is available in the predefined VDM support packages. While it would be easy enough to supply a user with a META-IV → Ada rule book (which in essence would be a VDM specification of all the Ada functions in the VDM support packages), automating transformations such as (4) above would not be so easy.

The argument could be carried further. The functions of the predefined Ada packages could be regarded as a set of predefined META-IV functions which the developer is recommended to use where possible.

For "simple" META-IV specifications, e.g. those not involving recursive domains and written in a functional or imperative (executable) style, it is possible to avoid or at least minimise the amount of explicit object and operation transformations which have to be performed and to code directly in Ada. This could be called "Ada programming in a VDM style" and it is this manual approach which has been applied at Generics thus far.

Acknowledgements

Part of this work was funded by the CEC under the ESPRIT programme, projects ToolUse (Software Technology 510) and Papillon (CIM 496).

References

[Barstow 79]   D.R. Barstow, "Knowledge-Based Program Construction," Elsevier, North-Holland, 1979.

[Bjørner 83]   D. Bjørner, "Software Engineering Aspects of VDM," Proceedings of the International Seminar on Software Engineering, Capri, North-Holland, 1983.

[Chedgey 87a]   C. Chedgey et al., "Developing Ada Software Using VDM in an Object-Oriented Framework", Proceedings EUUG Autumn '87 Conference, Trinity College, Dublin, September 1987.

[Chedgey 87b]   C. Chedgey et al., "Using VDM in an Object-Oriented Development Method for Ada Software," Proceedings VDM-Europe Symposium, Brussels, Lecture Notes in Computer Science, Vol. 252, Springer-Verlag, 1987.

[DDC 86]   C. Bjernaa and I. Hansen, "DDC META-IV Tool-Set User's Guide", Dansk Datamatik Center, No. DDC 164/RPT/31, December 1986.

[Foisseau 84]   J. Foisseau, R. Jacquart, M. Lemaitre, M. Lemoine and G. Zanon, "Le systeme SPRAC: expression et gestion de specifications, d'algorithmes et de representations," Rapport No 1/3619/DERI/CPAO/84/2, CERT, Toulouse, February 1984.

[Luckham 85]   D.C. Luckman and F.W. von Henke, "An Overview of Anna, a Specification Language for Ada", IEEE Software 2(2), March 1985, pp. 9-23.

[Moeller 84]   B. Moeller (ed.), "A Survey of the Project CIP: Computer-Aided, Intuition-Guided Programming - Wide Spectrum Language and Program Transformations," Technische Universitaet Muenchen, Institut fuer Informatik Report TUM-18406, July 1984.

[Prehn 83]   S. Prehn et al, "Formal Methods Appraisal", ESPRIT Preparatory Study, Dansk Datamatik Center, Document No. DDC 86/1983-06-24, 1983.

NUSL: AN EXECUTABLE SPECIFICATION LANGUAGE BASED ON DATA ABSTRACTION

XinJie Jiang
Computer Center
Nanjing Normal University
Nanjing, P.R.China

YongSen Xu
Dept. of Computer Science
Shantou University
Guangdong, P.R.China

ABSTRACT

It proves very useful to give a formal specification of the software to be developed before the development. To write formal specifications, a specification language is to be used. This paper describes the specification language NUSL which has a supporting system.

NUSL is an applicative executable specification language, centered around the concept of data abstraction, with module construct in it. Both the algebraic and the model-oriented specification techniques of abstract data types are embedded in the language. NUSL is an applicative language which is readable and mathematical. With the module construct, it is convenient to use NUSL to write large specifications. Because the language is executable, a specification in NUSL may be viewed as a prototype of the specified system and be executed on the supporting system.

The supporting system provides static checking and dynamic execution facilities.

1. INTRODUCTION

Specification is a crucial phase in the software life-cycle and more and more attention is paid to it. It is reported in [5] that over 60 percent of errors uncovered in several operational software systems were due to shortcomings in the specification themselves. This high percentage of errors contributes significantly to the unreliability and prohibitive cost of software. Therefore, the research for producing error-free specifications is a very important subject in software engineering.

Among the main causes that the specification phase are error-prone are

-- Natural language specifications are ambiguous, easy to misunderstand.

-- Specifications may be incomplete or contain conflict conditions.

-- User's requirement statements are vague, and it is hard to determine   whether a specification agrees with user's requirements.

One way to solve these problems is to introduce formal specification into software development. There are many advantages to give a formal specification of the developed software before the subsequent development. Formal specifications

(i) are precise, improbable to be misunderstood,

(ii) are the foundations of rigorous development,

(iii) can be processed by computers.

Data abstraction is a very important concept and method in formal specification techniques. Since C.A.R.Hoare discussed the correctness of data representations for the first time in 1972 [15], data abstraction and specification of abstract data types have been a very hot and active research field. Now there are mainly two approaches to specification of abstract data types. One is the so called property-oriented approach i.e. the algebraic specification method advocated by Goguen and Guttag et al. [9][10][11]. In this approach, data objects are characterized by operations of the data type and the semantics of the operations is described via algebraic equations. No representations of the data type is needed.

The other is the model-oriented approach, i.e. the constructive approach [15][16][18][23]. As to data abstraction, VDM is in the category of this approach. If an abstract data type is to be defined using this method, some meta constructs such as set, sequence etc., have to be used and an abstract representation of the type to be specified is given first using the meta constructs, then the operations of the type are defined as functions using the operations of the meta types.

Algebraic approach and model-oriented approach both have their advantages and disadvantages. Algebraic specifications are more abstract and mathematical, but more difficult to construct, especially for large software, and some times it is even impossible to specify in the algebraic approach [20]. The model-oriented approach is easier to learn and more feasible for the specification of large systems, but sometimes there is the problem of over-specification [19].

The introduction of formal specification into software development, however, introduces a new problem -- formal specifications may be too abstract for users to understand, so users are not able to make sure that formal specifications agree with their requirements. To solve this problem, the idea of rapid prototyping could be used. Before the development of the production software, a prototype software is produced for users to experiment with and suggest some changes [1][2].

To lower the cost for the development of prototypes, the languages used are often different from the language used for programming the final production software, e.g. if the language for programming a production software is an assembly language, the language used for prototyping might be PASCAL or PROLOG. It is most economical to use the same language for specifying and prototyping, i.e. to specify in an executable specification language, thus, when a specification is finished, it may be viewed as a prototype of the software to be developed [8][13][22].

In this paper the specification language NUSL is described which is designed by this author based on the study of current specification techniques and languages.

2. FEATURES AND STRUCTURE OF NUSL

Based on the analysis of the current specification languages [3][7] [12][13][22] and the experience we have got in the practice of software specification, we designed a specification language, NUSL, which, originally, we aimed to be small, flexible and executable.

NUSL is a specification language centered around the concept of data abstraction. Because the algebraic approach and the model-oriented approach of abstract data type specification both have their advantages and disadvantages, they are combined in NUSL.

The specification of stack is a classical example. The algebraic specification of stack in NUSL is

```
ALG astack
   TYPE
         Stack(elem);
   OPERATION
         empty:  -->Stack
         is_empty: Stack --> BOOL
         push: elem,Stack --> Stack
         pop: Stack --> Stack
         top: Stack --> elem
   EQUATION
         is_empty(empty)=TRUE;
         is_empty(push(e,s))=FALSE;
         pop(empty)=UNDEFINED;
         pop(push(e,s))=s;
         top(empty)=UNDEFINED;
         top(push(e,s))=e;
END astack
```

Here Stack is a parameterized type and it has a type parameter elem. Specified parameterized types can be used for abstract representation of types to be specified.

To facilitate model-oriented specification, four elementary structured parameterized types, set type SET, sequence SEQ, map type MAP and abstract tree are provided in NUSL. Each type has some basic operations.

Stack may be abstractly represented as a sequence,

Stack=SEQ(elem).

A model-oriented specification of Stack is

```
MOD mstack
    TYPE
        Stack(elem);
    ABSREP
        Stack=SEQ(elem)
    OPERATION
        empty:   -->Stack
        is_empty: Stack --> BOOL
        push: elem,Stack --> Stack
        pop: Stack --> Stack
        top: Stack --> elem
    FUNCTION
        empty()=<>;
        is_empty(s)= (s=<>);
        push(e,s)=<e>¦¦s ;
        pop(s)= IF is_empty(s) THEN UNDEFINED
                ELSE TL s FI;
        top(s)= IF is_empty(s) THEN UNDEFINED
                ELSE HD s FI;
    END mstack
```

A NUSL specification usually consists of a number of units (sometimes only one). There are two kinds of units in NUSL -- ALG units for algebraic specification and MOD units for model-oriented specification. The structures of these two kinds of units are as below:

```
ALG name                        MOD name
 USE segment                     USE segment
 TYPE segment                    TYPE segment
                                 ABSREP segment
 OPERATION segment               OPERATION segment
 LOCOP segment                   LOCOP segment
 EQUATION segment                FUNCTION segment
END name                        END name
```

USE segment indicates the names of the units which are used by this unit. TYPE segment indicates the names of the global types defined in this units (and formal parameters, if parameterized types). ABSREP segment of MOD unit gives abstract representation of global types and local types of this unit. Local types and local operations can not be used outside the unit. OPERATION segment and LOCOP segment indicate the names, parameter types and return types of global operations and local operations respectively. EQUATION segment of ALG unit is a group of algebraic equations to define the semantics of the operations. FUNCTION segment gives function definition for each operation. Some of the segments may be absent according to the situation.

The algebraic specification of Stack seems more elegant. As we indicated before, however, model-oriented specifications are more practical, easier to read and construct. So we might use ALG units to specify small components and use MOD units to construct larger specifications from these components (cf. section 3).

Since NUSL is a specification language centered around data abstraction, software systems are specified as abstract data types with various operations on them.

The Bill-of-Material problem may be an interesting example. Suppose a manufacturer builds a number of products each of which is either a base item (no-components) or a sub-assembly; sub-assemblies may be made up from a number of components which are themselves either basic or sub-assemblies; and so on. We may abstractly represented a bill of materials as a MAP from part numbers to SETs of part numbers,

        BOM=MAP(pat_no,SET(part_no))
and basic elements map onto empty sets or do not appear in the domain of the map.

The needed operations on BOM are:

explode: Compute the set of component units (basic or otherwise) for a stated unit.

enter: Enter a new unit description into BOM. If there has been a description of the unit in BOM, it is replaced.

delete: Delete a unit description in BOM if the unit is not a sub-component of any other units in BOM. Otherwise BOM is left unchanged.

add: Add an additional constituent unit to a composite unit.

erase: Erase a constituent unit from a composite unit.

```
MOD bill
  TYPE    Bom;
  ABSREP
    Bom=MAP(part_no, part_set);
    part_set=SET(part_no);
  OPERATION
    explode:part_no,Bom --> part_set
    enter: part_no,part_set,Bom --> Bom
    delete: part_no,Bom --> Bom
    add: part_no,part_no,Bom --> Bom
    erase: part_no,part_no,Bom --> Bom
  LOCOP
    exps:Bom,part_set --> part_set
  FUNCTION
```

```
      explode(p,b) = IF p <- DOM b THEN b^p U exps(b,b^p)
                        ELSE UNDEFINED  FI;
      exps(b,ps) = IF ps={ } THEN { }
                     ELSE LET p1=ELEM ps IN
                            explode(b,p1) U exps(b,ps-{p1})
                          TEL
                     FI;
      enter(p,ps,b) = IF ps < DOM b THEN b+[p¦->ps]
                        ELSE UNDEFINED  FI;
      delete(p,b) =  IF p <- UNION RNG b THEN b
                     ELSE b/{p}  FI;
      add(p,p1,b) = IF {p,p1} < DOM b THEN b+[p¦-> b^p U {p1}]
                      ELSE UNDEFINED  FI;
      erase(p,p1,b) = IF p <- DOM b  THEN  b+[p¦->b^p-{p1}]
                        ELSE  UNDEFINED FI;
  END bill
```

NUSL is also a pure applicative language without side effect.

3. INCREMENTAL SPECIFICATION IN NUSL

As stated in the previous section, NUSL is a modular language and a
specification in NUSL usually consists of a number of units. By the USE
segment, types and operations defined in other units could be used in
the current definition. Types and operations that do not appear in the
TYPE segment and OPERATION segment of a unit are hidden from outside
the unit. These features of NUSL facilitate large scale specification
in NUSL and incremental construction of specifications. The so- called
incremental construction runs two ways, top-down and bottom-up, which
is demonstrated by the following specification of symbol-table, a data
structure used by compilers of blocked languages.

The operations on symbol-table are:

init: Allocate and initialize the symbol table.

enterblock: Prepare a new local naming scope.

leaveblock: Discard entries from the most recent scope entered, and
           reestablish the next outer scope.

is_inblock: Has a specified identifier already been declared in this
           scope? (Used to avoid duplicate declarations.)

add: Add an identifier and its attributes to the symbol table.

retrieve: Return the attributes associated (in the most local scope
           in which it occurs) with a specified identifier.

The type symbol-table might be abstractly represented as Stack of
Layers:

        Symtab=Stack(Layer)

in which a Layer reserves the identifiers and their attributes of a
certain block. Stack has been specified before and we suppose that

Layer has the following operations:

new: Produce a new, empty Layer.

assign: Assign an identifier and its attribute to the Layer.

read: Read the attributes associated with a specified identifier in
        the Layer.

is_defined: Has a specified identifier already been defined in the
        Layer?

The specification of symbol-table is

```
MOD msymtab
  USE
    astack, dlayer;
  TYPE
    Symtab;
  ABSREP
    Symtab=Stack(Layer);
  OPERATION
    init:    -->Symtab
    enterblock:  Symtab --> Symtab
    leaveblock:  Symtab --> Symtab
    add:Symtab,Ident,Attr --> Symtab
    is_inblock:  Symtab,Ident --> BOOL
    retrieve:  Symtab,Ident --> Attr
  FUNCTION
    init()=push(new,empty);
    enterblock(s)=push(new,s);
    leaveblock(s)=IF is_empty(pop(s)) THEN UNDEFINED
                  ELSE pop(s)  FI;
    add(s,id,at)=push(assign(top(s),id,at),pop(s));
    is_inblock(s,id)= IF is_empty(s) THEN FALSE
                        ELSE is_defined(top(s),id) FI;
    retrieve(s,id)= IF is_empty(s) THEN UNDEFINED
                      ELSE
                        IF is_defined(top(s),id)
                        THEN read(top(s),id)
                      ELSE retrieve(pop(s),id) FI
                      FI;
  END msymtab
```

Now symbol-table has been specified, our   next   task   is   the
specification of Layer, which is trivial.

```
ALG dlayer
  TYPE
    Layer;
  OPERATION
    new:  --> Layer
    assign: Layer,Ident,Attr --> Layer
    read: Layer,Ident --> Attr
    is_defined: Layer,Ident --> BOOL
  EQUATION
    read(new,id)=UNDEFINED;
    read(assign(ar,id1,at),id)=
      IF id=id1 THEN at ELSE read(ar,id)  FI;
    is_defined(new,id)=FALSE;
    is_defined(assign(ar,id1,at),id)=
      IF id=id1 THEN TRUE ELSE is_defined(ar,id) FI;
  END dlayer
```

Ident and Attr are undefined type names. Since it is unnecessary to present all details in a specification sometimes, undefined type names are allowed in NUSL and the allowance of undefined types increase the flexibility of NUSL.

From the above example we might notice that the basic objects are better defined using ALG units and a model might be based on such ALG unit defined objects rather than only on the four basic types. In ALG units, however, functions defined in MOD units, basic types and operations, and constructs such as LET expression and CASE expression are also available in an ALG unit. That makes ALG units more powerful than usual algebraic definition mechanisms.

4. EXECUTION OF SPECIFICATIONS AND OVERVIEW OF THE SUPPORTING SYSTEM

NUSL is an executable specification language. Specification in NUSL may be executed on the supporting system and be viewed as a prototype of the production system. Since NUSL is a applicative language, the execution of NUSL specifications is facilitated by evaluation of expressions which contain operations defined in the specification to be executed resulting in object instances of the types defined in the specification. Let us examine the execution of mstack first. Contents showed by system are underlined.

```
Current Unit > mstack
Evaluate
    pop(pop(push(pop(<1,2,3,4>),5)))
Value is
    <1,2>
Evaluate
    push(push(pop(<'a','b','c'>),'d'),'e')
Value is
    <'a','b','d','e'>
Evaluate
    top(pop(<23,45,36>)
Value is
    45
```

Since an algebraically specified type has no representation, its object instances can only be constructed by applications of its constructing operations.

```
Current Unit > astack
Evaluate
    pop(push(push(pop(push(empty,4)),3),2))
Value is
    push(empty,4)
```

In the above evaluation, push and empty can not be eliminated, they are constructors of the type.

Evaluate
    top(pop(pop(push(empty,9))))
Value is
    UNDEFINED

If a tested data instance is not trivial and used in test for many times, We may assign it to an identifier using system function DEF.

Current Unit > bill
Evaluate
    DEF exmpbill=
     enter(12,{3,10},[10¦->{1,2},1¦->{4,6},2¦->{3,4},
                 4¦->{6,7},3¦->{},7¦->{},6¦->{}])
    FED
Value is
    [12¦->{3,10},
     10¦->{1,2},
     1¦->{4,6},
     2¦->{3,4},
     4¦->{6,7},
     3¦->{},
     7¦->{},
     6¦->{}]
Evaluate
    explode(10,exmpbill)
Value is
    {1,4,6,7,2,3}
Evaluate
    explode(10,erase(10,1,exmpbill))
Value is
    {2,3,4,6,7}

The execution of the msymtab is interesting in that all operations of type Symtab can be eliminated and a symbol-table instance is constructed by the operations of Stack and Layer.

Current Unit > msymtab
Evaluate
    DEF exsym=add(add(enterblock(add(enterblock(add(add(
           enterblock(add(init,'a','INT')),'b','BOOL')),
           'c','CHAR')),'d','RECORD')),'e','INT'),
           'f','ARRAY') FED
Value is
    push(assign(assign(new(),
                  'e',
                  'INT'),
        'f',
        'ARRAY'),
      push(assign(new(),
              'd',
              'record'),
        push(assign(assign(new(),
                   'b',
                   'BOOL'),
          'c',
          'CHAR'),
        push(assign(new(),
               'a',
              'INT'),
          empty()))))
Evaluate
    retrieve(exsym,'b')
Value is

```
     'BOOL'
Evaluate
     is_inblock(exsym,'b')
Value is
     FALSE
```

One of the major advantages of introducing formal specification into software development is that specifications may be processed with the help of computers, and NUSL is an executable specification language. We built the NUSL supporting system to provide NUSL users with facilities of static syntactic and semantic check and dynamic execution of NUSL specifications.

The structure of the system is demonstrated by the graph below:

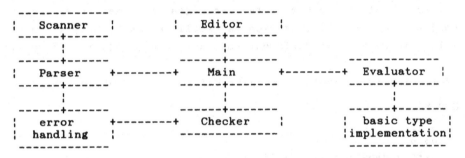

The system consists mainly of the following four parts:

Main: controls the execution of different parts; interacts with users;

Parser: scans source specification,check out syntax errors, if no, produces the internal syntax tree which will be used by Checker and Evaluator;

Checker: makes static semantic checks;

Evaluator: performs evaluation of expressions, therefor, provides the rapid prototyping facility.

Evaluation of expressions is like many other implementations of applicative languages [6][14] except evaluation of function applications, since the function names (operations) may be defined either in MOD units or by algebraic equations in ALG units. If the operation is defined in a model-based unit, the actual parameters are passed to the corresponding formal parameters using a lazy evaluation mechanism [6][14] and then the function body is evaluated.

If the operation is defined by algebraic equations in a ALG unit, the equations are viewed as rewrite rules. The arguments are evaluated (the result values may be expressions containing constructing operations, internally in the form of constant) and matched with left-hand sides of the equations defining the operation, one by one. In the process of matching, the variables appear in the equations get their values. If the match succeeds with the left-hand side of an equation, the right-hand side of the equation is evaluated. If no match succeeds, i.e. the expression can not be simplified, it is transformed to an internal constant record.

The system is programed in modula-2 and run on IBM-PC/XT,AT.

5. APPLICATION IN FORMAL DEFINITION OF PROGRAMMING LANGUAGES

NUSL can also be used for formal definition of programming languages. A formal definition of a programming language in NUSL is different from that in other meta languages in that they can be executed directly. In this section, a small language, SAL, which has been defined in Meta IV at different abstract levels [4], is defined in NUSL.

The following is a denotational-like definition of SAL in NUSL.

```
MOD SAL
 TYPE
   Expr;
 ABSREP
   *** Syntactic Domains ***
   Expr = Const|Var|Infix|Cond|Let|Rec|Lamb|Appl;
   Const :: INT;
   Var :: Id;
   Prefix :: Op Expr
   Infix :: Expr Op Expr;
   Cond :: Expr Expr Expr;
   Let :: Id Expr Expr;
   Rec :: Id Lamb Expr;
   Lamb :: Id Expr;
   Appl :: Expr Expr;
   *** Semantic Domains ***
   ENV = MAP(Id,VAL);
   VAL = FUN|REC|INT|BOOL;
   FUN :: Lamb ENV;
   REC :: Id Lamb ENV;
 OPERATION
   eval_prog: Expr --> VAL
   eval_expr: Expr,ENV --> VAL
 FUNCTION
   eval_prog(e) = eval_expr(e,[ ]);
   eval_expr(e,env)=
    CASE e: mk-Const(k)    --> k,
            mk-Var(id)    --> env^id,
            mk-Prefix(o,e1)   --> LET v1=eval_expr(e1,env) IN
                                    CASE o:
                                      '-'-->-v1,
                                      'Not'-->NOT v1
                                    ESAC,
            mk-Infix(e1,o,e2) --> LET v1=eval_expr(e1,env),
                                      v2=eval_expr(e2,env) IN
                                    CASE o:
                                      '+'-->v1+v2,
                                      '-'-->v1-v2,
```

```
                                          '*'-->v1*v2,
                                          '/'-->v1 / v2,
                                          'And'-->v1 AND v2,
                                          'Or'-->v1 OR v2,
                                          '='-->v1=v2,
                                          '#'-->v1#v2,
                                          '>'-->v1>v2,
                                          '<'-->v1<v2
                              ESAC
                              TEL,
            mk-Cond(t,c,a) --> IF eval_expr(t,env)
                               THEN eval_expr(c,env)
                               ELSE eval_expr(a,env)
                               FI,
            mk-Let(id,d,b) -->
                    LET env1=env+[id |-> eval_expr(d,env)] IN
                           eval_expr(b,env1) TEL,
            mk-Rec(g,d,b)-->
                    LET env1=env+[g |-> mk-REC(g,d,env)] IN
                           eval_expr(b,env1) TEL,
            mk-Lamb(id,ex)       --> mk-FUN(e,env),
            mk-Appl(f,a) -->
                  LET fun = eval_expr(f,env),
                      val = eval_expr(a,env) IN
                  CASE fun:
                      mk-FUN(mk-Lamb(id,expr),env1)-->
                        eval_expr(expr,env1+[id |-> val]),
                      mk-REC(g,mk-Lamb(id,expr),env1)-->
                        eval_expr(expr,(env1+[id |-> val])+
                                       [g |-> fun])
                  ESAC
                TEL
        ESAC
      END SAL
```

The abstract syntax of SAL is described in ABSREP segment and the semantic domains are also described in ABSREP segment, the semantic functions are given in FUNCTION segment and their signature in OPERATION and LOCOP segment.

We call this a denotational-like definition, because it looks denotational and satisfies the criterion of compositionality of denotational definitions, but strictly the denotations of Let or Rec defined functions of SAL are not real denotations. In fact, only the function bodies are reserved in ENVs.

With this definition and the NUSL supporting system, we are able to run SAL programs directly. Evaluation of

```
    eval_Prog(mk-Rec('f',
              mk-Lamb('n',
                mk-Cond(mk-Infix(Var('n'),'=',mk-Const(1)),
                      mk-Const(1),
                      mk-Infix(Var('n'),'*',
                          mk-Appl(Var('f'),
                                    mk-Infix(Var('n'),'-',
                                      mk-Const(1)))))),
              mk-Appl(Var('f'), mk-Const(5))))
```

results in 120. In the above expression, the argument of eval_Prog is the abstract syntax form of the following SAL program:

```
let f(x)=if x=0 then 1 else x*f(x-1) in
       f(5)
```

We will provide functional type in the next version of NUSL and implement high-order function evaluation in its supporting system, thus, denotational definition will be possible in NUSL and be executed on the supporting system.

6. REMARKS ON VDM AND OTHER RELATED WORK

Most constructs of model-based units are borrowed from Meta IV [3], and in a sense, the sublanguage of model-based units may be regarded as a subset of applicative Meta IV, but our different motivations, the embedding of algebraic method, the permission of parameterized types and many other language mechanisms make NUSL a fully different language.

We think it would make Meta IV more powerful if parameterized types were permitted in Meta IV. For example, having specified a parameterized type Stack, if we want to specify a type of integer Stack, IntStack, which has one more operation in addition to the operations of Stack, we may specify it as

```
IntStack = Stack(INT)
sum-stack: IntStack-->INT
sum-stack(s) = if is-empty(s) then 0
                    else top(s)+sum-stack(pop(s))
```

Otherwise, we have to take more effort in modelling IntStack on basic types and defining all of its operations.

The NUSL project is an experiment in putting formal specification techniques into productive use. To save the cost of syntax parsing, we adopt a syntax which makes the model-based subset of NUSL not as readable as applicative Meta IV. We will improve this aspect of NUSL in the next version.

The executability of specifications suggests that in a rigorous method like VDM, a specification may be examined through execution and testing on computers rather than only with human developer poring over it.

We think it is an advantage [21], but also a disadvantage of Meta IV that it is an open language, without standardization. It is hard for users to learn different dialects and sometimes users may be confused.

It is also an obstacle for producing generally used supporting tools.

Other projects which interest us are OBJ [7][8], Miranda [22], me-too [13], Larch [12] etc.

OBJ is an executable specification language based on algebraic specification of abstract data types. The OBJ system regards algebraic equations as rewrite rules for the evaluation of expressions, which gives us some ideas in the implementation of NUSL supporting system. The syntax for user defined operations in OBJ is very flexible, allowing infix, prefix, postfix, and in general, "mixfix".

Miranda and me-too are model-oriented specification languages, but the primitives provided by these two languages are not as powerful as Meta IV, thus, not as powerful as model-based units of NUSL.

Algebraic specification and model-oriented specification are also combined in Larch. Larch includes two sub-languages, shared language and interface language. We think there are two problems in the language:

1) The semantics of a trait (module) in shared language can not be decided on its own. It depends on the context the trait is in.

2) Interface language is programming language dependent. Users of Larch have the burden to learn different interface languages if different programming languages are used. Furthermore, specifications in Larch are programming language dependent, which makes understanding and reusing of specifications more difficult.

7. CONCLUSION

The introduction of formal specification into software engineering can increase the productivity and reliability of software. The experience of applying VDM in industry [17] shows that formal specification techniques are not as difficult to spread as some people imagine. The problem is that the applicable areas of current specification languages are relatively limited, waiting for further development. By using an executable specification language, it may be examined earlier whether a specification agrees with user's requirements, but unnecessary implementation details may be contained in such executable specifications. Since executable specification languages are different from traditional programming languages, new techniques have to be adopted in implementation.

REFERENCES

[1] ACM SIGSOFT Rapid Prototyping Workshop, Special Issue on Rapid Prototyping, Software Engineering Notes, Dec. 1982.

[2] Berry, D. M. and J. M. Wing, Specifying and Prototyping: Some Thoughts on Why They Are Successful, in Formal Methods and Software development, Vol. 2, H. Ehrig et al. eds., Springer-Verlag, 1985.

[3] Bjorner, D. and C. B. Jones, Vienna Development Method: The Meta Language, Springer-Verlag, 1978.

[4] Bjorner, D., Rigorous Development of Interpreters and Compilers, in Formal Specification and Software Development, D. Bjorner and C. B. Jones eds., Prentice-Hall, 1982.

[5] Boehm, B. K., Software Engineering: R and D Trends and Defense Needs, in Research Directions in Software Technology, P. Wegner ed., MIT Press, 1979.

[6] Darlington, J., Principle of Functional Programming, Prentice-Hall, 1983.

[7] Goguen, J. A., An Introduction to OBJ: A Language for Writing and Testing Formal Algebraic Program Specifications, in Proc. Specification of Reliable Software, 1979.

[8] Goguen, J. A. and J. Meseguer, Rapid Prototyping in the OBJ Executable Specification Language, in [1].

[9] Goguen, J. A. etc., Abstract Data Types as Initial Algebras and Correctness of Data Representations, Current Trends in Programming Methodology 4, R.Yeh ed., Prentice-Hall, 1978.

[10] Guttag, J. V., Notes on Type Abstraction, in Proc. Specification of Reliable Software, 1979.

[11] Guttag, J. V., E.Horowitz and D. R. Musser, Abstract Data Types and Software Validation, CACM, Dec. 1978.

[12] Guttag, J. V. and J. J. Horning, Report on the Larch Shared Language, Science of Computer Programming, Vol. 6, pp 103-134, 1986.

[13] Henderson, P., Functional Programming, Formal Specification and Rapid Prototyping, IEEE Trans. on Soft. Eng., Feb. 1986.

[14] Henderson, P., Functional Programming: Application and Implementation, Prentice-Hall, 1980.

[15] Hoare C. A. R., Proof of Correctness of Data Representations, in Programming Methodology, D. Gries ed., Springer-Verlag, 1978.

[16] Hoare, C. A. R., Notes on Data Structuring, in Structured Programming (O. J. Dahl et al.), Academic Press, 1972.

[17] Jackson, M.I. and B.T.Denvir, Experience of Introducing VDM into an Industrial Organization, in Formal methods and Software Development, Vol 2, H. Ehrig et al. eds., Springer-Verlag, 1985.

[18] Jones, C. B., Systematic Software Development Using VDM, Prentice-Hall, 1986.

[19] Jones, C. B., Implementation Bias in Constructive Specifications, Manuscript, 1977.

[20] Majster, M. E., Limits of the Algebraic Specifications of Abstract Data Types, SIGPLAN Notices, Oct. 1977.

[21] Oest, O. N., VDM from Research to Practice, Information Processing 86, H. J. Kugler ed., 1986.

[22] Turner, D. A., Functional Programs as Excutable Specifications, in Mathematical Logic and Programming Languages, C.A.R.Hoare ed., Prentice-Hall, 1985.

[23] Wulf, W. A. et al., An Introduction to the Construction and Verification of Alphard Programs, IEEE Trans. on Soft. Eng., Dec., 1976.

A Support System for Formal Reasoning: Requirements and Status

C.B. Jones and P.A.Lindsay

1 Introduction

FRIPSE is the formal reasoning sub-project of IPSE 2.5 being undertaken by staff at Manchester University and SERC-Rutherford Appleton Labs. The aim is to produce a rich environment for supporting formal reasoning of the kind arising in software engineering. We hope to create a synergy of human and machine in which each performs the tasks to which he, she or it is best suited: the human guiding proof creation using his or her insight into the problem domain; the computer effecting faultless symbolic manipulations, checking formal correctness, and making occasional (constrained) searches. This paper sets requirements for a computer-based proof assistant, and reports on the status of the FRIPSE project. The companion paper [28] in this volume describes an experimental design (called 'Muffin') of an improved user interface for a proof assistant.

IPSE 2.5 is an Alvey-funded project to build an *integrated project support environment (ipse)* with support for formal methods of software engineering. The "2.5" in its name reflects the intention (cf. [17][1]) that IPSE 2.5 be a second generation ipse with some third generation features. (The Alvey Software Engineering initiative proposed the notion of three generations of ipses with different sets of characteristics: see [51] for more details. In terms of data storage IPSE 2.5 will be "data-based" rather than "knowledge-based", which places it in the second generation. Support for formal methods, on the other hand, is a third generation feature.) The IPSE 2.5 project is divided into five closely interlinked but identifiable "themes" (cf. [49]), of which two are concerned with formal methods support: 'Theme B' is to provide general support, while 'Theme C' focuses on formal reasoning. FRIPSE is part of Theme C and stands for Formal Reasoning in an IPSE.

The Theme C members bring a large and useful diversity to the task of designing and building FRIPSE. Degrees held include ones in Psychology, Physics and Mathematics as well as Computer Science. An earlier SERC funded project at Manchester created a "structure editor generator" which became known as 'Mule'.[2] 'LCF' [20] has provided one of the most influential paradigms for formal reasoning, and we were fortunate to be able to learn from the first-hand involvement of Chris Wadsworth and Lockwood Morris about design of ML and LCF. Brian Ritchie's research at Edinburgh lead to 'IPE' [46] which provides a new "interactive proof editor" approach to formal reasoning. Finally, work at Manchester University on model-oriented specifications in general, and VDM in particular, provides a mass of examples of the sort of proofs which arise in the development of software.

Apart from the present authors, the people directly involved in the FRIPSE project are: Juan Bicarregui, Neil Dyer, Bob Fields, Jane Gray, Kevin Jones, Ralf Kneuper, Richard Moore, Brian Ritchie and Alan Wills. Past members include Ian Cottam, Mark van Harmelen, Lockwood Morris, Tobias Nipkow, Roy Simpson and Chris Wadsworth. Acting as consultant to the project, Michel Sintzoff has proven invaluable as an

---

[1]Readers wishing to obtain copies of IPSE 2.5 documents should apply to: Mr M.K. Tordoff, STL NW, Copthall House, Nelson Place, Newcastle-under-Lyme, Staffs ST5 1EZ.

[2]The distinction between "structure" and the more common "syntax-directed" editors is explained in [14] and [53]. Full documentation of the Mule project can be found in the final report [13]; some discussion of its relation to FRIPSE is to be found in [29].

external source of challenging questions. We are also grateful for the useful contributions from the rest of the IPSE 2.5 project, and especially to David Duce for facilitating the MU/RAL collaboration.

This paper is structured as follows: Section 2 looks at the motivation for FRIPSE, including the kinds of reasoning involved, the need for computer support, and what form that support should take. Section 3, comprising the main part of this paper, draws out requirements on FRIPSE and indicates the nature of the support we intend to supply. Section 4 describes the status of the work on FRIPSE at about two-thirds of the way through the project.

2 Why Support Formal Reasoning?

The aim of this section is to give some of the context in which FRIPSE is being built. Mathematics is a very diverse discipline, so diverse in fact that a single project could not hope to provide anything more by way of broad support, perhaps, than an editor for mathematical formulae. On the other hand, we believe we can provide useful support for the kind of mathematical reasoning involved in software engineering. Once the motivation for, and characteristics of, such reasoning are elucidated it's much easier to be specific about how computers can best be of assistance.

2.1 Mathematical Reasoning in Software Engineering

Let us take *formal methods* to mean the formal specification and verified development of software. There should be no need in a conference dedicated to one of the most widely used formal development methods to rehearse the arguments for their use; other papers in these proceedings or in [7] describe the use of VDM. This section sets out some of the ways in which mathematical statements—about which reasoning is required—arise in different formal methods.

2.1.1 Proofs about Specifications

There are, unfortunately, few examples of formal models of requirements[3] and it is inherently impossible to prove that a (formal) specification satisfies a user's informal requirements. Part of the FRIPSE effort is devoted to investigating techniques for "animation" of specifications (cf. [32, 33]). Of course, one (extreme) case of animation is to prove properties of a formal specification. Such proofs can both locate mismatches with requirements and deepen the understanding of a specification. Any redundancy in a specification can be exploited to check its consistency; abstractions or generalizations of an intended behaviour can be shown to capture such intentions.

There are also rather routine checks on the consistency of a specification. A structure editor system can support simple type checking, but the sub-typing mechanism brought about by (data type) invariants in [25] results in proof obligations even to show that terms are properly typed.

In many cases, the best way to check that a specification is *implementable* is to proceed with design. But, in some complex cases, the proof obligation of implementability (cf. [25]) should be addressed before any design is considered.

2.1.2 Verification in Design

The main role of formal reasoning is in establishing that a design satisfies a specification. VDM is typical of what is probably the most familiar "paradigm" of formal software development. It proceeds by iterating three steps: specification, design and verification. Careful choice of the design steps is essential. A step of development which fixes one clear design decision is both easy to verify and supportive of subsequent

---

[3]One such is the finite state automaton used to describe the security model in [10].

review (including consideration of design changes).[4] In VDM, a step of data reification (going from an abstract model of a state to a more concrete representation)—for example—gives rise to proof obligations like *adequacy* (cf. [25]). An example is presented in §2.2 below.

In a careful iterative design, the designer's experience in selecting the steps should extend to an intuitive idea of why a step is correct. The generated proof obligation is a completely formal statement of what has to be proved to establish certainty that the design satisfies its specification. There will normally be many mathematical details which need ironing out. The designer will want help with the mechanics of this task but be left as free as possible in the order in which sub-tasks are undertaken. One of the crucial advantages of methods like VDM is that verification of a single design step at a time often repays the effort involved— by revealing design errors before subsequent work begins.

2.1.3   Other Formal Approaches

A slightly different paradigm of formal software development is the so-called "constructive mathematics" approach, which combines the design and verification stages into one. Design takes the form of a constructive proof of the implementability of a specification; the computational content is then extracted from the proof to yield the required algorithm. For example, a proof by induction that

$$\forall x \in \mathsf{N} \cdot \exists y \in \mathsf{N} \cdot y^2 \leq x < (y+1)^2,$$

when done "constructively", gives a method for finding the integer square root of natural numbers by "applying" the induction step repetitively to the base case. NuPRL [12] and Manna and Waldinger's work [40] are examples of this approach. Programs synthesized in such a way are guaranteed to terminate correctly and in a finite number of steps. Unfortunately, the approach is currently hampered by the lack of suitable compilers.

Yet another approach is that of program transformation, transforming inefficient but clearly correct "implementations" into runable programs. CIP [11] is an example of this approach. Many transformations have associated "applicability conditions" which give rise to proof obligations when used.

2.1.4   Other Tasks

In addition to discharging the sort of proof obligations indicated above, the use of any formal method gives rise to more general mathematical reasoning tasks. It has long been clear (cf. [16, 24, 9, 19]) that the development of *theories* (in analogy with, for example, the algebraist's groups, rings and fields) of data types is essential if proofs are to be widely used in software development. The recording of knowledge as formal properties of bags, stacks, tree representations, and so on, looks a much more promising path to the much vaunted goal of *reuse* than the collection of millions of lines of code. Since these theories would consist of properties which would be used many times, completely formal proofs are likely to be required.

Another area where proofs arise is in showing that proof obligations are consistent with some underlying semantics: for example, [26] considers VDM's operation decomposition proof obligations, and [43] justifies a powerful data refinement rule. These rules are so central that their proofs really must be formally checked.

There are many other examples of the need to support formal reasoning and, as Computing Science matures, more and more of its corpus of results will be supported by machine checked proofs.

2.2   The Kinds of Reasoning Involved

Having seen how reasoning tasks arise in software engineering, we now turn to a closer analysis of the *kinds* of reasoning involved. After this analysis it will be clear where support can best be offered.

Let us start with an example from the companion paper [28] in this volume. A simple consistency condition on the Muffin specification (in Appendix B of that paper) might state that, under appropriate

---

[4]It is this careful decomposition which enables VDM to avoid the problems encountered in the "verification condition generator" approach, which many workers agree is unworkable even for modestly sized programs: cf. [15]. There, the step from specification to code is so large, and the level of discourse so low, that verification conditions become intractable.

validity constraints, a non-trivial instantiation of an expression results in a new expression. This consistency condition can be stated as the following proof obligation:

$$es \in Expstore, m \in (\text{map } Atom \text{ to } Expref), pre\text{-}expand\text{-}inst(y, m, es), leaves(y, es) \cap \text{dom } m \neq \{ \} \vdash$$
$$expand\text{-}inst(y, m, es) \neq expand(y, es)$$

The (inductive) structure of a proof of this sequent is not difficult to guess. But even a casual expansion of the sequent with all of the functions used (*inv-Expstore*, *is-closed*, *args*, *is-finite*, *trace*, *descendants*, *offspring*, *expand*) would produce a completely incomprehensible string of symbols.

The Muffin specification formally gives rise to more than 50 implementability proof obligations: some of these are trivial, some require a few moments thought to see that necessary assumptions have been captured in pre-conditions; but some—like those involved in checking the consistency of the *Proofstore*— give rise to sequents more complex than the consistency condition given above.

The verification of a design with respect to the Muffin specification might involve showing the adequacy of representations which differ greatly from the abstractions used in the abstract state: a text-book example would be the use of a reverse-Polish representation for *Texp*; far more difficult problems might arise in the representations of *Proofs*. Experience with VDM suggests that such adequacy proof obligations are worth tackling with care before subsequent design work is based on a possibly inadequate representation. (The cost-effectiveness comes from the fact that, unlike the domain and result rules, only one adequacy proof is required per step of reification.)

The textbook [25] contains many more examples of proofs arising in VDM.

In general, the proofs of the sort of sequents given as examples above are long but routine. Far from relying on some brilliant insight, *the proofs are intended as cross-checks on detail*. Given the sheer amount of detail[5] and the long and tedious nature of the proofs involved, mechanical checking of proofs is essential.

A *formal proof* is one in which every step can be checked mechanically—that is, without requiring any insight beyond what can be written down as a set of rules. Formal proof thus comes down to a game of pushing symbols around. The basic set of rules of the game is called a *logical calculus*, a proof theory, or often just a *logic* for short. There are many different calculi, although a glib logician might simply offer "ZF Set Theory with First Order Predicate Calculus" to the unsuspecting computer scientist. We do not regard this as adequate: logical calculi which are suited to the problem domain are required, so that reasoning is "natural" and concise. Proof theories (as, for example, in [23]) of program constructs and Temporal Logic (cf. [5]) are examples of calculi which are being used in software engineering. The design of more, and ever more relevant, calculi is a matter for ongoing research: one example is the decision to use 'LPF' (cf. [4]) in VDM as a way of handling nondenoting terms.

To a mathematician, the components of formal specifications are quite elementary: (labelled) cartesian products, finite maps, finite sets, relations, trees and so on. Unlike much of mathematics, these concepts are easily axiomatised and formal proof is at least feasible for them, particularly if an appropriate calculus is chosen. We recognise however that the effort spent constructing fully formal proofs is not realistically justifiable in all cases. Even if systems like FRIPSE succeed in reducing the effort required, the aim of mechanical formality—far beyond what is found in most mathematical papers—will always present a significant workload. The phrase *rigorous argument* is intended to suggest something closer to the normal informal proofs in mathematics. As part of the FRIPSE project we are considering ways in which formality can be relaxed while still providing useful support (cf. §3.2 below).

Our hope is that computer support will ease the construction of formal proofs. Above all, it is apparent that the sorts of sequents indicated above can best be handled after a rich theory of the underlying data types has been developed.

---

[5]Consider for example the range of languages involved in the verification of a compiler: cf. [27].

2.3 Mechanical support for reasoning

We observed above that, in software verification tasks, the sheer amount of detail makes mechanical checking of proofs essential. It's also obvious that machine support, particularly for symbol manipulation, would be extremely useful for *constructing* such proofs. For example, in verifying the condition on *leaves(expand-inst(...))*, it is important to perform the case distinctions before fully expanding the sequent. A mechanical system can check that all cases are considered and perform simplifications under each case assumption. Such support would relieve tedium and reduce the number of (possibly "fatal") transcription errors which would occur in a pencil-and-paper proof.

It is a tenet of the IPSE 2.5 plan that improved machine support will encourage the construction of formal proofs.[6] This statement is made with awareness of the current situation, brought home in most of the reported experiments (cf. [15, 50, 1]), that existing machine support provides at best very limited help with the construction of proofs.

The reader is referred to [35] for an extensive survey of mechanical support for formal reasoning. The situation is roughly the following: Some program verification environments have been built (e.g. Gypsy [18], Abstract Pascal [34]), but their reasoning support is generally not as well developed as that of "stand-alone" reasoning tools. The latter fall into two broad camps:

1. highly automated systems, such as resolution provers and the Boyer-Moore prover [8]

2. interactive proof checkers, such as LCF [20]

The former are characterized by (large) systematic searches, sometimes constrained by heuristics or user advice (typically in advance). Such systems are surveyed in [39].

In existing automated theorem provers the machine usually dictates (to greater or lesser extent) how the proof proceeds, and when—as often happens—it leads down an obscure path, the user is left to work out what is happening and how to get back on the right path.[7] This means in practice that the user must have a particularly good understanding of the system's search routines and heuristics, which are often very complicated. Proof becomes a challenge: to beat the machine at its own game.

Although much has been achieved in automating reasoning in certain problem domains, there is little hope that more broadly based reasoning can be automated. (And of course, there's always Church's Theorem on the undecidability of validity for even quite weak logics.) In our opinion, reasoning tools must be so designed that the human, rather than the program, is in control of proof creation. This is the philosophy of the second of the above camps.

By their very nature, interactive proof checkers involve a lot of work on the user's part. They support proof construction by allowing the user to experiment with choices, and to backtrack when poor choices become apparent. Unfortunately, many systems more or less force the user to commit to choices before the consequences can be explored—not just choices within proofs, but also the "style" of proof (e.g. whether bottom-up or top-down) and in other ways. Most are fairly inflexible in their style of proof, for example not allowing insertion of extra proof steps or small changes to earlier steps without losing all the later steps. (Proof editors such as IPE [46] overcome this to some extent.)

Probably the main criticism of interactive proof checkers, though, is that proof construction is still rather tedious. (LCF and its descendants relieve some of the tedium by allowing the user to program commonly occurring patterns of proof construction.) Their user interfaces are generally very poor and help facilities weak. In the few systems with "library facilities" for storing definitions, theorems, proofs, and so on, these facilities are fairly rudimentary.

In the next section we indicate how we would hope to improve on existing support.

---

[6]Of course, machine support is also very useful for teaching people formal logic: cf. the evaluation of Muffin in [28] in this volume.

[7]See for example §8.3 of [35].

2.4 The Goals Of FRIPSE

With existing systems the user typically works out a sketch proof with pencil and paper, and then tries to run it through the system, returning to pencil and paper when the attempt fails. The marriage of human intuition and mechanical support can only be consumated if a system facilitates *proof at the workstation*. The system must be easier to use than pencil and paper. (This is not a fanciful objective: pointing at a formula and a definition to be expanded is both easier and less error-prone than substitution by hand.) In fact, it is to be hoped—but is not yet shown—that mechanical help and a good user interface will lead to methods of discovering proofs which are an improvement upon the traditional pencil-and-paper approach. This seems a realistic goal for the routine proofs of §2.2.[8]

In the last section we noted how the machine could help with symbolic manipulations and with checking the formal ("syntactic") correctness of proofs, but there are other places where machine support is required before people can be weaned off pencil and paper. The process of proof construction, for example, is very much one of experimentation, with many unsuccessful attempts, blind alleys, and much "scratching out". The machine could keep track of parallel attempts, and could prepare and maintain an orderly summary of the "state of play". It could report on what remains to be proven and could search its store for relevant results. And it could profitably be used to track the impact of changes (e.g. to the statements and proofs of proof obligations when a design changes).

IPSE 2.5 is supposed to be a *generator* of ipses which would be customized to specific application domains: for example, to different formal methods, specification languages, target (implementation) languages, and so on. The aim is to provide "schematic" or "data-driven" support tools, which would be "instantiated". Perhaps the best analogy is with the Cornell Synthesizer Generator [52], which generates a language-based ("syntax-directed") editor from a grammar for the language. Another analogy is with the development of table-driven compiler-compliers.

The problems here are well known from many generators: for example, diagnostics can become incomprehensible. The target user of FRIPSE is a software engineer who has received some suitable education in formal methods and training in the use of the created system; the project will not be considered a success if it can only be used by people with a Ph.D. in mathematical logic.

In terms of support for formal reasoning, the logical calculus ("object language") is an obvious candidate for parametrization: as remarked earlier, different applications call for different logical calculi.[9] We believe that useful *logic-independent* support can be provided. The main ideas behind LCF proved to be largely logic independent, for example—as witnessed by the number of offspring systems differing from Edinburgh LCF almost only in their object language. More recently, Isabelle [44] and ELF [22] have provided logic-independent "generic" support. And although not in its brief, Muffin is generic to the extent that the axiomatic properties of propositional connectives are user-defined.

FRIPSE will be "configurable" for different logics. In order to demonstrate its effectiveness we plan to populate a FRIPSE instance with a calculus appropriate to BSI-VDM.

3 What Support Is Required?

Having set out the context in which FRIPSE is being built, we turn now to more detailed requirements.

3.1 Overview: The Basic Functionality

Assuming for the moment FRIPSE has been configured to allow reasoning in one of the target logics,[10] the applications in §2.1 call for the following (mathematical) abilities:

---

[8]The goal of "proof at the workstation" may still be beyond the deeper proofs of §2.1.4.

[9]See §2.1 of [35] for a more detailed list.

[10]See §3.7 below for the requirements imposed by genericity

- to extend the logical language with one's own primitives [11]

- to make abbreviations and definitions

- to postulate *axioms* (primitive inference rules)

- to conjecture new inference rules to be derived

- to sketch informal proofs of conjectures

- to "refine" informal proofs towards formal ones

- to construct and apply reasoning strategies

- to organise results into theories

The overall style of interaction called for is structure editor-like, with store searches and some other processes automated (cf. [53]). Note that the requirement is for *automated* tools rather than *automatic*: LCF is closer to what we have in mind than say the Boyer-Moore prover. The report [54] discusses architectural requirements for the FRIPSE system.

The user should not be (overly?) constrained in the order in which tasks are performed: e.g. it should be possible to use conjectured inference rules before they are completely justified. One of the design tenets of FRIPSE is to provide an "open" system in which the user can access any tools which are of use. Thus, it should be possible for the user to unfold a definition, or to ask for the (most general) unifier of any two expressions. But just exposing the data store is still not enough: the system should record all such mechanically derived relationships.

The system will be extensible on the fly, so that the user can customize his or her own environment. Of course, the ordinary user will not be allowed to change the kernel operations of FRIPSE, so that the logical soundness of the system is not compromised.

3.2 The Proof Model

The "style" of formal proof we intend to support is Gentzen's Natural Deduction, as described in chapter 2 of [25] for example.[12] There's a brief introduction to proof construction in §2 of the companion paper ([28] in these proceedings) which gives a feel for how one might interact with FRIPSE. Inference rules for the target logics are more complicated than those in Muffin of course, but take much the same form.[13]

For practical reasons we need to be able to incorporate certain forms of mathematical reasoning which are not based on inference rules: for example, arithmetical reasoning and other calculations which are best left to the machine. We imagine this would fit best into the model of proof described above in the form of "oracles" for checking side-conditions. (Such an idea has been used in theorem provers before now: e.g. the arithmetical unit of NuPRL [12] and the tautology checker of Veritas [21].) Oracles probably would not be supplied "generically", but nor would we expect the "ordinary user" to add such facilities, since they involve changing kernel operations.

A *complete* formal proof is one in which every non-hypothesis line is justified correctly. Since FRIPSE will support the *construction* of proofs, however, the requirement is for a data structure for incomplete proofs. We are presently considering a model which is quite different from that underlying the Muffin

---

[11]By primitives here we mean sort symbols, function symbols, predicate symbols, and quantifiers and other binding symbols, as well as the usual constant symbols.

[12]See [45] for a more formal treatment of Natural Deduction. Note that our derived rules are what Kleene calls "[derived] rules of the direct type" (p.94 of [31]). Such rules necessarily remain valid when a theory is extended, unlike say rules derived by induction over the structure of the theory.

[13]Some inference rule schemes have "side-conditions"—usually constraints on the possible syntactic form of instances. Certain side-conditions (e.g. variable occurrence) can be "caught at the level of the proof model" with static checks (cf. [22]), while others are probably best checked dynamically. In FRIPSE, derived rules with side-conditions will probably not be allowed (other than those caught at the level of the proof model, of course): case studies seem to suggest this will not be a problem.

state, but which will allow something like the Muffin style as a "projection". Muffin allows forwards and backwards reasoning, but yet finer granularity of operations is desirable. For example, it should be possible to insert proof steps, and forward steps should be carried into subproofs. In FRIPSE it should be possible to sketch the outline of a proof and refine it, say by first putting down the main conjectures involved, then linking them with justifications. It should also be possible to interact with linear projections of chains of equalities and inequalities, thereby simulating equational and inequational reasoning. These requirements call for a quite complex data model.

What can be done to provide support for rigorous—as opposed to fully formal—proof? One obvious idea, which has already been used in other verification systems, is to permit a user to *assert* some lines of a proof instead of formally justifying them. Lines might be justified by a "lemma" specially created to cover the case, but otherwise not proven. Or lines might have partial justifications: e.g. the claim "can be proved by structural induction on *T*" can be checked for overall applicability. At other times there would be merit[14] in recording the assumptions on which the asserted line is believed to depend, even though such a dependency would not be formally checked. At the extreme, a rigorous proof will be a stream of unanalyzed characters.

Even when no checking can be done, FRIPSE will store such arguments. Indeed, users should be encouraged to store some textual annotations to even fully formal proofs. The fact that the final result is relative to the truth of the unproven facts must be tracked; furthermore, the user must be able to return to such assertions and refine their justifications.

The correctness of software produced using formal methods obviously depends on the correctness of the reasoning involved, so it is vital that the formal reasoning tools be correct. (Of course, we are taking our own medicine: FRIPSE is being formally specified, as was Muffin.) How can the user have faith in the soundness[15] of the reasoning tools? The requirement is that any rule which the machine accepts as formally proven must be derivable from the axioms (in the relevant logic). The criteria for formal provability will be built into the kernel of FRIPSE and will not be modifiable by the ordinary user. In the rest of this section we briefly discuss one of the criteria: the others are described in the preliminary FRIPSE specification [41].

As mentioned above, we want the user to be able to use conjectures before their justifications are complete: the danger here is that circular arguments might slip in, so clearly FRIPSE must record dependencies of rules on rules and guard against circularities. Similarly, justifications of lines in a proof must be noncircular, as should definitions and abbreviations.

3.3 The Theory Store

After substantial use, the system will hold a richly interconnected collection of constant declarations, definitions and abbreviations, axioms, derived rules and conjectures, complete and incomplete proofs, proof strategies, and more, organised in *theories* in a *store*. The store tracks dependencies and guards against circularities. It also holds documentation for the various components. The main purpose of the store, however, is to promote reuse of work. It is vital that a mechanical proof assistant have the capacity to raise the level of reasoning above the "machine code" of primitive rules of inference. The efficacy of derived inference rules is stressed in the accompanying 'Muffin' paper [28]. Reuse of theories is also important, a point to which we shall return below. The ability to reuse proofs seems less useful (although cf. NuPRL's use of "transformation tactics" [12]).

To encourage reuse of derived rules, there should be some way of searching the store of results. No one search routine is believed to be sufficient: most routines should be constrained to search in the theory in which the conjecture is postulated, for example, but there will be other times when "any relevant rule" might be of interest. Some kind of pattern-matching is needed, to narrow the choice of applicable rules (cf. IPE [46] and Muffin's "matching rules"). It would also be useful for the user to be able to informally order the rules in a theory so that "most interesting" rules come up first. Lemmas which have served their

---

[14]e.g. to guard against circularities and to help with "version control": cf. §3.5 below.

[15]Of course, here we mean soundness *relative* to a given logical calculus and set of user-supplied axioms. There is no way of automatically precluding the user from adding an inconsistent set of axioms, even if we wanted to. On the contrary, proving that a specification is contradictory is one case where such a facility is even desirable.

purpose and are unlikely to be used again (e.g. because they have been superceded by a "more powerful" theorem) could be omitted from the list. These and related matters are discussed further in [48] and [47].

An important aspect of reuse is the ability to build new theories from existing theories, and to this end certain combinators should be available: for example, (1) the ability to extend a theory by adding new sorts, constants, binders and/or axioms; and (2) the ability to merge two theories possibly containing common elements. (There may be a need to rename other elements to avoid confusion.) Clearly one wants to be able to build general (parametrized) theories and then reuse instances; thus we also want (3) the ability to instantiate abstract parameters. Generalization (abstraction) is in some sense the dual operation to instantiation, and can be expected to arise in FRIPSE. It should be possible to abstract from existing theories, "linking" the new theory to the old theories so that the latter are instances of the former. The morphisms of [36] are proposed as the mechanism for linking theories in FRIPSE, and to achieve parametrization in a powerful CLEAR-like manner.

3.4 Proof Strategies

It has often been observed when using theorem provers that certain "patterns" of reasoning occur frequently, and that it would relieve tedium if such patterns could be "coded up". Of course, sometimes by making the right generalisation it is possible to capture the pattern as a derived rule, but usually this is not the case. The designers of LCF provided the user with a programmable metalanguage (ML) in which one writes proof tactics essentially as coded sequences of applications of inference rules. ML provides access to substitution, pattern-matching, a mechanism for raising and handling exceptions (so that tactics can backtrack), and combinators for combining tactics to form new tactics.

Our precise requirements are still hazy in this area, but basically we imagine having a way of coding up sequences of interactions. The tactic language should give access to (a subset of) the basic operations for building proofs and for searching and matching, and so on. Tactics should be able to ask questions of the user: e.g. which term to substitute, which occurrences to replace, which hypothesis should have an elimination rule applied to it, and so on. Of course, tactics must not be able to change the kernel operations, so that the logical soundness of the system is not compromised.

Where proof strategies should be stored is not always clear. Many are domain-specific and would best be stored in the relevant theory. Others (e.g. simplification parametrized with respect to a set of rewrite rules) are more general.

3.5 Versioning

For the most part, the store of a reasoning system grows monotonically: the user extends or adds new theories, adds new conjectures, builds new proofs and so on. There are a few exceptions: Often, the statement of a conjecture will change as its proof is refined, for example to add new hypotheses. Occasionally the user will want to delete (or disable?) dubious conjectures and proof attempts which are superceded or which have come to a dead-end. Less frequently, theories and rules will change. (For example, when a specification or a design changes—as is their wont—the corresponding theories and proof obligations must also change.)

We want to be able to recover work when "small" changes are made. Clearly FRIPSE must record and maintain dependencies between the various objects in its store. At Manchester University, John Fitzgerald has been investigating how one might change an axiomatization of Muffin to get from one Muffin instance to another. This is clearly not possible with the operations given in Appendix B of [28], but if a few extra deletion operations were added one could, for example, change the axioms of a logic to an equivalent set without losing all of its theorems.

Proofs are generally large objects, and we expect to have lots. FRIPSE will provide a "garbage collector" which extracts from a completed proof only those parts relevant to the conclusion of the proof. Even then, it cannot expect to be able to store all proofs. If proofs must be deleted, FRIPSE should at least record the rules on which the proofs depend. A hope for the future is that a lot of experience will be coded into proof strategies which will then be able to regenerate many simpler proofs.

3.6 User Interface

The relatively late placing of this section does not reflect any lack of importance; in fact, the user interface (UI) is regarded as crucial to the design of a FRIPSE system which meets the other objectives (notably "proof at the workstation"). The key role of user interfaces is widely recognised. One only has to observe the frequency of chess boards on SUN screens—relative to the few users who struggled with the same program on a VAX—to appreciate the general point. It would be easy to make a long list of important issues here, such as handling of long formulae, presentation of long lists of options, ellision of detail, interaction by pointing, navigation around the system, and presentation of information in forms appropriate to the task. To some extent, these requirements have been realized in the "Muffin" system; the reader is referred to [28] for a description and evaluation of that experiment.

The Muffin experiment brought less obvious UI issues to light. One such issue is *process modelling*, which is an important concept in the overall IPSE 2.5 project. The idea is that the processes of software creation can be better controlled by a system which has data about the desired mode of working.[16] There is a danger that the process model idea could be realized in a way which makes a project support environment very restrictive. In particular, a sequential *process modelling language* could force a user into a regime as rigid as that of the production line. At least for theorem proving tasks this is anathema to the academic part of the IPSE 2.5 project.

It is clear that a system which has more data about entities and their desired relations can provide more information about the development it is supporting. (Some would anthropomorphize and say "the system understands the state of the development".) Context conditions (cf. Appendix B of [28]) are used to require consistency conditions of the state which must always hold. Similar predicates can be used to record *desirable* states. A system can then be made to report on the imperfections of a state. Thus, in Muffin, it is desirable that every proof is complete; in a full support system for a formal method, a predicate could state it as desirable that all specifications had associated realizations. Notice that these desirable states can be nested and that different imperfections would be of interest to different classes of users. Although this idea is not easy to illustrate in a system as small as Muffin, it is believed that it would facilitate the design of a system which really did *support* the process of creating systems using formal methods.

3.7 Genericity

As remarked in §2.4 above, FRIPSE will be "generic" in the logical calculus it supports. Clearly it is too much to expect that useful support can be provided for *all* logics. The following have been identified as target logics: first order predicate calculus (in three varieties: classical, constructive and LPF [4]), Hoare Logic, and Temporal Logic. How far we go beyond these is unknown. Certainly we intend to restrict to logics which are presentable in Natural Deduction style. (This rules out for example non-monotonic reasoning.) The applications call for many-sorted logics. The most appropriate type structure is still unclear. Algebraic methods seem to make do with variations on Church's Simple Type Theory, with varying amounts of polymorphism. Case studies with VDM on the other hand, revealed the need for graceful handling of subsorts (induced by data-type invariants).

The requirement is for a "frame" within which a sufficiently wide class of logics can be described. Various possible approaches to the problem are outlined in [38]. The 'Edinburgh Logical Frame' [22] is a frame which has successfully been used to specify many logics (cf. [2]). We propose to use a frame of our own design, but resembling ELF on many points. A first attempt to design a logical frame for FRIPSE is presented in the working paper [37]. It adds a "subtype constructor" and inclusion polymorphism to a polymorphic λ-calculus; as a result type-checking is undecidable, but that seems to be the price which must be paid (just as determining whether a given state satisfies a VDM invariant is undecidable in principle).

To instantiate FRIPSE for a particular application domain, one would first create a set of "base theories" representing the desired logic and the "primitives" of the application. For example, to configure FRIPSE for VDM one would need to provide the axioms for LPF, a parametrized theory of finite sets (with axioms

---

[16]cf. [3]. This is connected with what Bjørner and his colleagues call a "project graph": cf. [6].

for ∪, ∩, etc.), and so on. The kernel of FRIPSE need not usually be changed, except perhaps to add oracles and methods for checking side-conditions (cf. §3.2).

4 How Far Have We Got?

We close this paper with a brief report on the history and status of the FRIPSE project up to the time of writing (June 1988).

The project began in October 1985 and is due to finish in September 1989. Early in the project the two present authors and Chris Wadsworth wrote a "concepts paper" which discussed many issues to do with mechanical support of formal reasoning for software engineering, and around which subsequent work was based. The concepts paper was followed by an extensive period spent investigating existing support, using as many of the systems as we could port to our equipment, and supplemented by site visits and a literature survey; the main results were published in [35]. Throughout the project, scenarios and case studies have been found to be very useful for formulating requirements.

We realised early on that an experimental implementation would be needed in order to clarify User Interface requirements and to test *Smalltalk-80* (ST-80) as an implementation language. (This is one of the few points where we diverged from the "specify before designing" methodology. In part we felt this was justified because of our inability to formally specify UI requirements such as "user friendly".) The result of this experiment was the Muffin proof assistant for propositional calculus described in [28] in this volume. We now believe that ST-80 is a good environment for prototyping FRIPSE: see [30] for a fuller evaluation. In particular, it's interesting to note that the specification work on Muffin took more than six months to complete, whereas the implementation in ST-80 took less than two, an observation made even more remarkable by the fact that the implementors were new to the language.

Work on the proof model (cf. §3.2), the logical frame (§3.7) and the theory store (§3.3) are major inputs into the task of producing the *specification for FRIPSE*. The team has produced a preliminary specification [41] in which the data model (the "state") and many primitive operations are specified in a fair amount of detail; work continues on more complex "higher level" operations. Later in the project we will produce a complete specification of FRIPSE.

It is perhaps as well to emphasise what is implicit in the foregoing discussion: we are striving to formally identify the major concepts in FRIPSE *before* implementation commences. The system is being specified in VDM.

The preliminary specification will be prototyped in ST-80. General principles for the "architecture" of the system—based on work on structure editor generators—are described in [54] and [53]. A limited amount of implementation work has already been undertaken: in particular, Lockwood Morris has proposed a way of representing expressions using a combination of de Bruijn indices and conventional variables when bindings are involved, and with lazy computation of β-normal forms (cf. [42]). Work is also progressing on adding methods for "versioning" to ST-80.

Finally, although this paper has concentrated on the formal reasoning aspects of FRIPSE we should mention two other areas where work is being undertaken as part of the FRIPSE project:

1. research into techniques for the animation of specifications [32], and symbolic execution in particular [33]

2. the specification and development of an editor for BSI-VDM specifications, including a "proof obligation generator" which will interface with the formal reasoning support

FRIPSE will be populated with theories corresponding to BSI-VDM's primitives, leading to an evaluation of the created FRIPSE instantiation. Of course, we are in an ideal environment to find both researchers who wish to instantiate FRIPSE with their own favourite logics and a source of slave labour (viz. students) to provide usage reports.

References

[1] J. Allen. *An Investigation into the IOTA Project Support Environment.* Technical Report UMCS 86-10-3, University of Manchester Computer Science Department, 1986.

[2] A. Avron, F. Honsell, and I. Mason. *Using Typed Lambda Calculus to Implement Formal Systems on a Machine.* Technical Report ECS-LFCS-87-31, University of Edinburgh LFCS, 1987.

[3] N. Barghouti and G. Kaiser. *Strategies in MARVEL: Object-Oriented and Rule-Based.* Technical Report, Columbia University Department of Computer Science, 1987.

[4] H. Barringer, J. Cheng, and C. Jones. A logic covering undefinedness in program proofs. *Acta Informatica*, 21:251–269, 1984.

[5] H. Barringer, R. Kuiper, and A. Pnueli. Now you may compose temporal logic specifications. In *Proceedings of the 16th ACM Symposium on the Theory of Computing*, Washington DC, 1984.

[6] D. Bjørner. The stepwise development of software developments: meta-programming vdm developments. In D. Bjørner et al, editors, *VDM '87: VDM — A Formal Method at Work*, pages 77–96, 1987. Lecture Notes in Computer Science Volume 252.

[7] D. Bjørner, C. Jones, M. Mac an Airchinnigh, and E. Neuhold, editors. *VDM '87: VDM — A Formal Method at Work (Proceedings of the VDM-Europe Symposium 1987, Belgium, March 1987)*, Springer-Verlag, 1987. Lecture Notes in Computer Science, Vol. 252.

[8] R. Boyer and J. Moore. *A Computational Logic.* Academic Press, 1979.

[9] R. M. Burstall and J. A. Goguen. Putting theories together to make specifications. In *Fifth International Joint Conference on A.I.*, Boston, 1977.

[10] M. Cheheyl, M. Gasser, G. Huff, and J. Millen. Verifying security. *Computing Surveys*, 13:279–339, 1981.

[11] CIP Language Group. *The Munich Project CIP—Volume 1: The Wide Spectrum Language CIP-L.* Volume 183 of *Lecture Notes in Computer Science*, Springer-Verlag, 1985.

[12] R. Constable et al. *Implementing Mathematics with the Nuprl Proof Development System.* Prentice-Hall, 1986.

[13] I. Cottam, C. Jones, T. Nipkow, A. Wills, M. Wolczko, and A. Yaghi. *Mule — An Environment for Rigorous Software Development (Final Report to SERC on Grant Number GR/C/05762).* Department of Computer Science, University of Manchester, 1986.

[14] I. Cottam, C. Jones, T. Nipkow, A. Wills, M. Wolczko, and A. Yaghi. Project support environments for formal methods. In J. McDermid, editor, *Integrated Project Support Environments*, chapter 3, Peter Peregrinus Ltd., 1985.

[15] D. Craigen. *A Technical Review of Four Verification Systems: Gypsy, Affirm, FDM and Revised Special.* Technical Report, I.P. Sharpe Associates Ltd, Ottawa, Canada, 1985.

[16] O. J. Dahl. Can program proving be made practical? In *EEC-Crest Course on Programming Foundations*, Toulouse, 1977. revised May 1978.

[17] B. Denvir, V. Downes, C. Jones, R. Snowdon, and M. Tordoff. *IPSE 2.5 Project Proposal*, February 1985.

[18] D. Good. Mechanical proofs about computer programs. In C. Hoare and J. Shepherdson, editors, *Mathematical Logic and Programming Languages*, pages 55–75, Prentice-Hall International, 1985.

[19] D. Good. *Reusable problem domain theories*. Technical Report 31, ICSCA, University of Texas at Austin, 1982.

[20] M. Gordon, R. Milner, and C. Wadsworth. *Edinburgh LCF*. Volume 78 of *Lecture Notes in Computer Science*, Springer-Verlag, 1979.

[21] F. Hanna and N. Daeche. Purely functional implementation of a logic. In *Proceedings of Eighth International Conference on Automated Deduction*, pages 598–607, 1986. Lecture Notes in Computer Science 230.

[22] R. Harper, F. Honsell, and G. Plotkin. A framework for defining logics. In *Proceedings of Second Symposium on Logic in Computer Science*, pages 194–204, 1987.

[23] C. Hoare. An axiomatic basis for computer programming. *Communications of the ACM*, 12:576–583, 1969.

[24] C. Jones. Constructing a theory of a data structure as an aid to program development. *Acta Informatica*, 11:119–137, 1979.

[25] C. Jones. *Systematic Software Development Using VDM*. Prentice-Hall International, 1986.

[26] C. Jones. VDM proof obligations and their justification. In D. Bjørner et al, editors, *VDM '87: VDM — A Formal Method at Work*, pages 260–286, 1987. Lecture Notes in Computer Science, Vol. 252.

[27] C. Jones. The Vienna Development Method: examples of compiler development. In M. Amirchahy and D. Neel, editors, *Le Point sur la Compilation*, pages 89–114, IRIA-SEFI, 1979.

[28] C. Jones and R. Moore. Muffin: a user interface design experiment for a theorem proving assistant. In *VDM–The Way Ahead*, 1988. This volume.

[29] K. Jones. Support environments for VDM. In D. Bjørner et al, editor, *VDM '87: VDM — A Formal Method at Work*, 1987. Lecture Notes in Computer Science Volume 252.

[30] K. D. Jones. The muffin prototype: experiences with smalltalk-80. Ipse Document 060/00066/1.1, August 1987.

[31] S. Kleene. *Introduction to Metamathematics*. North-Holland Publishing Co., 1967.

[32] R. Kneuper. Animation of specifications: a survey. Ipse Document 060/00069/1.2, December 1987.

[33] R. Kneuper. *Symbolic Execution of Specifications: UI and Scenarios*. Technical Report UMCS 87-12-6, University of Manchester Computer Science Department, 1987.

[34] J. Latham. *Abstract Pascal User and Reference Manual*. 1985.

[35] P. Lindsay. A survey of mechanical support for formal reasoning. *Software Engineering Journal*, 3(1):3–27, January 1988.

[36] P. Lindsay. Theory structuring for reuse. In *Proceedings of the Leeds Workshop on Logic Teaching Systems*, July 1987. to appear.

[37] P. A. Lindsay. A formal system with inclusion polymorphism. Ipse working document 060/pal014/2.3, December 1987.

[38] P. A. Lindsay. *Logical Frames for Interactive Theorem Proving*. Technical Report UMCS 87-12-7, University of Manchester Computer Science Department, 1987.

[39] D. Loveland. Automated theorem-proving: a quarter century review. In *Automated Theorem Proving: After 25 Years*, pages 1–45, American Mathematical Society, 1984. AMS Contemporary Mathematics Series Volume 29.

[40] Z. Manna and R. Waldinger. A deductive approach to program synthesis. *ACM TOPLAS*, 2:90–121, 1980.

[41] R. Moore. The bumper fripse spec. Ipse Document 060/00143/2.1, June 1988.

[42] F. Morris. Some low-level suggestions for expression representation. To appear as a University of Manchester technical report, 1988.

[43] T. Nipkow. *Behavioural Implementation Concepts for Nondeterministic Data Types*. PhD thesis, University of Manchester, May 1987.

[44] L. Paulson. Natural deduction proof as higher-order resolution. *Journal of Logic Programming*, 237–258, 1986.

[45] D. Prawitz. *Natural Deduction*. Almqvist and Wiskell, 1965.

[46] B. Ritchie. *The Design and Implementation of an Interactive Proof Editor*. PhD thesis, University of Edinburgh, 1988.

[47] B. Ritchie and J. C. Bicarregui. Theory store analysis. Ipse Document 060/00111/1.1, October 1987.

[48] B. Ritchie and J. C. Bicarregui. Theory store requirements study. Ipse Document 060/00063/1.4, October 1987.

[49] R. Snowdon. *Scope of the IPSE 2.5 Project*. IPSE Project Document 060/00002/4.1.

[50] V. Stavridou, H. Barringer, and D. Edwards. *Formal Specification and Verification of Hardware: A Comparative Case Study*. Technical Report UMCS 87-11-1, University of Manchester Computer Science Department, 1987.

[51] D. Talbot and R. Witty. Alvey programme for software engineering. November 1983. Published by the Alvey Directorate.

[52] T. Teitelbaum and T. Reps. CPS: a syntax-directed programming environment. *Communications of ACM*, 24:563–573, 1981.

[53] A. Wills. Structure of interactive environments. In *Software Engineering Environments, Proceedings of the 3rd Annual Conference on Software Engineering Environments, April 1987*, pages 174–188, Ellis Horwood, 1988.

[54] A. C. Wills. Fripse architectural requirements. Ipse Document 060/00113/2.1, January 1988.

THE USE OF VDM WITHIN THE ALVEY FLAGSHIP PROJECT

Graham Boddy

ICL Mainframe Systems,

West Gorton,

Manchester M12 5DR

1) Objectives of the project

The overall objective of the Alvey Flagship [1] project is to provide an extensible parallel machine to support the declarative programming languages - both functional and logic based. The design philosophy is one of languages first, meaning that the machine is tailored to these languages to provide the attributes that the languages require.

However, no matter how powerful the hardware or attractive the languages, the system will only be used by a devout few unless it is capable of providing a useful programming environment, of managing itself and its resources to a level expected in the 1990's and of adaptation to meet the rapidly advancing ideas and languages of the declarative world.

The responsibility for all these ideas lies with the system software.

2) Implementation of the system software

In order for the system software to run efficiently on the parallel hardware, it must itself exploit the parallelism available. This is achieved by implementing the code in a particular declarative language - the functional programming language - Hope+ [2] .

Very little work has been done on large-scale software projects with the declarative languages, but they seem very amenable to a development route that uses formal specification as a first step due to the languages' mathematical bases. The Flagship system software development route is using VDM as its specification language.

3) Design methodology

The principal aim of the design methodology was to adopt a rigorous approach to the development of the system software, placing particular emphasis on the design and specification stages of the software life-cycle.

The system software had already been decomposed into a structure of components designed to work concurrently with each other. Each of these components could then be specified in terms of their behaviour and structure. Obviously it would have been better if we could have taken a top-level VDM specification of the system and decomposed it, but that was impractical within the constraints of the project.

In order to gain some degree of confidence in our specifications, and in the absence of any automatic theorem-proving devices suited to our requirements, we decided to produce executable models which tested the constraints imposed by the specifications against candidate algorithms [4]. These constraints include automatic transformation of pre/post checks and tests for violation of data type invariants.

The models are developed in our target language - Hope+. The development process involves writing the predicates of the operations and the functions in a functional style without the usual presence of mathematical symbols as used in familiar VDM dialects. The very early stages of specification development may still involve using the traditional VDM syntax using tools developed on top of the STL VDM Reference language developed as part of another Alvey project [3]. These specifications may then be mapped onto the "Flagship VDM" style used for expressing specifications. At present this part of the process is mainly manual, but the potential for development of an automatic compilation system exists, given the time and resources.

It is intended that we will concentrate less on the STL level of VDM as we become more concrete with our requirements for the "Flagship VDM" language. This is partially because of the direction in which the STL VDM reference language is progressing, particularly in the way of the new additions to the language such as statements which make a declarative-style model of behaviour very difficult to produce.

4) Aspects of the design language

In order to explain the details of the transformation process, it is first necessary to understand the language aspects of the "Flagship VDM" mentioned earlier.

4.1) "Flagship VDM"

The unit of composition is defined to be the Abstract Data Type (ADT), although this is being extended to cope with the hierarchy of software development within the project by introducing notions such as "subsystem" and "layer". A specification written in FVDM consists of a set of data type definitions, a set of functions and a set of operations, all of which are grouped together to form ADT definitions. Thus the entire system may be viewed as a hierarchy of ADT's, each with different properties.

4.1.1) Data type definitions

In order to provide a close mapping between the FVDM specification and the final Hope+ implementation, we have created standard modules which provide ADT's for the built-in VDM types of **sets, maps** and **lists**. By using these modules, the FVDM user may express predicates and functions at the high level of abstraction required by the specification phase. In order to provide as rich a set of potential data types as possible, the FVDM user is not only provided with the standard VDM types, but also the facility to express data-types in Hope+. This provides the user with a powerful polymorphic type system which promotes software re-use by use of generic functions and library ADT's.

For example :

```
data flagrec1 == REC OF
    [
    ( SOFTWARE , S_type ),
    ( HARDWARE , H_type ),
    ( REST , R_type )
    ]; ! FVDM record definition !
data Mytree(alpha) == HOPEDATA OF tip(alpha) ++
        node ( Mytree(alpha) X alpha X Mytree(alpha) );
    ! Hope+ type definition !
```

4.1.2) Function definitions

Explicit functions are expressed as normal Hope+ functions, which represent functions as a set of equations, using pattern matching to select the required equation. These functions may, of course use any new or standard types provided as part of their signatures. There is also the capability for creating generic functions by means of the polymorphic type system. A facility for including implicit function definitions by means of quoting a **post** condition instead of a set of equations is also provided, but is seldom used within the transformation environment.

For example :

```
dec double : num -> num; ! Explicit functions !
--- double ( n ) <= n + n ;
dec is_double : num X num -> truval; ! Implicit function !
post is_double ( n , m ) <= m = ( n * 2 ) ;
```

4.1.3) Operation definitions

Due to the declarative nature of the Flagship machine architecture, it is particularly important to capture the behaviour of operations as they represent transformations on state, which has no obvious meaning in a declarative system. Operations may be viewed as state-transition functions that take the old state and any parameters, perform some operation upon them, and return a pair of the result and the new state, using copying semantics.

For example :

```
dec PUSH : alpha X Stack  -> Stack ;

---PUSH (a , s) <= a :: s ;
```

However, in order to achieve efficiency on the Flagship machine, it may be necessary to map operations down onto a more efficient aspect of the machine architecture, such as updating of state rather than copying. It is therefore important for operations not to be regarded just as functions, although this may be one possible implementation.

4.1.4 The use of functional notation

As previously stated, functions, operation predicates, etc. are written in a functional style using the declarative language Hope+. This means that all such expressions are written in a keyword style as opposed to the mathematical symbol style found in most VDM references. In most cases, the mathematical symbols used would represent some built-in operations such as the symbol † for the operation "map overwrite".

The standard modules that the FVDM system provides include built-in functions for all such operations, making specification writing as close to using normal predicate calculus as is practical. For example, the VDM expression :

($\forall$ x $\in$ ThisSet) (is_even (x))

becomes :

```
forall ( ThisSet , is_even )
```

4.1.5 The executable subset

The use of this functional notation does not seem to restrict us unduly in terms of its expressiveness or its degree of expression of abstraction. It is only when we come to consider the derivation of executable models from these specifications that we must consider any restrictions that should be placed upon these specifications.

- **Any use of quantifiers which range over infinite sets should be removed or modified to range over a finite set. This includes quantifiers which range over types.**

- **Any implicit functions should either be made explicit or reworked. These reworked functions could be explicit truth-valued functions whose bodies are identical to the post conditions of the original implicit functions.**

5) The transformation process

The purpose of developing executable model frameworks from specifications is to reinforce our confidence in the specifications, to a greater degree than might otherwise be achieved by formal inspections or the current, more limited, proof techniques. The executable model framework allows the user to slot potential algorithms into a testing framework, and validate those algorithms against the original specification. These can provide useful feedback in both directions.

- **The algorithm may cause a test condition such as pre/post/invariant to fail, indicating an error in the algorithm.**

- **A test case fed into the algorithm which should fail is allowed by the test conditions. In this case the specification test conditions must be made tighter.**

The framework that is generated is derived from the FVDM specification according to the rules described in the following sections. The actual transformation process works from an internal database structure used to hold all of the system software ADT's that will be described later. For the time being, it may be assumed that the FVDM -> Hope$^+$ transformation works very much like a conventional compiler system.

5.1) Data types and functions

Data types and functions are passed through into Hope$^+$ with very few changes. The only changes are the transformation of special VDM types such as records and their associated field selector functions into the appropriate Hope$^+$ type definitions. If any data types have invariants defined upon them, then the invariants are recorded. Function definitions are echoed exactly from FVDM into Hope$^+$.

5.2) Operations

The main work performed by the transformation process involves the use of operations. As stated previously, in the current system, operations map down onto state transition functions in order to model their behaviour in a declarative style. This is not always going to be the case, but it is true during the modelling phase being discussed here. In general, the behaviour of an ADT is specified in terms of the operations upon its state. We therefore perform the most significant degree of validation upon the action of these operations.

5.2.1 The structure of an operation

Each operation is considered to consist of :

- **A name and signature.**

- **A definition of what state this operation accesses and what mode of access to the state (read / write).**

- **A pre-condition Boolean expression.**

- **A post-condition Boolean expression.**

- **An errors clause which maps onto the Hope+ errors scheme.**

In order to validate that a user's algorithm satisfies these conditions, we build a framework program which tests all of these conditions at the appropriate stages. We must also test that invariants still hold for those states where the data-type has an invariant bound to it.

5.2.2) Operation transformation

In order to illustrate the transformation process at work, a simple example of a stack will be used. The complete definition of the stack would include an interface description, plus definitions for data types, functions and any operations defined upon the type "stack". Only those definitions declared in the interface section are made visible outside of the ADT. This example will only illustrate the behaviour of a single operation chosen from this ADT.

The operation POP may be defined in FVDM as follows :

```
OP POP : -> res : num;

ext wr st : Stack; ! Stack implemented as a list !

pre st /= nil;

err (1,"Pre fail in POP"),(2,"Post fail in POP");

post let (a :: x) == st in (res = a) and (st_new = x);
```

The transformation system would generate the following Hope⁺ code :

```
dec pre_POP : Stack -> truval;
--- pre_POP (st) <= st /= nil;
dec post_POP : num X Stack X Stack -> truval;
--- post_POP ( res , st , st_new ) <=
    let (a :: x) == st in (res = a) and (st_new = x);
dec POP : Stack -> num X Stack;
---POP ( s ) <=
    if   ! Test if pre_condition holds !
        pre_POP ( s )
    then
        let ( res , st_new ) ==
            alg_POP ( st ) in ! User-defined algorithm !
        if   ! Test if post_condition holds !
            post_POP ( res , st , st_new )
        then
            ( res , st_new )
        else
            error ([ ( 2 , "Post fail in POP" ) ])
    else
        error ([ ( 1 , "Pre fail in POP" ) ]);
```

The pre-condition check may be viewed as a test to be performed upon the validity of the parameters and the old value of the operation's state. Similarly the post-condition is used to check the consistency of the new state relative to the old state and any parameters. The function **alg_POP** is the user-defined algorithm function that the specification writer can slot into the framework. The following additional checks may also be generated by the transformation system depending upon context :

- If the type of any of the state items is bound by an invariant, then an additional check will be generated for each such type which ensures that the invariant of this object has not been violated. For example, if stack was declared with an invariant property - inv_Stack, then the following operation body would be generated : (Note - all pre/post as before)

```
dec POP : Stack -> num X Stack;

---POP ( s ) <=
    if
        pre_POP ( s )
    then
        let ( res , st_new ) ==
            alg_POP ( st ) in
        if
            post_POP ( res , st , st_new ) and
            inv_Stack ( st_new ) ! New - invariant check !
        then
            ( res , st_new )
        else
            error ([ ( 2 , "Post fail in POP" ) ])
    else
        error ([ ( 1 , "Pre fail in POP" ) ]);
```

- If any state item is declared as read-only, then an additional check is generated to ensure that the new state is identical to the old state. For example, take a different stack operation :

```
OP ISEMPTY : -> yes : truval;

ext rd st : Stack;

err ( 2 , "Post fail in ISEMPTY" );

post yes = ( st = nil );


dec post_ISEMPTY : truval X Stack X Stack -> truval;

---post_ISEMPTY ( yes , st , st_new ) <=

     yes = ( st = nil );

dec ISEMPTY : Stack -> truval X Stack;

---ISEMPTY ( st ) <=

          let ( res , st_new ) ==

               alg_ISEMPTY ( st ) in

          if

               post_ISEMPTY ( res , st , st_new ) and

               ( st = st_new ) ! New - consistency check !

          then

               ( res , st_new )

          else

               error ([ ( 2 , "Post fail in ISEMPTY" ) ])
```

6 Testing of the executable models

In order to test the executable models, we have developed an interactive command interpreter system which can be customised to accept a set of commands and drive the model accordingly. This interpreter has itself been developed using the FVDM system. The interpreter may be used interactively or in batch mode. This allows the user to develop test-scripts to drive the interpreter in order to test operations over multiple invocations with different parameter sets. Test-scripts are developed by careful analysis of the ranges of possible values that parameters may take.

The major headache of using the interpreter system in interactive mode is the repetition of typing in the same commands with marginally different parameters. This problem is alleviated by the development of a WIMP-based test harness system, written in 'C' using Sun's proprietary SunView™ package [5]. The test harness is customised to generate a set of commands which are fed into the standard interpreter system. The commands and their parameters may be selected via pointing with a mouse rather than explicit typing every time. This reduces the burden of testing to a fairly acceptable degree.

It is intended that the test-scripts used to drive the test-harness system are included as a part of the formal review of a sub-system. This should improve the rigour of what is actually a very informal process in the absence of any full-blown theorem-proving techniques.

7) The Development Route database

The process of specification capture and subsequent manipulation (including the transformation into Hope+ compilable code) is controlled via a central database application. This database stores specifications at a much finer level of granularity than conventional file-based systems. This allows a variety of detailed dependency information to be generated from the internal database structure.

Specifications are stored at the level of granularity of individual signatures and predicates, being represented by objects in a hierarchical structure. Dependency information between these objects such as "uses" or "used by" information is represented by relations between such objects. Detailed dependency reports on any level of object in the hierarchy are therefore easily available and are updated automatically as new objects are added to the database.

The transformation process described earlier can be viewed as just another tool working off the database structure in a similar fashion to the browsing or reporting tools. This allows a very clean orthogonal view of our specification information which can be manipulated in any chosen fashion, by plugging in the appropriate tools.

Existing tools include a window-based editor, various browsing / reporting tools and archiving facilities. Mechanisms for performing product builds from the database structure are being developed, as are more sophisticated version and change control facilities.

8) Difficulties using VDM on the project

- The general lack of supported tools forced us to develop our own tools internally (with the exception of the STL system).

- Any aspects related to concurrency and parallel behaviour are not suitably dealt with.

- Composition of modules / ADT's is difficult and cumbersome.

- We are attempting to use a currency style interface to our ADT's, whereby creating an instance of an ADT returns a set of partially-parameterised functions which are bound to this ADT instance. We can find no way of clearly expressing this in standard VDM.

- In general, the usage of other operations from within an operation is extremely painful owing to the contrived nature of quoting the target operation's post-conditions. This is particularly obvious when attempting to get a result from an operation where the result is not stored anywhere afterwards.

9) Summary

In Flagship, we have attempted to perform a very gradual introduction of the use of formal methods without proclaiming it to be the answer to all of our problems. Since this is not a formal methods project, our primary concern has been to gain some benefit from the use of formal methods, rather than to research their use in an industrial environment.

In particular, this led us to drive our development process towards a particular declarative environment which might not otherwise have been considered in a formal methods project. Hopefully this use of a declarative environment will give us great benefits in terms of fine-grain concurrency when we are able to develop our software on the Flagship parallel hardware.

10) References

[1]   ICL Technical Journal : The ICL Fifth Generation Programme
       International Computer Limited
       Volume 5 Issue 3 May 1987

[2]   Hope[+] -
       Nigel Perry, Imperial College, London.
       IC / FPR / LANG / 2.5.1 / 7

[3]   VDM Toolset -
       Alvey Project ALV / PRJ / SE / 016

[4]   Generating executable models from VDM specifications -
       G.S.Boddy
       Flagship FLAG / UD / 3DR . 020 (internal)

[5]   SunView™ Programmers Guide
       Sun Microsystems 800-1345-10

The Formal Definition of Modula-2 and Its Associated Interpreter

D.J.Andrews, A.Garg, S.P.A.Lau, J.R.Pitchers

Department of Computing Studies

University of Leicester

Leicester LE1 7RH, UK

Abstract

A three year research project is currently being undertaken at Leicester University, The National Physical Laboratory (NPL) and The British Standards Institution (BSI). The project aims to produce a formal definition of the syntax and semantics of the programming language Modula-2, written in VDM Meta IV, together with a rigorously verified interpreter derived directly from the definition. In the process of producing a good quality document of the formal definition of Modula-2, two by-products will also be developed and applied. They are a VDM structure editor and an environment to generate LaTeX files from the VDM structure editor.

1 Objectives of the Project

- To use the VDM meta-language to write a formal definition of the syntax and semantics of the programming language Modula-2.

- To demonstrate the feasibility of using formal methods in the production of a usable programming language standard.

- To develop an executable interpreter of Modula-2 derived from the formal definition.

- To provide a basis for the development of a Modula-2 compiler which can be formally verified against the formal definition.

- To establish the formal definition as the reference standard for Modula-2, within both the standards and implementor community.

2 Background

There are currently two approaches to the definition of a programming language that are used either separately or together. They are: (a) to write the definition of the language in a natural language and (b) to provide a reference implementation. The approach taken by most language developers of using a natural language as the specification tool leaves many unresolved questions about the semantics of the programming language being defined which are usually answered differently by each implementor. This problem can be resolved by producing a standard implementation to which everyone may refer. As for the reference implementation approach, it is likely to be machine dependent and certainly to be dependent upon the architecture of the compiler/interpreter that is used as the reference. The reference implementation approach has one advantage in that it will be a full implementation of the language (by definition) and thus will have no ambiguities or omissions.

Although the formal definition of programming languages and systems is well tried, no programming language standard exists which is written in a formal language. There is now sufficient experience with formal methods to provide a mathematical specification of the programming language Modula-2 that is suitable for use as a BSI/ISO standard.

3 The Formal Definition of Modula - 2

The formal definition of Modula-2 is written in the VDM meta-language (META-IV) with an accompanying commentary written in English. As the meta-language is similar to a programming language in both syntax and semantics, it will not be too difficult for the computing profession to read.

There are two major difficulties in producing a correct (i.e. the intended) definition. Firstly, the text of the definition must be syntactically correct and secondly, the semantics of the definition must define the required language. The project currently uses a VDM structure editor to check the syntax. It also provides a flexible environment for the development of the formal definition. The structure editor is able to store the definition in a tree form in one or many separate files. The same structure editor may then be used to modify the definition, as and when required. Furthermore, with suitable alternative unparsing schemes, the VDM structure editor may output the definition in different concrete syntaxes. One such unparsing scheme was designed to produce a concrete syntax suitable for typesetting by LaTeX. Thus, a high quality listing of the definition may be obtained. With appropriate translation algorithms, another unparsing scheme will be be designed to produce Pascal concrete syntax of the definition. This Pascal representation will form part of the Modula-2 Interpreter.

As for the semantics, this will be checked by an executable version of the formal definition—the interpreter. This interpreter can be tested with a suite of programs that are considered to be written in Modula-2. If the interpreter is rigorously developed from the formal definition, any errors that occur during the testing can be traced back to the appropriate part of the formal definition and corrected. Although the development of the interpreter will be rigorous rather than formal, the documentation will be such that formal proofs may easily be written and machine checked when the tools become available. The interpreter will be a direct translation of the formal definition where possible and only those parts which need to be implemented as algorithms will be done as such. Thus, the interpreter will be as close as possible to the formal definition.

There is a danger that the formal definition may be unduly influenced by the fact that it is to be translated into an executable form and this could lead to the probability of over specification. Although this trap has been avoided wherever possible, the formal definition of Modula-2 has probably been over specified for another reason concerned more with the expected audience rather than the production of an executable version of the specification. For example, it is customary in VDM to model declarations as mappings of identifiers to their properties and use a "declare before use" rule to guarantee that the normal fixed point equation for resolving declarations has a solution other than bottom. In the formal definition of Modula-2, declarations have been modelled as a sequence in the order that they occur in the problem and checks for "declared before use" have been specified. Although this is not the normal approach taken when specifying languages, it was considered more important to describe the rules for "declare before use" rather than use the simplification that fixed point equations allow.

4 The VDM Structure Editor

The abstract syntax which defines the meta language used by the VDM structure editor was derived from a proposed BSI standard for the VDM Meta-IV language, contained within documents: BSI/IST/5/50/D40-871206 and BSI/IST/5/50/D51-871215. It should be noted that at the time the VDM structure editor was developed, the VDM Meta-IV language had not been standardised.

The VDM structure editor was developed and runs under a Sun Unix system on a Sun 3/50 workstation.

This document now describes the process of configuration of the VDM structure editor using the Gandalf System (from Carnegie-Mellon University).

4.1 The Process of Configuration

The Gandalf system permits the implementor to develop structure editors with varying attributes; the simplest editor being a pure structure editor. The VDM structure editor discussed in this report is one such pure structure editor.

4.1.1 The Abstract Syntax

The VDM Meta-IV abstract syntax used to develop the VDM structure editor is itself written in VDM Meta-IV. However, the AloeGrammar used by the Gandalf system to build structure editors is based on the BNF style. Therefore, it was necessary to convert from a VDM description of a language into an equivalent BNF description and there were many different ways to achieve this. To build a pure structure, only syntactic information is required. Having said that, extra information is sometimes required in order to achieve unparsing to the desired concrete syntax. For low level constructs, such as:

$Text_literal = $ **seq of** $Char\_literal$

it was decided that Text_literal should be a terminal operator (leaf node) governed by a lexical routine to achieve the same result as defined by the abstract syntax above. This philosophy facilitates the user of the editor by allowing a whole string to be entered in one go rather than a character at a time.

4.1.2 The Concrete Syntax

Input of a specification (in VDM) into the VDM structure editor is achieved by selecting the required operator (terminal or non-terminal) from the displayed class list. In the case of terminal operators, it may be necessary to enter a value, as for an integer. In abstract terms, the representation of an integer is irrelevant. However, in order to enter an integer into the VDM structure editor it is necessary to have a particular concrete representation (Roman or Arabic, for instance). In the VDM structure editor, the concrete representation of inputting such values is governed by lexical routines. The concrete representation output by the VDM structure editor depends on the unparsing scheme used.

4.2 Unparsing Schemes

The VDM structure editor has several unparsing schemes that produce several different concrete representations of the specification (in VDM) stored in its abstract syntax trees.

There are currently two schemes designed to display VDM Meta-IV concrete syntax on the terminal screen. The first scheme uses only the standard seven bit ASCII character set and is incapable of displaying all of the special characters required by VDM concrete syntax. The second scheme uses an eight bit, extended ASCII character set to display these special characters.

A third scheme produces a concrete representation suitable for typesetting by LaTeX, to produce a high quality document in VDM Meta-IV concrete syntax.

A fourth scheme is to be designed that will produce a Pascal concrete syntax of the VDM abstract syntax tree.

There are several other minor unparsing schemes to display the abstract syntax tree in other concrete forms.

5 The Interpreter

Figure 1 contains the overall view of the Modula-2 Interpreter.

The interpreter will consist of the following components:

1. The **Parser** will take a Modula-2 program as input and produce an abstract syntax tree of that program. The format of the tree will be based on the abstract syntax of Modula-2 as defined in Meta-IV.

2. The **Static Checker** will take the abstract syntax tree of a Modula-2 program as input and decide whether the program is well-formed.

3. The **Dynamic Interpreter** will take the completed abstract syntax tree and execute the underlying Modula-2 program.

The development of this interpreter is divided into two different phases (testing and final) for the following reasons:

- Firstly, there is the advantage of permitting independent development and testing of each major program fragment of the interpreter.

- Secondly, a parser already exists written in Modula-2; the remaining program fragments of the interpreter are to be written in Pascal.

Figure 1 contains the overall picture of what the interpreter will look like when the testing phase is complete. It is intended that the initial version of the interpreter will handle the well-formedness conditions and meaning functions for a simple program module.

There shall be two separate forms of the abstract syntax tree: an internal version and a disk version. Two routines are to be produced: one will flatten the internal abstract syntax tree and write it to disk; the other will do the reverse process. Thus, the three major program fragments of the interpreter can interact with each other via the disk, or via store.

Figure 1   The Overall Structure of the Interpreter

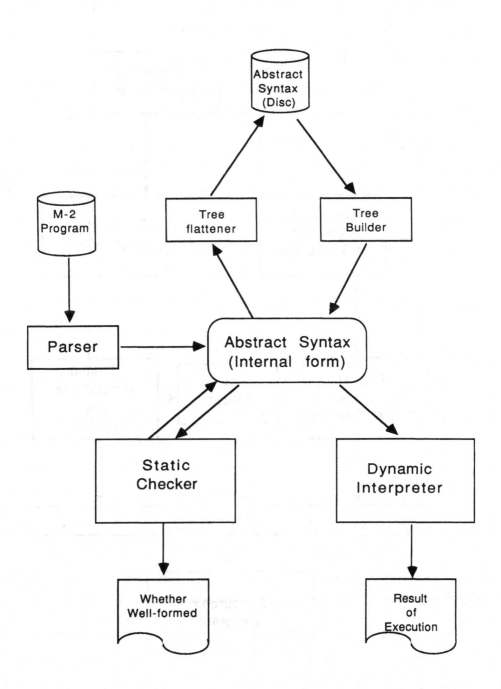

Figure 2 Type Model and ADT Library

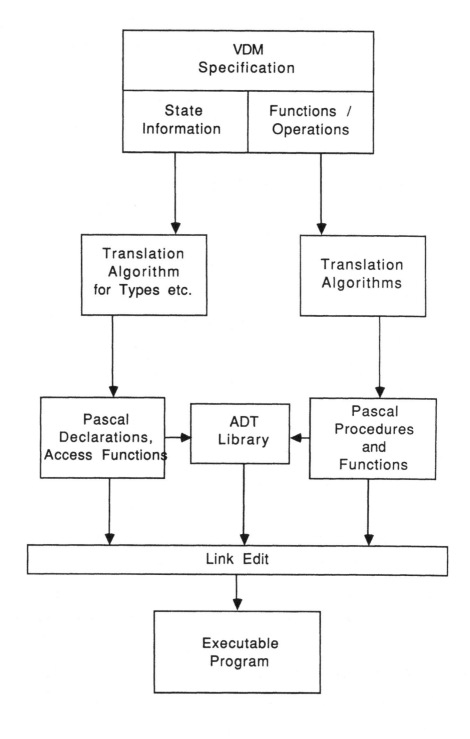

5.1 The Parser

The parser will consist of two components. The first component will read a Modula-2 program and generate an internal abstract syntax tree. Some type information will not be present in the abstract representation of a Modula-2 program. The second component is a tree flattener and it will dump an internal abstract syntax tree on disk in ASCII format.

In the final phase, the parser will be re-written in Pascal and can be combined with the static checker and dynamic interpreter to become one program.

5.2 Static Checker

The static checker will take the abstract syntax tree of a Modula-2 program produced by the parser and decide whether or not the underlying program is well-formed. It will also need to supply the missing type information during the checking process. Rules must be applied to decide whether or not the underlying program represented by an abstract syntax tree is well-formed or not, and these rules can be found in the formal definition of Modula-2. By applying a suitable translation algorithm to the well-formed functions in the definition, an executable version of the definition in the form of a series of Pascal functions can be obtained. Since the definition is in VDM which uses abstract data types, a Pascal abstract data type (ADT) library, which consists of the essential operations to manipulate abstract data types, is being developed.

5.2.1 Translation Algorithms

Work has been done to hand translate well-formed and meaning functions for the sections on Variables, Expressions, and Statements in the formal definition. The translation algorithms to translate all the specification for Modula-2 will be derived from the experience gained so far. Although it is possible to hand translate the rest of the definition, an automatic means is more preferable. The translation algorithms derived will be expressed as unparsing schemes in the VDM structure editor. By applying these unparsing schemes to the Modula-2 specifications held in the VDM structure editor, Pascal code can be generated. A major part of the code for the static checker will be produced by these translation algorithms.

5.2.2 The Type Model

The explicit operation definitions used in VDM specifications manipulate the state. The type model will form the basis of the translation of the state information contained in the VDM specification into Pascal. In addition, the type model is also required for type checking. All VDM types have to be translated into Pascal, and it will be necessary to have a one to one correspondence between the VDM specification and the Pascal equivalent. Once translated into Pascal, a direct implementation of data types: maps, sequences, composite objects and sets can be used to produce an executable version of a VDM specification. Figure 2 shows the relationship between the type model and the ADT library. The type model and the ADT library have been designed to allow easy expansion and change.

5.3 Dynamic Interpreter

The dynamic interpreter will read in an abstract syntax tree of a well-formed Modula-2 program and execute the underlying program. It consists of a series of functions and procedures produced by feeding the meaning functions in formal definition through the translation algorithm. Again, the translation algorithm will be expressed as unparsing schemes in the VDM structure editor to produce Pascal code. The Pascal code will be as close as possible to the VDM specification so as to expedite debugging and other necessary checks.

6 Current Status (June, 1988)

1. The formal definition of Modula-2 is almost complete and is at present being reviewed by the BSI/ISO standardization committees.

2. The ADT library is almost complete.

3. The translation algorithms are currently being designed and developed.

4. The VDM structure editor has been available for nearly a year and has since been modified to conform with the proposed BSI standard for VDM. As the standardization of VDM progresses, the VDM structure editor is expected to undergo a series of upgrades.

5. The draft version of the environment to produce LaTeX files from the VDM structure editor was completed last December. It is now capable of producing LaTeX files for good quality documents in a particular style. Attention is now drawn to the minor issues of spacing, fonts etc and further upgrading of the structure editor.

References

1. D.J. Andrews. *The Formal Definition of Modula-2*, The Department of Computing Studies, Leicester University, Leicester, June 1988.

2. Anjula Garg. *Design and Implementation of Abstract Data Types*, The Department of Computing Studies, Leicester University, Leicester, June 1988.

3. Anjula Garg. *Type Model for the Translation of the Definition of Modula-2 from VDM to Standard Pascal*, The Department of Computing Studies, Leicester University, Leicester, June 1988.

4. J.R. Pitchers. *The VDM Structure Editor V0.2n*, The Department of Computing Studies, Leicester University, Leicester, May 1988.

5. D. Notkin. The Gandalf Project. *The Journal of Systems and Software*, 5(2):91–105, May 1985.

6. B.J. Staudt, C.W. Krueger, A.N. Habermann and V. Ambriola. *The Gandalf System Reference Manuals*. Department of Computer Science, Carnegie-Mellon University, Pittsburgh, Pa. 15213, May 1986.

7. Leslie Lamport. *A Document Preparation System, User's Guide and Reference Manual.* Addison-Wesley, 1986.

TEST CASE SELECTION USING VDM

G.T.Scullard

ICL Defence Systems

West Gorton, Manchester, M12 5DR, United Kingdom

Abstract

This paper describes the design validation process adopted by the VLSI Distributed Array Processor (VDAP) Project. In this project structured, informal design techniques were used in the hardware design process, but the validation team used some of the tools and methods of VDM as a means of defining the testing strategy.

Introduction

The VDAP is a development of the ICL DAP Single Instruction Multiple Data architecture machines, details of which are described in [6] and consists of some 60 VLSI chips (eight different designs), each chip having up to 200,000 transistors. At the heart of the system is an array of (in this implementation) 16 processing elements, each capable of simple four bit arithmetic and logical operations and each having a local on-chip memory of 256 bits. The whole is controlled by a 16 bit control processor, responsible for instruction sequencing and address modification. In addition, each processing element is capable of local address modification using its own internal registers.

The testing of VLSI hardware is well documented in the literature and good descriptions of the standard techniques may be found in [1] and [8]. The problems encountered in large designs, where exhaustive testing is not possible, is considered in [3] and [7]. These methods, however, are concerned with the Silicon production process and assume that the design information, on which that process is based, is correct. We are here concerned with demonstrating the correctness of the VDAP design with respect to its specification, a process rather similar to software validation; we therefore apply some of the techniques of software testing to a VDM representation of the hardware specification.

Hardware Development Route

Since the bulk of the hardware was to be realised using VLSI technology, where the cost of fabrication was high, it was clear that design errors had to be reduced to a minimum (preferably zero). The design method was informal and was based on hierarchies of English language specifications and software models, as illustrated in Fig. 1.

The starting point is the so-called 'Primitive Level Interface' (PLI), a definition of the system which would be used by a software writer and which defines, for example, the order code and memory mappings, visible to such a user. Below this, hardware specifications are produced at the levels of system, functional unit and chip. To conclude the specification stage, each document is inspected against its parent. Two parallel activities are now based on the set of chip specifications, namely: logic design and modelling.

High level language (S3, an in-house language based on ALGOL68) models of the chips are written and collected together to form an executable system model which may be tested against the original PLI specification. This serves to check that the specification and modelling route is correct. When this has been established, input and output patterns are extracted from the system model, corresponding to chip boundaries; these patterns are then applied to chip logic simulations, which are automatically extracted from the logic design database, thus checking that this process is also correct.

Clearly, this process is wholly dependent on the quality of the tests; how we ensure that the tests are adequate is described below.

The Testing Problem

The objective of design validation is to show that, for all valid conditions, the object being validated behaves correctly. Clearly the easiest way to do this is simply to test every valid case;

this is exhaustive testing and for small, simple designs is sometimes possible. Unfortunately, in most real projects, the number of valid states is so large that it is impossible to visit them all, and so an alternative strategy is required. The selection of a suitable subset of the system state has traditionally been difficult and often a rather ad-hoc process, complicated by the fact that, where natural language specification is used, the total state is often not well defined. In this project, the use of VDM as a specification language clarifies the problem domain and allows relatively simple criteria to be applied to test set selection.

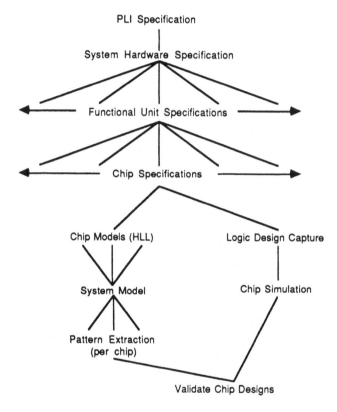

Fig 1. Hardware Development Route

The Test Development Route

Generation of tests, like the design process, starts from the English PLI Specification but, from then on, proceeds independently thus avoiding, as far as possible, 'common mode ' errors.

The first step is to translate the PLI Specification into VDM. This has two immediate benefits: first, it is a highly effective way of introducing the testing team to the system they are to test, and second, it quickly highlights deficiencies and ambiguities in the natural language specification. It is, of course, necessary to carry out a detailed inspection of the VDM before it is used as a basis for test case extraction.

The working specification consists of a single top level operation, representing the execution of a single instruction, which has access to the whole state. Below this is a hierarchy of functions and operations, describing the detailed functionality in an obvious way. In total there are 8 operations and some 150 functions, the whole specification running to some 3500 lines.

VDM proof obligations are of the form:

$$(\forall x \; \varepsilon \; X)(p(x))$$

where p is a truth valued function of x.

The process of testing is, in essence, to select samples from the set X and establish the truth of p(x) case by case. The quality of the tests is determined by the quality of the sampling process and the coverage is the ratio of sample size to domain size.

Test Case Extraction Procedure

The test case extraction in the case of the VDAP Project was carried out manually, but with the advent of reasonable VDM tools, it is easy to see how this process may be automated.

The procedure takes each function or operation separately and considers the structure of its domain in order that a reasonable sample may be identified. Typically, the domain set of a function is the cartesian product of a number of basic types (Int, Bool etc); in the case of VDAP all these basic types are finite sets and either totally ordered or unordered (it is possible to imagine partial orderings but these did not occur in practice).

The test case extraction process proceeds, for each function, as follows:

      a. Reduce the signature of the function to basic types only. This means that compound types are simply replaced by the cartesian product of their components.

b. Take into account the effect of any function pre-condition or data type invariants. This usually reduces the size and number of sets under consideration.

c. Where arguments are used only in the quotation of an embedded function, replace them by an object of the type returned by that function.

d. Repeat the above until the revised signature has been reduced to basic types only.

e. Analyse the domain of the reduced signature by taking each of the basic types and extracting a set of 'typical' values; in the case of unordered types all values are used, for ordered types extreme values and one or more central values are chosen. This identifies the 'external structure' of the function and in particular identifies the 'dark corners'.

f. By skolemizing the post condition of the function, identify all the different ways in which the post condition may be satisfied. This is the 'internal structure' of the function and is rather similar to the path testing ideas used in software testing (see [9] and [11]). Thus test cases are added to ensure that all sub-domains are visited and that the boundaries between them are correctly discriminated.

g. Analyse the structure of the range set in the same way as the domain.

The array control processor is a conventional von-Neumann architecture microprocessor having 16-bit registers. The following example is taken from its addition operation, which is unusual in that it may operate over less than 16 bits. Thus in addition to the usual address information, length (in bits) and location within the register must be provided. The specification of the function is as follows :-

add : Operand x Operand x Bool $\rightarrow$ Operand

pre-add(a,b,cin) == (LENGTH(a) = LENGTH(b)) $\wedge$ LENGTH(a) $\leq$ 16

post-add(a,b,cin,result) == ~cin $\Rightarrow$ N(result) = N(a) + N(b) $\wedge$

$$cin \Rightarrow N(result) = N(a) + N(b) +1 \wedge$$

$$N(result) \geq 2 \uparrow (LENGTH(a)) \Rightarrow LENGTH(result) = LENGTH(a) + 1 \wedge$$

$$N(result) < 2 \uparrow (LENGTH(a)) \Rightarrow LENGTH(result) = LENGTH(a)$$

Where

Operand :: N : Nat0

LENGTH : Nat

inv-Operand(x) == N(x) < 2 $\uparrow$ LENGTH(x)

This function is of course embedded within others concerned with operand fetching and storing.

Following our prescription, the signature of add is expanded into its basic types as follows :-

add : Nat0 x Nat x Nat0 x Nat x Bool → Nat0 x Nat

Hence, the domain of add consists of the cartesian product of five sets, four of which are ordered and one (Bool) unordered. Next the effects of pre-conditions and invariants are taken into account:

The function pre-condition and Operand invariant place limits on the sizes of the Nat and Nat0 sets, and consideration of the post-condition limits the range set. Thus:

add : $\{0 : 2^{len} - 1\}$ x $\{1 : 16\}$ x $\{0 : 2^{len} - 1\}$ x Bool → $\{0 : 2^{len+1}-1\}$ x $\{1 : 17\}$

Where $1 \leq len \leq 16$

This reduced signature defines the size and shape of the function domain, in this case the size of the domain is

$$2\ \Pi_{x=1,16}\ 2^{2x}$$

The next step is to identify an adequate subset of this domain which will give confidence in an implementation of the function. First, orderings are used to identify the 'dark corners' of the domain, in this case the three numeric sets. Thus, values of 1 and 16 are used for operand length and values of 0 and 1 or 0 and 65535 for operand value which, together with both values of the boolean set, give 16 cases. This is clearly inadequate, so now the internal structure of the function, as defined by the post-condition, is taken into account. Skolemisation of the post condition gives:

post-add(a,b,cin,result) ==

(~cin $\wedge$ N(result) = N(a) + N(b) $\wedge$

   N(result) < 2 ↑ (LENGTH(a)) $\wedge$ LENGTH(result) = LENGTH(a)) $\vee$

(~cin $\wedge$ N(result) = N(a) + N(b) $\wedge$

   N(result) $\geq$ 2 ↑ (LENGTH(a)) $\wedge$ LENGTH(result) = LENGTH(a) + 1) $\vee$

(cin $\wedge$ N(result) = N(a) + N(b) +1 $\wedge$

   N(result) < 2 ↑ (LENGTH(a)) $\wedge$ LENGTH(result) = LENGTH(a)) $\vee$

(cin $\wedge$ N(result) = N(a) + N(b) +1 $\wedge$

$$N(result) \geq 2 \uparrow (LENGTH(a)) \wedge LENGTH(result) = LENGTH(a) + 1)$$

Thus we conclude that the domain should be considered in four parts defined by the value of carry in and whether overflow occurs and values should be chosen which lead to these internal boundaries being examined. In fact cin has already been taken into account in the domain analysis, so the numerical value of the result is the only new information here.

Combining the following sets satisfies these requirements:

cin = {true,false}
length = {1,16}
a = $\{0,1,2^{length} - 1\}$
b = $\{0,1,2^{length} - 1\}$

Giving 26 cases in all (8 for length = 1, 18 for length = 16).

In this simple example their is no extra information supplied by the range set.

In practice, some non-boundary cases were added so, for example, length became {1,4,16} and arbitrary values were added to a and b.

Conclusions

As the size and complexity of VLSI continues to grow there is a clear need to develop design methods which will remove errors before designs are committed to Silicon. The obvious way forward in this area would seem to be the use of formal methods giving proof of correctness and no doubt in due course such methods will mature. In the meantime, however, we are left with testing as the only practical approach to large problems and in this project we have attempted to extract test cases in a systematic way using the formality of VDM as a framework within which to work.

It is difficult to assess the effectiveness of the approach; at the time of writing a high level model of the design, consisting of some 5000 lines of S3, has been tested and about 50 errors discovered (these are residual errors; the models are tested informally by the design team).

One obvious criticism is that this method is 'black box', since it is based on the specification rather than the implementation of the design. This is inevitable when top-down design methods are used, since many implementation details which may affect the testing stategy are not visible until late in the project but, to be of use, design validation tests are needed early. However, when one considers VDM as a design method rather than, as here, simply a specification language, the possibility of using the later, refined models as vehicles for test case generation suggests itself. In this case, the refinements introduced into the model are, in effect, the implementation details which we seek. Thus, as the specification is gradually refined into an implementation, the tests develop from 'black box' to 'white box'. Such a process would however lead to a large test set; the VDAP test generation produced some 8000 cases from the specification alone. Were refined models to be subjected to the same type of procedure, this number would grow rapidly.

The above arguments lead to the speculation that an automated test generation system would be useful. Such a system may well be possible using principles already used in automatic test generation systems for chip manufacture. Suppose, for example, a design process had produced an abstract specification, an implementation (both in, say, VDM) and a set of retrieve functions. The test set is generated by analysis of the structure of the implementation. The values thus obtained are then retrieved onto the data types defined in the abstraction and the abstract specification used to specify a suitable result set.

Acknowledgements

This work was jointly funded by the RSRE and DCVD divisions of MoD and ICL Defence Systems.

References

[1] Z.Barzilai, D.Coppersmith, A.L.Rosenberg, 'Exhaustive Generation of Bit Patterns with Applications to VLSI Self Testing' IEEE Trans Comp C-32 Feb 83.
[2] L.A.Clark, 'A System to Generate Test Data and Symbolically Execute Programs' IEEE Trans SE SE-2 1976.
[3] P.Golan, O.Novac, J.Hlavicka, 'Pseudoexhaustive Test Pattern Generator with Enhanced Fault Coverage' IEEE Trans Comp C-37 Apr 88.
[4] B.Goodenough, S.L.Gerhart, 'Towards a Theory of Test Data Selection' IEEE Trans SE SE-1 1975.
[5] J.C.King, 'Symbolic Execution and Program Testing' Comm ACM 19 1976.
[6] K.C.Lo, 'VDAP Primitive Level Interface' ICL Internal Document.
[7] E.J.McCluskey, 'Verification Testing - A Pseudoexhaustive Technique' IEEE Trans. Comp.

C-33 June 84.

[8] E.I.Muehldorf, A.D.Savkar, 'LSI Logic Testing - An Overview' IEEE Trans Comp C-30 Jan 81.

[9] S.C.Ntafos, S.L.Hakimi, 'On Structured Digraphs and Program Testing' IEEE Trans Comp C-30 Jan 81.

[10] C.V.Ramamoorthy, S.F.Ho, W.T.Chen, 'On the Automated Generation of Program Test Data' IEEE Trans SE SE-2 Dec 76.

[11] M.L.Shooman, 'Software Engineering' McGraw Hill 1983.

The VIP VDM Specification Language

Kees Middelburg*
PTT Dr. Neher Laboratories
P.O. Box 421, 2260 AK Leidschendam, The Netherlands

Abstract

VVSL is a VDM specification language of the 'British School' with modularisation constructs allowing sharing of hidden state variables and parameterisation constructs for structuring specifications, and with constructs for expressing temporal aspects of the concurrent execution of operations which interfere via state variables. VVSL was designed and is being used in the ESPRIT project 1283: VIP.

The modularisation and parameterisation constructs have been inspired by the 'kernel' design language COLD-K from the ESPRIT project 432: METEOR, and the constructs for expressing temporal aspects mainly by a linear, discrete time temporal logic from Lichtenstein, Pnueli and Zuck that includes operators referring to the past. VVSL is provided with a well-defined semantics by defining a translation to an extension of COLD-K (which has itself a well-defined semantics).

In this paper the syntax for the modularisation and parameterisation constructs of VVSL is outlined. Their meaning is informally described by giving an intuitive explanation and by outlining the translation to COLD-K. It is explained in some detail how sharing of hidden state variables is modelled. Examples of the use of the modularisation and parameterisation constructs are given too. These examples are based on a formal definition of the relational data model. With respect to the constructs for expressing temporal aspects, only the semantic ideas underlying the use of temporal formulae in VVSL are briefly outlined.

1 Introduction

VVSL is the VDM specification language used in the ESPRIT project 1283: "VDM for Interfaces of the PCTE" (usually abbreviated to VIP). This project is concerned with defining in a mathematically precise manner the PCTE interfaces [14], using a VDM specification language as far as possible. The PCTE interfaces aim to support the coordination and integration of software engineering tools. They address topics such as an object management system, a common user interface and distribution. The objectives in producing a formal definition of the PCTE interfaces can be summarised as follows:

- to support implementors of PCTE, tool builders using PCTE primitives, etc. by giving them access to a precise description of the interfaces;

- to identify weaknesses in the PCTE interfaces and to suggest improvements;

- to provide a basis for long-term evolution of PCTE.

A VDM specification language suitable for the formal definition of the PCTE interfaces should incorporate powerful features for *structuring* the specification of the interfaces and specifying *temporal* aspects of PCTE. Reasons for structuring the specification of the interfaces are:

- Unstructured, the specification will be too large to have any chance of being reasonably understandable by its intended 'users' (e.g. implementors of PCTE, tool builders using PCTE primitives, etc.). Division into 'functional units' with well-defined interfaces will enhance understandability.

- Weaknesses in the current design should be identified and improvements suggested. Composing the functional units from instantiations of a small number of orthogonal and generic 'underlying semantic units' will support such improvements.

*Supported by the European Communities under ESPRIT project 1283: VIP. The VIP consortium consists of Praxis Systems plc, Centre for Mathematics and Computer Science, Dr. Neher Laboratories, Océ Nederland bv and the University of Leicester.

- PCTE is currently rather language (C) and operating system (UNIX) oriented. Evolution away from these influences will improve PCTE. Isolating these language and operating system oriented parts will support such evolution.

For the formal definition of the PCTE interfaces, it is unrealistic to consider all operations *atomic*: some operations interfere via a global state. Due to this non-atomicity, temporal aspects of the concurrent execution of operations may be relevant details for users of the formal definition. Specifying these temporal aspects will enhance completeness.

VVSL is a VDM specification language of the '*British School*' with modularisation constructs allowing sharing of hidden state variables and parameterisation constructs for structuring specifications, and with constructs for expressing temporal aspects of the concurrent execution of operations which interfere via state variables. The modularisation and parameterisation constructs have been inspired by the 'kernel' design language COLD-K [3,6], and the constructs for expressing temporal aspects by a linear, discrete time temporal logic from Lichtenstein, Pnueli and Zuck that includes operators referring to the past [9].
VVSL is provided with a well-defined semantics by defining a translation to an extension of COLD-K, which has itself a well-defined semantics. For the time being, VVSL will have the restriction that functions can be only first-order functions. Higher-order functions does not seem to cause any fundamental problem, but require additional work on the semantical basis and actual formal definition of a 'higher-order' COLD-K to be done.
To the best of our knowledge, COLD-K is the only language with modularisation constructs allowing sharing of hidden variables in state-oriented styles of specification. COLD-K is meant to be used as the kernel of user-oriented versions of the language (attuned to e.g. different styles of specification or different implementation languages), each being an extension with features of a purely syntactic nature. VVSL without constructs for expressing temporal aspects can be considered a user-oriented version of COLD-K.
The abstract syntax of VVSL agrees for the greater part with the preliminary abstract syntax of the emerging BSI standard VDM specification language [1]. This VDM specification language will have a full formal definition, but at present the semantics is not fixed. The concrete syntax of VVSL is similar to the concrete syntax of the specification language used in Jones' book "Systematic Software Development Using VDM" [5]. The semantics of VVSL agrees for the greater part with the semantics of the STC VDM Reference Language [12,13], for which a full formal definition exists. Roughly speaking, the language used in [5] is the STC VDM Reference Language with a different concrete syntax.

In section 2 the syntax and semantics of VVSL modules are described. This includes a sketch of their translation to COLD-K (subsection 2.4) and an explanation of how sharing of hidden state variables is modelled (subsection 2.5). In section 3 examples of the use of the modularisation and parameterisation constructs are given. In section 4 the semantic ideas underlying the use of temporal formulae in VVSL are sketched.

2 Modules

2.1 General Aspects

The meaning of the modularisation and parameterisation constructs of VVSL is given by their translation to those of COLD-K. The translation is defined in [18, part I] and sketched in section 2.4 of this paper. Familiarity with COLD-K is necessary in order to grasp the meaning of the modularisation and parameterisation constructs of VVSL given in this way. The meaning of the COLD-K constructs is given by their translation to a formal language, called the *nucleus*, which is defined using standard mathematical techniques. The translation as well as the nucleus are defined in [3].
According to this translation, the modularisation constructs of COLD-K correspond to *class descriptions*. In this manner, the modularisation constructs of VVSL correspond indirectly to class descriptions of a special kind. Roughly speaking, such a class description[1] consists of:

---

[1] On a less intuitive level, a class description can be considered a theory presentation (of a special kind) extended with an encapsulating signature that indicates which names are the visible ones.

visible names: a collection of names for types, state variables, functions and operations[2] which may be used externally;

hidden names: a collection of names for types, state variables, functions and operations[2] which may <u>not</u> be used externally (special names, i.e. names which are not user-defined but added for technical reasons, can never be used externally);

formulae: a collection of formulae[3] representing the properties characterizing the types, state variables, functions and operations denoted by the visible names (both the visible and hidden names may occur in these formulae as symbols).

In section 2.3, the meaning of the modularisation constructs of VVSL will be informally explained in these terms.

The parameterisation constructs of COLD-K are abstraction constructs and application constructs. According to the translation from COLD-K to the nucleus, the abstraction constructs correspond roughly to higher-order functions on class descriptions[4] (i.e. functions mapping class descriptions to class descriptions, functions mapping class descriptions to functions from class descriptions to class descriptions, etc.). The domain of these functions always consists of the collection of *implementations* of another class description or function on class descriptions. Broadly speaking, one class description is considered to be an implementation of another one if the visible names of the latter are visible names of the former too and the properties represented by the formulae of the latter are properties represented by the formulae of the former too. Implementation in case of functions on class descriptions is the usual pointwise extension. According to the translation from VVSL to COLD-K, the abstraction constructs of VVSL correspond indirectly to higher-order functions on class descriptions of the special kind described above. Both in COLD-K and VVSL the application constructs describe applications of these functions to arguments. In section 2.3, the meaning of the parameterisation constructs of VVSL will be informally explained in terms of *higher-order class descriptions*, i.e. class descriptions and higher-order functions on class descriptions.

A module is intended for the specification of a 'system component'. The 'parts' of the system component are modelled by types, state variables, functions and operations. A basic module comprises type, variable, function and operation definitions. Each definition consists of (among other things) a name and a body. The body is either a *defining* body or a *free* body. In the former case, the name is a *defined name*; and in the latter case, the name is a *free name*. Herewith a distinction is made within any module between names denoting parts of the system component specified by means of the module itself, and names denoting parts of other system components. Free names are most commonly used in a situation where we want to use a name which is supposed to be specified somewhere else. Free and defined names are further discussed in section 2.5.

2.2 Syntax of Modules

The concrete syntax for the modularisation and parameterisation constructs of VVSL is outlined by the following production rules from the complete BNF-grammar given in [18, part II]:

```
<module> ::= module <types> <state> <functions> <operations> end
           | import <module-list> into <module>
           | export <signature> from <module>
           | rename <renaming> in <module>
           | abstract <module-parameter-list> of <module>
           | apply <module> to <module-list>
           | let <module-binding-list> in <module>
           | <module-name>

<module-list> ::= <module> | <module> , <module-list>
```

---

[2] For names of state variables, functions and operations, the associated type is considered part of the name; thus allowing 'overloading of identifiers'.

[3] The formulae are those from the language of the logic MPL$_\omega$ [3]. This is a many-sorted infinitary logic for partial functions with equality and definedness.

[4] The use of first-order functions (of multiple arguments) on class descriptions would lead to restrictions on the use of parameterised modules.

$<module\text{-}parameter\text{-}list> ::= <module\text{-}name> : <module>$
$\qquad | <module\text{-}name> : <module> , <module\text{-}parameter\text{-}list>$

$<module\text{-}binding\text{-}list> ::= <module\text{-}name> \triangleq <module>$
$\qquad | <module\text{-}name> \triangleq <module>$ and $<module\text{-}binding\text{-}list>$

$<signature> ::= <signature\text{-}element\text{-}list>$
$\qquad |$ signature $<module\text{-}list>$
$\qquad |$ add $<signature>$ to $<signature>$

$<signature\text{-}element\text{-}list> ::= <signature\text{-}element>$
$\qquad | <signature\text{-}element> , <signature\text{-}element\text{-}list>$

$<renaming> ::= <signature\text{-}element> \mapsto <identifier>$
$\qquad | <signature\text{-}element> \mapsto <identifier> , <renaming>$

$<signature\text{-}element> ::= <type\text{-}name>$
$\qquad | <variable\text{-}name> : <variable\text{-}type>$
$\qquad | <function\text{-}name> : <function\text{-}type>$
$\qquad | <operation\text{-}name> : <operation\text{-}type>$

The four 'sections' of a "module" construct are roughly lists of definitions of types, state variables (with associated state invariants, etc.), functions and operations respectively. The details of the concrete syntax for them is given in [18, part II]. The concrete syntax for the various definition constructs is similar to the one used in [5] (except for the "free" constructs), as can be seen from the examples in section 3.

Notice that modules comprise modularisation constructs ("module", "import", "export" and "rename" constructs), parameterisation constructs ("abstract" and "apply" constructs) and *abbreviation constructs* ("let" constructs). The abbreviation constructs of VVSL have a rather 'standard' syntax and semantics. The main difference with the abbreviation constructs of COLD-K is the relaxation of the 'define before use' condition of COLD-K: VVSL has the weaker 'no circularities' condition.

2.3 Informal Semantics of Modules

The meaning of the modularisation constructs of VVSL is informally explained in terms of visible names, hidden names and formulae. Notice that only the case that no parameterised modules are involved, is described. Afterwards the meaning of the parameterisation constructs of VVSL is explained. The meaning of the "import", "export" and "rename" constructs in the case that parameterised modules are involved is a straightforward generalisation of the non-parameterised case.

module $\mathcal{T} \; \mathcal{S} \; \mathcal{F} \; \mathcal{O}$ end: The visible names are the names introduced in the type definitions from $\mathcal{T}$, the variable definitions from $\mathcal{S}$, the function definitions from $\mathcal{F}$ and the operation definitions from $\mathcal{O}$. None of these names are hidden. The formulae represent the properties characterizing the types, state variables, functions and operations which may be associated with the names introduced in these definitions according to the normal VDM interpretation of the definitions.

import $M_1 , \ldots , M_n$ into M: The visible names are the visible names of the 'imported' modules $M_1 , \ldots , M_n$ as well as those of the 'importing' module M. Likewise, the hidden names are the hidden names of all these modules and the formulae are the formulae of all these modules[5].

export S from M: The visible names are the visible names of the 'exporting' module M that are also names of the 'exported' signature S. The hidden names are the hidden names of the exporting module M as well as its visible ones that are not names of the exported signature S. The formulae are the formulae of the exporting module M.

rename R in M: The visible names are the new names, according to the renaming R, for the visible ones of the module M. The hidden names are the hidden names of the module M. The formulae are the formulae of the module M with all occurrences of its visible names replaced by the new names for them.

---

[5] In case of name clashes, this may lead to undesirable changes in the properties represented by the formulae. The problem of name clashes in module composition is further discussed in section 2.5.

The meaning of the parameterisation constructs of VVSL is informally explained in terms of higher-order class descriptions, i.e. class descriptions and higher-order functions on class descriptions.

abstract $m_1 : M_1 , \ldots, m_n : M_n$ of M: If $n = 1$, the function sending each implementation c_1 of the higher-order class description denoted by the 'parameter restriction' module M_1 to the higher-order class description denoted by M when the module name m_1 is interpreted as c_1. Otherwise[6], the function sending each implementation c_1 of the higher-order class description denoted by the parameter restriction module M_1 to the higher-order class description denoted by **abstract** $m_2 : M_2 , \ldots, m_n : M_n$ of M when the module name m_1 is interpreted as c_1.

apply M to $M_1 , \ldots, M_n$: If $n = 1$, the higher-order class description resulting from applying the function denoted by M to the higher-order class description denoted by M_1 whenever it is in the domain of the function and undefined otherwise. Otherwise[6], the higher-order class description resulting from applying the function denoted by **apply** M to $M_1 , \ldots, M_{n-1}$ to the higher-order class description denoted by M_n whenever it is in the domain of the function and undefined otherwise.

The meaning of the abbreviation constructs of VVSL, which is straightforward, is explained last.

let $m_1 \triangleq M_1$ and ... and $m_n \triangleq M_n$ in M: If $n = 1$, the class description denoted by M when the module name m_1 is interpreted as the class description denoted by M_1. Otherwise, the class description denoted by **let** $m_{k_2} \triangleq M_{k_2}$ and ... and $m_{k_n} \triangleq M_{k_n}$ in M when the module name m_{k_1} is interpreted as the class description denoted by M_{k_1}; where the list $k_1, \ldots, k_n$ is some permutation of the list $1, \ldots, n$ such that if m_{k_i} occurs in M_{k_j} then $i < j$ (if such a permutation does not exist, the meaning of the abbreviation construct is undefined)[7].

2.4 Formal Semantics of Modules

In [18, part I] a translation from VVSL constructs to COLD-K constructs is defined by means of schematic production rules, called *translation rules*. Presenting the definition of the translation in this way, emphasizes the syntactic nature of the translation.

The left-hand side of a translation rule is a VVSL construct enclosed by the special brackets $\langle,\rangle$ or $\{\!|,|\!\}$ which may contain variables for subconstructs. The right-hand side is a COLD-K construct which may contain these variables enclosed by the special brackets $\langle,\rangle$ or $\{\!|,|\!\}$ for subconstructs (except for variables ranging over constructs solely consisting of an *identifier*, which may occur without enclosing brackets). The left-hand side and right-hand side of a translation rule are separated by the arrow $\Rightarrow$.

The translations of a VVSL construct C are the terminal productions of $\langle C \rangle$ (where it is the responsibility of the translator to add parentheses at the proper places). In general, the translation is not unique.

The special brackets $\langle,\rangle$ and $\{\!|,|\!\}$ denote *translation operators*. The translation operator denoted by the brackets $\langle,\rangle$ maps meaningful VVSL constructs (definition constructs included) to meaningful COLD-K constructs[8]. The auxiliary translation operator denoted by the brackets $\{\!|,|\!\}$ maps meaningful VVSL definition constructs to meaningful COLD-K constructs (its purpose is illustrated below).

The translation for the modularisation and parameterisation constructs of VVSL is outlined by the following translation rules from the complete definition of the translation from VVSL constructs to COLD-K constructs given in [18, part I]:

$\langle$module $\mathcal{T}\ S\ \mathcal{F}\ O$ end$\rangle$ $\Rightarrow$ export $\{\!|\mathcal{T}|\!\} + \{\!|S|\!\} + \{\!|\mathcal{F}|\!\} + \{\!|O|\!\}$ from
import **BOOL** into import **NAT** into
import **INT** into import **REAL** into import **TEXT** into
import $\langle\mathcal{T}\rangle$ into import $\langle S\rangle$ into import $\langle\mathcal{F}\rangle$ into class $\langle O\rangle$ end

$\langle$import $M_1 , \ldots, M_n$ into $M\rangle$ $\Rightarrow$ import $\langle M_1\rangle$ into $\cdots$ import $\langle M_n\rangle$ into $\langle M\rangle$

$\langle$export S from $M\rangle$ $\Rightarrow$ export $\langle S\rangle$ from $\langle M\rangle$

---

[6] For a global understanding of the parameterisation constructs of VVSL, the explanation of the case that $n > 1$ is not essential.

[7] If there exist several such permutations, the translation is not unique. However, all translations are semantically equivalent in COLD-K.

[8] The resemblance of the special brackets with the 'semantic brackets' $[\![,]\!]$ is intentional. It is meant to strengthen the intuition of translation operators as meaning functions.

⟨rename R in M⟩ $\Rightarrow$ rename $⦅R⦆$ in $⟨M⟩$

⟨abstract $m_1 : M_1 ,\ldots, m_n : M_n$ of M⟩ $\Rightarrow$ abstract $m_1 : ⦅M_1⦆$ of $\cdots$ abstract $m_n : ⦅M_n⦆$ of $⟨M⟩$

⟨apply M to $M_1 ,\ldots, M_n$⟩ $\Rightarrow$ apply $\cdots$ apply $⟨M⟩$ to $⟨M_1⟩$ $\cdots$ to $⟨M_n⟩$

⟨let $m_1 \triangleq M_1$ and ... and $m_n \triangleq M_n$ in M⟩ $\Rightarrow$ let $m_{k(1)} := ⟨M_{k(1)}⟩$; $\ldots$; let $m_{k(n)} := ⟨M_{k(n)}⟩$; $⟨M⟩$

where k is some bijection on $\{1,\ldots,n\}$ such that if $m_{k(i)}$ occurs in $M_{k(j)}$ then $i < j$

$⟨m⟩$ $\Rightarrow$ m

These translation rules show that the modularisation and parameterisation constructs of VVSL are very similar to those of COLD-K. Only the translation of "module" constructs is not straightforward. Its translation rule shows that modular schemes (i.e. COLD-K modules) specifying the *basic types* of VDM are imported into the modular scheme associated with the definitions from the "module" construct via the translation operator denoted by the brackets ⟨,⟩. Furthermore it shows that the COLD-K signature associated with these definitions via the auxiliary translation operator denoted by the brackets ⦅,⦆ is exported from the resulting scheme. Due to this, only the names introduced in the definitions are visible.

2.5 Name Clashes and Variable Sharing

Class descriptions can be viewed as descriptions of system components. System components consist of external and internal 'parts' which have a certain 'location'. The parts are modelled by types, state variables, functions and operations. The way the locations of parts are modelled is by giving *names* to parts. The external parts are indicated by the presence of their names in the collection of visible names and the internal parts by the presence of their names in the collection of hidden names.

In the abstraction from locations to names the information of the 'identity' of parts gets lost, in case names are just strings of characters. This leads to a problem with *name clashes* in the composition of class descriptions, since there is no way to tell whether parts denoted by the same name are intended to be identical. Any solution to this problem has to make some assumptions. Commonly it is assumed that external parts denoted by the same name are identical and internal parts are never identical. By these assumptions visible names (i.e. names of external parts) are allowed to clash, while clashes of hidden names (i.e. names of internal parts) with other names are avoided by automatic renamings. As far as hidden names are concerned, this solution seems the only one which is consistent with the intention of encapsulation. However it creates a new problem. In state-oriented specification, we are dealing with a state space where certain names denote variable parts of that state space. These *state variables* should not be duplicated by automatic renamings. This would make it impossible for two class descriptions (and hence modules) to *share* hidden state variables.

Origins

The root of the above-mentioned problems is that the information of the identity of parts is lost in the abstraction from locations to names. Therefore the solution is to endow each name with an *origin* uniquely identifying the location of the part denoted by the name. The use of combinations of a name and an origin rather than names in class descriptions solves the problem with name clashes in the composition of class descriptions. If two such *symbols*[9] have the same name while denoting different parts, their origins and thereby the symbols are different (and renaming is not necessary). If two symbols have the same name while denoting the same part, their origins and thereby the symbols are the same (and renaming is not necessary too).

The situation is in fact more complicated, due to the fact that we have to distinguish between two different kinds of names in a class description: those denoting parts of the system component described by the class description itself, called *defined names*, and those denoting parts of other system components, called *free names*. The meaning of the defined names is laid down in the class description, hence the origins for these names seem clear (at the module level, origins of names can be viewed as pointers to their definitions). The meaning of the free names is defined elsewhere, hence the origins for these names are not always clear. Free names often act as parameters in a class description, whereby their origins can not be known before

---

[9]If combinations of a name and an origin rather than names are used in class descriptions, then they must be interpreted as symbols of the underlying logic.

their instantiation. However, the definition of a defined name may 'use' such free names. In this case the meaning of the defined name, and thereby its origin, depends on the instantiation of the free names.

Therefore, first of all, an *origin variable* rather than a fixed origin is used for each free name in a class description. These origin variables can later be instantiated with fixed origins. Secondly, a tuple of the form $\langle c, x_1, \ldots, x_n \rangle$ is used for each defined name in a class description, where c is a fixed value (called an *origin constant*) uniquely identifying the definition of the defined name and $x_1, \ldots, x_n$ are the origin variables for the free names on which the defined name depends.

Origin Consistency

If, within a class description, the origins of visible symbols (i.e. symbols denoting external parts) with the same name can be *unified* (simultaneously for all such collections of origins) then the class description is called *origin consistent*.

For an origin consistent class description there is an unique correspondence between the visible names and the visible symbols. Hence abstraction from the origins associated with the visible names is possible.

Note that the requirement of origin consistency does not take hidden names into account. Since the hidden names of a class description may not be used outside that class description, there exists no identification problem for hidden names. However, by endowing each hidden name with an appropriate origin undesirable automatic renamings are no longer necessary and class descriptions may share hidden state variables.

At the level of modules (i.e. in the specification language), where there are only names, a sufficient condition for origin consistency is that in the composition of modules visible defined names never clash with other visible defined names. However, visible free names may always clash with other visible names. This condition is considered necessary for a sound style. If it is not satisfied, the meaning of the modularisation constructs is not intuitively clear (e.g. the informal explanation in section 2.3 does not suffice[10]).

2.6 Specification Documents

A complete VVSL text is a specification document. A specification document is intended for the specification of a 'system'. Like the specification of a 'system component', this is done by means of a module. In other words, specification documents are essentially modules. Within modules, abbreviations allow for local module definitions. The optional components part of a specification document allows for global module definitions.

The syntax and formal semantics (i.e. translation to COLD-K) of specification documents is outlined below.

Syntax of Specification Documents

\<specification-document\> ::= *\<components-option\>* system is *\<module\>*

\<components-option\> ::= | component *\<components\>*

\<components\> ::= *\<module-name\>* is *\<module\>*
    | *\<module-name\>* is *\<module\>* and *\<components\>*

Formal Semantics of Specification Documents

$\langle$ component m_1 is M_1 and ... and m_n is M_n system is $M \rangle$ $\Rightarrow$
 design
  let **BOOL** := $\cdots$; let **NAT** := $\cdots$; let **INT** := $\cdots$; let **REAL** := $\cdots$; let **TEXT** := $\cdots$;
  let **SET** := $\cdots$; let **SEQ** := $\cdots$; let **MAP** := $\cdots$; let $m_{k(1)}$:= $\langle M_{k(1)} \rangle$; $\ldots$; let $m_{k(n)}$:= $\langle M_{k(n)} \rangle$;
  system $\langle M \rangle$
 where k is some bijection on $\{1, \ldots, n\}$ such that if $m_{k(i)}$ occurs in $M_{k(j)}$ then $i < j$

The translation rule shows that in the translation of a specification document special scheme names are introduced for modular schemes specifying the *basic types* and the *type constructors* of VDM.

---

[10]Not enforcing origin consistency compels to extending class descriptions with an *origin partition* that indicates which origins in the symbols are considered equal and which ones are not.

3 Examples of Use: the Relational Data Model

In [10] and [18, part III] the modularisation and parameterisation constructs of VVSL are illustrated, using the 'Relational Data Model' (RDM) [2,15] as an example. The peculiarities of the main parts of PCTE do not make them very suitable for illustration of VVSL or any other specification language. Therefore something related, but more suitable for illustration, was looked for. RDM was found reasonably appropriate.

The structure of the formal definition of the RDM given in [10][11] is outlined in the appendix. This outline is obtained from the complete definition by replacing 'basic' modules by "module···end" and signature element sets by "···". In the following two subsections the modules **ATTRIBUTE**, **RELATION** (both in subsection 3.1) and **MANIPULATION** (in subsection 3.2) are presented to give examples of the use of the modularisation and parameterisation constructs as well as the closely related "free" constructs. The way in which the modularisation constructs and the parameterisation constructs are used in these modules (in particular the module **MANIPULATION**) seems typical for the use of this kind of constructs.

3.1 Relations

A relation can be conceived as a collection of rows of entries, each entry in the row addressed by an attribute. An entry must contain a value (e.g. a number or a string). The collection of attributes for addressing the entries must be the same for all rows in the relation. The rows in a relation are called tuples.

We do not have to commit ourselves to a particular choice of attributes and values. For attributes, this is expressed by the following VVSL module:

ATTRIBUTE is
  module
    types
      Attribute free
  end

The "module" construct above contains one type definition. By using "free" as 'body' of the type definition, the type *Attribute* has no a priori properties. This module plays the role of 'requirement' for modules by which various parameterised modules can be instantiated. For example, there is a parameterised module **TUPLE** in the complete definition of the RDM given in [10] (see the appendix for the outline of its structure), which can be instantiated by any two modules **x** and **y** provided that **x** contains more details (i.e. visible names and/or derivable properties) than the module **ATTRIBUTE** and **y** contains more details than a similar (but less trivial) module **VALUE**. Roughly speaking, this means that **x** and **y** must specify a particular choice of attributes and values respectively. The "free" constructs are often used in modules like **ATTRIBUTE**, which play the role of 'requirement' for modules by which a parameterised module can be instantiated.

A "module" construct can also be used to define functions working on values of introduced types, as is shown in the VVSL module **RELATION** on the next page. The type *Relation* is defined in this module according to the description of relations above. Furthermore, functions are defined for putting relations together. They are defined in the explicit 'applicative style' of VDM specification languages [5]. They could have been defined in the implicit 'pre- and post-condition style' of VDM specification languages too.

The "import" construct causes the types and functions introduced in the module **TUPLE** to be included in the module **RELATION**. Because **TUPLE** is parameterised by the modules **x** (restricted by **ATTRIBUTE**) and **y** (restricted by **VALUE**), this module is likewise. Another way of achieving this effect would be to apply **TUPLE** first to **x** and **y**, and abstract of them again:

RELATION' is
  abstract **x**: **ATTRIBUTE**,**y**: **VALUE** of
  import apply **TUPLE** to **x**,**y** into
  module···end

---

[11] In this definition, the complexity of what is specified by the modules increases gradually. If the reader wants to understand everything in detail, he can study the modules just in their textual order. For a global understanding, he may better browse on them in reverse order.

RELATION is
  import **TUPLE** into
  module
    types
      $Relation$ = set of $Tuple$
        where inv$(r) \triangleq$
          $\forall t_1 \in Tuple, t_2 \in Tuple \cdot (t_1 \in r \wedge t_2 \in r) \Rightarrow attributes(t_1) = attributes(t_2)$
      $Relations$ = set of $Relation$
      $Tuple\_constraint$ = map $Tuple$ to $\mathbf{B}$
        where inv$(tc) \triangleq$ dom $tc \in Relation$
      $Attribute\_renaming$ = map $Attribute$ into $Attribute$
    functions
      $empty()Relation$
        $\triangleq \{\}$

      $singleton(t: Tuple)Relation$
        $\triangleq \{t\}$

      $union(rs: Relations)Relation$
        pre $\forall r_1 \in Relation, r_2 \in Relation \cdot$
          $(r_1 \in rs - \{empty\} \wedge r_2 \in rs - \{empty\}) \Rightarrow attributes(r_1) = attributes(r_2)$
        $\triangleq \bigcup rs$

      $intersection(rs: Relations)Relation$
        pre $\forall r_1 \in Relation, r_2 \in Relation \cdot$
          $(r_1 \in rs - \{empty\} \wedge r_2 \in rs - \{empty\}) \Rightarrow attributes(r_1) = attributes(r_2)$
        $\triangleq \bigcap rs$

      $difference(r_1: Relation, r_2: Relation)Relation$
        pre $r_1 = empty \vee r_2 = empty \vee attributes(r_1) = attributes(r_2)$
        $\triangleq r_1 - r_2$

      $product(rs: Relations)Relation$
        pre $\forall r_1 \in Relation, r_2 \in Relation \cdot$
          $(r_1 \in rs \wedge r_2 \in rs \wedge r_1 \neq r_2) \Rightarrow attributes(r_1) \cap attributes(r_2) = \{\}$
        $\triangleq \{t \mid t \in Tuple \,;\, attributes(t) = as \wedge \forall r \in Relation \cdot r \in rs \Rightarrow attributes(r) \triangleleft t \in r\}$
        where $as: Attributes \triangleq \bigcup\{attributes(r) \mid r \in Relation \,;\, r \in rs\}$

      $projection(r: Relation, as: Attributes)Relation$
        pre $as \subseteq attributes(r)$
        $\triangleq \{as \triangleleft t \mid t \in Tuple \,;\, t \in r\}$

      $selection(r: Relation, tc: Tuple\_constraint)Relation$
        pre $r \subseteq$ dom tc
        $\triangleq \{t \mid t \in Tuple \,;\, t \in r \wedge tc(t)\}$

      $rename(r: Relation, ar: Attribute\_renaming)Relation$
        pre dom $ar = attributes(r)$
        $\triangleq \{\{ar(a) \mapsto t(a) \mid a \in Attribute \,;\, a \in attributes(r)\} \mid t \in Tuple \,;\, t \in r\}$

      $attributes(r: Relation)Attributes$
        pre $r \neq empty$
        $\triangleq \bigcap\{attributes(t) \mid t \in Tuple \,;\, t \in r\}$
  end

3.2 Relational Data Base Management Systems

A relational data base management system enables the user to manipulate relations. The basic facilities are defined in the VVSL module **MANIPULATION** on the next page, in which it is shown that a "module" construct can also be used to introduce state variables and to define operations which may consult and modify introduced state variables. Variables *curr_dbschema* and *curr_database* are introduced. The "free" constructs indicate that they are not parts of the system component specified by means of the module **MANIPULATION**. They constitute the 'state' of the data base management system as seen by this component. The "inv" construct characterizes the restriction on these states, which guarantees that the data base is always a valid instance of the data base schema. Furthermore, operations are defined for querying the current database and updating it. They are defined in the usual implicit 'pre- and post-condition style' of VDM specification languages [5].

The "import" construct causes the types and functions, which are introduced in the modules denoted by the "apply" constructs and may be used outside them, to be included in the module **MANIPULATION**. **QUERY**, **DATABASE_SCHEMA** and **DATABASE** are parameterised modules (see the appendix for the outline of their structure). The "apply" constructs instantiate these parameterised modules by the modules w,x and y. The "export" construct restricts the names which may be used outside the module **MANIPULATION** to the mentioned type and operation names[12]. The "abstract" construct turns **MANIPULATION** into a parameterised module, which can be instantiated by any three modules w, x and y provided they contain more details than the modules **RELATION_NAME**, **ATTRIBUTE** and **VALUE** respectively. Owing to this 'parameter mechanism' it is quaranteed that the type *Relation_name* can be used safely in the definitions of **MANIPULATION** (and that the parameterised modules **QUERY**, **DATABASE_SCHEMA** and **DATABASE** can be instantiated safely by w, x and y).

3.3 General Remark

The "module" construct within the module **RELATION** is only used to define types and functions working on values of these types, while the "module" construct within the module **MANIPULATION** is only used to define state variables and operations consulting and/or modifying these variables. This is a consequence of the idea elaborated in [10] to compose the 'functional units' (like **MANIPULATION**) from 'underlying semantic units' (like **RELATION**). It resulted in separation of the state independent aspects and the state dependent ones.

4 Temporal Formulae

In VVSL temporal formulae can be used as *dynamic constraints* in the state section of "module" constructs, and as *inter-conditions* in operation definitions. With dynamic constraints, global restrictions can be imposed on the set of possible histories of values taken by the state variables. With inter-conditions, restrictions can be imposed on the set of possible histories of values taken by the state variables during the execution of the operation being defined.

The temporal formulae of VVSL and their meaning have been inspired by a temporal logic from Lichtenstein, Pnueli and Zuck [9] that includes operators referring to the *past*. For details on the temporal formulae of VVSL and their use as dynamic constraints and inter-conditions, see [17], [18, part II] and [11]. In this section, only the underlying ideas are sketched.

Operational Interpretation of Interfering Operations

For *atomic* operations, it is appropriate to interpret them as roughly transition relations from initial states to final states. This is in accordance with the so-called *relational* semantics; which is the semantics of VDM specification languages of the 'British School'. For *non-atomic* operations[13], such an interpretation is no longer appropriate; since some of the intermediate states, via which the final state is reached from the initial state, may occur due to interference of concurrently executed operations. Non-atomic operations require a more *operational* interpretation as sets of possible histories of values taken by the state variables during execution of the operation concerned.

---

[12]The type names need not to be mentioned. Because it makes no sense to export a name of a state variable, function or operation without exporting the type names occurring in its type, these type names are always exported automatically.

[13]For the formal definition of the PCTE interfaces, it is unrealistic to consider all operations atomic.

MANIPULATION is
  abstract **w: RELATION_NAME, x: ATTRIBUTE, y: VALUE** of
  export
    Relation, Relation_name, Query,
    SELECT: Query ⇒ *Relation,*
    INSERT: Relation_name, Query ⇒,
    DELETE: Relation_name, Query ⇒,
    REPLACE: Relation_name, Query, Query ⇒
  from
  import
    apply **QUERY** to w, x, y ,
    apply **DATABASE_SCHEMA** to w, x, y ,
    apply **DATABASE** to w, x, y
  into
  module
    state
      curr_dbschema: Database_schema free *curr_database: Database* free
      inv *is_valid_instance(curr_database, curr_dbschema)*
    operations
      SELECT(q: Query)r: Relation
        ext rd *curr_dbschema: Database_schema,* rd *curr_database: Database*
        pre *is_wf(q, curr_dbschema)*
        post $r = eval(q, curr\_dbschema, curr\_database)$

      INSERT(rnm: Relation_name, q: Query)
        ext rd *curr_dbschema: Database_schema,* wr *curr_database: Database*
        pre *is_wf(mk-Union({mk-Reference(rnm), q}), curr_dbschema)*
        post let *dbsch: Database_schema* △ *curr_dbschema* and
              db: Database △ *curr_database* and
              r: Relation △ *eval(mk-Union({mk-Reference(rnm), q}), dbsch, db)* and
              db': Database △ *update(db, rnm, r)* in
           curr_database = if *is_valid_instance(db', dbsch)* then *db'* else *db*

      DELETE(rnm: Relation_name, q: Query)
        ext rd *curr_dbschema: Database_schema,* wr *curr_database: Database*
        pre *is_wf(mk-Difference(mk-Reference(rnm), q), curr_dbschema)*
        post let *dbsch* △ *curr_dbschema* and
              db: Database △ *curr_database* and
              r: Relation △ *eval(mk-Difference(mk-Reference(rnm), q), dbsch, db)* and
              db': Database △ *update(db, rnm, r)* in
           curr_database = if *is_valid_instance(db', dbsch)* then *db'* else *db*

      REPLACE(rnm: Relation_name, q_1: Query, q_2: Query)
        ext rd *curr_dbschema: Database_schema,* wr *curr_database: Database*
        pre *is_wf(mk-Difference(mk-Reference(rnm), q_1), curr_dbschema)* ∧
          is_wf(mk-Union({mk-Reference(rnm), q_2}), curr_dbschema)
        post let *dbsch: Database_schema* △ *curr_dbschema* and
              db: Database △ *curr_database* and
              r: Relation △ *eval(mk-Difference(mk-Reference(rnm), q_1), dbsch, db)* and
              r': Relation △ *eval(mk-Union({mk-Reference(rnm), q_2}), dbsch, db)* and
              db': Database △ *update(db, rnm, r)* and
              db'': Database △ *update(db', rnm, r')* in
           curr_database = if *is_valid_instance(db'', dbsch)* then *db''* else *db*

  end

The more operational interpretation of operations is irrelevant for atomic operations. Therefore the relational interpretation of operations is maintained in VVSL for all operations, i.e. for atomic and non-atomic ones. This interpretation is characterized by the pre- and post-condition in their definition. Non-atomic operations have in addition the operational interpretation, which is characterized mainly by the inter-condition in their definition.

However, this additional interpretation must 'agree' with the relational one. To be more precise, the transition relation according to the relational interpretation must hold between the first and last state of any possible *finite* history. Therefore, the inter-condition of VVSL expresses a restriction on the set of finite histories that have a first and last state between which the transition relation according to the relational interpretation holds.

Connection between Post- and Inter-condition

This has as a practical consequence that the post-condition of non-atomic operations will seem rather *weak* in general. For initial states must often be related to many final states which should only occur due to unavoidable interference. The inter-condition is meant to describe (among other things) which interference is required for the occurrence of such final states. The view that the post- and inter-condition constitute the relational and temporal part of a generalized post-condition may clarify this weakness issue[14]. The relational part describes how the final state depends on the initial state and the temporal part describes how the final state depends on the intermediate states (which may occur due to interference of concurrently executed operations). In general, the generalized post-condition will not be weak at all.

The operational interpretation is only related to the relational one as far as finite state sequences are concerned. Owing to this, the inter-condition has some power which was not revealed above: it may describe which interference is required for *non-termination*, i.e. how non-termination depends on the intermediate states, in case the initial state allows termination.

Role of Dynamic Constraints

The role of dynamic constraints is similar to that of state invariants. State invariants impose restrictions on what values the state variables can take. Therefore they should be preserved by the relational interpretation of all operations. Dynamic constraints impose restrictions on what histories of values taken by the state variables can occur. Likewise they should be preserved by the operational interpretation of all operations.

Interference and Exceptions

Often, operations have to be defined which are rather complex due to the many exceptional cases that can occur. The ability to separate exceptional cases from the normal case is an important aid in mastering complexity. In Jones' book "Systematic Software Development Using VDM" [5, page 193] a possible notation is introduced[15]. In that book, because of the assumed atomicity of operations, exceptional cases can arise due to exceptional initial states but not due to exceptional intermediate states, i.e. exceptional interference. Therefore the notation for exceptions had to be adapted for VVSL. Owing to the ability to describe exceptions caused by interference, the proposed notation allows to make the origin(s) of weak post-conditions clear. This notation may often avoid the need to write an inter-condition explicitly[16].

5   Conclusions and Final Remarks

VVSL is being used in the VIP project to produce a formal definition of the PCTE interfaces. The impression is that VVSL is suitable for the formal definition of the PCTE interfaces, but it is to early to draw firm conclusions. One remark may be in order. The PCTE interfaces can only be divided into functional units with complex interfaces. At best, the use of the modularisation and parameterisation constructs of VVSL will make this complexity explicit. It can not reduce the complexity that is inherent in PCTE. Although this seems obvious, it is not always realized.

---

[14] Actually the post-condition is superfluous, but it allows to distinguish the aspects of the execution of operations that do not inhere the temporal aspects.

[15] In [5], the meaning of this notation is explained by translation to the VDM specification language used in that book. Various other translations make sense too. For VVSL a slightly different translation has been chosen.

[16] The meaning of this adapted notation is likewise given by translation to VVSL without constructs for separating exceptional cases.

For writing VVSL specification documents, a new style option for use with LaTeX [8] was created. The macro set for this style option, called vvsl.sty [7,16], is a big enhancement of the macro set for an available style option for writing VDM specification documents, called vdm.sty [20].

VVSL was designed for use in the VIP project. Apart from the features for specifying temporal aspects (which may turn out too tailor-made), it seems to be a VDM specification language of general utility.

Because VVSL is provided with a well-defined semantics by defining a translation to COLD-K, it can be extended 'for free' with features:

- to define operations in the explicit 'imperative style' of VDM specification languages of the 'Danish School';

- to specify types and associated functions in the 'algebraic style' of many other specification languages (e.g. ASL [19] and the Larch Shared Language [4]).

Acknowledgements

Thanks go to L.M.G. Feijs and H.B.M. Jonkers from Philips Research Laboratories, Eindhoven, and G.R. Renardel de Lavalette from the University of Utrecht, for the enthusiastic help on COLD-related matters. Thanks also go to my colleagues in the VIP project. The work on VVSL has benifited from their critical feedback. Special thanks go to H. Goeman from the Centre for Mathematics and Computer Science and J. Bruijning from the Dr. Neher Laboratories for their comments on a draft of this paper and the latter additionally for his contribution to the intuitive explanation of the meaning of the modularisation constructs.

References

[1] *VDM Specification Language Proto-Standard.* BSI IST/5/50, Document No. 40, draft edition, December 1987.

[2] M.L. Brodie and J.W. Schmidt. *Final Report of the ANSI/X3/SPARC DBS-SG Relational Database Task Group.* Doc. No. SPARC-81-690, September 1981.

[3] L.M.G. Feys, H.B.M. Jonkers, C.P.J. Koymans, and G.R. Renardel de Lavalette. *Formal Definition of the Design Language COLD-K.* Preliminary Edition METEOR/t7/PRLE/7, METEOR, 1987.

[4] J.V. Guttag and J.J. Horning. Report on the Larch Shared Language. *Science of Computer Programming,* 6:103–134, 1986.

[5] C.B. Jones. *Systematic Software Development Using VDM.* Prentice-Hall, 1986.

[6] H.B.M. Jonkers. *Informal Description of the Design Language COLD-K.* Technical Report METEOR/t7/PRLE/2, METEOR, 1986.

[7] M. Kooij. *LaTeX macros for VVSL: Examples.* Working Paper VIP.T.D.MK7, VIP, April 1988.

[8] L. Lamport. *LaTeX: A Document Preparation System.* Addison-Wesley Publishing Company, 1984.

[9] O. Lichtenstein, A. Pnueli, and L. Zuck. The glory of the past. In *Logics of Programs,* pages 196–218, Springer-Verlag, LNCS 193, 1985.

[10] C.A. Middelburg. *Formal Definition of the Relational Data Model Using VVSL.* Working Paper VIP.T.D.KM12, VIP, February 1988.

[11] C.A. Middelburg. *Semantics of Temporal Constructs in VVSL.* Working Paper VIP.T.D.KM16, VIP, July 1988.

[12] B.Q. Monahan. *Abstract Syntax for the STC VDM Reference Language.* Technical Report 725 05306 Ed 1B, STC IDEC Ltd, 1985.

[13] B.Q. Monahan. *A Semantic Definition of the STC VDM Reference Language.* Technical Report, STC IDEC Ltd, 1985.

[14] *PCTE Functional Specifications.* ESPRIT, 4th edition, June 1986.

[15] J.D. Ullman. *Principles of Database Systems.* Computer Science Press, 1980.

[16] VIP Project Team. *Tool Extension Report.* Report VIP.T.E.7.1, VIP, May 1988.

[17] VIP Project Team. *VDM Extensions: Initial Report.* Report VIP.T.E.4.1, VIP, December 1987.

[18] VIP Project Team. *VDM Extensions: Interim Report.* Report VIP.T.E.4.2, VIP, May 1988.

[19] M. Wirsing. Structured algebraic specifications: a kernel language. *Theoretical Computer Science,* 42(2):123–249, 1986.

[20] M. Wolczko. Typesetting VDM with LaTeX. 1986.

Appendix

Structure of the Formal Definition of the RDM

```
component
    RELATION_NAME is
        module ··· end
    and

    ATTRIBUTE is
        module ··· end
    and

    VALUE is
        module ··· end
    and

    TUPLE is
        abstract x: ATTRIBUTE, y: VALUE of
        import x, y into
        module ··· end
    and

    RELATION is
        import TUPLE into
        module ··· end
    and

    DATABASE is
        abstract w: RELATION_NAME of
        import w, RELATION into
        module ··· end
    and

    RELATION_SCHEMA is
        import RELATION into
        module ··· end
    and

    DATABASE_SCHEMA is
        abstract w: RELATION_NAME, x: ATTRIBUTE, y: VALUE of
        import
            apply DATABASE to w, x, y ,
            apply RELATION_SCHEMA to x, y
        into
        module ··· end
    and
```

DOMAINS is
  export
    add · · · to signature **RELATION_SCHEMA**
  from
  import **RELATION_SCHEMA** into
  module · · · end
and

QUERY is
  abstract w: **RELATION_NAME**, x: **ATTRIBUTE**, y: **VALUE** of
  export · · · from
  import
    apply **DOMAINS** to x, y ,
    apply **DATABASE_SCHEMA** to w, x, y ,
    apply **DATABASE** to w, x, y
  into
  module · · · end
and

MANIPULATION is
  abstract w: **RELATION_NAME**, x: **ATTRIBUTE**, y: **VALUE** of
  export · · · from
  import
    apply **QUERY** to w, x, y ,
    apply **DATABASE_SCHEMA** to w, x, y ,
    apply **DATABASE** to w, x, y
  into
  module · · · end
and

DEFINITION is
  abstract w: **RELATION_NAME**, x: **ATTRIBUTE**, y: **VALUE** of
  export · · · from
  import
    apply **DATABASE_SCHEMA** to w, x, y ,
    apply **DATABASE** to w, x, y
  into
  module · · · end
and

system is
  abstract w: **RELATION_NAME**, x: **ATTRIBUTE**, y: **VALUE** of
  export · · · from
  import
    apply **DEFINITION** to w, x, y ,
    apply **MANIPULATION** to w, x, y ,
    apply **QUERY** to w, x, y ,
    apply **DATABASE_SCHEMA** to w, x, y ,
    apply **DATABASE** to w, x, y
  into
  module · · · end

SAMPLE - A Functional Language

M. Jäger, M. Gloger, S. Kaes
Fachgebiet Praktische Informatik, FB 20
Technische Hochschule Darmstadt
Magdalenenstr. 11 c, D-6100 Darmstadt

1. Introduction

With SAMPLE [1] we present a modern language incorporating well-established features like modularisation, strong typing, and a pattern-based definition mechanism.

Originally, SAMPLE was intended as a rapid prototyping tool (Specification and multi-purpose prototyping language) supporting constructive specifications in the sense of the Vienna Development Method [Bj/Jo78]. Since evaluation of specifications has turned out to be rather efficient, prototypes written in SAMPLE need not in any case be implemented in a (procedural) programming language. There are a lot of applications, where optimised prototypes fullfill the run-time and space requirements for the implementation very well. Thus, SAMPLE may also be used as a very high level programming language. The present version, which has been influenced by the VDM metalanguage META IV as well as by Miranda, is an applicative language, extended by nondeterminacy and file-I-O with side-effects.

As design and representation of data types are of essential importance for the specification of large programs, a powerful type system combines the benefits of compile-time type-checking with a natural and easily-readable notation. It is characterised by combination of classical typing concepts like polymorphism, subtypes, recursive types, overloading, and type abstraction. Thus, the well-known inference-based type systems for polymorphic languages (like ML or Miranda) are extended to avoid unnecessary restrictions on the expressional power of the language. Another important design aspect has been the consequent "emancipation" of recursive definitions (with respect to types and values).

In contrast to usual implementations of applicative languages through separate compiler and interpreter components, SAMPLE is implemented as a language-dependend prototyping environment, integrating a hybrid editor (combining text- and structure-editing facilities), a comfortable library manager, compiler and interpreter with a single user interface.

In this paper we introduce the language by means of some examples (chapter 2). The most interesting aspects of the typing system are discussed in more detail. We try to point out its flexibility and power and, on the other hand, the resulting implementation problems and the main ideas to their solution. We also deal with the evaluation strategy which is influenced by the language's nondeterminism and an appropriate treatment of recursively defined values.

Chapter 3 describes the SAMPLE-environment, which is partly generated from a formal definition by the PSG-system [Ba/Sn86]. Finally we discuss similarities and differences to other languages and outline the future development (chapter 4).

2. Language Overview

SAMPLE is characterised by an applicative language kernel with strongly typed expressions, modules, and pattern matching. Nondeterministic expressions (and also file-I-O functions which are not discussed here) extend this kernel. A modularisation concept wich enables type-checking across module boundaries and separate compilation supports the development of large systems in the language.

After introducing some basic notions in (2.1) we discuss the language's type concept (2.2) and the main typing problems (2.3). In (2.4) some interesting aspects of expression evaluation are considered.

[1] The development has been supported by Deutsche Forschungsgemeinschaft under grant He1170-3

2.1 Modules

A *module* is a collection of *top level declarations*. Identifiers declared on top level represent *types*, *typeparameters*, or *objects*. An object is an identifier denoting a value, e.g. an integer, or a higher-order function. (We shall frequently refer to a functional object as a function.) A block concept with statically scoped local declarations is realised through **let**- and **where**-abstractions embedding an expression into an environment of object-definitions.

Every declaration list, top level or local, is considered to be a set of systems of mutually recursive (type- or object-) definitions. An object-declaration may consist of several parts, one of which is a type assertion, the others form a list of defining equations, where patterns on the left-hand side represent the arguments of function applications.

The typing system is based on type inference. However, to achieve better readability, the types of top level declarations have to be given explicitly while local declarations can optionally be supplied with type assertions.

The *export* of declarations (**export** $id_1,...,id_k$) allows their usage in other modules. These can either use all exported identifiers of a module (**use** *modulename*) or only a subset thereof (**import** $id_1,..., id_k$ **from** *modulename*).

2.2 The typing concept

In this chapter the most important aspects of the language's type system are discussed. Particular typing problems are considered in (2.3).

The *base types* of SAMPLE represent booleans, integers, reals, characters, and strings with a set of suitable operations. Some of predefined *type constructors* (list-, sum-, product-, and function-types) are introduced below. Additionally, sets and finite mappings (adopted from the VDM metalanguage META IV) are predefined to provide a more comfortable notation as well as efficient evaluation. Also we deal with recursive types, type parameters and polymorphism, type coercion, and abstract types.

List types

A list type represents linear lists of a homogeneous component type. The predefined list operations

$\langle\rangle$	–	the empty list
$\wedge$	–	*append* a new head-component to a list
&	–	*concatenate* two lists
hd	–	select the *head* of a list
tl	–	select the *tail* of a list

and the list constructor brackets $\langle elem_1,...,elem_k\rangle$ (equivalent to $elem_1 \wedge...\wedge elem_k \wedge \langle\rangle$) provide a comfortable notation, which is necessary because of the frequent usage of lists. The list constructors are non-strict (cf 2.4).

Sum types

A sum type is constructed from a set of *variant types*. It represents the disjoint union of its variants' object sets. Every variant is identified by a *discriminant* (i and r in the example below).

       type arithmetic = **sum** i(int) | r(real) **end**

Type conversions from variant into sum-type (*injection*) or vice versa (*projection*) are always done explicitly using the discriminants:

```
real_value : real
a_value    : arithmetic
a_value = r(5.24)          ** injection of a real constant into the sum-type
real_value = a_value | r   ** projection of a sum-type value into it's variant type
a_value is r               ** variant test
```

Ex. 1:   A SAMPLE module with some list functions

```
module list_example
export reduce, map, filter, forall, exists
definitions
typepar A, B    ** A and B represent arbitrary types
** type assertions with higher-order functional types
reduce:    ((A, B) → B, B)       →  list(A) → B
map:       (A → B)               →  list(A) → list(B)
filter:    (A → bool)            →  list(A) → list(A)
forall:    (list(A), A → bool)   →  bool
exists:    (list(A), A → bool)   →  bool

** reduce is a curried version of the well-known APL list reduction operation
reduce (f,c) <> = c
reduce (f,c) (x^l) = f (x, reduce(f,c) l)

map f <> = <>
map f (x^l) = (f x)^(map f l)

** filter p constructs a list by throwing away all components of it's argument not satisfying p
filter p <> = <>
filter p (x^l) = let tl_filter = filter p l
                 in ( if p(x) then <x> else <> fi ) & tl_filter

** forall(l, p) - p holds for all components of l
forall(l, p) = reduce (cand, TRUE) (map l p)   ** cand is a non-strict and

** exists(l, p) - p holds for at least one component of l
exists(l, p) = reduce (cor, FALSE)(map l p)   ** cor is a conditional or

end
```

Product types

Product types are derived from the cartesian product of the involved object sets. Tuples (as in Miranda [Tu86]) or records (as in PASCAL) are the classical type constructors related to cartesian products. In contrast to the "anonymous" tuple components, record components are always referenced through identifiers.

SAMPLE product types integrate both concepts by allowing the optional definition of selectors for every product component. Type compatibility is given, if two product types with compatible component types don't have different selectors for the same component. Brackets serve as type- and object-constructors. We will refer to the SAMPLE producttype-values as tuples. Tuples with only one component are equivalent to their component, e.g. (5)= 5.

The question whether to define a product type with or without selectors is very much a matter of taste. As described above, SAMPLE provides constructor- as well as selectoroperations for lists, tuples, and sum-type values (considering the injection as a constructor and projection as a selector). Since definitions are pattern-based, all selections can be replaced by constructor applications within patterns (ex. 2). Although patterns usually improve readability and elegance of function definitions, there are counterexamples, where predefined selector functions should be used favourably. Thus the appropriate choice is left to the SAMPLE-user.

Like lists, tuples are constructed non-strictly (cf. 2.4).

Ex. 2: Two product types as variants of a sum type

type coordinate = **sum** cartesian (real, real) |

   polar   (angle: real, radius: real)

   end

Components of cartesian coordinates can only be referred through coordinate patterns, as in

   abscissa: coordinate → real

   abscissa(cartesian(x,y)) = x

Additionally, for products like the polar variant component selectors are defined and may be used in Pascal-like Notation (*expr.selector*):

   abscissa(polar(c)) = c.radius * cos c.angle

Function types and functions

A function type is defined by an argument-type and a result-type. A function with k≥0 arguments (or results) is represented in SAMPLE by a function with one k-tuple argument (or result respectively).

   The only operations predefined on function types are application and functional composition. The notation for function application is left associative, e.g. f x y is equivalent to (f x) y. The composition is denoted by the infix operation **o**:

typepar A, B, C

o: (B→C, A→B) → A→C   {The function type constructor → is right-associative}

f **o** g = λx. f(g x)

Functions are usually defined by a list of associated pattern-expression pairs. Pattern matching has already been proved to be useful in a lot of other languages (HOPE, ML, Miranda, PROLOG, etc.) A pattern represents its instances, i.e. expressions constructed by type-correct instantiation of the pattern's variables. In a function application the (textually) first definition part with a pattern that matches the actual argument, is evaluated. Matching means, roughly speaking, checking if the argument is equivalent to an instance of the pattern. In contrast to other languages the SAMPLE pattern mechanism also supports the definition of curried functions, as illustrated in Example 1 (reduce, map, filter).

The following curried map definitions are equivalent (see also ex. 1)

   map: (A→B) →   list(A)→list(B)

1. map f ⟨⟩   = ⟨⟩
   map f (x^l) = (f x)^(map f l)

2. map f = g **where** g ⟨⟩   = ⟨⟩
           g (x^l) = (f x)^(g l);

3. map = λf.g **where** g ⟨⟩   = ⟨⟩
           g (x^l) = (f x)^(g l);

In SAMPLE, functions are always non-strict. For a discussion of the evaluation strategy, see (2.4).

Recursive types

A characteristic feature of SAMPLE is that there are no restrictions with respect to the recursivity of definitions. One important aspect thereof is the possibility of combining type expressions to systems of mutually recursive types. The most important application is the adequate typing of recursively defined data structures such as trees, terms, graphs etc.

Ex. 3:   If we assume a representation of variables and operations as strings we can define terms with variables and integer constants in the following way:

type term1 = **sum** const(int) |

var(string) |

compound(functor: string

args: list(term1))

end

The set of values represented by term1 is not restricted to finite objects, it also includes all infinite terms. Infinite objects can be defined via generating recursive functions or by systems of mutually recursive defining equations. Each declaration list, i.e. the top level declarations of a module as well as local declarations (within **let**- or **where**-abstractions), is considered as a set of systems of mutually recursive defining equations.

Ex. 3 a: A circularly defined term1-value

cyclic_term1_object: term1
cyclic_term1_object = compound('op', ⟨const(1), var('X'), cyclic_term1_object⟩)

Parameterised types and polymorphism

Following other languages like ML and Miranda the SAMPLE type system supports the typing of polymorphic values. Informally, an object is polymorphic if it belongs to a whole class of types. The empty list ⟨⟩, e.g., is a constant of all list types, the type of $\lambda x.TRUE$ is representable by $\alpha \rightarrow bool$, the *type variable* α denoting an arbitrary type. The list functions of ex. 1 are also polymorphic as their definitions are independend from the list components' types. We need not go into details here, since the notion of (parametric) polymorphism has been thoroughly discussed elsewhere [e.g. Mi78, Da/Mi82]. However, we have to introduce parameterised types and explain their relation to polymorphism.

Type expressions with type parameters are called *parameterised types*. Every SAMPLE type-parameter represents a class of types, which are called instances. This class is defined by the set of overloaded functions defined on the instance types. Within the scope of its declaration each parameter is bound to an arbitrary subset of the predefined overloaded functions (in a future version this will extend to user-defined overloading), e.g.

typepar nonfunctional **ops** (=)

This typeparameter may be instantiated by any type T with a predefined operation

= :   (T,T)→bool .

In SAMPLE only functions and structures with functional components are not comparable (cf. 2.4), thus "nonfunctional" represents the class of all nonfunctional types.

```
Ex. 4:    A parameterised version of terms ( see also ex. 3 )
typepar constants, variables, operations ops (=)
type      term ( constants,variables,operations ) =
               sum const (constants ) |
                   var ( variables )    |
                   compound ( functor:operations
                             args:   list(term(constants,variables,operations ))
               end
```

A parameterised type serves two purposes independently. First, it can be used in type assertions of polymorphic definitions (see ex.5). Used in this way, it serves as an external representation of a polymorhic type and the user-declared type parameters correspond to type variables in the internal type representation. (For a further discussion, see (2.3)).

Second, it can be used as a type constructor, mapping each suitable set of its parameters' instances to a type. Note, that this language feature of user-defined type constructors is completely independend from the language's polymorphism. As an example we redefine the type term1 (example 3a) by applying the type constructor term defined above:

$$\text{type term1} = \text{term(int,string,string)}$$

```
Ex. 5:  Testing the occurrence of variables in terms with variables

occurs: variables → term(constants,variables,operations ) → bool

occurs x var(y ) ▪ x=y
{Here we use the overloaded equality test bound to the typeparameter variables}

occurs x compound(f,f_args ) ▪ exists(f_args, occurs x )

occurs x  t ▪ FALSE
```

A more "exotic" example showing the flexibility of the type system is the fixpoint operator

$$\text{fix} = \lambda f. (\lambda x. f (x \, x)) (\lambda x. f (x \, x))$$

mapping each function to its least fixpoint.

In most strongly typed languages H is not definable in this way, as the selfapplication x x cannot be typed correctly. (In fact, we don't know any other language with a sufficiently powerful inference-based type system.) However, all we need is a polymorphic as well as recursive type concept (cmp. [MQ/Pl/Se84]):

$$\text{type}(x) = \alpha \to \beta \qquad \text{as x is a function,}$$
$$\text{type}(x) = \alpha \qquad\qquad \text{as x is the argument,}$$

thus: $\text{type}(x) = \text{type}(x) \to \beta$.

In SAMPLE a suitable type assertion for x is:

```
typepar beta
type    x_type(beta ) = x_type(beta ) → beta
```

Type coercion

We speak of coercion if predefined or user-defined type conversions need not be applied explicitly but are performed automatically whenever this is necessary for a correct typing. As a well-known and practically important example integer-real coercion is implemented in a lot of programming languages.

Type coercions can easily be integrated into non-polymorphic type systems. In a polymorphic language, however, they cause severe typing problems, especially in the presence of recursive types. In SAMPLE type coercion is, for the time being, restricted to integer-real conversion. It has been integrated as an experimental feature of the type system. Since the problems have now shown to be manageable (as discussed in 2.3), the next language version will make further use of the advantages of coercion. The conversion of characters into strings and the conversion of finite mappings to functions are other straightforward applications. Though going into details here would lead too far, let us remark, that one of our goals is a uniform handling of overloaded operations bound to polymorphic types by a type coercion system. We have also considered user-defined coercions.

Type abstraction

An abstract type consists of a system of mutually recursive types and a suitable set of functions and objects. The SAMPLE **datatype** constructor, which allows the definition of abstract types, is an encapsulation construct supplied with special visibility rules to hide type representations from the user. Thus, any user of a datatype is guaranteed to be independend from the concrete representations of the involved types.

Syntactically, a datatype definition is divided into a signature part (listing the types involved and the type assertions for the datatype's objects) and a representation part giving the concrete definitions of all types and objects belonging to the datatype. The visibility of the concrete type representation is limited to the representation part.

```
Ex. 6:  A parameterised abstract set type with a non-standard representation

typepar A ops ( = )
datatype set( A ) with emptyset: set( A )
                      is_elem:  ( A, set( A ))  → bool
                      insert:   ( A, set( A ))  → set( A )
                      union:    ( set( A ), set( A ))  → set( A )
                      intersect: ( set( A ), set( A ))  → set( A )
end

rep   set( A ) = A→bool       **A set is represented by the function is_elem defined below
      emptyset = λx. FALSE
      is_elem( x,s ) = s x
      insert( x,s )   = λy. x=y cor s y
      union( s1, s2 ) = λy. ( s1 y ) cor ( s2 y )
      intersect( s1, s2 ) = λy. ( s1 y ) cand ( s2 y )
end
```

If an exported datatype identifier is imported from another module, the whole signature part becomes visible.

2.3 Typing problems

The concept of parametric polymorphism, originally introduced by Strachey [St68] and theoretically worked up by Milner [Mi78], has strongly influenced the type systems of ML [Mi84] and several more recently designed languages, e.g Miranda [Tu86] and SAMPLE.

It is well-known today, how to treat ML-like polymorphism in inference-based typing systems. The SAMPLE type concept introduced in (2.2), however, is more general with respect to recursive types, type coercion, and overloaded operations in polymorphic definitions. It turns out, that especially the combination of polymorphic recursive types with coercions complicates type analysis considerably. As this paper is not intended as a systematic presentation of the SAMPLE type analysis we have to confine ourselves to the discussion of some examples.

Overloaded operators in polymorphic definitions

As mentioned in (2.2) (parametric) polymorphic types can be represented by means of *type variables*. This is illustrated by some simple examples: If α and β are type variables, (α,α) is a polymorphic 2-tuple type of all pairs with components of the same, arbitrary type. (α,β) is more general as its instances are not required to have two identical component types. The identity function $ID=\lambda x.x$ can be typed by the polymorphic function type $\alpha\rightarrow\alpha$ (for simplicity our notation contains no binding constructs for type variables).

The use of overloaded operations, e.g. =, +, *, -, >, <, etc., causes representation problems: What is the type of the function f, defined as $f(x,y)=x=y$, in a language, where equality is defined on all nonfunctional types ? The problem is, that the typing $(\alpha,\alpha)\rightarrow bool$ allows arbitrary instantiation of α, even by a functional type. Hence, an application like $f(\lambda x.x, \lambda x.x)$ is considered type-correct. As the evaluation leads to a run-time error, the typing is not as safe as it should be. On the other hand prohibiting the usage of any overloaded functions is also unsatisfying.

To preserve the flexibility and guarantee safe typing nevertheless, in SAMPLE polymorphism is internally represented by pairs, e.g. $\alpha_{\{=,<,>,+,-\}}$, each consisting of a type variable and a set of overloaded functions. Thus a safe typing for f is given by $(\alpha_{\{=\}}, \alpha_{\{=\}})\rightarrow bool$, with $\alpha_{\{=\}}$ denoting the class of all types t with an equality $= : (t,t)\rightarrow bool$.

Explicit type assertions are possible through the similar mechanism of binding sets of operations to type parameters discussed in (2.2). A type assertion for f is

typepar alpha **ops** (=)
f: (alpha, alpha)$\rightarrow$bool

(Note, however, that the relation between type parameters in the external and type variables in the internal type representation is generally rather complicated. (For details, consult [Jä87]).

Therefore the type inference algorithm has to deal with sets of operations used in polymorphic definitions, e.g. compute the set of operators used in a definition, check if operators are defined for an instance, or check if a type assertion restricts the polymorphism of a definition in this regard. [Ka88] contains a more detailed treatment of overloading.

Problems with coercion

If values of a type A are automatically converted into a type B this relation between the two types induces a (partial) conversion order $\leqslant$ on the types of the language. Some of the rules defining this order are

$$A \leqslant B \qquad (A \text{ "is convertible to" } B)$$
$$\alpha \leqslant \beta \qquad\qquad \Rightarrow \qquad list(\alpha) \leqslant list(\beta)$$
$$\alpha_i \leqslant \beta_i, \; i=1, ..., k \qquad \Rightarrow \qquad (\alpha_1,...,\alpha_k) \leqslant (\beta_1,...,\beta_k)$$
$$\alpha \leqslant \beta, \gamma \leqslant \delta \qquad \Rightarrow \qquad \beta\rightarrow\gamma \;\; \leqslant \; \alpha\rightarrow\delta$$

(Note, that function type conversion is antimonotonic in the argument types. For illustration, consider the expression $f(3)=2.15$ in which f is expected to be of type int$\rightarrow$real. If f were actually of type real$\rightarrow$int, the coercion of argument and result would lead to a correct typing.)

In a polymorphic type system two types are represented by type expressions x and y possibly containing type variables. Type compatibility in the absence of coercion is checked by unifying x and y, as they are compatible if and only if there is a substitution ρ of type variables, such that $\rho(x)=\rho(y)$.

With coercion the situation is more complicated. To make two types (e.g. the expected and the actual parameter type of a function) fit together, not only instantiations of type variables, but also automatic conversions are to be considered: x and y are compatible if and only if there is a substitution ρ and a type z, s.t. $\rho(x) \leqslant z$ and $\rho(y) \leqslant z$. The problem is, that failure in unifying x and y no longer indicates a type error, while on the other side the existence of z can, in general, neither be proved nor disproved as long as x or y contain variables.

Now we try to illustrate the appropriate typing strategy by a simple example. We represent type conversions graphically, an edge from type x to type y means x $\not\leq$ y. (In fact, this graph representation for conversions is very close to our implementation.)

In a bottom-up typing of the let-abstraction

$$\textbf{let } a=(1, 3.6)$$
$$b=(7.21, 2)$$
$$\textbf{in } a=b$$

the following type information can be deduced from the body a=b:

type(a)=α
type(b)=β
type(=)=(γ,γ)$\rightarrow$bool

conversion graph

(Note, that a pairwise unification of α, β, and γ is successful, but leads to the false result, that a and b must have identical types.)

Regarding the definition of *a* next, one can instantiate α to (int, real). As the conversion order is defined inductively over the type structure, all nodes in a connected component of the conversion graph must have the same structure, i.e. γ and β are 2-tuples as well. Hence, these variables have to be instantiated by product types and the appropriate conversion informations have to be passed to the component types. This corresponds to the instantiations $\gamma\rightarrow(\gamma_1,\gamma_2)$, $\beta\rightarrow(\beta_1,\beta_2)$ and the graph transformations:

Additionally, as real is only convertible into itself, γ_2, the type of the second component of the equality operands, can be instantiated to real. In a similar way the definition of b is treated, leading to the instantiation of β_2 to int, of β_1 to real, and consequently of γ_1 to real.

As demonstrated in the example, unification of two types – the basic operation for checking compatibility in languages without coercion – is no longer adequate in our case. Instead, generalised algorithms are necessary, which operate on connected components of conversion graphs.

An early discussion of coercions in polymorphic type systems is to be found in [Le83]. Our implementation is based on some ideas of [Le86]. But also [Mit84] deals with coercions in polymorphic languages.

<u>Recursive types again</u>

Without coercions recursive type definitions don't cause severe complications of the type analysis. Recursive definitions should be detected anyway to guarantee the termination of the typing algorithm. However, the type representation must be generalised to cyclic terms or graphs. Recursion is detected whenever a term to be substituted for a variable X, contains X again.

The main problem coming along with coercions is that recursive dependencies may be hidden in the set of conversion relations represented by the conversion graph. The following conversion graph may serve as example:

Note, that the graph itself is not cyclic. However, the strategy of reducing the conversions to relations between the tuple components (described above) must fail. Since all types connected in the conversion graph, particularly β and (β, real), must have the same structure, the instance types are recursive. A set of correct variable substitutions corresponds to this conversion graph. All three variables may be substituted into one of the recursive types **fix** t.(t, real) or **fix** t.(t, int) (**fix** denotes the fixpoint operator on type expressions). The substitutions for each variable are restricted as follows:

$$\alpha = \textbf{fix } t.(t, real) \Rightarrow \alpha=\beta=\gamma , \quad \beta = \textbf{fix } t.(t, real) \Rightarrow \beta=\gamma .$$

Another interesting situation arises, when the conversion graph becomes cyclic during type analysis. In this case all involved types have to be unified, since they must be identical.

Thus the simple occur-check has to be replaced by a generalised mechanism that keeps track of the transitive closure of the conversion relations, i.e. operates on connected components of the conversion graph.

2.4 Evaluation of expressions

In this chapter we want to show, why nondeterminism and infinite objects determine the evaluation strategy to a great extend. We also discuss a problem arising from the equal treatment of recursive and non-recursive object definitions: How to define and implement the equality test.

Infinite objects

Infinite objects are defined by circular definitions (as in ex. 3a) or by generating recursive functions, e.g.:

```
Ex. 7 :   The infinite list of prime numbers ( a so-called "stream"-object )

          integers_from( i ) = i^integers_from( i+1 )
          primes = sieve( integers_from( 2 ) )
                  where sieve ( x^l ) = x^filter( λy. y mod x = 0 );
```

To allow the definition of infinite objects, all constructors, i.e. tuple constructor, the list constructor functions ^, <...>, and the sum-type injection constructors, must not evaluate their arguments. Additionally, the treatment of parameters in function applications and the evaluation of object definitions is characterised by a lazy, demand-driven strategy. As a third aspect, object definitions are also evaluated only, if necessary.

Nondeterministic expressions

In SAMPLE a nondeterministic choice expression is defined, which can be considered the applicative variant of Dijkstra's guarded commands:

```
abs( x ) = if  x≤0  then -x
           ▯  x≥0  then  x  fi
```

Though abs relies on a nondeterministic language construct, it is actually a deterministic function always returning the same result for a certain argument.

```
typepar t
choose: list( t ) → t
choose <x> = x
choose ( x^y^l ) = if TRUE then x
                   ▯ TRUE then choose( y^l ) fi

one_or_two = choose <1,2>
```

In contrast to the definition of abs above, choose might nondeterministically return different values in identical applications.

Rather than discussing the way of evaluating a nondeterministic language construct, we want to emphasise the influence of nondeterminism on the evaluation of arbitrary SAMPLEexpressions. (In fact, our actual implementation of the nondeterministic choice expression is deterministic, but in a future version the implementation should be able to generate all possible values.)

To preserve the clearness of expression semantics in the presence of nondeterminism, identifiers representing uniquely determined objects are necessary. Otherwise expressions which are equivalent in a deterministic language, would be different. As an example, consider:

$$(\text{one\_or\_two} + \text{one\_or\_two}) \quad \text{and} \quad (2 * \text{one\_or\_two}).$$

If one_or_two is evaluated twice in the first expression, 3 is a possible result and thus both expressions differ. As a consequence, proofs and program transformations become extremely difficult, the semantics of expressions too complex.

This is the reason why in SAMPLE <u>every</u> identifier represents a determined value within its whole scope. This extends from top level objects over locally defined identifiers to formal parameters in function definitions. It follows, that all these objects have to be evaluated at most once. Hence call-by-name parameter evaluation is impossible as well as textual replacement semantics for object definitions (which would be restricted to nonrecursive values anyhow).

Note, however, that evaluation of a SAMPLE object cannot be considered as a single step operation. As the object constructors are nonstrict a representation of a value may contain unevaluated substructures (implemented by closures). In the case of recursively defined objects the evaluation can be regarded as a sequence of approximations of the "infinite" least fixpoint of some recursive equations. An evaluation step transforms an approximation A of a structured value into another approximation B which may be better in that it contains more information about some substructure of the value (an approximation step of an infinite list could be the computation of another component value, e.g.). As substructures may always be bound to nondeterministic expression we must require that every substructure of a structured value is evaluated at most once. As a consequence, call-by-need parameter evaluation and shared representation of all objects are necessary.

Equality test

In SAMPLE equality testing is predefined on all non-functional types. Two lists or tuples are equal if all their components are equal, two values of a sum-type are equivalent iff they belong to the same variant and their values projected to this variant are equal.

An interesting aspect is the equality test for recursively defined objects, since it is impossible to evaluate all their components. Nevertheless there is an important class of objects which can be compared. We call these objects "regular" objects. An object is regular if it can be represented by a regular tree (having only a finite number of different subtrees) or, equivalently, by a finite graph where the nodes are constructors or constants of the object's type or arbitrary expressions of its components' types.

In contrast to a regular object a stream is defined by a nonterminating sequence of function applications. Thus, equivalence of streams is not decidable. A stream example is the list of prime numbers defined in Example 6.

Testing the equality of regular objects requires a normal form representation based on a minimal set of constructor operations. The normalisation algorithm (see ex. 7) is based on [Ru86]. Termination is guaranteed for all "reasonable" definitions of regular objects. The algorithm does not terminate if a list to be normalised is defined by a concatenation with an infinite left operand, e.g. l1 = 1^l1 & <2>.

Two normalised object representations can be compared using a straightforward graph equivalence algorithm. For efficiency reasons, however, normalisation and equivalence test are interleaved. Any representation of a structured value is normalised only so far, that another component value can be computed. Hence, if two corresponding components are different, any further normalisation is unnecessar y as the objects are yet recognised to be different. The difference of the two lists l1=1^f(2) and l2=2^tl(l1 & l2) is recognised without expanding f(2) or reducing the right append-operand in the definition of l2. The following list example contains nonnormalised list definitions:

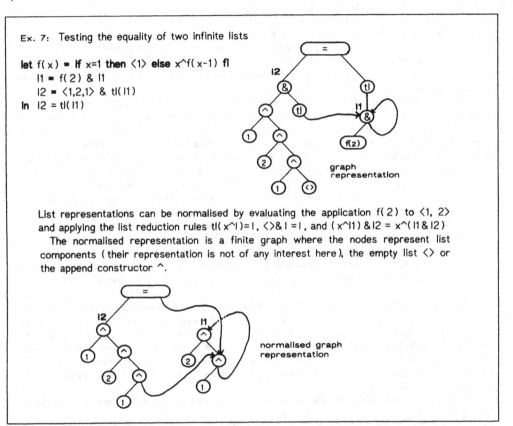

Ex. 7: Testing the equality of two infinite lists

```
let f( x ) = If x=1 then <1> else x^f( x-1) fl
    l1 = f( 2 ) & l1
    l2 = <1,2,1> & tl( l1 )
In  l2 = tl( l1 )
```

graph representation

List representations can be normalised by evaluating the application f(2) to <1, 2> and applying the list reduction rules tl(x^l)=l, <>&l =l, and (x^l1) &l2 = x^(l1 & l2)

The normalised representation is a finite graph where the nodes represent list components (their representation is not of any interest here), the empty list <> or the append constructor ^.

normalised graph representation

By interleaving normalisation and componentwise comparison differences between structured objects are detected without unnecessary evaluation. Thus, considering the efficiency of equality test, there is no reason to apply different algorithms to finite and infinite values.

Generally, recursive and non-recursive values need not be (and are not) distinguished at all, neither in their syntactical representation, nor with respect to typing and evaluation. (This is another aspect of what we called "emancipation of recursive definitions").

As a practical application consider that a type-checker for SAMPLE must unify recursively defined terms. This unification can easily be defined using the "="-Operator to test for cycles.

3. The SAMPLE environment

The SAMPLE system is an integrated prototyping environment consisting of editor, typechecker, compiler, interpreter, and library manager. In the following we briefly characterise the system, emphasizing the user's viewpoint.

The editor's top level menu is the user's interface to the whole system. The main functions available to the user are editing and evaluating a module. (In every module, following the list of declarations, an expression to be evaluated may be specified.)

The editor combines the advantages of a modern bitmap-oriented multi-window text editor and a language dependend menu-driven syntax editor (*hybrid editor*). It was generated by the PSG programming system generator [Jä84, Ba/Sn86] from formal syntax and formatting rules definitions. The most important characteristic of the editor is the choice between free text editing and menu-driven refinement- or modification steps, which is possible in any phase of an editing session (without the need of explicit modeswitching).

While in free input mode syntax-analysis as well as the prettyprinting mechanism are always available on keystroke, menu-guided editing prevents any syntactical errors from the beginning. If syntactical errors are detected, an error-recovery dialogue supports the user in correcting his program. The parser is incremental, allowing for proper handling of incomplete modules.

Inter-module dependency as well as status information is stored in a global *dependency graph*, which is automatically adapted after editing a module. In order to guarantee type consistency between modules, the library management system employs a "lazy recompilation" algorithm (somewhat similar to the UNIX - *make*). As a possible recompilation strategy one could, after editing, enforce subsequent recompilation of all affected modules (directly or indirectly using definitions from the edited module). On the contrary, lazy recompilation means, that the evaluation of a module entails the recompilation of all needed modules, which have become inconsistent by some previous editing session. Additionally, the user has the option of forcing the library to be consistent.

Thus, type consistence between modules and all compilation is controlled automatically. The user need not keep track of module dependencies, in fact, he even need not know, that a compiler exists at all.

A module library consists of different kinds of information. The module representation construc-ted by the editor is an *abstract syntax tree* enriched by the local type information, whereas global type information is stored separately in *interface files*. If a module is compiled, *code files* have to be stored. These files include symbol tables and machine code for an abstract machine. For the details of the compiler and the abstract machine ("E-machine") the reader is referred to [GI/Th87]. Furthermore, transformations of *text-files* into abstract trees and vice versa are available in the editor's menu.

We are currently extending the library manager to a module database handler, additionally supporting concurrent access to module libraries.

The SAMPLE prototyping environment is implemented on a Siemens BS2000 machine, the portation to PCS-Cadmus and SUN workstations will, however, be completed soon.

For more detailed information about the SAMPLE environment the reader is referred to [Jä88].

4. Conclusion

We are convinced, that model-based specifications in the VDM sense become much more attractive if the underlying language has a powerful type system and if a sophisticated prototyping environment offers different kinds of support tools like the ones embedded into the SAMPLE environment. From our first practical experiences (using SAMPLE for prototyping a Pascal-Compiler) we learned, that executable specifications may be very useful for recognising conceptual mistakes early. However, the experienced programmer must be a little careful to keep in mind that prototype specifications in contrast to programs should *not* be based on trade-offs between run-time efficiency on one hand and clearness on the other.

Comparing SAMPLE with other functional languages it turns out that, in the general approach, SAMPLE is related to Miranda ([Tu86]). With polymorphic type systems and pattern-based definitions both languages stand in the tradition of HOPE ([Bu/MQ/Sa80], and ML ([Mi84]) differing from ML in many aspects, from HOPE in particular by the non-strict semantics.

Compared to these languages the most important difference is the more general type system of SAMPLE. The combination of polymorphism, user-defined type constructors, recursive types, overloading, and coercion allows for elegant design and safe usage of data types for all kinds of applications.

The Miranda feature of algebraic types appears in SAMPLE as a special class of sum types. In SAMPLE, however, one is free to use constructors within patterns on the left or, alternatively, predefined selectors on the right hand side of definitions, while Miranda does not support the latter.

Comparing the implementations we claim that the SAMPLE environment provides a lot of extra user-support which is essential for the development of large software systems.

As a future perspective, we want to support user-defined overloading by the type system (in particular to allow the use of predefined operators for abstract datatypes). The theoretical basis is to be found in [Ka88]. Furthermore we want to extend the interpreter to a comfortable debugging system. A more critical aspect is the replacement of current file-I-O (which we left out in this paper, since we are not very satisfied with the current solution) by a more general concept of objects with states on a seperate language level to be defined.

References

Ba/Sn86   R. Bahlke, G. Snelting
               The PSG System: From formal Language Definitions to Interactive
               Programming Environments
               ACM Transactions on Programming Languages,
               Vol. 8, No. 4 10/86 p. 547-576

Ba/Hu87   R. Bahlke, M. Hunkel
               The User Interface of PSG Programming Environments
               Proceeding of the INTERACT 87 - IFIP Conference on
               human-computer interaction
               North-Holland 9/87, p. 311-316

Bj/Jo78   Bjørner, D., Jones, C.B. (Eds.)
               The Vienna Development Method: The Metalanguage
               LNCS Vol. 61, Springer 1978

Bu/MQ/Sa80   R. Burstall, D.B. McQueen, D. Sanella
               HOPE: An experimental applicative language
               in: Proceedings of the 1st Intern. LISP conference, Stanford 1980

Da/Mi82   L. Damas, R. Milner
               Principal Type Schemes for Functional Programs
               in: Proceedings of the 9th ACM Symposion on Principles of Programing
               languages, 1982

Gl/Th87   M. Gloger, C. Thies
               The E-machine
               Report PI-R6/87, FB20, TH. Darmstadt, 1987

GI/Th86   M. Gloger, C. Thies
Entwurf und Implementierung eines Compilers und
Interpretierers für die Spezifikationssprache SPL
Diploma thesis, FB20, TH Darmstadt, 1986

Jä84   M. Jäger et al.
PSG - Programming System Generator
in: Proceedings of the Programming Environments and Compiler
Conference, Munich 1984
Teubner Verlag, Stuttgart 1984, p. 285-291

Jä87   M. Jäger
SAMPLE (Sprachbeschreibung)
Report PI-R1/87, FB20, TH Darmstadt, 1987

Jä88   M. Jäger
The SAMPLE Environment
in: Proceedings of the GI-Workshop 1988 on language dependend
programming environments, edited by G. Snelting
Technical University Darmstadt, 1988

Ka88   S. Kaes
Parametric Overloading in Polymorphic Languages
in: Proceedings of the European Symposium on Programming,
ESOP 88, Nancy, France
Springer LNCS, Vol. 300, 1988

Le83   T. Letschert
Type Inference in the Presence of Polymorphism, Overloading, and
Coercions
in: Proceeding of the 8th Conference on Programming Languages
and Program Development, Zürich, 1984

Le86   T. Letschert
Typinferenzsysteme
Dissertation, TH Darmstadt, 1986

MQ/Pl/Se84 D.B. McQueen, G.D. Plotkin, R. Sethi
An Ideal Model for Recursive Polymorphic Types
Proceedings of the 11th ACM Symposion on Principles of Programing
languages 1984, p. 165 - 174

Mi78   R. Milner
A Theory of Type Polymorphism in Programming
Journal of Computer and System Sciences 17
p. 348-375, 1978

Mi84   R. Milner
A proposal for standard ML
Proceedings 1984 Symposium on LISP and Functional Programming
ACM, 8/84

Mit84   J.C. Mitchell
Coercion and Type Inference
Proceedings of the 11th ACM Symposion on Principles of Programing
languages 1984, p. 175-185

St67   C. Strachey
            Fundamental Concepts in Programming Languages
            International Summer School in Computer
            Programming, Kopenhagen 1967

Tu86   D.A. Turner
            Miranda: A non-strict functional language with polymorphic
            types
            in: SIGPLAN Notices, 9/86

A three-valued logic
for
software specification and validation

Tertium tamen datur[1]

Beata Konikowska, Andrzej Tarlecki, Andrzej Blikle

Project MetaSoft
Institute of Computer Science
Polish Academy of Sciences
PKiN, P.O.Box 22, 00-901 Warsaw

Abstract

Different calculi of partial or three-valued predicates have been used and studied by several authors in the context of software specification, development and validation. This paper offers a critical survey on the development of three-valued logics based on such calculi.

In the first part of the paper we review two three-valued predicate calculi, based on, respectively, McCarthy's and Kleene's propositional connectives and quantifiers, and point out that in a three-valued logic one should distinguish between two notions of validity: *strong validity* (always true) and *weak validity* (never false). We define in model-theoretic terms a number of consequence relations for three-valued logics. Each of them is determined by the choice of the underlying predicate calculus and of the weak or strong validity of axioms and of theorems. We discuss mutual relationships between consequence relations defined in such a way and study some of their basic properties.

The second part of the paper is devoted to the development of a formal deductive system of inference rules for a three-valued logic. We use the method of semantic tableaux (slightly modified to deal with three-valued formulas) to develop a Gentzen-style system of inference rules for deriving valid sequents, which in turn is used to obtain a sound and complete system of natural deduction rules. We have chosen to study the consequence relation determined by the predicate calculus with McCarthy's propositional connectives and Kleene's quantifiers and by the strong interpretation of both axioms and theorems. Although we find this choice appropriate for applications in the area of software specification, verification and development, we regard this logic merely as an example and use it to present some general techniques of developing a sequent calculus and a natural deduction system for a three-valued logic.

---

[1] *Non-(tertium non datur)*

1   Introduction

Tertium non datur — a law of classical logic — states that every hypothesis is either true or false. Nevertheless, sentences which people use in formulating thoughts may be meaningless and therefore neither true nor false. "This paper is tall" or "$0^{-1} > 1$" are two such examples.

In every deductive reasoning we can recognize and reject meaningless sentences and therefore every hypothesis which can be proved at all can be proved using only meaningful sentences. This makes a two-valued logic an adequate tool for proving facts. The situation changes if sentences with free variables are evaluated dynamically in the process of running an algorithm. Formulas like "x is tall" or "$x^{-1} > 1$" may be true, false or undefined depending on the value of x. Of course, if an algorithm runs across an undefined formula, then it either aborts, or loops or produces an incorrect result. In order to avoid such situations we must be able to describe them formally, and therefore we have to assume that our formulas (Boolean expressions) represent either partial functions with values in the two-element set $\{tt, ff\}$ or total functions with values in a three-element set $\{tt, ff, ee\}$, where ee represents an "abstract error" or "undefinedness". It turns out that the latter solution is more convenient since it allows us to treat undefinedness in a lazy, non-strict way (cf. [Blikle 87]).

When we admit a third logical value, we have a variety of choices in formalizing and in using three-valued Boolean expressions in software specification and validation. First, there are several ways of extending the classical two-valued predicate calculus to the three-valued case. Three major candidates for such extensions have been proposed in the literature: a calculus described by S.C.Kleene [Kleene 38, 52], a calculus described by J.McCarthy [McCarthy 61], and a combination of these calculi described in [Blikle 87]. Second, for each such extension we have two major strategies of using three-valued predicates in the specification and in the validation of software. One strategy consists in constructing a special algebra of three-valued predicates which is later used at the level of a second-order two-valued logic. This strategy has been chosen in [Blikle 87] where it was applied to the McCarthy-Kleene calculus in the context of a particular software-specification language. It was discussed later in [Blikle 88] in a more general setting.

Another strategy consists in developing a three-valued formal logic. Here we have again several possibilities. First we choose the underlying predicate calculus. Besides the choice between Kleene's and McCarthy's (or yet different) propositional connectives and quantifiers, we also have to decide whether we accept non-monotone propositional connectives. Second, we choose the concept of the validity of a formula. In a three-valued logic we distinguish between *strongly valid* (always true) and *weakly valid* (never false) formulas. When we construct a logic, i.e. an axiomatic theory of a consequence relation, we can talk about strong and weak axioms (in the above sense) and strong and weak theorems. This yields four possibilities. Finally, we can develop a sequent deduction system or a natural deduction system.

The issue of three-valued logic in the context of software specification and validation has recently attracted much attention. Of the most important contributions we should mention [Hoogewijs 79, 83] where the author discussed a three-valued logic over Kleene's connectives (including a non-monotone connective) and quantifiers, with strong axioms and weak theorems. Another logic over Kleene's calculus, with a non-monotone connective, strong axioms and strong theorems has been presented in [Barringer, Cheng & Jones 84] and its applications were discussed in [Jones 86, 87]. [Hoogewijs 87] gives a comparison of the two systems. [Owe 85] develops a formal logic with weak axioms and weak theorems based on a rather unusual predicate calculus which is a mixture of strict logical connectives, *if*-expressions (under the assumptions in [Owe 85] this is sufficient to define both Kleene's and McCarthy's connectives) Kleene's existential quantifier and a "weak" universal quantifier. A more complete discussion of different three-valued logics may be found in [Cheng 86].

In this paper we attempt to tackle two issues. First, we give a general comparative analysis of semantic consequence relations corresponding to various three-valued logics. In this way we come up with a number of conclusions about three-valued logics without even starting to think about the proof-theoretic machinery of deduction rules. We compare these consequence relations with each other and with the classical consequence. For instance, we point out that a three-valued consequence relation based on any of the two calculi we consider (both without non-monotone operators) with strong axioms and weak theorems, is equivalent to the classical consequence relation (Sec. 4), and we discuss where we can and where we cannot expect the rule of detachment and the deduction theorem to hold (Sec. 5).

The second objective of this paper is to develop a system of inference rules for a three-valued logic. We develop two sets of proof rules, two formal systems (a sequent calculus and a natural deduction system) for the Kleene-McCarthy logic without non-monotone operators, with strong axioms and strong theorems. We have chosen these parameters for our logic following motivation given in [Blikle 87, 88], but to a large extent we regard this logic merely as an example which we use to discuss some general techniques of developing sequent proof rules and natural-deduction proof rules for an arbitrary three-valued logic.

We have tried to make our paper possibly self-contained for a reader who is not a logician. However, we could not make it a complete tutorial. Therefore we skip some standard technical details (trying to outline all the ideas, though) which may be found in the literature.

To keep this version of the paper within a reasonable size we omit all the proofs and some discussion and examples. A full version of the paper will be published elsewhere.

Acknowledgements
We are grateful to A.Hoogewijs, J.H.Cheng, O.Owe and N.Haichu for their comments on an early version of the paper, which helped to improve the presentation and discussion of many points here.

2 Introductory concepts

In this section we define and discuss the predicate calculi of Kleene and of McCarthy. We also define a combination of these caluli which is to be used later as a basis for our logic. Let us start by introducing some notation.

If A and B are sets, then by $A \to B$ we denote the set of all total functions from A to B. By $f : A \to B$ we denote the fact that f is a total function from A to B. $g : A \to B \to C$ abbreviates $g : A \to (B \to C)$. Instead of $f(a)$ we write $f.a$ and instead of $(g.a).b$ we write $g.a.b$. For any $a \in A$, $b \in B$ and $f : A \to B$, by $f[b/a]$ we denote a modification of f defined as follows:

$$f[a/b].x = \text{if } x = a \text{ then } b \text{ else } f.x$$

Let

$$Boolerr = \{tt, ff, ee\}$$

be our three-element set of logical values (*Boolerr* stands for *Boolean + Error*). We introduce McCarthy's conditional operator:

$$\xrightarrow{\text{MC}} : Boolerr \times Boolerr \times Boolerr \to Boolerr$$

where for any $a, b, c \in Boolerr$,

$$
\begin{aligned}
a \xrightarrow{\text{MC}} b, c \ &= \ b \quad &&\text{for } a = tt, \\
& \ c \quad &&\text{for } a = ff, \\
& \ a \quad &&\text{for } a = ee.
\end{aligned}
$$

McCarthy's propositional connectives are defined as follows:

$$\begin{aligned}
\textbf{not } a & = a \xrightarrow{\text{MC}} \mathit{ff}, \mathit{tt} && - \textit{negation,} \\
a \textbf{ or } b & = a \xrightarrow{\text{MC}} \mathit{tt}, b && - \textit{disjunction,} \\
a \textbf{ and } b & = a \xrightarrow{\text{MC}} b, \mathit{ff} && - \textit{conjunction,} \\
a \textbf{ implies } b & = a \xrightarrow{\text{MC}} b, \mathit{tt} && - \textit{implication.}
\end{aligned}$$

In all the above definitions "=" denotes the identity in *Boolerr*.

McCarthy's connectives have four important properties:

1. They extend classical connectives, i.e. coincide with them on the logical values *tt* and *ff*. They also satisfy the classical mutual relationships such as for example:

$$a \textbf{ implies } b = (\textbf{not } a) \textbf{ or } b \tag{1}$$
$$a \textbf{ and } b = \textbf{not}((\textbf{not } a) \textbf{ or } (\textbf{not } b)) \tag{2}$$

However, not all classical identities hold. For example, neither of the following is true in general:

- $a \textbf{ or } b = b \textbf{ or } a$
- $a \textbf{ or } (\textbf{not } a) = \mathit{tt}$

2. They allow for a lazy evaluation of expressions and in that case they again coincide with classical operators. For example, if we evaluate $exp_1 \textbf{ or } exp_2$ and if exp_1 evaluates to *tt*, then we can abandon the evaluation of exp_2, since independently of its value (even if it is *ee*) the value of the whole expression is *tt*.

3. They are monotone in the usual cpo over *Boolerr*:

That is, if in a propositional expression we replace one of its current arguments by *ee*, then the value of that expression either remains unchanged, or becomes *ee*. This is in contrast with some other three-valued calculi. For example, [Hoogevijs 79, 83, 87] and [Barringer, Cheng & Jones 84] study a calculus similar to Kleene's calculus as presented below, but with a total non-monotone unary connective Δ which determines whether or not its argument is "defined" (i.e. $\neq ee$).

4. They are strict with respect to their left argument, i.e. assume value *ee* whenever their left argument is *ee*.

Properties 2 and 3 guarantee that the third logical value *ee* may be interpreted not only as an abstract error (i.e. as an error signal generated by the system), but also as true undefinedness resulting from a nonterminating computation. Due to property 4, McCarthy's Boolean expressions may be implemented on a sequential machine.

As the reader has probably already noticed, McCarthy's disjunction and conjunction are not commutative. This is the price which we have to pay for a propositional calculus which has properties 1, 2 and 3 and which is sequentially implementable at the same time. If we do not care about the latter property, we can select the propositional calculus of Kleene, where negation (**not**) is the same as above, disjunction (**or**$_K$) is the following extension of the classical connective:

$tt \text{ or}_K ee = ee \text{ or}_K tt = tt$

$a \text{ or}_K ee = ee \text{ or}_K a = ee$ for $a \neq tt$,

and the remaining operators are defined by identities (1) and (2). Now we have the commutativity of conjunction and of disjunction, but in order to implement expressions in the case where ee may correspond to a nonterminating computation, we need unbounded parallelism. Indeed, when we compute

$$exp_1 \text{ or}_K \ldots \text{ or}_K exp_n$$

we have to compute all exp_i $(i = 1, \ldots, n)$ in parallel in order to determine whether one of them evaluates to tt.

Now, let us talk about predicates and quantifiers. In this section we discuss them on semantic, model-theoretic grounds. The corresponding formalized language of logic is defined in the next section.

Let Ide be an arbitrary nonempty set of *identifiers* (variables) and let $Value$ be an arbitrary nonempty set of *values*. A *state* is a total function from identifiers to values; a *predicate* is a total function from states to logical values:

$State \quad\ = Ide \rightarrow Value$
$Predicate = State \rightarrow Boolerr$

Logicians would have probably preferred to say *valuations* rather than *states*. We use the latter term since it is more common in the field where our logic is to be applied.

The elements of $State$ will be denoted by sta, the elements of Ide by $x, y, z, \ldots$, the elements of $Value$ by v, val, and the elements of $Predicate$ by $p, q, \ldots$, all possibly with indices, primes etc.

In this framework quantifiers may be regarded as functions that assign predicate transformers to identifiers:

Forall: $Ide \rightarrow Predicate \rightarrow Predicate$
Exists: $Ide \rightarrow Predicate \rightarrow Predicate$

In this paper we define quantifiers after [Kleene 52] by extending the corresponding classical definitions to the three-valued case. For all $p \in Predicate$, $x \in Ide$ and $sta \in State$ we set:

Forall.$x.p.sta =$ tt if for all values $val \in Value$, $p.(sta[val/x]) = tt$;
                     ff if for some value $val \in Value$, $p.(sta[val/x]) = ff$;
                     ee otherwise, i.e.
                            if for no value $val \in Value$, $p.(sta[val/x]) = ff$,
                            but for some value $val \in Value$, $p.(sta[val/x]) = ee$.

Exists.$x.p.sta =$ tt if for some value $val \in Value$, $p.(sta[val/x]) = tt$;
                     ff if for all values $val \in Value$, $p.(sta[val/x]) = ff$;
                     ee otherwise, i.e.
                            if for no value $val \in Value$, $p.(sta[val/x]) = tt$,
                            but for some value $val \in Value$, $p.(sta[val/x]) = ee$.

These quantifiers satisfy de Morgan's laws and generalize Kleene's conjunction and disjunction. However, they are not the generalizations of McCarthy's respective connectives. Quantifiers which attempt to generalize McCarthy's connectives have been defined in [McCarthy 61]. In that case:

Exists$_{Mc}$.$x.p.sta = tt$ if for some value $val \in Value$, $p.(sta[val/x]) = tt$,
                              and for all values $val \in Value$, $p.(sta[val/x]) \neq ee$,

all other cases are changed accordingly, and the universal quantifier is then defined by the de Morgan laws.

In the sequel our predicate calculus, based on McCarthy's propositional connectives and Kleene's quantifiers, will be referred to as the *MK-calculus* (for "McCarthy-Kleene") and the calculus based on Kleene's propositional connectives and quantifiers as the *K-calculus*.

3 Consequence relations based on three-valued predicate calculi

A formalized logic may be regarded as an axiomatic theory of a consequence relation between formulas (we refer to [Avron 87] for an expository presentation of this point of view). In this section we define a certain scheme of such a relation (based on a model-theoretic view of three-valued predicate calculi) and we instantiate it later to different logical systems. We start from the concept of a formalized language and of its semantic interpretation. Let:

Ide	be a countably infinite set of identifiers (variables),
Fun_m	be a set of m-ary function symbols, $m = 0, 1, \ldots,$
$Fun = \bigcup_{m=0}^{\infty} Fun_m,$	
$Pred_m$	be a set of m-ary predicate symbols, $m = 1, 2, \ldots,$
$Pred = \bigcup_{m=1}^{\infty} Pred_m,$	

and let

$Term$	denote the set of all terms constructed in the usual way over Fun, Ide and appropriate auxiliary symbols such as parentheses, commas, etc.
$Form$	denote the set of all formulas constructed in the usual way over $Term$, $Pred$, appropriate auxiliary symbols and the following special logical symbols: $\neg, \vee, \wedge, \supset, \forall, \exists.$

The two sets $Term$ and $Form$ constitute our formalized logical language. Throughout the rest of the paper we will consider an arbitrary (but fixed) language of such a form. For technical reasons we assume that at least one $Pred_m$, $m = 1, 2, \ldots,$ is nonempty.

It should be pointed out that in this paper we deal with one-sorted logics, rather than with many-sorted logics which are more general and more appropriate for applications to software specification and validation. This, however, is only for the technical convenience of the presentation. All the notions and results we present carry over directly to the many-sorted case.

A *logical structure*, or simply *structure* (sometimes also called a *model*, but we reserve this term for a somewhat different concept) for a given logical language consists of a nonempty set $Value$ of *values* and of two families of functions:

$$F_m : Fun_m \to Value^m \to Value \qquad \text{for } m = 0, 1, \ldots$$
$$P_m : Pred_m \to Value^m \to Boolerr \qquad \text{for } m = 1, 2, \ldots$$

(Recall that $Boolerr = \{tt, ff, ee\}$ is our set of three logical values.)

We say that a structure is *classical* if for $m = 1, 2, \ldots,$ for all $p \in Pred_m$ and $\vec{v} \in Value^m$, $P_m.p.\vec{v} \neq ee$.

The careful reader has probably noticed that we use the term *predicate* in this paper to name both functions mapping *states* into $Boolerr$ (as introduced in the previous section) as well as predicates in the more traditional sense, i.e. functions mapping *values* into $Boolerr$. We hope that this will never lead to any ambiguity.

Observe that from the formal point of view the meanings of all function and predicate symbols are total functions. However, since the set $Boolerr$ contains the "undefined element" ee, we can interpret our predicates as partial. The same, of course, may be applied to functions. Each time we wish to do so, we may assume that the set $Value$ of values contains a special element representing "undefinedness". The only additional requirement would be that all functions and predicates are monotone w.r.t. the obvious flat ordering with the "undefined element" at the bottom. In this sense our model covers partial functions as well. We are not going to discuss this explicitly here, since contrary to the case of propositional connectives over *Boolerr*, we do not consider any specific functions or predicates. In particular, in order to keep our paper within a reasonable size, the equality predicate will not be discussed at all. Let us just point out that in the case of partial functions the requirement of monotonicity mentioned above excludes the so-called strong equality (cf. e.g. [Barringer, Cheng & Jones 84]) which is not monotone.

One more general comment is perhaps appropriate here: we have introduced in our model only one "undefined value". This means that we have identified two different kinds of undefinedness:

- the undefinedness resulting from an infinite computation, and

- the undefinedness resulting from a computable error signal (an abstract error in the sense of [Goguen 77]).

We believe that this is appropriate at the logical level, where we describe and prove properties of states, and so indirectly software properties as well (we sketch this view in more in detail Section 10). This is, of course, in contrast with the situation at the level of software semantics, where it is necessary not only to distinguish between these two kinds of undefinedness, but in fact to distinguish between different error messages and perhaps describe some operations which model the "error handling" in the software system. In our view, however, this should be modelled at the level of "data" for our logic, via the functions of the structure that describes the software system, and should not affect directly the logical part. Thus, in the set *Value* of values, but not in the set *Boolerr* of logical values, we would normally replace a single "undefined element" by a set of error elements

$$Error = \{inf, err_1, \ldots, err_n\}$$

where *inf* represents the "true undefinedness" resulting from an infinite computation and $err_1, \ldots,$ err_n represent computable error signals. Notice that from the abstract point of view the computable error signals are as much "normal elements" of the structure we describe as any other data and they should be treated as such in our theory. In particular, we would require that the functions and predicates of the structure we deal with are monotone w.r.t. the flat ordering where the "true undefinedness elelment" *inf* is at the bottom, and all the other error elements are incomparable (and incomparable with other data). This allows a natural description of "error handling" without affecting the logical issues we discuss in this paper.

For every structure we define the set of states (over this structure):

$$State = Ide \rightarrow Value$$

and the semantic function for terms:

$$T : Term \rightarrow State \rightarrow Value$$

(the obvious definition is omitted — *T.t.sta* is the value of term *t* in the structure in state *sta*).

A semantic function for formulas will map them to predicates (i.e. functions from states to the set of logical values). Such a function is unambiguously determined by any interpretation of the special logical symbols, i.e. by any (three-valued) predicate calculus (together with a semantic function for terms). Since in the previous section we introduced two such calculi, with every structure we associate two semantic functions for formulas:

$$F_{MK} : Form \rightarrow Predicate$$

determined by the *MK*-calculus, and

$$F_K : Form \rightarrow Predicate$$

determined by the K-calculus, where

$$Predicate = State \rightarrow Boolerr.$$

Thus, for example, for any formulas $\varphi_1, \varphi_2 \in Form$ and $sta \in State$:

$$F_{MK}.(\varphi_1 \vee \varphi_2).sta = F_{MK}.\varphi_1.sta \text{ or } F_{MK}.\varphi_2.sta$$
$$F_K.(\varphi_1 \vee \varphi_2).sta = F_K.\varphi_1.sta \text{ or}_K F_K.\varphi_2.sta$$

and for any formula $\varphi \in Form$ and identifier $x \in Ide$:

$$F_{MK}.(\exists x)\varphi = \textbf{Exists}.x.(F_{MK}.\varphi)$$
$$F_K.(\exists x)\varphi = \textbf{Exists}.x.(F_K.\varphi)$$

(again, a complete formal definition is omitted).

Clearly, if the considered logical structure is classical then the two semantic functions for formulas coincide, which we will make explicit by using a common name for them: in classical structures we define $F_C = F_{MK} = F_K$.

Let A be an arbitrary structure with the semantics of formulas F_{MK} and F_K, $sta \in State$ be an arbitrary state (over A) and let $\varphi \in Form$ be an arbitrary formula. The following definitions are analogous for the MK-calculus and for the K-calculus, so we give them in a schematic form for $\nabla \in \{MK, K\}$.

We say that A *strongly* ∇-*satisfies* φ in sta (or that φ *strongly* ∇-*holds in* $\langle A, sta \rangle$), written $\langle A, sta \rangle \models_s^\nabla \varphi$, if $F_\nabla.\varphi.sta = tt$.

We say that A *weakly* ∇-*satisfies* φ in sta (or that φ *weakly* ∇-*holds in* $\langle A, sta \rangle$), written $\langle A, sta \rangle \models_w^\nabla \varphi$, if $F_\nabla.\varphi.sta \neq ff$.

If A is classical then the above notions coincide (and coincide with the classical definition) and we simply say then that A *satisfies* φ in sta (or that φ *holds in* $\langle A, sta \rangle$).

Further, let $Ax \subseteq Form$ be an arbitrary set of formulas, which we shall refer to as axioms. We say that $\langle A, sta \rangle$ is a *strong* (respectively, *weak*) ∇-*model of* Ax, or that it *strongly* (respectively, *weakly*) ∇-*satisfies* Ax, if each $\varphi \in Ax$ strongly (respectively, weakly) ∇-holds in $\langle A, sta \rangle$. We say that $\langle A, sta \rangle$ is a *classical model of* Ax if A is classical and each $\varphi \in Ax$ holds in $\langle A, sta \rangle$.

Now we can introduce a parametric class of consequence relations:

$$\models_{\beta\gamma}^\nabla \subseteq 2^{Form} \times Form$$

where $\nabla \in \{C, K, MK\}$ and $\beta, \gamma \in \{s, w\}$.

We say that a formula $\varphi \in Form$ is a β-γ-∇-*consequence of* Ax, in symbols:

$$Ax \models_{\beta\gamma}^\nabla \varphi$$

if the formula φ γ-∇-holds in every β-∇-model of Ax[2].

(In examples we write $\varphi_1, \ldots, \varphi_n \models_{\beta\gamma}^\nabla \varphi$ instead of $\{\varphi_1, \ldots, \varphi_n\} \models_{\beta\gamma}^\nabla \varphi$.)

For each $\nabla \in \{MK, K\}$ we have four corresponding consequence relations, depending on whether we are considering strong or weak models and strong or weak theorems. In the sequel, however, we exclude w-s-∇-consequences from our considerations, since they lead to theories where an axiom does not need to be a theorem.

As to the other papers on three-valued logics, which we mentioned earlier, [Hoogewijs 79, 83] deals with s-w-K-consequence, [Barringer, Chang & Jones 84] probably with s-s-K-consequence (although in that paper the authors restrict their attention to syntactic proof rules leaving the

---

[2] We hope that this notation, although not quite formal, is understandable; for example, by "w-K-holds" we mean "weakly K-holds", by "s-MK-model" we mean "strong MK-model", etc.

semantics of their logic completely undefined) and [Owe 85] with *w-w-(yet different calculus)*-consequence.

β-γ-∇-consequences of an empty set of axioms are called β-γ-∇-*tautologies*. However, we do not have to mention the β parameter when dealing with tautologies, since every w-model of the empty set of formulas is also an s-model of that set and vice versa. The fact that a formula φ is a γ-∇-tautology is denoted by $\models_\gamma^\nabla \varphi$.

When we consider the classical consequence relation we may omit both the β and γ parameters, since strong satisfaction and weak satisfaction mean the same in classical structures. We write, therefore, $Ax \models^C \varphi$ and $\models^C \varphi$ with the obvious meaning.

The consequence relations introduced above may be referred to as the consequence relations of *truth*, as opposed to the consequence relations of *validity* where open formulas are always (implicitly) universally quantified (cf. [Avron 87] where this distinction is made explicit and discussed). For example, the classical consequence relation of validity is defined as follows:

$Ax \models^C_{validity} \varphi$ if for every classical structure A:

    if for every state sta over A, $\langle A, sta \rangle$ is a model of Ax

    then for every state sta' over A, formula φ holds in $\langle A, sta' \rangle$.

Clearly, the difference occurs only if we allow open formulas to be used as axioms, and so we consider it irrelevant for practical purposes. Although it seems more convenient to deal with the consequence relations of truth here, the technical analysis and results presented in the rest of the paper carry over with little modification to the case of the consequence relations of validity.

4   A comparison of β-γ-∇-consequence relations

In the previous section we have introduced a number of (apparently) different consequence relations on the same set of formulas of a formalized language. We have already mentioned some trivial facts about their mutual relationships, for example that all the consequence relations determined by the classical notion of a structure coincide. In this section we will have a closer look at the somewhat less obvious relationships between the consequence relations based on three-valued calculi.

Let us start by pointing out some facts connecting the different notions of satisfaction we consider.

Fact 4.1 For any structure A and state sta over A, for any formula $\varphi \in Form$, if $F_{MK}.\varphi.sta \neq ee$ then $F_K.\varphi.sta = F_{MK}.\varphi.sta$.

Fact 4.2 For any structure A, state sta over A and formula φ:

1. $\langle A, sta \rangle \models_s^{MK} \varphi$ implies $\langle A, sta \rangle \models_s^K \varphi$ (not reversible in general).
2. $\langle A, sta \rangle \models_s^K \varphi$ implies $\langle A, sta \rangle \models_w^{MK} \varphi$ (not reversible in general).
3. $\langle A, sta \rangle \models_w^K \varphi$ implies $\langle A, sta \rangle \models_w^{MK} \varphi$ (not reversible in general).

Lemma 4.1 Let $\nabla \in \{MK, K\}$. Consider two structures A and A', which have a common set $Value$ of values and common semantics of function symbols (hence, a common semantics of terms as well). Further, assume that predicates of A' are more defined than the corresponding ones of A, i.e. that for $m = 1, 2, \ldots$, for $p \in Pred_m$ and $\vec{v} \in Value^m$, if $P_m.p.\vec{v} \neq ee$ then $P'_m.p.\vec{v} = P_m.p.\vec{v}$. Let F_∇ and F'_∇ be the semantics of formulas in A and A' respectively.

Then: for any formula $\varphi \in Form$ and state sta over A (which is a state over A' as well),

$$F_\nabla.\varphi.sta \neq ee \quad \text{implies} \quad F_\nabla.\varphi.sta = F'_\nabla.\varphi.sta$$

It should be pointed out that the above lemma (and its consequences, like Corollary 4.1 and Theorem 4.1.4 below) holds only because all the propositional connectives and quantifiers of the calculus we use are monotone.

Corollary 4.1 Let $\nabla \in \{MK, K\}$. If a set of formulas $Ax \subseteq Form$ has a strong ∇-model then it has a classical model.

Notice that the above corollary implies that under strong interpretation of axioms we have no way to ensure that a formula is undefined. More precisely:

Corollary 4.2 Let $\nabla \in \{MK, K\}$. For any set of formulas $Ax \subseteq Form$ and formula $\varphi \in Form$, if $Ax \models_{ss}^{\nabla} \varphi \wedge \neg\varphi$ then Ax has no strong ∇-model.

We are ready now to state the main theorem of this section, which fully describes the relationship between the consequence relations we consider.

Theorem 4.1 For any $Ax \subseteq Form$, $\varphi \in Form$, $\nabla \in \{MK, K\}$ and $\beta, \gamma \in \{s, w\}$:

1. $Ax \models_{ww}^{\nabla} \varphi$ implies $Ax \models_{sw}^{\nabla} \varphi$ (not reversible in general)
2. $Ax \models_{ss}^{\nabla} \varphi$ implies $Ax \models_{sw}^{\nabla} \varphi$ (not reversible in general)
3. $Ax \models_{\beta\gamma}^{\nabla} \varphi$ implies $Ax \models^{C} \varphi$
4. $Ax \models^{C} \varphi$ iff $Ax \models_{sw}^{\nabla} \varphi$
5. In general neither $Ax \models_{ss}^{MK} \varphi$ implies $Ax \models_{ss}^{K} \varphi$, nor $Ax \models_{ss}^{K} \varphi$ implies $Ax \models_{ss}^{MK} \varphi$. That is, the s-s-K-consequence and s-s-MK-consequence are incomparable.
6. In general neither $Ax \models_{ss}^{\nabla} \varphi$ implies $Ax \models_{ww}^{\nabla} \varphi$, nor $Ax \models_{ww}^{\nabla} \varphi$ implies $Ax \models_{ss}^{\nabla} \varphi$. That is, the s-s-∇-consequence and the w-w-∇-consequence are incomparable.
7. In general neither $Ax \models_{ww}^{K} \varphi$ implies $Ax \models_{ww}^{MK} \varphi$, nor $Ax \models_{ww}^{MK} \varphi$ implies $Ax \models_{ww}^{K} \varphi$. That is, the w-w-K-consequence and the w-w-MK-consequence are incomparable.

The above theorem may be summarized by the following picture, where the arrows represent all the inclusions (except those that follow by transitivity) between the consequence relation:

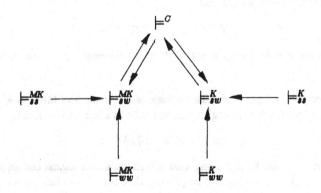

For tautologies we have the following analog of the former theorem:

Corollary 4.3 For any $f \in Form$ and $\nabla \in \{MK, K\}$:

1. $\models_{s}^{\nabla} \varphi$ implies $\models_{w}^{\nabla} \varphi$ (not reversible)

2. $\models_w^\nabla \varphi$ iff $\models^C \varphi$

Notice, however, that the first part of the above corollary holds trivially:

Fact 4.3 Let $\nabla \in \{MK, K\}$. In our logical language there are no strong ∇-tautologies. That is, for no formula $\varphi \in Form$, $\models_s^\nabla \varphi$.

Although s-s-∇-consequence and w-w-∇-consequence are incomparable (by Theorem 4.1.6) there is an intrinsic relationship between them:

Fact 4.4 Let $\nabla \in \{MK, K\}$. For any formulas $\varphi, \psi \in Form$

$$\varphi \models_{ss}^\nabla \psi \quad \text{iff} \quad \neg\psi \models_{ww}^\nabla \neg\varphi$$

5 Some logical properties of β-γ-∇-consequence relations

By a logic over a (semantic) consequence relation $\models$ we mean a set of syntactic inference rules which define a syntactic consequence relation $\vdash$ (sometimes referred to as syntactic entailment). This new relation must be at least consistent with the former, i.e. $Ax \vdash \varphi$ must imply $Ax \models \varphi$. If the underlying formalized language is of first order (as in our case), then we should also try to make this new relation complete, i.e. such that $Ax \models \varphi$ implies $Ax \vdash \varphi$. As is known from the famous Gödel incompleteness theorem, we cannot expect a complete $\vdash$ for a second-order logic.

Although we have not yet presented a logic for any of our consequence relations, we nevertheless can investigate the properties of such logics, since if $\vdash$ is consistent and complete, then it coincides with $\models$. We consider below some basic properties of classical logic: the rule of detachment, the deduction theorem and the relationship between the consistency of a theory and the existence of a model. We check which of these properties are satisfied by our consequence relations.

It turns out that from this point of view MK-calculus and K-calculus are quite similar. Let $\nabla \in \{MK, K\}$ throughout this section. Recall that by Theorem 4.1 the s-w-∇-consequences coincide with the classical consequence. Thus, we will consider below only s-s-∇-consequence and w-w-∇-consequence.

In classical logic, one of the most frequently used inference rules is the *rule of detachment* also known as *modus ponens*. This rule says that

$$Ax \models \varphi \supset \psi \text{ and } Ax \models \varphi \text{ implies } Ax \models \psi.$$

Theorem 5.1 The rule of detachment is satisfied by s-s-∇-consequence, but is not satisfied by w-w-∇-consequence.

Another very important property of classical logic is the *deduction theorem* which establishes the following relationship between the logical consequence relation and implication:

$$Ax \models \varphi \supset \psi \text{ iff } Ax \cup \{\varphi\} \models \psi$$

If the deduction theorem holds, then proving that a formula ψ is a logical consequence of a finite set of axioms $\{\varphi_1, \ldots, \varphi_n\}$ may be reduced to proving that the implication $\varphi_1 \wedge \ldots \wedge \varphi_n \supset \psi$ is a tautology; and vice versa: proving that the implication $\varphi_1 \wedge \ldots \wedge \varphi_n \supset \psi$ is a tautology may be reduced to proving that ψ is a logical consequence of $\{\varphi_1, \ldots, \varphi_n\}$.

Theorem 5.2 For any set $Ax \subseteq Form$ of axioms and formulas $\varphi, \psi \in Form$:

1. $Ax \models_{ss}^\nabla \varphi \supset \psi$ implies $Ax \cup \{\varphi\} \models_{ss}^\nabla \psi$, but the implication is not reversible in general.

2. $Ax \cup \{\varphi\} \models^\nabla_{ww} \psi$ implies $Ax \models^\nabla_{ww} \varphi \supset \psi$, but the implication is not reversible in general.

For any consequence relation $\models$ and a set of axioms Ax, by a theory over Ax we mean the set

$$Cn.Ax = \{\varphi \mid Ax \models \varphi\}$$

of all the consequences of Ax. We say that Ax is *inconsistent* if there exists a formula φ such that both φ and $\neg\varphi$ belong to $Cn.Ax$. Otherwise we say that Ax is *consistent*.

In the framework of classical logic the following properties of a set Ax of formulas are equivalent:

1. Ax is consistent,

2. $Cn.Ax \neq Form$, i.e. there is a formula φ such that $Ax \not\models \varphi$,

3. Ax has a model.

Theorem 5.3 Let $Ax \subseteq Form$.

1. For s-s-∇-consequence the following properties are equivalent:

    (a) Ax is consistent,

    (b) $Cn.Ax \neq Form$,

    (c) Ax has a strong ∇-model.

2. For w-w-∇-consequence:

    (a) if Ax is consistent then $Cn.Ax \neq Form$,

    (b) if $Cn.Ax \neq Form$ then Ax has a weak ∇-model,

    (c) Ax may have a weak ∇-model and be inconsistent.

6 Sequents and signed formulas

In the rest of the paper we will present a formalized logic corresponding to the s-s-MK-consequence relation defined in the previous sections. In fact, we are going to develop two equivalent deduction systems for this consequence relation: a Gentzen-style sequent calculus and a natural deduction system.

Let us begin with a sequent calculus of Gentzen's type (see e.g. [Beth 59]). Recall that we are dealing with an arbitrary but fixed formalized logical language as presented in Section 2.

As usual for Gentzen-style calculi, we will formalize not just s-s-MK-consequence, but its generalization to the multi-conclusion case defined as follows: for any two sets of formulas $Ax, \Phi \subseteq Form$, we define

$$Ax \models^{MK}_{ss} \Phi$$

to mean that at least one formula $\varphi \in \Phi$ strongly MK-holds in every strong MK-model of Ax.

By a *sequent* we mean any pair $\langle \Gamma, \Delta \rangle$ of finite sets Γ and Δ of formulas, $\Gamma, \Delta \subset Form$. Sequents are traditionally written in the form $\Gamma \vdash \Delta$. Also traditionally, comma appearing in a sequent denotes the set-theoretic union; for example $\varphi, \Gamma \vdash \Delta$ should be read as $\{\varphi\} \cup \Gamma \vdash \Delta$.

Notice that since from now on we are dealing with only one consequence relation, we omit any decoration on the entailment symbol $\vdash$. Similarly, we omit any decoration on the semantic consequence and write simply $\models$ for $\models^{MK}_{ss}$, "satisfies" for "strongly MK-satisfies", "model" for "strong MK-model", etc.

A sequent $\Gamma \vdash \Delta$ is *valid* if for every model $\langle A, sta \rangle$ of Γ at least one formula $\delta \in \Delta$ holds in $\langle A, sta \rangle$.

Thus, for any (finite) set of formulas $Ax \subset Form$ and formula $\varphi \in Form$, the sequent $Ax \vdash \{\varphi\}$ is valid if and only if $Ax \models \varphi$. This implies that the syntactic entailment $\vdash$ in a valid sequent may indeed be viewed as a formal counterpart of (the generalization to the multi-conclusion case of) the semantic consequence relation we are studying.

The main problem we have to cope with to develop a formalized logic for the s-s-MK-consequence is, of course, that we are dealing with a three-valued calculus. One way of reducing this three-valued case to the standard situation is to introduce so-called signed formulas.

A *signed formula* has the form either $T\varphi$ or $NT\varphi$ (to be read "φ is true" and "φ is not true", respectively) where $\varphi \in Form$ is an arbitrary formula. Thus, the set of all signed formulas is defined as follows:

$$SForm = \{T\varphi, NT\varphi \mid \varphi \in Form\}.$$

Let A be any logical structure with the semantics of formulas F_{MK}. The semantic function for signed formulas

$$SF: SForm \to State \to Bool$$

where $Bool = \{tt, ff\}$, is defined in a rather obvious way: for any formula $\varphi \in Form$ and state sta over A

$$\begin{aligned} SF.T\varphi.sta &= tt && \text{if } F_{MK}.\varphi.sta = tt, \\ &\quad ff && \text{otherwise,} \end{aligned}$$

and

$$\begin{aligned} SF.NT\varphi.sta &= ff && \text{if } F_{MK}.\varphi.sta = tt, \\ &\quad tt && \text{otherwise.} \end{aligned}$$

It is easy to see that we can always recover the value (in $Boolerr$) of any formula just by considering the truth of appropriate signed formulas:

Fact 6.1 For any formula $\varphi \in Form$, for any structure A and state sta over A:

1. $F_{MK}.\varphi.sta = tt$ iff $SF.T\varphi.sta = tt$,
2. $F_{MK}.\varphi.sta = ff$ iff $SF.T\neg\varphi.sta = tt$,
3. $F_{MK}.\varphi.sta = ee$ iff $SF.NT\varphi.sta = SF.NT\neg\varphi.sta = tt$.

Consider any structure A and state sta over A. Just as for formulas, for any signed formula $\rho \in SForm$ we say that A *satisfies* ρ in sta, or that ρ *holds in* $\langle A, sta \rangle$ if $SF.\rho.sta = tt$. For any set $\Omega \subseteq SForm$ of signed formulas, we say that $\langle A, sta \rangle$ is a *model of* Ω if each $\rho \in \Omega$ holds in $\langle A, sta \rangle$; we say that Ω is *satisfiable* if it has a model.

For any set $\Phi \subseteq Form$ we write $T\Phi$ for $\{T\varphi \mid \varphi \in \Phi\}$ and $NT\Phi$ for $\{NT\varphi \mid \varphi \in \Phi\}$.

Theorem 6.1 A sequent $\Gamma \vdash \Delta$ is valid if and only if the set $T\Gamma \cup NT\Delta$ of signed formulas is not satisfiable.

7 Semantic tableaux

Theorem 6.1 ensures that we can consider (non-)satisfiability of sets of signed formulas instead of considering validity of sequents. A classical tool for verifying whether a set of signed formulas is satisfiable is the method of semantic tableaux introduced originally in [Beth 59] and then modified to cover the non-standard three-valued case in [Koletsos 76], where it was used to develop a sound and complete Gentzen-style formalization of the three-valued Kleene calculus.

In the sequel we follow the general line of [Koletsos 76], although we have a somewhat different set of rules, as we are dealing with a different calculus here. Therefore we omit most technicalities which may be found in [Koletsos 76] (this includes some technical lemmas and detailed proofs) and concentrate on explaining the general idea, highlighting the key points of the reasoning and discussing some details specific to the calculus we are formalizing.

Let us start with an informal description of the method.

A semantic tableau for a finite set Ω of signed formulas is a binary tree of signed formulas (to be more precise: of their occurrences) which may be used to determine whether Ω is satisfiable. It is built downwards (i.e. from the root towards the leaves) starting from a chain containing all the formulas in Ω. The basic idea is that each branch of the tree should contain all formulas which must be simultaneously satisfied if Ω is to be satisfied. Thus, each maximal branch represents an alternative "way" of satisfying Ω. A branch B is expanded downwards or split into two branches by appending new formula(s) which must hold in order that some formula $\rho \in B$ hold. If, for example, $\rho \cong T(\alpha \wedge \beta)$, then B is expanded by appending $T\alpha$ (and $T\beta$) since the only way to make $T(\alpha \wedge \beta)$ true is to make both $T\alpha$ and $T\beta$ true. If $\rho \cong NT(\alpha \wedge \beta)$ then B is split at the end, with one subbranch containing $NT\alpha$ and the other containing $NT\beta$, since there are two ways to make $NT(\alpha \wedge \beta)$ true: one is to make $NT\alpha$ true, and the other is to make $NT\beta$ true. The semantics of formulas may be used to determine a whole set of such rules for expanding and splitting branches. We refer to these rules as *tableau rules*. In fact, we have just mentioned three such tableau rules for the calculus we are formalizing:

$$\frac{T(\alpha \wedge \beta)}{T\alpha} \qquad \frac{T(\alpha \wedge \beta)}{T\beta} \qquad \frac{NT(\alpha \wedge \beta)}{NT\alpha \mid NT\beta}$$

Each branch is expanded until we encounter a contradiction, i.e. discover a pair of signed formulas that cannot be simultaneously true. Then the branch is *closed* by applying one of the following two closure rules:

$$\frac{T\varphi}{T\neg\varphi} \qquad \frac{T\varphi}{NT\varphi}$$

which list the "forbidden" pairs of fomulas. Such a branch (traditionally marked by a double line at its end) is not expanded further, as it does not represent any possible way of satisfying Ω. The lack of what one might think to be a closure rule

$$\frac{NT\varphi}{NT\neg\varphi}$$

expresses the fact that the law of excluded middle does not hold for the logic we formalize.

With this ideas in mind let us try to give a bit more formal definition.

A *semantic tableau* for a set $\Omega = \{\rho_1, \ldots, \rho_n\}$ of signed formulas is a downward progressing tree of signed formulas which is either of the form

$$\rho_1$$
$$\rho_2$$
$$\vdots$$
$$\rho_n$$

or has been obtained from another semantic tableau for Ω by applying one of the tableau rules given in Section 11, where a tableau rule of the form

$$\frac{\rho}{\sigma} \qquad \text{or} \qquad \frac{\rho}{\sigma_1 \mid \sigma_2}$$

may be applied to a branch B of a tableau if B contains ρ and then

- as a result of applying the rule $\dfrac{\rho}{\sigma}$ to B, this branch is expanded by attaching σ to its end, and

- as a result of applying the rule $\dfrac{\rho}{\sigma_1 \mid \sigma_2}$ to B, this branch is split at the end into two sub-branches with σ_1 added at the end of the left subbranch and σ_2 added at the end of the right subbranch.

Some of the rules given in Section 11 deserve special attenion, as they reflect the specific pecularities of McCarthy's connectives. For example, the rule

$$\frac{T(\alpha \vee \beta)}{T\alpha \mid T(\neg\alpha \wedge \beta)}$$

indicates the characteristic asymmetry of McCarthy's disjunction. Indeed, $\alpha \vee \beta$ is true if and only if either α is true (for the evaluation is "lazy") or $\neg\alpha \wedge \beta$ is true, i.e. α is false (but defined) and β is true.

By a dual analysis we obtain the rules:

$$\frac{NT(\alpha \vee \beta)}{NT\alpha} \quad \text{and} \quad \frac{NT(\alpha \vee \beta)}{NT\neg\alpha \mid NT\beta}$$

Indeed, if $\alpha \vee \beta$ is not true then certainly α cannot be true, and moreover, either $\neg\alpha$ or β must not be true.

Since we use Kleene's quantifiers, the rules for quantified formulas are the same as in [Koletsos 76] and we do not discuss them here.

It should be pointed out, though, that similarly as in [Koletsos 76] for each connective (or quantifier) we have two sets of tableau rules: one for formulas formed using this connective, and another for negations of such formulas. This, of course, is a consequence of the fact that we are dealing with a three-valued calculus here, and hence we have to know the truth of both a formula and its negation to recover its original value (in the three-valued case, $T\neg\varphi$ and $NT\varphi$ are not equivalent — cf. Fact 6.1). Thus, the above rules describing disjunction must be considered together with the following:

$$\frac{T\neg(\alpha \vee \beta)}{T\neg\alpha} \qquad \frac{T\neg(\alpha \vee \beta)}{T\neg\beta} \qquad \frac{NT\neg(\alpha \vee \beta)}{NT\neg\alpha \mid NT\neg\beta}$$

It is perhaps worth pointing out that alternatively we could have used here de Morgan's law in the form of the rules:

$$\frac{T\neg(\alpha \vee \beta)}{T(\neg\alpha \wedge \neg\beta)} \qquad \frac{NT\neg(\alpha \vee \beta)}{NT(\neg\alpha \wedge \neg\beta)}$$

We would need fewer tableaux rules then (as well as fewer rules in the formal logical systems we derive from them) but we feel that the overall justification of the soundness and completeness of the resulting systems would be less clear.

A branch of a semantic tableau is *closed* if it contains a pair of formulas appearing in one of the closure rules given in Section 11:

$$\begin{array}{cc} T\varphi & T\varphi \\ T\neg\varphi & NT\varphi \end{array}$$

A semantic tableau is *closed* if all its branches are closed.

A semantic tableau is *complete* if none of its open branches can be expanded any further by applying any of the rules.

Intuitively, a set of signed formulas with a closed semantic tableau cannot be satisfiable, as each of the alternative ways leading to its satisfiability results in a contradiction. The opposite implication is true as well:

Theorem 7.1 A finite set $\Omega \subset SForm$ of signed formulas is not satisfiable if and only if it has a closed semantic tableau.

Theorems 6.1 and 7.1 directly imply the following key fact.

Corollary 7.1 A sequent $\Gamma \vdash \Delta$ is valid if and only if the set $T\Gamma \cup NT\Delta$ of signed formulas has a closed tableau.

8 A complete deduction system for valid sequents

Corollary 7.1 hints at a certain method of obtaining a deduction system for valid sequents out of the set of tableau rules. This method was discussed in [Koletsos 76], although we find the presentation there far from clear. Moreover, that paper is not easily available, and since we certainly feel that the method is worth popularising, we will outline it in this section, giving in addition explicit forms of inference rules for the sequent calculus corresponding to the basic types of tableau rules (in [Koletsos 76] each inference rule was derived separately, which obscured the general pattern of reasoning).

First some notation: for any finite set $\Omega \subset SForm$ of signed formulas, by $seq.\Omega$ we denote the sequent $\Gamma \vdash \Delta$ where $\Omega = T\Gamma \cup NT\Delta$. Notice that Corollary 7.1 may be rephrased as follows: for any finite set $\Omega \subset SForm$ of signed formulas, $seq.\Omega$ is valid if and only if Ω has a closed tableau.

Now, consider a tableau rule of the form $\dfrac{\rho}{\sigma}$.

Then, by the definitions of Section 7, any branch of a semantic tableau that contains ρ may be expanded by adding σ to it. Consequently, for any finite set $\Omega \subset SForm$ of signed formulas, $\Omega \cup \{\rho\}$ has a closed tableau provided that $\Omega \cup \{\rho, \sigma\}$ has a closed tableau. Hence, by Corollary 7.1, the sequent $seq.(\Omega \cup \{\rho\})$ is valid whenever the sequent $seq.(\Omega \cup \{\rho, \sigma\})$ is. For example, taking $\rho \cong T\varphi$ and $\sigma \cong T\psi$, the tableau rule of the form

$$\frac{T\varphi}{T\psi}$$

gives rise to the following inference rule for deriving valid sequents:

$$\frac{\Gamma, \varphi, \psi \vdash \Delta}{\Gamma, \varphi \vdash \Delta}$$

In other words, if we have a tableau rule $\dfrac{T\varphi}{T\psi}$ then the inference rule $\dfrac{\Gamma, \varphi, \psi \vdash \Delta}{\Gamma, \varphi \vdash \Delta}$ leads from valid sequents to valid sequents.

In particular, since one of our tableau rules is $\dfrac{T(\alpha \wedge \beta)}{T\alpha}$, we can include in the deduction system for valid sequents the following inference rule:

$$\frac{\Gamma, \alpha \wedge \beta, \alpha \vdash \Delta}{\Gamma, \alpha \wedge \beta \vdash \Delta}$$

The situation with the splitting rules of the form $\dfrac{\rho}{\sigma_1 \mid \sigma_2}$ is quite similar. Here we know that for any finite set $\Omega \subset SForm$ of signed formulas, $\Omega \cup \{\rho\}$ has a closed tableau provided that both $\Omega \cup \{\rho, \sigma_1\}$ and $\Omega \cup \{\rho, \sigma_2\}$ have closed tableaux. Hence, the sequent $seq.(\Omega \cup \{\rho\})$ is valid whenever the sequents $seq.(\Omega \cup \{\rho, \sigma\})$ and $seq.(\Omega \cup \{\rho, \sigma_1\})$ are. For example, taking $\rho \cong NT\varphi$, $\sigma_1 \cong NT\psi_1$ and $\sigma_2 \cong NT\psi_2$, the tableau rule

$$\frac{NT\varphi}{NT\psi_1 \mid NT\psi_2}$$

gives rise to the following inference rule for deriving valid sequents:

$$\frac{\Gamma \vdash \Delta, \varphi, \psi_1 \quad \Gamma \vdash \Delta, \varphi, \psi_2}{\Gamma \vdash \Delta, \varphi}$$

In particular, since one of our tableau rules is $\dfrac{NT(\alpha \wedge \beta)}{NT\alpha \mid NT\beta}$, we can include in the deduction system for valid sequents the following inference rule:

$$\frac{\Gamma \vdash \Delta, \alpha \wedge \beta, \alpha \quad \Gamma \vdash \Delta, \alpha \wedge \beta, \beta}{\Gamma \vdash \Delta, \alpha \wedge \beta}$$

What is not very elegant here is that apparently we are forced to include φ and $\alpha \wedge \beta$, respectively, in the top sequents of the above rules, although intuitively they should not be necessary. In fact, we can get rid of them in the presence of the universally accepted *thinning rules*:

$$\frac{\Gamma \vdash \Delta}{\Gamma, \varphi \vdash \Delta} \qquad\qquad \frac{\Gamma \vdash \Delta}{\Gamma \vdash \Delta, \varphi}$$

which clearly lead from valid sequents to valid sequents. It is easy to see that in the presence of the thinning rules the four rules of we have mentioned above are equivalent to, respectively:

$$\frac{\Gamma, \psi \vdash \Delta}{\Gamma, \varphi \vdash \Delta} \qquad\qquad \frac{\Gamma \vdash \Delta, \psi_1 \quad \Gamma \vdash \Delta, \psi_2}{\Gamma \vdash \Delta, \varphi}$$

and

$$\frac{\Gamma, \alpha \vdash \Delta}{\Gamma, \alpha \wedge \beta \vdash \Delta} \qquad\qquad \frac{\Gamma \vdash \Delta, \alpha \quad \Gamma \vdash \Delta, \beta}{\Gamma \vdash \Delta, \alpha \wedge \beta}$$

The above considerations are summarized in the following table which gives the inference rules for deriving valid sequents induced by tableau rules of the form we are using:

Tableau rule	Inference rule for sequents
$\dfrac{T\varphi}{T\psi}$	$\dfrac{\Gamma, \psi \vdash \Delta}{\Gamma, \varphi \vdash \Delta}$
$\dfrac{NT\varphi}{NT\psi}$	$\dfrac{\Gamma \vdash \Delta, \psi}{\Gamma \vdash \Delta, \varphi}$
$\dfrac{T\varphi}{T\psi_1 \mid T\psi_2}$	$\dfrac{\Gamma, \psi_1 \vdash \Delta \quad \Gamma, \psi_2 \vdash \Delta}{\Gamma, \varphi \vdash \Delta}$
$\dfrac{NT\varphi}{NT\psi_1 \mid NT\psi_2}$	$\dfrac{\Gamma \vdash \Delta, \psi_1 \quad \Gamma \vdash \Delta, \psi_2}{\Gamma \vdash \Delta, \varphi}$

It seems even more obvious how the closure rules for tableaux give rise to axioms of the sequent calculus. By the closure rules, for any finite set $\Omega \subset SForm$ of signed formulas, the sets $\Omega \cup \{T\varphi, T\neg\varphi\}$ and $\Omega \cup \{T\varphi, NT\varphi\}$ have closed tableaux, and so the corresponding sequents:

$$\Gamma, \varphi, \neg\varphi \vdash \Delta \qquad \text{and} \qquad \Gamma, \varphi \vdash \Delta, \varphi$$

may be taken as axioms of the calculus for deriving valid sequents.

Applying the above schema to each of the tableau rules (given in Section 11, the first column) we obtain a set of inference rules for deriving valid sequents induced by the tableau rules. These inference rules are listed in Section 11 (second column) together with the extra thinning rules and the axioms.

We have obtained thus a deductive system for our sequent calculus. From now on it will be denoted by SC. For any sequent $\Gamma \vdash \Delta$, we will write $\Gamma \vdash_{SC} \Delta$ if the sequent $\Gamma \vdash \Delta$ is derivable in SC, i.e. if it can be derived from the axioms of SC by means of the rules of SC (applied finitely many times).

Theorem 8.1 A sequent $\Gamma \vdash \Delta$ is valid if and only if it is derivable in SC, that is, $\Gamma \models \Delta$ if and only if $\Gamma \vdash_{SC} \Delta$.

9 A natural deduction system

Intuitively, by a natural deduction we mean the process of deducing conclusions from assumptions used in everyday life. Such a process is formalized by two types of logical systems: Gentzen-style sequent calculi (like that discussed in Section 8) and so-called *natural deduction systems*. An extensive classical study of natural deduction systems may be found in [Prawitz 65]. Here we will only give a brief description of such systems and develop such a system for the logic we are studying.

A natural deduction system is composed solely of inference rules, used for drawing immediate conclusions from given assumptions. The inference rules are of the form

$$\frac{\begin{matrix}(\Gamma_1) & & (\Gamma_n)\\ \varphi_1 & \cdots & \varphi_n\end{matrix}}{\varphi}$$

where $\varphi_1, \ldots, \varphi_n$ and φ are formulas and $\Gamma_1, \ldots, \Gamma_n$ are finite sets of formulas. Such a rule should be read: if we have derived $\varphi_1, \ldots, \varphi_n$ from $\Gamma_1, \ldots, \Gamma_n$, respectively, then φ is true without any additional assumptions, i.e. we can derive φ from $\varphi_1, \ldots, \varphi_n$ "discharging" assumptions $\Gamma_1, \ldots, \Gamma_n$ used to derive $\varphi_1, \ldots, \varphi_n$, respectively.

A typical simple form of such a rule is, of course, when all the sets $\Gamma_1, \ldots, \Gamma_n$ are empty. We write such rules simply as follows:

$$\frac{\varphi_1 \cdots \varphi_n}{\varphi}$$

which should be read: if all $\varphi_1, \ldots, \varphi_n$ are true then φ is true as well.[3]

A standard example of a rule where some assumptions are indeed discharged is the following rule of classical logic

$$\frac{\begin{matrix} & (\alpha) & (\beta)\\ \alpha \vee \beta & \varphi & \varphi\end{matrix}}{\varphi}$$

which should be read: if $\alpha \vee \beta$ is true, we have derived φ from α, and we have derived φ from β, then φ is true without any additional assumptions (that is, we can "discharge" assumptions α and β previously used to prove φ).

The notion of a *derivation tree* in such a natural deduction system is defined inductively. Any (occurrence of a) formula is such a tree. More complex trees are formed using the inference rules of the system in the obvious way. For example, if we have an inference rule $\dfrac{\varphi_1 \cdots \varphi_n}{\varphi}$ and we have built derivation trees $T_1, \ldots, T_n$ with formulas $\varphi_1, \ldots, \varphi_n$, respectively, at their roots, then we can use this rule to form a derivation tree with the formula φ at its root and with the trees $T_1, \ldots, T_n$ as the immediate subtrees.

---

[3] Natural deduction systems with all inference rules of this form are sometimes referred to as *Hilbert-style systems*. In fact, Gentzen-style sequent calculi may be viewed as Hilbert-style systems over a formal language where sequents are viewed as individual formulas.

The case of a rule like

$$\frac{\alpha \vee \beta \quad \overset{(\alpha)}{\varphi} \quad \overset{(\beta)}{\varphi}}{\varphi}$$

is a bit more complex. Namely, given derivation trees T_1, T_2 and T_3 with formulas $\alpha \vee \beta$, φ, and φ, respectively, at their roots, we can use this rule to form a new derivation tree with the formula φ at its root and T_1, T_2 and T_3 as its immediate subtrees (as before) but additionally we are allowed to mark occurrences of the formula α at the leaves of T_2 and occurrences of β at the leaves of T_3 as "discharged".

In general, given an inference rule

$$\frac{\overset{(\Gamma_1)}{\varphi_1} \quad \dots \quad \overset{(\Gamma_n)}{\varphi_n}}{\varphi}$$

and derivation trees T_1, ..., T_n with formulas φ_1, ..., φ_n, respectively, at their roots, we can use this rule to form a derivation tree with the formula φ at its root, with the trees T_1, ..., T_n as its immediate subtrees, and with the occurrences of formulas in Γ_1,...,Γ_n at the leaves of the trees T_1, ..., T_n, respectively, marked as "discharged".

Now, a derivation of a formula φ from assumptions Γ in a natural deduction system is any derivation tree in this system with the formula φ at its root and all the formulas at its leaves that are not marked as "discharged" in the set Γ.

There is an obvious way to compare natural deduction systems with Gentzen-style systems (over the same logical language). For example, we say that a Gentzen-style system is equivalent to a natural deduction system whenever a sequent of the form $\Gamma \vdash \{\delta\}$ is derivable in the Gentzen-style system if and only if there is a derivation of δ from Γ in the natural deduction system.

Notice that we have to consider here again only single-conclusion sequents, as there is no obvious way of generalizing natural deduction systems to the multi-conclusion case. From now on, single-conclusion sequents as above will be written in the form $\Gamma \vdash \delta$. In this context it is important to realize that, roughly, in the Gentzen-style sequent calculus we have defined in the previous section a single-conclusion sequent may be derived if and only if it may be derived using only single-conclusion sequents.

In the rest of this section we will develop a natural deduction system NDS equivalent to the sequent calculus for deriving valid sequents, SC, defined in the previous section.

There can be no uniform way to define a natural deduction system equivalent to a given Gentzen-style sequent calculus. There is, however, an obvious strategy which we will try to employ here. Roughly:

- for each axiom $\Gamma \vdash \delta$ of SC, there must be a rule of NDS allowing us to derive δ from Γ;

- for each inference rule of SC of the form

$$\frac{\Gamma_1 \vdash \delta_1 \ \dots \ \Gamma_n \vdash \delta_n}{\Gamma \vdash \delta}$$

  there must be a rule of NDS allowing us to construct a derivation of δ from Γ given derivations of δ_1, ..., δ_n from, respectively, Γ_1, ..., Γ_n.

There is no uniform recipe for finding an NDS rule corresponding in the above sense to a given SC rule. We must simply examine the rules of SC (in their single-conclusion versions) and guess an appropriate NDS rule. We will discuss a few typical cases.

The simplest case is that of an inference rule of SC of the form

$$\frac{\Gamma \vdash \varphi_1 \ \dots \ \Gamma \vdash \varphi_n}{\Gamma \vdash \psi}$$

which clearly corresponds to a natural deduction inference rule of the form

$$\frac{\varphi_1 \dots \varphi_n}{\psi}$$

Then, an *SC* inference rule of the form

$$\frac{\Gamma, \varphi \vdash \delta}{\Gamma, \psi \vdash \delta}$$

induces in the above sense an *NDS* rule $\frac{\psi}{\varphi}$. Indeed, given a derivation of δ from $\Gamma \cup \{\varphi\}$ we can replace the leave(s) holding the formula φ by derivation(s) of φ from ψ built in the trivial way using this rule and then we obtain a derivation of δ from $\Gamma \cup \{\psi\}$.

The most complicated case is that of the *SC* rules like

$$\frac{\Gamma, \alpha \vdash \delta \quad \Gamma, \neg\alpha \wedge \beta \vdash \delta}{\Gamma, \alpha \vee \beta \vdash \delta} \qquad \frac{\Gamma, \neg\alpha \vdash \delta \quad \Gamma, \alpha \wedge \neg\beta \vdash \delta}{\Gamma, \neg(\alpha \wedge \beta) \vdash \delta}$$

Then, the corresponding natural deduction rules are:

$$\frac{\begin{array}{ccc} & (\alpha) & (\neg\alpha \wedge \beta) \\ \alpha \vee \beta & \delta & \delta \end{array}}{\delta} \qquad \frac{\begin{array}{ccc} & (\neg\alpha) & (\alpha \wedge \neg\beta) \\ \neg(\alpha \wedge \beta) & \delta & \delta \end{array}}{\delta}$$

It is clear how the axioms of *SC* translate to the rules of *NDS*: the axiom $\Gamma, \neg\varphi, \varphi \vdash \delta$ induces the rule $\frac{\varphi \quad \neg\varphi}{\delta}$. The other axiom, $\Gamma, \varphi \vdash \varphi$ needs no natural deduction rule, since by definition there is always a derivation of φ from any set that contains φ.

It remains to consider the thinning rules. The rule $\frac{\Gamma \vdash \delta}{\Gamma, \varphi \vdash \delta}$ needs no natural deduction rule, as any derivation of δ from Γ is a derivation of δ from any set that includes Γ.

The other thinning rule, $\frac{\Gamma \vdash \Delta}{\Gamma \vdash \Delta, \varphi}$, deserves some special attention (although it does not require any natural deduction rule either) as it is the only rule that allows us to derive a single-conclusion sequent from a non-single-conclusion one. This is the case if we take $\Delta = \emptyset$. However, it is quite clear then that the only way to derive the sequent $\Gamma \vdash \emptyset$ is using the axiom $\Gamma', \neg\varphi, \varphi \vdash \Delta$, and then we can apply the rule $\frac{\varphi \quad \neg\varphi}{\delta}$ to obtain a derivation of δ from Γ.

We can apply the above ideas to all the rules of the *SC* calculus listed in Section 11 (second column) to obtain the set of natural deduction rules listed in Section 11, third column. We will refer to this natural deduction system as *NDS*, and write $\Gamma \vdash_{NDS} \delta$ if there is a derivation of δ from Γ in *NDS*.

Theorem 9.1 If a sequent $\Gamma \vdash \delta$ is derivable in *SC* then there is a derivation of δ from Γ, that is,

$$\Gamma \vdash_{SC} \delta \qquad \text{implies} \qquad \Gamma \vdash_{NDS} \delta$$

Theorem 9.2 For any finite set $\Gamma \subset Form$ of formulas and formula $\delta \in Form$,

$$\Gamma \models \delta \qquad \text{iff} \qquad \Gamma \vdash_{NDS} \delta$$

10 Final remarks

To conclude the paper, let us try to indicate briefly how the logical system presented here may be used in program specification and verification. Very roughly, we have the following model in mind:

Most programming languages used nowadays are parameterised by an underlying structure consisting of data the programs of the language operate on and of functions and predicates the programs may use as elementary operations and predicates on the data. Given such a structure, the (semantics of) programs are usually presented in terms of their input/output behaviour as state transformations. Three-valued predicates over this structure may be defined in our formalized logic by (open) formulas. Now, in our view, they may be used to describe adequately properties of states. Consequently, properties of state transformations (i.e., properties of programs) may be formulated in terms of so-called *superpredicates*, i.e. relations between predicates. This view has been developed and presented in detail in [Blikle 81a, 81b] where four such superpredicates were discussed (cf. also [Blikle 88]). Since they are all mutually definable in terms of each other, let us concentrate on one of them.

Let A be a structure and let $p, q: State \rightarrow Boolerr$ be two predicates over A. We say that p *is stronger than* q, written $p \Rightarrow q$, if $q.sta = tt$ whenever $p.sta = tt$ for every state sta over A. The superpredicate

$$\Rightarrow: Predicate \times Predicate \rightarrow \{tt, ff\}$$

is not expressible in our formalized language: roughly, there is no formula $st(\_, \_)$ with two "holes" such that for any structure A (with the semantics of formulas F_∇, $\nabla \in \{MK, K\}$) and any two formulas $\varphi, \psi \in Form$, $F_\nabla.\varphi \Rightarrow F_\nabla.\psi$ if and only if the formula $st(\varphi, \psi)$ strongly (resp., weakly) holds in A (cf. [Blikle 87]). It is easy to see that to build such a formula we need a non-monotone propositional connective. For example, if the definedness operator Δ (cf. Sec. 2) were added to our formalized language then

$$st(\varphi, \psi) \cong \Delta\varphi \supset (\varphi \supset (\Delta\psi \wedge \psi))$$

There is, however, another possibility which is more in the spirit of the system we present here. Namely, we can use the s-s-∇-consequence relation (which itself may be viewed as a non-monotone superpredicate):

Let us assume that the class of data structures on which the considered programs are expected to operate is definable by a set Ax of closed formulas. In fact, this in turn may be viewed as a specification of programs that implement the "primitive" functions and predicates of the data structure. Then, for any two formulas $\varphi, \psi \in Form$, for any structure A (with the semantics of formulas F_∇, $\nabla \in \{MK, K\}$) in this class (i.e., strongly satisfying Ax)

$$F_\nabla.\varphi \Rightarrow F_\nabla.\psi \quad \text{iff} \quad Ax, \varphi \models_{ss}^\nabla \psi$$

Of course, the latter fact may be proved using the formal logics we have presented here (for $\nabla = MK$).

It should be emphasized, however, that yet another approach is possible. Superpredicates are total, yielding always true or false, and so they may be viewed as classical predicates of a classical second-order theory we are working in. Thus, this classical second-order theory may be used directly to prove relationships between partial predicates, and hence properties of programs as well. In this approach, suggested in [Blikle 88], the need for a special three-valued logic disappears at all.

Much more experience is necessary to decide which of the approaches outlined above is best suited for practical applications.

11 Appendix: The three formal systems

Tableau rules	Sequent calculus SC	Natural deduction system NDS
$\dfrac{T(\alpha \wedge \beta)}{T\alpha}$	$\dfrac{\Gamma,\alpha \vdash \Delta}{\Gamma,\alpha \wedge \beta \vdash \Delta}$	$\dfrac{\alpha \wedge \beta}{\alpha}$
$\dfrac{T(\alpha \wedge \beta)}{T\beta}$	$\dfrac{\Gamma,\beta \vdash \Delta}{\Gamma,\alpha \wedge \beta \vdash \Delta}$	$\dfrac{\alpha \wedge \beta}{\beta}$
$\dfrac{NT(\alpha \wedge \beta)}{NT\alpha \mid NT\beta}$	$\dfrac{\Gamma \vdash \Delta,\alpha \quad \Gamma \vdash \Delta,\beta}{\Gamma \vdash \Delta,\alpha \wedge \beta}$	$\dfrac{\alpha \quad \beta}{\alpha \wedge \beta}$
$\dfrac{T\neg(\alpha \wedge \beta)}{T\neg\alpha \mid T(\alpha \wedge \neg\beta)}$	$\dfrac{\Gamma,\neg\alpha \vdash \Delta \quad \Gamma,\alpha \wedge \neg\beta \vdash \Delta}{\Gamma,\neg(\alpha \wedge \beta) \vdash \Delta}$	$\dfrac{\neg(\alpha \wedge \beta) \quad \begin{matrix}(\neg\alpha)\\ \delta\end{matrix} \quad \begin{matrix}(\alpha \wedge \neg\beta)\\ \delta\end{matrix}}{\delta}$
$\dfrac{NT\neg(\alpha \wedge \beta)}{NT\neg\alpha}$	$\dfrac{\Gamma \vdash \Delta,\neg\alpha}{\Gamma \vdash \Delta,\neg(\alpha \wedge \beta)}$	$\dfrac{\neg\alpha}{\neg(\alpha \wedge \beta)}$
$\dfrac{NT\neg(\alpha \wedge \beta)}{NT\alpha \mid NT\neg\beta}$	$\dfrac{\Gamma \vdash \Delta,\alpha \quad \Gamma \vdash \Delta,\neg\beta}{\Gamma \vdash \Delta,\neg(\alpha \wedge \beta)}$	$\dfrac{\alpha \quad \neg\beta}{\neg(\alpha \wedge \beta)}$
$\dfrac{T(\alpha \vee \beta)}{T\alpha \mid T(\neg\alpha \wedge \beta)}$	$\dfrac{\Gamma,\alpha \vdash \Delta \quad \Gamma,\neg\alpha \wedge \beta \vdash \Delta}{\Gamma,\alpha \vee \beta \vdash \Delta}$	$\dfrac{\alpha \vee \beta \quad \begin{matrix}(\alpha)\\ \delta\end{matrix} \quad \begin{matrix}(\neg\alpha \wedge \beta)\\ \delta\end{matrix}}{\delta}$
$\dfrac{NT(\alpha \vee \beta)}{NT\alpha}$	$\dfrac{\Gamma \vdash \Delta,\alpha}{\Gamma \vdash \Delta,\alpha \vee \beta}$	$\dfrac{\alpha}{\alpha \vee \beta}$
$\dfrac{NT(\alpha \vee \beta)}{NT\neg\alpha \mid NT\beta}$	$\dfrac{\Gamma \vdash \Delta,\neg\alpha \quad \Gamma \vdash \Delta,\beta}{\Gamma \vdash \Delta,\alpha \vee \beta}$	$\dfrac{\neg\alpha \quad \beta}{\alpha \vee \beta}$
$\dfrac{T\neg(\alpha \vee \beta)}{T\neg\alpha}$	$\dfrac{\Gamma,\neg\alpha \vdash \Delta}{\Gamma,\neg(\alpha \vee \beta) \vdash \Delta}$	$\dfrac{\neg(\alpha \vee \beta)}{\neg\alpha}$
$\dfrac{T\neg(\alpha \vee \beta)}{T\neg\beta}$	$\dfrac{\Gamma,\neg\beta \vdash \Delta}{\Gamma,\neg(\alpha \vee \beta) \vdash \Delta}$	$\dfrac{\neg(\alpha \vee \beta)}{\neg\beta}$
$\dfrac{NT\neg(\alpha \vee \beta)}{NT\neg\alpha \mid NT\neg\beta}$	$\dfrac{\Gamma \vdash \Delta,\neg\alpha \quad \Gamma \vdash \Delta,\neg\beta}{\Gamma \vdash \Delta,\neg(\alpha \vee \beta)}$	$\dfrac{\neg\alpha \quad \neg\beta}{\neg(\alpha \vee \beta)}$
$\dfrac{T\neg\neg\alpha}{T\alpha}$	$\dfrac{\Gamma,\alpha \vdash \Delta}{\Gamma,\neg\neg\alpha \vdash \Delta}$	$\dfrac{\neg\neg\alpha}{\alpha}$
$\dfrac{NT\neg\neg\alpha}{NT\alpha}$	$\dfrac{\Gamma \vdash \Delta,\alpha}{\Gamma \vdash \Delta,\neg\neg\alpha}$	$\dfrac{\alpha}{\neg\neg\alpha}$

continued on the next page

Tableau rules	Sequent calculus SC	Natural deduction system NDS
$\dfrac{T((\forall x)\varphi[x])}{T\varphi[t]}$ (*)	$\dfrac{\Gamma, \varphi[t] \vdash \Delta}{\Gamma, (\forall x)\varphi[x] \vdash \Delta}$ (*)	$\dfrac{(\forall x)\varphi[x]}{\varphi[t]}$ (*)
$\dfrac{NT((\forall x)\varphi[x])}{NT\varphi[y]}$ (**)	$\dfrac{\Gamma \vdash \Delta, \varphi[y]}{\Gamma \vdash \Delta, (\forall x)\varphi[x]}$ (**)	$\dfrac{\varphi[y]}{(\forall x)\varphi[x]}$ (**)
$\dfrac{T\neg((\forall x)\varphi[x])}{T\neg\varphi[y]}$ (**)	$\dfrac{\Gamma, \neg\varphi[y] \vdash \Delta}{\Gamma, \neg(\forall x)\varphi[x] \vdash \Delta}$ (**)	$\dfrac{\neg(\forall x)\varphi[x]}{\neg\varphi[y]}$ (**)
$\dfrac{NT\neg((\forall x)\varphi[x])}{NT\neg\varphi[t]}$ (*)	$\dfrac{\Gamma \vdash \Delta, \neg\varphi[t]}{\Gamma \vdash \Delta, \neg(\forall x)\varphi[x]}$ (*)	$\dfrac{\neg\varphi[t]}{\neg(\forall x)\varphi[x]}$ (*)
$\dfrac{T((\exists x)\varphi[x])}{T\varphi[y]}$ (**)	$\dfrac{\Gamma, \varphi[y] \vdash \Delta}{\Gamma, (\exists x)\varphi[x] \vdash \Delta}$ (**)	$\dfrac{(\exists x)\varphi[x]}{\varphi[y]}$ (**)
$\dfrac{NT((\exists x)\varphi[x])}{NT\varphi[t]}$ (*)	$\dfrac{\Gamma \vdash \Delta, \varphi[t]}{\Gamma \vdash \Delta, (\exists x)\varphi[x]}$ (*)	$\dfrac{\varphi[t]}{(\exists x)\varphi[x]}$ (*)
$\dfrac{T\neg((\exists x)\varphi[x])}{T\neg\varphi[t]}$ (*)	$\dfrac{\Gamma, \neg\varphi[t] \vdash \Delta}{\Gamma, \neg(\exists x)\varphi[x] \vdash \Delta}$ (*)	$\dfrac{\neg(\exists x)\varphi[x]}{\neg\varphi[t]}$ (*)
$\dfrac{NT\neg((\exists x)\varphi[x])}{NT\neg\varphi[y]}$ (**)	$\dfrac{\Gamma \vdash \Delta, \neg\varphi[y]}{\Gamma \vdash \Delta, \neg(\exists x)\varphi[x]}$ (**)	$\dfrac{\neg\varphi[y]}{\neg(\exists x)\varphi[x]}$ (**)
—	(thinning rules) $\dfrac{\Gamma \vdash \Delta}{\Gamma, \varphi \vdash \Delta}$ $\quad$ $\dfrac{\Gamma \vdash \Delta}{\Gamma \vdash \Delta, \varphi}$	—
Closure rules	Axioms	
$\begin{array}{c} T\varphi \\ \underline{\underline{T\neg\varphi}} \end{array}$	$\Gamma, \varphi, \neg\varphi \vdash \Delta$	$\dfrac{\varphi \quad \neg\varphi}{\delta}$
$\begin{array}{c} T\varphi \\ \underline{\underline{NT\varphi}} \end{array}$	$\Gamma, \varphi \vdash \Delta, \varphi$	—

(*) t is an arbitrary term;

(**) y is a new variable (i.e., respectively, y does not occur free in the formulas in the branch of the tableau where this rule is applied, y does not occur free in the formulas of Γ and of Δ, y does not occur free in non-discharged assumptions).

In the above table, α, β, φ and δ stand for arbitrary formulas, Γ and Δ for arbitrary finite sets of formulas, and x for an arbitrary identifier.

12 References

[Avron 87]
Simple consequence relations.
Report ECS-LFCS-87-30, Laboratory for Foundations of Computer Science, University of Edinburgh, June 1987.

[Barringer, Cheng & Jones 84]
Barringer, H., Cheng, J.H., Jones, C.B.
A logic covering undefinedness in program proofs.
Acta Informatica 21(1984), 251-269.

[Beth 59]
Beth, E.W.
The Foundations of Mathematics.
North-Holland 1959.

[Blikle 81a]
Blikle, A.
On the development of correct specified programs.
IEEE Transactions on Software Engineering SE-7(1981), 251-169.

[Blikle 81b]
Blikle, A.
The clean termination of iterative programs.
Acta Informatica 16(1981), 199-217.

[Blikle 87]
Blikle, A.
MetaSoft Primer: Towards a Metalanguage for Applied Denotational Semantics.
LNCS vol.288, Springer-Verlag 1987.

[Blikle 88]
Blikle, A.
A calculus of three-valued predicates for software specification and validation.
in: Proc. VDM-Europe Symposium 1988, LNCS, Springer-Verlag 1988, this volume.

[Cheng 86]
Cheng, J.H.
A logic for partial functions.
PhD thesis, Department of Computer Science, University of Manchester 1986; Report UMCS-86-7-1.

[Goguen 77]
Goguen, J.A.
Abstract errors for abstract data types.
in: Proc. IFIP Working Conference on the Formal Description of Programming Concepts, St.Andrews 1977 (E.Neuhold, ed.), North-Holland 1978.

[Hoogewijs 79]
Hoogewijs, A.
On a formalization of the non-definedness notion.
Zeitschrift f. Math. Logik u. Grundlagen d. Math. 25(1979), 213-221.

[Hoogewijs 83]
Hoogewijs, A.

A partial predicate calculus in a two-valued logic.
Zeitschrift f. Math. Logik u. Grundlagen d. Math. 29(1983), 239-243.

[Hoogewijs 87]

Hoogewijs, A.
Partial-predicate logic in computer science.
Acta Informatica 24(1987), 381-393.

[Jones 86]

Jones, C.B.
Systematic Software Development Using VDM.
Prentice-Hall 1986.

[Jones 87]

Jones, C.B.
VDM proof obligations and their justification.
in: VDM – A Formal Method at Work, Proc. VDM-Europe Symposium 1987, LNCS vol.252,
Springer-Verlag 1987, 260-286.

[Kleene 38]

Kleene, S.C.
On notation for ordinal numbers.
Journal of Symbolic Logic 3(1938), 150-155.

[Kleene 52]

Kleene, S.C.
Introduction to Mathematics.
North Holland 1952, then republished in 1957, 59, 62, 64, 71.

[Koletsos 76]

Koletsos, G.
Sequent calculus and partial logic.
MSc thesis, The University of Manchester 1976.

[McCarthy 61]

McCarthy, J.
A basis for a mathematical theory of computation.
Western Joint Computer Conference, May 1961; then published in: Computer Programming
and Formal Systems (P.Braffort, D.Hirshberg, eds.) North-Holland 1967, 33-70.

[Owe 85]

Owe, O.
An approach to program reasoning based on a first-order logic for partial functions.
Research Report 89, Institute of Informatics, University of Oslo, February 1985.

[Prawitz 65]

Prawitz, D.
Natural Deduction.
Almquist & Wiksell, Stockholm 1965.

THREE—VALUED PREDICATES FOR SOFTWARE SPECIFICATION AND VALIDATION

Andrzej Blikle
Project MetaSoft
Institute of Computer Science
Polish Academy of Sciences
PKiN P.O.Box 22, 00—901 Warsaw

ABSTRACT

Partial functions, hence also partial predicates, cannot be avoided in algorithms. Although the former fact has been accepted in the theory of software very early, the latter is still not quite commonly recognized. In many programming- and software—specification languages the partiality of predicates (Boolean expressions) is treated only semiformally. On the other hand it is quite well known today that an explicit formal treatment of partial predicates substantially improves the discipline of software specification, programming and validation.

Partial predicates are usually formalized as three—valued functions where the third value corresponds to an undefinedness. This leads, of course, to the necessity of developing a new calculus of predicates and new rules of proving facts expressed by three—valued predicates. One possible approach to the latter problem, which has been already explored by several authors, consists in developing a three-valued logic which is used later in proving properties of software. In this paper we are surveying and analyzing another approach. We show how to combine a calculus of three-valued predicates — to be used in the construction of algorithms — with a two—valued logic — to be used in proving facts about these algorithms. We briefly discuss the possible applications of this approach in the construction of software and of software—specification metalanguages. In the opinion of the author our approach has the advantage of using classical techniques of proofs which are better understood by the majority of users and which are supported by many existing soft- ware systems such as e.g. LCF or MIZAR.

1. INTRODUCTION

This paper has been addressed to readers interested in the mathematical aspects of software specification, development and validation. Together with its companion paper [Konikowska,Tarlecki,Blikle 88] it offers a critical survey on the formalization and application of partial predicates in that context.

The partiality of predicates, both in mathematics and in software, is a fact which has been recognized by many authors (see e.g. [Lukasiewicz 20], [Kleene 38,52], [McCarthy 61], [Hoogevijs 79,83], [Blikle 81a,81b,87], [Barringer,Cheng,Jones 84], [Owe 85], [Jones 86,87], and many others). In the three following examples:

$$y < x + z$$
$$a[i] < a[i+1]$$
$$FAC.x > x^2 \quad \text{where} \quad FAC.x = x=0 \rightarrow 1, \ x*FAC.(x-1).$$

we see three sources of such a partiality which are typical for the context of programming languages. In the first case the value of a predicate becomes undefined whenever the values of x and z are too large to make their sum representable in a machine arithmetics. In the second case, the predicate has an undefined value whenever i goes beyond the range of the array a. In the third case the undefinedness results from the fact that for x<0 the procedure FAC.x enters an infinite loop of recursive calls.

Partial predicates cannot be avoided in algorithms. On the other hand, any attempt to the evaluation of a predicate outside of the domain of its definedness leads to a failure. In order to cope with this problem we have to formally introduce partial predicates into the semantics of programming— and software-specification languages and into logic where we carry out software validation.

Usually partial predicates are formalized as three-valued predicates with the third value corresponding to undefinedness. As we shall see later, this solution has a technical advantage since it allows for a "lazy" treatment of undefinedness (Sec.2).

The formalization of three-valued predicates requires the solution of two groups of problems:

1) We have to establish the semantics of three-valued formulas (Boolean expressions, assertions, etc.), i.e. we have to construct a calculus of three-valued predicates.

2) We have to establish a mechanism of proving facts expressed in terms of three-valued formulas, i.e. we have to construct a logic suitable for handling three-valued hypotheses.

The former problem consists of defining a three-valued extension of classical propositional connectives – **and, or, implies** and **not** and of quantifiers. Here we can either assume that the new connectives are strict (i.e. return an undefined value whenever at least one of its arguments is undefined) or that they are not strict, i.e. can be evaluated "lazily". As we shall argue in Sec.2 the latter solution is more convenient, and therefore we discuss it in the paper. Here we may choose between the calculi defined by S.C.Kleene [Kleene 38,52] or by J.McCarthy [McCarthy 61]. We can also construct their combinations.

The latter problem is more difficult. Here two essentially different approaches are possible.

One approach consists of constructing a three-valued logic corresponding to an earlier chosen calculus of three-valued predicates. That approach has been explored in [Hoogewijs 79,83,87], [Barringer,Chang,Jones 84], [Owe 85], [Jones 86,87] and then surveyed, analyzed and further developed in [Konikowska,Tarlecki,Blikle 88]. It leads to a logic where proving theorems requires a little more than a usual mathematical skill since many proof-rules and proof-techniques known from two-valued logic are not applicable.

An alternative approach has been proposed in [Blikle 81a,81b,87]. It consists in enriching the calculus of three-valued predicates by two-valued predicates on predicates which we call **superpredicates**. In the enriched calculus we can conveniently express all these facts about data and algorithms which are relevant for software specification and validation. In particular, we can express partial and total correctness of programs and the soundness of program-transformation rules. The proofs of these facts are carried out in the classical logic. We do not need, therefore, to abandon our "two-valued intuition" in reasoning and we can support our proofs by many existing computer systems which support the use of two-valued logic such as e.g. LCF or MIZAR. We return to this comment later in Sec.6

The latter idea is surveyed, analyzed and further developed in this paper. We start from a general discussion about the non-strict treatment of undefinedness (Sec.2).

This is followed by the comparison of three non-strict propositional calculi: of J.Lukasiewicz, of S.C.Kleene and of J.McCarthy (Sec.3). For a further discussion we choose only the second and the third calculus, since the first is not implementable.

In Sec.4 we briefly describe and analyze four predicate calculi which result from the former two propositional calculi and from two corresponding definitions of quantifiers. For further investigations we choose two of them: a calculus with Kleene's propositional connectives and quantifiers and a calculus with McCarthy's propositional connectives and Kleene's quantifiers. The former has been used as a basis for different three-valued logics developed in [Hoogewijs 79,83] and in [Barringer,Chang, Jones 84]. It was also applied to software specification and validation in [Jones 86,87]. The latter was primarily developed as a stand-alone calculus for software specification, development and validation in [Blikle 81a,81b, 87]. The corresponding three-valued logics for that calculus has been described in [Konikowska,Tarlecki,Blikle 88].

In Sec.5 we show how to enrich a calculus of three-valued predicates by two-valued superpredicates and how to use these superpredicates in defining partial and total correctness of programs and in formulating the corresponding proof rules. We do not go too far into these applications since they have been already discussed in [Blikle 81a,81b,87].

Sec.6 contains remarks about the possible applications of our method in software design and in the construction of software-specification languages.

2. REMARKS ABOUT THE STRICTNESS OF PROPOSITIONAL CONNECTIVES

As we have mentioned already in the former section partial predicates are usually formalized by "replacing" the undefinedness by a third logical value. We do so in order to be able to introduce non-strict propositional connectives where the undefinedness of one argument does not necessarily lead to the undefinedness of the result. The present section is devoted to the discussion of that problem.

We start by introducing two domains of logical values:

    Bool   = {tt,ff}
    Boolerr = {tt,ff,ee}

"Boolerr" stands for Bool+Error and ee may be regarded as an abstract error. As we shall see later, our propositional calculi will be constructed in such a way that ee may be interpreted either as a computed error-signal or as a true undefinedness resulting from an infinite computation. Therefore tt and ff are referred to as **defined values** and ee as an **undefined value**.

By a **three-valued propositional calculus** we mean an algebra over Boolerr with four **propositional operators** also called **propositional connectives**:

$$\textbf{not} : \text{Boolerr} \rightarrow \text{Boolerr}$$
$$\textbf{and, or, implies} : \text{Boolerr} \times \text{Boolerr} \rightarrow \text{Boolerr}$$

Sometimes it contains also a fifth operator:

$$\textbf{def} : \text{Boolerr} \rightarrow \text{Bool}$$

such that **def** tt = **def** ff = tt and **def** ee = ff. At present, however, we exclude this operator from our calculi and we return to it in Sec.7.

We say that a three-valued propositional calculus is an extension of the classical calculus if the first four operators coincide with the classical operators on Bool. For obvious reasons we shall not go beyond such extensions in our applications.

In extending propositional connectives from Bool to Boolerr an apparently very natural solution is to assume that all connectives are **strict**, i.e. that they evaluate to ee, whenever at least one of their arguments is ee. That solution corresponds directly to the situation where instead of considering three-valued total predicates we are considering two-valued partial predicates. As we are showing below that solution is rather inconvenient for our applications, although it may be convenient in other cases (cf. [Colmerauer,Pique 81]).

Assume that we are given two predicates p:A→Boolerr and q:B→Boolerr, where A and B are disjoint domains. Assume further that on the ground of our calculus we want to define a third predicate r:(A∪B)→Boolerr, such that r = p∪q, where "∪" is the usual union of sets (functions are sets of pairs and therefore p q makes sense; moreover, since the domains of p and q are disjoint, p∪q is a function). The predicate r tests the property expressed by p in A and the property expressed by q in B. In programming languages this corresponds to the use of a case constructor.

In the first attempt to solve our problem we may try to write the following equation:

$$r.x = (x \epsilon A \text{ implies } p.x) \text{ and}$$
$$(x \epsilon B \text{ implies } q.x) \tag{2.1}$$

where "=" is the equality in Boolerr. Unfortunately, if our propositional connectives are strict, then this is an incorrect solution. Indeed, r.x=ee for all $x \epsilon A \cup B$ since for any x in $A \cup B$ either p.x=ee or q.x=ee. As is easy to show, r cannot be defined as a propositional combination of p and q if we use strict propositional connectives

The strictness of abstract functions corresponds to a so called **eager evaluation** of expressions. When we eagerly evaluate "$x \epsilon A$ **implies** p.x", we first evaluate both subexpressions "$x \epsilon A$" and "p.x" and only when this step is successfully completed we compute the final value of implication. In our case, if $x \epsilon A$ evaluates to ff, then p.x is undefined and therefore the whole computation fails. The eager evaluation of expressions is what mathematicians believe that they do, and therefore – although this is not a very convenient evaluation strategy – it has been chosen in several programming languages. For instance, the **and** and **or** in many Pascal compilers and in the standard of ADA have been implemented in that way.

An alternative to eager evaluation is **lazy evaluation**. Informally speaking when we lazily evaluate an expression we assume that all its subexpressions have defined values and we only evaluate as many of them as it is necessary to establish the value of the whole expression. For instance, we can lazily evaluate "$x \epsilon A$ **implies** p.x" in such a way that we first evaluate $x \epsilon A$ and if this yields ff, then we abandon the evaluation of p.x and we set the value of the expression to tt, since ff **implies** a = tt for any aϵBool. Of course if $x \epsilon A$ evaluates to ee (e.g. because A is not a set), then the value of the implication is ee. Examples of programming languages, where boolean expressions are lazily evaluated, are Algol-W, Euclid and C. Also the special operators **and then** and **or else** of Ada, called "the short circuit control forms", are evaluated lazily.

On the formal ground the suggested above lazy evaluation of implication leads to the following non-strictness property of **implies**:

$$ff \text{ implies } bb = tt \quad \text{for any } bb \ \epsilon \ \text{Boolerr} \tag{2.2}$$

As is easy to check, if we assume this property, then (2.1) becomes equivalent to the equation $r = p \cup q$.

The principle of lazy evaluation may be applied to all binary propositional connectives. To see another example consider the following program:

```
INTEGER ARRAY a[1..10];
i:=1;
WHILE i<10 and a[i] < a[i+1] DO i:=i+1 OD
```

Of course, if **and** is strict, i.e. if **and** is evaluated eagerly, then our program
will abort for every array which is ordered increasingly since if i reaches the
value 10, then i<10 is false but a[1]<a[i+1] is undefined. However, if we assume
the following non-strictness of conjunction:

    ff **and** bb = ff   for any bb ε Boolerr   (2.3)

then **and** may be evaluated lazily in which case our program will always terminate
properly.

In the next section we describe and compare three non-strict propositional calculi
which satisfy both (2.2) and (2.3).

3. THREE NON-STRICT PROPOSITIONAL CALCULI

The first known non-strict three-valued propositional calculus is due to a Polish
logician Jan Lukasiewicz [Lukasiewicz 20]. The first such a calculus investigated
in the context of computational mathematics has been described by an American
logician Stephen Cole Kleene [Kleene 38]. A calculus oriented for programming has
been proposed by an American computer scientists John McCarthy [McCarthy 61].

All three calculi are the extensions of the classical calculus and in all of them
not ee = ee. In the calculi of Kleene and McCarthy **and** and **or** are expressible
by **not** and **implies** in the following classical way:

    a **and** b = **not** (a **implies** (**not** b))   (3.1)
    a **or** b = **not** ((**not** a) **and** (**not** b))

Moreover, the **and** and **or** of Lukasiewicz and Kleene are the same. Therefore, in
order to compare the three calculi, it is sufficient to compare each of the
corresponding **implies** operators. Since all these operators are the extensions of

the classical **implies**, we may restrict our attention to the case where at least
one of the arguments is ee:

LUKASIEWICZ	KLEENE	McCARTHY
1) tt **implies** ee = ee	tt **implies** ee = ee	tt **implies** ee = ee
2) ff **implies** ee = tt	ff **implies** ee = tt	ff **implies** ee = tt
3) ee **implies** tt = tt	ee **implies** tt = tt	ee **implies** tt = ee
4) ee **implies** ff = ee	ee **implies** ff = ee	ee **implies** ff = ee
5) ee **implies** ee = tt	ee **implies** ee = ee	ee **implies** ee = ee

Fig.3.1

As we see the three operators coincide whenever the premise has a defined value
(first two cases). In particular (case 2)) they all satisfy our lazy-evaluation
principle (2.2). Below we discuss the differences between the calculi.

In the case of Lukasiewicz, ee represents an unknown (but defined) logical value –
an "I do not know" of a philosopher – and if there is more than one ee in a
formula, then they all represent the same (unknown) value.

In the calculi of Kleene and McCarthy ee may correspond to an infinite computation.
With this interpretation the calculus of Lukasiewicz is not implementable, since
the property of non-termination is not computable and therefore, if the
computations of the arguments have not terminated (yet), we cannot decide whether
they will or will not terminate and therefore we cannot obey to 5). In the two
remaining calculi, if both arguments of an implication are undefined, then so is
the result. This makes them implementable. Also, if the evaluation of the
conclusion has terminated with ff but the evaluation of the premise has not
terminated, we cannot establish the value of the implication and therefore it must
be ee again (case 4)).

The calculi of Kleene and McCarthy differ only in 3). In the Kleene's case,
whenever the conclusion evaluates to tt, we do not care about the value (and the
termination) of the premise and we yield tt as a result. We yield the same result,
if the premise evaluates to ff. Observe that in order to satisfy 2) and 3) in an
implementation, the evaluations of arguments must be executed in parallel in order
to allow for the abortion of one of them, when the other yields an appropriate
value. Of course, this concerns not only **implies** but also **and** and **or**
(cf.3.1). Since in a propositional expression we may have many nested propositional

operators, we need an unbounded parallelism in order to implement the calculus of Kleene.

From the mathematical viewpoint the **implies** of Kleene is "more strict" than that of Lukasiewicz, since it differs from the former in 5), where the value ee is yielded in the place of tt. This makes the **implies** of Kleene lazily implementable, although with the requirement of parallelism. When we further strengthen the strictness of implication, by putting ee instead of tt in 3), we get the calculus of McCarthy which is sequentially implementable. In that calculus we evaluate the premise in the first place and therefore, if this leads to an infinite computation, then the value of the whole expression must be ee (cases 3)-5)). In the opposite case we (lazily) yield tt if the premise yields ff (case 2)) and we proceed to the evaluation of conclusion, if the premise yields tt (case 1)).

Since the calculus of Lukasiewicz is not implementable, we exclude it from the further discussion. In the sequel we analyze and compare the calculi of Kleene and McCarthy giving a little more attention to the latter since, in the opinion of the author, it is more appropriate for the specification of software and for programming. In fact, McCarthy's **and** and **or** have been chosen in Euclid, Algol-W and C. In Ada they correspond to **and then** and **or else**. In E.Dijkstra's famous book [Dijkstra 76] they are used under the names of **cand** and **cor**. They have also been used by the author in the context of software specification, development and validation [Blikle 81a, 81b,87]. The calculus of Kleene has been used in the same context in [Jones 86,87].

That the calculus of McCarthy is implementable on a sequential machine may be seen quite clearly if we express McCarthy's propositional connectives by the following equations:

not a	= a —Mc→ ff, tt	where a —Mc→ b,c =	b for a=tt
a **or** b	= a —Mc→ tt, b		c for a=ff
a **and** b	= a —Mc→ b, ff		a for a=ee
a **implies** b = a —Mc→ b, tt			

As we see, all binary operators of McCarthy are left-strict, i.e. assume the value ee whenever a=ee. They are not right-strict, however, and therefore **or** and **and** are not commutative. This is the price which we pay for the sequential implementability. The operators of Kleene are commutative and therefore their implementation requires parallelism. The logical arrays of Kleene's **and** and **or** are the following:

or|	tt	ff	ee
tt	classical		tt
ff	values		ee
ee	tt	ee	ee

and|	tt	ff	ee
tt	classical		ee
ff	values		ff
ee	ee	ff	ee

The calculus of Kleene inherits many nice algebraic properties of the classical case. The calculus of McCarthy, a little less. For instance:

1) **and** and **or** are commutative   (Kleene)
2) **and** is right distributive over **or**   (Kleene)
3) **or** is right distributive over **and**   (Kleene)
5) **or** is left distributive over **and**   (Kleene & McCarthy)
4) **and** is left distributive over **or**   (Kleene & McCarthy)
4) **and** and **or** are associative   (Kleene & McCarthy)
3) the laws of de Morgan hold   (Kleene & McCarthy)

Of course, there are also such classical laws, as e.g. p **or** (**not** p) = tt, known as *tertium non datur*, which do not hold in none of the calculi.

An important property of all Kleene's and McCarthy's operators is their monotonicity with respect to the partial ordering in Boolerr defined by ee<tt and ee<ff. A one-argument function f:Booler→Booler is called **monotone** if a<b implies f.a<f.b. In our case this is equivalent to the fact that

f.ee < f.b for any b ≠ ee

A two- or more-argument function is monotone, if it is monotone in each argument separately with other arguments arbitrarily fixed.

Each monotone function in Boolerr has the property that if we replace one of its arguments by ee, then the value of the function either remains unchanged or becomes ee. Moreover, the former case is possible only if the function is constant on that argument, i.e. if the evaluation of that argument may be lazily omitted. This means that all functions which are monotone in Boolerr are implementable even if ee corresponds to an infinite computation. The converse implication is also true – a function which is not monotone is not implementable.

4. THREE-VALUED CALCULI OF PREDICATES

In mathematical logic predicates are defined as the denotations of formulas, i.e. as functions from some states (in logic we say *valuations of variables*) into some values. Since in this paper we do not introduce the technical machinery of logic, we do not need to talk about the syntax of predicates. We define predicates as abstract functions from states into Boolerr and then we show how to construct an algebra (a calculus) of such predicates with operations corresponding to the propositional connectives and quantifiers.

We start by introducing some auxiliary notation which we use throughout the paper. If A and B are sets, then by A-set we denote the set of all subsets of A, by A→B we denote the set of all total functions from A into B and by A⇸B we denote the set of all partial functions from A into B. By f:A→B (f:A⇸B) we denote the fact that f is a total (partial) function from A into B. By g:A→B→C we abbreviate g:A→(B→C). Instead of f(a) we write f.a and instead of (g.a).b we write g.a.b. Observe that in the traditional notation we should have written (g(a))(b) instead of g.a.b. For any aεA, bεB and f:A→B, by f[b/a] we denote a modification of function f defined by:

    f[b/a].x = if x=a then b else f.x

Let Ide denote an arbitrary nonempty set of **identifiers** (variables) and let Value denote an arbitrary nonempty set of **values**. By a **state** we mean any mapping from identifiers to values and by a **predicate** we mean any total function from states to logical values:

    State   = Ide → Value
    Predicate = State → Boolerr

The elements of State will be denoted by sta, the elements of Ide by x,y,z,..., the elements of Value by val and the elements of Predicate by p,q,r,... . If we wish to express the fact (which is usual in the models of software) that each state associates only a finite number of identifiers to values, then we may assume that states are finite-domain partial functions (called **mappings** in VDM). Such an assumption does not change any relevant properties of our subsequently defined calculi of predicates.

By a **three-valued predicate calculus** we mean a two-sorted algebra over Predicate and Ide with six following **predicative operators** which are also called **predicate constructors:**

$$\underline{not} : \text{Predicate} \rightarrow \text{Predicate}$$
$$\underline{and}, \underline{or}, \underline{implies} : \text{Predicate} \times \text{Predicate} \rightarrow \text{Predicate}$$
$$\exists : \text{Ide} \rightarrow \text{Predicate} \rightarrow \text{Predicate}$$
$$\forall : \text{Ide} \rightarrow \text{Predicate} \rightarrow \text{Predicate}$$

We assume that the first four operators correspond in the usual way to respective propositional operators of a chosen propositional calculus. E.g.:

$$(p \ \underline{and} \ q).sta = p.sta \ \underline{and} \ q.sta$$

Two remaining predicate constructors are quantifiers. The existential quantifiers are defined as follows:

Kleene:

$\exists.x.p.sta =$ tt   if for some $val \varepsilon Value$, $p.(sta[val/x]) = tt$;

            ff   if for any $val \varepsilon Value$, $p.(sta[val/x]) = ff$;

            ee   otherwise, i.e. if for no $val \varepsilon Value$, $p.(sta[val/x]) = tt$,
                 but for some $val \varepsilon Value$, $p.(sta[val/x]) = ee$.

McCarthy:

$\exists.x.p.sta =$ tt   if for some $val \varepsilon Value$, $p.(sta[val/x]) = tt$
                 and for any $val \varepsilon Value$, $p.(sta[val/x]) \neq ee$

            ff   if for any $val \varepsilon Value$, $p.(sta[val/x]) = ff$;

            ee   otherwise, i.e. if for some $val \varepsilon Value$, $p.(sta[val/x]) = ee$

The general quantifiers are defined in both cases by de Morgan equations:

$$\forall.x.p = \underline{not} \ (\exists.x.(\underline{not} \ p))$$

Observe that in McCarthy's case in order to claim the existence of a value of x such that p is satisfied, we have to make sure that p is defined for any value of x. For instance, $(\exists x)(\sqrt{x} > 2)$ is not true, since for some x, $\sqrt{x} > 2$ is undefined. It is true, however, that $(\exists x)(x > 0 \ \textbf{and} \ \sqrt{x} > 2)$. The proof of that fact requires an additional argument that the quantified predicate is always well defined. In the Kleene's case both $(\exists x)(\sqrt{x} > 2)$ and $(\exists x)(x > 0 \ \textbf{and} \ \sqrt{x} > 2)$ are true and none requires a definedness argument in the proof. The quantifiers of Kleene seem therefore more appropriate for applications.

With two sets of propositional connectives and two sets of quantifiers we have four basic candidates for a predicate calculus:

K-calculus: the calculus of Kleene,
M-calculus: the calculus of McCarthy,
KM-calculus: Kleene's propositional operators and McCarthy's quantifiers,
MK-calculus: McCarthy's propositional operators and Kleene's quantifiers.

It should be mentioned in this place that there are even more three-valued predicate calculi which may be investigated in the context of software specification and programming [Owe 85]. In the sequel, however, we shall analyze only two of them: the MK-calculus and the K-calculus. The former has been applied in [Blikle 81a,81b,87] and a corresponding three-valued logic has been constructed in [Konikowska, Tarlecki,Blikle 88]. The latter, in a version extended by a non-monotone propositional connective **def** (see Sec.2), has been used and investigated in [Hoogewijs 79,83,87], [Barringer,Cheng,Jones 84] and [Jones 86,87].

As a convenient technical vehicle for proofs we introduce a set-theoretic interpretation of predicates by characteristic sets. Each three-valued predicate may be unambiguously represented by two sets:

T.p = {sta | p.sta=tt }
F.p = {sta | p.sta=ff }

We call these sets the **positive characteristic set** and the **negative characteristic set** respectively. The following equations describe our two calculi:

	Kleene		McCarthy	
1) T.(**not** p)	= F.p		F.p	(4.1)
F.(**not** p)	= T.p		T.p	
2) T.(p **or** q)	= T.p ∪ T.q		T.p ∪ (F.p ∩ T.q)	
F.(p **or** q)	= F.p ∩ F.q		F.p ∩ F.q	
3) T.(p **and** q)	= T.p ∩ T.q		T.p ∩ T.q	
F.(p **and** q)	= F.p ∪ F.q		F.p ∪ (T.p ∩ F.q)	

4) T.(p **implies** q) = F.p u T.q   F.p u (T.p ∩ T.q)

   F.(p **implies** q) = T.p ∩ F.q   T.p ∩ F.q

5) T.($\forall$.x.p) = $\bigcap_{val\varepsilon Value}$\{sta | sta[val/x]$\varepsilon$T.p\}

   F.($\forall$.x.p) = $\bigcup_{val\varepsilon Value}$\{sta | sta[val/x]$\varepsilon$F.p\}

6) T.($\exists$.x.p) = $\bigcup_{val\varepsilon Value}$\{sta | sta[val/x]$\varepsilon$T.p\}

   F.($\exists$.x.p) = $\bigcap_{val\varepsilon Value}$\{sta | sta[val/x]$\varepsilon$F.p\}

Observe how the commutativity of Kleene's **and** and **or** is reflected in the symmetry of corresponding equations for characteristic sets.

5. SUPERPREDICATES

Superpredicates are binary relations between predicates. They constitute a bridge between our calculus of three-valued predicates and a classical two-valued logic. By their means we can formulate and prove theorems about data and programs on the classical ground.

We introduce four superpredicates:

   $\equiv$, <=>, $\sqsubseteq$, => : Predicate x Predicate $\rightarrow$ Bool

defined as follows:

   p => q   iff   for all sta, if p.sta=tt, then q.sta=tt   (stronger then)

   p $\sqsubseteq$ q   iff   p => q   and **not** p => **not** q   (less defined then)

   p <=> q   iff   p => q   and   q => p   (weakly equivalent)

   p $\equiv$ q   iff   p <=> q   and **not** p <=> **not** q   (strongly equivalent)

As is easy to check, for classical predicates the relations $\equiv$, <=> and $\sqsubseteq$ coincide. In the three-valued case they are, however, different. E.g.:

1) x>0 **and** $\sqrt{x}$>2 $\equiv$ x>4   (5.1)

2) $\sqrt{x}$>2   <=>   x>4   but neither "$\equiv$" nor "$\sqsupseteq$" holds

3) $\sqrt{x}$<2 $\sqsubseteq$ x<4   but neither "$\equiv$" nor "<=>" holds

4) $\sqrt{x}$>4   =>   x>3   but neither "$\sqsubseteq$" nor "<=>" holds

Of course, "≡" is the strongest of our four relations (this is simply the identity of predicates) and "=>" is the weakest. Two remaining are mutually independent. The relation "⊑" is a cpo ordering induced in the set of predicates by the ordering in Boolerr, where ee<tt and ee<ff.

The major field where the superpredicates are applied is the validation of software including software development by sound transformations [Blikle 81a, 81b]. In order to describe the corresponding proof-rules and transformation- rules we introduce two additional constructors of predicates. For any partial function F:State⇸State (which may be regarded as an I/O function of a program) and any predicate p:State→Boolerr, by pF and Fp we denote two predicates which are defined as follows (dom.F denotes the domain of F):

    pF.sta = tt   p.sta=tt and sta∊dom.F
             ff   p.sta=ff
             ee   otherwise

    Fp.sta = tt   sta∊dom.F and p.(F.sta)=tt
             ff   sta∊dom.F and p.(F.sta)=ff
             ee   otherwise

We say that F is **partially correct** wrt a precondition p and a postcondition q, in symbols

   parpre p: F **parpost** q   (5.2)

if pF => Fq and we say that F is **totally correct** wrt a precondition p and a postcondition q, in symbols

   totpre p: F **totpost** q   (5.3)

if p => Fq.

Proof rules for partial and total correctness of programs expressed in these terms are discussed in [Blikle 81b] and [Blikle 87] we shall not, therefore, repeat this discussion here. We give only one example of such a proof rule for total correct- ness (see (5.4)). It is understood that _iff_ is a two-valued propositional connective and that 1), 2) and 3) are connected by two-valued _and_. Observe also that in the classical Hoare's proof-rule we do not have the condition 1). Here, however, it expresses the fact that the satisfaction of p guarantees a successful evaluation of r.

totpre p: IF r THEN F ELSE G FI **totpost** q   (5.4)

iff

  1) p => [r **or** (**not** r)]

  2) **totpre** [p **and** r]: F **totpost** q

  3) **totpre** [p **and** (**not** r)]: G **totpost** q

Superpredicates are also used in expressing transformation rules of specified programs, where by a specified program we mean – roughly speaking – a total-correctness statement about a program [Blikle 81a]. For instance, two specified programs:

  totpre p_1: WHILE r_1 DO F OD **totpost** q_1
  totpre p_2: WHILE r_2 DO F OD **totpost** q_2

are equivalent – i.e. both correct or both incorrect – whenever

  p_1 <=> p_2 **and** $r_1 \equiv r_2$ **and** q_1 <=> q_2 (5.5)

and the correctness of the first implies the correctness of the second if

  p_2 => p_1 **and** $r_1 \sqsubseteq r_2$ **and** q_1 => q_2 (5.6)

As we see, for the sake of such applications our superpredicates may be split into two groups: {$\equiv$, $\sqsubseteq$ } and {<=>,=>}. The former are used to talk about branching conditions of algorithms. In that case when we replace one predicate by another, the new one must be either strongly equivalent to the former, in which case we do not change the meaning of the algorithm, or only better defined than the former, in which case our new algorithm has a not smaller domain of termination. If, however, we replace a branching condition of a program by a weakly equivalent one, then we risk that the new program will abort where the old did not. For instance, of three following programs (cf.(5.1)):

  1) WHILE x>4 DO x:=x-1 OD
  2) WHILE x>0 **and** √x>2 DO x:=x-1 OD
  3) WHILE √x>2 DO x:=x-1 OD

1) behaves exactly as 2) does, but 3) aborts for all x<0, whereas 1) and 2) only exit the loop in that case.

Strong equivalence need not be observed if we use predicates to represent sets.

Typical applications are well-formedness conditions of domains in denotational semantics or pre-conditions, post-conditions and assertions in the correctness statements of programs. In all such cases a predicate p represents only the set T.p and therefore all modifications of p may be performed up to weak equivalence. For instance:

$\{x \mid \sqrt{x} > 2\} = \{x \mid x > 4\}$.

Now a few words about the algebraic properties of our calculus. First observe that the relations "≡" and "<=>" are equivalence relations. The former is simply an identity and therefore it is a congruence with respect to all predicate constructors. For instance, if p ≡ q, then **not** p ≡ **not** q. The weak equivalence is a congruence with respect to only **and** and to both quantifiers. For instance, $\sqrt{x} > 2$ <=> x>4 is true, but $\sqrt{x} < 2$ <=> x<4 is not.

Using equations (4.1) we can easily derive basic calculation rules. For instance we may show that in the MK-calculus:

    1) **and** and **or** are associative,
    2) **and** is left distributive over **or** and vice versa,
    3) usual de Morgan's laws hold for **and**, **or** and both quantifiers,
    4) p **and** q <=> q **and** p, i.e. **and** is weakly commutative

Observe that since McCarthy's **and** is weakly commutative, we can commute its arguments in the assertions although we cannot commute them in branching conditions. In the K-calculus 1)-4) are also satisfied and besides both **and** and **or** are strongly commutative. More properties of our calculi are discussed in [Blikle 87].

In the set of superpredicates a central role is played by => which we shall call a **predicate implication**. First, the other superpredicates are definable in its terms, second - it appears in the definitions of the partial and the total correctness of programs. As can be seen the Hoare's method of proving program correctness consists in reducing correctness statements of the form (5.2) or (5.3) to formulas of the form p => q. It should be observed in this place that if we deal with two-valued predicates, then the correctness statements are reduced to formulas of the form p **implies** q rather than p => q. It is so since in the classical case predicate implication is expressible by the validity of propositional implication, i.e.:

    |= p **implies** q iff p => q,

where $|= r$ iff(def) $r \equiv tt$ and tt denotes a predicate which is always true. In the three-valued case we have two concepts of the validity of a predicate:

$|=_s$ iff $p \equiv tt$;   the **strong validity** of p,

$|=_w$ iff $p \sqsubseteq tt$;   the **weak validity** of p.

and none of them allows for a reduction of predicate implication to propositional implication. As is easy to check, for both Kleene's and McCarthy's propositional implication we have:

$$|=_s(p \text{ \textbf{implies} } q) \text{ implies } p => q \qquad (5.7)$$

$$p => q \text{ implies } |=_w(p \text{ \textbf{implies} } q) \qquad (5.8)$$

but none of the converse (meta) implications is true. The counterexample for (5.7) is any pair of predicates such that $p => q$ and for some staεState, p.sta=ee and q.sta=ff. and the counterexample for (5.8) is any pair of predicates such that $|=_w(p \text{ \textbf{implies} } q)$, but for some sta$\varepsilon$State, p.sta=tt and q.sta=ee. For instance, $|=_w$ x<0 **implies** $\sqrt{x}<0$, but   x<0 => $\sqrt{x}<0$ does not hold and $\sqrt{x}>2 => x>4$, but $|=_s\sqrt{x}>2$ **implies** x>4 does not hold. As is not difficult to show, => cannot be expressed by any combination of McCarthy's or Kleene's propositional connectives and validity since it required nonmonotone connectives in the definition. In the three-valued case the introduction of the predicate implication is, therefore, the matter of necessity.

6. REMARKS ABOUT FUTURE APPLICATIONS

Our calculus of three-valued predicates has been thought as a tool for the designers of software. In particular it is to be applied in project MetaSoft, devoted to the construction of tools for software design, specification and development [Blikle 87,88].

When we are talking about the applications of our calculus we should distinguish between four following conceptual levels:

    (1) the level of a software system (SS),
    (2) the level of a logic of a software system (LSS),
    (3) the level of a definitional metalanguage (ML),
    (4) the level of a logic of a definitional metalanguage (LML)

At each level we may use a different version or a different incarnation of the calculus.

The lowest conceptual level is that of a software system, i.e. of a programming language, an operating system, a data-base-menagment system, etc. When we design an object of that level we usually define a many-sorted algebra of data-types where, among other sorts, we introduce a sort Boolerr with constructors corresponding to McCarthy's or Kleene's propositional connectives (Sec.3). Of course, we may introduce more than only one version of each constructor. E.g. in Ada we have both, the strict and the McCarthy's **and** and **or**.

The algebra of data usually serves as an initial step in the definition of an algebra of denotations of the system. In the latter we define the sort Predicate with predicate constructors corresponding to propositional connectives (Sec.4). Since predicates constitute at the level of SS the denotations of boolean expressions we in general do not allow for the quantification of identifiers since this would lead to non-computabilities.

When we are done with the definition of SS we may think of a logic where to formulate and prove the properties of objects definable in SS, such as programs, procedures, tasks, etc. This brings us to LSS, which constitutes the second conceptual level. The language of LSS comprises the whole language of SS plus a new sort called **formulas**. Formulas may be atomic or compound. Atomic formulas are constructed from the boolean expressions of SS (which play the role of terms in this logic) by means of superpredicates and correctness-statements constructors. Typical examples of atomic formulas are:

$(x>0$ **and** $\sqrt{x}>2) \equiv x>4$

$x>y \Rightarrow x>z$

totpre $x^2>4$; IF $x>0$ THEN $y:= \sqrt{x}$ ELSE $y:= \sqrt{-x}$ FI **totpost** $y>2$

Compound formulas are constructed from atomic formulas by means of two-valued propositional connectives <u>and</u>, <u>or</u>, <u>implies</u>, etc. An example of a compound formula may be:

$[(x^2>4 \Rightarrow x>0$ **or** $x<0)$ <u>and</u>   (6.1)

  $(x^2>4$ **and** $x>0) \Rightarrow \sqrt{x}>2)$ <u>and</u>

  $(x^2>4$ **and** $x<0) \Rightarrow \sqrt{-x}>2)]$

  <u>implies</u>

totpre $x^2>4$; IF $x>0$ THEN $y:=\sqrt{x}$ ELSE $y:= \sqrt{-x}$ FI **totpost** $y>2$

Here we should emphasize that the identifiers x,y,z,... are not variables in LSS and therefore they cannot be quantified. In LSS they are constants in the same sense as 1,2,3,... are constants in arithmetics. The formula (6.1) contains, therefore, no free variables. E.g. x is a constant whose value is a function on states f_x:State$\rightarrow$Value, such that f_x.sta = sta.x. Therefore a quantified formula, like e.g. $(\forall x)(x^2 > 4 \Rightarrow x > 0$ or $x < 0)$ does not make sense in LSS.

A logic without variables is, of course, of a little expressive power and therefore we in general introduce variables into LSS. Since the models of LSS are many-sorted algebras, each variable must be given a sort. For instance, if we assume that p,q,r are variables of sort Predicate and F,G are variables ranging over the denotations of commands Com-den = State$\rightarrow$State, then (5.4) is an example of a formula of LSS with free variables. These variables can, of course, be quantified. We may also introduce variables e,f,g,... ranging over the denotations of arithmetic expressions Arith-exp-den = State$\rightarrow$Real in which case we can write the following quantified formula:

$(\forall e)(e^2 > 4 \Rightarrow e > 0$ or $e < 0)$

In LSS we may also wish to start the construction of the set of formulas from a set of boolean expressions larger then that of SS. While it is reasonable to assume that all objects expressible in SS are computable, there is no particular reason why to make the same assumption at the level of LSS, the more that superpredicates make our formulas non-computable anyway. For instance, if at the level of SS we have functions as objects, then we may wish to introduce the inclusion or the equality of such functions in the extended boolean expressions to be used in LSS. Of course, in most cases we shall not do the same at the level of SS. We may also allow for the quantification of identifiers in the extended boolean expressions. For instance, we may wish to write a formula of the form:

totpre *is-an-array-of-integers*(ar)

    (a program that is sorting ar)

totpost $(\forall x,y \in dom.ar)(x < y$ **implies** ar[x] < a[y])

For readers who know LCF [Gordon,Milner,Wadsworth 79] it may be of interest to observe that the way in which we construct LSS over SS is to a certain extend in the spirit of PPλ. In the latter logic we also have three-valued boolean terms and two-valued formulas constructed over them. Moreover, since among the terms we have tt, ff and ee (the last denoted by uu) and we have the equality in Boolerr (denoted by $\equiv$) we can define our superpredicates. E.g. we define p $\Rightarrow$ q by p$\equiv$tt **implies** q$\equiv$tt.

SS and LSS constitute two linguistic levels associated to a software system. Of course, in order to describe (design) both these levels and in order to prove them correct, we need an appropriate metalanguage ML with its own logic LML. This leads to two further levels. The construction of ML and LML is in principle analogous to the construction of SS and LSS, although there are some technical differences. First, in ML we may admit quantifiers in boolean expressions – i.e. the quantification of x,y,z,... – and in general we may admit some non-computable costructions. Second, in ML – a language where we should be able to define SS – the domains of SS and the operations on these domains must belong to the set of objects. Therefore, the domain Boolerr and the corresponding propositional constructors from the level of SS are the _elements_ of the algebra of ML. Independently, since ML should allow for conditional definitions of objects, it must have its own sort of three-valued boolean expressions, and therefore we must have Boolerr also as a _carrier_ of this algebra and propositional constructors as operations. Of course, we have to carefully distinguish between the former and the latter incarnations of these objects giving them different names in the corresponding syntax.

When we talk about logic of programs we must not forget about the problem of supporting it by a computer. Here again the solution may depend on the level where we are carrying out proofs and on the field of applications. In a typical LSS we shall have a system supporting the reduction of program-correctness statements to strong implications, and a separate system for proving strong implications. Whereas the former part is rather obvious (when we have our proof-rules) the latter requires such an axiomatization of the underlying data-types, where strong implications are provable. At the moment there seem to be two different ways of solving this problem. One consists in carrying the proofs on the ground of a theory which is rich enough to define in it the semantics of SS and the superpredicates. Some successful experiments in this field were described in [Woronowicz 86], where a proof-checker MIZAR [Trybulec,Blair 85a,85b] has been used to support formalized proofs of program correctness. Another possibility consists in reducing strong implications to metaformulas involving a superpredicate of a **logical consequence**. This solution is briefly discussed in [Konikowska, Tarlecki,Blikle 88].

For LML the possible solutions are analogous although technically more difficult since in that case the underlying algebra of data-types is far richer than in a usual software system. In any of these two levels more research is needed before practical solutions may be thought.

Another problem associated to applications which we want to briefly discuss in this section is the nature of the third logical value ee. As we explained in Sec.1 the element ee is handled by propositional connectives in such a way that it may be interpreted not only as a computable error signal (an abstract error) but also as a "true undefinedness" resulting from a nonterminating computation. Of course, in the applications we shall rather prefer to explicitly distinguish between these two cases as well as between different computable abstract errors. This leads to a model where ee is replaced by a set of error values. Formally we introduce a set:

$$Error = \{inf, err_1, \ldots, err_n\}$$

where inf corresponds to an infinite computation and err_i's represent computable error signals, and we define the set Boolerr by:

$$Boolerr = Bool \mid Error$$

Now we have to redefine all propositional connectives. We again assume that they are the extensions of classical connectives and we construct our definition analogously to the former case. For instance in the case of McCarthy's implication we set:

(1) ff **implies** bb = tt for any bb ε Boolerr
(2) tt **implies** ee = ee for any ee ε Error
(3) ee_1 **implies** ee_2 = ee_1 for any ee_1, ee_2 ε Error

Other choices in the case of (3) are also possible but the present one seems the closest to McCarthy's laziness.

ACKNOWLEDGMENTS

The author wishes to acknowledge many useful comments which were conveyed to him (in the alphabetic order) by: Jen H. Chang, Ni Haichu, Albert Hoogevijs, Beata Konikowska, Jacek Leszczyłowski, Olaf Owe and Andrzej Tarlecki.

REFERENCES

BARRINGER H., CHENG J.H., JONES C.B.

[84] **A logic covering undefinedness in program proofs,** Acta Informatica 21 (1984), 251–269

BLIKLE A.

[81a] **On the development of correct specified programs,** IEEE Trans. on Soft. Eng. SE-7 (1981), 519–527
[81b] **The clean termination of iterative programs,** Acta Informatica 16 (1981), 199–217
[87] **MetaSoft Primer, Towards a Metalanguage for Applied Denotational Semantics,** LNCS 288, Springer-Verlag 1987
[88] **A guided tour of the mathematics of MetaSoft'88,** Information Processing Letters (to appear in 1988)

COLMERAUER A., PIQUE J.F.

[81] **About natural logic,** in: Advances in Data Base Theory (H.Gallaire and J.Minker, eds.), Vol.1 (1981), 343–365

DIJKSTRA E.W.

[76] **A Discipline of Programming,** Prentice Hall 1976

HOOGEWIJS A.

[79] **On a formalization of the non-definedness notion,** Zeitschrift f. Math. Logik u. Grundlagen d. Math. Vol.25 (1979), 213–221
[83] **A partial predicate calculus in a two-valued logic,** ibid. Vol.29 (1983), 239–243
[87] **Partial-predicate logic in computer science,** Acta Informatica 24, 381–393 (1987)

JONES C.B.

[86] **Systematic Software Development Using VDM,** Prentice-Hall International Series in Computer Science 1986
[87] **VDM proof obligations and their justification,** in: VDM – A Formal Method at Work, Proc. VDM-Europe Symposium 1987, LNCS 252, Springer- -Verlag 1987

KLEENE S.C.

[38] **On notation for ordinal numbers,** Journal of Symb. Logic, Vol.3 (1938), 150–155

[52] **Introduction to Metamathematics**, North Holland 1952; since then
republished in 1957, 59, 62, 64, 67, 71

KONIKOWSKA B., TARLECKI A., BLIKLE A.

[88] **A three-valued logic for software specification and validation**, a
manuscript submitted to VDM'88

LUKASIEWICZ J.

[20] **O logice trojwartosciowej** (On three-valued logic), Ruch Filozoficzny,
Vol.5, Lwow 1920, 169-171

McCARTHY J.

[61] **A basis for a mathematical theory of computation.** Western Joint
Computer Conference, May 1961, since then published in Computer Programming
and Formal Systems (P.Braffort, D.Hirshberg eds.), North Holland 1967, 33-70

OWE, O.

[85] **An approach to program reasoning based on a first order logic for
partial functions**, Res.Rep. Institute of Informatics, University of Oslo,
no.89 1985

TRYBULEC A., BLAIR H.

[85a] **Computer assisted reasoning with Mizar**, Proc. International Joint
Conference on Artificial Intelligence 1985, Los Angeles 1985
[85b] **Computer aided reasoning**, in: Logic of programs 1985, LNCS 193,
Springer-Verlag 1985

WORONOWICZ E.

[86] **Wspomaganie procesu konstrukcji programow poprawnych w eksperymentalnym
srodowisku programistycznym** (Supporting the process of correct-program
derivation in an experimental programming environment), Ph.D. dissertation,
Bialystok Branch of Warsaw University 1986

A Set-Theoretic Model
for a Typed Polymorphic Lambda Calculus
A Contribution to MetaSoft

Andrzej Borzyszkowski
Ryszard Kubiak
Stefan Sokołowski

Project MetaSoft[1]

1 Introduction

The Reader who knows that polymorphism is not set-theoretic (cf. [16]) is nevertheless implored not to quit reading out of hand. We are aware that the complexity of full polymorphism escapes a set-theoretic description. The situation, however, is not as hopeless with many restricted forms. This includes shallow polymorphism such as in ML. The aim of this paper is to define precisely the set-theoretic interpretation of the ML-like polymorphic system of types. The aim of this Introduction is to convince the Reader that this is worthwhile to try.

1.1 The use of set-theoretic interpretations

One reason for defining semantics of a formal system is to enhance its understanding. A typical semantic function should give a meaning of syntax within a world one knows well beforehand. For instance, a definition of semantics which interpretes computer programs as functions (that transform states) is useful to people with a good understanding of the concept of function.

If an attempt to define semantics within a given world fails one may want to replace this world by a different one; one may even want to construct a special domain of denotations for the particular formal system. But while doing so one may end up with a consistent but unintuitive model with little explaining power.

The authors of this paper, and in fact the MetaSoft group, are convinced that this happens to many formal systems in the computer science.

[1]Polish Academy of Sciences, Institute of Computer Science, Group for the Mathematical Methods of Programming, c/o Gdańsk Division of the PAS, ul. Jaśkowa Dolina 31, P.O.Box 562, 80–252 Gdańsk, POLAND

The simplest example is the untyped λ-calculus. Originally designed to investigate the ways functions apply to objects, it turned out to have no set-theoretic model, i.e. no model in which λ-expressions were interpreted as functions and the operation of application as the genuine application of a function to an argument.

However, there are numerous models of λ-calculus, for instance $P\omega$, the powerset of natural numbers, proposed by D.Scott [17]. Unfortunately, all these models are highly unintuitive. For example, to explain the meaning of "$((\lambda x)x + 1).2$" in $P\omega$ a subset of Nat is assigned to "$(\lambda x)x + 1$" and another subset to "2", the both subsets are treated by the special "application" operation that has nothing to do with the true function application; finally a subset of Nat is yielded as result.

We think it possible to develop the "naive" semantics that respects the intuitive understanding of such basic mathematical concepts as function and function application, set and set belonging, equality, etc. We cannot construct such a model for the full untyped λ-calculus because it involves self-application which is not set-theoretic. But we do believe a user has always in mind its typed version without self-application. We cannot solve *any* type equations but we are happy with the *useful* ones that do not require reflexive domains. This "naive" approach has been presented in [4].

In this paper we give a set-theoretic model for polymorphism. We hope the model is both consistent and intuitive. We believe our approach is adequate for discussing polymorphism and also for explaining the concept to uninitiated.

1.2 Discussion of models for polymorphism

We understand (parametric) polymorphism as a dependence of objects and types on types. The concept appears in a number of programming languages in one form or another, for instance in ML (cf. [11]) and in ADA (cf. [1]). The distinction between the *explicit* polymorphism of ADA and the *implicit* one of ML is not essential for our considerations: whether type parameters are explicitly present in expressions or inferred automatically using Milner's algorithm from [13] is a syntax issue; we assume they are around whenever we need them to discuss semantics.

When we say that a polymorphic type is a dependence of types on types, i.e. a function

$$T : Types \to Types$$

we have to be careful to properly define the *Types*. In particular, it is important to realize whether polymorphic types, such as T above, belong themselves to *Types*.

In Girard's and Reynold's second order polymorphic λ-calculus [9,15] a polymorphic type may be instantiated by itself. This causes non-existence of set-theoretic model for it (cf. [16]) similarly to the case of the untyped λ-calculus. The construction of a model by Pitts [14] does not falsify this result since it is done under a non-standard view of the set-theory. In [6] Scott's denotational model is given, this model, however, is highly unintuitive and not "naive" in our sense.

The typed λ-calculus does have a simple set-theoretic model (cf. [12]). We have chosen the same remedy, i.e. strong typing, to enable a set-theoretic model for polymorphism; we have thus "typed the types". This gives rise to an infinite hierarchy of objects, types, supertypes,... etc., all of which may be polymorphic, superpolymorphic,... etc., and still with a set-theoretic model (see [5]).

This report presents a more conventional version. The polymorphism studied here is the shallow explicit one. "Shallow" means that polymorphic types may only depend on monomorphic ones, like in ML (cf. [10] or [11]). "Explicit" means that, unlike in ML, the dependence on types has to be explicitly pointed at in expression or type expression rather than be inferred from an occurence of type variables. Along with the syntax for polymorphic types and objects we give their naive denotational semantics.

In [5] we consider non-shallow polymorphism and dependent types.

1.3   Types and expressions in MetaSoft

MetaSoft is intended as a system for designing, developing and reasoning about programs (see [2] and [3]). It is based on the naive denotational semantics (see [4]) which attempts to describe in terms of the classical set theory what one may reasonably require from a computer. The authors gave up self-application, an item unlikely to be mourned over by programmers, and for this price they got a nice and uniform set-theoretic model of high-order typed computations where types translate to sets; $A \to B$ is the set of all functions from A to B and equality is equality rather than an isomorphism.

One of the components of MetaSoft is a formalized metalanguage intended as a means to talk about software. It must be sufficiently expressive not to limit people's creativity, and in the same time sufficiently unambiguous to allow computer support.

In the core of the definition of the language lies a high-order polymorphic type system similar to the one described in this paper. Types may be composed using the function space constructor and recursion; polymorphic types may be set up and instantiated only with monomorphic ones to retain the shallowness of polymorphism. Other type constructors may be introduced or defined but this is out of the scope of this presentation and will be treated separately.

All the notions involved are given a natural set-theoretic meaning. In particular, $A \to B$ stands for the set of all total functions from A to B; and a polymorphic function is assigned a family of monomorphic functions indexed with types. A care is taken to avoid paradoxes: no function takes itself as an argument and there is no set of all sets. This does not however preclude recursive types.

Expressions are uniquely typed and may denote individual primitive elements, or composed data such as Cartesian pairs, or functions, or polymorphic objects.

We try to make this presentation sufficiently formal to enable its use as a meeting point between man and computer. It may seem a little too detailed for a man but it defines the notions with enough precision to enable an unambiguous implementation.

2 Set theoretic system of types

To define a denotational semantics within the set theory following [4] one needs a set large enough to include all things one may ever need to talk about: numbers, truth values, trees, ..., functions over numbers, functions over truth values, ..., functions over functions over numbers, ...and so forth. This universal set is bound to be much larger than a programmer will ever need; for instance, it contains *all* functions on numbers while a programmer will only use *recursive* functions.

One may wonder whether such a universal set exists. There can be no set that contains everything (it cannot contain itself; cf. the Russell's paradox). It turns out, however, that the existence of a universal set is consistent with the classical Zermelo-Fraenkel set theory, therefore it may be added as another axiom. An alternative approach, satisfactory for our needs, is to construct the required set strictly within the Zermelo-Fraenkel set theory. Below we show how to do this.

The construction is split in two parts: making a sufficiently large family *Types* of sets to handle all we need except polymorphism and building shallow polymorphic types and objects on top of *Types*. We start with the latter construction since it is simpler.

Let *Types* be a family of sets (hereafter referred to as monomorphic types). Let

$$Elems = \bigcup Types$$

be the set of all members of sets belonging to *Types*, hereafter referred to as monomorphic objects. The family *PolTypes* of polymorphic types is defined as follows:

(1) $\quad PolTypes_0 \quad = \quad Types$

$\qquad PolTypes_{n+1} \quad = \quad Types \rightarrow PolTypes_n \qquad$ for any $n \in Nat$

$\qquad PolTypes \quad = \quad \bigcup_{n=0}^{\infty} PolTypes_n$

The family *PolElems* of polymorphic objects is defined analogously:

$\qquad PolElems_0 \quad = \quad Elems$

$\qquad PolElems_{n+1} \quad = \quad Types \rightarrow PolElems_n \qquad$ for any $n \in Nat$

$\qquad PolElems \quad = \quad \bigcup_{n=0}^{\infty} PolElems_n$

This is a different view of polymorphism than the one commonly used, for instance in [16], where all types, polymorphic or not, are treated alike. By our approach a polymorphic type is a family of types indexed with monomorphic types; no possibility of self-application and hence also no danger of paradoxes is around. The polymorphism treated in this paper is the shallow one, precisely the kind encountered in, say, ML. For the existence of set-theoretic model the adherence to shallow polymorphism is not necessary (see [5]) but it is always necessary to avoid self-application. In this report we stick to shallowness for simplicity.

In the sequel we show how to construct the domain *Types* that is sufficiently universal for our needs (though smaller than the one discussed in a similar context by [4] after [7]). We start from a certain collection of sets *Prim* considered primitive. This collection is one of the parameters of the whole approach and it should correspond to user's needs. For instance, for numerical applications it might consist of

$\{tt, ff\}$	truth values
$\{0, 1, 2, \ldots\}$	natural numbers
$\{\ldots, -5.0, \ldots, 3.14, \ldots\}$	real numbers

but without arrays that are non-primitive.

The set constructors we need, however, are somewhat different than those in the standard set theory. All of them have one element in common, called a bottom and denoted by $\perp$. It should not be viewed as a denotation of various abstract errors but rather as a result of an erroneous computation in cases where the presence of the error is not detectable. One example is non-termination; another is given in the definition of the semantic function *semexp* in Sec. 4.3. We reserve another element ?? for a denotation of ill-typed expressions. The presence of bottom forces us to redefine standard set-theoretic operations.

Cartesian product:
$$A \bar{\times} B = (A \backslash \{\perp\}) \times (B \backslash \{\perp\}) \cup \{\perp\}$$

In the above the Cartesian product $\times$ is taken in its traditional sense.

Disjoint union:
$$A \mp B = (A \backslash \{\perp\}) \times \{tt\} \cup (B \backslash \{\perp\}) \times \{ff\} \cup \{\perp\}$$

Here tt and ff are the truth values. The disjoint union $\mp$ should not be confused with the non-disjoint union $\cup$.

Function space:
$$A \overset{.}{\rightarrow} B = (A \rightarrow B) \cup \{\perp\}$$

Here → denotes the constructor of the set of total functions.

The disjoint union is defined as one may expect — with bottoms glued together. In the Cartesian product all pairs with either coordinate equal to bottom are glued together. The set $A \dot{\to} B$ needs a special attention. We distinguish between the non-bottom function yielding the bottom for all arguments, and the bottom itself. Our set theory is not extensional since these two elements of $A \dot{\to} B$ are distinguished even though both yield $\perp$ for any argument, in view of the following operation of function application that we use

$$\_.\_ \; : \; (A \dot{\to} B) \times A \to B$$
$$f.a \; = \; \text{IF } f = \perp \text{ THEN } \perp$$
$$\text{ELSE } f(a)$$

Note also that we allow for non-strict functions. In the literature these three constructions are sometimes referred to as strict product, strict union and lifted function space.

This is different then in the classical set theory. But the classical set theory does not deal with partial functions so we need special ways to reflect partiality by total functions.

In all applications we will assume the following sets are primitive, i.e. belong to $Prim$:

$$\text{Empty} \; = \; \{\perp\}$$
$$\text{Unit} \; = \; \{\perp, ()\}$$
$$\text{Bool} \; = \; \{\perp, tt, ff\}$$
$$\text{TypeErr} \; = \; \{\perp, ??\}$$

We can formulate a number of laws on the behavior of these sets under the above defined set-theoretic operations. In most cases they are analogous to the classical set theory.

Theorem 2.1

$$A \bar{\times} Empty \; = \; Empty$$
$$\text{and} \quad Empty \bar{\times} A \; = \; Empty$$

$$A \bar{\times} Unit \; \approx \; A$$
$$\text{and} \quad Unit \bar{\times} A \; \approx \; A$$

(where $\approx$ means that both sets are in a natural 1–1 correspondence)

$$A \bar{+} Empty \; \approx \; A$$
$$\text{and} \quad Empty \bar{+} A \; \approx \; A$$

$$A \bar{\times} (B \cup C) = (A \bar{\times} B) \cup (A \bar{\times} C)$$

and $\quad (B \cup C) \bar{\times} A = (B \bar{\times} A) \cup (C \bar{\times} A)$

All the proofs are straightforward. There is however no full analogy to the classical set theory:

Theorem 2.2

$$A \overset{.}{\to} Empty \approx Unit$$

and $\quad Empty \overset{.}{\to} A \approx A \overset{.}{\to} Unit$

Below we present a number of properties that are not satisfied in the calculus of sets with bottom:

- functions are not subsets of Cartesian product, i.e. from $f : A \overset{.}{\to} B$ we cannot infer that f is in any sense a subset of $A \bar{\times} B$;

- there is no natural embedding of functions $A \overset{.}{\to} B$ into relations, the latter defined as elements of $A \bar{\times} B \overset{.}{\to} Bool$;

- there is no natural 1–1 correspondence between $Bool \overset{.}{\to} A$ and $A \bar{\times} A$; the former contains many more elements that involve $\perp$;

- there is no natural 1–1 correspondence between $A \overset{.}{\to} B \overset{.}{\to} C$ and $A \bar{\times} B \overset{.}{\to} C$; thus the curried functions may not be in any sense identified with the uncurried ones.

All the above claims may be justified by taking $A = Empty$.

Now we are ready to define *Types*.

Definition: Let *Prim* be a family of primitive sets containing at least the following sets: *Empty*, *Unit*, *Bool*, *TypeErr*. Then *Types* is the least family of sets such that:

- *Prim* is contained in *Types*;

- *Types* is closed under Cartesian products, disjoint unions and total functions, that is for any A and B that belong to *Types*:

    $A \bar{\times} B$

    $A \overline{+} B$

    $A \overset{.}{\to} B$

    also belong to *Types*;

- *Types* is closed under enumerable unions, that is for any enumerable family $\{A_i \mid i = 0, 1, 2, \ldots\}$ of sets that belong to *Types* its union $\bigcup_{i=0}^{\infty} A_i$ also belongs to *Types*.

As we have already said there are sets in *Types* which are far too large for programmer's needs. But how much larger?

Since *Prim* contains *Bool* and since *Types* is closed under the (barred) arrow and under countable union, there are in *Types* sets of cardinalities

$$
2, 2^2, 2^{2^2}, \ldots, k = \bigcup_{i=0}^{\infty} 2^{2^{2^{\cdot^{\cdot^{2}}}}} \left. \right\} (height\ i),
$$

$$
2^k, 2^{2^k}, \ldots, l = \bigcup_{i=0}^{\infty} 2^{2^{2^{\cdot^{\cdot^{k}}}}} \left. \right\} (height\ i),
$$

$$
2^l, 2^{2^l}, \ldots,
$$

Thus the cardinality of *Types* is not less than $\aleph_1$, the least uncountable cardinal, and the cardinality of *Elems* is not less than $beth_\Omega$ where Ω is the least uncountable ordinal.

The model contains everything a programmer may define in a reasonable programming language. On top of this it contains non-programmable types and functions, such as

$$(\lambda x)\text{IF } x = \perp \text{ THEN } \ldots \text{ ELSE } \ldots$$

(halting problem) that may prove useful for discussing programs' properties. And it also contains enormously many other things that bear no correspondence to anything a programmer will ever need.

Why do we consider the sets that are too big for the purposes of programming? Why not to confine ourselves to the really needed minimum? Well, it turns out that an easy to understand construction introduces large sets while other models (say, the Scott's theory) are much more complex although admittedly smaller.

The reason for having the family *Types* closed under enumerable unions is the need for recursive type definitions. In section 3.4 we are going to use the following operation:

(2) $Rec : (Types \to Types) \to Types$

$Rec.F = \bigcup_{i=0}^{\infty} A_i \quad$ where $\quad A_0 = Empty, \quad A_{i+1} = F(A_i) \quad$ for $i = 0, 1, 2, \ldots$

In case $F : Types \to Types$ is a continuous function Rec provides the least wrt set inclusion solution of the equation

$$X = F(X).$$

Nevertheless, $Rec.F$ is defined also for any non-continuous F.

Note that in the definition of *Types* we cannot go much further than enumerable unions. If we required that it be closed under arbitrary unions, this could not be realised consistently with the Zermelo-Fraenkel set theory.

3 Syntax and semantics of type expressions

We give below the definition of type expressions and their interpretations as types from Sec. 2. As announced in the Introduction, type expressions are "typed" themselves to avoid self-application. In this respect the calculus of type expressions presented below may be viewed as a version of the typed λ-calculus (cf. [12]). Two points however need highlighting.

First of all, the "type structure" over the type expressions is poorer than could be expected. This is because our system is confined to shallow polymorphism only. A type expression may depend on a certain number of monomorphic types and this number is its "supertype". For non-shallow polymorphism this supertype structure is bound to be more complex (cf. [5]).

The other point worth a comment is that there is only one family of type expressions, some of which are well-formed, i.e. may be consistently "typed" to a natural number, while some other are ill-formed. Alternatively, we could have adopted a system with a countable family of syntactic domains, one for each natural number. This would have brought us closer to [12]. We prefer however to have the type (supertype) checking within the system rather than in a metasystem.

3.1 Type expressions

At the bottom of our hierarchy of type expressions lies a family

(3) $tc : TypeCon = \{\mathbf{Fun}, \ldots\}$

of *type constants*. This is one of the parameters of our construction: one may put there various types that she/he wishes to consider primitive: Nat, or Bool, or Real, or whatever. Polymorphic types are eligible as well, such as

   Fun

which is the polymorphic type of functions: after instantiating with a concrete type A and with another concrete type B it becomes the type of all functions from A to B. We require that Fun be in *TypeCon*; the rest of the family is arbitrary and the presentation does not depend on a particular selection of its members.

Another syntactic domain involved

(4) $tv : TypeVar$

consists of *type variables*. This is not a parameter of the approach, we consider it the same for all applications. *TypeVar* is assumed countable; actually, sometimes we will treat it as an infinite sequence with a fixed order. It is required that the elements of the two domains be syntactically distinguishable. The type variables are an auxiliary means to define polymorphism and recursion on types.

Now we define the domain of *type expressions* by the following domain equation:

(5) $te : TypeExpr$ ::= $TypeCon$ type constant

                | $TypeVar$ type variable

                | $((\text{POLY } TypeVar) TypeExpr)$ polymorphic abstraction

                | $(TypeExpr \; @ \; TypeExpr)$ polymorphic instantiation

                | $((\text{REC } TypeVar) TypeExpr)$ recursive type

Informally, the meaning of the last three clauses is as follows.

$((\text{POLY } tv)te)$ is the polymorphic type that can be instantiated with a monomorphic type expression for tv yielding te.

$(te_1 @ te_2)$ is the polymorphic type te_1 instantiated with the monomorphic type te_2. For instance, the polymorphic type Fun may be instantiated twice, say with te_1 and te_2, resulting in the type $((\text{Fun } @ te_1) @ te_2)$ of functions from te_1 to te_2. Instantiation is opposite to abstraction in the sense that e.g. Fun should be considered semantically equivalent to

$$((\text{POLY } tv_1)((\text{POLY } tv_2)((\text{Fun } @ tv_1) @ tv_2)))$$

This will be made precise later on.

We intend $((\text{REC } tv)te)$ to be the recursive type, or the least solution of the equation

$$tv = te$$

But the equality need not always to hold, namely, in order that the above equation have a unique least solution the semantic meaning of its right-hand side has to be continuous with respect to tv. This will be also made precise later on (cf. Sec. 3.4).

We adopt the general convention that the external parentheses in type expressions may be skipped under the following precedences: @ binds stronger than both POLY and REC and it associates to the left; the other two syntactic type constructors are never in conflict.

There is no special constructor for mutual recursion since it may be defined using REC. There is also no special constructor for Cartesian product of types but to its effect one may include in *TypeCon* a polymorphic type constant Cart analogous to Fun. The same holds for, say, disjoint union constructor.

Not all type expressions consistent with (5) are considered well-formed. For instance

$$\text{Fun } @ \text{ Fun}$$

is not, see Sec. 3.2.

3.2 Syntactic check on type expressions

As we said in Introduction and in Sec. 2 we are going to deal only with the shallow polymorphism which means polymorphic type expressions may be instantiated only by the monomorphic ones. The correctness of the use of polymorphism is controlled by the syntactic function that "types" the type expressions:

$$arity : TypeExpr \rightarrow Nat \cup Message$$

that may yield either a natural number indicating the number of monomorphic type expressions the given type expression is waiting for, or a message saying that it is ill-constructed. In the above Nat is the domain of natural numbers and the other involved domain

$$msg : Message$$

will also be used in other parts of this paper.

To define $arity$ we have to start with another function

(6) $aricon : TypeCon \rightarrow Nat$

that gives the arities of type constants. This function is another parameter of the theory; notably, everything that concerns constants has to be a parameter since it is imported into the theory. It is required from $aricon$ that

$$aricon[\textbf{Fun}] = 2$$

i.e. Fun is a polymorphic type constant that needs two arguments to yield a monomorphic type expression. If one extends $TypeCon$ with, say, Real or Bool, it is reasonable to make $aricon$ assign them zeros. Note that $aricon$ must never yield an error message.

The definition of arity is now:

(7) $arity[tc] = aricon[tc]$

   $arity[tv] = 0$

   $arity[(\textbf{POLY tv})te] =$
   $= \text{LET } n = arity[te]$
   $\quad \text{IN IF } n \in Message \text{ THEN } n$
   $\quad\quad\quad \text{ELSE } n + 1$

$arity[te_1 \; @ \; te_2] =$

$\quad = \text{LET } n_1 = arity[te_1] \text{ AND } n_2 = arity[te_2]$

$\qquad \text{IN CASES}$

$\qquad\qquad n_1 \in Message \implies n_1$

$\qquad\qquad n_2 \in Message \implies n_2$

$\qquad\qquad n_1 = 0 \qquad\quad \implies$ "INSTANTIATION IN MONOMORPHIC TYPE"

$\qquad\qquad n_2 > 0 \qquad\quad \implies$ "NON-SHALLOW POLYMORPHISM"

$\qquad\qquad \text{OTHERWISE} \implies n_1 - 1$

$\qquad \text{END}$

$arity[(\text{REC } tv)te] =$

$\quad = \text{LET } n = arity[te]$

$\qquad \text{IN CASES}$

$\qquad\qquad n \in Message \implies n$

$\qquad\qquad n > 0 \qquad\quad \implies$ "RECURSION ON POLYMORPHIC TYPE"

$\qquad\qquad \text{OTHERWISE} \implies 0$

$\qquad \text{END}$

For instance

$$arity[\text{Fun}] = 2$$
$$arity[\text{Fun} \; @ \; tc_1] = 1$$
$$arity[\text{Fun} \; @ \; tc_1 \; @ \; tc_2] = 0$$
$$arity[\text{Fun} \; @ \; \text{Fun}] = \text{"NON-SHALLOW POLYMORPHISM"}$$

Note that recursion is allowed only on monomorphic types. This does not however preclude recursive type expressions to denote polymorphic types. For instance, the recursive type expression to denote polymorphic sequences is as follows:

$(\text{POLY } tv_1)(\text{REC } tv_2)\text{Disj} \; @ \; \text{Unit} \; @ \; (\text{Cart} \; @ \; tv_1 \; @ \; tv_2)$

provided the type constants: Unit (one-element type), Cart (Cartesian product) and Disj (disjoint union) with respective arities 0, 2 and 2 have been previously introduced. In a more conventional infix notation for Cart and Disj this can be expressed as

(8) $\quad \text{Seq} = (\text{POLY } tv_1)(\text{REC } tv_2)\text{Unit} + tv_1 \times tv_2$

A type expression *te* is said to be *well-formed* if *arity*[*te*] is a number rather than a message. As the Reader will see in Sec. 4 the ill-formed type expressions will be interpreted to the set *TypeErr* containing a special symbol ?? that denotes an error.

There is another syntactic function

$$free : TypeExpr \rightarrow TypeVar\text{--FINSET}$$

that detects all free type variables in a type expression. It is defined as usually:

$$
\begin{aligned}
(9) \qquad\qquad free[tc] &= \{\} \\
free[tv] &= \{tv\} \\
free[(\texttt{POLY } tv)te] &= free[te] \setminus \{tv\} \\
free[te_1 \; \bullet \; te_2] &= free[te_1] \cup free[te_2] \\
free[(\texttt{REC } tv)te] &= free[te] \setminus \{tv\}
\end{aligned}
$$

A special class of type expressions is *closed type expressions*, i.e. the ones that have no free variables:

$$(10) \quad ClTypeExpr = \{te : TypeExpr \mid free[te] = \{\}\}$$

They can be characterized as semantically meaningful on their own while the other type expressions need environments to assign types to their free type variables. This is treated in length in Sec. 3.4.

3.3 Syntactic operations on type expressions

As is customary for any calculus that involves variable binding operators, we introduce equivalence relations on type expressions: α-, β- and η- conversions. In Sec. 3.4 we show that these relations are congruences with respect to the semantic meaning of type expressions; in other words that the semantics glues together type expressions that are convertible to each other. It should be however emphasized that we do not treat $\alpha\beta\eta$-convertible type expressions as equal. In particular we insist that the expressions denoting individual objects (see Sec. 4) be typed to type expressions rather than to their equivalence classes. There are two variable binding operators in the syntax for type expressions: POLY and REC.

We start the discussion on conversions with the definition of the operation of syntactic substitution: $te'[te/tv]$ is meant to stand for the result of substituting the type expression *te* for all free occurrences of the variable *tv* in the type expression *te'* with all due renaming of bound variables. This is done alike for both POLY and REC since it is only important that they both bind variables. In the definition of the syntactic substitution that follows we call both operators BIND (the syntactic substitution is assumed to bind stronger than all other syntactic operations). The definition is that of [12] transcribed to our syntax given by (5).

(11) $tc[te/tv] = tc$

$tv[te/tv] = te$

$tv'[te/tv] = tv'$

provided tv' and tv are distinct type variables

$(te_1 \; @ \; te_2)[te/tv] = te_1[te/tv] \; @ \; te_2[te/tv]$

$((\text{BIND} \; tv)te')[te/tv] = (\text{BIND} \; tv)te'$

$((\text{BIND} \; tv')te')[te/tv] = (\text{BIND} \; tv')te'[te/tv]$

provided tv' and tv are distinct type variables and $tv \notin free[te']$ or $tv' \notin free[te]$

$((\text{BIND} \; tv')te')[te/tv] = (\text{BIND} \; tv'')te'[tv''/tv'][te/tv]$

where tv'' is the least type variable not in $free[te] \cup free[te']$; provided tv' and tv are distinct type variables and $tv \in free[te']$ and $tv' \in free[te]$

In the last clause of this definition we have made use of the assumption from Sec. 3.1 that the type variables are arranged in a sequence; the phrase: "least variable" refers to the order in this sequence.

Two type expressions are called *α-convertible* to each other if they are related by $\sim$ which is the least binary relation on type expressions such that:

(12) $tc \sim tc$

$tv \sim tv$

IF $(te_1 \sim te_1')$ & $(te_2 \sim te_2')$ THEN $te_1 \; @ \; te_2 \sim te_1' \; @ \; te_2'$

IF $(te \sim te'[tv/tv'])$ & $(tv \notin free[te'])$ THEN $(\text{BIND} \; tv)te \sim (\text{BIND} \; tv')te'$

The only non-trivial case in this definition is the last. It says that a bound type variable may be renamed within a type expression. It should be obvious that $\sim$ is an equivalence relation; moreover it is a congruence with respect to syntactic type constructors defined in (5).

Two other syntactic operations, the β-reduction and the η-reduction apply only to POLY. They may be given informally by:

$\beta[((\text{POLY} \; tv)te) \; @ \; te'] = te[te'/tv]$

$\eta[(\text{POLY} \; tv)te \; @ \; tv] = te$ \quad provided $tv \notin free[te]$

More precisely, these reductions are performed by the syntactic function

$$reduce : TypeExpr \rightarrow TypeExpr \cup Message$$

given by

(13) $reduce[tc] = tc$

$reduce[tv] = tv$

$reduce[(\textbf{POLY}\ tv)te] =$
    $= \text{IF}\ arity[te] \in Message\ \text{THEN}\ arity[te]$
      $\text{ELSE LET}\ te' =\ reduce[te]$
          $\text{IN IF}\ te' = te''\ \textbf{@}\ tv\ \text{for some}\ te''\ \text{such that}\ tv \notin free[te'']\ \text{THEN}\ te''$
             $\text{ELSE}\ (\textbf{POLY}\ tv)te'$

$reduce[te_1\ \textbf{@}\ te_2] =$
    $= \text{IF}\ arity[te_1\ \textbf{@}\ te_2] \in Message\ \text{THEN}\ arity[te_1\ \textbf{@}\ te_2]$
      $\text{ELSE LET}\ te_1' = reduce[te_1]$
          $\text{IN IF}\ te_1' = (\textbf{POLY}\ tv)te_1''\ \text{for some}\ tv\ \text{and}\ te_1\ \text{THEN}\ reduce[te_1[te_2/tv]]$
             $\text{ELSE}\ te_1'\ \textbf{@}\ reduce[te_2]$

$reduce[(\textbf{REC}\ tv)te] =$
    $= \text{IF}\ arity[(\textbf{REC}\ tv)te] \in Message\ \text{THEN}\ arity[(\textbf{REC}\ tv)te]$
      $\text{ELSE}\ (\textbf{REC}\ tv)reduce[te]$

In the above definition non-trivial are only the clauses for POLY and for **@**. The η-reduction is performed in the THEN clause of the inner conditional in $reduce[(\textbf{POLY}\ tv)te]$ and the β-reduction is performed in the THEN clause of the inner conditional in $reduce[te_1\ \textbf{@}\ te_2]$. For instance

$reduce[((\textbf{POLY}\ tv)\textbf{Fun}\ \textbf{@}\ tv\ \textbf{@}\ tv)\ \textbf{@}\ \textbf{Nat}] =$

(η-reduction is not applicable because **tv** is free in **Fun @ tv**, hence only the β-reduction is performed:)

$= \textbf{Fun @ Nat @ Nat}$

We define the relation of $\alpha\beta\eta$-convertibility as the least equivalence $\approx$ such that

$te \approx reduce[te]$

for any well-formed type expression te.

Note that prior to any β-reduction it is indispensable to verify the arity-correctness of $te_1 \text{ @ } te_2$, otherwise the reduction procedure may loop:

$$reduce[((\text{POLY tv})\text{tv @ tv}) \text{ @ } ((\text{POLY tv})\text{tv @ tv})] =$$

(η-reduction is not applicable since tv is free in tv, hence only the β-reduction is performed right away:)

$$= \quad reduce[(\text{tv @ tv})((\text{POLY tv})\text{tv @ tv/tv})] =$$
$$= \quad reduce[((\text{POLY tv})\text{tv @ tv}) \text{ @ } ((\text{POLY tv})\text{tv @ tv})] =$$
$$= \quad \ldots$$

Such infinite self-applications are disabled by the arity checking:

Theorem 3.1

$reduce[te]$ is defined for any $te : TypeExpr$

Proof: See [12] for a proof of the strong normalization theorem for the typed λ-calculus. This proof may be transformed into the proof that for any well-formed type expression any sequence of $\beta\eta$-reductions must be finite. To do this replace our well-formed type expressions for their terms and our arities for their types; any time [12] refers to an atomic type this should be read as *arity* 0, and structural induction over types should become the induction over natural arities.

Now the proof that the definition (13) of *reduce* halts relies on the following:

- it obviously halts for ill-formed type expressions;

- it gives the value of $reduce[te]$ for any well-formed te either with no recursive call of *reduce*, or in terms of $reduce[te']$ for some proper subexpression te' of te or in terms of $reduce[te']$ for some expression te' that results from te by a $\beta\eta$-reduction.

$\square$

To end this Section we give three theorems on the consistency of the introduced syntactic operations and conversions.

The first of these theorems states that the arity of a type expression depends only on the arities of its subexpressions rather than on the subexpressions themselves:

Theorem 3.2   For any type expressions te and te_1 such that $arity[te_1] = 0$ and for any type variable tv

$$arity[te] = arity[te[te_1/tv]]$$

Proof: Induction on length of te. □

The second theorem states that the α-convertibility relation is a congruence with respect to syntactic functions:

Theorem 3.3 For any type expressions $te_1, te_2 : TypeExpr$ such that $te_1 \sim te_2$ the following properties hold:

- $arity[te_1] = arity[te_2]$

- $free[te_1] = free[te_2]$

- if te_1, hence also te_2, are well-formed then $reduce[te_1] \sim reduce[te_2]$

Proof: For the proof of the first property introduce the following relation R on type expressions:

$$te_1 \, R \, te_2 \Longleftrightarrow arity[te_1] = arity[te_2]$$

and prove that all the four clauses of the definition (12) of α-convertibility are satisfied with R replaced for $\sim$. Since $\sim$ is the least relation that satisfies (12), this implies that $\sim$ is contained in R, which ends the proof of the property. □

The two other properties are proved alike with appropriate definitions of R.

The last theorem gives the invariance of $arity$ along $\beta\eta$-reductions:

Theorem 3.4

For any well-formed type expression $te : arity[te] = arity[reduce[te]]$

For any ill-formed type expression $te : arity[te] = reduce[te]$

Proof: First prove that a single β- or η- reduction does not change $arity$; then generalize to the function $reduce$. □

3.4 Semantics of type expressions

One would like to interpret type expressions as elements of *PolTypes* defined in Sec. 2. In general, type expressions can be ascribed meanings only in the presence of an environment in which their free type variables are given meaning. We call the assignment of sets to type variables a *type environment* to distinguish it from static and dynamic environments used in Sec. 4:

$$ten : TypeEnv = TypeVar \rightarrow Types$$

Note that an environment assigns to each type variable an element from *Types* rather than from *PolTypes* since we do not allow for polymorphic variables, as this could lead to non-shallow polymorphism. Below the symbol [_/_] will stand for operation of updating of environments. Although it was already used to denote syntactic substitution its meaning should be clear from the context.

Now the semantics of type expressions will be the function

$$semtyp : TypeExpr \rightarrow TypeEnv \rightarrow \text{PolTypes}$$

the definition of which will follow. This definition starts with the function

$$semtycon : TypeCon \rightarrow PolTypes$$

that gives the meaning of constant type expressions. This function is another parameter of the theory and, as is apparent, the semantic meaning of type constants is to be independent of a type environment. To make the function *semtyp* consistent with the function *arity* (defined in Sec. 3.2) we require the following consistency for the type constants:

(14) $semtycon.tc \in PolTypes_{aricon[tc]}$

For the only obligatory type constant Fun (of *arity* 2) the function *semtycon* yields the value:

$$semtycon.\text{Fun} = (\text{FN } A)(\text{FN } B)A \rightarrow B$$

Above and hereafter we skip the bar in the set constructors introduced in Sec. 2 and $\times$ $+$ $\rightarrow$ mean $\bar{\times}$ $\bar{+}$ $\rightarrow$ unless stated explicitly otherwise. In the above FN denotes the abstraction operator over sets: given two sets A and B, *semtycon*.Fun becomes the (lifted) space of all functions from A to B.

The function *semtyp* is defined by the structural induction on type expressions in the following way:

(15) $semtyp.tc.ten = semtycon.tc$

$semtyp.tv.ten = ten.tv$

$semtyp.((\text{POLY } tv)te).ten =$
   $= \text{IF } arity[(\text{POLY } tv)te] \in Message \text{ THEN } TypeErr$
      $\text{ELSE } (\text{FN } A)semtyp.te.ten[A/tv]$

$semtyp.(te_1 \bullet te_2).ten =$
   $= \text{IF } arity[te_1 \bullet te_2] \in Message \text{ THEN } TypeErr$
      $\text{ELSE } (semtyp.te_1.ten).(semtyp.te_2.ten)$

$$semtyp.((\textbf{REC }\ tv)te).ten =$$

$$= \text{IF }\ arity[(\textbf{REC }\ tv)te] \in Message \text{ THEN } TypeErr$$

$$\text{ELSE } Rec.(semtyp.((\textbf{POLY }\ tv)te).ten)$$

Note that the type assigned by *semtyp* to any type expression may be different from *TypeErr* (see Sec. 2) only if the type expression is well-formed (i.e. its arity is non-error). This fulfills our announcement from Sec. 3.2 about the desirable relation between the syntactic function *arity* and the semantics of type expressions. It is apparent in (15) that the polymorphic abstraction and instantiation translate to the abstraction and application of functions $Types \rightarrow PolTypes_n$ for appropriate n. Finally, *Rec* is the enumerable union operator defined by (2).

An alternative approach to the definition of *semtyp* would be to define type environments as partial functions with finite domains. As a matter of fact, the value of *semtyp* over a type expression *te* and a type environment *ten* depends only on the values of *ten* for the finite set of free type variables in *te*:

Theorem 3.5   If type environments ten_1 and ten_2 coincide over the set *free[te]* of free variables of a type expression *te* then

$$semtyp.te.ten_1 = semtyp.te.ten_2$$

Proof: Straightforward from the definition (15) of *semtyp*.   □

To give the Reader more familiarity with the function *semtyp* that plays a central role for our notion of types we now formulate several properties of this function. The following theorem states that it is consistent with the function *arity*:

Theorem 3.6   For any well-formed type expression *te* and for any type environment *ten*:

$$semtyp.te.ten \in PolTypes_{arity[te]}$$

Proof: By the structural induction starting from (14) that establishes the claim for constant type expressions.   □

Analogously to theorems 3.2, 3.3 and 3.4 that describe the behavior of *arity*, the next three theorems describe the behavior of *semtyp*. Their proofs are analogous to the respective proofs in Sec. 3.3

Theorem 3.7   For any type expressions *te* and te_1 such that $arity[te_1] = 0$, any type variable *tv* and any type environment *ten*:

$$semtyp.te[te_1/tv].ten = semtyp.te.ten[semtyp.te_1.ten/tv]$$

Theorem 3.8 If the type expressions te_1 and te_2 are α-convertible to each other then for any type environment ten:

$$semtyp.te_1.ten = semtyp.te_2.ten$$

Theorem 3.9 For any well-formed type expression te and any type environment ten:

$$semtyp.te.ten = semtyp.(reduce[te]).ten$$

The defined meaning of (REC tv)te is often the least solution (wrt to set inclusion) of the equation

$$tv = te$$

but this is not always the case. For instance the equation

(16) $tv = Fun \, @ \, tv \, @ \, Bool$

has no solution in *Types* because the cardinality of any set is strictly less than the cardinality of the set of functions from this set to *Bool*. On the other hand, for any $ten : TypeEnv$

(17) $semtyp.((REC \, tv)Fun \, @ \, tv \, @ \, Bool).ten =$

$$= Rec.(semtyp.((POLY \, tv)Fun \, @ \, tv \, @ \, Bool).ten)$$
$$= \bigcup_{i=0}^{\infty} A_i \quad \text{where} \quad A_0 = \{\bot\}, \quad A_{i+1} = A_i \rightarrow Bool \quad \text{for } i = 0, 1, 2, \ldots$$

is a well defined element of *PolTypes* but not a solution of (16). The key is of course the noncontinuity of the set constructor Fun. In general, we do not require that the meaning assigned by *semtycon* to a polymorphic type constant be a continuous function on *Types*. But if it is then our construction does not introduce any new non-continuity. This is stated in the following two theorems:

Theorem 3.10 Let *ContPolTypes* be the family of sets built over *Types* in analogy to the construction (1) of *PolTypes* but using the continuous functions operator rather than $\rightarrow$, where continuity is understood with respect to the set inclusion in *Types* and the vertical order derived from it in *PolTypes_n*. Assume te is a well-formed type expression such that

$$semtycon.tc \in ContPolTypes$$

for every type constant tc that occurs in te.

Then for any type variable tv and any type environment ten:

$$semtyp.((POLY \, tv)te).ten \in ContPolTypes$$

Proof: Structural induction on te using the recursive definition (15) of *semtyp* and the fact that a function of two arguments is continuous if and only if it is continuous with respect to each of its arguments separately. $\square$

Theorem 3.11 For any type variable tv, any type expression te of arity 0 and any type environment ten, if the function

$$semtyp.((\text{POLY } tv)te).ten : Types \rightarrow Types$$

is continuous (equivalently: belongs to $ContPolTypes$) then

$$semtyp.((\text{REC } tv)te).ten$$

is the least fixed point of this function.

Proof: Structural induction again, and a standard construction of the least fixed point for a continuous function. □

4 Object expressions

While type expressions discussed in the previous Section describe sets, object expressions describe individual elements of these sets, e.g. numbers, truth values, functions. For non-polymorphic expressions and type expressions the relation "...*is of type...*" translates to the set-theoretic "...*belongs to...*". Expressions are strongly typed, i.e. every expression is assigned a unique type expression and this assignment turns the relation "...*is of type...*" into a function. The assignment of types to expressions stratifies the expressions in a similar way the arity function stratifies the type expressions. The semantic functions defined in Sec. 3.4 may have use the typing to check whether an expression is well-formed.

4.1 Syntax of object expressions

At the bottom of the construction of expressions lies a primitive domain of constants

$$con : Constant$$

that makes another parameter of the theory. Also an infinite countable collection

$$var : Variable$$

of variables is given. Variables are not a parameter, they are granted once for ever as has been the case with the type variables. The four primitive syntactic domains introduced so far: *TypeCon*, *TypeVar*, *Constant* and *Variable* are to be mutually disjoint and their elements syntactically distinguishable.

In our approach variables do not have fixed types, instead they are typed by static environments discussed in Sec. 4.2. This is different than standardly done in typed λ-calculus (cf. [12]) but we think this approach has its advantages.

The syntactic domain of expressions is defined by the following equation:

(18) $ex : Expr$ $::=$ *Constant*   constant

             | *Variable*   variable

             | $((\texttt{POLY}\ TypeVar)\ Expr)$ polymorphic abstraction

             | $(Expr\ @\ TypeExpr)$ polymorphic instantiation

             | $((\texttt{LAMBDA}\ Variable : TypeExpr)\ Expr)$ functional abstraction

             | $(Expr.Expr)$ functional application

             | $((\texttt{ABS}\ TypeVar)\ TypeExpr)$ abstraction into a recursive type

             | $((\texttt{REP}\ TypeVar)\ TypeExpr)$ representation of a recursive type

The superfluous parentheses in expressions may be skipped under the following precedences: the type instantiation @ binds stronger than the function application, which in turn binds stronger than other operators. Further, instantiation and application are left associative. When two @-s, one from type expressions and the other from expressions meet, they are still considered left-associative; thus $ex\ @\ te_1\ @\ te_2$ is $(ex\ @\ te_1)\ @\ te_2$.

The intended meaning of all but the last two clauses should be clear. The last two clauses are related to recursive types and they serve as conversion functions between a type and its recursive definition. Semantically they come down to identity functions on appropriate sets but they are essential for type checking. To better understand their role consider the type of sequences, first introduced in (8), instantiated with natural numbers Nat:

(19) $(\texttt{REC}\ \texttt{tv})\texttt{Unit+Nat}\times\texttt{tv}$

This should be semantically equivalent to

(20) $\texttt{Unit+Nat}\times((\texttt{REC}\ \texttt{tv})\texttt{Unit+Nat}\times\texttt{tv})$

because (19) is meant to be the least solution of

    $\texttt{tv} = \texttt{Unit+Nat}\times\texttt{tv}$

Still syntactically (19) and (20) are different types and should be supplied with explicit conversion functions

    $(\texttt{ABS}\ \texttt{tv})\texttt{Unit+Nat}\times\texttt{tv} : (20) \rightarrow (19)$

and

    $(\texttt{REP}\ \texttt{tv})\texttt{Unit+Nat}\times\texttt{tv} : (19) \rightarrow (20)$

The abbreviations ABS (abstraction) and REP (representation) originate from ML (see [10]).

4.2 Strong typing of object expressions

We want to assign a type expression to every well-formed expression. But as it may contain free variables it may be typed only in the presence of an environment. Such an environment we call *static:*

(21) *sen* : *StatEnv* =

$$= \{ s : Variable \rightarrow TypeExpr \cup Message \mid$$

$$(\forall var : Variable)(s.var = \text{"UNTYPED VARIABLE"}) \vee (arity[s.var] = 0) \}$$

The function *arity* has been defined in (7). We allow for variables with no type at all but if a variable is typed then its type has to be monomorphic.

Now, the type of an expression is given by the function

$$typing : Expr \rightarrow StatEnv \rightarrow TypeExpr \cup Message$$

The definition of *typing* starts with a function that assigns type expressions to constants:

$$typingcon : Constant \rightarrow \{ cte : ClTypeExpr \mid arity[cte] \notin Message \}$$

(for the definition of *ClTypeExpr* see (10). Note that we require that *typingcon.con* be well-formed for any *con* : *Constant*.

This function is another parameter of the theory. Note that constants are well-typed expressions (no typing errors) and are typed to closed type expressions only. In the following definition of typing the typing errors propagate i.e. all clauses start with checking whether subexpressions are well-formed, if not a message signalling an error is passed further up as the value of the function *typing*. This resembles the definition of *arity* that does the same to type expressions. The function *typing* is defined by:

(22) *typing.con.sen* = *reduce*[*typingcon.con*]

(function *reduce* is defined in (13))

$$typing.var.sen = reduce[sen.var]$$

$$typing.((\text{POLY } tv)ex).sen =$$

$$= \text{LET } te = typing.ex.sen$$

$$\text{IN IF } arity[te] \in Message \text{ THEN } arity[te]$$

$$\text{ELSE } reduce[(\text{POLY } tv')te[tv'/tv]]$$

where tv' is the least type variable not in $free[sen.var]$ for any variable var that occurs freely in ex (function $free$ is defined by (9)); see below for an explanation of this requirement

$typing.(ex \bullet te).sen =$

    $= \text{LET } te_1 = typing.ex.sen$

       $\text{IN IF } arity[te_1] \in Message \text{ THEN } arity[te_1]$

          $\text{ELSE } reduce[te_1 \bullet te]$

$typing.((\text{LAMBDA } var : te) ex).sen =$

    $= \text{LET } te_1 = typing.ex.sen[te/var]$

      IN CASES

            $arity[te] \in Message \quad \Longrightarrow \quad arity[te]$

            $arity[te] > 0 \qquad\qquad \Longrightarrow \quad \text{"NON-SHALLOW POLYMORPHISM"}$

            $arity[te_1] \in Message \quad \Longrightarrow \quad arity[te_1]$

            $arity[te_1] > 0 \qquad\qquad \Longrightarrow \quad \text{"NON-SHALLOW POLYMORPHISM"}$

            $\text{OTHERWISE} \qquad\qquad \Longrightarrow \quad reduce[\text{Fun} \bullet te \bullet te_1]$

          END

$typing.(ex_1.ex_2).sen =$

    $= \text{LET } te_1 = typing.ex_1.sen \text{ AND } te_2 = typing.ex_2.sen$

      IN CASES

            $arity[te_1] \in Message \qquad\qquad\qquad \Longrightarrow \quad arity[te_1]$

            $arity[te_2] \in Message \qquad\qquad\qquad \Longrightarrow \quad arity[te_2]$

            $arity[te_1] > 0 \text{ OR } arity[te_2] > 0 \quad\; \Longrightarrow \quad \text{"NON-SHALLOW POLYMORPHISM"}$

            $reduce[te_1] = Fun \bullet te_2' \bullet te$

            for some type expressions te and te_2'

            where $te_2' \sim te_2 \qquad\qquad\qquad\quad\; \Longrightarrow \quad te$

            $\text{OTHERWISE} \qquad\qquad\qquad\qquad\; \Longrightarrow \quad \text{"IMPROPER APPLICATION"}$

          END

(relation $\sim$ is defined in (12)).

$typing.((\text{ABS } tv) te).sen =$

$$= \text{IF } arity[te] \in Message \text{ THEN } arity[te]$$

$$\text{ELSE IF } arity[te] > 0 \text{ THEN "RECURSION ON POLYMORPHIC TYPE"}$$

$$\text{ELSE LET } te_1 = (\text{REC } tv)te$$

$$\text{IN } reduce[\text{Fun} \bullet te[te_1/tv] \bullet te_1]$$

$$typing.((\text{REP } tv)te).sen =$$

$$= \text{IF } arity[te] \in Message \text{ THEN } arity[te]$$

$$\text{ELSE IF } arity[te] > 0 \text{ THEN "RECURSION ON POLYMORPHIC TYPE"}$$

$$\text{ELSE LET } te_2 = (\text{REC } tv)te$$

$$\text{IN } reduce[\text{Fun} \bullet te_2 \bullet te[te_2/tv]]$$

Several comments concerning the above definition are due.

The typing of the polymorphic abstraction $(\text{POLY } tv)ex$ requires renaming the type variable tv so as to make it unrelated to any type expression that might be involved in typing ex via the static environment sen. Violation of this requirement may yield undesired effects, such as the following. Let

$$sen.var = tv_1$$

then the types of the following two expressions

$$(\text{POLY } tv_1)var \quad \text{and} \quad (\text{POLY } tv_2)var$$

that are intended to be α-convertible to each other, are not α-convertible themselves (cf. [8]).

The polymorphism under the operator LAMBDA of functional abstraction is prohibited. But this does not preclude our capability to deal with polymorphic functions; for example the polymorphic function null that verifies the emptiness of a sequence is typed and defined as follows (for Seq see (8)):

```
null  :   (POLY tv)(Seq • tv→Bool)
null  =   (POLY tv)(LAMBDA var:Seq • tv)......
```

while

```
null  :   Seq → Bool
null  =   (LAMBDA var:Seq)......
```

is intended as meaningless.

By analogy to the LAMBDA case, there can also be no polymorphism under the functional application. The message "IMPROPER APPLICATION" refers to the situation where ex_1 is not applicable to *ex* because of a type incompatibility. Note that this compatibility is checked modulo the α-renaming and between the reduced forms of type expressions.

We say that an expression *ex* is *well-formed* in a static environment *sen* if *typing.ex.sen* is a type expression rather than a message. This is analogous to the notion of well-formedness of type expressions introduced in Sec. 3.2. Note however that the reference to a static environment must not be omitted: for instance the expression

$$var_1 . var_2$$

is well-formed in any static environment *sen* such that both variables are typed and

$$reduce[sen.var_1] \sim \textbf{Fun} \; @ \; reduce[sen.var_2] \; @ \; te$$

for some *te* : *TypeExpr* and is ill-formed in any static environment that does not meet this requirement.

It is important to note that *typing.ex.sen* is always in its $\beta\eta$-reduced form provided it is not an error message, i.e.

$$typing.ex.sen = reduce[typing.ex.sen]$$

for any *ex* : *Expr* and *sen* : *StatEnv*.

This ends our remarks on the way the expressions are typed. To summarize, we give the following theorem on the relation between the syntactic substitution and the updating of static environments, an analogous statement for type expressions has been the Theorem 3.7:

Theorem 4.1   For any *ex, ex$_1$* : *Expr* and any *sen* : *StatEnv* such that *typing.ex$_1$.sen* $\in$ *Message* :

$$typing.ex[ex_1/var].sen = typing.ex.sen[typing.ex_1.sen/var]$$

Proof: By induction on length of *ex* using the definition (22) of typing and a definition analogous to (11) of syntactic substitution for object expressions (this time the variable binding operator **BIND** can only be **LAMBDA**).   □

Note that an expression may involve both object and type variables (the latter may occur in its **LAMBDA**, **ABS** and **REP** subexpression). Operator **LAMBDA** binds object variables while **POLY**, **ABS** and **REP** bind type variables. It is straightforward to define the notion of a closed expression — the one in which neither object nor type variables occur free. It may be then proved that *typing.ex.sen* is a closed type expression for any closed object expression *ex* and any static environment *sen* (in fact it does not depend on *sen*).

4.3 Semantics of object expressions

Now, we proceed to the semantics of expressions, or the evaluation rules. The semantics will be given by the function

$$semexp : Expr \rightharpoonup Env \rightharpoonup PolElems$$

(for *Elems* and *PolElems* see Sec. 2) but before its definition is brought we have to discuss its desirable properties and to choose an appropriate domain for the environment *Env*.

If *ex* is an expression then the function *typing* assigns to it a type expression

(23) $te = typing.ex.sen$

(see (22)). Now, the function *semtyp* defined by (15) assigns to this type expression an element

(24) $A = semtyp.te.ten$

from $PolTypes_{arity[te]}$ (cf. Theorem 3.6). In case the expression *ex* is monomorphic (i.e. $arity[te] = 0$) it is reasonable to expect that the element

$$a = semexp.ex.env$$

assigned to it by *semexp* be in A; i.e. that the following "diagram" commutes:

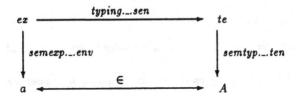

In general, provided $arity[te] = n$, we require

$$semexp.ex.env.A_1 \ldots . A_n \in A.A_1 \ldots . A_n \qquad \text{for any } A_1, A_2, \ldots, A_n \in Types$$

This makes the content of the theorem in the end of this Section.

In order that all this make sense the environment *env* has to be defined so that it contain both the *sen* needed for (23) and the *ten* needed for (24). It should also contain an assignment of values from *Elems* to object variables. This assignment we call the *dynamic environment*:

$$den : DynEnv = Variable \rightharpoonup Elems$$

$$env : Env =$$

$$= \{\langle ten, sen, den \rangle : TypeEnv \times StatEnv \times DynEnv \mid$$

$$(\forall var : Variable)\text{IF } sen.var = \text{"UNTYPED VARIABLE" THEN } den.var = ??$$

$$\text{ELSE } den.var \in semtyp.(sen.var).ten$$

$$\}$$

Let us recall that $sen.var$ is a monomorphic type expression (cf. the definition (21) of static environment) hence $semtyp.(sen.var).ten$ is an element of $Types$ (cf. Theorem 3.6). The definition of Env says that the value assigned to a variable in an environment has to be consistent with the type assigned to it in the same environment. In particular the THEN clause requires that if the type of a variable is undefined then so be the value.

The definition of $semexp$ starts with the function

$$semcon : Constant \rightarrow PolElems$$

that makes another parameter of our theory. We require that $semcon$ be consistent with the function $typingcon$ from Sec. 4.2 that types the constants. This means that for every constant con and for every type environment $ten : TypeEnv$ the following holds

(25) LET $te = typingcon.con$

IN LET $n = arity[te]$

IN $(semcon.con \in PolElems_n)$ &

$$((\forall A_1, \ldots, A_n \in Types)semcon.con.A_1 \ldots . A_n \in semtyp.te.ten.A_1 \ldots . A_n)$$

Recall that according to the definition of $typingcon$ the n above is a natural number (i.e. $arity$ does not yield an error message) and te is a closed type expression, hence in fact $semtyp.te.ten$ does not depend on ten.

Function $semexp$ is now defined by structural recursion on expressions:

(26) $semexp.con.\langle ten, sen, den \rangle = semcon.con$

$semexp.var.\langle ten, sen, den \rangle = den.var$

$semexp.((\text{POLY } tv)ex).\langle ten, sen, den \rangle =$

$= \text{IF } typing.((\text{POLY } tv)ex).sen \in Message \text{ THEN } ??$

$\text{ELSE } (\text{FN } A)semexp.ex.\langle ten[A/tv], sen, den \rangle$

$semexp.(ex \bullet te).\langle ten, sen, den \rangle =$

$\quad = $ IF $typing.(ex \bullet te).sen \in Message$ THEN ??

$\quad$ ELSE $semexp.ex.\langle ten, sen, den \rangle.(semtyp.te.ten)$

(note that in the ELSE clause above te has to be monomorphic and thus it denotes a set from $Types$)

$semexp.((\text{LAMBDA } var:te)ex).\langle ten, sen, den \rangle =$

$\quad = $ IF $typing.((\text{LAMBDA } var:te)ex).sen \in Message$ THEN ??

$\quad$ ELSE $(\text{FN } x : semtyp.te.ten)semexp.ex.\langle ten, sen[te/var], den[x/var]\rangle$

$semexp.(ex_1 . ex_2).\langle ten, sen, den \rangle =$

$\quad = $ IF $typing.((ex_1 . ex_2).sen \in Message$ THEN ??

$\quad$ ELSE $semexp.ex_1.\langle ten, sen, den \rangle . (semexp.ex_2.\langle ten, sen, den \rangle)$

$semexp.((\text{ABS } tv)te).\langle ten, sen, den \rangle =$

$\quad = $ IF $typing.((\text{ABS } tv)te).sen \in Message$ THEN ??

$\quad$ ELSE LET $(A = semtyp.((\text{REC } tv)te).ten)$ & $(B = semtyp.te[(\text{REC } tv)te/tv].ten)$

$\qquad$ IN IF $A = B$ THEN $(\text{FN } x : A)x$

$\qquad\qquad$ ELSE $\perp$

$semexp.((\text{REP } tv)te).\langle ten, sen, den \rangle =$

$\quad = $ IF $typing.((\text{REP } tv)te).sen \in Message$ THEN ??

$\quad$ ELSE LET $(A = semtyp.te[(\text{REC } tv)te/tv].ten)$ & $(B = semtyp.((\text{REC } tv)te).ten)$

$\qquad$ IN IF $A = B$ THEN $(\text{FN } x : A)x$

$\qquad\qquad$ ELSE $\perp$

Some comments concerning the *semexp* of ABS and REP are necessary. The semantic equality $A = B$ after the IF is in both cases satisfied whenever only continuous type constructors are used in te (cf. the end of Sec. 2); then the identity function belongs to $A \to B$ and is the desired semantical meaning of the expression. If this is not the case, we still want the semantic meaning of the expression to belong to $A \to B$, and $\perp$ is our only choice.

In analogy to the case of the function *semtyp*, the value assigned by *semexp* to any expression may be different from both $\perp$ and ?? only if the expression is well-formed.

The following theorem is responsible for the integrity of our *typing* and evaluating system.

Theorem 4.2　Given $ex : Expr$ and $env = \langle ten, sen, den \rangle : Env$ let $te = typing.ex.sen$. Then the following holds:

IF $te \in Message$ THEN $semexp.ex.env = ??$

ELSE LET $n = arity[te]$

  IN $(semexp.ex.env \in PolElems_n)$ &

   $((\forall A_1, \ldots, A_n \in Types)semexp.ex.env.A_1.\ldots.A_n \in semtyp.te.ten.A_1.\ldots.A_n)$

Proof: Structural induction on ex starting from (25) which is an analogous condition imposed on constants, and from the definition of Env that contains an analogous condition imposed on variables.

□

To end our considerations, note that the syntax of expressions involves the operators that bind type variables (POLY, ABS and REP) and one operator that binds individual variables (LAMBDA). Thus the notions of α- and $\alpha\beta\eta$- conversions are more complex in this case. We do not give here respective theorems since, unlike the ones quoted in Sec. 3, they are irrelevant for our purposes.

5 Final remarks

We have defined the basic syntax and semantics for the system of types and their elements that makes the core of a high-order polymorphic specification language. The semantic part has been defined in the naive set theory thus its understanding does not require any specialized concepts such as the Scott's theory.

The definition is open to extensions, in the sense that one may provide a syntax and semantics for her/his own type and object constants and thus obtain a language oriented towards her/his needs. In our paper-and-pencil experiments we have extended the collection of type constants to include continuous functions, Cartesian products, disjoint unions, etc. along with necessary constructors and destructors (for instance the least fixed point operator and conversion from continuous to all functions may be viewed as destructors for continuous functions). This will be presented in a separate paper (cf. [5]). We have also studied a way to turn the system into a programming and/or specification language. This also will be presented separately.

The point worth clarification is the "implementability" of our definition. Actually, Sec. 4 contains a complete interpreter of the system for an imaginary computer in which the whole set theory were hard-wired. This is very much in the spirit of the MetaSoft and other VDM-like specification systems.

Notably, there is just one feature that stands in the way of implementing the stuff on a more realistic computer: the equality check on sets A and B in the definition of $semexp$ for (ABS tv)te and (REP tv)te (see Sec. 4.3). But a user's extension may introduce new objects that may be unimplementable, for instance the strong equality. As long as the system is viewed as a VDM-like specification device the implementability is however not an issue.

Acknowledgements

The problems addressed in this paper have been extensively discussed at MetaSoft meetings. The authors are also grateful to anonymous referees whose comments and criticism have contributed to the clarity of exposition.

References

[1] *The Programming Language ADA. Reference Manual* LNCS 106, Springer-Verlag, 1981

[2] Andrzej Blikle *A Guided Tour of Naive Denotational Semantics and the Mathematics of Meta-Soft* internal report of the Dept. of Comp. Sci., Techn. Univ. of Denmark, Lyngby, 1986

[3] Andrzej Blikle *MetaSoft Primer: Towards a Metalanguage for Appplied Denotational Semantics* LNCS 288, Springer-Verlag, 1987

[4] Andrzej Blikle, Andrzej Tarlecki *Naive Denotational Semantics* in "Information Processing 83" Proc. of IFIP-Congress, North- Holland, pp. 345–355, 1983

[5] Andrzej Borzyszkowski, Ryszard Kubiak, Jacek Leszczyłowski, Stefan Sokolowski *Set-Theoretic Type Theory* in preparation

[6] Kim B. Bruce, Albert R. Meyer *The Semantics of Second-Order Polymorphic Lambda Calculus* in "Semantics of Data Types" Proc. of International Symposium, Sophia-Antipolis, LNCS 173, pp. 131–144, Springer-Verlag, 1984

[7] P. M. Cohn *Universal Algebra* D. Reidel Publishing Co., 1981

[8] S. Fortune, D. Leivant, M. O'Donnell *The Expressiveness of Simple and Second-Order Type Structures* JACM (30), pp. 151–185, 1983

[9] J-Y. Girard. *Interprétation fonctionelle et élimination des coupures dans l'aritmétique d'ordre supérieure* Thèse d'Etat, Université Paris VII, 1972.

[10] Michael J. Gordon, Robin J. Milner, Christopher P. Wadsworth *Edinburgh LCF* LNCS 78, Springer-Verlag, 1979

[11] Robert Harper, David B. Macqueen, Robin Milner *Standard ML* Edinburgh University Internal Report ECS-LFCS-86-2, March 1986

[12] J. Roger Hindley, Jonathan P. Seldin *Introduction to Combinators and λ-Calculus* Cambridge University Press, 1986

[13] Robin Milner *A Theory of Polymorphism in Programming* Journal of Computer and System Sciences, Vol.17, pp. 348–375, 1978

[14] Andrew M. Pitts *Polymorphism is Set Theoretic, Constructively* in "Category Theory in Computer Science", LNCS 283, pp. 12–39, Springer-Verlag, 1987

[15] J. C. Reynolds *Towards a theory of type structure* in B. Robinet, ed. Colloquium sur la programmation, pp. 408–425, LNCS 19, Springer-Verlag, 1974.

[16] John C. Reynolds *Polymorphism Is Not Set-Theoretic* in "Semantics of Data Types" Proc. of International Symposium, Sophia-Antipolis, LNCS 173, pp. 145–156, Springer-Verlag, 1984

[17] Dana Scott *Data types as lattices* Programming Research Group Technical Monographs, PRG-5, Oxford University, 1974

Mutually Recursive
Algebraic Domain Equations

Anne Elisabeth Haxthausen*
Department of Computer Science
Technical University of Denmark
DK-2800 Lyngby, Denmark

Abstract

A theory of *mutually recursive algebraic domain equations* is developed. The theory may provide algebraic interpretation of domain equations as known from VDM's specification language Meta-IV. A set of *mutually recursive algebraic domain equations* is roughly spoken a set of parameterized algebraic specifications applying instances of each other in a recursive fashion. A solution to a set of algebraic domain equations can be constructed by using a new parameter passing technique called *recursive parameter passing*. It is sketched how the theory makes sense under an arbitrary institution.

1 Introduction

Recursive definitions of syntactic and semantic domains play an important role in Meta-IV specifications. For instance, if we want to define a programming language having statements which are either while statements or assignments, where a while statement consists of a boolean and a statement, the domain *Stmt* of statements and the domain *While* of while statements may be defined (using the notation in [BJ82]) by the simultaneous domain equations:

$$Stmt \ = \ While \mid Ass$$
$$While \ = \ Bool \times Stmt$$

Now, a very interesting question is how to give semantics to these mutually recursive domain equations. This is the theme of this paper. There may be different approaches to this, depending on which mathematical model data types (domains) are given.

There have been two main approaches to data types. The one is Scott-Stracheys denotational/model oriented approach ([Sto77]) in which data types are certain partial ordered sets. The other is the (standard) algebraic approach in which data types are (discrete) algebras, i.e. not just sets, but operations on these as well. Accordingly, there have been two different methods for specifying data types. In Scott-Stracheys denotational/model oriented approach data types are, as in Meta-IV, constructed from a given set of basic domains and domain constructors, as solutions of domain equations, which may be recursive. The solution of a recursive domain equation may be constructed using inverse limits or universal domains. Algebraic specifications define the sets implicitly by the

---

*Address from May 1988: Dansk Datamatik Center, Lundtoftevej 1C, DK-2800 Lyngby, Denmark.

operations available to them and define the operations by their behaviour (axioms they must satisfy).

Different attempts to combine ideas (mathematical models and specification methods) from the two approaches have been made. The ideas of algebraic specification have been brought into the denotational/model oriented approach by the theory of continuous algebras [GTWW77], [MD84]. In [EL83] a specification method for algebraic data types using an algebraic analogue to Meta-IV's domain equations has been discussed.

In this paper we will try to combine the algebraic model of data types with the denotational/model oriented specification method of Meta-IV, that is we take the approach that domains denote algebras, and try to give semantics to recursive domain equations.

Our method is the following: First we transform the domain equations to an algebraic analogue called *algebraic domain equations*, and then we find the solution to these by using a new parameter passing technique called *recursive parameter passing*. We believe that this solution can serve as semantics for the Meta-IV domain equations. The algebraic analogue to domain equations is obtained by replacing the basic domains like *Bool* and N in the Meta-IV domain equations by algebraic specifications of *booleans* and *natural numbers*, and by replacing domain constructors like | and × by parameterized algebraic specifications of them. The equations obtained in this way are called *algebraic domain equations*. Below we will illustrate our method on the example above.

Our theory of mutually recursive algebraic domain equations is a generalization of the theory in [EL83] which only treats the case of *one* recursive algebraic domain equation. By our generalization specifications may be defined by an *arbitrary* number of *mutually recursive* algebraic domain equations, and the parameterized specifications of the right-hand sides of the equations may have an *arbitrary* number of parameters. Furthermore, we do not put any restrictions on which kind of semantics (initial, loose or ...) specifications are given. Finally, our theory is defined in the framework of an *arbitrary* institution.

We shall now try to give an algebraic interpretation of the domain equations of the example above. Assume we have given an algebraic specification ASS of assignments having the sort *ass* and a specification $BOOL$ of booleans having the sort *bool*. Furthermore, two parameterized specifications $UNION$ and $PROD$ (the algebraic analogues to the domain constructors | and ×) are given (using the notation in [EM85]):

$UNION(X, Y)$
$\quad = X + Y +$
      sorts   *union*
      opns   *inj1: x → union*
                inj2: y → union

$PROD(Z, V)$
$\quad = Z + V +$
      sorts   *prod*
      opns   *pair: z v → prod*
                first: prod → z
                second: prod → v
      axioms   *first(pair(a,b)) = a*
                 second(pair(a,b)) = b

where the formal parameter specifications are given by:
$X = $ **sorts** x, $Y = $ **sorts** y, $Z = $ **sorts** z, and $V = $ **sorts** v.

Above, x, y, z and v are the parameter sorts, *union* the sort of the union of elements of sort x and y, $inj1$ and $inj2$ the associated injections, *prod* the sort of pairs of elements of sort z and v, *pair* the pairing operation and *first* and *second* the associated projections.

Now we want to give a specification $STMT$ of statements as $UNION$ instantiated with a specification $WHILE$ of while statements and the specification ASS of assignments. The specification $WHILE$ is $PROD$ instantiated with $BOOL$ and $STMT$. This can be formulated as two mutually recursive equations:

$$STMT = UNION(WHILE[x \rightarrow prod], ASS[y \rightarrow ass])$$

$$WHILE = PROD(BOOL[z \rightarrow bool], STMT[v \rightarrow union])$$

However it is not possible to find the solution for $STMT$ and $WHILE$ (specifications of the data types denoted by $STMT$ and $WHILE$) using the standard parameter passing technique - each requires the other to be defined first. In this paper a new parameter passing technique *recursive parameter passing* is introduced. By this, the solution to two mutually interdependent equations of the form above can be found. The resulting specification $STMT$ has $WHILE$ as subspecification and vice versa (value specifications have the actual parameter specifications as subspecifications), i.e. $STMT = WHILE$. In general the solution to a set of recursively interdependent algebraic domain equations is *one* new specification.

The paper is organized as follows:
Section 2 presents some fundamental concepts and notation. Section 3 defines the concept of algebraic domain equations and an operation for combining specifications by recursive parameter passing. It is shown how to solve algebraic domain equations by use of recursive parameter passing. Finally some semantical properties of the solution is given. Section 4 generalizes this to the more general case, where the parameterized specifications may have multiple parameters, informally this means that there may be an arbitrary number of "unknowns" on each right-hand side of the equations. Finally, in section 5 it is explained how the theory given so far in the standard algebraic framework makes sense under a fixed but arbitrary institution (logical system).

The reader is assumed to be familiar with basic concepts of category theory such as *category*, *cocomplete category*, *full sub-category*, *functor*, *contra variant functor*, *cocontinuous functor*, *left adjoint*, *coequalizer*, *coproduct*, and *colimit*, (see [AM75]).

2 Fundamental Concepts and Notation

Any approach to algebraic specification must be based on some logical system. The notion of a logical system has been formalized by Goguen and Burstall [GB85], who introduced the notion of *institution*. In section 2.1 we will give the definition of the *institution* concept, and, in section 2.2, we will define the notions of *specification*, *specification morphism* and *parameterized specification* in the framework of a fixed, but arbitrary institution. Finally, in section 2.3, we will define the particular institution and some operations on specifications used in the standard algebraic framework.

2.1 Definition of the Institution Concept

Definition 2.1
An *institution* consists of:

1. A category *Sign* of signatures and signature morphisms.

2. A functor $Sen : Sign \rightarrow Set$
   which to each signature Σ in *Sign* associate the set of Σ-sentences and to each signature morphism $\sigma{:}\Sigma \rightarrow \Sigma'$ associate a function which translates Σ-sentences to Σ'-sentences.

3. a (contra variant) functor $Mod : Sign \rightarrow Cat^{op}$
   which to each signature Σ in *Sign* associate the category of Σ-models and Σ-model morphisms and to each signature morphism $\sigma{:}\Sigma \rightarrow \Sigma'$ associate a functor which translates Σ'-models and Σ'-model morphisms to Σ-models and Σ-model morphisms respectively.

4. A satisfaction relation $\models_\Sigma \; \subseteq \; |Mod(\Sigma)|^1 \times |Sen(\Sigma)|$ for each signature Σ in *Sign*.

such that for each signature morphism $\sigma{:}\Sigma \rightarrow \Sigma'$ in *Sign* the translations $Sen(\sigma)$ of sentences and the translations $Mod(\sigma)$ of models and model morphisms satisfy the following condition, called *the satisfaction condition*:
for each Σ'-model m' in $|Mod(\Sigma')|$ and for each Σ-sentence e in $|Sen(\Sigma)|$

$$m' \models_\Sigma e' \text{ iff } m \models_\Sigma e$$

where $e' = Sen(\sigma)(e)$ and $m = Mod(\sigma)(m')$

2.2 Specifications in Arbitrary Institutions

Given a fixed but arbitrary institution.

Definition 2.2
A *specification* $SPEC = (\Sigma, E)$ consists of a signature Σ and a set of Σ-sentences E $(E \subseteq Sen(\Sigma))$.

Definition 2.3
Given a specification $SPEC = (\Sigma, E)$ a *SPEC-model* is a Σ-model m $(m \in |Mod(\Sigma)|)$ satisfying all the sentences in E, i.e. $(\forall e \in E)(m \models_\Sigma e)$.

The full sub-category of $Mod(\Sigma)$ having all *SPEC-models* as objects is denoted $Cat(SPEC)$.

Definition 2.4
Given specifications $SPEC_1 = (\Sigma_1, E_1)$ and $SPEC_2 = (\Sigma_2, E_2)$ a *specification morphism* $\sigma{:}SPEC_1 \rightarrow SPEC_2$ is a signature morphism $\sigma{:}\Sigma_1 \rightarrow \Sigma_2$ such that all $SPEC_2$-models m when "forgotten" by $Mod(\sigma)$ to a Σ_1-model is a $SPEC_1$-model, i.e.
$(\forall m \in |Cat(SPEC_2)|)(Mod(\sigma)(m) \in |Cat(SPEC_1)|)$.

---

[1]Notation: $|C|$ denotes the class of objects in the category C.

Specifications and specification morphisms are defining a category $Spec$ of specifications.

The functor $Mod(\sigma)$ restricted to a functor from $Cat(SPEC_2)$ to $Cat(SPEC_1)$ is denoted V_σ and called the *forgetful functor* associated with σ.

We let $Cat : Spec \rightarrow Cat^{op}$ denote the functor sending a specification $SPEC$ to the category $Cat(SPEC)$ and a specification morphism σ to the corresponding forgetful functor V_σ.

Definition 2.5
A *multiparameterized specification* with multiplicity n consists of n specifications PAR_j, $j = 1, \ldots, n$ called *parameter specifications*, a specification $SPEC$ called the *target specification* and of n specification morphisms $\sigma_j : PAR_j \rightarrow SPEC$, $j = 1, \ldots, n$.

It is denoted by $SPEC((PAR_1, \sigma_1), \ldots, (PAR_n, \sigma_n))$ or just $(\sigma_1, \ldots, \sigma_n)$ leaving the specifications implicit.

A usual parameterized specification is a multiparameterized specification with $n = 1$. For $n = 0$ a multiparameterized specification degenerates to a usual specification.

2.3 The Standard Algebraic Framework

In this section we define the particular institution and some operations on specifications used in the standard algebraic framework. First we have to define some notions:

Definition 2.6
An *algebraic signature* Σ is a pair (S, OP) where S is a set of *sorts* (names) and OP is a family $(OP_{w,s})_{w \in S^*, s \in S}$ of *operation symbols*. An operation symbol $N \in OP_{\langle s_1, \ldots, s_n \rangle, s}$ is written $N : s_1 \ldots s_n \rightarrow s$ ($\in OP$).

Let (S, OP) and (S', OP') be algebraic signatures.

Definition 2.7
An *algebraic signature morphism* $\sigma : (S, OP) \rightarrow (S', OP')$ is a pair $(\sigma_{sorts}, \sigma_{opns})$ where $\sigma_{sorts} : S \rightarrow S'$ and σ_{opns} is a family $(OP_{w,s} : OP_{w,s} \rightarrow OP'_{\sigma_{sorts}(w,s)})_{w \in S^*, s \in S}$, where $\sigma_{sorts}((s_1, \ldots, s_n), s) = \langle \sigma_{sorts}(s_1), \ldots, \sigma_{sorts}(s_n) \rangle, \sigma_{sorts}(s))$. We write $\sigma(s)$ for $\sigma_{sorts}(s)$ and $\sigma(N : s_1 \ldots s_n \rightarrow s)$ for $\sigma_{\langle s_1, \ldots, s_n \rangle, s}(N)$.

Let $\Sigma = (S, OP)$ be an algebraic signature.

Definition 2.8
A Σ-*algebra* A consists of

1. a set A_s for each sort $s \in S$, and

2. a function $A_{op} : A_{s_1} \times \ldots \times A_{s_n} \rightarrow A_s$ for each $op = N : s_1 \ldots s_n \rightarrow s \in OP$

Let $\Sigma = (S, OP)$ be an algebraic signature, and let A and B be Σ-algebras.

Definition 2.9
A Σ-*homomorphism* $h : A \to B$ is a family of functions $(h_s : A_s \to B_s)_{s \in S}$ such that for any
$op = N : s_1 \ldots s_n \to s \in OP$ and $a_1 \in A_{s_1} \ldots a_n \in A_{s_n}$ $h_s(A_{op}(a_1, \ldots, a_n)) = B_{op}(h_{s_1}(a_1), \ldots, h_{s_n}(a_n)))$.

Let $\sigma : \Sigma \to \Sigma'$ be an algebraic signature morphism and A' be a Σ'-algebra.

Definition 2.10
The σ-*reduct* of the algebra A' is the the Σ-algebra A defined by: $A_s = A'_{\sigma(s)}$ for each $s \in S$, and
$A_{op} = A'_{\sigma(op)}$ for each $op \in OP$, where $(S, OP) = \Sigma$.

The σ-reduct may be extended to a functor by in a similar way defining the σ-reduct of Σ'-homomorphisms.

The notions defined above form the standard algebraic institution in which signatures are algebraic signatures; signature morphisms are algebraic signatures; for any signature Σ, the Σ-sentences are Σ-equations between Σ-terms, the Σ-models are the Σ-algebras, and the Σ-model morphisms are the Σ-homomorphisms:

1. The category *Sign* has as objects algebraic signatures and algebraic signature morphisms; the composition of the signature morphisms is the function composition of their components.

2. For each algebraic signature Σ in *Sign*, $Sen(\Sigma)$ is the set of Σ-equations between Σ-terms. For each algebraic signature morphism $\sigma : \Sigma \to \Sigma'$, $Sen(\sigma : \Sigma \to \Sigma')$ is the obvious function which translates Σ-equations to Σ'-equations.

3. For each algebraic signature Σ in *Sign*, $Mod(\Sigma)$ is the category of Σ-algebras and Σ-homomorphisms. For each algebraic signature morphism $\sigma : \Sigma \to \Sigma'$, $Mod(\sigma : \Sigma \to \Sigma')$ is the *reduct*-functor.

4. For any algebraic signature Σ, $A \models_\Sigma e$ iff the Σ-algebra A *satisfies* the Σ-equation e. For a precise definition of *satisfies*, see [EM85].

The operations $\cup$, $\subseteq$, *sorts* and *opns* on specifications in the standard algebraic framework are defined by:

$$((S_1, OP_1), E_1) \cup ((S_2, OP_2), E_2) \triangleq (S_1 \cup S_2, OP_1 \cup OP_2, E_1 \cup E_2)$$

$$((S_1, OP_1), E_1) \subseteq ((S_2, OP_2), E_2) \triangleq S_1 \subseteq S_2 \wedge OP_1 \subseteq OP_2 \wedge E_1 \subseteq E_2$$

$$sorts((S, OP), EQ) \triangleq S$$

$$opns((S, OP), EQ) \triangleq OP$$

Let $h : SPEC \to SPEC'$ be a specification morphism. We define the image of a specification $((S, OP), E)$ by h to be

$$h(((S, OP), E)) \triangleq ((h(S), h(OP)), Sen(h)(E))$$

3   Algebraic Domain Equations

This section gives an algebraic analogue to domain equations, i.e. a method for defining algebraic specifications as solutions to set of mutually recursive equations. *Algebraic domain equations* are first studied at the level of specifications and then at the level of models (algebras). The theory in this and next section is given in the standard algebraic framework.

3.1 Specification Level

This section defines the concept of *algebraic domain equations* and a parameter passing technique called *recursive parameter passing* by which the syntactic solution to a set of algebraic domain equations may be constructed.

Informally, a set of n *mutually recursive algebraic domain equations* is a set of simultaneous specification definitions of the form

$$X_1 = G_1(X_{l(1)}, p_1)$$
$$\vdots$$
$$X_n = G_n(X_{l(n)}, p_n)$$

where $l(j) \in \{1, \ldots, n\}$, $j = 1, \ldots, n$.
The right-hand sides are actualizations of parameterized specifications $G_1, \ldots, G_n$ by the specification variables $X_1, \ldots, X_n$ which are going to be defined. More formally:

Definition 3.1
A set of n *mutually recursive algebraic domain equations* is a set of n pairs

$$(SPEC_j(PAR_j, \iota_j), p_j), \; j = 1, \ldots, n$$

each consisting of a parameterized specification with

$$\iota_j : PAR_j \rightarrow SPEC_j$$

and a parameter passing morphism (a specification morphism)

$$p_j : PAR_j \rightarrow SPEC_{l(j)}, \; l(j) \in \{1, \ldots, n\}$$

Notice that ι_j and p_j have the same source but not necessary the same target. The target of p_j is the target of the specification morphism $\iota_{l(j)}$ of the $l(j)$'th parameterized specification.

The solution to a set of simultaneous algebraic domain equations is a specification which is the union of the target specifications with certain sorts and operation symbols identified. Technically this is obtained by a colimit construction in the category *Spec* of specifications:

Definition 3.2
A *(syntactic) solution* to a set of n mutually recursive algebraic domain equations $(SPEC_j(PAR_j, \iota_j), p_j)$, $j = 1, \ldots, n$ is the colimit object RES of $(\iota_1, \ldots, \iota_n, p_1, \ldots, p_n)$, i.e. there exists morphisms $h_j : SPEC_j \rightarrow RES$, $j = 1, \ldots, n$ such that $(RES, h_1, \ldots, h_n)$ is a colimit of $(\iota_1, \ldots, \iota_n, p_1, \ldots, p_n)$, that is

1.
$$h_j \circ \iota_j = h_{l(j)} \circ p_j, j = 1, \ldots, n \tag{1}$$

2. for all specifications $SPEC$ and specification morphisms $h'_j : SPEC_j \rightarrow SPEC$,
$j = 1, \ldots, n$ with
$$h'_j \circ \iota_j = h'_{l(j)} \circ p_j \tag{2}$$
there is a unique morphism $f{:}RES \rightarrow SPEC$ such that $h'_j = f \circ h_j$ for $j = 1, \ldots, n$.

Remarks:

- The solution is uniquely determined up to isomorphism.

- The solution exists since *Spec* in the standard algebraic framework is cocomplete, cf. [EL83].

We will now define an operation *recursive parameter passing* which informally spoken instantiates a set of parameterized specifications by instances of each other in a recursive manner.

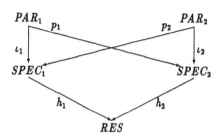

Figure 1: Recursive parameter passing diagram for the case $n = 2, l(1) = 2, l(2) = 1$

Definition 3.3
The diagram (for the case $n = 2$, $l(1) = 2$, $l(2) = 1$: see figure 1) consisting of the specifications

- PAR_j, $j = 1, \ldots, n$

- $SPEC_j$, $j = 1, \ldots, n$

- RES

and the specification morphisms

- $\iota_j : PAR_j \rightarrow SPEC_j$, $j = 1, \ldots, n$

- $p_j : PAR_j \rightarrow SPEC_{l(j)}$, $j = 1, \ldots, n$

- $h_j : SPEC_j \rightarrow RES$, $j = 1, \ldots, n$

such that $(RES, h_1, \ldots, h_n)$ is a colimit of $(\iota_1, \ldots, \iota_n, p_1, \ldots, p_n)$, is called a *recursive parameter passing diagram*, p_j, $j = 1, \ldots, n$ are called the *parameter passing morphisms*, h_j, $j = 1, \ldots, n$ the *induced morphism* and RES is called the *value specification*. The operation taking the parameterized specifications and the parameter passing morphisms to the value specification is called *recursive parameter passing*.

From definition 3.2 and 3.3 it follows that the solution to a set of algebraic domain equations may be found by recursive parameter passing.

In the special case where formal parameters are not passed by other formal parameters, i.e. $p_j(PAR_j) \subseteq BODY_{l(j)}$, where $SPEC_j = PAR_j + BODY_j$, we may give the following explicit definition of the recursive parameter passing operation *recpas* assuming the bodies $BODY_j$, $j = 1, \ldots, n$ are disjoint:

Definition 3.4

$$recpas(\iota_1, \ldots, \iota_n, p_1, \ldots, p_n) = h_1(SPEC_1) \cup \ldots \cup h_n(SPEC_n) \tag{3}$$

where h_j, $j = 1, \ldots, n$ are defined by:

$$h_j(s) = \begin{cases} p_j(s) & \text{for } s \in sorts(PAR_j) \\ s & \text{for } s \in sorts(BODY_j) \end{cases} \tag{4}$$

$$h_j(N : type) = \begin{cases} p_j(N : type) & \text{for } (N : type) \in opns(PAR_j) \\ N : h_j(type) & \text{for } (N : type) \in opns(BODY_j) \end{cases} \tag{5}$$

Remark:
The operation *recpas* is well-defined (is a recursive parameter passing operation), since it may be proved that h_j, $j = 1, \ldots, n$ become specification morphisms with sources $SPEC_j$ and target RES $= recpas(\iota_1, \ldots, \iota_n, p_1, \ldots, p_n)$ and $(RES, h_1, \ldots, h_n)$ is a colimit of $(\iota_1, \ldots, \iota_n, p_1, \ldots, p_n)$.

Remark:
Standard parameter passing can be considered as the special case of recursive parameter passing where $n = 2$, and one of the parameter specifications is the empty specification Φ. To be more precise the standard parameter passing operator *replace* given in [EM85] is related to *recpas* by:

$$replace(PAR, SPEC, p:PAR \rightarrow ACT)$$
$$= recpas(\iota_1:PAR \rightarrow SPEC, \iota_2:\Phi \rightarrow ACT, p:PAR \rightarrow ACT, \varphi:\Phi \rightarrow SPEC)$$

where Φ is the empty specification, ι_1, ι_2 and φ are inclusions.

Example 3.5
We shall now show how a solution to the problem in the introduction can be found by use of recursive parameter passing.

After partial instantiation of $UNION$ and $PROD$ by ASS and $BOOL$ respectively we get two parameterized specifications $\iota_1 : PAR_1 \rightarrow SPEC_1$ and $\iota_2 : PAR_2 \rightarrow SPEC_2$ with:

PAR_1 = **sorts** x

$SPEC_1$ = $PAR_1 + ASS +$
         sorts   *union*
         opns   *inj1*: $x \rightarrow union$
                inj2: *ass* $\rightarrow union$

PAR_2 = **sorts** v

$$SPEC_2 \quad = PAR_2 + BOOL +$$

sorts   *prod*

opns   *pair: bool v → prod*

        first: prod → bool

        second: prod → v

axioms   *first(pair(a,b)) = a*

          second(pair(a,b) = b

Let $p_1 : PAR_1 \to SPEC_2$ and $p_2 : PAR_2 \to SPEC_1$ be the parameter passing morphisms $[x \to prod]$ and $[v \to union]$.

Then (ι_1, p_1) and (ι_2, p_2) are two algebraic domain equations, whose solution RES can be found as the value specification $recpas(\iota_1, \iota_2, p_1, p_2)$ of the recursive parameter passing.

The induced morphisms h_1 and h_2 are defined by:

$h_1(x) = p_1(x) = prod$,

$h_1(inj1: x \to union) = inj1: prod \to union$,

$h_2(v) = p_2(v) = union$,

$h_2(pair:bool\ v \to prod) = pair:bool\ union \to prod$

$h_2(second:prod \to v) = second:prod \to union$

and on all other sorts and operation symbols they are the identity.

The resulting specification is

$$RES \quad = h_1(SPEC_1) \cup h_2(SPEC_2)$$
$$= ASS + BOOL +$$

sorts   *union*

        prod

opns   *inj1: prod → union*

        inj2: ass → union

        pair: bool union → prod

        first: prod → bool

        second: prod → union

axioms   *first(pair(a,b)) = a*

          second(pair(a,b) = b

3.2   Model Level

In last section we treated algebraic domain equations at the level of specifications. We saw that the solution to a set of algebraic domain equations is a specification and it may be found by the operation *recursive parameter passing*. The connection between the components to a set of algebraic domain equations and their solution is given by a *recursive parameter passing diagram*. This section studies the semantical properties of algebraic domain equations, and in particular it investigates how the loose respectively initial semantics of the solution to a set of mutually recursive algebraic domain equations is related to the loose respectively initial semantics of the parameterized specifications of the equations. This is done by studying the semantical properties of *recursive parameter passing diagrams*. The main result is that the recursive parameter passing is compositional, i.e. the semantics of the result may be expressed in terms of the semantics of its arguments, or equivalently the semantics of the solution to a set of algebraic domain equations may be expressed in terms of the semantics of its components (the morphisms).

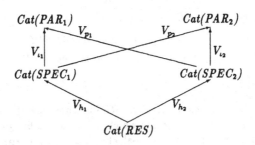

Figure 2: Diagram for the case $n = 2, l(1) = 2, l(2) = 1$.

Let be given a *recursive parameter passing diagram* as in definition 3.3.

Consider the corresponding diagram in the category Cat^{op} of categories. (For the case $n = 2, l(1) = 2, l(2) = 1$: see figure 2). It consists of the objects $Cat(PAR_j)$, $Cat(SPEC_j)$ and $Cat(RES)$ (the categories of PAR_j- , $SPEC_j$- and RES-algebras respectively) and the morphisms V_{i_j}, V_{p_j} and V_{h_j}, $j = 1,\dots,n$ (the forgetful functors induced by the specification morphisms ι_j, p_j and h_j). This diagram has the following limit property:

Theorem 3.6
$(Cat(RES), V_{h_1}, \dots, V_{h_n})$ is a limit for the diagram $(V_{i_1}, \dots, V_{i_n}, V_{p_1}, \dots, V_{p_n})$, i.e.

1. the subdiagrams $(V_{i_j}, V_{h_j}, V_{p_j}, V_{h_{l(j)}})$, $j = 1,\dots,n$ are commutative, i.e.

$$V_{i_j} \circ V_{h_j} = V_{p_j} \circ V_{h_{l(j)}} \tag{6}$$

2. for all categories $Cat(SPEC)$ and functors $h_j':Cat(SPEC_j) \to Cat(SPEC)$, $j = 1,\dots,n$ with $V_{i_j} \circ h_j' = V_{p_j} \circ h_{l(j)}'$ there is a unique functor $f:Cat(SPEC) \to Cat(RES)$
such that $h_j' = V_{h_j} \circ f$ for $j = 1,\dots,n$.

Proof:
Follows from the colimit property of the recursive parameter passing diagram and the fact that the functor $Cat:Spec \to Cat^{op}$ is cocontinuous, cf. [ST85].
□

From the theorem above we conclude the loose semantics of algebraic domain equations is *compositional*, since the loose semantics $Cat(RES)$ of the solution is given in terms of the loose semantics V_{i_j} of the parameterized specifications.

We will now define a construction *amalgamated sum* by which algebras of the solution specification may be constructed from target specification algebras with the same parameter reducts.

Definition 3.7

For all algebras $A_j \in Cat(SPEC_j)$, $j = 1, \ldots, n$ with

$$V_{\iota_j}(A_j) = V_{p_j}(A_{l(j)})$$

the *amalgamated sum*

$$A_1 + \ldots + A_n$$

of $A_1, \ldots, A_n$ is the algebra $A \in Cat(RES)$ defined by:

$$A_s = (A_j)_{s'} \text{ for } s = h_j(s') \text{ and } s' \in sorts(SPEC_j) \tag{7}$$
$$A_{op} = (A_j)_{op'} \text{ for } op = h_j(op') \text{ and } op' \in opns(SPEC_j) \tag{8}$$

From the following theorem we conclude that the RES-algebras are the amalgamated sums of $SPEC_j$-algebras $j = 1, \ldots, n$, i.e. those algebras which can be found by 'gluing together' $SPEC_j$-algebras with the same PAR_j-reducts. Each RES-algebra has a *unique* representation as an amalgamated sum.

Theorem 3.8

For all algebras $A \in Cat(RES)$ and for all algebras $A_j \in Cat(SPEC_j)$ $j = 1, \ldots, n$ with

$$V_{\iota_j}(A_j) = V_{p_j}(A_{l(j)}) \tag{9}$$

we have

$$A = A_1 + \ldots + A_n \Leftrightarrow (A_1 = V_{h_1}(A)) \wedge \ldots \wedge (A_n = V_{h_n}(A))$$

i.e. A is the amalgamated sum of $A_1, \ldots, A_n$ if and only if A_j is the h_j-reduct of A for $j = 1, \ldots, n$.

The proof is given in [Hax88a].

From the following theorem we conclude that the initial semantics is *compositional* as the initial semantics T_{RES} of the solution is given in terms of the initial semantics F_j of the parameterized specifications.

Theorem 3.9

Assume that the free functors (left adjoints) F_j w.r.t. V_{ι_j}, $j = 1, \ldots, n$ are persistent. Then the initial RES-algebra T_{RES} has the property that $A_j = V_{h_j}(T_{RES})$, $j = 1, \ldots, n$ are the initial solutions to the fixpoint equations

$$F_j \circ V_{p_j}(A_{l(j)}) \simeq A_j, \; j = 1, \ldots, n$$

The proof is given in [Hax88a].

From the theorems 3.9 and 3.8 we conclude:

Theorem 3.10

Assume that the free functors (left adjoints) F_j w.r.t. V_{ι_j}, $j = 1, \ldots, n$ are persistent. Then the initial RES-algebra T_{RES} is the amalgamated sum of $SPEC_j$-algebras A_j which are the initial solutions to the fixpoint equations

$$F_j \circ V_{p_j}(A_{l(j)}) \simeq A_j, \; j = 1, \ldots, n$$

4 The Multiparameter Case

Until now we have been looking at the case where the parameterized specifications had only one parameter specification. We will now generalize the theory to the case, where each of the parameterized specifications may have an arbitrary and distinct number of parameter specifications.

4.1 Specification Level

Informally a set of n *mutually recursive algebraic domain equations* is a set of simultaneous specification definitions of the form

$$X_1 \;=\; G_1(X_{l(1,1)}, P_{(1,1)}, \ldots, X_{l(1,m(1))}, P_{(1,m(1))})$$
$$\vdots$$
$$X_n \;=\; G_n(X_{l(n,1)}, P_{(n,1)}, \ldots, X_{l(n,m(n))}, P_{(n,m(n))})$$

where $l(j,i) \in \{1, \ldots, n\}$, $i = 1, \ldots, m(j)$, $j = 1, \ldots, n$.
The right-hand sides are actualizations of parameterized specifications $G_1, \ldots, G_n$ by the specification variables $X_1, \ldots, X_n$ which are going to be defined. More formally:

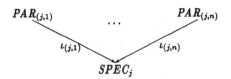

$$PAR_{(j,1)} \qquad \cdots \qquad PAR_{(j,n)}$$
$$\iota_{(j,1)} \qquad\qquad \iota_{(j,n)}$$
$$SPEC_j$$

Figure 3: A multiparameterized specification

Definition 4.1
A set of n *mutually recursive algebraic domain equations*
is a set of n pairs

$$(SPEC_j((PAR_{(j,1)}, \iota_{(j,1)}), \ldots, (PAR_{(j,m(j))}, \iota_{(j,m(j))})), (p_{(j,1)}, \ldots, p_{(j,m(j))})), \; j = 1, \ldots, n$$

each consisting of a multi-parameterized specification of multiplicity $m(j)$ with

$$\iota_{(j,i)} : PAR_{(j,i)} \rightarrow SPEC_j, \; i = 1, \ldots, m(j)$$

and a list of $m(j)$ parameter passing morphisms

$$p_{(j,i)} : PAR_{(j,i)} \rightarrow SPEC_{l(j,i)}, \; l(j,i) \in \{1, \ldots, n\}, \; i = 1, \ldots, m(j)$$

Definition 4.2

The *(syntactic) solution* to a set of algebraic domain equations is a colimit object RES of the diagram consisting of the specifications:

- $PAR_{(j,i)}$, $i = 1, \ldots, m(j)$, $j = 1, \ldots, n$

- $SPEC_j$, $j = 1, \ldots, n$

and the morphisms:

- $\iota_{(j,i)} : PAR_{(j,i)} \to SPEC_j$, $i = 1, \ldots, m(j)$, $j = 1, \ldots, n$

- $p_{(j,i)} : PAR_{(j,i)} \to SPEC_{l(j,i)}$, $i = 1, \ldots, m(j)$, $j = 1, \ldots, n$

Definition 4.3

The diagram consisting of the specifications:

- $PAR_{(j,i)}$, $i = 1, \ldots, m(j)$, $j = 1, \ldots, n$

- $SPEC_j$, $j = 1, \ldots, n$

- RES

and the specification morphisms:

- $\iota_{(j,i)} : PAR_{(j,i)} \to SPEC_j$, $i = 1, \ldots, m(j)$, $j = 1, \ldots, n$

- $p_{(j,i)} : PAR_{(j,i)} \to SPEC_{l(j,i)}$, $i = 1, \ldots, m(j)$, $j = 1, \ldots, n$

- $h_j : SPEC_j \to RES$, $j = 1, \ldots, n$

such that $(RES, h_1, \ldots, h_n)$ is a colimit of the diagram consisting of the specifications:

- $PAR_{(j,i)}$, $i = 1, \ldots, m(j)$, $j = 1, \ldots, n$

- $SPEC_j$, $j = 1, \ldots, n$

and the morphisms:

- $\iota_{(j,i)} : PAR_{(j,i)} \to SPEC_j$, $i = 1, \ldots, m(j)$, $j = 1, \ldots, n$

- $p_{(j,i)} : PAR_{(j,i)} \to SPEC_{l(j,i)}$, $i = 1, \ldots, m(j)$, $j = 1, \ldots, n$

is called a *recursive parameter passing diagram*, $p_{(j,i)}$, $i = 1, \ldots, m(j)$, $j = 1, \ldots, n$ are called the *parameter passing morphisms*, h_j, $j = 1, \ldots, n$ the *induced morphism* and RES is called the *value specification*. The operation taking the parameterized specifications and the parameter passing morphisms to the value specification is called *recursive parameter passing*.

In the special case where formal parameters are not passed by other formal parameters, i.e. $p_{(j,i)}(PAR_{(j,i)}) \subseteq BODY_{l(j,i)}$, where $SPEC_j = PAR_{(j,1)} + \ldots + PAR_{(j,m(j))} + BODY_j$, we may give the following explicit definition of the recursive parameter passing operation $recpas$ assuming the bodies $BODY_j$, $j = 1, \ldots, n$ are disjoint:

Definition 4.4

Let $PSPEC_j = SPEC_j((PAR_{(j,1)}, \iota_{(j,1)}), \ldots, (PAR_{(j,m(j))}, \iota_{(j,m(j))}))$
and $p_j = (p_{(j,1)}, \ldots, p_{(j,m(j))})$ in

$$recpas(PSPEC_1, \ldots, PSPEC_n, p_1, \ldots, p_n) = h_1(SPEC_1) \cup \ldots \cup h_n(SPEC_n) \tag{10}$$

where h_j, $j = 1, \ldots, n$ are defined by:

$$h_j(s) = \begin{cases} p_{(j,i)}(s) & \text{for } s \in sorts(PAR_{(j,i)}) \\ s & \text{for } s \in sorts(BODY_j) \end{cases} \tag{11}$$

$$h_j(N : type) = \begin{cases} p_{(j,i)}(N : type) & \text{for } (N : type) \in opns(PAR_{(j,i)}) \\ N : h_j(type) & \text{for } (N : type) \in opns(BODY_j) \end{cases} \tag{12}$$

Remark:
It may be proved that the operation $recpas$ is well-defined.

Example 4.5
We shall now see how the problem in the introduction can be expressed as a set of 4 simultaneous algebraic domain equations (the case $n = 4$) with $m(1) = m(2) = 2$, $m(3) = m(4) = 0$ and $l(1,1) = 2$, $l(1,2) = 3$, $l(2,1) = 4$, $l(2,2) = 1$ without a preceding partial instantiation as in example 3.5.

Let the four parameterized specification (the two of them are degenerated) be given by:

$PAR_{(1,1)}$ = **sorts** x

$PAR_{(1,2)}$ = **sorts** y

$SPEC_1$ = $PAR_{(1,1)} + PAR_{(1,2)}$ +
     sorts $union$
     opns $inj1: x \to union$
            $inj2: y \to union$

$PAR_{(2,1)}$ = **sorts** z

$PAR_{(2,2)}$ = **sorts** v

$SPEC_2$ = $PAR_{(2,1)} + PAR_{(2,2)}$ +
     sorts $prod$
     opns $pair: bool\ v \to prod$
            $first: prod \to z$
            $second: prod \to v$
     axioms $first(pair(a,b)) = a$
                 $second(pair(a,b) = b$

$$SPEC_3 \quad = ASS$$

$$SPEC_4 \quad = BOOL$$

Let $p_{(1,1)}$, $p_{(1,2)}$, $p_{(2,1)}$ and $p_{(2,2)}$ be the parameter passing morphisms $[x \rightarrow prod]$, $[y \rightarrow ass]$, $[z \rightarrow bool]$ and $[v \rightarrow union]$.

The solution RES which can be found by recursive parameter passing is the same as in example 3.5.

4.2 Model Level

Theorem 4.6
$(Cat(RES), V_{h_1}, \ldots, V_{h_n})$ is a limit for the diagram consisting of the categories

1. $Cat(PAR_{(j,i)})$, $i = 1, \ldots, m(j)$, $j = 1, \ldots, n$

2. $Cat(SPEC_j)$, $j = 1, \ldots, n$

and of the functors

1. $V_{t_{(j,i)}}$, $i = 1, \ldots, m(j)$, $j = 1, \ldots, n$

2. $V_{p_{(j,i)}}$, $i = 1, \ldots, m(j)$, $j = 1, \ldots, n$

Definition 4.7
For all algebras $A_j \in Cat(SPEC_j)$, $j = 1, \ldots, n$ with

$$V_{t_{(j,i)}}(A_j) = V_{p_{(j,i)}}(A_{l(j,i)})$$

the *amalgamated sum*

$$A_1 + \ldots + A_n$$

of A_1, ..., A_n is the algebra $A \in Cat(RES)$ defined by:

$$A_s = (A_j)_{s'} \text{ for } s = h_j(s') \text{ and } s' \in sorts(SPEC_j) \tag{13}$$
$$A_{op} = (A_j)_{op'} \text{ for } op = h_j(op') \text{ and } op' \in opns(SPEC_j) \tag{14}$$

Theorem 4.8
For all algebras $A \in Cat(RES)$ and for all algebras $A_j \in Cat(SPEC_j)$ $j = 1, \ldots, n$ with

$$V_{t_{(j,i)}}(A_j) = V_{p_{(j,i)}}(A_{l(j,i)}) \tag{15}$$

we have

$$A = A_1 + \ldots + A_n \Leftrightarrow (A_1 = V_{h_1}(A)) \wedge \ldots \wedge (A_n = V_{h_n}(A))$$

i.e. A is the amalgamated sum of A_1, ..., A_n if and only if A_j is the h_j-reduct of A for $j = 1, \ldots, n$.

We will now give the theorem corresponding to theorem 3.9.

Let $(\eta_{(j,1)}, \ldots, \eta_{(j,m(j))}, PAR_j)$ be the coproduct of the $m(j)$ parameters of the j'th parameterized specification $PAR_{(j,1)}, \ldots, PAR_{(j,m(j))}$

$$\eta_{(j,i)} : PAR_{(j,i)} \rightarrow PAR_j$$

Let for each j, $j = 1, \ldots, n$ $\iota_j : PAR_j \rightarrow SPEC_j$ be the unique morphism satisfying

$$\iota_j \circ \eta_{(j,i)} = \iota_{(j,i)} \text{ for all } i = 1, \ldots, m(j)$$

i.e. the diagram below commutes:

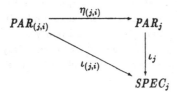

Theorem 4.9

Assume that the free functors (left adjoints) F_j w.r.t. V_{ι_j} $j = 1, \ldots, n$ are persistent. Then the initial RES-algebra T_{RES} has the property that $A_j = V_{h_j}(T_{RES})$, $j = 1, \ldots, n$ are the initial solutions to the fixpoint equations

$$F_j(V_{P_{(j,1)}}(A_{l(j,1)}) + \ldots + V_{P_{(j,m(j))}}(A_{l(j,m(j))})) \simeq A_j, \ j = 1, \ldots, n$$

where the argument of F_j is the unique object B_j in $Cat(PAR_j)$ with $V_{\eta_{(j,i)}}(B_j) = V_{P_{(j,i)}}(A_{l(j,i)})$.

Theorem 4.10

Assume that the free functors (left adjoints) F_j w.r.t. V_{ι_j} $j = 1, \ldots, n$ are persistent. Then the initial RES-algebra T_{RES} is the amalgamated sum of $SPEC_j$-algebras A_j which are the initial solutions to the fixpoint equations

$$F_j(V_{P_{(j,1)}}(A_{l(j,1)}) + \ldots + V_{P_{(j,m(j))}}(A_{l(j,m(j))})) \simeq A_j, \ j = 1, \ldots, n$$

where the argument of F_j is the unique object B_j in $Cat(PAR_j)$ with $V_{\eta_{(j,i)}}(B_j) = V_{P_{(j,i)}}(A_{l(j,i)})$.

5   Generalization to Arbitrary Institutions

The theory has been made in the standard algebraic framework, however the definitions of algebraic domain equations, their solutions and the recursive parameter passing have been made independent of the underlying logical system and may hence be used in the framework of an arbitrary institution, i.e. in a variety of logical systems.

We must require the category $Sign$ of signatures is cocomplete in order to be sure that the solution to any set of mutually recursive algebraic domain equations exists.

The compositionality property of the loose semantics (theorem 3.6 and 4.6) holds only for institutions having a cocontinuous model functor Mod.

The definition 3.7 and 4.7 of amalgamated sum should now be defined as the unique model (algebra) having the universal property of theorem 3.8 and 4.8 in order to be institution independent.

The fixpoint theorems 3.9 and 4.9 are valid for liberal institutions, i.e. institutions for which there exists a left adjoint (free construction) to every 'forgetful' functor $Mod(\sigma)$ associated with a signature morphism σ in $Sign$.

6 Conclusion

The notion of *algebraic domain equations* introduced by [EL83] has been extended to the case of an arbitrary number of simultaneous equations and generalized to the framework of an arbitrary institution. Furthermore, a new algebraic specification building operation for combining specifications by recursive parameter passing has been defined. It gives a syntactic method for solving algebraic domain equations. Its usefulness has been demonstrated by an example. It does not increase the expressive power of algebraic specifications, but gives the possibility of combining specifications in a recursive fashion, which in many cases corresponds to a natural way of structuring. The recursive parameter passing operation is shown to be compositional wrt. as well the loose as the initial semantics.

It is explained how the theory may provide an algebraic interpretation of Meta-IV's domain equations. Using the standard algebraic framework we may interpret domain equations not involving the function space arrow. The theory may also provide interpretation of recursive definitions of Meta-IV specification units in a structured version of Meta-IV, (see [Hax86] and [Hax88b]).

The theory may easily be extended to also covering *parameterized domain equations*: A *parameterized domain equation* is like a (non-parameterized) domain equation but with some of the parameter passing morphisms $p_{(j,i)}$ missing. The solution is found by partial recursive parameter passing. It is a parameterized specification having as parameters those parameters which are not instantiated, and as target specification the solution which may be found by usual recursive parameter passing using $\iota_{(j,i)}$ for the missing parameter passing morphisms.

A remaining issue is the question about how to handle shared subspecifications in connection with algebraic domain equations. This will be covered in [Hax88b].

Acknowledgements

The author is grateful to Professor Dines Bjørner for giving the idea of making an algebraic version of Meta-IV and to Hans Rischel for many helpful discussions. The author is indebted to H.-J. Kreowski for important suggestions and comments and to Professor H. Ehrig, M. Löwe, W. Fey and H. Hansen for inspiring discussions and valuable suggestions and comments to an earlier version of this paper. Finally, the author would like to thank Mogens Nielsen and Ma Qing Ming for helpful comments to the paper.

References

[AM75]   M. A. Arbib and E. G. Manes. *Arrows, Structures and Functors. The Categorical Imperative*. Academic Press, Inc., 1975.

[BJ82]   D. Bjørner and C. B. Jones. *Formal Specification and Software Development*. Prentice-Hall International, Inc., 1982.

[EL83]   H-D. Ehrich and U. Lipeck. Algebraic domain equations. *Theoretical Computer Science*, (27):167–196, 1983.

[EM85]   H. Ehrig and E. Mahr. *Fundamentals of Algebraic Specification 1: Equations and Initial Semantics*. Springer-Verlag, 1985.

[GB85]   J.A. Goguen and R.M. Burstall. *Institutions: Abstract Model Theory for Computer Science*. SRI International, 1985.

[GTWW77] J.A. Goguen, J.W. Thatcher, E.G. Wagner, and J.B. Wright. Initial Algebra Semantics and Continuous Algebras. *Journal of Association Computing Machinery*, (24):68–95, 1977.

[Hax86]   A. E. Haxthausen. *Meta-IV in an Algebraic Framework*. Technical Report, Department of Computer Science, Technical University of Denmark, December 1986. Revised April 1988.

[Hax88a] A. E. Haxthausen. Mutually recursive algebraic specifications. 1988. To appear.

[Hax88b] A. E. Haxthausen. *Structuring Mechanisms in Formal Specification Languages*. Technical Report, Department of Computer Science, Technical University of Denmark, May 1988.

[MD84]   B. Möller and W. Dosch. On the algebraic specification of domains. In *Proceedings of 3rd Workshop on Specification of Abstract Data Types*, Bremen, 1984.

[ST85]   D. Sannella and A. Tarlecki. *Specifications in an Arbitrary Institution*. Technical Report, Department of Computer Science, University of Edinburgh, 1985.

[Sto77]   J. E. Stoy. *Denotational Semantics: The Scott-Strachey Approach to Programming Language Theory*. MIT Press, 1977.

Proof rules for VDM statements

Robert Milne

STC Technology Ltd, London Road, Harlow, Essex, CM17 9NA, United Kingdom

1 Introduction

1.1 Scope

Certain dialects of VDM include constructive declarations of operations using statements, as well as implicit declarations using pre-conditions and post-conditions. This note concerns how such statements are to be understood for a language in which the primary stress is not on transformations of states but on assertions about states.

In the absence of a standard for VDM, the dialect considered is the STC VDM Reference Language [1,2]. This is based on the VDM of Jones [6] and intended for use in the STC group of companies. Most of the note should be equally applicable to other dialects.

1.2 Why statements are needed

Much teaching material for VDM deals with implicit declarations of functions and operations in terms of pre-conditions and post-conditions. Some deals with constructive declarations of types using maps (which are general arrays), lists and sets, and with the formation of subtypes using invariants. Only very little deals with the constructive declaration of functions and operations using expressions and statements, presumably because expressions and statements are thought to be familiar to users already.

This emphasis in the teaching material does not mean that statements can be omitted from VDM. Without statements, VDM would be unable to provide a clear development path from implicit specifications to constructive ones. Though it would let users make assertions about operations it would not let them compose operations from other operations. (Combinations of pre-condition and post-condition 'quotations' can serve as compositions of operations but they are often long-winded and sometimes unimplementable.)

In fact without statements VDM would be curiously lop-sided. For control flow it would permit only implicit declarations, whilst for data structuring it would permit at least:

- implicit declarations (in which a type would be marked as not yet defined and would be constrained by the pre-conditions and post-conditions of functions and operations acting on its elements);

- constructive declarations (in which a type would be described using maps, lists and sets and would be subject to an invariant);

- proof rules for justifying the refinement of implicit declarations of types into constructive ones.

The first of these usually has a counterpart for operations in VDM. Statements provide a counterpart to the second. Proof rules like those in this note provide a counterpart to the third: they allow implicit declarations of operations to be refined into constructive ones. They can also be viewed as defining conditions in which combinations of pre-condition and post-condition 'quotations' are implementable (which here means essentially that they are monotonic with respect to theory inclusion [10]).

1.3   How the proof rules are expressed

The proof rules need to be expressed in a compositional manner: for a composite statement the pre-condition and post-condition must be composed from the pre-conditions and post-conditions of its components. When this is done, the proof rules can be used to justify the refinement of an implicit declaration of an operation into a constructive one by decomposing the pre-condition and post-condition of the operation into pre-conditions and post-conditions of statements.

Here pre-conditions and post-conditions are formulated using equations which are like those for synthesised attributes in attributed grammars: there are functions *pre* and *post* which calculate a pre-condition and post-condition for a statement in terms of pre-conditions and post-conditions of the components of the statement. These components are not necessarily themselves statements, so *pre* and *post* are overloaded.

An equivalent formulation of the pre-conditions and post-conditions could be based on inference rules. These would let a pre-condition and a post-condition for a composite statement be inferred from pre-conditions and post-conditions for the components.

Either of these formulations produces rather untidy results. This is due partly to the emphasis on variables in the proof rules and partly to the VDM distinction between pre-conditions and post-conditions. Two somewhat different approaches to proof rules for statements are described in 2.1 and 2.2; these can produce quite tidy results when they are applied to languages that have been designed suitably.

The proof rules given here differ from those suggested before for VDM [6,7], because, for example:

- they rely on 'syntactic' entities such as variables instead of 'semantic' entities such as states (as exemplified in the treatment of assignment statements in 6.1.3, conditional statements in 6.1.4, and sequencing statements in 6.5.3);

- they handle loops by introducing general induction rules (given in 6.1.6) that avoid explicit uses of well-founded relations;

- they deal with a crude modularity mechanism (discussed in 6.2.2).

2 Related work

2.1 Equational axioms

There is a technique for specifying operations using equational axioms, analogous to that for specifying functions using equational axioms [8]. This technique generalises the use of pre-conditions and post-conditions like those of VDM. It involves the introduction of a notion of equality between statements; this notion is very straightforward and useful, but as it is missing from most dialects of VDM it is adopted here only to provide the following explanation of pre-conditions and post-conditions.

If 'u_1', ..., 'u_m' are the variables which may be read from but not written to by 'statement' and if 'v_1', ..., 'v_n' are the variables which may be read from and written to by 'statement', then the claim that the statement 'statement' has pre-condition 'proposition$_1$' and post-condition 'proposition$_2$' can be formalised as

$$(\forall\ y_1 \in type[\![\ u_1\ ]\!], \ldots, y_m \in type[\![\ u_m\ ]\!])$$
$$(\forall\ z_1 \in type[\![\ v_1\ ]\!], \ldots, z_n \in type[\![\ v_n\ ]\!])$$
$$(proposition_1\ [y_1, \ldots, y_m, z_1, \ldots, z_n/u_1, \ldots, u_m, v_1, \ldots, v_n] \Rightarrow$$
$$(\exists\ z_1' \in type[\![\ v_1\ ]\!], \ldots, z_n' \in type[\![\ v_n\ ]\!])$$
$$((\textbf{begin}\ u_1 := y_1 \ldots u_m := y_m\ v_1 := z_1 \ldots v_n := z_n\ statement\ \textbf{end} =$$
$$\textbf{begin}\ u_1 := y_1 \ldots u_m := y_m\ v_1 := z_1' \ldots v_n := z_n'\ \textbf{end})\ \wedge$$
$$proposition_2[y_1, \ldots, y_m, z_1, \ldots, z_n, z_1', \ldots, z_n'/u_1, \ldots, u_m, v_1, \ldots, v_n, v_1', \ldots, v_n'])).$$

The equality between statements in the above indicates that the effect of executing the statement on a state in which certain variables have particular values is to replace some of those values by others. The rest of the notation is explained in 3.1 and 3.2.

For any statement 'statement' the propositions $pre[\![$ statement $]\!]$ and $post[\![$ statement $]\!]$ formulated in this note are respectively a pre-condition and a post-condition of 'statement' in the above sense. The equations for $pre[\![$ statement $]\!]$ and $post[\![$ statement $]\!]$ are accompanied by other equations, for $write[\![$ statement $]\!]$, to describe the set of variables that may be written to by 'statement'.

In the equations for $post[\![$ statement $]\!]$ it is convenient to ignore variables which must not written to; consequently the post-condition of 'statement', as sometimes understood, is not $post[\![$ statement $]\!]$ but

$$(w_1' = w_1) \wedge \ldots \wedge (w_o' = w_o) \wedge post[\![\text{ statement }]\!],$$

where 'w_1', ..., 'w_o' are the variables that are declared in the module enclosing 'statement' and that must not be written to by 'statement'. (In a post-condition, expressions like 'w_1', ..., 'w_o' refer to values 'before' the execution of a statement and expressions like 'w_1'', ..., 'w_o'' refer to values 'after' the execution of a statement.)

2.2 Modal assertions

One technique for proving properties of statements is to introduce modal assertions [4,5], like

proposition$_1$ $\Rightarrow$ [statement]proposition$_2$,

which generalises the common assertion of partial correctness,

proposition$_1$ {statement} proposition$_2$.

The pre-conditions and post-conditions of VDM are not modal assertions; moreover, they may refer to the states present both 'before' and 'after' a statement is executed (by contrast with modal assertions). Nonetheless the common basic modal assertions can be interpreted in terms of pre-conditions and post-conditions by using the following equations, in which 'statement' is any statement, 'proposition' is any proposition and '$v_1, \ldots, v_n$' are the variables that may be written to by 'statement'.

[statement]proposition =
    $pre[\![$ statement $]\!] \Rightarrow$
    $(\exists\, v_1' \in type[\![\, v_1\,]\!], \ldots, v_n' \in type[\![\, v_n\,]\!])$
    $(post[\![$ statement $]\!] \wedge$ proposition$[v_1', \ldots, v_n'/v_1, \ldots, v_n])$

<statement>proposition =
    $pre[\![$ statement $]\!] \wedge$
    $(\forall\, v_1' \in type[\![\, v_1\,]\!], \ldots, v_n' \in type[\![\, v_n\,]\!])$
    $(post[\![$ statement $]\!] \Rightarrow$ proposition$[v_1', \ldots, v_n'/v_1, \ldots, v_n])$

For these versions of the modal assertions the usual properties of such assertions can be established from the equations governing pre-conditions and post-conditions. Accordingly the rest of this note will concentrate on pre-conditions and post-conditions and ignore modal assertions.

3 Notation

3.1 The metalanguage

The proof rules are formulated using recursive pattern matching equations (and induction rules for loops), in a style reminiscent of attributed grammars. The emphasis in them is on clarity rather than full formality; for example, '...' and subscripts will be used.

These recursive pattern matching equations may be preceded by 'environments', which are conjunctions of equations that match sets or lists of names with the names used in particular constructs; these sets and lists are always used in ways which make the results deterministic. Environments identify the names used in particular constructs in order that one proposition may be turned into another by substituting expressions for names in it. They are separated from the equations which form their scopes by '⊢' (as is illustrated in 6.1.3).

3.2   Substitution

The proposition

proposition[expression$_1$, ..., expression$_k$/name$_1$, ..., name$_k$]

signifies the result of simultaneously substituting 'expression$_1$' for 'name$_1$', ..., 'expression$_k$' for 'name$_k$' in 'proposition', renaming bound variables where necessary. The substitution takes effect throughout the smallest possible term to its left; for instance

$$(x' = x//y) \Rightarrow ((y \neq 0) \wedge (x//y \neq 0))[x'/x]$$

is actually

$$(x' = x//y) \Rightarrow ((y \neq 0) \wedge (x'//y \neq 0))$$

(where x and y denote integers and // is the integer division operator).

3.3   The logic

Expressions in VDM may not denote values, because they may, for instance, contain function applications in which the pre-conditions of the functions are not satisfied. There are several ways of overcoming the difficulties that such non-denoting expressions introduce. For the present purposes it is enough to suppose that the metalanguage provides a 'strong' equality (as in LPF [3,7]): expression$_0$ = expression$_1$ if and only if expression$_0$ and expression$_1$ both denote values and the values that they denote are the same. (Quantifier introduction and elimination use the further assumption that bound variables denote values, though free variables may not do so.)

A concomitant of this treatment of equality is that there can be an existence predicate: the expression 'expression' denotes a value if and only if expression = expression. Of course usually

$$pre[\![\text{ expression }]\!] \Rightarrow (\text{expression} = \text{expression}).$$

A general discussion of an appropriate logic is given by Scott [9].

3.4   The presentation of the grammar

The dialect used here differs from the STC VDM Reference Language only in that it ignores distinctions between the upper case and lower case uses of the same name and omits certain statements and constant declarations (detailed in 4.1 and 4.3). These differences raise no matters of principle.

The syntax is presented in a style which helps with the formulation of pre-conditions and post-conditions, rather than in one which helps with general matters of teaching or tooling.

4   Syntax

4.1   Statements

statement ::=
  operation_application |
  variable:= expression |
  variable:= operation_application |
  if expression **then** statement$_1$ **else** statement$_2$ |
  let constant_declaration$_1$ ... constant_declaration$_m$ **within** statement |
  while expression **do** statement |
  begin variable_declaration_or_statement_list **end**

An operation application used as a statement on its own must not return a result.

An assignment may have on its right hand side either an expression or an operation application. If it has an expression, it is conventional in effect. If it has an operation application, the operation application must return a result, which is assigned to the variable on the left hand side of the assignment.

An 'if' statement is a commonplace conditional statement.

A 'let' statement contains constant declarations that have scopes extending to the end of the statement. The names thus declared must be different from each other and from the names that are written to in the statement.

A 'while' statement contains an expression and an statement which are respectively the test and the body of a loop.

A 'begin' statement contains variable declarations and statements which together constitute a block. The variable declaration or statement list in it is not itself a statement, but it can be treated largely as if it were one. The statements above deviate from those in the STC VDM Reference Language only through ignoring 'if' statements without 'else' (which are just abbreviations for 'if' statements with 'else' followed by an empty variable declaration or statement list), 'where' statements (which are just rearrangements of 'let' statements using different reserved words) and 'cases' statements.

4.2   Operation applications

operation_application ::=
  operation(expression$_1$, ..., expression$_m$) |
  operation(expression$_1$, ..., expression$_m$, instance)

The operation application

operation(expression$_1$, ..., expression$_m$)

is used inside the module in which the operation is declared. The variables which are read from and written to by it are those declared in that module.

The operation application

operation(expression$_1$, ..., expression$_m$, instance)

is used outside the module in which the operation is declared. The variables which are read from and written to by it are those declared in the particular instance of a module. The module concerned is the one which contains the operation declaration and the declarations of the variables 'v_1', ..., 'v_n' (say) used in that declaration. The instance concerned is the one to which this particular operation application is applied; it is identified above by 'instance'. The instance has its own variables, which are 'copies' of 'v_1', ..., 'v_n'. For the purposes of formulating the post-condition of the operation application, these copies are written as 'v_1(instance)', ..., 'v_n(instance)' and the instance is regarded as a record variable which has these copies as its components.

4.3   Constant declarations

constant_declaration ::=
    constant: type $\triangleq$ expression

A constant declaration provides a constant which may be read from but not written to. The constant should be different from the names that are declared in the enclosing module and are used in declarations of functions or operations.

The constant declarations above deviate from those in the STC VDM Reference Language only through ignoring pattern matching declarations, function declarations, and constant declarations in which the constants are not yet defined.

4.4   Variable declarations

variable_declaration ::=
    variable: type

A variable declaration provides a variable which may be both read from and written to. The variable should be different from the names that are declared in the enclosing module and are used in declarations of functions or operations.

4.5 Variable declaration or statement lists

variable_declaration_or_statement_list ::=
|
variable_declaration variable_declaration_or_statement_list |
statement variable_declaration_or_statement_list

A variable declaration or statement list which is empty provides a statement having no effect.

A variable declaration or statement list which begins with a variable declaration makes the scope of the declaration extend through the rest of the list.

A variable declaration or statement list which begins with a statement has as its effect the sequential composition of the effect of that statement with the effect of the rest of the list. (The peculiarities of the syntax of this dialect for VDM lead to the omission of ';' in variable declaration and statement lists.)

5 The pre-conditions and post-conditions

5.1 Statements

Describing a statement 'statement' uses:

- *pre*[[statement]], the pre-condition of the statement;
- *post*[[statement]], the post-condition of the statement;
- *write*[[statement]], the set of variables that the statement may write to.

Formulating these entails introducing, for any expression 'expression', any module 'module', any constant 'constant', and any variable 'variable':

- *pre*[[expression]], the pre-condition of the expression;
- *var*[[module]], the set of variables that are declared in the module;
- *type*[[constant]], the type associated with the constant;
- *type*[[variable]], the type associated with the variable.

There should also be a proposition giving the post-condition of an expression, but as it raises complications in the naming of the results of expressions it will be ignored.

5.2   Operation applications

Describing an operation application 'operation_application' uses:

- *pre*⟦ operation_application ⟧, the pre-condition of the operation application;
- *post*⟦ operation_application ⟧, the post-condition of the operation application;
- *write*⟦ operation_application ⟧, the set of variables that the operation application may write to;
- *result*⟦ operation_application ⟧, the variable that the operation application may regard as the result (if it exists).

These can be calculated using the information given in the declaration of the operation (and, in particular, the pre-condition and post-condition defined or constructed from the declaration). Expressing this information entails introducing, for any operation 'operation':

- *pre*⟦ operation ⟧, the pre-condition of the operation;
- *post*⟦ operation ⟧, the post-condition of the operation;
- *write*⟦ operation ⟧, the set of variables that the operation may write to;
- *argument*⟦ operation ⟧, the list of arguments that the operation must take as its parameters;
- *result*⟦ operation ⟧, the variable that the operation may regard as the result (if it exists);
- *module*⟦ operation ⟧, the module that contains the declaration of the operation.

5.3   Constant declarations

Describing a constant declaration 'constant_declaration' uses:

- *pre*⟦ constant_declaration ⟧, the pre-condition of the constant declaration;
- *post*⟦ constant_declaration ⟧, the post-condition of the constant declaration;
- *const*⟦ constant_declaration ⟧, the set of constants that are declared in the constant declaration.

5.4   Variable declarations

Describing a variable declaration 'variable_declaration' uses:

- *var*⟦ variable_declaration ⟧, the set of variables that are declared in the variable declaration.

5.5 Variable declaration or statement lists

Describing a variable declaration or statement list 'variable_declaration_or_statement_list' uses:

- *pre*⟦ variable_declaration_or_statement_list ⟧, the pre-condition of the variable declaration or statement list;
- *post*⟦ variable_declaration_or_statement_list ⟧, the post-condition of the variable declaration or statement list;
- *write*⟦ variable_declaration_or_statement_list ⟧, the set of variables that the variable declaration or statement list may write to.

6 The proof rules

6.1 Statements

6.1.1 Statements formed from operation applications that do not return results

In these equations, the overloading of *pre*, *post* and *write* produces an apparent circularity. It is resolved by noting that *pre*, *post* and *write* are applied to a statement on the right of '=' and to an operation application on the left of '='.

pre⟦ operation_application ⟧ =
    pre⟦ operation_application ⟧

post⟦ operation_application ⟧ =
    post⟦ operation_application ⟧

write⟦ operation_application ⟧ =
    write⟦ operation_application ⟧

6.1.2 Statements assigning to variables using expressions

Expressions are not allowed to contain assignments. Hence the only variable written to by an assignment having an expression on its right hand side is the variable on the left hand side.

pre⟦ variable:= expression ⟧ =
    pre⟦ expression ⟧

post⟦ variable:= expression ⟧ =
    (variable$'$ = expression)

$write[\![$ variable:= expression $]\!] =$
  {variable}

6.1.3 Statements assigning to variables using operation applications that return results

Operation applications are allowed to contain assignments. Indeed the variables written to by an assignment having an operation application on its right hand side are the variable on the left hand side and the variables 'v_1', ..., 'v_n' (say) which are written to by the operation application (excluding the result, which has its scope confined to the operation declaration). The result returned by the operation application is written to the variable on the left of the assignment. This variable may have been given a value in the operation application, if it is one of 'v_1', ..., 'v_n'; in this case that value must be hidden by existential quantification.

$pre[\![$ variable:= operation_application $]\!] =$
  $pre[\![$ operation_application $]\!]$

r = $result[\![$ operation_application $]\!] \vdash$
  $post[\![$ variable:= operation_application $]\!] =$
    $(\exists$ variable$'' \in type[\![$ variable $]\!])$
      $(post[\![$ operation_application $]\!][$variable$''$, variable$'/$variable$'$, r$'])$

$write[\![$ variable:= operation_application $]\!] =$
  $(write[\![$ operation_application $]\!] \setminus \{result[\![$ operation_application $]\!]\}) \cup \{$variable$\}$

6.1.4 'if' statements

The only complication in the treatment of 'if' statements is that the post-conditions of the statements following 'then' and 'else' must be augmented to ensure that the variables written to by one statement but not by the other are properly constrained. If the version of $post$ used here dealt with all the variables in scope, rather than just with those to which its argument may write, this complication would not be necessary, but many of the other proof rules would become more intricate.

$pre[\![$ if expression then statement$_1$ else statement$_2$ $]\!] =$
  $pre[\![$ expression $]\!] \wedge$
  $((\text{expression} = \textbf{true}) \Rightarrow pre[\![$ statement$_1$ $]\!]) \wedge$
  $((\text{expression} = \textbf{false}) \Rightarrow pre[\![$ statement$_2$ $]\!])$

$(\{v_1, \ldots, v_n\} = write[\![$ statement$_2$ $]\!] \setminus write[\![$ statement$_1$ $]\!]) \wedge$
$(\{w_1, \ldots, w_o\} = write[\![$ statement$_1$ $]\!] \setminus write[\![$ statement$_2$ $]\!]) \vdash$
  $post[\![$ if expression then statement$_1$ else statement$_2$ $]\!] =$
    $((\text{expression} = \textbf{true}) \Rightarrow (v_1' = v_1 \wedge \ldots \wedge v_n' = v_n \wedge post[\![$ statement$_1$ $]\!])) \wedge$
    $((\text{expression} = \textbf{false}) \Rightarrow ((w_1' = w_1) \wedge \ldots \wedge (w_o' = w_o) \wedge post[\![$ statement$_2$ $]\!]))$

$write[\![\ \textbf{if}\ \text{expression}\ \textbf{then}\ \text{statement}_1\ \textbf{else}\ \text{statement}_2\ ]\!] =$
    $write[\![\ \text{statement}_1\ ]\!]\ \cup\ write[\![\ \text{statement}_2\ ]\!]$

6.1.5 'let' statements

The treatment of constant declarations resembles that of sequencing statements (variable declaration or statement lists that start with statements, discussed in 6.5.3). The constant declarations may be mutually recursive, as a name declared in one of them may be used in the others; however, they are not assumed to provide a least fixed point, as (by contrast with the position for 'while' statements, outlined in 6.1.6) they may not depend continuously on the names.

$\{c_1, \ldots, c_m\} = const[\![\ \text{constant\_declaration}_1\ ]\!]\ \cup \ldots \cup\ const[\![\ \text{constant\_declaration}_m\ ]\!]\ \vdash$
    $pre[\![\ \textbf{let}\ \text{constant\_declaration}_1\ \ldots \text{constant\_declaration}_m\ \textbf{within}\ \text{statement}\ ]\!] =$
        $(\exists\ c_1 \in type[\![\ c_1\ ]\!], \ldots, c_m \in type[\![\ c_m\ ]\!])$
            $(pre[\![\ \text{constant\_declaration}_1\ ]\!]\ \wedge \ldots \wedge\ post[\![\ \text{constant\_declaration}_m\ ]\!])\ \wedge$
        $(\forall\ c_1 \in type[\![\ c_1\ ]\!], \ldots, c_m \in type[\![\ c_m\ ]\!])$
            $((post[\![\ \text{constant\_declaration}_1\ ]\!]\ \wedge \ldots \wedge\ post[\![\ \text{constant\_declaration}_m\ ]\!])\ \Rightarrow\ pre[\![\ \text{statement}\ ]\!])$

$\{c_1, \ldots, c_m\} = const[\![\ \text{constant\_declaration}_1\ ]\!]\ \cup \ldots \cup\ const[\![\ \text{constant\_declaration}_m\ ]\!]\ \vdash$
    $post[\![\ \textbf{let}\ \text{constant\_declaration}_1\ \ldots \text{constant\_declaration}_m\ \textbf{within}\ \text{statement}\ ]\!] =$
        $(\exists\ c_1 \in type[\![\ c_1\ ]\!], \ldots, c_m \in type[\![\ c_m\ ]\!])$
            $((post[\![\ \text{constant\_declaration}_1\ ]\!]\ \wedge \ldots \wedge\ post[\![\ \text{constant\_declaration}_m\ ]\!])\ \wedge\ post[\![\ \text{statement}\ ]\!])$

$write[\![\ \textbf{let}\ \text{constant\_declaration}_1\ \ldots \text{constant\_declaration}_m\ \textbf{within}\ \text{statement}\ ]\!] =$
    $write[\![\ \text{statement}\ ]\!]$

6.1.6 'while' statements

The 'while' statement is intepreted in terms of conditional statements and sequencing statements, so the proof rules for it depend mainly on those for 'if' statements (given in 6.1.4) and on those for variable declaration or statement lists that start with statements (given in 6.5.3).

The 'while' statement can be regarded as a fixed point of a function acting on statements. Thus

while expression **do** statement

can be expanded into

if expression
then begin statement **while** expression **do** statement **end**
else begin end.

As *pre* and *post* for the '**while**' statement can be viewed similarly, the following equations hold.

$\{v_1, \ldots, v_n\} = write[\![\text{ statement }]\!] \vdash$
  $pre[\![\textbf{ while } \text{expression } \textbf{do} \text{ statement }]\!] =$
    $pre[\![\text{ expression }]\!] \wedge$
    $((\text{expression} = \textbf{true}) \Rightarrow$
    $(pre[\![\text{ statement }]\!] \wedge$
    $(\forall v_1{}' \in type[\![v_1]\!], \ldots, v_n{}' \in type[\![v_n]\!])$
      $(post[\![\text{ statement }]\!] \Rightarrow$
      $pre[\![\textbf{ while } \text{expression } \textbf{do} \text{ statement }]\!][v_1{}', \ldots, v_n{}'/v_1, \ldots, v_n])))$

$\{v_1, \ldots, v_n\} = write[\![\text{ statement }]\!] \vdash$
  $post[\![\textbf{ while } \text{expression } \textbf{do} \text{ statement }]\!] =$
    $((\text{expression} = \textbf{true}) \Rightarrow$
    $(\exists v_1{}'' \in type[\![v_1]\!], \ldots, v_n{}'' \in type[\![v_n]\!])$
    $(post[\![\text{ statement }]\!][v_1{}'', \ldots, v_n{}''/v_1{}', \ldots, v_n{}'] \wedge$
    $post[\![\textbf{ while } \text{expression } \textbf{do} \text{ statement }]\!] [v_1{}'', \ldots, v_n{}''/v_1, \ldots, v_n])) \wedge$
    $((\text{expression} = \textbf{false}) \Rightarrow ((v_1{}' = v_1) \wedge \ldots \wedge (v_n{}' = v_n)))$

$write[\![\textbf{ while } \text{expression } \textbf{do} \text{ statement }]\!] =$
  $write[\![\text{ statement }]\!]$

The '**while**' statement can even be regarded as the least fixed point of a continuous function acting on statements; the statements are ordered by '$\sqsubseteq$' and the least statement is

while true do begin end.

Since this is so, *pre* and *post* for the '**while**' statement can be viewed as the least fixed points of two continuous functions acting on propositions. These functions rely on different orderings on propositions: that for *pre* relies on '$\Leftarrow$' (for which the least proposition is **true**) and that for *post* relies on '$\Rightarrow$' (for which the least proposition is **false**). This view of *pre* and *post* for the '**while**' statement is reflected in the following two induction rules. In the first of these 'proposition' is any proposition that mentions the variables which the '**while**' statement may read from. In the second 'proposition' is any proposition that mentions the variables which the '**while**' statement may read from and the variables which the '**while**' statement may write to.

$\{v_1, \ldots, v_n\} = write[\![\text{ statement }]\!] \vdash$
  $(pre[\![\text{ expression }]\!] \wedge$
  $((\text{expression} = \textbf{true}) \Rightarrow$
  $(pre[\![\text{ statement }]\!] \wedge$
  $(\forall v_1{}' \in type[\![v_1]\!], \ldots, v_n{}' \in type[\![v_n]\!])$
    $(post[\![\text{ statement }]\!] \Rightarrow$
    $proposition[v_1{}', \ldots, v_n{}'/v_1, \ldots, v_n])))) \Rightarrow$
  $proposition$

$\{v_1, \ldots, v_n\} = write[\![\text{ statement }]\!] \vdash$
  $pre[\![\textbf{ while } \text{expression } \textbf{do} \text{ statement }]\!] \Rightarrow proposition$

$\{v_1, \ldots, v_n\} = write[\![$ statement $]\!] \vdash$
  (proposition $\Rightarrow$
  ((expression = **true**) $\Rightarrow$
    ($\exists\, v_1'' \in type[\![\, v_1\,]\!], \ldots, v_n'' \in type[\![\, v_n\,]\!]$)
      ($post[\![$ statement $]\!][v_1'', \ldots, v_n''/v_1', \ldots, v_n'] \wedge$
        proposition$[v_1'', \ldots, v_n''/v_1, \ldots, v_n])) \wedge$
    ((expression = **false**) $\Rightarrow ((v_1' = v_1) \wedge \ldots \wedge (v_n' = v_n)))$

$\{v_1, \ldots, v_n\} = write[\![$ statement $]\!] \vdash$
  proposition $\Rightarrow post[\![$ **while** expression **do** statement $]\!]$

6.1.7 'begin' statements

In these equations, the overloading of *pre*, *post* and *write* avoids an apparent circularity purely because a variable declaration or statement list is not on its own a statement. Hence *pre*, *post* and *write* are applied to a statement on the right of '=' and to a variable declaration or statement list on the left of '='.

$pre[\![$ **begin** variable_declaration_or_statement_list **end** $]\!] =$
  $pre[\![$ variable_declaration_or_statement_list $]\!]$

$post[\![$ **begin** variable_declaration_or_statement_list **end** $]\!] =$
  $post[\![$ variable_declaration_or_statement_list $]\!]$

$write[\![$ **begin** variable_declaration_or_statement_list **end** $]\!] =$
  $write[\![$ variable_declaration_or_statement_list $]\!]$

6.2 Operation applications

6.2.1 Operation applications that are inside the modules where the operations are declared

Inside the module in which an operation is declared, an application of the operation is simple, as there is immediate access to all the individual variables declared in the module.

$\ll a_1, \ldots, a_m \gg = argument[\![$ operation $]\!] \vdash$
  $pre[\![$ operation(expression$_1, \ldots,$ expression$_m$) $]\!] =$
    $pre[\![$ expression$_1\,]\!] \wedge \ldots \wedge pre[\![$ expression$_m\,]\!] \wedge$
    $pre[\![$ operation $]\!][$expression$_1, \ldots,$ expression$_m/a_1, \ldots, a_m]$

$\ll a_1, \ldots, a_m \gg = argument[\![$ operation $]\!] \vdash$
  $post[\![$ operation(expression$_1, \ldots,$ expression$_m$) $]\!] =$
    $post[\![$ operation $]\!][$expression$_1, \ldots,$ expression$_m/a_1, \ldots, a_m]$

$write[\![$ operation(expression$_1$, ..., expression$_m$) $]\!] =$
   $write[\![$ operation $]\!]$

$result[\![$ operation(expression$_1$, ..., expression$_m$) $]\!] =$
   $result[\![$ operation $]\!]$

6.2.2 Operation applications that are outside the modules where the operations are declared

The presence of 'v_1(instance)', ..., 'v_n(instance)' in the proof rules below arises because the variables written to in an operation declaration are not individually available outside the module enclosing the declaration. Instead, the variables are treated as some components of a record variable, which names the instance of the module to which the operation is being applied (as described in 4.2). There may be other variables declared in the module which are not written to in the declaration of the operation; these form the remaining components of the record variable, 'w_1(instance)', ..., 'w_o(instance)'. The entire record variable, not an individual component, may be written to, so '$'$ is attached to 'instance', not to any of 'v_1', ..., 'v_n', 'w_1', ..., 'w_o'.

$(\ll a_1, ..., a_m \gg = argument[\![$ operation $]\!]) \wedge$
$(\{v_1, ..., v_n\} = var[\![$ module$[\![$ operation $]\!]$ $]\!] \cap write[\![$ operation $]\!]) \wedge$
$(\{w_1, ..., w_o\} = var[\![$ module$[\![$ operation $]\!]$ $]\!] \setminus write[\![$ operation $]\!]) \vdash$
   $pre[\![$ operation(expression$_1$, ..., expression$_m$, instance) $]\!] =$
      $pre[\![$ expression$_1$ $]\!] \wedge ... \wedge pre[\![$ expression$_m$ $]\!] \wedge$
      $pre[\![$ operation $]\!]$
         $[$expression$_1$, ..., expression$_m$,
         v_1(instance), ..., v_n(instance),
         w_1(instance), ..., w_o(instance)/
         a_1, ..., a_m, v_1, ..., v_n, w_1, ..., $w_o]$

$(\ll a_1, ..., a_m \gg = argument[\![$ operation $]\!]) \wedge$
$(\{v_1, ..., v_n\} = var[\![$ module$[\![$ operation $]\!]$ $]\!] \cap write[\![$ operation $]\!]) \wedge$
$(\{w_1, ..., w_o\} = var[\![$ module$[\![$ operation $]\!]$ $]\!] \setminus write[\![$ operation $]\!]) \vdash$
   $post[\![$ operation(expression$_1$, ..., expression$_m$, instance) $]\!] =$
      $(w_1($instance$') = w_1($instance$)) \wedge ... \wedge (w_o($instance$') \doteq w_o($instance$)) \wedge$
      $post[\![$ operation $]\!]$
         $[$expression$_1$, ..., expression$_m$,
         v_1(instance), ..., v_n(instance),
         w_1(instance), ..., w_o(instance),
         v_1(instance$'$), ..., v_n(instance$'$)/
         a_1, ..., a_m, v_1, ..., v_n, w_1, ..., w_o, v_1', ..., $v_n']$

$write[\![$ operation(expression$_1$, ..., expression$_m$, instance) $]\!] =$
   $\{$instance$\} \cup \{result[\![$ operation $]\!]\}$

$result[\![$ operation(expression$_1$, ..., expression$_m$, instance) $]\!] =$
   $result[\![$ operation $]\!]$

6.3   Constant declarations

pre⟦ constant: type $\triangleq$ expression ⟧ =
   pre⟦ expression ⟧

post⟦ constant: type $\triangleq$ expression ⟧ =
   constant = expression

const⟦ constant: type $\triangleq$ expression ⟧ =
   {constant}

6.4   Variable declarations

var⟦ variable: type ⟧ =
   {variable}

6.5   Variable declaration or statement lists

6.5.1   Variable declaration or statement lists that are empty

Executing the empty variable declaration or statement list has no effect on the state.

pre⟦   ⟧ =
   true

post⟦   ⟧ =
   true

write⟦   ⟧ =
   {}

6.5.2   Variable declaration or statement lists that start with variable declarations

A variable declaration or statement list that starts with a variable declaration makes the names thus declared available for reading from or writing to in the remainder of the list. The precondition and post-condition of the list must not assume any initial values for the variables, so these values are universally quantified. The post-condition of the list must not reveal the final values of the variables, so these values are existentially quantified. The variables have scopes confined to the list, so they are not among the variables to which the list as a whole may write.

$\{v_1, \ldots, v_n\} = var[\![$ variable_declaration $]\!] \vdash$
   $pre[\![$ variable_declaration variable_declaration_or_statement_list $]\!] =$
     $(\forall\, v_1 \cdot \in type[\![\, v_1\,]\!], \ldots, v_n \in type[\![\, v_n\,]\!])$
      $(pre[\![$ variable_declaration_or_statement_list $]\!])$

$\{v_1, \ldots, v_n\} = var[\![$ variable_declaration $]\!] \vdash$
   $post[\![$ variable_declaration variable_declaration_or_statement_list $]\!] =$
     $(\forall\, v_1 \in type[\![\, v_1\,]\!], \ldots, v_n \in type[\![\, v_n\,]\!])$
      $(\exists\, v_1{}' \in type[\![\, v_1\,]\!], \ldots, v_n{}' \in type[\![\, v_n\,]\!])$
       $(post[\![$ variable_declaration_or_statement_list $]\!])$

$write[\![$ variable_declaration variable_declaration_or_statement_list $]\!] =$
   $write[\![$ variable_declaration_or_statement_list $]\!] \setminus var[\![$ variable_declaration $]\!]$

6.5.3 Variable declaration or statement lists that start with statements

A variable declaration or statement list that starts with a statement has as its effect the composition of the effect of that statement with the effect of the rest of the list. The post-condition describes this effect by asserting that a state 'before' the statement is executed may be related to a state 'after' the rest of the list is executed only if there is a state 'after' the statement is executed and 'before' the rest of the list is executed to which both states are related. A sufficient condition for the existence of such a state is provided by the pre-condition. A further complication is that, just as for '**if**' statements (discussed in 6.1.4), the post-conditions of the statement and of the rest of the list must be augmented to ensure that the variables written to by one but not by the other are properly constrained.

$(\{v_1, \ldots, v_n\} = write[\![$ statement $]\!] \cap write[\![$ variable_declaration_or_statement_list $]\!]) \wedge$
$(\{w_1, \ldots, w_o\} = write[\![$ statement $]\!] \setminus write[\![$ variable_declaration_or_statement_list $]\!]) \vdash$
   $pre[\![$ statement variable_declaration_or_statement_list $]\!] =$
     $pre[\![$ statement $]\!] \wedge$
     $(\forall\, v_1{}' \in type[\![\, v_1\,]\!], \ldots, v_n{}' \in type[\![\, v_n\,]\!])$
      $(\forall\, w_1{}' \in type[\![\, w_1\,]\!], \ldots, w_o{}' \in type[\![\, w_o\,]\!])$
       $(post[\![$ statement $]\!] \Rightarrow$
       $pre[\![$ variable_declaration_or_statement_list $]\!]$
        $[v_1{}', \ldots, v_n{}', w_1{}', \ldots, w_o{}'/v_1, \ldots, v_n, w_1, \ldots, w_o])$

$(\{v_1, \ldots, v_n\} = write[\![$ statement $]\!] \cap write[\![$ variable_declaration_or_statement_list $]\!]) \wedge$
$(\{w_1, \ldots, w_o\} = write[\![$ statement $]\!] \setminus write[\![$ variable_declaration_or_statement_list $]\!]) \vdash$
   $post[\![$ statement variable_declaration_or_statement_list $]\!] =$
     $(\exists\, v_1{}'' \in type[\![\, v_1\,]\!], \ldots, v_n{}'' \in type[\![\, v_n\,]\!])$
      $(post[\![$ statement $]\!][v_1{}'', \ldots, v_n{}''/v_1{}', \ldots, v_n{}'] \wedge$
      $post[\![$ variable_declaration_or_statement_list $]\!]$
       $[v_1{}'', \ldots, v_n{}'', w_1{}', \ldots, w_o{}'/v_1, \ldots, v_n, w_1, \ldots, w_o])$

$write[\![$ statement variable_declaration_or_statement_list $]\!] =$
   $write[\![$ statement $]\!] \cup write[\![$ variable_declaration_or_statement_list $]\!]$

7 Example

Because *pre* is sometimes expressed in terms of *post* and *post* is sometimes expressed in terms of *write*, the equations for them are best used in the following order: first that for *write*, then that for *post*, and last that for *pre*. Also, the pre-conditions and post-conditions of variable declaration or statement lists are best found by proceeding from the tails of the lists to their heads. This is illustrated below for

x:= x//y y:= x//y x:= x//y

when x and y denote integers and // is the integer division operator (though // could be any operator which has as its pre-condition the assertion that its second argument is non-zero).

$write[\![\ \text{x:= x//y}\ ]\!]$
$= \{x\}$

$post[\![\ \text{x:= x//y}\ ]\!]$
$= (x' = \text{x//y})$

$pre[\![\ \text{x:= x//y}\ ]\!]$
$= pre[\![\ \text{x//y}\ ]\!]$
$= (y \neq 0)$

$write[\![\ \text{y:= x//y x:= x//y}\ ]\!]$
$= write[\![\ \text{y:= x//y}\ ]\!] \cup write[\![\ \text{x:= x//y}\ ]\!]$
$= \{y\} \cup \{x\}$
$= \{x, y\}$

$post[\![\ \text{y:= x//y x:= x//y}\ ]\!]$
$= post[\![\ \text{y:= x//y}\ ]\!] \wedge post[\![\ \text{x:= x//y}\ ]\!][y'/y]$
$= (y' = \text{x//y}) \wedge (x' = \text{x//y})[y'/y]$
$= (y' = \text{x//y}) \wedge (x' = \text{x//y})[\text{x//y}/y]$
$= (y' = \text{x//y}) \wedge (x' = \text{x//(x//y)})$

$pre[\![\ \text{y:= x//y x:= x//y}\ ]\!]$
$= pre[\![\ \text{y:= x//y}\ ]\!] \wedge (\forall\ y' \in \text{Int})(post[\![\ \text{y:= x//y}\ ]\!] \Rightarrow pre[\![\ \text{x:= x//y}\ ]\!][y'/y])$
$= pre[\![\ \text{x//y}\ ]\!] \wedge (\forall\ y' \in \text{Int})((y' = \text{x//y}) \Rightarrow (y \neq 0)[y'/y])$
$= (y \neq 0) \wedge (\forall\ y' \in \text{Int})((y' = \text{x//y}) \Rightarrow (y \neq 0)[y'/y])$
$= (y \neq 0) \wedge (\text{x//y} \neq 0)$

$write[\![\ \text{x:= x//y y:= x//y x:= x//y}\ ]\!]$
$= write[\![\ \text{x:= x//y}\ ]\!] \cup write[\![\ \text{y:= x//y x:= x//y}\ ]\!]$
$= \{x\} \cup \{x, y\}$
$= \{x, y\}$

$post[\![\ x:= x//y\ y:= x//y\ x:= x//y\ ]\!]$
$= (\exists\ x'' \in \text{Int})(post[\![\ x:= x//y\ ]\!][x''/x'] \wedge post[\![\ y:= x//y\ x:= x//y\ ]\!][x''/x])$
$= (\exists\ x'' \in \text{Int})((x' = x//y)[x''/x'] \wedge ((y' = x//y) \wedge (x' = x//(x//y)))[x''/x])$
$= (\exists\ x'' \in \text{Int})((x'' = x//y) \wedge (y' = x''//y) \wedge (x' = x''//(x''//y)))$
$= (y' = (x//y)//y) \wedge (x' = (x//y)//((x//y)//y))$

$pre[\![\ x:= x//y\ y:= x//y\ x:= x//y\ ]\!]$
$= pre[\![\ x:= x//y\ ]\!] \wedge (\forall\ x' \in \text{Int})(post[\![\ x:= x//y\ ]\!] \Rightarrow pre[\![\ y:= x//y\ x:= x//y\ ]\!][x'/x])$
$= (y \neq 0) \wedge (\forall\ x' \in \text{Int})((x' = x//y) \Rightarrow ((y \neq 0) \wedge (x//y \neq 0))[x'/x])$
$= (y \neq 0) \wedge ((y \neq 0) \wedge (x//y \neq 0))\ [x/y/x]$
$= (y \neq 0) \wedge (y \neq 0) \wedge ((x//y)//y \neq 0)$
$= (y \neq 0) \wedge ((x//y)//y \neq 0)$

8   References

[1] *Concrete Syntax for the STC VDM Reference Language (Edition 4)*, STC (1987).

[2] *Development Advice for the STC VDM Reference Language (Edition 2)*, STC (1987).

[3] Barringer, H., Cheng, J.H., and Jones, C.B., *A Logic Covering Undefinedness in Program Proofs*, **Acta Informatica 21** (1984), 251-259.

[4] Goldblatt, R., **Axiomatising the Logic of Computer Programming, Lecture Notes in Computer Science 130** (Springer-Verlag, 1982).

[5] Harel, D., **First-Order Dynamic Logic, Lecture Notes in Computer Science 68** (Springer-Verlag, 1979).

[6] Jones, C.B., **Software Development: A Rigorous Approach** (Prentice-Hall, 1980).

[7] Jones, C.B., **Systematic Software Development Using VDM** (Prentice-Hall, 1986).

[8] Milne, R.E.,*The sequential imperative aspect of the RAISE specification language,* RAISE/STC/REM/2/V1, STC (1987).

[9] Scott, D.S., *Identity and Existence in Intuitionistic Logic,* **Lecture Notes in Mathematics 735** (Springer-Verlag, 1979), 660-696.

[10] Turski, W., and Maibaum, T.S.E., **The Specification of Computer Programs** (Addison-Wesley, 1987).

Muffin:
A User Interface Design Experiment for a Theorem Proving Assistant

Cliff B. Jones and Richard Moore
Department of Computer Science,
The University,
Manchester M13 9PL

Abstract

A Theorem Proving Assistant is a computer program which can be used interactively to keep track of, and automate some steps of, attempts to prove theorems. Muffin is an experiment in the design of a user interface to a theorem proving assistant. A formal description of Muffin is given from which the program has been implemented in Smalltalk-80.

1 Introduction

The overall status of the Formal Reasoning work in the IPSE 2.5 project is described in a companion paper (cf. [7]). The overriding objective of the project is to design a Theorem Proving Assistant which provides enough support for the activity in hand that a user would prefer to use the system rather than pencil and paper. Some computer scientists doubt the wisdom of this objective; many more question its feasibility. It is, therefore, worth trying to give some indication of why the group believe the goal to be worthy of pursuit. Nearly all of the proof obligations which arise in, for instance, the examples discussed in [6] are provable in rather simple steps. They can be characterized as being rather shallow results: their purpose is not to extend mathematics but rather to provide a cross-check between a specification and its putative design. Experience in constructing large numbers of such proofs by hand suggests that a system providing powerful symbol manipulation facilities could help remove the tedious aspects of the process.

The aim is to build a system which leaves the user free to provide the insight which steers the proof in as natural a way as possible. Section 3 explores some of the user interface questions prior to the specification being developed in Section 4.

Before embarking on this, it is necessary to clarify the (rather limited) objectives of the current experiment. Several members of the FRIPSE team were involved in earlier projects to write systems which supported formal methods. In particular, the "Mule" project (cf. [2], [18], [3], [4]) built a "Structure Editor" which went significantly beyond the then current "Syntax Directed Editors". This work helped identify the following objectives for the experiment described in this paper:

- we believe that formal specifications help fix many aspects of such projects—this belief should be tested;

- in particular, the underlying data structures of the implementation are crucial—could these be fixed ahead of implementation;

- the experience of developing parts of "Mule" from their specifications encouraged us to want to extend this mode of work;

- it was appreciated that we do not yet know how to (formally) specify good properties of user interfaces (and develop designs which provably fulfil them) – to what extent do these underlying data structures dictate what is referred to below as "deep User Interface" and leave the "surface User Interface" open to experimentation;

- specifically, we wanted to find ways of letting a user focus on the essential details of one part of a proof at a time;

- one possible way of limiting the length of proofs is to use derived rules—we wanted to experiment with their efficacy;

- it was *not* an objective to handle any specific logic—the experiment could be undertaken with something as simple as propositional calculus.

It was therefore decided that some experimentation was necessary in the User Interface area. The internals of the system were described in VDM specification style (see [14]) before any code was written. Furthermore, the implementation language chosen to provide the underlying data structures was Smalltalk-80. A lack of familiarity with this language provided another argument for an experimental system.

In order to simplify the task, a trivial logic was chosen as the basis. Our experimental system (known as "Muffin") supports proofs in Propositional Calculus only—we could clearly have written a decision procedure but the experiment in interactive use has been revealing even in such a simple problem domain[1]. Furthermore, in the final system, it will be necessary to construct a proof that a specification like that given in Appendix B has operations which are consistent with a formal notion of proof: this has not been attempted for Muffin. This limitation made it possible to postpone questions about, for example, bound variables and substitution. None of the limitations is such that it invalidates the use of the interaction style with other logics. In fact, it is hoped that the proof style will be readily extendible to other domains.

2 Proofs

It is a fact that, given the classical[2] meaning of $\land$ (and) and $\lor$ (or), the two expressions $(p \lor q) \land (p \lor r)$ and $p \lor q \land r$ are equivalent. In other words, whatever Boolean values are given to p, q and r, both expressions evaluate to the same value, or, equivalently, "or (left) distributes over and". For simple logical systems like the propositional calculus, such facts can be checked by evaluation of "all possible values" and truths can be established in the model theory. For richer systems, on the other hand, it is essential, and even for propositional calculus it is convenient, to establish the truth of claims by proof. This section pinpoints some facts about *natural deduction* proofs for the propositional calculus in order to make the examples in the remainder of the paper easier to follow. It is *not* intended to teach the topic here, however, and the reader who is unfamiliar with the propositional calculus is referred to one of many excellent textbooks (e.g. [17, 5]) on the subject.

Expressions in the propositional calculus (P.C.) can be built up from the constants (true, false), letters for propositions and the operators[3] $\neg$ (not), $\land$ (and), $\lor$ (or), $\Rightarrow$ (implies) and $\Leftrightarrow$ (equivalence). The fact that one expression follows from another can be recorded as a *sequent*, for example:

$$(p \lor q) \land (p \lor r) \vdash p \lor q \land r$$

---

[1] Actually, Muffin has to be seeded with a set of axioms and we have used the Logic of Partial Functions of [1] as well as classical Propositional Logic. In fact, a range of logics could be supported. It would be interesting to characterize exactly what assumptions on this class of logics have been made in the design of Muffin: this task is left for the work on the (full) FRIPSE (cf. [10]).

[2] It is also true in the "Logic of Partial Functions" presented in [1]. The proof given in Fig. 2 is prompted by that system; classical proofs often use the "law of the excluded middle" which can be seen from Fig. 2 not to be necessary.

[3] The operators are listed in order of decreasing priority.

This sequent records one half of the information about the distribution of **or** over **and**. Such sequents denote the fact that the term on the right of the "turnstile" ($\vdash$) can be deduced from that on the left. There is an infinity of such valid deductions, however, so they cannot all be recorded, but any of their proofs can be formed by using a small number of "inference rules". In general, an inference rule has one or more *hypotheses* and a *conclusion* separated by a horizontal line. One such rule is written:

$$\wedge\text{-}E_r \qquad \frac{E_1 \wedge E_2}{E_1}$$

This states that if $E_1 \wedge E_2$ is known, then E_1 can be deduced, for any E_1, E_2. This rule can be used to prove results like:

$$(p \vee q) \wedge (p \vee r) \vdash p \vee q$$

Notice how the schema-like variables (E_i) match sub-expressions.

Another obvious rule is:

$$\vee\text{-}I_r \qquad \frac{E_1}{E_1 \vee E_2}$$

which states that if E_1 is known, then $E_1 \vee E_2$ can be deduced. A particular instance of this justifies:

$$p \vdash p \vee q \wedge r$$

A more complicated rules states that if $E_1 \vee E_2$ has been established and, furthermore, some conclusion follows from each of the disjuncts E_1 and E_2, then this conclusion can be deduced. This rule, known here as $\vee\text{-}E$, can be thought of as providing a way of reasoning by cases:

$$\vee\text{-}E \qquad \frac{E_1 \vee E_2; \quad E_1 \vdash E; \quad E_2 \vdash E}{E}$$

Notice here how the second and third hypotheses are sequents. An example of the use of this rule would be the deduction of $p \vee q \wedge r$ from the three "knowns" $p \vee q$, $p \vdash p \vee q \wedge r$ and $q \vdash p \vee q \wedge r$.

	from $(p \vee q) \wedge (p \vee r)$	
1	$p \vee q$	$\wedge\text{-}E_r(\text{h})$
2	from p	
	infer $p \vee q \wedge r$	$\vee\text{-}I_r(\text{h2})$
3	from q	
	infer $p \vee q \wedge r$	?
	infer $p \vee q \wedge r$	$\vee\text{-}E(1,2,3)$

Figure 1: A Partial Proof

A useful way of presenting proofs built up from these simple steps is illustrated in Fig. 1. This illustrates well the power of the method—although the individual rules, such as $\wedge\text{-}E_r$, might not in themselves appear to be particularly useful, combinations of these rules can be used to build larger proofs and thus establish non-trivial results. Notice how the instances of rules above have been slotted into this proof but that the step from q to $p \vee q \wedge r$ has not yet been justified. Filling out the missing detail, makes the rôle of this nested box style of presentation clearer. Within box 3, the following facts are available:

- q—its local hypothesis

- $(p \vee q) \wedge (p \vee r)$—the global hypothesis

- $p \lor q$—a conclusion which depends only on *outer* assumptions

- $p \vdash p \lor q \land r$—another such conclusion

The conclusion of box 2 ($p \lor q \land r$) is *not* available because that relies on an assumption p which does not hold in box 3.

It should not surprise the reader that there is a rule ($\land$-E_l), analogous to $\land$-E_r, which permits elimination of the left conjunct of some conjunction:

$$\land\text{-}E_l \qquad \frac{E_1 \land E_2}{E_2}$$

This can be applied to the overall hypothesis to create the new line 3.1 in box 3 with $p \lor r$. This now suggests that another $\lor$-E can be used. In fact, box 2 already yields one of the two subsidiary deductions. All that is needed is to establish $r \vdash p \lor q \land r$. Clearly, in isolation, this sequent is not provable: its hypothesis is too weak. But, again, box 3.2 (cf. Fig. 2) is in an environment where other facts are available. In particular, the hypothesis of box 3 gives q. The rule now needed ($\land$-I) facilitates the formation of a conjunction from two facts:

$$\land\text{-}I \qquad \frac{E_1; E_2}{E_1 \land E_2}$$

This creates line 3.2.1 and the conclusion of box 3.2 follows by:

$$\lor\text{-}I_l \qquad \frac{E_2}{E_1 \lor E_2}$$

The reader should now be able to check all of the steps in Fig. 2. Notice, in particular, how box 3 justifies the second subsidiary conclusion ($q \vdash p \lor q \land r$) via a series of steps contained within the box.

One final point—which is important for the understanding of Muffin—is the fact that this proof justifies a new *derived* inference rule which can be used in subsequent proofs. Using E_i as schema variables to emphasize the point, this can be given as:

$$\frac{(E_1 \lor E_2) \land (E_1 \lor E_3)}{E_1 \lor (E_2 \land E_3)}$$

	from $(p \lor q) \land (p \lor r)$	
1	$p \lor q$	$\land$-E_r(h)
2	from p	
	infer $p \lor q \land r$	$\lor$-I_r(h2)
3	from q	
3.1	$p \lor r$	$\land$-E_l(h)
3.2	from r	
3.2.1	$q \land r$	$\land$-I(h3,h3.2)
	infer $p \lor q \land r$	$\lor$-I_l(3.2.1)
	infer $p \lor q \land r$	$\lor$-E(3.1,2,3.2)
	infer $p \lor q \land r$	$\lor$-E(1,2,3)

Figure 2: Proof (one direction) that $\lor$ distributes over $\land$

3 User Interface Issues

We now approach the main point of the paper. Muffin is a system which aims to make it easy to prove theorems at the workstation (cf. aims in [7]). The claim is that User Interface (UI) considerations are crucial if this aim is to be achieved. A distinction can be made between "surface UI" questions, which concern the appearance of the screen of the workstation, and "deep UI" issues, which govern the sort of interactions which are possible.

3.1 Surface User Interface

The evolution of workstation technology has brought to the user both significant computation speed and screens larger than the old "24 by 80" character displays. One of the reasons for believing that "proof at the workstation" might be possible is the change to the surface UI brought about by the workstations now available.

Apart from specifications and designs which give rise to a proof obligation, one might want to look both at results from the theories of data types in use and at derived inference rules in the logic itself. It might be argued that a screen as large as the desk on which one might do proofs by hand should be available. To some extent, multi-windowing systems, with their ability to overlay and collapse windows to icons, ameliorate the constraint to "A3 screens", and the speed of the processor means that even complex rearrangements of windows can be carried out extremely rapidly. Unfortunately, the need to rearrange the screen can be distracting to a user, so the size of the screen is still of some concern.

Very early in the FRIPSE project it was realised that different users would want to be able to project the information held in the system in different ways. It has subsequently become clear that a single user might also wish to view the same information in different ways. That the design of Muffin was based on an underlying abstract state was a great advantage here as it meant that this facility could be provided simply by designing alternative "projection functions".

It was originally envisaged that a user would interact with a theorem proving assistant via the natural deduction proof style used in [6] (cf. Figure 2). Experimentation with longer proofs has shown, however, that, for such proofs, the amount of information presented to the user in this natural deduction style display is more that can comfortably be assimilated. This prompted (cf. [3]) the design of an alternative projection in Muffin (Muffin's "prover"—see Section 4.4 for more details), which focuses on one "box" of such a proof at a time and which attempts to reduce the information presented to the user to essentials. The natural deduction style projection is also available, and it is sometimes useful to look at both views side by side (though not one on top of the other!). Modification of the proof can, however, only be made via the single box view.

3.2 Deep User Interface

A bad surface UI can mar a good design; it cannot redeem a poor one. The deep UI questions are the real concern of the Muffin experiment. Experience with many other, in themselves excellent, theorem proving systems gives rise to a deep sense of frustration. One has the feeling that, with a huge body of code embodying many clever algorithms, the user is limited to a very restricted, pre-planned, menu of options: much of the functionality of the system is hidden from the user. The ground rule of our UI design has been to expose the whole state of the system both to view and to modification.

The idea of projection functions is mentioned above. This must be extended to allow the user to interact with the state through these projections, thus invoking changes to the state. For example, either forward or backward proof steps are catered for, and in a more powerful system, one would be able to unify two arbitrary expressions or to instantiate any definition with chosen arguments. Of course, the alterations that can be made to the state must be such that the logical soundness and consistency of the system, achieved in LCF-like systems by careful use of the type structure of ML, is preserved.

4 Muffin

4.1 Beyond Trees

It is almost axiomatic that (abstract) syntaxes of things like *Expressions* define a set of "Trees". It would be possible to extend this to cope with *Proofs* etc. but a difficulty arises which makes it worth considering an alternative. In the specification developed in Section 4.2, references are introduced in a way which permits (acyclic) graph-like structures to be created. This section motivates that development.

A first guess at the underlying state of Muffin might lead one to view Theorems and Axioms as subsets of *Problems*. Thus the database might be:

$Db_1 = $ set of $Problem_1$

$$Problem_1 :: hyp \quad : \text{ set of } Exp_1$$
$$con \quad : Exp_1$$
$$proofs : [\text{set of } Proof_1]$$

Axioms would have nil proofs; unproven theorems would have empty sets; whilst proven theorems would have one, or more, proofs in the set. When attention is turned to *Proofs* it is clear that individual steps could be justified by appeal to other *Problems* (be they axioms or proven theorems). This means that a series of *Problems*/*Proofs* constitute a graph-like structure which is more general than can be represented by a tree. This sort of "sharing" is inevitable and it is normal in formal descriptions to model it by the use of some "reference" object[4]. Introducing *Problemref*, one might define the proof database as:

$$Db_2 :: pm \; : \; \text{map } Problemref \text{ to } Problem_2$$
$$jm \; : \; \text{map } Problemref \text{ to (set of } Proof_2)$$

$$Problem_2 :: hyp : \text{ set of } Exp_2$$
$$con : Exp_2$$

Here, references to axioms are simply omitted from the domain of the justification map jm. The reader should be able to picture how graph-like structures can be built; acyclicity can be defined by an invariant. The next section shows how even expressions can be treated as graphs.

4.2 Muffin's Underlying State

This section contains a description of the state underlying the actual Muffin system. The interested reader can find full details of the formal specification of Muffin, including the invariant on the state and the operations for changing the state, in Appendix B. The overall state (*Muffin*) is given below. Before that, each component of *Muffin*, together with the appropriate validity conditions that it has to satisfy, are dealt with in turn. At the same time, and under the assumption that the state contains exactly the statement of the problem *or-and-dist* (viz. $(p \vee q) \wedge (p \vee r) \vdash p \vee q \wedge r$) together with the six axioms (or and and introduction and elimination) used in its proof (see Figs. 2 and 3), concrete examples of what objects exist in each store component are built up. This process is continued in Section 4.5, where the actual construction of the proof *or-and-dist* shown in Fig. 3 together with the attendant changes to the state at each step are described.

The fundamental entities in Muffin are expressions. These are either meta-variables (*Atoms* in the specification) or are built up of some logical connective having other expressions for its operand(s). In order to make the specification and the description clearer, a particular set of logical connectives

---

[4]The archetypal example being *Locations* in the denotational semantics of imperative programming languages.

has been chosen and is built into Muffin, though the particular choice made is unimportant to the specification. (The extension to an arbitrary collection of operators is described in [16].)

A particular expression may, of course, be a subexpression of many different expressions (though not of itself) and it is therefore appropriate to make use of the acyclic graphs described in the preceding section and to use references to other expressions as the components of expressions. The *Expstore* records the relationship between expressions and their references. For ease of testing of equality on expressions, we make the *Expstore* 1–1; this means that any two expressions are the same if and only if their references are the same.

Other conditions are imposed on the *Expstore* for consistency. First, all subexpressions of any expression in the *Expstore* must also be in the *Expstore* (*closedness*), and second, the graphical structure representing the *Expstore* must be acyclic (*finiteness*). This latter condition is equivalent to saying that no expression can be a subexpression of itself. The syntax for expressions is therefore given by:

$Exp = And \mid Or \mid Atom \mid \cdots$

$And :: andl : Expref$
$\qquad\quad andr : Expref$

$Or :: orl : Expref$
$\qquad\ orr : Expref$

The *Expstore* is defined[5]:

$Expstore = \mathsf{map}\ Expref\ \mathsf{into}\ Exp$

where

$inv\text{-}Expstore(es) \quad \triangleq \quad is\text{-}closed(es) \wedge is\text{-}finite(es)$

The *Expstore* for the sample state will contain exactly the associations:

$d_1 \mapsto mk\text{-}Or(a_p, a_q), \qquad d_2 \mapsto mk\text{-}Or(a_p, a_r), \qquad g \mapsto mk\text{-}Or(a_p, c_1),$
$h \mapsto mk\text{-}And(d_1, d_2), \qquad c_1 \mapsto mk\text{-}And(a_q, a_r), \qquad c \mapsto mk\text{-}And(a_1, a_2),$
$a_p \mapsto p, \qquad a_q \mapsto q, \qquad a_r \mapsto r,$
$d \mapsto mk\text{-}Or(a_1, a_2), \qquad a_1 \mapsto E_1, \qquad a_2 \mapsto E_2, \qquad e \mapsto E$
$\{p, q, r, E, E_1, E_2\} \subseteq Atom$

Some inference rules (e.g. ∨-*E*) permit a sequent, rather than just an expression, to be present in their hypothesis. This is handled by bringing in the notion of a *subsequent* (written $a \rightsquigarrow b$) to restrict the nesting to one level. A subsequent (*Subseq*) has a *left-hand side*, which is a set of expressions, and a *right-hand side*, which is a single expression. Again, references to the expressions rather than the expressions themselves are used for the arguments of subsequents. Notice that a subsequent with an empty left-hand side can be identified with the expression on its right-hand side. This suggests an invariant on subsequents which prohibits empty left-hand sides:

$Subseq :: lhs : \mathsf{set\ of}\ Expref$
$\qquad\qquad rhs : Expref$

where

$inv\text{-}Subseq(mk\text{-}Subseq(lhs, rhs)) \quad \triangleq \quad lhs \neq \{\ \}$

---

[5] Note that *Atom* and *Expref* are (disjoint) infinite sets of structureless tokens.

Expressions and subsequents, collectively referred to as *Nodes*, form the building blocks for *Problems*, which represent many similar entities, such as *axioms, (derived) rules of inference, lemmas, theorems* and *conjectures*, in Muffin. Problems have a set of *hypotheses* to the left of their turnstile, and a single *conclusion* to the right. The arbitrary nesting of turnstiles is avoided by restricting the hypotheses to be nodes and the conclusion to be an expression. Subsequents and problems are stored respectively in the *Subseqstore* and the *Problemstore*, with both stores being taken to be 1–1 mappings as for the *Expstore*. The validity condition on the *Subseqstore* states that any expression which forms part of some subsequent in the *Subseqstore* must be in the *Expstore*; the one on the *Problemstore* that any expression or subsequent forming part of some problem in the *Problemstore* must be in, respectively, the *Expstore* or the *Subseqstore*[6].

$Subseqstore = $ map $Subseqref$ into $Subseq$

$Node = Expref \mid Subseqref$

$Problem ::\ hyp\ :\ $ set of $Node$
$\qquad\qquad con\ :\ Expref$

$Problemstore = $ map $Problemref$ into $Problem$

In the sample state, the *Subseqstore* contains just the two subsequents needed for the $\lor$-E rule:

$ss_1 \mapsto mk\text{-}Subseq(\{a_1\}, e),$
$ss_2 \mapsto mk\text{-}Subseq(\{a_2\}, e),$

whilst the *Problemstore* contains the statement of the problem *or-and-dist* together with the statements of the six axioms mentioned above:

$p_0 \mapsto mk\text{-}Problem(\{h\}, g),$
$p_{OrIr} \mapsto mk\text{-}Problem(\{a_1\}, d),$
$p_{OrIl} \mapsto mk\text{-}Problem(\{a_2\}, d),$
$p_{OrE} \mapsto mk\text{-}Problem(\{d, ss_1, ss_2\}, e)$
$p_{AndEr} \mapsto mk\text{-}Problem(\{c\}, a_1),$
$p_{AndEl} \mapsto mk\text{-}Problem(\{c\}, a_2),$
$p_{AndI} \mapsto mk\text{-}Problem(\{a_1, a_2\}, c)$

At this basic level, the notions of *substitution* and *matching* can also be introduced. Thus, one is allowed to build an *instance* of, for example, some expression e by substituting expressions for any meta-variables occurring in e. In the formal specification a map $Atom$ to $Expref$ represents such a substitution. If the result of making some substitution m in an expression A yields the expression B then the expression A is said to *match* the expression B. Alternatively, B is an instance of A, with the particular instance being given by the substitution m (thus, this is essentially one direction unification). The notions of matching and substitution extend trivially to both subsequents and problems.

Problems can be divided into several different categories. They may be assumed true without proof (corresponding to the axioms of the system), proved (corresponding to derived inference rules, lemmas and theorems) or unproven (corresponding to conjectures). The first two categories together will be referred to as *solved* problems, the third as *unsolved* problems. Some subset of the solved problems is designated as the *rules of inference* of the system.

Given some existing set of solved problems, there are essentially two ways of creating a new solved problem. First, one can simply build an instance of some existing rule of inference by replacing some or all of the variables appearing in the statement of the rule with expressions. The new solved problem so created then has a proof which is simply an *Instantiation*, consisting of a reference to

---

[6] *Subseqref* and *Problemref* are both infinite sets of structureless tokens, assumed disjoint from each other and from both *Expref* and *Atom*.

the problem which is the statement of the rule together with a map recording the necessary variable substitution. Thus:

$$Instantiation :: of : Problemref$$
$$by : \text{map } Atom \text{ to } Expref$$

where

$$inv\text{-}Instantiation(mk\text{-}Instantiation(of, by)) \quad \triangleq \quad by \neq \{\}$$

Notice that the case in which the substitution map is the empty map is excluded—building an instance of something with a null substitution does nothing.

The second way of creating new solved problems is by combining existing solved problems together in some order as a *Composite-proof*. This is represented in Muffin simply as a sequence of solved problems and is used to describe proofs like the one shown in Fig. 2. Further details of this can be found below and in Section 4.5.

$$Composite\text{-}proof = \text{seq of } Problemref$$

Proofs as a whole are then just the union of *Instantiations* and *Composite-proofs*:

$$Proof = Instantiation \mid Composite\text{-}proof$$

For a composite proof c, the *knowns* of some problem p with respect to c are the set of things deducible from the hypotheses of p via the elements of c taken in order. Thus, if c is empty, the knowns of p are the same as the hypotheses of p. Otherwise, the $i + 1$ *th* element v of c contributes an expression or a subsequent to the knowns as follows: if the hypotheses of v are all contained in the knowns collected with the first i elements of c, then v contributes its conclusion to the knowns; if not, but if there is some subsequent s in the *Subseqstore* whose right-hand side is the same as the conclusion of v and whose left-hand side added to the hypotheses of p gives the hypotheses of v, then v contributes s to the knowns; if neither of these two conditions is satisfied, v contributes nothing to the knowns. A composite proof c is therefore a *complete proof* of a problem p if the knowns of p with respect to c contains the conclusion of p; otherwise c is an *incomplete proof* of p.

The method by which the knowns of the problem p with respect to the composite proof c are generated also forms the basis for the full natural deduction style display of Figure 3[7]. Taking the elements of the proof c in turn, if a particular element e adds an expression to the knowns, that element adds a line like line 1 to the display, with the line showing the new known generated and the justification of the new known. If the element e adds a subsequent to the knowns, this generates a from–infer box in the display, the from line listing the elements of the left-hand side of the subsequent, the infer line the right-hand side. The lines of the proof internal to that box or subproof are generated similarly by displaying the proof of the problem e between the from and the infer lines.

Each proof is associated with a reference via the *Proofstore*[8]:

$$Proofstore = \text{map } Proofref \text{ to } Proof$$

where

$$inv\text{-}Proofstore(fs) \quad \triangleq \quad \forall p, q \in \text{dom } fs \cdot fs(p) = fs(q) \land is\text{-}Instantiation(fs(p)) \Rightarrow p = q$$

The sample state has an empty *Proofstore*.

The invariant states that each *Instantiation* is assigned a unique reference via the *Proofstore*. This restriction turns out to be impractical for composite proofs in general, however—new complete proofs are going to be built by editing existing incomplete proofs, so sometimes different references to the same proof might be required (for example, it may not be clear to a user how exactly to proceed from the current state of some proof in order to complete the proof, and he might wish to try several different possibilities, thus necessitating duplicating the current state of the proof). In Muffin, this

---

[7]Note that extra steps (over Figure 2) are required: this is explained in Section 4.5.

[8]*Proofref* is yet another infinite set of structureless tokens, disjoint from all the others.

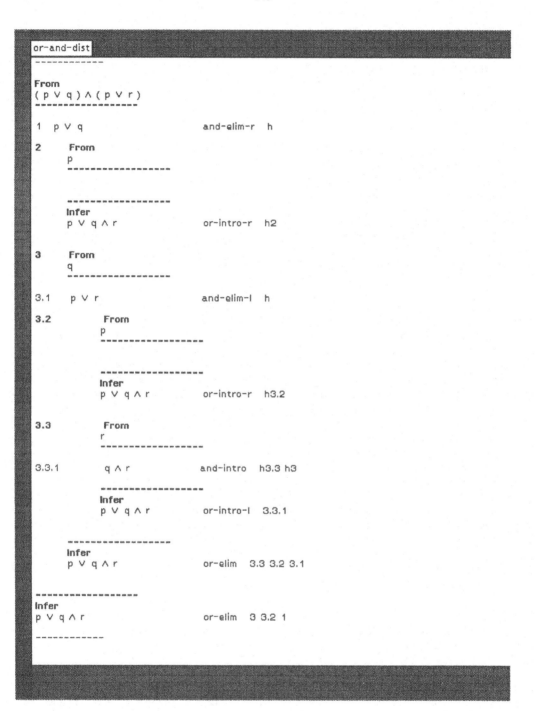

Figure 3: Muffin Projection of *or-and-dist* Proof

restriction is in fact taken to the other extreme and *no* composite proof is shared. The difficulties only really occur in the case of incomplete proofs, however, so it would in fact be possible to extend the invariant here so that all complete proofs were assigned unique references.

The validity condition on the *Proofstore* states simply that any component of any proof in the *Proofstore* has to be in the *Expstore*, the *Subseqstore* or the *Problemstore* as appropriate.

In order to associate proofs with problems, the *Proofmap* and the *Incomplete-proofmap* are introduced. The first of these associates problems with complete proofs, the second with incomplete proofs.

$Proofmap = $ map *Problemref* to set of *Proofref*

$Incomplete\text{-}proofmap = $ map *Problemref* to set of *Proofref*

where

$inv\text{-}Incomplete\text{-}proofmap(im)\quad \underline{\Delta}$
$\quad \{\,\} \notin \text{rng}\, im \wedge \forall k, m \in \text{dom}\, im \cdot im(k) \cap im(m) \neq \{\,\} \;\Rightarrow\; k = m$

The first part of the invariant on the *Incomplete-proofmap* says that it does not record the fact that a given problem has no incomplete proofs as this can be inferred from the absence of the problem in question from the domain of the *Incomplete-proofmap*. The second part of the invariant occurs as a result of the restriction that no composite proof is shared (note that only composite proofs can be incomplete—instantiations are by definition always complete).

Those problems occurring in the domain of the *Proofmap* are the solved problems, those not, the unsolved problems. The axioms of Muffin are made to conform to this definition by mapping them to the empty set under the *Proofmap*. In addition, some of the solved problems are designated as the *rules of inference* of the system, and these are given names via the *Rulemap*:

$Rulemap = $ map *String* into *Problemref*

Again no two rules may have the same name, and the empty string is not a valid rule name.

The sample state therefore has a *Proofmap* containing the associations:

$p_{OrIr} \mapsto \{\,\}$
$p_{OrIl} \mapsto \{\,\}$
$p_{OrE} \mapsto \{\,\}$
$p_{AndEr} \mapsto \{\,\}$
$p_{AndEl} \mapsto \{\,\}$
$p_{AndI} \mapsto \{\,\}$

and a *Rulemap* containing

$\textit{or-intro-r} \mapsto p_{OrIr}$
$\textit{or-intro-l} \mapsto p_{OrIl}$
$\textit{or-elim} \mapsto p_{OrE}$
$\textit{and-elim-r} \mapsto p_{AndEr}$
$\textit{and-elim-l} \mapsto p_{AndEl}$
$\textit{and-intro} \mapsto p_{AndI}$

Its *Incomplete-proofmap* is empty.

The validity condition on the *Rulemap* states that all rules are solved problems, all axioms are rules, and all *Instantiations* are instantiations of rules. The condition on the *Proofmap* is, however, somewhat more complicated. First, all the solved problems must be in the *Problemstore* and all the complete proofs in the *Proofstore*. Second, any proof attached to some problem via the *Proofmap* must not only *be* a complete proof of that problem but may itself only contain solved problems. Thirdly, it must be possible to associate exactly one of its complete proofs with each solved problem other than the axioms in such a way that there are no circularities of reasoning amongst this set of associations, that is the system must be logically sound. Note however, that circularities *can* exist due to a problem being allowed to have multiple complete proofs. Thus, for instance, a user might prove result A from the basic axioms, then prove B making use of A as a derived rule, then prove A again using B as a derived rule, without destroying the logical soundness of the system. Finally, no two solved problems share a complete composite proof.

The validity condition on the *Incomplete-proofmap* is built up similarly. First, any problem in its domain must be in the *Problemstore* and any incomplete proof attached to that problem in the *Proofstore*. In fact, this condition is extended to state that the *Proofstore* contains only those proofs which are attached to some problem via either the *Proofmap* or the *Incomplete-proofmap*. Here, however, the proof must *not* be a complete proof of the problem, though it must still consist only of solved problems. There should be no *Instantiations* occurring in any element in the range of the *Incomplete-proofmap*, and no proof is both an incomplete proof of some problem and a complete proof of some other.

Incomplete proofs consist effectively of two parts, the *forward proof* and the *backward proof*, with the proof as a whole being the concatenation of the backward proof onto the forward proof. When attempting to convert an incomplete proof of some problem into a complete proof thereof, new elements can be added either to the tail of the forward proof or to the head of the backward proof, corresponding respectively to *forward inferencing* and *backward inferencing*. In order to be able to insert new elements into a proof at the correct point, it is therefore necessary to record for each incomplete proof the position in the sequence which marks the division between the forward and backward proofs. The last component of Muffin, the *Indexmap*, does this by recording the index of the last element of the forward proof:

$$Indexmap = \mathsf{map}\ Proofref\ \mathsf{to}\ \mathbb{N}$$

The *Indexmap* is empty in the sample state.

The elements of the forward proof give rise to all the knowns, with part of the validity condition on the *Indexmap* being that each element of the forward proof should actually contribute to the knowns. Thus, by adding a new element to the tail of the forward proof which satisfies one of the conditions for adding to the knowns it is possible to increase the current knowns (forward inferencing).

The elements of the backward proof, on the other hand, provide a proof of the conclusion of the relevant problem from some set of subgoals. Proving all these subgoals would be sufficient to complete the proof. In this case, a new element can be added to the head of the backward proof if the conclusion of that element is amongst the current subgoals. (This condition also forms part of the validity constraint.) The conclusion of the element is then removed from the subgoals and all its hypotheses are added to get the new subgoals, that is, one of the existing subgoals is itself reduced to subgoals. This is backward inferencing.

Another part of the validity condition on the *Indexmap* states that the backward proof should contain no element all of whose hypotheses are among the current knowns—such an element would correctly contribute its conclusion to the knowns and should therefore be positioned at the tail of the forward proof. After every forward inferencing step, therefore, any such elements in the backward proof must be removed therefrom and transferred to the tail of the forward proof, then any spurious elements in what remains of the backward proof must be discarded (this latter is necessary because the new forward element might have added something to the knowns which had previously been reduced to subgoals by some backward step). If the new knowns contains the conclusion of the problem, the new forward proof forms a complete proof of it and so the problem—proof association can be removed from the *Incomplete-proofmap* and added to the *Proofmap*, at the same time removing the proof—index association from the *Indexmap*. Otherwise, the new incomplete proof becomes the new forward proof concatenated with the new backward proof, with the appropriate change to the *Indexmap*. Note that this reorganisation is unnecessary for backward inferencing as this does not alter the knowns.

The remaining parts of the validity condition on the *Indexmap* say that it records an index for each incomplete proof but for no complete proof, and that the value of the index lies somewhere between zero and the number of elements in the proof.

Any *Expression*, *Subseq*, *Problem* or *Proof* can be given a name[9], so that the user of Muffin can more readily identify those objects of particular interest. The names are stored in a name store for each of the basic types of object, though no two objects of the same type may have the same name, and the empty string is not a valid name. It is possible, however, for objects of different types to have identical names. These names are stored in mappings.

It is now possible to turn to the full description of the Muffin state (*Muffin*). The first four components are object stores for each of the basic types of object in Muffin, that is, *expressions*, *subsequents*, *problems* and *proofs*. Next come name stores for each type of object. The *Proofmap* associates problems with complete proofs, and some solved problems are designated as rules of inference via the *Rulemap*. The *Incomplete-proofmap* associates problems with incomplete proofs. As has been mentioned above, Muffin supports both forward and backward inferencing, which, in terms of the state, means that an incomplete proof effectively consists of two parts, a forward proof and a backward proof. Elements can be added either to the tail of the forward proof or to the head of the backward proof, as explained in more detail later in Section 4.4. The remaining component of the state, the *Indexmap*, therefore records the last element of the forward proof for each incomplete proof, that is the point in the sequence at which new elements can be inserted.

$$
\begin{array}{lll}
Muffin :: & es & : & Expstore \\
& ss & : & Subseqstore \\
& ps & : & Problemstore \\
& fs & : & Proofstore \\
& en & : & ExpNames \\
& sn & : & SubseqNames \\
& pn & : & ProblemNames \\
& fn & : & ProofNames \\
& jm & : & Proofmap \\
& rm & : & Rulemap \\
& im & : & Incomplete\text{-}proofmap \\
& xm & : & Indexmap
\end{array}
$$

where

$$
inv\text{-}Muffin(mk\text{-}Muffin(es, ss, ps, fs, en, sn, pn, fn, jm, rm, im, xm)) \;\triangleq\; \ldots
$$

4.3 Granularity of Operations

The state outlined in the previous section supports a view of what a proof is; it is now possible to envisage operations at different granularities. At one extreme, an operation for inserting a whole proof could be provided; at the other, one could specify operations which dealt with single operands (or even key strokes). In deciding to choose operations between these two extremes, one is saying more about the current focus of concern than about the final program: the implementation has to handle single key strokes and, in a sense, has to have a state change which corresponds to the insertion of a whole proof. It would, of course, be possible to write specifications at different levels of operation granularity. Although this would be connected with the likely implementation, it is important to see that the level of granularity chosen in *the specification* takes a position about the sort of interactions supported by *transactions* within the system. Here, operations (cf. Appendix B) for adding forward and backward steps to evolving proofs were judged to be the right level of concern for the Muffin specification. The "operation" of adding a whole proof can, in this specification, be thought of as a composition of simpler operations some of which involve the human user of the system.

---

[9]Strictly, the name is associated with the reference.

4.4 Muffin's User Interface

The various components of the surface UI can be conveniently divided into three categories, the *browser*, the *builder* and the *prover*.

The *browser* essentially allows the user to inspect the current state of Muffin. The user selects the type of object to be inspected from the list *axioms*, *proofs*, *rules*, *problems*, *subsequents* and *expressions*. The browser will then show all objects of the selected type. Where the particular type selected has multiple subtypes, e.g. *complete* and *incomplete* for proofs, *and*, *or*, etc. for expressions, the user can additionally select one of these subtypes and the browser will then show only those objects of the selected subtype. Objects can be accessed via their names or via some textual representation of the objects themselves. When the particular object selected is a problem, the browser shows additionally either the status of any existing proofs of that problem or that the selected problem is an axiom. In the latter case, the axiom name is also shown. Figure 4 shows the browser where the selection is the unsolved problem named *or-and-dist* and its incomplete proof of the same name, the completed version of which is shown in Figure 3.

In addition, the browser allows a few simple changes to be made to the state of Muffin, such as naming and renaming of objects, conversion of an unsolved problem to an axiom, conversion of a solved problem to a (derived) rule, and addition of a new empty composite proof to the set of incomplete proofs of some problem. The interested reader can find the specification of these actions amongst the operations on the Muffin state given in Appendix B.

Finally, the browser acts as a controller for the other components of Muffin. Thus, for instance, it allows the user to start up either a builder or a prover, to inspect the current status of some existing proof, to remove incomplete proofs and unsolved problems from Muffin's store, and to restart some abandoned proof at the point at which it was abandoned.

The *builder*, of which there are several different forms, allows the user to create new expressions, subsequents and problems and add them to the relevant object stores. The operations for updating the object stores can also be found in Appendix B.

Lastly, the *prover* allows the user to edit an incomplete proof with a view to converting it into a complete proof. Both forward and backward inferencing are supported, together with the ability to undo proof steps (by removing them either from the tail of the forward proof or from the head of the backward proof).

Proofs in the style of [6], an example of which is given in Figure 2, contain much information which is in general of little help to someone actually in the process of constructing such a proof. Muffin's prover therefore attempts to reduce the information presented to the user to essentials in two ways. First, proof steps internal to some subproof or "box" in such a proof are only meaningful within that subproof and not within the containing proof. Muffin therefore restricts attention to one box at a time, with any subproof of that box being represented as a subsequent. A set containing all the expressions appearing on the from line of the box forms the left-hand side of the subsequent, whilst the right-hand side is what appears on the infer line of the box.

Second, the prover hides all of the details of ordering of lines and justification of proofsteps within a box by using the knowns and the goals as described above as the basis for its display. The prover thus displays the problem the user is attempting to solve, the current knowns, and the *visible goals*, where the visible goals are those current goals (as obtained via the elements of the backward proof) not amongst the current knowns. Figure 5 shows a prover at that point during the construction of the proof of Figure 3 at which the proof is complete apart from the subproof at box 3.

The full natural deduction style display of Figure 3 is also available, however, and the user can additionally display any complete or incomplete proof in this style if so desired.

In addition, the user can choose to further reduce the amount of information displayed by the prover by making use of the facility of *elision* of knowns. Thus, if the user decides that a particular element of the knowns is not going to be of any use in the remainder of the proof, it can be designated as *hidden* and it will be removed from the display. When a prover has hidden knowns, Muffin reminds the user of this by displaying ellipsis points at the foot of the list of displayed knowns. Any hidden

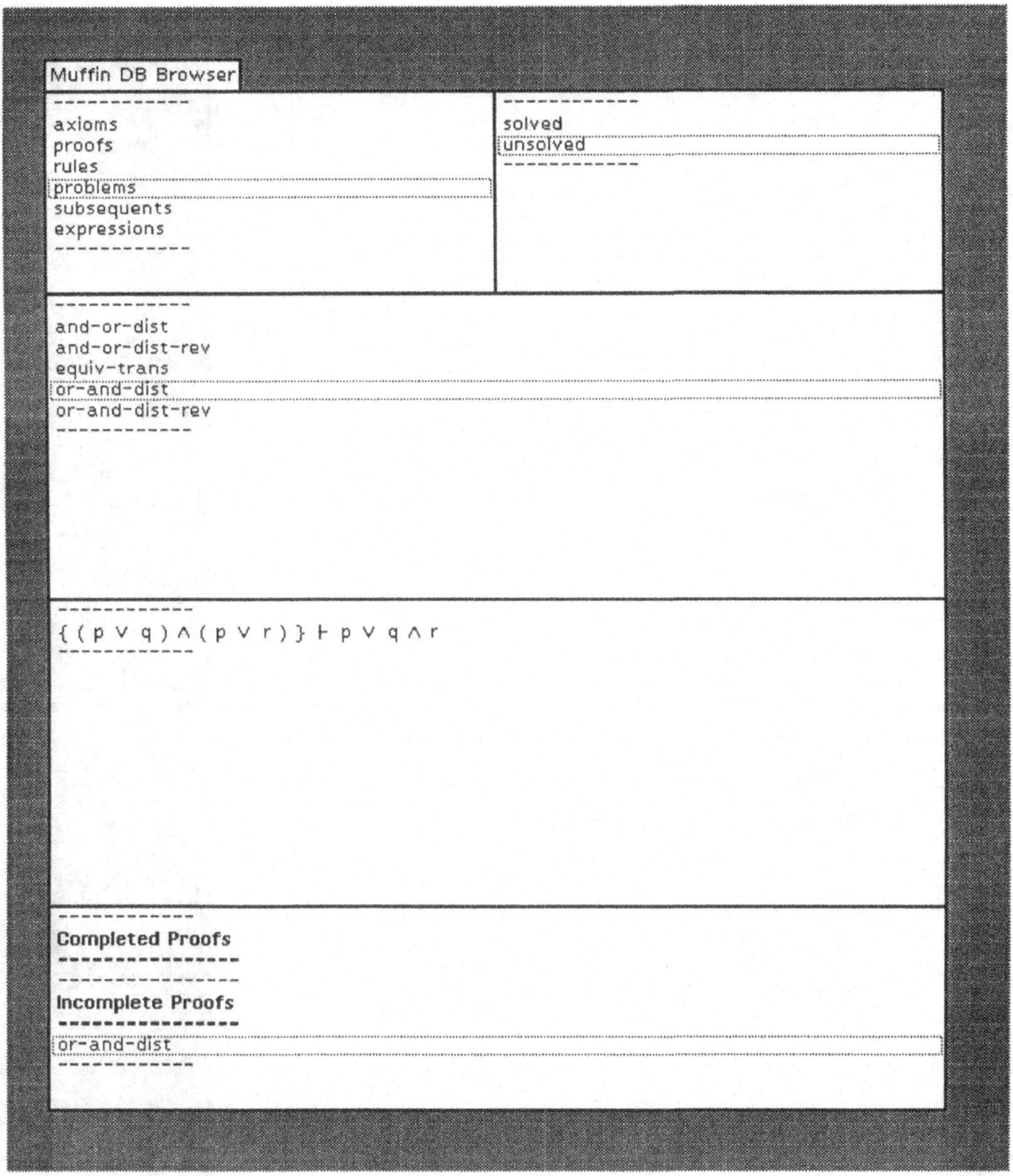

Muffin DB Browser

```
------------
axioms
proofs
rules
problems
subsequents
expressions
------------
```

```
------------
solved
unsolved
------------
```

```
------------
and-or-dist
and-or-dist-rev
equiv-trans
or-and-dist
or-and-dist-rev
------------
```

```
------------
{ ( p ∨ q ) ∧ ( p ∨ r ) } ⊢ p ∨ q ∧ r
------------
```

```
------------
Completed Proofs
------------------
------------------
Incomplete Proofs
------------------
or-and-dist
------------
```

Figure 4: Muffin's Browser

352

Figure 5: Muffin's Prover

known remains a known of the proof, of course, and the reverse operation of redisplaying hidden knowns is available to the user at any time.

The prover offers the user three ways of adding a new element to an incomplete proof. First, if it is possible to build some instance i of some rule of inference such that all hypotheses of i are amongst the current knowns, then i can be added to the tail of the forward proof. If, on the other hand, the user can build such an i such that the conclusion of i is amongst the current goals, then i can be added to the head of the backward proof. Finally, if there is a subsequent $a \rightsquigarrow b$ amongst the current goals and if the problem p is solved and has hypotheses $h \cup a$ and conclusion b, where h represents the hypotheses of the problem the user is currently trying to solve, then p can be added to the tail of the forward proof (the conditions on p are exactly those that must be satisfied in order for it to contribute the subsequent $a \rightsquigarrow b$ to the knowns).

Muffin offers assistance with each of these three processes. In the first two cases, the user can select an expression from either the knowns or the goals and ask Muffin to provide a menu of rules matching the selection. When matching to a goal, Muffin returns the list of rules whose conclusions match the selected goal; when matching to a known, it returns the list of rules which have amongst their hypotheses something which matches the selected known. Selecting a rule from the list returned then causes Muffin to try to build the relevant instance of the selected rule and add this to the proof.

The variable substitution deduced from the initial matching process is not always complete, however. For instance, more than one element of the hypotheses of the selected rule might match the selected known, or the rule might contain more variables than the expressions which were matched do. In such circumstances, Muffin prompts the user to complete the parts of the variable substitution it was unable to deduce for itself (this is done via the *substitution editor*—see Section 4.5). Then, when the instantiation is complete, it adds the new element to the proof.

The assistance offered with the third method of adding a new element to a proof is less sophisticated. Here, the user can select a subsequent from the current goals and ask Muffin to search through the solved problems to see whether the problem p which would have to be added to the tail of the forward proof in order for the selected subsequent to be added to the knowns is amongst them. If it is, Muffin automatically adds p to the forward proof. If not, the user is given the opportunity to open a new prover in order to attempt to solve the problem p.

The user may have as many provers, browsers and builders as desired active and displayed on the screen at once and can switch the focus of attention between them at will. In particular, there may be provers in which different problems are being proved as well as provers showing different attempted proofs of the same problem. Thus, for example, if, while working on some proof, the user decides that the proof would be more straightforward if some new derived rule were proved first, the current proof can be abandoned and the problem stating that derived rule can be built in a builder, proved in some other prover, then designated as a derived rule, maybe in a browser. On returning to the original proof, the new rule will now be available and it can be used there as desired.

Finally in this section, it is worth noting that any window appearing on the screen is simply a *view* of the current underlying Muffin state. Closing a window simply removes a particular view from the display; it *never* changes the state. Thus, if the user is unable to complete a particular proof, the prover showing that proof can be safely deleted from the display; it can later be retrieved via the browser in exactly the same form as it had when deleted.

4.5   A Sample Muffin Session

This section explains in some detail the sequence of actions a user of Muffin would typically perform in order to prove the theorem *or-and-dist* of Figure 3. For the purposes of this exercise, it is assumed that the session begins with the state as described in Section 4.2, that is, it contains the statement of the problem *or-and-dist* together with all the rules of inference used to justify the steps of the proof as shown in Figure 3.

The problem p_0 will at this stage appear in the browser as an unsolved problem (cf. Figure 4). By selecting it there, the user can give it a name (*or-and-dist* in Figure 4), associate a new empty incomplete proof with it, and give the new proof a name (also *or-and-dist* in Figure 4). The effect of these actions on the Muffin state is as follows. The first adds the association *or-and-dist* $\mapsto p_0$ to *ProblemNames*. The second begins by adding the association $f_0 \mapsto [\,]$ to the *Proofstore*, where f_0 is some new *Proofref*, then adds $p_0 \mapsto \{f_0\}$ to the *Incomplete-proofmap* and $f_0 \mapsto 0$ to the *Indexmap*. The third adds *or-and-dist* $\mapsto f_0$ to the *ProofNames*.

A side effect of adding the new proof f_0 is that Muffin automatically opens a prover on f_0. Initially, this shows the problem p_0 in its top pane, and there is a single known $(p \lor q) \land (p \lor r)$ (i.e. the hypothesis of p_0), and a single goal, $p \lor q \land r$ (i.e. the conclusion of p_0).

As the first step of the proof, the user might select the known $(p \lor q) \land (p \lor r)$ and ask Muffin to display the matching rules. One of these will be the rule called *and-elim-r*, which is mapped to the *Problemref* p_{AndEr} under the *Rulemap*. Selection of this rule causes several changes to be made to the state. First, Muffin builds the problem *mk-Problem*$(\{h\}, d_1)$ (i.e. $(p \lor q) \land (p \lor r) \vdash p \lor q$) and adds the association $p_1 \mapsto$ *mk-Problem*$(\{h\}, d_1)$ to the *Problemstore*. This problem is, of course, just an instance of the *and-elim-r* rule. It is therefore solved, its proof being simply the relevant instantiation. The next step is therefore to build the instantiation and add the new proof to the *Proofstore*. This is done by adding the association $f_1 \mapsto$ *mk-Instantiation*$(p_{AndEr}, \{E_1 \mapsto d_1, E_2 \mapsto d_2\})$ to the *Proofstore*. The fact that the problem p_1 is solved is then recorded by adding the association $p_1 \mapsto \{f_1\}$ to the *Proofmap*. Finally, the problem p_1 has to be added to the forward proof of the proof f_0. Thus, in the *Indexmap*, the association $f_0 \mapsto 0$ is replaced by $f_0 \mapsto 1$, and in the *Proofstore* $f_0 \mapsto [\,]$ is replaced by $f_0 \mapsto [p_1]$. Since the backward proof is empty, no reorganisation of the backward proof is necessary.

All this behind the scenes activity is, of course, hidden from the user, and the sole visible effect of all the above is the addition of $p \lor q$ to the knowns of p_0.

As the next step in the proof f_0, the user might select the goal $p \lor q \land r$ and choose the rule *or-elim* from the menu of matching rules. In concrete terms, this rule has the form $E_1 \lor E_2; E_1 \rightsquigarrow E; E_2 \rightsquigarrow E \vdash E$. From the matching so far performed, Muffin can deduce that it must instantiate E to $p \lor q \land r$ but not the required instantiations of E_1 and E_2. It therefore prompts the user for these substitutions by opening a *substitution editor*. The user elects to replace E_1 by p and E_2 by q. Muffin then builds the instance of the *or-elim* rule defined by this substitution, namely $p \lor q; p \rightsquigarrow p \lor q \land r; q \rightsquigarrow p \lor q \land r \vdash p \lor q \land r$.

The two subsequents appearing in this problem are new, so must first be added to the *Subseqstore*, achieved by adding to it the associations:

$$ss_1 \mapsto mk\text{-}Subseq(\{a_p\}, g),$$
$$ss_2 \mapsto mk\text{-}Subseq(\{a_q\}, g),$$

where ss_3 and ss_4 are new *Subseqrefs*. Now it is possible to add the association:

$$p_4 \mapsto mk\text{-}Problem(\{d_1, ss_3, ss_4\}, g),$$

and thus the new *Problem*, to the *Problemstore*. Again, this is a solved problem, the proof of which is an instantiation. These facts are recorded by adding the association:

$$f_4 \mapsto mk\text{-}Instantiation(p_{OrE}, \{E_1 \mapsto a_p, E_2 \mapsto a_q, E \mapsto g\})$$

to the *Proofstore*, and the association

$$p_4 \mapsto \{f_4\}$$

to the *Proofmap*. Finally, the new proof step is added to the proof f_0 by replacing the association $f_0 \mapsto [p_1]$ with $f_0 \mapsto [p_1, p_4]$ in the *Proofstore*. In this case, the value of the index of f_0 in the *Indexmap* remains unchanged (i.e. 1) as this was a backward proof step.

The goals pane of the prover now shows the two subsequents $p \rightsquigarrow p \lor q \land r$ and $q \rightsquigarrow p \lor q \land r$. The subgoal $p \lor q$ doesn't appear there as it is amongst the current knowns (that is, it is a current goal but not a visible goal).

Next, the user selects the subsequent $p \rightsquigarrow p \vee q \wedge r$ in the goals pane and chooses the menu option "search for solved problems". Muffin checks through all solved problems to see whether the problem $(p \vee q) \wedge (p \vee r); p \vdash p \vee q \wedge r$ (i.e. the problem which would contribute the required subsequent to the knowns of the proof f_0) is among them. In this case, the problem has not already been solved, and Muffin offers the user the chance to open a new prover to try to solve it. Accepting this offer causes the new problem to be added to the *Problemstore* via the association $p_2 \mapsto mk\text{-}Problem(\{h, a_p\}, g)$, adds a new empty proof to the *Proofstore* via $f_2 \mapsto [\,]$, and designates f_2 as an incomplete proof of p_2 by adding $p_2 \mapsto \{f_2\}$ to the *Incomplete-proofmap* and $f_2 \mapsto 0$ to the *Indexmap*.

The user now switches attention to the new problem p_2, corresponding to box 2 of Fig. 3, and tries to solve it. This is very easy – selecting the goal $p \vee q \wedge r$ and the *or-intro-r* rule from the menu of matching rules is, in fact, sufficient to complete the proof. Behind the scenes, Muffin adds the association $p_{21} \mapsto mk\text{-}Problem(\{a_p\}, g)$ to the *Problemstore*, adds $f_{21} \mapsto mk\text{-}Instantiation(p_{OrIr}, \{E_1 \mapsto a_p, E_2 \mapsto c_1\})$ to the *Proofstore*, and marks p_{21} as solved by adding $p_{21} \mapsto \{f_{21}\}$ to the *Proofmap*. In the *Proofstore*, the association $f_2 \mapsto [\,]$ is replaced with $f_2 \mapsto [p_{21}]$. Since f_2 is now a complete proof of p_2, the association $p_2 \mapsto \{f_2\}$ is moved from the *Incomplete-proofmap* to the *Proofmap* and $f_2 \mapsto 0$ is deleted from the *Indexmap*.

Having completed the proof of p_2, the user can now return to the proof f_0 and ask Muffin to search again for the solved problem it failed to find earlier. Now, of course, the problem is solved, and Muffin duly finds it and adds p_2 to the tail of the forward proof of f_0. Thus, in the *Proofstore*, $f_0 \mapsto [p_1, p_4]$ is replaced by $f_0 \mapsto [p_1, p_2, p_4]$ and in the *Indexmap* $f_0 \mapsto 1$ is replaced by $f_0 \mapsto 2$. On the screen, the subsequent $p \rightsquigarrow p \vee q \wedge r$ vanishes from the goals pane and appears in the knowns pane.

The user completes the proof f_0 by selecting the remaining subsequent $q \rightsquigarrow p \vee q \wedge r$ in the goals pane, setting up the new problem to be solved as before (thus adding the association $p_3 \mapsto mk\text{-}Problem(\{h, a_q\}, g)$ to the *Problemstore*) and proving it using steps entirely analogous to those already described. Note, however, that the process of setting up and solving subproblems is in fact repeated during the proof of p_3, corresponding to the inner boxes 3.2 and 3.3 of Fig. 3. The goals pane of the proof f_0 finally shows *"Q.E.D."* to indicate that the proof is complete. At this point, the association $f_0 \mapsto 2$ is removed from the *Indexmap*, and $p_0 \mapsto \{f_0\}$ is moved from the *Incomplete-proofmap* to the *Proofmap*, with the *Proofstore* now containing $f_0 \mapsto [p_1, p_2, p_3, p_4]$. Full details (in concrete form) of the complete proof structure behind the proof *or-and-dist* can be found in Appendix A.

5 Evaluation

As stated earlier, one of the main aims of the Muffin exercise was to develop both a proof style and an interaction style which would encourage a user to use the system to actually discover formal proofs rather than just as a proof checker. Ideas on what form this proof style would take were initially somewhat nebulous, of course, so the first stage of the process consisted simply of designing and specifying a theorem store for simple propositional calculus. The resulting specification [14] then formed the basis for a prototype working system possessing a rudimentary user interface (see [15]).

This prototype system was implemented in Smalltalk–80, a language with which we were totally unfamiliar prior to our using it as the implementation language for Muffin. The second of the main aims of the exercise was therefore to assess the suitability or otherwise of Smalltalk–80 as an implementation language for formal reasoning systems.

One of the main reasons for choosing Smalltalk–80 as opposed to, say, standard ML, was that a lot of basic UI components are already built into the basic Smalltalk system. It is therefore very easy to construct a user interface simply by combining these existing primitives as desired. Moreover, it is also very easy to experiment with different user interface designs by simply combining these primitives in different ways. In fact, it turned out that the choice of language was even more fortuitous, due to the strong natural parallel between on the one hand the abstract data types and the operations and functions defined thereon of the formal specification and on the other hand the object classes and the messages acting thereon of the language. Exploiting this parallel made it possible to progress from the formal specification of the theorem store to a working prototype of Muffin with an expenditure of only two man-months of effort. Such rapid progress was no doubt partly due to the fact that much of the design of the system had been carried out at the specification level, which probably accounted for approximately three quarters of the total effort expended on Muffin. Nevertheless, we do not believe that such rapid progress would have been made had, for instance, standard ML been chosen as the implementation language, because it would not have offered the pre-packaged user interface components. The availability of Smalltalk–80 classes corresponding to VDM's type formation operators (e.g. sets, maps, etc.) made it very easy to implement the specification in this language. We therefore conclude that Smalltalk–80 is eminently suited not only to the implementation of formal reasoning systems but also to the implementation of formally specified systems. For a fuller assessment of these points see [8].

Following the completion of the prototype system, an attempt was made to evaluate the rudimentary interface it possessed by inviting people to come and try to prove theorems using Muffin. Those who took part in this evaluation exercise covered the whole spectrum, from rank novice to complete expert, in terms of familiarity with each of workstation technology and propositional logic, and came from a wide variety of backgrounds.

To our surprise, the most important factor influencing the ease with which a given person managed to complete his proof seemed to be his familiarity with the workstation, with the depth of knowledge of propositional calculus being far less significant. Indeed, those expert in workstation technology but having little or no knowledge of propositional logic generally managed to complete their proofs successfully simply by making extensive use of Muffin's pattern matching facilities. Familiarity with Smalltalk–80 was, of course, an extra bonus as the functionality of the mouse parallels that in the standard Smalltalk system closely. Most participants felt that the proof style of Muffin's prover was easier to understand than the natural deduction style of Figure 3. It is clear that one cannot simply extrapolate from this experience: more difficult proofs are bound to be more demanding of the user's knowledge of the underlying mathematics.

The evaluation exercise also provided a large and varied range of opinions as to how the prototype Muffin might be modified to make it easier to use. Some of these suggested modifications (e.g. the provision of a parser) went beyond Muffin's stated aim of investigating novel proof and interaction styles for formal reasoning systems, though some of these will undoubtedly be relevant to the design of the general FRIPSE user interface. Those suggested modifications lying within Muffin's scope, along with opinions similarly elicited from colleagues within the FRIPSE project, provided extremely useful input, however, and some of these have since been incorporated into the distributed version[10] of Muffin.

It was observed above that it is not possible to formally specify (and reason about) properties like "user-friendliness". In keeping with this observation, our development path can be viewed as one of evolution of the user-interface aspects. It should, however, be noted that the changes made during this process were mainly at the level of the surface UI and that the (formally specified) deep UI aspects remained largely constant.

Whilst this evaluation exercise was underway, one of us (RM) was invited to give a talk ([13]) on and a demonstration of the prototype Muffin at the Workshop on Programming for Logic Teaching, held at the University of Leeds, 6-8 July 1987. The participants at this workshop were in the main academics drawn from philosophy, computer science and pure mathematics (with particular emphasis on mathematical logic) departments. Their reactions, as well as the other talks and demonstrations presented at the workshop, also provided much useful input to the considerations of how to modify the prototype. In addition, many of the participants expressed an interest in acquiring a copy of Muffin for their own experimentation and use. This caused us to reconsider our original conception of Muffin as an essentially throwaway experiment within the wider FRIPSE project, and led to our decision to make the new version generally available for research purposes.

---

[10]This "Alvey deliverable" is available via: M.K.Tordoff, STL NW, Copthall House, Nelson Place, Newcastle-under-Lyme, Staffs ST5 1EZ

Up to this point, only the theorem store of Muffin had been formally specified, and all the higher level interactive mechanism had simply been coded on top of that, due mainly to the uncertainty as to the exact form it would take. Having fixed on the version of the system for general release, it was decided that, for the purpose of this exercise of documenting Muffin, the formal specification should be extended to cover the whole of the system as it then stood (apart, of course, from the actual surface UI which we still don't know how to describe formally, but see [11]). It is interesting to note that this additional specification exercise led to the discovery of a couple of bugs in the code!

The importance of the "derived rule" feature cannot be too strongly emphasised. Even in the very simple domain of propositional calculus to which Muffin restricts attention, it soon becomes extremely tedious if a user has to prove everything from the basic axioms. The ability to store a proved result and make use of it in later proofs, thus augmenting the set of rules, makes what might be a very long proof when proved from first principles much shorter, and hence much easier to understand. In fact, it is obvious from the Muffin experiment that a theorem proving system would be unusable without concepts such as derived rules which bring the level of interaction closer to that of normal mathematical reasoning.

If we ourselves look at the evaluation exercise, we cannot help but think Muffin's proof style(s) are a significant step towards the objective of proof discovery at the terminal. People who have never written a proof in a formal logic before have proved theorems using Muffin; what's more they have enjoyed the experience!

6 Beyond Muffin

Within the FRIPSE project as a whole, the Muffin exercise has always been looked upon as a simple experiment aimed at providing input to the eventual design of the general FRIPSE user interface, with the result that it was assigned only limited resources and a fixed duration. These limitations have meant that some issues, which will obviously be important in FRIPSE, remain unexplored, though after the Muffin exercise some aspects of these are perhaps clearer.

A couple of these issues have, in fact, already been explored in Muffin terms. The first of these is the generalisation of the syntax of expressions to allow for an essentially user-defined set of logical operators as opposed to the specific set built into Muffin. The modifications which have to be made to the specification of Muffin as given in Appendix B in order to achieve this generalisation can be found in [16].

The same document also explores a second important way in which the syntax of expressions could be extended, namely by introducing the notions of commutativity and associativity of binary operators. The original idea behind this was that such an extension would permit the automation of certain proofsteps (such as commuting the operands of some commutative binary operator), perhaps by storing expressions built from commutative and associative operators in some normal form. More recent work has, however, led us to believe that this issue is best treated as an extension to the pattern matching facilities rather than as a modification to the syntax of expressions as described in [16].

Another issue where further sophistication is going to be required is that of rules of inference. Here, Muffin essentially adopted the simplest solution and displayed all possible matching rules whenever the user selected the relevant menu option in the prover. Although the relatively small size of the Muffin system means that this approach was quite adequate there, there are (at least!) two things wrong with it. The first of these is that the matching technique used in Muffin is very simple–minded. Thus, any rule whose goal is simply a meta–variable (e.g. the *not-not-elim* rule, $\neg\neg E \vdash E$) will match for every backward proof step and any rule with a meta–variable amongst its hypotheses (e.g. the *or-intro-l* rule) will match for every forward proof step.

The second problem is that, even in a system as small as Muffin, the persistant user, given sufficient stamina, will eventually be able to create so many derived rules that the menu of matching rules will contain more items than can comfortably be assimilated at one go ("lemma explosion").

It is, therefore, clear that some much more sophisticated matching criteria are going to be required in FRIPSE to try to alleviate these difficulties.

One possibility here would be an extension of the mechanism by which matching rules are determined to allow the user to match to more than one expression at a time, for instance to a goal and/or a set of knowns. This, it is believed, could go a long way towards reducing the number of rules presented to the user, thus making the choice of rule that much easier. Some structuring of the menu of matching rules could also be introduced, for instance ordering the matching rules according to how closely they match the current selection(s) then presenting them a few at a time according to this ordering.

Another feature which is expected to be important in helping the user of the more general FRIPSE system with the task of proving theorems is proof tactics. Some thought has been given to how tactics might be incorporated into Muffin, with the conclusion that it would be relatively straightforward to include a simple tactic language consisting of a set of combinators for derived rules, with a tactic being applied in much the same way as a derived rule, but that it was unclear how to deal with anything more sophisticated.

The "official" work on Muffin has, in fact, now ceased, and attention has been switched to the formal specification of the more general FRIPSE system, with work on some of the outstanding issues, such as the general treatment of tactics, informal user–defined structuring of formal entities (e.g. designating some subset of all theorems as your "favourite" theorems), structuring of menus of matching rules, etc. proceeding in parallel with this. Some details of this work can be found in [12] and [9]. Muffin, of course, remains available as a test bed on which we can easily try out any new ideas arising from this more general FRIPSE work.

Acknowledgements

Our thanks to all our colleagues in the FRIPSE project at Manchester and RAL for many useful discussions and comments as the work on Muffin progressed, and to those members of the wider IPSE 2.5 project who provided useful contributions. Michel Sintzoff consults for the project and has been the instigator of many stimulating discussions. Thanks also to both the Alvey Directorate and the SERC for financial support, and to John Derrick of Leeds University for inviting one of us (RM) to present our work at the Workshop on Programming for Logic Teaching held there. Finally, we are grateful for the useful comments from the referees.

A The Proof of *or-and-dist*

This appendix gives the full proof structure arising from the proof of
$\{(p \vee q) \wedge (p \vee r)\} \vdash p \vee q \wedge r$ as dealt with in Section 4.5. For clarity, objects are written here in concrete (dereferenced) form, though it should be borne in mind that all are stored internally as references to objects[11]. Following the session described in Section 4.5, the overall problem will be stored in the *Problemstore* as:

$$p_0 \mapsto \{(p \vee q) \wedge (p \vee r)\} \vdash p \vee q \wedge r$$

Its complete proof, in the *Proofstore*, will be a *Composite-proof* consisting of four elements:

$$f_0 \mapsto [p_1, p_2, p_3, p_4]$$

In turn, their entries in the *Problemstore* will be:

$$p_1 \mapsto \{(p \vee q) \wedge (p \vee r)\} \vdash p \vee q$$
$$p_2 \mapsto \{(p \vee q) \wedge (p \vee r), p\} \vdash p \vee q \wedge r$$
$$p_3 \mapsto \{(p \vee q) \wedge (p \vee r), q\} \vdash p \vee q \wedge r$$
$$p_4 \mapsto \{p \vee q, \{p\} \rightsquigarrow p \vee q \wedge r, \{q\} \rightsquigarrow p \vee q \wedge r\} \vdash p \vee q \wedge r$$

Each of p_1 to p_4 is a solved problem, and therefore itself has a proof. The problems p_1 and p_4 are simply instances of rules: their proofs, f_1 and f_4, in the *Proofstore* are thus *Instantiations*:

$$f_1 \mapsto \textit{mk-Instantiation}(\{E_1 \wedge E_2\} \vdash E_1, \{E_1 \mapsto p \vee q, E_2 \mapsto p \vee r\})$$
$$f_4 \mapsto \textit{mk-Instantiation}(\{E_1 \vee E_2, \{E_1\} \rightsquigarrow E, \{E_2\} \rightsquigarrow E\} \vdash E,$$
$$\{E_1 \mapsto p, E_2 \mapsto q, E \mapsto p \vee q \wedge r\})$$

The elements p_2 and p_3 have, themselves, *Composite-proofs*, f_2 and f_3 respectively:

$$f_2 \mapsto [p_{21}]$$
$$f_3 \mapsto [p_{31}, p_{32}, p_{33}, p_{34}]$$

where:

$$p_{21} \mapsto \{p\} \vdash p \vee q \wedge r$$
$$p_{31} \mapsto \{(p \vee q) \wedge (p \vee r)\} \vdash p \vee r$$
$$p_{32} \mapsto \{(p \vee q) \wedge (p \vee r), q, p\} \vdash p \vee q \wedge r$$
$$p_{33} \mapsto \{(p \vee q) \wedge (p \vee r), q, r\} \vdash p \vee q \wedge r$$
$$p_{34} \mapsto \{p \vee r, \{p\} \rightsquigarrow p \vee q \wedge r, \{r\} \rightsquigarrow p \vee q \wedge r\} \vdash p \vee q \wedge r$$

Again, p_{21} and each of p_{31} to p_{34} is a solved problem and has a proof. The proofs f_{21}, f_{31} and f_{34} are simply *Instantiations*:

$$f_{21} \mapsto \textit{mk-Instantiation}(\{E_1\} \vdash E_1 \vee E_2, \{E_1 \mapsto p, E_2 \mapsto q \wedge r\})$$
$$f_{31} \mapsto \textit{mk-Instantiation}(\{E_1 \wedge E_2\} \vdash E_2, \{E_1 \mapsto p \vee q, E_2 \mapsto p \vee r\})$$
$$f_{34} \mapsto \textit{mk-Instantiation}(\{E_1 \vee E_2, \{E_1\} \rightsquigarrow E, \{E_2\} \rightsquigarrow E\} \vdash E,$$
$$\{E_1 \mapsto p, E_2 \mapsto r, E \mapsto p \vee q \wedge r\})$$

The elements p_{32} and p_{33} themselves have *Composite-proofs*:

$$f_{32} \mapsto [p_{21}]$$
$$f_{33} \mapsto [p_{331}, p_{332}]$$

where:

$$p_{331} \mapsto \{q, r\} \vdash q \wedge r$$
$$p_{332} \mapsto \{q \wedge r\} \vdash p \vee q \wedge r$$

---

[11]The completely formal story is that given in the running examples of Sections 4.2 and 4.5.

Note here how the sharing of problems comes in, the proof f_{32} consisting of the problem p_{21}, solved earlier as part of the proof f_2.

Finally, each of p_{331} and p_{332} is a solved problem and has a proof which is simply an *Instantiation*:

$f_{331} \mapsto mk\text{-}Instantiation(\{E_1, E_2\} \vdash E_1 \wedge E_2, \{E_1 \mapsto q, E_2 \mapsto r\})$

$f_{332} \mapsto mk\text{-}Instantiation(\{E_2\} \vdash E_1 \vee E_2, \{E_1 \mapsto p, E_2 \mapsto q \wedge r\})$

B Formal Specification

B.1 Muffin

$Muffin$ :: es : $Expstore$
ss : $Subseqstore$
ps : $Problemstore$
fs : $Proofstore$
en : $ExpNames$
sn : $SubseqNames$
pn : $ProblemNames$
fn : $ProofNames$
jm : $Proofmap$
rm : $Rulemap$
im : $Incomplete\text{-}proofmap$
xm : $Indexmap$

where

$inv\text{-}Muffin(mk\text{-}Muffin(es, ss, ps, fs, en, sn, pn, fn, jm, rm, im, xm))$ $\underline{\triangle}$

$is\text{-}valid\text{-}subseqstore(ss, es) \wedge is\text{-}valid\text{-}problemstore(ps, ss, es) \wedge$
$is\text{-}valid\text{-}proofstore(fs, ps, ss, es) \wedge is\text{-}valid\text{-}expnames(en, es) \wedge$
$is\text{-}valid\text{-}subseqnames(sn, ss) \wedge is\text{-}valid\text{-}problemnames(pn, ps) \wedge$
$is\text{-}valid\text{-}proofnames(fn, fs) \wedge is\text{-}valid\text{-}proofmap(jm, fs, ps, ss, es) \wedge$
$is\text{-}valid\text{-}rulemap(rm, jm, fs) \wedge is\text{-}valid\text{-}incomplete\text{-}proofmap(im, jm, fs, ps, ss, es) \wedge$
$is\text{-}valid\text{-}indexmap(xm, im, jm, fs, ps, ss, es)$

$add\text{-}exp$ (x: Exp) y: $Expref$
ext wr es : $Expstore$
pre $args(x) \subseteq$ **dom** es
post $x \in$ **rng** $\overleftarrow{es} \wedge y \in$ **dom** $\overleftarrow{es} \wedge \overleftarrow{es}(y) = x \wedge es = \overleftarrow{es}$ $\vee$
$x \notin$ **rng** $\overleftarrow{es} \wedge y \notin$ **dom** $\overleftarrow{es} \wedge es = \overleftarrow{es} \cup \{y \mapsto x\}$

$add\text{-}subseq$ (z: **set of** $Expref$, y: $Expref$) g: $Subseqref$
ext rd es : $Expstore$
    wr ss : $Subseqstore$
pre $z \cup \{y\} \subseteq$ **dom** $es \wedge y \notin z \wedge z \neq \{\}$
post let $t = mk\text{-}Subseq(z, y)$ **in**
$t \in$ **rng** $\overleftarrow{ss} \wedge g \in$ **dom** $\overleftarrow{ss} \wedge \overleftarrow{ss}(g) = t \wedge ss = \overleftarrow{ss}$ $\vee$
$t \notin$ **rng** $\overleftarrow{ss} \wedge g \notin$ **dom** $\overleftarrow{ss} \wedge ss = \overleftarrow{ss} \cup \{g \mapsto t\}$

add-problem $(n: \textbf{set of } Node, y: Expref)$ $u: Problemref$

ext rd es : $Expstore$
$\quad\quad ss$: $Subseqstore$
$\quad$ **wr** ps : $Problemstore$

pre $y \in \text{dom } es \land n \subseteq \text{dom } es \cup \text{dom } ss \land y \notin n$

post let $t = mk\text{-}Problem(n, y)$ **in**
$\quad\quad t \in \text{rng } \overleftarrow{ps} \land u \in \text{dom } \overleftarrow{ps} \land \overleftarrow{ps}(u) = t \land ps = \overleftarrow{ps} \lor$
$\quad\quad t \notin \text{rng } \overleftarrow{ps} \land u \notin \text{dom } \overleftarrow{ps} \land ps = \overleftarrow{ps} \cup \{u \mapsto t\}$

instantiate-exp $(y: Expref, m: \textbf{map } Atom \textbf{ to } Expref)$ $r: Expref$

ext wr es : $Expstore$

pre $y \in \text{dom } es \land is\text{-}substitution(\{y\}, m, \{\,\}, es)$

post $\overleftarrow{es} \subseteq es \land r \in \text{dom } es \land is\text{-}exp\text{-}match(y, r, m, es) \land$
$$\text{dom } es = \text{dom } \overleftarrow{es} \cup descendents(\{r\}, es)$$

instantiate-exp-set $(y: \textbf{set of } Expref, m: \textbf{map } Atom \textbf{ to } Expref)$ $r: \textbf{set of } Expref$

ext wr es : $Expstore$

pre $y \subseteq \text{dom } es \land is\text{-}substitution(y, m, \{\,\}, es)$

post $\overleftarrow{es} \subseteq es \land r \subseteq \text{dom } es \land is\text{-}exp\text{-}set\text{-}match(y, r, m, es) \land$
$$\text{dom } es = \text{dom } \overleftarrow{es} \cup descendents(r, es)$$

instantiate-subseq $(y: Subseqref, m: \textbf{map } Atom \textbf{ to } Expref)$ $r: Subseqref$

ext wr es : $Expstore$
$\quad\quad ss$: $Subseqstore$

pre $y \in \text{dom } ss \land is\text{-}substitution(\{y\}, m, ss, es)$

post $\overleftarrow{ss} \subseteq ss \land \text{dom } ss = \text{dom } \overleftarrow{ss} \cup \{r\} \land$
$\quad\quad post\text{-}instantiate\text{-}exp\text{-}set(exps(ss(y)), m, \overleftarrow{es}, exps(ss(r)), es) \land$
$$is\text{-}subseq\text{-}match(y, r, m, ss, es)$$

instantiate-node $(n: Node, m: \textbf{map } Atom \textbf{ to } Expref)$ $r: Node$

ext wr es : $Expstore$
$\quad\quad ss$: $Subseqstore$

pre $n \in \text{dom } es \cup \text{dom } ss \land is\text{-}substitution(\{n\}, m, ss, es)$

post $n \in \text{dom } ss \land post\text{-}instantiate\text{-}subseq(n, m, \overleftarrow{es}, \overleftarrow{ss}, r, es, ss) \lor$
$\quad\quad n \in \text{dom } es \land post\text{-}instantiate\text{-}exp(n, m, \overleftarrow{es}, r, es) \land \overleftarrow{ss} = ss$

instantiate-node-set $(n: \textbf{set of } Node, m: \textbf{map } Atom \textbf{ to } Expref)$ $r: \textbf{set of } Node$

ext wr es : $Expstore$
$\quad\quad ss$: $Subseqstore$

pre $n \subseteq \text{dom } es \cup \text{dom } ss \land is\text{-}substitution(n, m, ss, es)$

post $\overleftarrow{ss} \subseteq ss \land \overleftarrow{es} \subseteq es \land r \subseteq \text{dom } es \cup \text{dom } ss \land is\text{-}node\text{-}set\text{-}match(n, r, m, ss, es) \land$
$\quad\quad \text{dom } es = \text{dom } \overleftarrow{es} \cup descendents(components(r, ss, es), es) \land$
$\quad\quad \text{dom } ss = \text{dom } \overleftarrow{ss} \cup (r \cap \text{dom } ss)$

instantiate-problem (*p*: *Problemref*, *m*: map *Atom* to *Expref*) *r*: *Problemref*

ext wr *es* : *Expstore*
 ss : *Subseqstore*
 ps : *Problemstore*

pre $p \in \text{dom } ps \wedge \textit{is-substitution}(nodes(ps(p)), m, ss, es)$

post $\overleftarrow{ps} \subseteq ps \wedge \text{dom } ps = \text{dom } \overleftarrow{ps} \cup \{r\} \wedge \textit{is-problem-match}(p, r, m, ps, ss, es) \wedge$
 $\textit{post-instantiate-node-set}(nodes(ps(p)), m, \overleftarrow{es}, \overleftarrow{ss}, nodes(ps(r)), es, ss)$

name-exp (*n*: *String*, *e*: *Expref*)

ext wr *en* : *ExpNames*
 rd *es* : *Expstore*

pre $e \in \text{dom } es \wedge (n \in \text{dom } en \Rightarrow en(n) = e)$

post $n \in \text{dom } \overleftarrow{en} \wedge en = \overleftarrow{en} \vee n = [\,] \wedge en = \overleftarrow{en} \rhd \{e\} \vee$
 $n \notin \text{dom } \overleftarrow{en} \wedge n \neq [\,] \wedge en = (\overleftarrow{en} \rhd \{e\}) \cup \{n \mapsto e\}$

name-subseq (*n*: *String*, *s*: *Subseqref*)

ext wr *sn* : *SubseqNames*
 rd *ss* : *Subseqstore*

pre $s \in \text{dom } ss \wedge (n \in \text{dom } sn \Rightarrow sn(n) = s)$

post $n \in \text{dom } \overleftarrow{sn} \wedge sn = \overleftarrow{sn} \vee n = [\,] \wedge sn = \overleftarrow{sn} \rhd \{s\} \vee$
 $n \notin \text{dom } \overleftarrow{sn} \wedge n \neq [\,] \wedge sn = (\overleftarrow{sn} \rhd \{s\}) \cup \{n \mapsto s\}$

name-problem (*n*: *String*, *p*: *Problemref*)

ext wr *pn* : *ProblemNames*
 rd *ps* : *Problemstore*

pre $p \in \text{dom } ps \wedge (n \in \text{dom } pn \Rightarrow pn(n) = p)$

post $n \in \text{dom } \overleftarrow{pn} \wedge pn = \overleftarrow{pn} \vee n = [\,] \wedge pn = \overleftarrow{pn} \rhd \{p\} \vee$
 $n \notin \text{dom } \overleftarrow{pn} \wedge n \neq [\,] \wedge pn = (\overleftarrow{pn} \rhd \{p\}) \cup \{n \mapsto p\}$

name-proof (*n*: *String*, *f*: *Proofref*)

ext wr *fn* : *ProofNames*
 rd *fs* : *Proofstore*

pre $f \in \text{dom } fs \wedge (n \in \text{dom } fn \Rightarrow fn(n) = f)$

post $n \in \text{dom } \overleftarrow{fn} \wedge fn = \overleftarrow{fn} \vee n = [\,] \wedge fn = \overleftarrow{fn} \rhd \{f\} \vee$
 $n \notin \text{dom } \overleftarrow{fn} \wedge n \neq [\,] \wedge fn = (\overleftarrow{fn} \rhd \{f\}) \cup \{n \mapsto f\}$

remove-problem (*p*: *Problemref*)

ext wr *ps* : *Problemstore*
 fs : *Proofstore*
 im : *Incomplete-proofmap*
 xm : *Indexmap*
 pn : *ProblemNames*
 fn : *ProofNames*
 rd *jm* : *Proofmap*

pre $p \in \text{dom } ps \wedge p \notin \text{dom } jm$

$$\text{post } ps = \{p\} \mathbin{\underline{\triangleleft}} \overleftarrow{ps} \wedge pn = \overleftarrow{pn} \mathbin{\underline{\triangleright}} \{p\} \wedge$$
$$(p \in \text{dom } \overleftarrow{im} \wedge im = \{p\} \mathbin{\underline{\triangleleft}} \overleftarrow{im} \wedge fs = \overleftarrow{im}(p) \mathbin{\underline{\triangleleft}} \overleftarrow{fs} \wedge xm = \overleftarrow{im}(p) \mathbin{\underline{\triangleleft}} \overleftarrow{xm} \wedge fn = \overleftarrow{fn} \mathbin{\underline{\triangleright}} \overleftarrow{im}(p)$$
$$\vee \; p \notin \text{dom } \overleftarrow{im} \wedge im = \overleftarrow{im} \wedge fs = \overleftarrow{fs} \wedge xm = \overleftarrow{xm} \wedge fn = \overleftarrow{fn})$$

remove-proof $(f: Proofref)$

ext wr fs : $Proofstore$
$\quad\quad im$: $Incomplete\text{-}proofmap$
$\quad\quad xm$: $Indexmap$
$\quad\quad fn$: $Proofnames$

pre $f \in incomplete\text{-}proofs(im)$

$$\text{post } fs = \{f\} \mathbin{\underline{\triangleleft}} \overleftarrow{fs} \wedge xm = \{f\} \mathbin{\underline{\triangleleft}} \overleftarrow{xm} \wedge fn = \overleftarrow{fn} \mathbin{\underline{\triangleright}} \{f\} \wedge p \in \text{dom } \overleftarrow{im} \wedge f \in \overleftarrow{im}(p) \wedge$$
$$(\overleftarrow{im}(p) = \{f\} \wedge im = \{p\} \mathbin{\underline{\triangleleft}} \overleftarrow{im} \vee \overleftarrow{im}(p) \neq \{f\} \wedge im = \overleftarrow{im} \dagger \{p \mapsto \overleftarrow{im}(p) - \{f\}\})$$

name-rule $(n: String, p: Problemref)$

ext wr rm : $Rulemap$
$\quad\quad\text{rd } jm$: $Proofmap$

pre $n \neq [\,] \wedge p \in \text{dom } jm \wedge (n \in \text{dom } rm \Rightarrow rm(n) = p)$

$$\text{post } rm = (\overleftarrow{rm} \mathbin{\underline{\triangleright}} \{p\}) \cup \{n \mapsto p\}$$

make-axiom $(p: Problemref, n: String)$

ext wr im : $Incomplete\text{-}proofmap$
$\quad\quad jm$: $Proofmap$
$\quad\quad rm$: $Rulemap$
$\quad\quad xm$: $Indexmap$
$\quad\quad fs$: $Proofstore$
$\quad\quad fn$: $ProofNames$

pre $n \neq [\,] \wedge [p \in axioms(jm) \wedge (n \in \text{dom } rm \Rightarrow rm(n) = p) \vee p \notin \text{dom } jm]$

$$\text{post } p \notin \text{dom } \overleftarrow{jm} \wedge jm = \overleftarrow{jm} \cup \{p \mapsto \{\}\} \wedge rm = \overleftarrow{rm} \cup \{n \mapsto p\} \wedge im = \{p\} \mathbin{\underline{\triangleleft}} \overleftarrow{im} \wedge$$
$$(p \in \text{dom } \overleftarrow{im} \wedge xm = \overleftarrow{im}(p) \mathbin{\underline{\triangleleft}} \overleftarrow{xm} \wedge fs = \overleftarrow{im}(p) \mathbin{\underline{\triangleleft}} \overleftarrow{fs} \wedge fn = \overleftarrow{im}(p) \mathbin{\underline{\triangleleft}} \overleftarrow{fn} \vee$$
$$p \notin \text{dom } \overleftarrow{im} \wedge xm = \overleftarrow{xm} \wedge fs = \overleftarrow{fs} \wedge fn = \overleftarrow{fn}) \vee$$
$$p \in \text{dom } \overleftarrow{jm} \wedge im = \overleftarrow{im} \wedge xm = \overleftarrow{xm} \wedge jm = \overleftarrow{jm} \wedge rm = (\overleftarrow{rm} \mathbin{\underline{\triangleright}} \{p\}) \cup \{n \mapsto p\} \wedge$$
$$fs = \overleftarrow{fs} \wedge fn = \overleftarrow{fn}$$

add-instantiation $(p: Problemref, m: \text{map } Atom \text{ to } Expref, q: Problemref)$

ext wr fs : $Proofstore$
$\quad\quad jm$: $Proofmap$
$\quad\text{rd } rm$: $Rulemap$
$\quad\quad ps$: $Problemstore$
$\quad\quad ss$: $Subseqstore$
$\quad\quad es$: $Expstore$

pre $p \in \text{rng } rm \wedge m \neq \{\,\} \wedge \text{dom } m \subseteq vars(nodes(ps(p)), ss, es) \wedge$
$\quad is\text{-}substitution(nodes(ps(p)), m, ss, es) \wedge is\text{-}problem\text{-}match(p, q, m, ps, ss, es) \wedge$
$\quad q \notin axioms(jm)$

post let $i = mk\text{-}Instantiation(p, m)$ in
$$[i \in \text{rng}\ \overleftarrow{fs} \wedge f \in \text{dom}\ \overleftarrow{fs} \wedge \overleftarrow{fs}(f) = i \wedge \overleftarrow{fs} = fs\ \vee$$
$$i \notin \text{rng}\ \overleftarrow{fs} \wedge f \notin \text{dom}\ \overleftarrow{fs} \wedge fs = \overleftarrow{fs} \cup \{f \mapsto i\}] \wedge$$
$$[q \in \text{dom}\ \overleftarrow{jm} \wedge s = \overleftarrow{jm}(q) \cup \{f\} \vee q \notin \text{dom}\ \overleftarrow{jm} \wedge s = \{f\}] \wedge$$
$$jm = \overleftarrow{jm} \dagger \{q \mapsto s\}$$

add-assumption (p: *Problemref*)

ext wr fs : *Proofstore*
$\quad\quad jm$: *Proofmap*
$\quad$ rd ps : *Problemstore*
pre $p \in \text{dom}\ ps \wedge p \notin axioms(jm) \wedge con(ps(p)) \in hyp(ps(p))$
post $f \notin \text{dom}\ \overleftarrow{fs} \wedge fs = \overleftarrow{fs} \cup \{f \mapsto []\} \wedge$
$$(p \in \text{dom}\ \overleftarrow{jm} \wedge jm = \overleftarrow{jm} \dagger \{p \mapsto \overleftarrow{jm}(p) \cup \{f\}\} \vee p \notin \text{dom}\ \overleftarrow{jm} \wedge jm = \overleftarrow{jm} \cup \{p \mapsto \{f\}\})$$

add-empty-proof (p: *Problemref*)

ext wr im : *Incomplete-proofmap*
$\quad\quad xm$: *Indexmap*
$\quad\quad fs$: *Proofstore*
$\quad$ rd jm : *Proofmap*
$\quad\quad ps$: *Problemstore*
pre $p \notin axioms(jm) \wedge p \in \text{dom}\ ps \wedge con(ps(p)) \notin hyp(ps(p))$
post $f \notin \text{dom}\ \overleftarrow{fs} \wedge fs = \overleftarrow{fs} \cup \{f \mapsto []\} \wedge xm = \overleftarrow{xm} \cup \{f \mapsto 0\} \wedge$
$$(p \in \text{dom}\ \overleftarrow{im} \wedge im = \overleftarrow{im} \dagger \{p \mapsto \overleftarrow{im}(p) \cup \{f\}\} \vee p \notin \text{dom}\ \overleftarrow{im} \wedge im = \overleftarrow{im} \cup \{p \mapsto \{f\}\})$$

spawn-proof (p: *Problemref*, f: *Proofref*)

ext wr im : *Incomplete-proofmap*
$\quad\quad xm$: *Indexmap*
$\quad\quad fs$: *Proofstore*
pre $p \in \text{dom}\ im \wedge f \in im(p)$
post $g \notin \text{dom}\ \overleftarrow{fs} \wedge fs = \overleftarrow{fs} \cup \{g \mapsto \overleftarrow{fs}(f)\} \wedge xm = \overleftarrow{xm} \cup \{g \mapsto \overleftarrow{xm}(f)\} \wedge$
$$im = \overleftarrow{im} \dagger \{p \mapsto \overleftarrow{im}(p) \cup \{g\}\}$$

add-fwd-step (p: *Problemref*, f: *Proofref*, s: *Problemref*)

ext wr fs : *Proofstore*
$\quad\quad im$: *Incomplete-proofmap*
$\quad\quad xm$: *Indexmap*
$\quad\quad jm$: *Proofmap*
$\quad$ rd ps : *Problemstore*
$\quad\quad ss$: *Subseqstore*
$\quad\quad es$: *Expstore*
pre let $k = knowns(p, hyp(ps(p)), forward\text{-}proof(f, fs, xm), ps, ss)$ in
$\quad p \in \text{dom}\ im \wedge f \in im(p) \wedge s \in \text{dom}\ jm \wedge adds\text{-}known(p, k, s, ps, ss)$

post let $y = forward\text{-}proof(f, \overleftarrow{fs}, \overleftarrow{xm}) \curvearrowright [s]$,

$\qquad z = backward\text{-}proof(f, \overleftarrow{fs}, \overleftarrow{xm})$,

$\qquad k = knowns(p, hyp(ps(p)), y, ps, ss)$,

$\qquad l = new\text{-}fwd\text{-}steps(k, z, ps)$,

$\qquad bwd = new\text{-}bwd\text{-}steps(\{con(ps(p))\}, reverse(z \rhd rng\, l), ps)$,

$\qquad fwd = y \curvearrowright l$,

$\qquad new\text{-}proof = fwd \curvearrowright bwd$

$\qquad$ **in**

$\quad \neg is\text{-}complete\text{-}proof(fwd, p, ps, ss, es) \wedge fs = \overleftarrow{fs} \dagger \{f \mapsto new\text{-}proof\} \wedge$

$\quad jm = \overleftarrow{jm} \wedge im = \overleftarrow{im} \wedge xm = \overleftarrow{xm} \dagger \{f \mapsto \overleftarrow{xm}(f) + len\, l + 1\} \vee$

$\quad is\text{-}complete\text{-}proof(fwd, p, ps, ss, es) \wedge xm = \{f\} \lhd \overleftarrow{xm} \wedge$

$\quad (\overleftarrow{im}(p) = \{f\} \wedge im = \{p\} \lhd \overleftarrow{im} \vee \overleftarrow{im}(p) \neq \{f\} \wedge im = \overleftarrow{im} \dagger \{p \mapsto \overleftarrow{im}(p) - \{f\}\})$

$add\text{-}bwd\text{-}step$ $\;(p: Problemref, f: Proofref, s: Problemref)$

ext wr fs : $Proofstore$

$\quad$ **rd** im : $Incomplete\text{-}proofmap$

$\qquad xm$: $Indexmap$

$\qquad jm$: $Proofmap$

$\qquad ps$: $Problemstore$

$\qquad ss$: $Subseqstore$

pre let $k = knowns(p, hyp(ps(p)), forward\text{-}proof(f, fs, xm), ps, ss)$,

$\qquad g = goals(\{con(ps(p))\}, reverse(backward\text{-}proof(f, fs, xm)), ps)$

$\qquad$ **in**

$\quad p \in dom\, im \wedge f \in im(p) \wedge s \in dom\, jm \wedge \neg(hyp(ps(s)) \subseteq k) \wedge con(ps(s)) \in g - k$

post let $new\text{-}proof = forward\text{-}proof(f, \overleftarrow{fs}, xm) \curvearrowright [s] \curvearrowright backward\text{-}proof(f, \overleftarrow{fs}, xm)$ **in**

$\quad fs = \overleftarrow{fs} \dagger \{f \mapsto new\text{-}proof\}$

$undo\text{-}fwd\text{-}step$ $\;(p: Problemref, f: Proofref)$

ext wr fs : $Proofstore$

$\qquad xm$: $Indexmap$

$\quad$ **rd** im : $Incomplete\text{-}proofmap$

pre $p \in dom\, im \wedge f \in im(p) \wedge xm(f) \neq 0$

post $xm = \overleftarrow{xm} \dagger \{f \mapsto \overleftarrow{xm}(f) - 1\} \wedge fs = \overleftarrow{fs} \dagger \{f \mapsto \overleftarrow{xm}(f) \lhd \overleftarrow{fs}(f)\}$

$undo\text{-}bwd\text{-}step$ $\;(p: Problemref, f: Proofref)$

ext wr fs : $Proofstore$

$\qquad xm$: $Indexmap$

$\quad$ **rd** im : $Incomplete\text{-}proofmap$

pre $p \in dom\, im \wedge f \in im(p) \wedge xm(f) \neq len\, fs(f)$

post $xm = \overleftarrow{xm} \wedge fs = \overleftarrow{fs} \dagger \{f \mapsto (xm(f) + 1) \lhd \overleftarrow{fs}(f)\}$

B.2 Expressions

$Texp = Tnot \mid Tand \mid Tor \mid Timpl \mid Tequiv \mid Tdelta \mid Atom$

$Tnot :: tn : Texp$

$Tand$ :: $tandl$: $Texp$
$tandr$: $Texp$

Tor :: $torl$: $Texp$
$torr$: $Texp$

$Timpl$ :: $tant$: $Texp$
$tcon$: $Texp$

$Tequiv$ :: $teql$: $Texp$
$teqr$: $Texp$

$Tdelta$ :: td : $Texp$

$Exp = Not \mid And \mid Or \mid Impl \mid Equiv \mid Delta \mid Atom$

Not :: not : $Expref$

And :: $andl$: $Expref$
$andr$: $Expref$

Or :: orl : $Expref$
orr : $Expref$

$Impl$ :: ant : $Expref$
con : $Expref$

$Equiv$ :: eql : $Expref$
eqr : $Expref$

$Delta$ :: del : $Expref$

$Expstore = $ map $Expref$ into Exp

where

$inv\text{-}Expstore(es) \quad \triangle \quad is\text{-}closed(es) \land is\text{-}finite(es)$

$args : Exp \rightarrow$ set of $Expref$

$args(x) \quad \triangle \quad$ cases x of
$mk\text{-}And(l, r) \;\; \rightarrow \{l, r\}$
$mk\text{-}Or(l, r) \;\;\; \rightarrow \{l, r\}$
$mk\text{-}Impl(l, r) \;\; \rightarrow \{l, r\}$
$mk\text{-}Equiv(l, r) \rightarrow \{l, r\}$
$mk\text{-}Not(l) \;\;\;\;\; \rightarrow \{l\}$
$mk\text{-}Delta(l) \;\;\; \rightarrow \{l\}$
$Atom \;\;\;\;\;\;\;\;\; \rightarrow \{\}$
end

$is\text{-}closed :$ map $Expref$ to $Exp \rightarrow \mathbf{B}$

$is\text{-}closed(m) \quad \triangle \quad \forall x \in \text{rng}\, m \cdot args(x) \subseteq \text{dom}\, m$

$offspring :$ set of $Expref \times$ map $Expref$ to $Exp \rightarrow$ set of $Expref$

$offspring(z, m) \quad \triangle \quad \bigcup\{args(m(y)) \mid y \in \text{dom}\, m \cap z\} \cup z$

descendents : set of *Expref* × map *Expref* to *Exp* → set of *Expref*

descendents(*z*, *m*) $\triangleq$
    let *l* = *offspring*(*z*, *m*) in
    if *l* = *z* then *z* else *descendents*(*l*, *m*)

trace : set of *Expref* × map *Expref* to *Exp* → map *Expref* to *Exp*

trace(*z*, *m*) $\triangleq$ *descendents*(*z*, *m*) ◁ *m*

is-finite : map *Expref* to *Exp* → **B**

is-finite(*m*) $\triangleq$ ∀*y* ∈ dom *m* · ¬∃*x* ∈ rng *trace*({*y*}, *m*) · *y* ∈ *args*(*x*)

leaves (*z*: set of *Expref*, *es*: *Expstore*) *r*: set of *Atom*
pre *z* ⊆ dom *es*
post *r* = {*x* | *x* ∈ rng *trace*(*z*, *es*) ∧ *is-Atom*(*x*)}

expand (*y*: *Expref*, *es*: *Expstore*) *t*: *Texp*
pre *y* ∈ dom *es*
post *t* = cases *es*(*y*) of
      mk-Not(*l*)   → *mk-Tnot*(*expand*(*l*, *es*))
      mk-And(*l*, *r*) → *mk-Tand*(*expand*(*l*, *es*), *expand*(*r*, *es*))
      mk-Or(*l*, *r*)   → *mk-Tor*(*expand*(*l*, *es*), *expand*(*r*, *es*))
      mk-Impl(*l*, *r*) → *mk-Timpl*(*expand*(*l*, *es*), *expand*(*r*, *es*))
      mk-Equiv(*l*, *r*)→ *mk-Tequiv*(*expand*(*l*, *es*), *expand*(*r*, *es*))
      mk-Delta(*l*)   → *mk-Tdelta*(*expand*(*l*, *es*))
      Atom   → *es*(*y*)
      end

expand-inst (*y*: *Expref*, *m*: map *Atom* to *Expref*, *es*: *Expstore*) *t*: *Texp*
pre *y* ∈ dom *es* ∧ *is-substitution*({*y*}, *m*, { }, *es*)
post let *x* = *es*(*y*) in
   t = if *x* ∈ dom *m*
      then *expand*(*m*(*x*), *es*)
      else cases *x* of
        mk-Not(*l*)   → *mk-Tnot*(*expand-inst*(*l*, *m*, *es*))
        mk-And(*l*, *r*) → *mk-Tand*(*expand-inst*(*l*, *m*, *es*), *expand-inst*(*r*, *m*, *es*))
        mk-Or(*l*, *r*)   → *mk-Tor*(*expand-inst*(*l*, *m*, *es*), *expand-inst*(*r*, *m*, *es*))
        mk-Impl(*l*, *r*) → *mk-Timpl*(*expand-inst*(*l*, *m*, *es*), *expand-inst*(*r*, *m*, *es*))
        mk-Equiv(*l*, *r*)→ *mk-Tequiv*(*expand-inst*(*l*, *m*, *es*), *expand-inst*(*r*, *m*, *es*))
        mk-Delta(*l*)   → *mk-Tdelta*(*expand-inst*(*l*, *m*, *es*))
        Atom   → *x*
        end

is-exp-match (*x*: *Expref*, *y*: *Expref*, *m*: map *Atom* to *Expref*, *es*: *Expstore*) *r*: **B**
pre *x*, *y* ∈ dom *es* ∧ *is-substitution*({*x*}, *m*, { }, *es*)
post *r* ⇔ *expand-inst*(*x*, *m*, *es*) = *expand*(*y*, *es*)

$is\text{-}exp\text{-}set\text{-}match$ $(z\colon \text{set of } Expref, a\colon \text{set of } Expref, m\colon \text{map } Atom \text{ to } Expref, es\colon Expstore)$ $r\colon \mathbf{B}$
$\text{pre } (z \cup a) \subseteq \text{dom } es \land is\text{-}substitution(z, m, \{\,\}, es)$
$\text{post } r \Leftrightarrow \{\,expand\text{-}inst(x, m, es) \mid x \in z\,\} = \{\,expand(y, es) \mid y \in a\,\}$

B.3 Subsequents

$Tsubseq \ ::\ tlhs\ :\ \text{set of } Texp$
$\qquad\qquad trhs\ :\ Texp$
where
$inv\text{-}Tsubseq(mk\text{-}Tsubseq(l, r)) \ \triangleq\ l \neq \{\,\}$

$Subseq \ ::\ lhs\ :\ \text{set of } Expref$
$\qquad\qquad rhs\ :\ Expref$
where
$inv\text{-}Subseq(mk\text{-}Subseq(z, y)) \ \triangleq\ z \neq \{\,\}$

$Subseqstore = \text{map } Subseqref \text{ into } Subseq$

$exps : Subseq \rightarrow \text{set of } Expref$
$exps(q) \ \triangleq\ lhs(q) \cup \{rhs(q)\}$

$is\text{-}valid\text{-}subseqstore : Subseqstore \times Expstore \rightarrow \mathbf{B}$
$is\text{-}valid\text{-}subseqstore(ss, es) \ \triangleq\ \forall q \in \text{rng } ss \cdot exps(q) \subseteq \text{dom } es$

$expand\text{-}subseq$ $(q\colon Subseqref, m\colon \text{map } Atom \text{ to } Expref, ss\colon Subseqstore, es\colon Expstore)$ $t\colon Tsubseq$
$\text{pre } q \in \text{dom } ss \land is\text{-}substitution(\{q\}, m, ss, es) \land is\text{-}valid\text{-}subseqstore(ss, es)$
$\text{post } \text{let } r = expand\text{-}inst(rhs(ss(q)), m, es),$
$\qquad l = \{\,expand\text{-}inst(y, m, es) \mid y \in lhs(ss(q))\,\} \text{ in}$
$\quad t = mk\text{-}Tsubseq(l, r)$

$is\text{-}subseq\text{-}match$ $(g\colon Subseqref, q\colon Subseqref,$
$\qquad\qquad\qquad m\colon \text{map } Atom \text{ to } Expref, ss\colon Subseqstore, es\colon Expstore)$ $r\colon \mathbf{B}$
$\text{pre } g, q \in \text{dom } ss \land is\text{-}valid\text{-}subseqstore(ss, es) \land is\text{-}substitution(\{g\}, m, ss, es)$
$\text{post } r \Leftrightarrow expand\text{-}subseq(g, m, ss, es) = expand\text{-}subseq(q, \{\,\}, ss, es)$

B.4 Nodes

$Tnode = Texp \mid Tsubseq$

$Node = Expref \mid Subseqref$

$parts$ $(n\colon Node, ss\colon Subseqstore, es\colon Expstore)$ $r\colon \text{set of } Expref$
$\text{pre } n \in \text{dom } ss \cup \text{dom } es$
$\text{post } (n \in \text{dom } es \land r = \{n\}) \lor (n \in \text{dom } ss \land r = exps(ss(n)))$

components (*n*: set of *Node*, *ss*: *Subseqstore*, *es*: *Expstore*) *r*: set of *Expref*
pre $n \subseteq$ dom *ss* $\cup$ dom *es*
post $r = \bigcup \{ parts(k, ss, es) \mid k \in n \}$

vars (*n*: set of *Node*, *ss*: *Subseqstore*, *es*: *Expstore*) *r*: set of *Atom*
pre *is-valid-subseqstore*(*ss*, *es*) $\wedge$ *n* $\subseteq$ dom *es* $\cup$ dom *ss*
post $r = leaves(components(n, ss, es), es)$

is-substitution (*n*: set of *Node*, *m*: map *Atom* to *Expref*, *ss*: *Subseqstore*, *es*: *Expstore*) *r*: **B**
pre *is-valid-subseqstore*(*ss*, *es*) $\wedge$ *n* $\subseteq$ dom *es* $\cup$ dom *ss*
post $r \Leftrightarrow \forall x \in$ dom $m \cdot x \in vars(n, ss, es) \Rightarrow m(x) \in$ dom *es* $\wedge es(m(x)) \neq x$

expand-node (*n*: *Node*, *m*: map *Atom* to *Expref*, *ss*: *Subseqstore*, *es*: *Expstore*) *t*: *Tnode*
pre $n \in$ dom *ss* $\cup$ dom *es* $\wedge$ *is-valid-subseqstore*(*ss*, *es*) $\wedge$ *is-substitution*($\{n\}$, *m*, *ss*, *es*)
post $n \in$ dom *ss* $\wedge t = expand$-*subseq*(*n*, *m*, *ss*, *es*) $\vee$
    $n \in$ dom *es* $\wedge t = expand$-*inst*(*n*, *m*, *es*)

is-node-match (*n*: *Node*, *k*: *Node*, *m*: map *Atom* to *Expref*, *ss*: *Subseqstore*, *es*: *Expstore*) *r*: **B**
pre $\{n, k\} \subseteq$ dom *es* $\cup$ dom *ss* $\wedge$ *is-valid-subseqstore*(*ss*, *es*) $\wedge$ *is-substitution*($\{n\}$, *m*, *ss*, *es*)
post $r \Leftrightarrow expand$-*node*(*n*, *m*, *ss*, *es*) $= expand$-*node*(*k*, $\{\ \}$, *ss*, *es*)

is-node-set-match (*n*: set of *Node*, *k*: set of *Node*, *m*: map *Atom*
                    to *Expref*, *ss*: *Subseqstore*, *es*: *Expstore*) *t*: **B**
pre $n \cup k \subseteq$ dom *ss* $\cup$ dom *es* $\wedge$ *is-valid-subseqstore*(*ss*, *es*) $\wedge$ *is-substitution*(*n*, *m*, *ss*, *es*)
post $t \Leftrightarrow \{ expand$-*node*(*l*, *m*, *ss*, *es*) $\mid l \in n \} = \{ expand$-*node*(*r*, $\{\ \}$, *ss*, *es*) $\mid r \in k \}$

B.5 Problems

Problem :: *hyp* : set of *Node*
            con : *Expref*

Problemstore = map *Problemref* into *Problem*

nodes : *Problem* $\rightarrow$ set of *Node*
nodes(*o*) $\triangleq$ *hyp*(*o*) $\cup \{con(o)\}$

is-valid-problemstore : *Problemstore* $\times$ *Subseqstore* $\times$ *Expstore* $\rightarrow$ **B**
is-valid-problemstore(*ps*, *ss*, *es*) $\triangleq$ $\forall o \in$ rng *ps* $\cdot$ *nodes*(*o*) $\subseteq$ dom *ss* $\cup$ dom *es*

is-problem-match (*o*: *Problemref*, *u*: *Problemref*,
                    m: map *Atom* to *Expref*, *ps*: *Problemstore*, *ss*: *Subseqstore*,
                    es: *Expstore*) *r*: **B**
pre *o*, *u* $\in$ dom *ps* $\wedge$ *is-valid-subseqstore*(*ss*, *es*) $\wedge$
                is-valid-problemstore(*ps*, *ss*, *es*) $\wedge$ *is-substitution*(*nodes*(*ps*(*o*)), *m*, *ss*, *es*)
post let $l = ps(o), t = ps(u)$ in
    $r \Leftrightarrow$
            is-exp-match(*con*(*l*), *con*(*t*), *m*, *es*) $\wedge$ *is-node-set-match*(*hyp*(*l*), *hyp*(*t*), *m*, *ss*, *es*)

B.6 Proofs

$Instantiation$ :: of : $Problemref$
by : map $Atom$ to $Expref$

where

$inv\text{-}Instantiation(mk\text{-}Instantiation(o, m))$ $\triangleq$ $m \neq \{\}$

$Composite\text{-}proof$ = **seq of** $Problemref$

$Proof$ = $Instantiation$ | $Composite\text{-}proof$

$Proofstore$ = map $Proofref$ to $Proof$

where

$inv\text{-}Proofstore(fs)$ $\triangleq$ $\forall p, q \in \text{dom } fs \cdot fs(p) = fs(q) \land is\text{-}Instantiation(fs(p))$ $\Rightarrow$ $p = q$

$new\text{-}known$ (u: $Problemref$, k: set of $Node$, q: $Problemref$,
$\qquad\qquad$ ps: $Problemstore$, ss: $Subseqstore$) r: set of $Node$
pre $\{u, q\} \subseteq \text{dom } ps$
post r = if $hyp(ps(q)) \subseteq k$
$\qquad$ then $\{con(ps(q))\}$
$\qquad$ else if $\exists g \in \text{dom } ss \cdot lhs(ss(g)) \cup hyp(ps(u)) = hyp(ps(q)) \land rhs(ss(g)) = con(ps(q))$
$\qquad\qquad$ then $\{g\}$
$\qquad\qquad$ else $\{\}$

$adds\text{-}known$ (u: $Problemref$, k: set of $Node$, q: $Problemref$,
$\qquad\qquad$ ps: $Problemstore$, ss: $Subseqstore$) r: $\mathbb{B}$
pre $\{u, q\} \subseteq \text{dom } ps$
post r $\Leftrightarrow$ $new\text{-}known(u, k, q, ps, ss) \neq \{\}$

$knowns$ (u: $Problemref$, n: set of $Node$, c: seq of $Problemref$,
$\qquad\qquad$ ps: $Problemstore$, ss: $Subseqstore$) r: set of $Node$
pre $\{u\} \cup \text{rng } c \subseteq \text{dom } ps$
post r = if $c = []$
$\qquad$ then n
$\qquad$ else let $y = new\text{-}known(u, n, \text{hd } c, ps, ss)$ in
$\qquad\qquad$ $knowns(u, n \cup y, \text{tl } c, ps, ss)$

$problems$: $Proof$ $\rightarrow$ set of $Problemref$

$problems(v)$ $\triangleq$ **cases** v **of**
$\qquad\qquad$ $mk\text{-}Instantiation(o, m) \rightarrow \{o\}$
$\qquad\qquad$ **otherwise rng** v
$\qquad\qquad$ **end**

is-valid-instantiation (*i*: *Instantiation*, *ps*: *Problemstore*, *ss*: *Subseqstore*, *es*: *Expstore*) *r*: B
pre *is-valid-subseqstore*(*ss*, *es*) ∧ *is-valid-problemstore*(*ps*, *ss*, *es*)
post let *mk-Instantiation*(*o*, *m*) = *i* in
    let *n* = *nodes*(*ps*(*o*)) in
    r ⇔ *problems*(*i*) ⊆ dom *ps* ∧ dom *m* ⊆ *vars*(*n*, *ss*, *es*) ∧ *is-substitution*(*n*, *m*, *ss*, *es*)

is-valid-composite : *Composite-proof* × *Problemstore* → B
is-valid-composite(*c*, *ps*) △ *problems*(*c*) ⊆ dom *ps*

is-valid-proofstore (*fs*: *Proofstore*, *ps*: *Problemstore*, *ss*: *Subseqstore*, *es*: *Expstore*) *r*: B
pre *is-valid-subseqstore*(*ss*, *es*) ∧ *is-valid-problemstore*(*ps*, *ss*, *es*)
post *r* ⇔
        ∀*v* ∈ rng *fs* · (*is-Instantiation*(*v*) ⇒ *is-valid-instantiation*(*v*, *ps*, *ss*, *es*)) ∧
                               (*is-Composite-proof*(*v*) ⇒ *is-valid-composite*(*v*, *ps*))

new-fwd-steps (*n*: set of *Node*, *c*: *Composite-proof*,
               ps: *Problemstore*) *v*: *Composite-proof*
pre rng *c* ⊆ dom *ps*
post *v* = if ∃*g* ∈ rng *c* · *hyp*(*ps*(*g*)) ⊆ *n*
        then [*g*] ⌢ *new-fwd-steps*(*n* ∪ *con*(*ps*(*g*)), *c* ▷ {*g*}, *ps*)
        else [ ]

new-bwd-steps (*n*: set of *Node*, *c*: *Composite-proof*, *ps*: *Problemstore*) *v*: *Composite-proof*
pre rng *c* ⊆ dom *ps*
post *v* = if *c* = [ ]
        then *c*
        else let *y* = *con*(*ps*(hd *c*)), *z* = *hyp*(*ps*(hd *c*)) in
           if *y* ∈ *n*
           then *new-bwd-steps*((*n* − {*y*}) ∪ *z*, tl *c*, *ps*) ⌢ hd *c*
           else *new-bwd-steps*(*n*, tl *c*, *ps*)

B.7   Names

ExpNames = map *String* into *Expref*
where

inv-ExpNames(*en*) △ [ ] ∉ dom *en*

SubseqNames = map *String* into *Subseqref*
where

inv-SubseqNames(*sn*) △ [ ] ∉ dom *sn*

ProblemNames = map *String* into *Problemref*
where

inv-ProblemNames(*pn*) △ [ ] ∉ dom *pn*

$ProofNames = $ map $String$ into $Proofref$

where

$inv\text{-}ProofNames(fn) \quad \triangleq \quad [\,] \notin \text{dom } fn$

$String = $ **seq of** $Character$

$is\text{-}valid\text{-}expnames : ExpNames \times Expstore \rightarrow \mathbf{B}$

$is\text{-}valid\text{-}expnames(en, es) \quad \triangleq \quad \text{rng } en \subseteq \text{dom } es$

$is\text{-}valid\text{-}subseqnames : SubseqNames \times Subseqstore \rightarrow \mathbf{B}$

$is\text{-}valid\text{-}subseqnames(sn, ss) \quad \triangleq \quad \text{rng } sn \subseteq \text{dom } ss$

$is\text{-}valid\text{-}problemnames : ProblemNames \times Problemstore \rightarrow \mathbf{B}$

$is\text{-}valid\text{-}problemnames(pn, ps) \quad \triangleq \quad \text{rng } pn \subseteq \text{dom } ps$

$is\text{-}valid\text{-}proofnames : ProofNames \times Proofstore \rightarrow \mathbf{B}$

$is\text{-}valid\text{-}proofnames(fn, fs) \quad \triangleq \quad \text{rng } fn \subseteq \text{dom } fs$

B.8   Solved and Unsolved Problems and Rules of Inference

$Proofmap = $ **map** $Problemref$ **to set of** $Proofref$

$Incomplete\text{-}proofmap = $ **map** $Problemref$ **to set of** $Proofref$

where

$inv\text{-}Incomplete\text{-}proofmap(im) \quad \triangleq$
$\quad \{\,\} \notin \text{rng } im \land \forall k, m \in \text{dom } im \cdot im(k) \cap im(m) \neq \{\,\} \;\Rightarrow\; k = m$

$Rulemap = $ **map** $String$ **into** $Problemref$

where

$inv\text{-}Rulemap(rm) \quad \triangleq \quad [\,] \notin \text{dom } rm$

$solved\text{-}problems : Proofmap \rightarrow $ **set of** $Problemref$

$solved\text{-}problems(jm) \quad \triangleq \quad \text{dom } jm$

$rules : Rulemap \rightarrow $ **set of** $Problemref$

$rules(rm) \quad \triangleq \quad \text{rng } rm$

$axioms : Proofmap \rightarrow $ **set of** $Problemref$

$axioms(jm) \quad \triangleq \quad \{u \mid u \in solved\text{-}problems(jm) \land jm(u) = \{\,\}\}$

$complete\text{-}proofs : Proofmap \rightarrow$ set of $Proofref$

$complete\text{-}proofs(jm) \quad \triangleq \quad \bigcup rng\, jm$

$is\text{-}valid\text{-}rulemap : Rulemap \times Proofmap \times Proofstore \rightarrow \mathbf{B}$

$is\text{-}valid\text{-}rulemap(rm, jm, fs) \quad \triangleq$
$\quad axioms(jm) \subseteq rules(rm) \wedge rules(rm) \subseteq solved\text{-}problems(jm) \wedge$
$\quad \forall p \in complete\text{-}proofs(jm) \cdot$
$$p \in \text{dom}\, fs \Rightarrow (is\text{-}Instantiation(fs(p)) \Rightarrow of(fs(p)) \in rules(rm))$$

$derivable\text{-}results \quad (jm: Proofmap, fs: Proofstore,$
$\qquad\qquad\qquad w: \text{set of } Problemref)\ r: \text{set of } Problemref$
pre $complete\text{-}proofs(jm) \subseteq \text{dom}\, fs \wedge w \subseteq solved\text{-}problems(jm)$
post let $l = \{b \mid b \in axioms(jm) \vee b \in solved\text{-}problems(jm) \wedge$
$\quad \exists v \in jm(b) \cdot problems(fs(v)) \subseteq w)\} \cup w$ in
$r = $ if $l = w$ then w else $derivable\text{-}results(jm, fs, l)$

$is\text{-}self\text{-}consistent \quad (jm: Proofmap, fs: Proofstore)\ r: \mathbf{B}$
pre $complete\text{-}proofs(jm) \subseteq \text{dom}\, fs$
post $r \Leftrightarrow solved\text{-}problems(jm) = derivable\text{-}results(jm, fs, axioms(jm))$

$is\text{-}complete\text{-}proof \quad (v: Proof, u: Problemref, ps: Problemstore, ss: Subseqstore,$
$\qquad\qquad\qquad es: Expstore)\ r: \mathbf{B}$
pre $u \in \text{dom}\, ps \wedge is\text{-}valid\text{-}subseqstore(ss, es) \wedge is\text{-}valid\text{-}problemstore(ps, ss, es) \wedge$
$\quad (is\text{-}Instantiation(v) \Rightarrow is\text{-}valid\text{-}instantiation(v, ps, ss, es)) \wedge$
$\quad (is\text{-}Composite\text{-}proof(v) \Rightarrow is\text{-}valid\text{-}composite(v, ps))$
post let $t = $ cases v of
$\qquad mk\text{-}Instantiation(o, m) \rightarrow is\text{-}problem\text{-}match(o, u, m, ps, ss, es)$
$\qquad$ otherwise $con(ps(u)) \in knowns(u, hyp(ps(u)), v, ps, ss)$
$\qquad$ end
$\quad$ in
$\quad r \Leftrightarrow t$

$is\text{-}valid\text{-}proofmap \quad (jm: Proofmap, fs: Proofstore, ps: Problemstore,$
$\qquad\qquad\qquad ss: Subseqstore, es: Expstore)\ r: \mathbf{B}$
pre $is\text{-}valid\text{-}subseqstore(ss, es) \wedge is\text{-}valid\text{-}problemstore(ps, ss, es) \wedge$
$$is\text{-}valid\text{-}proofstore(fs, ps, ss, es)$$
post $r \Leftrightarrow$
$\quad solved\text{-}problems(jm) \subseteq \text{dom}\, ps \wedge complete\text{-}proofs(jm) \subseteq \text{dom}\, fs \wedge$
$\quad is\text{-}self\text{-}consistent(jm, fs) \wedge$
$\quad \forall u \in solved\text{-}problems(jm) \cdot$
$\qquad \forall v \in jm(u) \cdot problems(fs(v)) \subseteq \text{dom}\, jm \wedge is\text{-}complete\text{-}proof(fs(v), u, ps, ss, es) \wedge$
$\quad \forall k, m \in \text{dom}\, jm \cdot (\exists v \in jm(k) \cap jm(m) \cdot is\text{-}composite\text{-}proof(fs(v))) \Rightarrow k = m$

$incomplete\text{-}proofs : Incomplete\text{-}proofmap \rightarrow$ set of $Proofref$

$incomplete\text{-}proofs(im) \quad \triangleq \quad \bigcup rng\, im$

$is\text{-}valid\text{-}incomplete\text{-}proofmap$ (im: $Incomplete\text{-}proofmap$, jm: $Proofmap$, fs: $Proofstore$,
$\qquad\qquad\qquad\qquad\qquad$ ps: $Problemstore$, ss: $Subseqstore$, es: $Expstore$) r: **B**
pre $is\text{-}valid\text{-}subseqstore(ss, es) \wedge is\text{-}valid\text{-}problemstore(ps, ss, es) \wedge$
$\quad is\text{-}valid\text{-}proofstore(fs, ps, ss, es) \wedge is\text{-}valid\text{-}proofmap(jm, fs, ps, ss, es)$
post $r \Leftrightarrow \operatorname{dom} im \subseteq \operatorname{dom} ps \wedge axioms(jm) \cap \operatorname{dom} im = \{\,\} \wedge$
$\quad complete\text{-}proofs(jm) \cup incomplete\text{-}proofs(im) = \operatorname{dom} fs \wedge$
$\quad complete\text{-}proofs(jm) \cap incomplete\text{-}proofs(im) = \{\,\} \wedge$
$\quad \forall u \in \operatorname{dom} im \cdot \forall v \in im(u) \cdot problems(fs(v)) \subseteq solved\text{-}problems(jm) \wedge$
$\quad is\text{-}Composite\text{-}proof(fs(v)) \wedge \neg is\text{-}complete\text{-}proof(fs(v), u, ps, ss, es)$

$Indexmap = \mathsf{map}\ Proofref\ \mathsf{to}\ \mathbb{N}$

$forward\text{-}proof$ (h: $Proofref$, fs: $Proofstore$, xm: $Indexmap$) v: $Composite\text{-}proof$
pre $h \in \operatorname{dom} fs \cap \operatorname{dom} xm \wedge is\text{-}Composite\text{-}proof(fs(h)) \wedge 0 \leq xm(h) \leq \operatorname{len} fs(h)$
post $v = \{n \in \mathbb{N} \mid 1 \leq n \leq xm(h)\} \lhd fs(h)$

$backward\text{-}proof$ (h: $Proofref$, fs: $Proofstore$, xm: $Indexmap$) v: $Composite\text{-}proof$
pre $h \in \operatorname{dom} fs \cap \operatorname{dom} xm \wedge is\text{-}Composite\text{-}proof(fs(h)) \wedge 0 \leq xm(h) \leq \operatorname{len} fs(h)$
post $fs(h) = forward\text{-}proof(h, fs, xm) \curvearrowright v$

$goals$ (n: set of $Node$, c: seq of $Problemref$, ps: $Problemstore$) r: set of $Node$
pre rng $c \subseteq \operatorname{dom} ps$
post $r = $ if $c = [\,]$
$\qquad\quad$ then n
$\qquad\quad$ else let $k = hyp(ps(\operatorname{hd} c)), y = con(ps(\operatorname{hd} c))$ in
$\qquad\qquad\quad$ if $y \in n$ then $goals((n - \{y\}) \cup k, \operatorname{tl} c, ps)$ else $goals(n, \operatorname{tl} c, ps)$

$is\text{-}valid\text{-}indexmap$ (xm: $Indexmap$, im: $Incomplete\text{-}proofmap$, jm: $Proofmap$, fs: $Proofstore$,
$\qquad\qquad\qquad\qquad$ ps: $Problemstore$, ss: $Subseqstore$, es: $Expstore$) r: **B**
pre $is\text{-}valid\text{-}subseqstore(ss, es) \wedge is\text{-}valid\text{-}problemstore(ps, ss, es) \wedge$
$\quad is\text{-}valid\text{-}proofstore(fs, ps, ss, es) \wedge is\text{-}valid\text{-}proofmap(jm, fs, ps, ss, es) \wedge$
$\quad is\text{-}valid\text{-}incomplete\text{-}proofmap(im, jm, fs, ps, ss, es)$
post $\operatorname{dom} xm = incomplete\text{-}proofs(im) \wedge \forall u \in \operatorname{dom} im \cdot \forall v \in im(u) \cdot$
$\quad$ let $fp = forward\text{-}proof(v, fs, xm),$
$\qquad bp = backward\text{-}proof(v, fs, xm),$
$\qquad gp = reverse(bp)$ in
$\quad 0 \leq xm(v) \leq \operatorname{len} fs(v) \wedge$
$\quad \neg \exists z \in \operatorname{rng} bp \cdot hyp(ps(z)) \subseteq knowns(u, hyp(ps(u)), fp, ps, ss) \wedge$
$\quad \forall g \in \operatorname{dom} gp \cdot con(ps(gp(g))) \in goals(\{con(ps(u))\}, \{g, \ldots, \operatorname{len} gp\} \lhd gp, ps) \wedge$
$\quad \forall b \in \operatorname{dom} fp \cdot$
$\qquad adds\text{-}known(u, knowns(u, hyp(ps(u)), \{b, \ldots, \operatorname{len} fp\} \lhd fp, ps, ss), fp(b), ps, ss)$

References

[1] H. Barringer, J.H. Cheng, and C.B. Jones. A logic covering undefinedness in program proofs. *Acta Informatica*, 21:251–269, 1984.

[2] I.D. Cottam, C.B. Jones, T. Nipkow, and A.C. Wills. Mule: a support system for formal specification and rigorous software development. March 1983. BCS-FACS/SERC Conference on Program Specification and Verification, University of York, Proceedings not published.

[3] I.D. Cottam, C.B. Jones, T. Nipkow, A.C. Wills, M.I. Wolczko, and A. Yaghi. Project support environments for formal methods. In J. McDermid, editor, *Integrated Project Support Environments*, chapter 3, Peter Peregrinus Ltd., 1985.

[4] I.D. Cottam, C.B. Jones, T.N. Nipkow, A.C. Wills, M. Wolczko, and A. Yaghi. *Mule — An Environment for Rigorous Software Development (Final Report to SERC on Grant Number GR/C/05762)*. Technical Report, Department of Computer Science, University of Manchester, 1986.

[5] T. Denvir. *Introduction to Discrete Mathematics for Software Engineering*. Macmillan Education Ltd, 1986.

[6] C.B. Jones. *Systematic Software Development Using VDM*. Prentice Hall International, Englewood Cliffs, NJ, 1986. 300 pages.

[7] C.B. Jones and P.A. Lindsay. A mid-term report on FRIPSE. In R.Bloomfield and L.S. Marshall, editors, *VDM—The Way Ahead*, page ??, Springer-Verlag, 1988. Lecture Notes in Computer Science, Vol. This!

[8] Kevin D. Jones. *The Muffin Prototype: Experiences with Smalltalk-80*. Ipse Document 060/00066/1.1, August 1987. University of Manchester.

[9] Peter A. Lindsay. *A Draft Specification of FRIPSE*. Ipse Document 060/pal017, March 1988. University of Manchester.

[10] Peter A. Lindsay. *A Formal System with Inclusion Polymorphism*. Ipse Document 060/pal014/2.3, December 1987. University of Manchester.

[11] L.S. Marshall. *A Formal Description Method for User Interfaces*. PhD thesis, University of Manchester, October 1986.

[12] Richard Moore. *The Bumper FRIPSE Spec*. Ipse Document 060/00143/2.1, June 1988. University of Manchester.

[13] Richard Moore. *The Design of a User Interface to a Formal Reasoning System*. Ipse Document 060/rm002, July 1987. University of Manchester.

[14] Richard Moore. *The Muffin Database*. Ipse Document 060/00060/1.3, February 1987. University of Manchester.

[15] Richard Moore. *The Muffin Prototype*. Ipse Document 060/00065/1.1, June 1987. University of Manchester.

[16] Richard Moore. *Towards a Generic Muffin*. Ipse Document 060/00140/2.1, December 1987. University of Manchester.

[17] W.H. Newton-Smith. *Logic: An Introductory Course*. Routledge and Kegan Paul, 1985.

[18] T. Nipkow. Mule: persistence and types in an IPSE. In *Persistance and Data Types*, pages 1–25, 1986.

The RAISE Language, Method and Tools

Mogens Nielsen,
Klaus Havelund,
Kim Ritter Wagner
Dansk Datamatik Center
Lundtoftevej 1C
DK-2800 Lyngby,
Denmark

Chris George
STC Technology Limited
London Road, Harlow
Essex CM17 9NA
United Kingdom

Abstract

This paper presents the RAISE software development method, its associated specification language, and the tools supporting it. The RAISE Method enables the stepwise development of both sequential and concurrent software from abstract specification through design to implementation. All stages of RAISE software development are expressed in the wide-spectrum RAISE Specification Language. The RAISE Tools forms an integrated tool environment supporting both language and method.

The paper surveys RAISE and furthermore, more detailed presentations of major RAISE results are provided. The subjects of these are (1) an example of the use of the RAISE method and language, and (2) a presentation of the mathematical semantics of the RAISE specification language.

1 Introduction

As described in [Prehn87], the starting point for RAISE[1] is VDM ([Bjørner82],[Jones86]) – the Vienna Development Method – probably the most widely used "formal" method for software development. Experience from various applications has revealed a number of problems which seem to complicate the use of VDM in full scale industrial software development projects:

- VDM has until now been a largely paper-and-pencil approach. Real life software development requires a number of powerful, computerized tools supporting the development process.

- The VDM specification language does not have a satisfactory facility for the specification of concurrency. Many applications need to deal with concurrency, in specification, development, and implementation.

---

[1]RAISE is an acronym for "Rigorous Approach to Industrial Software Engineering".

- VDM does not have facilities for modulerisation of specification and development in such a way, that the development of large software systems can be divided into blocks of a reasonable size, which can then be combined in a well-defined way.

- The VDM specification language has never been given a satisfactory mathematical semantics. Such a semantics is a pre-requisite for a thorough understanding of the language, and for a proof theory allowing reasoning about specifications written in the language.

- The VDM specification language lacks abstraction facilities. The developments of formalisms for property oriented specification of abstract data types ([Futatsugi85],[CIP85],[Guttag85]) have shown the feasibility and usefulness of employing more abstraction than the domain equations in the VDM specification language provide.

These problems have been the motivation for designing a "second generation" formal method for software development. The aim of the RAISE project is to construct a mathematically well-founded software development method, supported by a comprehensive computer based tools which forms an environment for the method and language. RAISE extends and improves VDM in the areas mentioned above. The outcome of the RAISE project is termed the RAISE product and it consists of the following components:

- The RAISE Method for software development,

- the RAISE Specification Language in which the stages of software development can be expressed,

- the RAISE Tools consisting of the tools supporting method and language, and

- the RAISE Documentation, including manuals and educational material for language, method and tools.

RAISE is intended to be used for industrial development of large and complex software systems, an area in which the need for the extensions and improvements of VDM, removing the above mentioned problems, are commonly acknowledged. RAISE is designed to be applicable to the development of a wide variety of software systems. Examples are: embedded real-time systems, network software, data base management systems, application generators, expert system generators, operating systems, compilers, and control and robotic systems.

As it is the case for VDM, the RAISE focus is on supporting the specification, design, and implementation stages of the software development process. There are, however, important implications on most of the remaining development stages from using RAISE, e.g. the maintenance stage will be improved considerably by the precence of a formal recording of the development of the software system to be maintained.

The development of software using RAISE is a stepwise process in which all stages are expressed in the RAISE Specification Language, RSL. Each stage in the process is called a specification and represents the knowledge of the problem and its solution at that stage. The number of steps may vary according to the nature of the problem to be solved and the project organisation.

A RAISE specification is often derived from the preceding specification by constraining the description (commitment), reflecting the fact that a degree of freedom or indeterminacy has been removed. A specification can also be constructed from the preceding specification by taking further requirements into account. In the last step the specification will be transformed into a program written in the programming language chosen for the project.

Within this framework, the use of RAISE can be varied according to the nature of the software project in question and the people involved in the development. RAISE allows the user several styles of expression through a wide-spectrum language with the possibility of implementation in a range of programming languages, and allows the application of a user-defined degree of formalism ranging from systematic via rigorous to formal.

In this paper, the main characteristics of the RAISE product are surveyed. It should be noted that RAISE is an ongoing project, and that the method, language and tools might undergo changes during the remaining year and a half of the project. In particular the results so far are being evaluated in "industrial trials" where project partners are applying them to real projects. Their evaluations will be an important input to the final product. The paper is organised as follows: Section 2 surveys the RAISE method and section 3 the RAISE Specification Language. These two sections are conceptual, as the method and language is exemplified in section 5. The mathematical semantics of RSL is discussed in section 6. Section 4 presents the RAISE Tools and finally section 7 contains information on the RAISE project organisation and discusses the current state of the project.

2 The RAISE Method

In this section we survey the RAISE method. An example of its use is given in section 5, and for a more complete documentation of the method, the reader is refered to the report [George88].

2.1 RAISE – A rigorous method

The aim of the RAISE Method is to enable the construction of reliable software by formalising the software development process. By a formal method we mean a method in which properties of specifications can be mathematically proved and in which the development steps can be mathematically proved to maintain desired, recorded properties. Insisting on complete formality would render the method unsuitable for industrial usage (at present at least). But many of the benefits of formal development can be obtained without actually carrying out the proofs completely, and a good notation for development steps is useful in itself.

Software development can be characterised by a sequence of increasingly strict development styles: (1) ad hoc, (2) systematic, (3) rigorous, (4) formal.

Rigorous methods and formal methods differ from ad hoc and systematic ones, in having a specification language and a notion of development with a mathematical description (semantics), such that specification and development of software can be subject to mathematical reasoning. The process of software development then produces the obligation to prove the well–definedness and correctness of the specifications written and the development steps carried out, mathematically. Whereas a formal method would insist on the formal proof of all such obligations, a rigorous method allows a level of formality which fits the actual situation. This notion of rigour is central to the RAISE Method, and allows users to select the level of formality that is appropriate to particular circumstances, project standards, etc. Since there is an underlying mathematical semantics, a correctness argument that is challenged can always be proved in more detail.

2.2 The development process

As it is the case for VDM, the RAISE Method is based on the notion of stepwise refinement ([Dijkstra76],[Wirth71],[Jones86]). The basis of stepwise refinement can be summarised as follows:

- Software is constructed by a series of steps – it is an iterative procedure.

- Each step starts with a description of the software and produces a new one, which is in some way more detailed (or more concrete).

- The result of each step is not only more detailed but also in some way conforms to the previous one, so that it can be used to replace it.

- Refinement typically involves both algorithm and data, since a change in one normally involves a change in the other.

This basis is taken into account in RAISE developments where initial abstract specifications are successively developed by a process of commitment in which degrees of freedom or indeterminacy are removed. Thus the top level specification is developed to give a more committed specification which in turn may be subject to the same development process. In each step data structures and/or control structures are elaborated. Such elaboration may take place within one specification or it may involve the creation of specifications to be developed separately, but whose combination satisfies the properties posed by the previous specification. Development steps also involves justification that each new specification, or combination, in some sense is a correct development of the previous one.

In RAISE the term *development step* is used for the process of performing each step and *development level* for its result. A development level records the specification constructed, the abstract specification it is a development of, and information about separate developments on which the present level depends. A *development* is a sequence of development levels.

The last development step produces a program or a collection of programs written in the programming language chosen for the project. Since the last development level containing specifications written in RSL should be very implementation oriented, the task of producing a program will be automated or semi-automated.

The software development process using RAISE can be illustrated as follows:

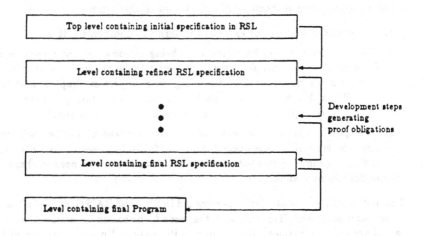

Note that the requirement to be able to support such a development process, places several requirements on RSL. It must provide a structuring concept so that specifications can be encapsulated and so that presentation details can be hidden. Without the possibility of abstracting from particular presentations the ability to provide different implementations and prove them correct would be lost. Secondly, RSL must allow for abstraction and underdeterminacy to be expressed, to allow e.g. design decisions to be postponed until appropriate, and to allow re-use. This leads to such notions as parameterisation, specification by property, and underspecification. Thirdly, the RSL needs a range of definition styles – imperative as well as applicative, concurrent as well as sequential, concrete types as well as abstract ones, implicit as well as explicit definition of entities – to enable specifications at different levels of development.

2.2.1 The initial specification

Initial specifications are intended to both capture the functionality of a system (or, for subsidiary developments, of part of it) and at the same time be as abstract as possible, i.e. make as few design decisions as possible. These are frequently contradictory objectives as many statements of requirements give too much detail — they are expressed in terms that assume the system will be designed in a certain way. Thus the early development stages typically involve a mixture of implementing incomplete specifications by making design decisions and enriching them to include more of the functionality, so that there is no specification that is both complete and fully abstract. The initial specification is then taken to be the first one recorded as part of a development. Thus RAISE allows developers some freedom in how much of the early development work is recorded and retained as part of the development history. The overall guidelines are that the initial specification should say something significant about the system, such as its breakdown into major components, and subsequent development steps should also each have a particular purpose in making and recording a particular design decision.

2.3 Managing the development process

Since RAISE is concerned with industrial application the method must also cater for 'programming in the large', for large projects with many people working in parallel on different parts. Hence there are a number of 'software engineering' requirements:

- It should be possible to record not only the RSL specifications at each stage, but also the relations between them. Such relations take one of three forms:

    1. One specification may be expressed in terms of another, i.e. it may *use* it

    2. One specification may be recorded as being in some *semantic* relation to another. In particular, one may *implement* another by preserving all its properties, or there may be some logical statement relating their properties. Implementation is defined formally as theory inclusion (possibly also including a *fitting* to express how named entities in one specification are implemented by entities in another).

    3. One specification may be regarded as a *development* of another, whether or not a semantic relation has also been recorded. Ideally there should be such a relation and it should be implementation, but in practice we sometimes need to change properties in development steps.

The first of these forms of relation is recorded in RSL; the RAISE method allows the others to be recorded as well. Together with the second, the semantic relations, we may want to record not only the precise relation but also its (rigorous) proof. Together with the third, the development relations, we may wish to record the purpose behind the development step — what details we are elaborating on, what design decisions are being taken and why, etc. The underlying purpose of such recording is the usual one of recording the design process — to make it manageable. In particular it is intended to help maintenance and reuse. If certain features are to be changed we need to find where the original development needs changing, and what other changes are required as a result.

- It should be possible to divide systems into pieces, to develop these pieces separately, and then to combine the results again in such a way that the properties of the result are the same as those of the original (the ideal situation, and guaranteed if the developed pieces are implementations of their initial specifications), or bear some known, stated relation to them. This is a natural extension of the notion that formal specification and rigorous development are intended to discover and deal with problems as early as possible. There should be no unpleasant surprises at system integration time!

- It should be possible to identify key milestones in the development process so that progress can be checked against plans. It seems to be the case that, compared with more traditional models of the development process, the use of formal methods extends the analysis and design phases but shortens the coding and testing phases. If progress is only measured by lines of target code produced the process appears slow and unmanageable.

In order to do development in practice, standard paradigms for development steps, and the conditions under which they produce implementations, are also part of the method description. The method also involves quality assurance procedures applicable to the various activities, notions of how changes of one part affect others, and guidelines for managing the process.

2.4   Proof obligations

In a RAISE development, proof obligations will arise in two ways.

Firstly, almost any specification on its own will produce proof obligations because it must be shown to be consistent, i.e. have a possible implementation. It must be shown, for example, that a partial function is not called with a parameter outside its domain of definition. Such obligations are not in general decidable and will not always be provable by tools. However, the tools are capable of identifying what needs to be proven in the form of proof obligations for the user to discharge. Simple checks such as ordinary type checking will be carried out by the tools.

Secondly, we have noted that development involves proving the existence of certain development relations between specifications. The RAISE environment allows the recording of such relations together with the appropriate proof obligations and whatever proofs are given to discharge them.

As discussed earlier, the notion of rigour in RAISE entails the user being able to choose an appropriate level of formality in discharging each proof obligation. This may range from a completely informal statement that the proof is "obvious" or "immediate", over sketching some reasons, to a completely formal proof. To support users in recording proofs in such a range of styles, a proof is regarded as a formal object in RAISE. This will enable tools to assist users in the development and presentation of proofs.

2.5   The role of transformation

Note that the notion of stepwise development in RAISE may be distinguished from design by transformation. In RAISE there is a cycle of construction (which generates proof obligations) followed by justification (which involves discharging these obligations). Thus each successive specification must be shown to implement the previous one. Implementation is in this way justified *post hoc*.

By a transformational design method is generally meant one in which each step is a transformation where the justification is included in the step. Part of this justification is *a priori* – the transformation has been shown to be correct – and part is usually particular to the specification to which it is being applied, since transformations are frequently only correct if certain semantic conditions are met (such as associativity of an operator).

Since transformational design frequently involves proving the applicability of a transformation, the difference between transformational design and the RAISE method may be small; they share the notion of stepwise development. There is a difference, however, in that the user perceives them differently. In RAISE the user constructs the next development step; in a transformational system the user selects a transformation and then applies it.

The decision not to attempt a transformational design system is purely pragmatic. We suspect that future methods may well be based on a transformation paradigm, and there are projects like CIP ([CIP85]) actively pursuing this approach. There are, however, problems of providing a sufficiently general and complete set of transformations, and of helping users choose the appropriate ones. It seems unlikely that this approach is adequate for RAISE, which is intended for use in large-scale industrial projects.

3 The RAISE Specification Language

In this section, the basic concepts of the RAISE Specification Language, RSL, are described. Examples of specifications in RSL are shown in section 5 and the mathematical semantics of RSL is discussed in section 6. A more complete documentation of RSL can be found in the report [Jørgensen88]. Here, we survey the language from a conceptual point of view.

The starting point for RSL was experiences with model based approaches to specification, mainly gained from the VDM meta language ([Bjørner82]). However, RSL derived inspiration from many other sources, the most prominent being Clear ([Burstall77],[Burstall80]), OBJ ([Futatsugi85]), ML ([Harper86]), CSP ([Hoare85]), and Occam ([Inmos84]).

RSL is a wide-spectrum language, complete with facilities for structuring and concurrency; it offers facilities for implicit and explicit specifications, as well as the possibility of expressing these specifications applicatively or imperatively. We therefore claim, that RSL is a major improvement compared to the VDM meta language, removing the criticism mentioned in the introduction.

RSL is intended to provide mathematical abstractions functional specifications of software. Therefore certain aspects of the description of software systems are outside the scope of RSL. Among these are performance requirements and real-time constraints. However, through the method and tools such requirements can be recorded and associated with the relevant part of a specification or development for later verification. The RAISE proof system will, however, not be able to support such verification.

Software developed using RAISE will in many cases be part of a system containing components which were not developed using RAISE. To achieve integration in these cases, the developer will need to construct interface descriptions in RSL. Such interfaces express the system characteristics on which a piece of software depends. RSL has facilities for abstract description of interfaces.

3.1 Structures

The fundamental structuring unit in RSL is the *structure*. Structures are the building blocks and abstraction units of RSL. Structures constitute the frame in which the RSL entities *types*, *values*, *variables*, *operations* and *processes* are defined. Semantically a structure consists of a *signature* associating type information to the entities in the structure, and a class of *models* where each model is an association of mathematical objects to the entities in the structure. A model constitutes an environment in which the expressions and statements of the structure can be interpreted. The reason for having a model class rather than just a single model is the possible presence of *underspecification*. Each model can be considered as an abstraction of one possible implementation.

Structures can be defined in a number of ways in RSL:

- As a *flat structure* which is just the encapsulation of a number of entities (types, values, variables, operations, and processes).

- as a *layered structure* which uses previously defined structures to define new entities. A layered structure can be considered as *parameterised* with respect to the structures on which it is building, due to the construct for defining structures by structure substitution,

- as a result of *structure substitution* where a structure S_2 is derived from a structure S_1 by substituting another structure for one that is used by S_1.

- as a *fitted structure* which is the result of renaming, hiding, and copying entities in a structure.

3.2 Types

Semantically, types should be thought of as characterising non-empty sets of values. RSL provide two styles of type definitions:

1. *Abstract type definitions*, where a type is named without explicitly indicating which values it characterises. These are characterised via the entities (constants, functions, operations and processes) who operate on the type.

2. *Explicit type definitions*, where a type is defined by expressing its equivalence with a type expression. The basic type equivalence is structural, but name equivalence can be obtained through *labeled type definitions*, where a type is defined whose values are labeled copies of the values characterised by a type expression. Recursive type definitions in the style of VDM are allowed.

Type expressions can be either names denoting predefined or abstract types (e.g. integers, Booleans, and characters), or type constructions where the type is constructed from other types (e.g. Cartesian products, disjoint sums, and function spaces), or sub-types of other types consisting of values satisfying additional constraints.

3.3 Values

A *value definition* serves to name a value and to state its type. Values can either be defined explicitly as the semantic meanings of *value expressions*, or they can be characterised implicitly using axioms.

RSL has a rich language of value expressions, including value expressions corresponding to atomic values, to composing and decomposing values of constructed type, applying operations and functions to other values, to expressing values using locally defined entities, and to conditionals.

A subset of the value expressions corresponding to the expressions resulting in values of Boolean type constitute the language of axioms. This is a very powerful language for property oriented specification, offering most of what is known from predicative specification languages.

3.4 States and operations

A structure may introduce a *state* through the declaration of variables, and different instantiations of the state of a structure can be created through copying of such a structure. A state is an association of values to variables. The state of a structure is not directly accessible outside the structure. Instead, manipulations of the state of a structure are performed by calls of *operations* defined in the structure.

In addition to the value expressions which can be used for specifying value returning operations, RSL has a language of *statements* for specifying proper operations. There are statements assigning values to variables, composing other statements, applying operations to argument values, statements defining operations using locally defined entities, and loop statements.

Additionally, operations can be specified axiomatically by pre- and post-conditions.

3.5 Processes

Parallel activities can be specified via the RSL *process* concept. It is based on CSP, Communicating Sequential Processes ([Hoare85]) and the language Occam ([Inmos84]).

A process can be considered as an entity capable of (1) communicating with other processes along (uni-directional) *channels*, and (2) accessing variables. The semantics of processes is based on the failure set model of [Roscoe84].

Processes can be specified by the statements described above and additionally the so-called *process statements*. These include atomic processes (SKIP, STOP, RUN, CHAOS), communication between processes, choices between processes, parallel composition of processes, interleaving of processes, hiding of communications, application of parameterised processes, renaming of channels, and alphabet extensions.

4 The RAISE tools

Support tools play an important role in RAISE. The aims of the RAISE Tools are to provide a software development environment specifically supporting the RAISE Method and Language, and to interface to tools supporting the software development aspects outside the scope of RAISE. At the symposium, a trial version of the basic syntax directed editor, and database facilities of the RAISE Tools is demonstrated. In this section we concentrate on outlining the facilities of the final RAISE Tools.

The RAISE Tools will be of professional quality and will include documentation enabling its maintenance (and adaptation to specific organisations); since the tools is developed using the RAISE method, the documentation will be in the RAISE style.

The tools is primarily designed to run on SUN[2] workstations, it will be based on the UNIX[3] operating system, and the X Window System[4] is chosen as the screen interface. There will be rudimentary support for the interface of character terminals. The language related components will all be based on the CSG (Cornell Synthesizer Generator [Reps87]) which provides the RAISE tools with a uniform user interface. The RAISE Tools will use LaTeX ([Lamport86]) as a document preparation system.

4.1 The RAISE database

The basis of all tools is the RAISE database. This allows recording of information about RSL structures, semantic relations between structures, and RAISE developments. It is capable of

---

[2] trademark of SUN Microsystems
[3] trademark of Bell Laboratories
[4] trademark of Massachusetts Institute of Technology

recording all parts of RAISE developments, and additionally it can be adapted so that information specific to a given RAISE application area or an organisation can be stored. The database responds to commands of the usual sort – add, delete, rename, etc. – and it handles version control. It allows several users to work against it at the same time.

A number of tools have a close relation to the database:

The Configuration Control Tool which provides facilities for connecting and maintaining related objects (in RAISE this includes RSL structures, relations between structures, and developments). The tool will provide possibilities for both static and dynamic building of configurations.

The Database Browser which can be used to display the contents of the database in various ways. The browser provides a query language facility allowing users to define which information should be extracted from the database.

The Change Propagation Tool which can be used to (1) propagate changes in the database, and (2) analyse the effects of changes.

4.2 The RSL editor

Another basic tool is the RSL editor. It is a syntax-directed editor, including visibility- and type-checking. There are facilities for multi-window, multi-buffer editing. The editor unparses with extended character sets, such that the RSL specifications shown on the screen, are identical to the ones prepared by LATEX (allowing boldface characters, underscoring, mathematical symbols etc.). As mentioned the editor is constructed using CSG and with XWindows as the screen interface.

Closely related to the editor is the:

Text Formatting Tool which, for the structures created by the editor, generates LATEX output suitable for incorporation in other documents prepared in LATEX.

4.3 The proof tools

The proof tools are the part of the RAISE tools which supports reasoning about properties of RSL specifications and RAISE developments. Together, the proof tools constitute an interactive assistant for theorem proving and specification transformation, with some limited facilities for automatic theorem proving.

The proof tools consist of:

The Proof Editor with proof well-formedness checks and automatic proof simplification. The editor is syntax directed over the syntax of RAISE proofs and theorems. It is generated by CSG.

The RSL Context Condition Tool which performs semantic analysis of specification correctness, and generates proof obligations for checks which cannot be carried out automatically. This tool can also be considered part of the RSL editor, as it extends the checks on RSL specifications, carried out there (syntax-, visibility-, type-, etc. checks).

The Transformation Tool which supports transformation of RSL specifications according to a set of transformation rules. As mentioned previously (section 2) only a few simple rules are defined in RAISE, but the tool will be extensible with respect to new transformation rules. The tool generates proof obligations when the proof of applicability of a transformation cannot be carried out automatically.

The Semantic Relation Tool which supports establishment of semantic relations between RSL structures. The tool generates proof obligations when checks, that a certain relation (e.g. an implementation relation) exists between structures, cannot be carried out automatically.

4.4   The translation tools

The translation tools support the translation from an executable, implementation oriented subset of RSL to various programming languages. The translation tools generate target code of a high quality and is not to be considered primarily as prototyping tools.

The basic translation tool will be generic and translators to C, Modula-2, and possibly Ada will be constructed as instantiations of the generic translation tool.

5   An example development — evaluating reverse Polish expressions

This section aims to describe the main features of the RAISE development method by means of a fairly simple example — the evaluation of reverse Polish expressions using a stack. The example is small to allow it to be developed within the confines of a short paper. It might be part of a much larger system. While describing the method as applied to the example some features of RSL are also illustrated.

First we give a brief note for those not familiar with the example. An expression like '$(1+2)*3$' may be converted into a 'reverse Polish' expression which is a list, in this case '$<1,2,+,3,*>$'. The reason for the conversion is that such a list can now be evaluated using a stack. The list is read from left to right. Any number is pushed onto the stack; any operator is applied to the top two elements on the stack, the two values are removed from the stack, and the result pushed onto it. At the end the number at the top of the stack is the result of the evaluation.

5.1   Planning the example

We can define the following milestones in the development:
- the evaluation of expressions

- the generation of reverse Polish lists and the applicative evaluation of such expressions using an applicative stack

- an imperative version of the previous milestone

5.2   Evaluating expressions

We start with a structure EVAL0 (figure 2) defining the function *eval* to evaluate expressions. We use a subsidiary structure CALC (figure 1) defining the type *Exp* of expressions and the function *calc*. For simplicity we take expressions with operators *plus* and *minus* only.

Some comments on the features of RSL displayed so far are in order. An RSL specification takes the form of a *structure*, which may in turn use other structures, just as EVAL0 uses CALC. Other possible constituents of structures include *type* and *value* definitions. In CALC are defined two types, *Exp* and *Op*. Each are union types, where a union type is expressed as a collection of (tag:type) pairs (as in *Exp*) or just of tags (as in *Op*). Thus an expression of type *Exp* is either a simp(le) expression which is an integer, or a comp(ound) expression

```
CALC = structure
         type
           Exp = [|simp:Int,comp:Exp × Op × Exp|],
           Op = [|plus,minus|]
         value
           calc (l:Int,opn:Op,r:Int) ≜
             match opn with
               [|plus|] then l+r,
               [|minus|] then l−r
             end
       end CALC
```

Figure 1: The structure CALC

```
EVAL0 = structure
          use CALC
          value
            eval (e:Exp) :Int ≜
              match e with
                [|simp=i|] then i,
                [|comp=(l,opn,r)|] then calc(eval(l),opn,eval(r))
              end
        end EVAL0
```

Figure 2: The structure EVAL0

which is a cartesian product of two expressions of type *Exp* and an operator of type *Op*. An operator is either *plus* or *minus*. In CALC is also defined a function *calc* used to evaluate a pair of integers and an operator. Note how the constituents of a union type (in this case *Op*) may be discriminated by a **match** expression. Another match expression is employed in the definition of *eval* in the structure EVAL0. The match is used here not only to discriminate the constituents in the union but also to bind identifiers to the component values of the matched value.

5.3 Generating reverse Polish expressions

To show that the function, *eval_rp*, say, that evaluates reverse Polish expressions is equivalent to *eval* we will need to define the function, *make_rp*, say, to convert from expressions to reverse Polish expressions. We can then prove that the composition of *eval_rp* and *make_rp* computes the same result as *eval*. We first, then, define reverse Polish expressions in a new structure RP (figure 3).

A reverse Polish expression is represented as a non-empty list (indicated by the type 'Rp_el$^+$') of either integers or operators. '^' is the concatenation symbol and '<...>' is the list constructor.

5.4 An abstract stack

Evaluation of reverse Polish expressions requires a stack. We can define a stack abstractly in the structure STACK0 (figure 4).

Several things are worth noting about STACK0. Firstly we have used a structure ELEMENT

```
RP = structure
      use CALC
      type Rp_el = [|intel:Int,opel:Op|]
      value
         make_rp (e:Exp) :Rp_el⁺ ≜
           match e with
              [|simp=i|] then <[|intel=i|]>,
              [|comp=(l,opn,r)|] then make_rp(l)^make_rp(r)^<[|opel=opn|]>
           end
      end RP
```

Figure 3: The structure RP

```
STACK0 = structure
            use ELEMENT
            type
              Stack,
              Stack1 = those st:Stack . ~is_empty(st)
            value
              empty: Stack,
              is_empty: Stack → Bool,
              push: El × Stack → Stack1,
              pop: Stack1 → Stack,
              top: Stack1 → El
            axiom
              ∀ st:Stack, x:El .
                 pop(push(x,st)) = st ∧
                 top(push(x,st)) = x ∧
                 is_empty(empty) ∧
                 ~is_empty(push(x,st))
          end STACK0
```

Figure 4: The structure STACK0

that does nothing other than define a type name *El* (figure 5).

We can regard STACK0 as parameterised, since we can substitute for the use of ELEMENT the use of any structure that implements it. In particular we shall want stacks of integers. But the development of STACK0 in which we introduce various representations of stacks (as lists, arrays or whatever) can proceed quite separately from developments of other structures using stacks of integers, etc.

Secondly we note that the type *Stack* in STACK0 has no definition — we say it is 'abstract' as opposed to our previous types like *Exp* which are 'concrete'. When employing such abstract types we typically use axioms rather than definitions to define the values (including functions) involving these types.

Lastly note we have used the 'subtype' notion (those ...) to define the type *Stack1* of non-empty stacks. This allows us to record that *pop* and *top* are defined for all non-empty stacks and that *push* produces a non-empty stack.

```
ELEMENT = structure
            type El
         end ELEMENT
```

Figure 5: The structure ELEMENT

5.5   A concrete stack

We can also define a structure *STACK1* using a concrete type definition for *Stack* as a list of elements (figure 6).

```
STACK1 = structure
            use ELEMENT
            type
               Stack = El*,
               Stack1 = those st:Stack . ~is_empty(st)
            value
               empty:Stack = <>,
               is_empty (st:Stack) :Bool ≜ st = empty,
               push (x:El,st:Stack) :Stack1 ≜ <x>^st,
               pop (st:Stack1) :Stack ≜ tl st,
               top (st:Stack1) :El ≜ hd st
         end STACK1
```

Figure 6: The structure STACK1

We can easily show that STACK1 implements STACK0 (it amounts to little more than showing the axioms in STACK0 are true in STACK1) and hence that any structure using STACK0 can safely use STACK1 instead. So why do we produce two versions? The abstract STACK0 is useful when used in other structures. They can use the properties expressed in the axioms without having to be concerned with any particular representation of the data structures that will eventually be developed as the stack implementation. Hence we describe STACK0 as the 'view' of the stack development. This development can now proceed quite independently of that of the evaluator. It is in general the case that axiomatic specifications like STACK0 are harder to write than those like STACK1, particularly for those brought up in the VDM tradition. But it is possible, of course, to formulate STACK1 first and then abstract from it to produce STACK0 as containing precisely those properties that the stack developer intends to maintain. It should also be the case that such axiomatic specifications will be written comparatively rarely because they are easy to re-use. Indeed we would expect in practice to find our stack development in the RAISE library.

5.6   Evaluating reverse Polish expressions applicatively

We are now ready to formulate the structure EVAL1 defining the function *eval_rp* and a new *eval* function, hopefully equivalent to the original one in EVAL0 (figure 7).

There are two things to notice about EVAL1. Firstly, the use clause

   ST = STACK0 with INT providing fit Int for El in ELEMENT

means that instead of using STACK0 we are using a structure ST obtained by substituting the built-in structure INT for ELEMENT. At the same time we use a 'fitting' (fit ...) to replace the

```
EVAL1 = structure
           use
             RP,
             ST = STACK0 with INT providing fit Int for El in ELEMENT
           value
             eval_rp (st:Stack, rp:Rp_el*) :Int ≜
               match rp with
                 <> then top(st),
                 <[|intel=i|]>^t then eval_rp(push(i,st),t),
                 <[|opel=opn|]>^t then
                   let v = calc(top(pop(st)),opn,top(st))
                   in eval_rp(push(v,pop(pop(st))),t) end
               end omit,
             eval (e:Exp) :Int ≜ eval_rp(empty,make_rp(e))
        end EVAL1
```

Figure 7: The structure EVAL1

type name *El* with the name of the built-in type **Int**. Thus we have obtained integer stacks from the generic ones. Secondly, note that the definition of *eval_rp* is regarded as local to EVAL1 and so is 'omitted'. A structure using EVAL1 can mention *eval* but not *eval_rp*.

We can now prove that EVAL1 implements EVAL0, because EVAL1`eval (the full name of the 'eval' defined in EVAL1) computes the same result as EVAL0`eval. (A rigorous proof can be found in [George88].) Thus we have completed our second milestone.

5.7   Evaluating reverse Polish expressions imperatively

We will firstly need our stack developers to provide an imperative stack structure IMP_STACK0 (figure 8).

```
IMP_STACK0 = structure
                use STACK0
                variable stack : Stack
                operation
                  empty_op write stack is stack := empty end,
                  is_empty_op :Bool read stack ≜ is_empty(stack) end,
                  push_op (x:El) write stack is stack := push(x,stack) end,
                  pop_op write stack pre stack ≠ empty is stack := pop(stack) end,
                  top_op :El read stack pre stack ≠ empty ≜ top(stack) end,
                  tpop_op :El write stack pre stack ≠ empty ≜
                    let r = top(stack) in stack := pop(stack) return r end
                end
             end IMP_STACK0
```

Figure 8: The structure IMP_STACK0

Note that we have used STACK0 in IMP_STACK0 so that we can define the imperative stack in terms of the applicative one. We have also added an operation *tpop_op* that both pops the stack and returns the old head value — this is useful in our imperative evaluator IMP_EVAL0 (figure 9).

```
IMP_EVAL0 = structure
            use
              RP,
              S = IMP_STACK0 with INT providing fit Int for El in ELEMENT
            operation
              eval_op (rp:Rp_el⁺) :Int write S ≙
                block
                  variable rp1:Rp_el* := rp,  x,y :Int
                in loop
                    match hd rp1 with
                      [|intel=i|] then push_op(i),
                      [|opel=opn|] then
                            x := tpop_op;
                            y := tpop_op;
                            push_op(calc(y,opn,x))
                    end;
                    rp1 := tl rp1
                  until rp1 = <>
                  return tpop_op
                end
              end eval_op
            end IMP_EVAL0
```

Figure 9: The structure IMP_EVAL0

It is not the case that IMP_EVAL0 implements EVAL0 because we have changed from an applicative function *eval* to an imperative operation *eval_op*. But there is, we hope, a relation between the function and the operation — they should return the same value. So we want to record and prove the semantic relation between IMP_EVAL0 AND EVAL0, namely

$$\forall \ e{:}Exp \ . \ eval\_op(make\_rp(e)) = EVAL0`eval(e) \tag{1}$$

We describe how this is done in section 5.9.

5.8 A stack process

There is insufficient space in this paper to describe the features of RSL dealing with concurrency, but to give at least a flavour of what is involved figure 10 shows a stack process.

The concurrency features of RSL are based on those of CSP. The stack process has two input channels *empty* and *push*, the second of which also inputs a value, and an output channel *tpop* that outputs a value. The process *stack* is a non-terminating loop that in each cycle can set the stack to empty or push a value on to it or, provided it is not empty, pop the stack and output the previous top value.

Note the form of use clause employed in this structure. If we had written 'use IMP_STACK0' we would have shared IMP_STACK0 with any other structures having a similar use clause. When we write instead 'use ST = IMP_STACK0' we make a local copy of IMP_STACK0, called ST, that can only be accessed in PROC_STACK0 or structures using it in turn. Thus in this case we have prevented our stack being shared accidentally with any other processes.

```
PROC_STACK0 = structure
                 use ST = IMP_STACK0
                 process
                     stack in [|empty,push:El|] out [|tpop:El|] write ST
                     is while true loop
                         empty? → empty_op;SKIP
                         []
                         push?x → push_op(x);SKIP
                         []
                         when ~is_empty_op do tpop!tpop_op → SKIP
                     end
                 end stack
             end PROC_STACK0
```

Figure 10: The structure PROC_STACK0

5.9 Recording the development

We will not take this example any further in this paper, but we will consider how the collection of structures formulated so far are organised in the RAISE library. Firstly, of course, all the structures are stored against their names, so that they can be referred to in other places, such as in use clauses. Secondly we want to record some semantic relations between structures. Thirdly we want to record the development relations.

5.9.1 Recording semantic relations

You will recall that semantic relations are relations between the properties of structures. The relation may be the general one of implementation, or it may be one or more particular properties like (1) above. For each relation we can record the name of the source structure, the name of the target structure (where if A implements B then A is the source and B the target), the fitting (if any), the property or properties being asserted, and the (rigorous) proof. We have established those shown in table 1.

Source	Target	Fitting		Property
INT	ELEMENT	Int for El		Implementation
STACK1	STACK0	—		Implementation
EVAL1	EVAL0	—		Implementation
IMP_EVAL0	EVAL0	—	$\forall$ e:Exp .	
				$eval\_op(make\_rp(e)) = EVAL0\`eval(e)$

Table 1: Semantic relations

Each of these relations may be stored as an item in the library, indexed by the (source,target) pair.

5.9.2 Recording development relations

We have assumed for our example that there are two separate developments, one for stacks and one for the evaluator. We want to record the sequence of development steps, the rationale behind the step and the connections, called 'contracts' between developments. We also need to distinguish between structures used as 'views', which are the specifications seen by other developments while the development work is proceeding, and structures used as 'bodies', which contain the current state of the developing specification. Developments will also have a set of requirements to be met, by which we mean an informal statement of both the non-functional and functional requirements. For a main development these requirements will be the original system requirements; for subsidiary developments (like that for the stack) they will be the requirements relevant to the subsidiary development. To capture all this the RAISE library contains named objects called 'developments'. These consist of the set of requirements and a sequence of 'levels'. Each level consists of a triple — a 'body' (which is a structure name), a 'view' (also a structure name) and a (possibly empty) set of 'contracts' (which are names of other developments on which this development is immediately dependent). There is a requirement that the body and view are either the same or the source and target of a semantic relation which is an implementation. This is necessary because it must be possible for structures in developments having a contract with this one to be able to substitute a body for a view. There is no necessary relation between the bodies and views of successive levels, but the same view appearing in them suggests that implementation is being maintained; a different view suggests that implementation has not been maintained and some change in contracts may be necessary.

In our example there are two developments, which we shall call STACK_DEV (table 2) and EVAL_DEV (table 3) respectively.

Level	Body	View	Contracts
1	STACK1	STACK0	{}
2	IMP_STACK0	IMP_STACK0	{}

Table 2: The development STACK_DEV

Level	Body	View	Contracts
1	EVAL0	EVAL0	{}
2	EVAL1	EVAL0	{STACK_DEV}
3	IMP_EVAL0	IMP_EVAL0	{STACK_DEV}

Table 3: The development EVAL_DEV

Note that it is always possible to make the first level have the same body and view, as with EVAL_DEV, if we want to establish the development with its name, requirements and initial view before we have actually done any development of that view.

This notion of developments is quite separate from the other relations in the library; projects may establish as many or as few separate developments as they find convenient. For example, we could have established IMP_STACK_DEV as a separate development for imperative stacks, with a contract to STACK_DEV. IMP_STACK_DEV would then have appeared as the contract in level 3 of EVAL_DEV instead of STACK_DEV.

6 The semantics of the RAISE Specification Language

This section presents some of the principles used to give a semantics to RSL. The semantics is written in a combination of a transformational and denotational style, where certain constructs are transformed into a kernel, which is then given a denotational semantics. The kernel is, however, quite large compared to the complete RSL and the semantics is thus mainly written in a denotational style.

This approach differs somewhat from an earlier attempt, where we attempted to base the semantics on a very small, purely applicative, kernel language. The transformation of processes into this kernel, however, became too complex, and we seemed to loose the advantage of a small kernel language: clarity.

This section is organised as follows. Section 6.1 presents an applicative subset of RSL, large enough to illustrate the major semantic techniques used in the semantics of RSL. Section 6.1 contains the syntax of the RSL subset, an example of a specification and a summary of intrinsic characteristics. Then follows an outline of the semantics of the RSL subset in the form of the semantic domains and the major semantic functions. We then illustrate the semantics of the example in section 6.1.2. Finally, we discuss the semantics of types and the choice of logic, and we give the semantic domains for states, operations and processes in RSL.

We would like to thank the following persons for encouragement and inspiration: C.B. Jones, M. Broy, D. Sannella, A. Blikle and B. Monahan.

6.1 An RSL subset

6.1.1 Syntax

The syntax is written in a BNF-like formalism:

1.	spec	::= id where struc-def-list
2.	struc-def-list	::= struc-def
.2		| struc-def struc-def-list
3.	struc-def	::= id = struc
4.	struc	::= structure
		def-list
		end
.2		| ...
5.	def-list	::= def
.2		| def def-list
6.	def	::= use id
.2		| type id
.3		| type id = type
.4		| value id : type
.5		| axiom exp
.6		| ...

A specification (1) is a list of structure definitions (2) together with an identification of a main structure (the name of one of the structures in the structure definition list).

A structure definition (3) names a structure (4), which in the atomic version is build from a list of definitions. A definition (6) can (here) have one of five forms: an import of another named structure (6.1), a type definition (6.2, 6.3), the introduction of a value (6.4) or the restriction of such a value by an axiom (6.5). Note that types can be given without a type equation (6.2) corresponding to sorts in algebraic specification languages.

6.1.2 Example

The following example consists of two structures, where the one (*ELEM*) is imported into the other (*BOXES*).

BOXES where

ELEM =
  structure
    type
      Elem
    value
      eq : Elem × Elem → Bool
    axiom
      ∀ e1, e2, e3 : Elem .
        eq(e1,e1) ∧
        (eq(e1,e2) ⇒ eq(e2,e1)) ∧
        (eq(e1,e2) ∧ eq(e2,e3) ⇒ eq(e1,e3))
  end

BOXES =
  structure
    use
      ELEM
    type
      Box
      Boxes = Box*
    value
      empty : Box
      add : ELEM`Elem × Box → Box
      isin : ELEM`Elem × Box → Bool
    axiom
      ∀ e1, e2 : ELEM`Elem . ∀ b : Box .
        isin(e1,empty) = false ∧
        isin(e1,add(e2,b)) = (ELEM`eq(e1,e2) ∨ isin(e1,b))
    value
      exists : ELEM`Elem × Boxes → Bool
    axiom
      ∀ e : ELEM`Elem . ∀ bs : Boxes .
        exists(e,bs) = (isin(e,hd(bs)) ∨ exists(e,tl(bs)))
  end

The *ELEM* structure specifies a type *Elem* and an equivalence relation *eq* on the elements of that type. An equivalence relation must be reflexive, symmetric and transitive. These properties are specified by 'algebraic equations'.

The *BOXES* structure specifies boxes of these elements (a box could for example be represented as a set, a bag or a list) and sequences of such boxes. Note the mixture of sorts (*Box*) and type equations (*Boxes*). Note also how one of the functions (*isin*) is specified in an algebraic style, while the specification of the other (*exists*) looks more like what is usually called a definition.

6.1.3 Semantic characteristics

RSL has, among others, the following semantic characteristics.

- The denotation of a specification is the denotation of the main structure, which is the set of models satisfying the axioms of the main structure and the structures used transitively by the main structure.

- Name clashes introduced by combining structures (by use clauses) are avoided by prefixing entities from imported structures.

- Types can be given as sorts (without a defining equation) as well as with a defining equation. Sorts are defined indirectly through the functions defined over them.

- A value is defined by a signature and possibly one or more axioms.

- Since recursive function definitions are just special axioms, we don't find least fixed points for these. A recursive function definition may thus have more than one solution (fixed point).

- The logic for interpreting an axiom in a model is a two valued logic with existential equality.

6.2 Semantic domains

The denotation of a specification is a set of models, where a model is a mapping from identifiers to components:

$$\text{Model} = \text{Id} \xrightarrow{\hspace{0.3em}\sim\hspace{0.3em}} \text{Component}$$

A component can be of one of four kinds depending on whether the identifier represents a type, a value, an operation or a process:

$$\text{Component} = \text{Carrier} \mid \text{Value} \mid \text{Operation} \mid \text{Process}$$

The domains *Carrier*, *Value*, *Operation* and *Process* will be elaborated in succeeding sections.

In obtaining the denotation of a specification consisting of a structure definition list and the name of a main structure, the first step is to evaluate the structure definition list to give a set of environments. Each environment maps each structure name to a model:

$$\text{Env} = \text{Id} \xrightarrow{\hspace{0.3em}\sim\hspace{0.3em}} \text{Model}$$

6.3 Semantic functions

The semantics of RSL is given in a denotational style where semantic functions map syntactic objects into semantic (mathematical) objects. Each semantic function is defined by a signature and a defining equation.

The semantics of a specification is as follows:

$$\text{Spec} : \text{spec} \rightarrow \text{Model-set}$$

$$
\begin{aligned}
&\text{Spec}[\![\text{id } \textbf{where } \text{struc-def-list}]\!] = \\
&\quad \textbf{let } \text{envs} = \{\text{env} : \text{Env} \mid \text{Struc-Def-List}[\![\text{struc-def-list}]\!]\text{env}\} \textbf{ in} \\
&\quad \{\text{env(id)} \mid \text{env} \in \text{envs}\}
\end{aligned}
$$

The first step in constructing the denotation of a specification is to obtain all environments that satisfy the structure definition list. This is perhaps an untraditional way to regard 'declarations' when comparing with programming language semantics, where a declaration usually denotes some function taking an environment and giving a new environment. In our approach, which is inspired by [Monahan85], a declaration denotes a function that takes an environment and gives a Boolean which is true if and only if the environment satisfies the declaration.

Having obtained the set of environments, a new set of all models denoted by the main structure name in each environment is returned.

The semantics of a structure definition list is just the conjunction of the semantics of the structure definitions in it:

Struc−Def−List : struc−def−list → Env → **Bool**

Struc−Def−List[|struc−def|]env =
    Struc−Def[|struc−def|]env

Struc−Def−List[|struc−def struc−def−list|]env =
    Struc−Def[|struc−def|]env ∧
    Struc−Def−List[|struc−def−list|]env

In the semantics of a structure definition, it should be noted that the structure expression denotes a set of models in the given environment, and that the structure identifier on the left hand side in that environment is supposed to denote one of these models:

Struc−Def : struc−def → Env → **Bool**

Struc−Def[|id = struc|]env =
    env(id) ∈ Struc[|struc|]env

One could say that the equality sign in the syntax is misleading syntax, since it really means 'belongs to'.

In the semantics of a structure expression, observe the same view on declarations (here *def-list*) as seen above for *struc-def-list*: a definition (whether it is a structure import, a type definition, a value signature or an axiom) denotes a function that takes a model and gives a Boolean which is true if and only if the model satisfies the definition:

Struc : struc → Env → Model−set

Struc[|**structure** def−list **end**|]env =
    let ms = {m : Model | Def−List[|def−list|]env m} **in**
    let new−concrete−types = New−Concrete−Types[|def−list|] **in**
    find−least−fixed−points(ms,new−concrete−types)

In the first line all models satisfying the definitions are obtained. This would be the result, if we were not to find least fixed points for type equations. The next two lines are concerned with exactly this. First the names of those newly introduced types which have been defined by equations are selected. An auxiliary function then throws those models away that do not represent least fixed points.

The semantics of a definition list is the conjunction of the semantics of the definitions it contains:

Def−List : def−list → Env → Model → **Bool**

Def−List[|def|]env m =
  Def[|def|]env m

Def−List[|def def−list|]env m =
  Def[|def|]env m ∧
  Def−List[|def−list|]env m

Definitions have the following semantics:

Def : def → Env → Model → **Bool**

Def[|**use** id|]env m =
  prefix(id,env(id)) ⊆ m

Def[|**type** id|]env m =
  m(id) ∈ Carrier

Def[|**type** id = type|]env m =
  m(id) = Type[|type|]m

Def[|**value** id : type|]env m =
  m(id) ∈ Type[|type|]m

Def[|**axiom** exp|]env m =
  Exp[|exp|]m = <u>true</u>

Note that the environment is only used for giving semantics to use clauses. A sort is just required to denote some arbitrary carrier in our type universe (section 6.5). A type equation must be satisfied in the obvious way. Note that least fixed points for type equations are found in *Struc* above. An axiom is just a Boolean expression.

The following auxiliary function prefixes all names in a model which have not already been prefixed:

prefix : Id × Model → Model

prefix(id,m) =
  m + [id`x → m(x) | x ∈ **dom**(m) ∧ not−prefixed(x)]

Avoiding prefixing already prefixed names implies that the prefix of an entity is always just the name of its defining structure. This principle makes sharing of one structure between several structures possible. Note, however, that RSL allows for copying of structures also, and in this case entities may get longer prefixes.

The following functions are only defined here by their signature:

Type : type → Model → Carrier
Exp : exp → Model → Value
New−Concrete−Types : def−list → Id−set
find−least−fixed−points : Model−set × Id−set → Model−set
not−prefixed : Id → **Bool**

6.4   Semantics of example

In this section we illustrate the semantics of the example from section 6.1.2. We do not show the semantics of the entire specification, but rather the last part of it, viz the sequence of structure definitions. In the semantic functions this point is reached in the function *Spec*:

Spec[|id **where** struc−def−list|] =
   let envs = {env : Env | Struc−Def−List[|struc−def−list|]env} **in**
   {env(id) | env ∈ envs}

where *envs* is created. It is *envs* we show in the following denotation.

envs maps structure names (here *ELEM* and *BOXES*) to possible models. There is one environment for each possible choice of combination of models for the structures in the *struc−def−list*. Here we have only shown one of the environments, one where the type *Elem* is bound to the natural numbers.

Another choice that is specific for the shown environment is the representation of the abstract type *Box*. *Box* is bound to a function domain (a function being a set of pairs) mapping elements from *Elem* (which are natural numbers in this environment) to a natural number saying how many times the element occurs in the box. If the element does not occur in a box, however, it is not mapped into 0, but absent from the domain of the function representing the box. The first element shown in *Box* is the box containing two 0'es and a 1. Many other representations could have been chosen, as long as they fulfil the axioms. These other choices are present in other environments in *envs*.

There is a difference for *Boxes* which is constructed explicitly. Its representation is fixed as a list of whatever the representation of *Box* elements are.

Note, how the elements from *ELEM* are prefixed with their structure name when imported into *BOXES*, in order to resolve possible name clashes.

```
envs =
  { ...,
    [ELEM →
       [Elem → {0,1,2,...},
       eq → {(0,0),(1,1),(2,2),...}
       ],
    BOXES →
       [ELEM`Elem → {0,1,2,...},
       ELEM`eq → {(0,0),(1,1),(2,2),...},
       Box → {{(0,2),(1,1)},...},
       Boxes → {< >, <{(0,2),(1,1)}>,...},
       empty → { },
       add → {((5,{ }),{(5,1)}),...},
       isin → {((5,{(5,1)}),true ),...},
       exists → {((5,< >),false ),...}
       ]
    ],
    ...
  }
```

6.5   Semantics of types

Since we do not find least fixed-points of recursive definitions of values, but are happy with the presence in the models of all values satisfying the axioms, we need not order values according to content of information, and types need not be cpo's. They are just sets.

Types are different in this respect. We wish that (recursive) type definitions have unique solutions, apart from the part that depends on abstract types (which range over the whole type universe). We have ordered types according to size in a subset ordering. Some type operators are continuous with respect to that ordering, others are not. We allow recursive type definitions with recursion through the continuous type operators, but not through the non-continuous ones. The following type operators are continuous:

- Cartesian product,

- Finite subsets (-finset),

- Finite lists (*),

- Finite, non-empty lists ($^+$),

- Finite functions ($\xrightarrow{f}$),

- Union type (|| ||),

- Record type ({| |}),

- Optional (| |)

The type constructors for infinite lists, infinite subsets, total functions and partial functions are not continuous, and types must not be defined recursively through these operators. They can however be used in recursive type definitions if the recursion does not go through them, such as in this example.

> **type** T = T × (**Bool** → (**Bool−set**))

The following, however, is not legal.

> **type** T = T → **Bool**

The semantic domain corresponding to types is called *Carrier*. *Carrier* is thus the type universe. It is a set of sets of values, and its elements (the carriers) are ordered subsetwise. *Carrier* is closed under arbitrary applications of type operators and recursion through continuous type operators (i.e. under least upper bounds of chains).

6.6   Semantics of axioms

The denotation of an axiom is a model filter: it maps a model into either **true** or **false** according to whether the model satisfies the axiom or not. Axioms are logical expressions and we have the following semantic function:

> Def : def → Env → Model → **Bool**

> Def|| **axiom exp** ||env m =
>   Exp|| exp ||m = <u>true</u>

The environment is not essential here. It is used for other kinds of definitions (uses).

There is a problem with undefined expressions. In general expressions can be undefined in a model. For instance the expression 1/0 is undefined in every model, and the expression 1/x is undefined in models binding x to 0. The question is how to handle such expressions, and our solution (highly inspired by the PROSPECTRA approach [Breu88]) can be sketched in the following way.

1. All user defined functions are strict, so if a user defines a function f : **Int** $\rightarrow$ **Int** then the expression $f(1/0)$ is always undefined.

2. Predefined operators (like **hd**, **card** etc.) are all strict except **if-then-else**.

3. Boolean expressions are treated separately:

    (a) We imagine that every Boolean expression, b say, is understood as if the expression were $b =$ **true**. Together with the notion of equality explained in the next point this ensures that all Boolean expressions in effect evaluate to either **true** or **false**. This means that we can employ a two valued logic for axioms. They are never undefined.

    (b) We employ existential equality, so that the expression $x = y$ is **true** if both x and y are defined and equal. Otherwise the expression is **false**.

The example from section 6.1.2 illustrates some of the points behind the scheme. Consider the axiom for *exists*:

$\forall$ e : ELEM`Elem . $\forall$ bs : Boxes .
  exists(e,bs) = (isin(e,hd(bs)) $\vee$ exists(e,tl(bs)))

According to (3a) we should interpret this axiom as if '=true' was appended everywhere a Boolean expression occurs. It is only the innermost occurrences of '=true' that make a difference, so we can rewrite the axiom to the following:

$\forall$ e : ELEM`Elem . $\forall$ bs : Boxes .
  (exists(e,bs) = true) =
  ((isin(e,hd(bs)) = true) $\vee$ (exists(e,tl(bs)) = true))

Now, if bs is non-empty everything works as usual – the '=true' means nothing. If however, bs is the empty list $hd(bs)$ is undefined according to (2), and according to (1), so is $isin(e,hd(bs))$ for every e. With existential equality the expression $isin(e,hd(bs))$ = **true** then becomes **false**, according to (3b). So does $exists(e,tl(bs))$ = **true**, and, to make the axiom **true**, $exists(e,bs)$ must be either undefined or **false** for bs =<>. According to the signature of *exists* in the example, *exists* is a total function, so it can only be **false**. Thus, only models in which $exists(e, <>)$ is **false** for every e are accepted.

If one wants to allow the axiom for *exists*, then we think that the chosen interpretation is the desired one. However, one could get the feeling that the rather indirect way undefined expressions are treated here suggests a too 'clever' style of programming, where undefinedness is treated in a rather subtle manner.

6.7 Operations and processes

In this presentation we have concentrated on the applicative part of RSL for the sake of brevity. However, in RSL one can specify states, operations on states, and processes, possibly reading and writing states. Processes and operations are bound in models just like values. This is reflected in the semantic domain *Model* that maps names into components which include operations and processes.

The semantic domains for states, operations, and processes are as follows:

State = Id $\xrightarrow{f}$ Value

Operation = (State × Value) $\xrightarrow{\sim}$ (State × Value)

Processes are modeled by failure sets like in [Roscoe84]:

Process = (State × Value) $\xrightarrow{\sim}$ Failures × Termination

Failures = Failure−set

Failure = Trace × Refusal

Trace = Value*

Refusal = (Value × {tick})−set

Termination = Trace → (State−finset ∪ {div})

For the sake of brevity we do not elaborate on this, but refer to [Roscoe84].

6.8 Conclusion

We have presented a subset of the RAISE Specification Language, RSL, and illustrated its semantics. In order to keep the presentation to a reasonable size we have dealt only with the applicative aspects of RSL.

We have focused on points that we think characterize RSL or its semantics. These points include the structuring and naming scheme of RSL, the mixture of abstract types (sorts) and types specified by equations, the axiomatic style of defining values (in contrast to the 'definitional' style of VDM) implying that we do not find least fixed-points of recursive value definitions, and finally, the way in which we treat undefined expressions, using a two-valued logic for axioms together with existential equality.

7 The RAISE project

The RAISE project is being carried out by a consortium formed by:

Dansk Datamatik Center (DDC)
Lundtoftevej 1C
2800 Lyngby
Denmark

STC Technology Limited (STL)
London Road, Harlow
Essex CM17 9NA
Great Britain

Asea Brown Boveri A/S (ABB)
Ved Vesterport 6
1612 København V
Denmark

International Computer Limited (ICL)
ICL House, Putney
London SW15 1SW
Great Britain

Dansk Datamatik Center is the main contractor. The RAISE project is part of the ESPRIT programme (ESPRIT 315) partly funded by the Commission of the European Communities. The project has a size of 115 staff-years. The project was started 1 January 1985 and runs for five years.

The project is divided into two phases. Phase I involves 64 staff-years of effort over (roughly) the first three project years. Phase I is concerned with research and development of the method, language and prototype tools, while phase II is concerned with development of the final tools and training and technology transfer material. The industrial trial applications link the two phases. The trial applications will be carried out in the industrial environments of ICL and ABB. These trials ensure that RAISE meets the requirements of the software producing industry.

The project plan can be illustrated as follows:

	Phase I			*Phase II*	
	1985	1986	1987	1988	1989
Fundamental issues					
Method, language and tool specification					
Industrial trial					
Final tools and technology transfer					

The project is approaching the second year of phase II, and the definitions of the method and the language are undergoing the final revision. The industrial trial projects, based on the preliminary method, language, and tools, have been going on for some time now, and the feedback has been encouraging. The experience gained from these industrial trials has and will provide input to the final revision of method and language.

Acknowledgements

The work described here is the result of a collective effort by the RAISE project team.

References

[Bjørner82]
: Dines Bjørner and Cliff B. Jones. *Formal Specification and Software Development*. Prentice Hall International, 1982.

[Breu88]
: Michael Breu, Manfred Broy, Thomas Grünler, and Friederike Nickl. *PA^{mm}dA-S Semantics*. PROSPECTRA Study Note M.2.1.S1-SN-1.3, Universität Passau, Fakultät für Mathematik und Informatik, 1988.

[Burstall77]
: R.M. Burstall and J.A. Goguen. Putting theories together to make specifications. In *Proceedings, Fifth International Joint Conference on Artificial Intelligence. Cambridge, Mass.*, pages 1045–1058, 1977.

[Burstall80]
    R.M. Burstall and J.A. Goguen. The semantics of clear, a specification language. In *Proceedings, 1979 Copenhagen Winter School on Abstract Software Specifications. Lecture Notes In Computer Science, 86*, pages 292–332, Springer-Verlag, 1980.

[CIP85]
    The Munich CIP Group. *The Munich Project CIP, The Wide Spectrum Language CIP-L.* Volume 183 of *Lecture Notes in Computer Science*, Springer-Verlag, 1985.

[Dijkstra76]
    E.W. Dijkstra. *A Discipline of Programming.* Prentice-Hall International, 1976.

[Futatsugi85]
    K. Futatsugi, J.A. Goguen, J-P. Jouannaud, and J. Meseguer. Principles of obj2. In *Eleventh Annual ACM Symposium on Principles of Programming Languages*, Association for Computing Machinery, Inc., 1985.

[George88]
    C. W. George. *Practical aspects of development.* RAISE Report CWG/28/V4, STC Technology Limited, April 1988.

[Guttag85]
    J.V. Guttag, J.J. Horning, and J.M. Wing. *Larch in Five Easy Pieces.* Digital Systems Research Center, 1985. Report 5.

[Harper86]
    Robert Harper, David MacQueen, and Robin Milner. *Standard ML.* LFCS Report Series ECS-LFCS-86-2, Laboratory for Foundations of Computer Science, Department of Computer Science, University of Edinburgh, 1986.

[Hoare85]
    C.A.R. Hoare, editor. *Communicating Sequential Processes.* P-H Series in Computer Science, Prentice/Hall International, 1985.

[Inmos84]
    Inmos Ltd. *Occam Programming Manual.* Prentice/Hall International, 1984.

[Jones86]
    C.B. Jones. *Systematic Software Development Using VDM.* P-H Series in Computer Science, Prentice Hall International Ltd., 1986.

[Jørgensen88]
    Jesper Jørgensen, Steen Ulrik Palm, Palle Christensen, Peter Haff, Lars Wilkens Henriksen, and Peter Sestoft. *Preliminary Definition of the RAISE Specification Language.* RAISE Report JJ/14/V6, Dansk Datamatik Center, February 1988.

[Lamport86]
    Leslie Lamport. $\text{\LaTeX}$: *A Document Preparation System.* Addison–Wesley Publishing Company, 1986.

[Monahan85]
    Brian Monahan. A semantic definition of the stc vdm reference language. November 1985. Hand written notes.

[Prehn87]

Søren Prehn. From vdm to raise. In D. Bjørner and C. B. Jones, editors, *Proceedings of the VDM '87 Symposium, Lecture Notes in Computer Science 252*, pages 141 – 150, Springer-Verlag, March 1987.

[Reps87]

T.W. Reps and T. Teitelbaum. The synthesizer generator reference manual. Cornell University, Dept. of Computer Science, July 1987. Second Edition.

[Roscoe84]

A.W. Roscoe. Denotational semantics for Occam. In G. Winskel S.D Brookes, A. W. Roscoe, editor, *Seminar on Concurrency, Lecture Notes in Computer Science 197*, Springer-Verlag, July 1984.

[Wirth71]

N. Wirth. Program development by stepwise refinement. *Communications of the ACM*, (14):221 – 227, 1971.

CORRECTNESS PROOFS FOR META IV WRITTEN CODE GENERATOR
SPECIFICATIONS USING TERM REWRITING

Bettina and Karl-Heinz Buth
Institut für Informatik und Praktische Mathematik
Christian-Albrechts-Universität zu Kiel
Olshausenstraße 40-60
D-2300 Kiel 1

Abstract:

In recent years, computer scientists have become more and more convinced that verification is an important part of software development. We give an example for formal verification of "realistic" software: we show how to prove correctness of code generators that are developed within the compiler generating system CAT. Such code generators are large and involved programs specified in META IV. The proofs that are necessary become even larger and more involved, and to carry them out by hand seems to be an unfeasible task. Therefore automatic proof support is needed. We demonstrate that it is possible to give this support; we have written a proof support system which does essential parts of the proof. It is based on term rewriting and on specification by pre- and postconditions.

1. INTRODUCTION

Since the 1960's it is undisputed that verification of software is an essential part of software development, not only for software of theoretical interest but also for software that is practically used for industrial purposes. In recent years the employment of term rewriting methods in this field has been considered (cf. e.g. [Thatcher/Wagner/Wright 1981]), but up to now it has not been tried to a greater extent. The main obstacles are, on the one hand, the very high number of rewrite rules necessary, and on the other hand, that software usually is not given in an appropriate form.

In this paper, we want to demonstrate that term rewriting systems can be an effective support for the verification of large software systems, as in this case for the verification of code generators.

In the compiler generating system CAT, the essential part of a code generator is defined by a specification written in META IV. In the

main, such a specification is a system of recursive function definitions with one main function which is responsible for the translation
of single source instructions into target code. Each of these specification functions is equipped with a pre- and a postcondition describing
its characteristics. Proving the correctness of a code generator means
to prove its partial and total correctness. For partial correctness, we
use fixpoint induction; it turns out that it is sufficient to show that
each specification function is partially correct with respect to its
pre- and postcondition. Total correctness in addition demands that the
main function is defined for all wellformed source instructions.

For the proof of partial correctness, we have found it quite natural
to employ term rewriting. We transform the postcondition according to
certain laws (arithmetical and logical rules, semantics definitions for
source and target language and META IV, ...) using the information we
have about the function.

The proofs that arise this way can be carried out very systematically, and we succeeded in automating them by developing a proof support system. This system makes use of special term rewriting systems
for each code generator specification and organizes the proof according
to the requirements of fixpoint induction. The term rewriting systems
are conditional ones; furthermore, their rules are applied according to
a fixed order ("priority").

As an example, we use a code generator for the MC 68000 micro processor and a subset of PASCAL as target language (without functions and
procedures, *real* arithmetic and sets).

This paper is organized as follows:

Section 2 briefly describes the CAT system.

Section 3 contains descriptions of the specifications we have to deal
with, i.e. the language and machine specifications.

In section 4, we introduce our proof principles, and in
section 5, term rewriting aspects are discussed.

Section 6 contains a larger example of a proof with our system, and in
section 7, we briefly compare our system with other approaches.

2. THE CAT SYSTEM

The CAT compiler system has originally been designed to be a multi-
language multi-target system and is now used for compiler generation.
It has been developed by U. Schmidt and R. Völler at the University of

Kiel between 1980 and 1983. Here, we will only give a very brief survey of it; for details, cf. [Schmidt 1983], [Völler 1983], [Schmidt/Völler 1984], [Schmidt/Völler 1987].

The basic idea of the system is to compile a program of a high level imperative language in two separated steps. In the first step, the programs of the source language (e.g. PASCAL, C, BASIC) are compiled by language dependent "frontends" into a common intermediate language called **CAT** ("<u>C</u>ommon <u>A</u>bstract <u>T</u>ree Language"). In the second step, CAT programs are translated by machine dependent "backends" or code generators into the target language (assembler format, linker format, machine code, etc.). [In principle, functional languages could also be compiled in this way. But up to now, only imperative languages have been considered.]

In the following, we only consider the code generator. Hence, we start from a given CAT program and deal with its translation into the target language for a target machine M.

This phase is separated into several subphases: At first, declarations and higher level statements are evaluated (machine independent up to the memory structure of M). The result of this subphase are programs of another intermediate language called **CAL**$_{CAT}$. CAL ("<u>C</u>AT <u>A</u>ssembly <u>L</u>anguage") is a language scheme parameterized with a signature the programs of which consist only of assignments (of arbitrary complexity), conditional and unconditional jumps, and procedure and label statements. The signature of CAL$_{CAT}$ is derived from the source language CAT and is therefore mainly machine independent.

In the next phase, CAL$_{CAT}$ is translated into **CAL**$_M$, the signature of which is determined by the target machine M. At first, the machine independent CAL$_{CAT}$ operators are replaced by suitable machine dependent CAL$_M$ operators ("substitution"), and then the resulting complex CAL$_M$ expressions are split into sequences of simple CAL$_M$ expressions ("decomposition") that afterwards can be translated 1-1 into the target language. This 1-1 translation forms the third phase of code generation.

Summing up the structure of a compiler in the CAT system gives the following diagram:

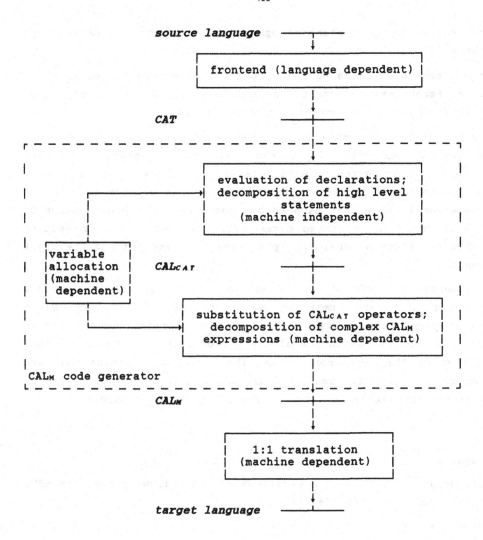

3. THE SPECIFICATIONS

In this section, we briefly describe the format of the specifications we have to consider in our proofs. We begin with a description of the two languages we have to deal with.

3.1 META IV'

META IV' is the subset of META IV that is used to specify the code generation algorithms. Actually, it is a very small subset. The language constructs that are allowed are
- conditional expressions,
- _let_ expressions,
- sequences, and
- terms (of arbitrary complexity).

Furthermore, we use two standard operators to denote (forward) jumps and labels.

Out of these constructs we build up a set of recursive function definitions. Parameters for these functions may only be of a basic type; especially, functional parameters are not allowed.

In order to keep the structure of the proof simple, we do not allow arbitrarily complex META IV' expressions. The essential additional restriction is that nested conditionals are not allowed. If such nestings do not occur, it is easy to split up functions written in META IV' into the several cases that have to be considered in a proof. Since it suffices to treat one of these cases at a time (cf. below in section 4.1), this restriction considerably reduces the overhead for the proof management.

The semantics of META IV' is defined in a denotational way. In order to cope with labels and jumps, we use a continuation semantics. Since the use of jumps is very restricted, fixpoint operators only occur in the definition of the semantics of the set of recursive functions, but not in that of the basic constructs. The semantic functions that are assigned to the primitive operators are defined to be strict. (This is important for the theoretical foundation of our proof method.)

3.2 CAL

3.2.1 Syntax

A CAL program consists of expressions of the following form (in META IV notation, cf. [Schmidt 1983]):

```
Expr      =   Te | Tv
Te        =   ( Op Mode Expr* )          "typed expression"
Op        =   QUOT
Tv        =   ( Val Mode )               "typed value"
Mode      =   ( Len Str )
Str       =   Subr_str | Array_str | ...
Subr_str ::   Lb Ub
Array_str::   Lb Ub Mode
Lb, Ub    =   INTG
Len       =   NAT₀
Val       =   Subr_val | Array_val | Ptr_val | ...
Subr_val =    INTG
Array_val=    Val*
```

```
Ptr_val  =    ( Memid NAT0 )
Memid    =    QUOT
```

Remarks

1) The quotations for the operators (Op) are selected according to the signature supplied. This also holds for the memory identifiers (Memid); the signature contains information about the memory structure of M.
   In general, the sets of operators of CAL_{CAT} and CAL_M are not disjoint.

2) We use the following abbreviations for the selector functions:
   s-m   for   *s-Mode*,
   s-ml   for   *s-Len*,
   s-e1   selects the first *Expr* argument of a *Te*,
   s-e2   the second *Expr* argument and so on.
   mk-exp0 is the constructor function for an object of type *Te* with 0 subtrees of type *Te*, *mk-exp1* that for objects with 1 such subtree and so on.
   Furthermore we abbreviate *s-ml (s-m (e))* by *s-1 (e)*.

3) Not all possible combinations of CAL operators yield a legal CAL expression. In order to keep the CAL syntax simple, these restrictions are not given in the syntax, but by *is-wellformed*-predicates that define the exact context conditions for each operator.

3.2.2 Semantics

In [Schmidt 1983], the semantics of a CAL expression is defined by a function *e_expr*, the type equation of which is
   type e_expr : Te $\Rightarrow$ Tv.
Hence, to each "typed expression" a "typed value" is assigned. During this evaluation, side effects on the memory state can occur (which is indicated by "$\Rightarrow$").

We express this function using the semantic functions that are used for the definition of the semantics of META IV'. For this, we have to state the semantics of all CAL operators.

For an example, let ρ be an environment and κ a continuation. $\mathcal{E}$ is the semantic function for expressions. Then the semantics of the CAL operator *ADDI* is defined as follows:

.1 $\mathcal{E}$ ⟦<u>mk-</u>exp2 (ADDI, mode, op₁, op₂)⟧ρκ

.2   = $\mathcal{E}$ ⟦op₁⟧ρ

.3   {λδ. $\mathcal{E}$ ⟦op₂⟧ρ

.4   {λε. ofl_test (<u>s-</u>val(δ) + <u>s-</u>val(ε), mode) κ}}

ofl_test is an auxiliary function that generates an overflow if necessary:

    ofl_test (*val*, *mode*) κ =

      <u>if</u> "*val* is representable in *mode*"

         <u>then</u> κ (<u>mk-</u>Tv (*val*, *mode*))

         <u>else</u> κ (overflow()).

An overflow is represented by the special *Tv*-object *overflow()* which is not further defined here.

Hence, the semantics of an *ADDI* expression is the following: First, the first operand is evaluated (.2), then the second (.3), and finally both values are added (.4). Result of the expression is either the sum or an overflow.(For a closer explanation of the notation, cf. [Stoy 1977].)

3.3 The Code Generator Specification

A special META IV' compiler (cf. [Schmidt 1983]) generates the code generator from a specification which consists of the following parts:

- the definition of the functions describing the substitution of CAL_CAT operators by CAL_M operators ("substitution functions"),
- the definition of the functions describing the decomposition of complex CAL_M expressions into well-formed CAL_M expressions ("*generate-wellformed*-functions" or "decomposition functions"),
- the definition of non-primitive predicates controlling substitution and decomposition,
- the type declaration of primitive META IV' operators.

In the following, we comprise the substitution and the decomposition functions under the notion "specification functions".

Example:

As an example for a specification function, we give part of the definition of the function *subst_addi*. It is part of our example specification and is used to substitute the CAL_CAT addition operator *ADDI* by appropriate CAL_M68 operators.

```
.1   subst_addi (e) =
.2    let e₁  = s-e1(e)
.3      , e₂  = s-e2(e)
.4      , m   = s-m(e)
.5      , len = maxi(s-l(e₁), s-l(e₂))
.6    in
.7     ( is_quick_pos (e₁)
.8        -> mk-exp2( ADDQ, s-m(e₂)
.9                  , e₁, mk_eq_int(e₂, s-l(e₂)) )
         ...
.10     , is_quick_neg (e₂)
.11        -> mk-exp2( SUBQ, s-m(e₁)
.12                  , c_neg(e₂), mk_eq_int(e₁, s-l(e₁)) )
         ...
.13     , (is_subrmode(s-m(e₁)) ∧ is_subrmode(s-m(e₂)))
.14        -> mk-exp2( ADD, set_ml(m, len)
.15                  , mk_eq_int(e₁, len)
.16                  , mk_eq_int(e₂, len) )

.17     , true
.18        -> wrong (8)
        )
.19  type : Te → Te
```

Remarks:

If one operand is a constant with a value between 1 and 8, the "add quick" operator may be used (.7-.9). The constant needs no further substitution, but this does not hold for the other operand as well. So, a recursive call of the substitution functions is necessary; here, it is hidden in the call of the function *mk_eq_int*. This call has the second effect that the "length" (size) of the argument is not changed by the substitution.

Similar operations take place, if one operand is a constant with a value between −8 and −1. In this case, "subtract quick" may be used. The constant only has to be negated for this purpose (.10 −.12). In the general case, the standard addition operator "add" is used (.13-.16). Here, both operands have to be substituted further. The last clause is the error clause (.17-.18).

3.4 **The Machine Specification**

By "machine specification" we mean:

1. The description of the context conditions for each CAL_M operator (i. e. the main part of the syntax description for CAL_M); these are expressed in the so called *is-well-formed*-predicates.

2. The definition of the semantics of the CAL_M operators.

Since the syntax of CAL given in section 2.2.1 is very simple, and since the semantics of a CAL expression entirely depends upon the operators contained, the "machine specification" is nothing but the complete definition of CAL_M.

3.4.1 The *is-well-formed*-Predicates

For most of the CAL_M operators, the statement of the context conditions is very simple, since they are directly derived from certain machine operators (cf. the example in section 3.1.3: the conditions for *ADDQ*). For these operators, the allowed formats of their operands can be found in a processor description of the target machine M.

But this is different for those operators that do not directly represent a machine operator. Here, we have a certain freedom how to define the *well-formed*-conditions. They will mainly depend on the actual implementation of the system, for instance on the structure of the runtime library. Examples for such operators are all those that are translated into calls of runtime system routines, e.g. the program entry and exit operators (*MGLBENTRY* and *MEXIT*), operators for arithmetical operations not available on M (like operators for *real* arithmetic on the MC 68000), and so on.

Since code generation is split into two phases (substitution and decomposition), it is reasonable to specify *well-formed*-conditions for both phases (otherwise it seems hard to prove the correctness of the substitution phase). Since only expressions are substituted and not whole instructions, a predicate for wellformed expressions is sufficient.

3.4.2 The Definition of the Semantics

The definition of the semantics for those operators representing certain machine operators is as simple as the definition of the *well-formed*-conditions.

For the other operators there are two possible ways of definition:

- Either their semantics is expressed by the composition of the semantics of existing machine operators,
- or, if this is not possible or not reasonable, their semantics is expressed in terms of "primitive" semantic functions (an example for this way of definition is given in section 3.2.2 for the operator *ADDI* using the primitive function *ofl_test*). For the correctness proof, these functions only need to be specified by rules that are part of the term rewriting systems used.

4. THE PROOF

4.1 The Theoretical Background

The specification functions form a recursive program P_{CS} given by a set of equations

$$f_1(x_{11},\ldots,x_{1,n(1)}) \Leftarrow term_1[x_{11},\ldots,x_{1,n(1)},f_1,\ldots,f_m]$$

$$\cdot$$
$$\cdot$$
$$\cdot$$

$$f_m(x_{m1},\ldots,x_{m,n(m)}) \Leftarrow term_m[x_{m1},\ldots,x_{m,n(m)},f_1,\ldots,f_m],$$

where, for $i=1,\ldots,m$, $term_i[\ldots]$ denotes some META IV' expression that is built up using the constructs described in section 3, the formal parameters of f_i, and calls of the functions $f_1,\ldots,f_m$.

Here, we want to prove the partial correctness of P_{CS} (with respect to certain pre- and postconditions). Termination (for total correctness) must be proved by other techniques than term rewriting (cf. [Buth /Wenzel 1987]).

Each proof for a recursive program makes use of invariant properties of the functions included. But since there is no general algorithm that can compute all necessary invariants all by itself, at least some of them have to be stated beforehand as an input to the proof. To be on the safe side, we demand that each specification function must be equipped with a pre- and a postcondition. Proving the correctness of P_{CS} then means to prove it with respect to the pre- and postconditions of the main function f_N.

For this proof we want to employ Scott's "Fixpoint Induction Principle". But we cannot do so without some preceding considerations, because the recursive programs to which this proof method is applied in literature are purely functional programs (cf. [Manna 1974], [Loeckx/ Sieber/Stansifer 1984]), which is a property P_{CS} does not possess. Each decomposition function, for example, produces a string of CAL_M expressions; but this string is not the functional result: its construction is just a side effect.

Nevertheless, however, we do use Fixpoint Induction; we construct a program equivalent to Pcs named Pcs' which possesses the property of functionality. For the transformation from Pcs into Pcs', we utilize the fact that the evaluation order in META IV' is fixed. All expressions are evaluated form left to right and from inside to outside (the latter is a result of the *call by value* strategy). So we know about the order in which the side effects arise. The transformation principle is quite simple:

We introduce a new "state" domain; then to each parameter list an additional state parameter is added, and each function is made to yield not its "normal" result *res* but a pair consisting of *res* and the state that results from executing the function. Since, in our case, we can express all possible side effects of a function f in Pcs by changes of the "state" component of the corresponding function f' in Pcs', Pcs and Pcs' are semantically equivalent.

For our proof, we need to know about the semantics of Pcs (or Pcs', equivalently). It turns out that a denotational definition is most suitable for this purpose. So, let I be the standard interpretation for the signature of META IV'. Then the semantics of Pcs' is defined by the least fixpoint $\mu\tau$ of the semantic functional

$$\tau = (\tau_1, \ldots, \tau_m)$$

associated with Pcs' and I (employing *call by value* parameter passing).

For each $i \in \{1, \ldots, m\}$, τ_i computes the semantics of the "body" of f_i' from the semantics of the META IV' constructs occurring inside and from the semantics of $(f_1', \ldots, f_m')$. Let S be the flat cpo corresponding to the domain of "states". There exist flat cpo's

$$D_{11}, \ldots, D_{1,n(1)}, E_1,$$

such that

$$\tau_1 : [D_{11} \times \ldots \times D_{1,n(1)} \times S \to (E_1 \times S)] \times \ldots \times$$
$$[D_{m1} \times \ldots \times D_{m,n(m)} \times S \to (E_m \times S)] \to$$
$$[D_{11} \times \ldots \times D_{1,n(1)} \times S \to (E_1 \times S)].$$

With

$$F_i =_{df} [D_{11} \times \ldots \times D_{1,n(1)} \times S \to (E_1 \times S)], \quad i=1,\ldots,m, \text{ and}$$
$$F =_{df} F_1 \times \ldots \times F_m,$$

we have $\tau_i : F \to F_i$, $i=1,\ldots,m$, and $\tau : F \to F$.

Now let for each function f_i, $i=1,\ldots,m$, and for each $x_i \in D_{11} \times \ldots \times D_{1,n(1)} \times S$ $pre_i[x_i]$ and $post_i[x_i, f_i(x_i)]$ denote the given pre- and post-conditions for this function. We assume that all these predicates are META IV' expressions of type BOOL.

The pre- and postconditions for the functions f_i', i=1,...,m, from P_{cs}' (pre_i' and $post_i$') can be derived from the corresponding conditions for f_i quite easily. The precondition pre_i' is exactly the same as pre_i (or possibly extended by a condition demanding that the state parameter is "legal"). The postcondition $post_i$ normally contains two parts: a "syntactical" one concerning the functional result of f_i and a condition concerning the semantics of f_i. Both parts can be adopted directly for $post_i$' (only that the syntactical part has to reference the "non-state" part of the result of f_i'). As an additional condition we only need the demand that the state part of the result of f_i' is "legal". This especially means that all CAL_M expressions generated inside of f_i' and appended to the part of the state representing the code file meet the corresponding *wellformed*-conditions.

Given all these predicates, we have to prove that the following claim holds for the least fixpoint $\mu\tau$ of τ:

$$P(\mu\tau) \qquad\qquad (4.1)$$

where

$$P(g) =_{df} \bigwedge_{i=1,\ldots,m} \forall x_i \in D_{i\,1} \times \ldots \times D_{i,n(i)} \times S:$$
$$def(x_i) \wedge def(g_i(x_i)) \Rightarrow_s$$
$$(pre_i'[x_i] \Rightarrow_s post_i'[x_i,g_i(x_i)])$$

for $g = (g_1,\ldots,g_m) \in F$,

and def(x) holds iff x is not $\bot$. $\Rightarrow_s$ is the sequential implication operation:

$a \Rightarrow_s b \Leftrightarrow_{df}$ **if** a **then** b **else** true **fi**.

[In words: If "proper" arguments are supplied to a function g_i and if its result is "defined" ($\neq\bot$), the result satisfies the postcondition of g_i, if the precondition is valid for the arguments. This claim means partial correctness of g_i with respect to pre_i' and $post_i$'.]

Note that P is a two-valued predicate (P: F → BOOL), even though pre_i' and $post_i$' are three-valued, i.e. yielding values out of $BOOL^+$ (the flat cpo of the Booleans).

We want to use fixpoint induction to prove properties of $\mu\tau$. As prerequisite for this, we first need the following lemmata (for the proofs, cf. [Buth/Wenzel 1987]):

Lemma 1

The semantic functional τ associated with our concrete P_{cs}' and I is continuous.

Lemma 2

P is an admissible predicate, i.e. for every chain C in F the following condition holds:

$(\forall f \epsilon C: P(f)) \implies P(\sqcup C)$

(The proof of Lemma 2 mainly depends on the flatness of our finite number of domains.)

Now we are in a position to use the

Fixpoint Induction Principle (cf. [Loeckx/Sieber/Stansifer 1984])

Let $(D, \sqsubseteq)$ be a cpo, $h\epsilon[D \rightarrow D]$ a continuous function and $\tau:D \rightarrow BOOL$ an
admissible predicate. If

(a) *Induction basis* $\tau(\bot)$ holds and

(b) *Induction step* $\forall d \epsilon D: \tau(d)$ implies $\tau(h(d))$,

then $\tau(\mu h)$ holds.

In our case, we have $D = F$, $h = \tau$, and $\tau = P$.

In the <u>induction basis</u>, we have to consider $P(\bot_F)$. Since
$def(\bot_{F i}(x_i))$ is always <u>false</u> and $\implies_s$ is sequential, $P(\bot_F)$ holds
trivially.

In the <u>induction step</u>, we have as induction hypothesis $P(g)$, where
$g = (g_1, \ldots, g_m) \epsilon F$, and we have to prove $P(\tau(g))$.

This means that for $i=1, \ldots, m$ we have to show that
$\forall x_i \epsilon D_{i\,1} \times \ldots \times D_{i,\,n(i)} \times S: def(x_i) \wedge def(\tau_i(g)(x_i)) \implies_s$

$\qquad\qquad\qquad (pre_i{}'[x_i] \implies_s post_i{}'[x_i, \tau_i(g)(x_i)])$ (4.2)

Now we assume that all prerequisites of (4.2) are valid; so we have
to show

$post_i{}'[x_i, \tau_i(g)(x_i)] = $ <u>true</u>. (4.3)

$\tau_i(g)$ is represented by $term_i{}'$, the converted (side effect free) version of $term_i$ which is a conditional expression. The possible values of
$\tau_i(g)(x_i)$ correspond to the possible leaves of this expression. In
order to prove (4.3), all these values have to be examined in consideration of the conditions that lead to the corresponding leaf of
$term_i{}'$. If calls of a function $f_j{}'$ occur inside these conditions or
inside this leaf, we have to make use of the induction hypothesis for
the corresponding (semantic) function g_j. If we want to use that the
postcondition holds for this function, we first have to show the
appropriate prerequisites, i.e. the corresponding precondition and the
definedness of the arguments and the result. Since the leaf has actually been reached and since all language constructs correspond to strict

semantic functions (except for the conditional which does not occur inside leaf or condition), the definedness follows from the assumption $def(\tau_1(g)(x_1))$. So it only remains to show the validity of the preconditions for all recursive calls in order to be allowed to use the postconditions for the proof of (4.3). Since it is easy to convert $post_1'$ into $post_1$, it suffices to consider P_{CS}; the explicit construction of P_{CS}' is not necessary.

4.2 Summary of the Proofs Necessary

In order to prove the partial correctness of the code generator specification, the following proofs have to be carried out:

1) The proof of the correctness of the specification functions with respect to their pre- and postconditions;

2) The proof of the correctness of the register management. The register management differs from the "normal" memory management in so far as only a small number of registers is available, some of which may furthermore be reserved for special purposes. Hence, it cannot be assumed that each call of an allocation function for these registers yields a new cell; a register may only be allocated, if its old contents are not needed any more.

3) The proof of the termination of the code generation algorithm, i.e. the proof that the main function is defined for all proper CAL_{CAT} expressions.

Our proof support system uses term rewriting methods for the proofs of 1). It does not yet handle 2) and 3); for these proofs, other methods are necessary (for first ideas, cf. [Buth/Wenzel 1987]).

4.3 The Input for the Proof

For the proof of the correctness of the codegenerator specification we need:

1) the specification itself;

2) the pre- and postconditions for all specification functions;

3) the *well-formed*-conditions for CAL:
   - *is_wf_operation*$_{CAT}$ (for CAL_{CAT});
   - *is_wf_expr_sub*$_M$ (for CAL_M expressions after the substitution) and
   - *is_wf_operation*$_M$ (for the "real" CAL_M);

4) the semantics definition of CAL and of META IV';

5) the specification of the primitive operators (like selector, constructor and arithmetical operators) by rules defining their characteristic properties (expressed by pre- and postconditions).

Our example specification for the MC 68000 and a restricted source language has a size of about 3200 lines of META IV' code. For our proof, we needed additional specifications (points 2 to 5) of about 2800 lines. Of these, one third is machine independent (like the definition of CAL$_{CAT}$ and META IV') and thus has to be written only once for all code generator proofs.

4.4 The Organization of the Proof

As said before (cf. section 3.1), the specification functions mainly consist of one conditional (possibly with a preceding *let*-part). The proof for each such function proceeds clause by clause: Let *fct* be a specification function and *k* = *cond* -> *body* the actual clause. If *fct* does not contain a conditional, *cond* is supposed to be true; the transformation of *if..then..else* into a conditional is obvious. (Therefore, every function can be considered as a conditional.)

Let *pre_fct* and *post_fct* denote the pre- and postcondition for *fct*. Then we have to prove the following for *k*:

1. If a call of a specification function occurs inside *body*, the corresponding precondition holds.
2. If *pre_fct* holds, *fct* satisfies *post_fct*.

As an additional assumption we have the negations of all clauses of *fct* preceding *k* and the condition *cond* of *k* itself. The induction hypothesis is the validity of the postconditions for all calls of specification functions inside of *body*.

If a call of a non-primitive predicate *pred* occurs inside a supposition or inside an assertion, it is substituted by the body of that clause of *pred* that is valid under the actual supposition if this clause can be determined. Such substitutions are carried out as often as possible; the process terminates because the non-primitive predicates form a terminating system of recursive function definitions (which, of course, is a fact that has to be proved!).

After all substitutions have taken place, the assertions are transformed using the conditional term rewriting systems described in the next section. The rewriting process stops, if true is reached (success) or if no more rule can be applied (failure).

5. TERM REWRITING AND ITS APPLICATION IN OUR SPECIAL CASE

5.1 Definitions

Before we describe the rewriting system that we actually use, we informally introduce some basic notions (for more details, cf. [Kaplan 1986]).

Σ stands for a finite set of ranked symbols, X for an enumerable set of variables. $T(\Sigma, X)$ is the set of terms built out of elements of Σ and X in the usual way. We take for granted the notions of **occurrences** in terms and of **substitutions**. $t|_w$ is the subterm of a term t starting at occurrence w, $t[w \leftarrow u]$ is t where $t|_w$ is replaced by u.

A **conditional term rewriting system** (CTRS for short) is a finite set R of triples (β, λ, ρ), where $\lambda, \rho \epsilon T(\Sigma, X)$ and $\beta = (u_1 = v_1 \wedge \ldots \wedge u_n = v_n)$, $u_i, v_i \epsilon T(\Sigma, X)$, $n \epsilon N$, or $\beta = \underline{true}$. The variables occurring inside β and ρ have to form a subset of the set of variables occurring inside λ. A triple of this kind is interpreted as a conditional rewrite rule: $\beta \implies \lambda \rightarrow \rho$.

The **rewriting relation** is defined as the smallest relation $\rightarrow_R$ on $T(\Sigma, X)$ that satisfies the following condition:

$t \rightarrow_R t' \iff$ There exists a $(\beta, \lambda, \rho) \epsilon R$, an occurrence w in t and a substitution σ such that $t|_w = \lambda\sigma$, $t' = t[w \leftarrow \rho\sigma]$ and $\beta\sigma \rightarrow_R *\underline{true}$.

R is **finitely terminating** $\iff_{df}$ There exists no infinite sequence $t_1 \rightarrow_R t_2 \rightarrow_R \ldots$ for any $t_1 \epsilon T(\Sigma, X)$.

R is **confluent** $\iff_{df}$

$$\forall t_1, t_2, t_3 \epsilon T(\Sigma, X): [t_1 \rightarrow_R *t_2 \wedge t_1 \rightarrow_R *t_3) \implies$$
$$\exists t_4 \epsilon T(\Sigma, X): (t_2 \rightarrow_R *t_4 \wedge t_3 \rightarrow_R *t_4)]$$

5.2 The Rewriting Systems Used

The rewriting systems we use are CTRS's in which the rules are ordered (CTRS's "with priorities"): If there are two rules applicable for a special term, that rule is chosen that comes first in the set of rules; the sets of rules are in fact lists of rules. The rules originate from
- the specifications of the primitive operators,
  e.g. _s-op (mk-expl (op, m, e)) → op;_
- the suppositions valid at present,
  e.g. _is_quick_pos (s-el (e)) → true;_
- general arithmetical and logical rules;
  e.g. _a - b → a + (-b), ¬ (¬e) → e;_
- the semantical definitions of META IV', CALᴄᴀᴛ and CALᴍ,

e.g. $\mathcal{E}$ $[e_1;e_2]\rho$ κ → $\mathcal{E}$ $[e_1]\rho$ $(\mathcal{E}$ $[e_2]\rho$ $\kappa)$ (the semantics definition for the META IV' sequence);
- the postconditions of the specification functions,
  e.g. $is\_wf\_expr\_sub_{N6B}$ $(subst\_addi$ $(e))$ → _true_.

5.2.1 The Ordering among the Rules

For most of the rules confluence holds, that is, the order in which they are applied does not affect the result. Thus, for each term there exists a unique normal form with respect to these rules (provided that this set of rules is finitely terminating), and there is no need for an ordering among these rules.

But there are two reasons for the introduction of an ordering:
1. There are rules for which confluence does not hold.
2. Some orders of application are more efficient than others.

Example for 1.:

We want to evaluate semantic expressions that virtually cannot be evaluated any further. For this we use a special "substitution rule":
  e $\{\lambda\varepsilon.e_1\}$ = e_1 $['e$ -> $\varepsilon]$. $\qquad$ (λ)

(Here, e may also be an expression like $\mathcal{E}[e']\rho$.)
' is a symbol that prevents its argument from being evaluated by the term rewriting process. $[.\to.]$ denotes a syntactical substitution.

Of course, this rule may only be applied if all other possible rules have been tried, especially, if no semantic definition is applicable. Otherwise, the other rules cannot be applied at all, since the argument e is not scheduled for evaluation after being passed on to the continuation. Therefore, the rule (λ) and the semantical definitions form a non-confluent set of rules.

Example for 2.:

The rules specifying the primitive selector functions should be the first to be applied in order to keep the terms as small as possible and to prevent the rewriting of terms that will disappear by selection anyhow.

5.2.2 Special Rules, Handling of Equations

Some laws that could be described by rules are handled separately. Among these are:
1) associative and commutative rules and
2) concrete evaluation of arithmetical and logical terms.

In most cases, the rules for 1) can be stated easily, but they should not be applied without special control, since otherwise it is possible that the system starts to loop. This problem could be handled with some extra precautions, but we want to keep our system as simple as possible, and therefore, we deal with these rules in a different way: these rules can only be applied to a term if no other rule is applicable, and they may only be applied once for each term. (Of course, this information has to be stored somehow; "ordinary" rewriting could hardly cope with this requirement.)

The rules for 2) can be stated only in theory. If we wanted to evaluate the sums of arbitrary pairs of integers in a purely symbolic way, we would need a rule for *plus(a,b)* for every possible value of *a* and *b*. Obviously, this is not possible, since it would mean to state an infinite (or at least very large) set of rules. This problem is avoided by simply adding *a* and *b*. [Of course, this means that we only prove correctness relative to the correctness of the implementation of arithmetics on the computer we use for our proof.]

All equations that appear in the supposition are transformed into an "equality normal form": For each of the corresponding equivalence classes one representative is chosen, and temporary rules are generated that replace each other element of the equivalence class by this special representative. Of course, the orientation of equations must not be reverted by this process.

5.3 Application of Term Rewriting

In section 4.4, we have listed the claims that have to be proved during the treatment of the single clauses of the specification functions. These claims are given as META IV' expressions of type BOOL. We may assume that only literals (primitive formulas) are negated. The treatment of conjunctions and disjunctions is straightforward and has nothing to do with term rewriting. But for the proof of the individual literals inside the claims, term rewriting is used.

We may assume that each literal is given in the form $a = b$ or $a \neq b$ (otherwise, it can be extended: *p(x)* can be written as *p(x)* = *true*). So, let a literal $a = b$ be given. Then the aim is to transform both sides of the equation until syntactically equal expressions are reached. In order to reach this aim, we use suitable CTRS's to generate the normal forms of *a* and *b*. (How to treat a literal $a \neq b$ is obvious.) So, except for the management of disjunctions and conjunctions, the goal of proving the partial correctness of our specification is replaced by a set of subgoals each of which is a term rewriting problem.

Since we do not have confluence for all of our rules (cf. section 5.2.1), we use more than one CTRS. For each of these, we assume confluence and finite termination. This means that we can avoid the problem of several different normal forms for one single term. For the automatic check of confluence and termination of the individual systems (which is not yet implemented), we do not take into account that the rules contained are ordered: for this purpose, our CTRS's are treated as usual.

Since environments, continuations, and states occur in the semantic definitions, these are higher order equations. This fact has two consequences:

1. The rewriting systems containing semantical rules do not quite fit into the theoretical framework of "ordinary" (first order) term rewriting as presented above. Especially, the result that confluence and finite termination together guarantee a unique normal form for each term cannot be adopted without some new considerations.

2. Since higher order logic is incomplete (cf. [Hermes 1978]), it is impossible to deduce all valid formulas using the calculus defined by our rewriting systems.

Both points lead to the result that there may be cases in which an assertion arising in the proof of a semantic postcondition cannot be proved. But up to now, it seems that one can cope with this theoretical problem in a practical way. If the system terminates (the automatic proof of which, as said before, is not yet implemented), one can check the result of the attempted proof manually and decide whether a real error in the specification has been detected or whether the system went wrong (e.g. because a rule is missing). It must be mentioned in this context that we consider all of our rewrite rules as correct. Therefore, we cannot obtain actually wrong results by rewriting.

6. EXAMPLE PROOFS

In this section, we demonstrate the use of our rewriting system in the proof of the correctness of two clauses of the specification function *subst_addi* that was defined above (in section 3.3).

Pre- and postcondition for this function read as follows:

```
.1  pre_subst_addi (e) =
.2    (is_wf_expr_cat (e) ∨ is_wf_expr_sub_m68 (e))
.3  type :  Te  →  BOOL

.4  post_subst_addi (e) =
.5    let e1 = subst_addi (e)
.6    in
.7     (is_wf_expr_sub_m68 (e1) ∧
.8      ( mode_cond (s-m (e), s-m (e1)) ∧
.9         is_eq (Ɛ ⟦e1⟧ρκ, Ɛ ⟦e⟧ρκ )))
.10 type :  Te  →  BOOL
```

The argument *e* must be a well-formed CAL$_{CAT}$ or substituted CAL$_M$ expression (.2). The result must be a well-formed substituted expression (.7); its mode may at most be changed in its length (.8), and the semantics must be the same as that of the argument (.9).

The auxiliary predicate *mode_cond* tests, whether the two modes that are its arguments have the same structure:

```
mode_cond (m1 , m2) =
  ( is_submode (m1)  -> is_submode (m2)
  , is_arraymode (m2) -> is_arraymode (m2)
  , ...
  )
type :  Mode  Mode  →  BOOL
```

Since *s_op (e) = ADDI*, and since *ADDI* is not a CAL$_{M68}$ operator, *is_wf_expr_sub_m68 (e)* is false; thus, *is_wf_expr_cat (e)* is known to be true, and it can be expanded to the following additional supposition:

```
(is_wf_expr_cat (s-e1 (e)) ∧ (is_wf_expr_cat (s-e2 (e)) ∧
 (is_submode (s-m (e)) ∧ (is_submode (s-m (s-e1 (e))) ∧
 (is_submode (s-m (s-e2 (e))) ∧ ... )))))
```

(The suppositions omitted are of no interest for this proof.)

6.1 Proof of the Third Clause of *subst_addi*

For the proof of each clause C_n, n≥2, the condition has to be extended by the conjunction of the negations of the conditions of the preceding clauses C_1,..., C_{n-1}, since these conditions are known to be false.

Thus, the complete third clause (the second that was completely specified above) is the following:

```
.1 C₃ = (is_quick_neg (s-e2 (e)) ∧
.2        (is_not (is_quick_pos (s-e1 (e))) ∧
.3         is_not (is_quick_pos (s-e2 (e))) ))
.4      -> mk-exp2 ( SUBQ, s-m (s-e1 (e))
.5                 , c_neg (s-e2 (e))
.6                 , mk_eq_int (s-e1 (e), s-1 (s-e1 (e))) )
```

If the second operand is a negative "quick"-constant (i.e. a constant with a value out of $\{-8,\ldots,-1\}$) (.1), the operation "sub quick" available on the processor can be used (.4). (Lines .2 and .3 are the negations of the conditions of the first two clauses.) The constant only has to be negated (.5). The first operand is substituted, and its length is not changed (.6); furthermore, the operands are reversed, since the first operand is subtracted from the second one by the machine operation which is reflected in the semantics of the corresponding CAL$_{M68}$ operator called *SUBQ*. The mode of the whole expression is chosen as the mode of the non-constant operand, since the result should not be of longer size than the longest operand (.4).

Let e' be the right-hand side of C_3. Then we have to show:

(is_wf_expr_sub_m68 (e') ∧   (6.1)

(mode_cond (s_m (e), s_m (e')) ∧   (6.2)

is_eq (ℭ ⟦e'⟧ρκ, ℭ ⟦e⟧ρκ)))   (6.3)

In the following, we will only demonstrate the proof of assertion (6.3); the other assertions are proved in very much the same way.

Assertion (6.3) says that the result of the substitution e' must be semantically equivalent to the original expression e. The variables ρ and κ occurring in (6.3) denote an environment and a continuation, respectively (hence, they denote functions, cf. section 5.3); all pre- and postconditions are interpreted as implicitly universally quantified.

Due to the deliberate choice of the mode mentioned above, semantical equivalence can only be proved up to the result mode. If the method is to be correct, this difference must be noticed (and in fact, it will be noticed, see below).

The first step in the proof is to rewrite the right-hand side of the desired equation. Since $s\text{-}op(e) = ADDI$, we get from the semantics definition for CAL$_{CAT}$:

$\mathcal{E}[e]\rho\kappa$

   $= \mathcal{E}[\underline{s}\text{-e1}(e)]\rho$

       $\{\lambda\varepsilon_1 .\ \mathcal{E}[\underline{s}\text{-e2}(e)]\rho$

              $\{\lambda\varepsilon_2 .\ \text{ofl\_test}(\ \underline{s}\text{-val}(\varepsilon_1) + \underline{s}\text{-val}(\varepsilon_2)$

                        $,\ \underline{s}\text{-m}(e)\ )\ \ \ \ \ \ \ \ \ \ \ \ \ \ \kappa\}\}$

.1 $= \text{ofl\_test}(\ \underline{s}\text{-val}('\mathcal{E}[\underline{s}\text{-e1}(e)]\rho) + \underline{s}\text{-val}('\mathcal{E}[\underline{s}\text{-e2}(e)]\rho)$

       $,\ \underline{s}\text{-m}(e))\ \ \ \ \ \ \ \ \ \ \ \ \ \ \ \ \ \kappa$

Now, no more rules are applicable. In step (.1), the "substitution rule" (λ) is applied twice (cf. section 5.2.1):

e $\{\lambda\varepsilon.\ e_1\}$ = $e_1\ ['e \to \varepsilon]$.   ($\lambda$)

For this rule, our strategy demands an evaluation order "from outside to inside", because for other strategies there are cases in which not all postconditions can be exploited, and thus the proof fails.

Next, the left-hand side of the desired equation is rewritten. From the definitions of the CAL$_{M68}$ semantics we get:

$\mathcal{E}[e']\rho\kappa$

.1 $= \mathcal{E}[\underline{mk}\text{-exp2}(\ \text{SUBQ},\ \underline{s}\text{-m}(\underline{s}\text{-e1}(e))$

              $,\ \text{c\_neg}(\underline{s}\text{-e2}(e))$

              $,\ \text{mk\_eq\_int}(\underline{s}\text{-e1}(e),\ \underline{s}\text{-ml}(\underline{s}\text{-m}(\underline{s}\text{-e1}(e)))))]\rho\kappa$

.2 $= \mathcal{E}[\text{c\_neg}(\underline{s}\text{-e2}(e))]\rho$

      $\{\lambda\varepsilon_1 .\ \mathcal{E}[\text{mk\_eq\_int}(...)]\rho$

             $\{\lambda\varepsilon_2 .\ \text{ofl\_test}(\ \underline{s}\text{-val}(\varepsilon_2) - \underline{s}\text{-val}(\varepsilon_1)$

                     $,\ \underline{s}\text{-m}(\underline{s}\text{-e1}(e))\ \ \ \ \ \ \ \ \ )\ \kappa\}\}$

.3 $= \mathcal{E}[\underline{s}\text{-e2}(e)]\rho$

      $\{\lambda\varepsilon.\ (\lambda\varepsilon_1 .\ ...)\ (\text{neg}(\varepsilon))\}$

.4 $= \mathcal{E}[\underline{s}\text{-e2}(e)]\rho$

      $\{\lambda\varepsilon.\ \mathcal{E}[\text{mk\_eq\_int}(...)]\rho$

             $\{\lambda\varepsilon_2 .\ \text{ofl\_test}(\ \underline{s}\text{-val}(\varepsilon_2) - \underline{s}\text{-val}(\text{neg}(\varepsilon))$

                    $,\ \underline{s}\text{-m}(\underline{s}\text{-e1}(e))\ \ \ \ \ \ \ \ \ \ )\ \kappa\}\}$

.5 $= \mathcal{E}[\underline{s}\text{-e2}(e)]\rho$

      $\{\lambda\varepsilon.\ \mathcal{E}[\underline{s}\text{-e1}(e)]\rho$

             $\{\lambda\varepsilon_4 .\ (\lambda\varepsilon_2 .\ ...)$

                $(\underline{mk}\text{-Tv}(\ \underline{s}\text{-val}(\varepsilon_4)$

                     $,\ \underline{mk}\text{-Mode}(\ \underline{s}\text{-str}(\underline{s}\text{-m}(\underline{s}\text{-e1}(e)))$

                          $,\ \text{len})))\ \ \ \ \ \ \ \ \ \ \}\}$

.6 $= \mathcal{E}[\underline{s}\text{-e2}(e)]\rho$

      $\{\lambda\varepsilon.\ \mathcal{E}[\underline{s}\text{-e1}(e)]\rho$

             $\{\lambda\varepsilon_4 .\ \text{ofl\_test}(\ \underline{s}\text{-val}(\underline{mk}\text{-Tv}(...)) - \underline{s}\text{-val}(\text{neg}(\varepsilon))$

                     $,\ \underline{s}\text{-m}(\underline{s}\text{-e1}(e))\ )\ \ \kappa\}\}$

```
.7  = Ɛ[s-e2(e)]ρ
        {λε. Ɛ[s-e1(e)]ρ
                {λε₄. ofl_test( s-val(mk-Tv(...)) +
                                  ( -(s-val(neg(ε))) )
                                , s-m(s-e1(e))          ) κ}}
.8  = Ɛ[s-e2(e)]ρ
        {λε. Ɛ[s-e1(e)]ρ
                {λε₄. ofl_test( s-val(ε₄) + ( -(s-val(neg(ε)))) 
                                , s-m(s-e1(e))          ) κ}}
.9  = Ɛ[s-e2(e)]ρ
        {λε. Ɛ[s-e1(e)]ρ
                {λε₄. ofl_test( s-val(ε₄) + s-val(ε)
                                , s-m(s-e1(e))          ) κ}}
.10 = ofl_test( s-val('Ɛ[s-e1(e)]ρ) + s-val('Ɛ[s-e2(e)]ρ)
                , s-m(s-e1(e)) )                                 κ
```

Used rules:

```
.1  s-l (e) = s-ml (s-m(e))                 (primitive)
.2  semantics definition for SUBQ
.3  is_intconst (e) ⟹
        Ɛ[c_neg(e)]ρκ = Ɛ[e]ρ {λε. κ(neg(ε))}
```

In order to apply this primitive rule, the condition has to be rewritten to __true__ first.

In our special case, we get:

```
    is_intconst (c_neg (s-e2 (e))) =
      is_intconst (s-e2 (e)) =
      true
```

by applying first the primitive rule

```
    is_intconst (c_neg (e)) = is_intconst (e)
```

and then the consequences of the premise

```
    is_quick_neg (s-e2(e)) ( = is_intconst (s-e2(e)) ∧ ... ).
```

```
.4  the application rule (β-reduction): (λε.e) (x) = e[x→ε]
.5  the postcondition of mk_eq_int
.6  the application rule
.7  a - b = a + (-b)                        (primitive)
```

Rules of this kind are used to build up a kind of "normal form" for arithmetical terms (such terms do not contain subtraction and division operators). This is useful to reduce the set of rules that are necessary.

```
.8  s-val (mk-Tv (val, mode)) = val         (primitive)
.9  - (s-val(neg(e))) = s-val(e)            (primitive)
.10 (λ) twice
```

Remark: *neg* is the negation operator for objects f type *Tv* and *c_neg* that for those of type *Te*.

Again, no more rules can be applied. The desired term has nearly been reached; the only difference are the modes that occur in *ofl_test* as second argument. But this is exactly what we required above: The different modes should be noticed.

What remains to be shown now is that the mode on the rewritten left-hand side is "reasonable"; it can be checked, for instance, if the result has at least the length of the longest operand. But this requirement is then part of the corresponding *wellformed*-predicate and is shown during the proof of this predicate. So, nothing remains to be proved here.

6.2 Proof of the Error Clause

The error clause is given as

true -> wrong (8),

where *wrong* is a function that stops compilation and writes out a message that depends on the error code which is its argument.

Of course, we cannot prove that the postcondition holds for an expression like *wrong (8)*. But we have to prove that there is no chance that this clause comes to execution whenever arguments are supplied to *subst_addi* that fulfil its precondition. This means that we must prove that the conjunction of the precondition and the negations of the selector conditions of all other clauses are a contradiction, i.e. equivalent to false.

In our case, among other things the precondition contains the condition *is_wf_expr_cat (e)*. Since *s-op (e) = ADDI*, this especially means

is_subrmode (s-m (s-e1 (e))) ∧ is_subrmode (s-m (s-e2 (e))).

But this is exactly the condition of the last clause before the error clause. The required result follows immediately. □

The proof can also be done by term rewriting, using the rule

p ∧ is_not (p) = false.

We only have to consider that several proofs are necessary, since the negation of the selector conditions is generally a disjunction, which means that several cases have to be proved separately.

7. RELATED WORK, CONCLUSION

In this paper, we demonstrated that with the support of term rewriting methods, it is possible to prove the partial correctness of even a large program. At the time being, the implementation of a prototype of the proof system is nearly accomplished. In order to keep the system portable, it is completely written in PASCAL (with only slight deviations from the standard).

There is still much work to be done: The proof system has to be applied to some other code generator specifications to make it more reliable; the proofs of total correctness and of the correctness of the register management need some extra considerations; the properties of term rewriting systems with conditional rules and priorities should be examined. (First ideas concerning these points can be found in [Buth/ Wenzel 1987].) Furthermore, investigations in the direction of higher order rewriting are necessary.

Another important task is to classify the type of programs for which proofs of this kind are possible. We suppose that modularity of the kind occurring in our specifications (which can be decomposed into the individual functions) is an essential condition because it facilitates the VDM-inspired employment of pre- and postconditions which is crucial for our method.

There already exist some proof support systems that make use of term rewriting, e.g. the *AFFIRM* system (cf. [Gerhart et al. 1980]) and the Boyer-Moore prover (cf. [Boyer/Moore 1979]). (For an overview, cf. [Lindsay 1988].) Furthermore, there exist "rewrite rule laboratories" like *REVE* (cf. [Lescanne 1983]) or *ASSPEGIQUE* (cf. [Kaplan 1987], [Bidoit/Choppy 1985]) that could probably be used as a basis for a proof support system. In comparison with our system, it seems that the other systems' approaches are too general to allow an easy adaption to our problem. But we have not had practical experiences with any of these system yet; there may be ways either to build a suitable environment on top of them or to "squeeze" our problem into their formalisms (which should be done as automatically as possible if the real problem is not to be buried under adaption problems). Experiments in this direction should be one of the next steps in our investigations.

Much work has already been done in the field of compiler proofs. But most of these approaches are quite different from ours. In one part of them, only correct transformations are performed until, finally, correct code is emitted; cf. e.g. [Mosses 1980] or [Polak 1981]. (In the latter work, the Hoare calculus built in to the Stanford Verifier (cf.

[Nelson/Oppen 1979]) is used to force the compiler program to be correct.) Another part of the approaches presents proofs that do not seem to be easily automated because of their mathematical style that does not only make use of simple term transformations (cf. e.g. [Milne/Strachey 1976], [Dybjer 1985], [Despeyroux 1986] and [Nielson/Nielson 1988]). The work of the ADJ group seems more related to ours, since the proofs carried out in [Thatcher/Wagner/Wright 1981] resemble more the use of rewrite rules. Here, the difference is the algebraic approach contrasted with our use of the λ-calculus.

To conclude, an experience we have made: Each time, our system could not prove an assertion that intuitively seemed to be correct, this incompleteness could be repaired either by stating additional rules or by correction of pre- or postconditions. That it to say that if only all knowledge about the specification is made explicit (in an appropriate way), all assertions that actually arise seem to be provable.

8. ACKNOWLEDGEMENTS

We would like to thank A. Bockmayr and U. Martin for important hints on the term rewriting aspects of our work, the referees for their critical comments, and especially H. Langmaack for various valuable discussions about the topics of this paper.

This work was supported in part by the *Deutsche Forschungsgemeinschaft* under grant La 426/8-1.

9. REFERENCES

[Bidoit/Choppy 1985]: Bidoit, M., Choppy, C., "Asspegique: an Integrated Environment for Algebraic Specifications", in: Ehrig, H. et al. (eds.), *Proceedings of the TAPSOFT '85 Conference*, pp. 246-260, LNCS 186, Springer, 1985

[Bjørner/Jones 1978]: Bjørner, D., Jones, C.B., *The Vienna Development Method: The Meta-Language*, LNCS 61, Springer, 1978

[Boyer/Moore 1979]: Boyer, R.S., Moore, J.S., *A Computational Logic*, Academic Press, 1979

[Buth/Wenzel 1987]: Buth, K.H., Wenzel, B., *Proving the Correctness of a Code Generator Specification Using Term Rewriting Techniques*, Bericht Nr. 8719, Institut für Informatik und Praktische Mathematik, Christian-Albrechts-Universität Kiel, 1987

[Despeyroux 1986]: Despeyroux, J., "Proof of Translation in Natural Semantics", in: *Proceedings Of The IEEE 1986 Symposium On Logic In Computer Science*, pp. 193-205, IEEE Computer Society Press, Washington, D.C., 1986

[Dybjer 1985]: Dybjer, D., "Using Domain Algebras to Prove the Correctness of a Compiler", in: Mehlhorn, K. (ed.), *Proceedings of the STACS 1985*, pp. 98-108, LNCS 182, Springer, 1985

[Floyd 1967]: Floyd, R.W., "Assigning meanings to programs", in: Schwartz, J.T. (ed.), *Mathematical Aspects of Computer Science*, pp. 19-32, *Proceedings of Symposia in Applied Mathematics*, 19, American Mathematical Society, Providence, R.I., 1967

[Gerhart et al. 1980]: Gerhart, S.L. et al., "An Overview of AFFIRM: a Specification and Verification System", in: Lavington, S. (ed.), *Information Processing '80*, pp. 343-347, North Holland, 1980

[Hoare 1969]: Hoare, C.A.R., "An Axiomatic Basis of Computer Programming", *Communications of the ACM*, 12 (10), pp. 576-583, 1969

[Huet/Oppen 1980]: Huet, G., Oppen, D.C., "Equations and Rewrite Rules: A Survey", in: Book, R.V. (ed.), *Formal Languages: Perspectives and Open Problems*, pp. 349-405, Academic Press, New York, 1980

[Kaplan 1986]: Kaplan, S., *Simplifying Conditional Term Rewriting Systems*, Report No. CS 86-08, Weizmann Institute of Science, Rehovot (Israel), 1986

[Kaplan 1987]: Kaplan, S., "A Compiler for Conditional Term Rewriting Systems", in: Lescanne, P. (ed.), *Proceedings of the Second International Conference on Rewriting Techniques and Applications*, pp. 25-41, LNCS 256, Springer, 1987

[Koch 1983]: Koch, J., *Der 16bit-Mikroprozessor SC 68000: Befehlsvorrat*, Boysen + Maasch, Hamburg, 1983

[Lescanne 1983]: Lescanne, P., "Computer experiments with the REVE term rewriting system generator", in: *Proceedings of the 10th ACM Symposium on Principles of Programming Languages*, Austin, Texas, pp. 99-108, 1983

[Lindsay 1988]: Lindsay, P.A., "A Survey of Mechanical Support for Formal Reasoning, *Software Engineering Journal*, 3 (1), pp. 3-27, Jan. 1988

[Loeckx/Sieber/Stansifer 1984]: Loeckx, J., Sieber, K., Stansifer, R.D., *The Foundations of Program Verification*, Teubner/Wiley, 1984

[Manna 1974]: Manna, Z., *Mathematical Theory of Computation*, McGraw-Hill, New York, 1974

[Milne/Strachey 1976]: Milne, R., Strachey, C., *A theory of programming language semantics*, Chapman and Hall, London, 1976

[Mosses 1980]: Mosses, P.D., "A constructive approach to compiler correctness", in: de Bakker, J.W., van Leeuwen, J. (eds.), *Proceedings of the ICALP 1980*, pp. 449-462, LNCS 85, Springer, 1980

[Nelson/Oppen 1979]: Nelson, G., Oppen, D.C., "Simplification by Cooperating Decision Procedures", *ACM Transactions on Programming Languages and Systems*, 1 (2), pp. 245-257, 1979

[Nielson/Nielson 1988]: Nielson, F., Nielson, H.R., "Two-level semantics and code generation", *Theoretical Computer Science*, 56, pp. 59-133, 1988

[Polak 1981]: Polak, W., *Compiler Specification and Verification*, LNCS 124, Springer, 1981

[Schmidt 1983]: Schmidt, U.: *Ein neuartiger, auf VDM basierender Codegenerator-Generator*, Dissertation, Christian-Albrechts-Universität Kiel, 1983

[Schmidt/Völler 1984]: Schmidt, U., Völler, R., "A Multi-Language Compiler System with Automatically Generated Codegenerators", in: *Proceedings of the SIGPLAN '84 Symposium on Compiler Construction*, pp. 202-212, *ACM SIGPLAN Notices*, 19 (6), 1984

[Schmidt/Völler 1987]: Schmidt, U., Völler, R., "Experience with VDM in Norsk Data", in: Bjørner, D. et al. (eds.): *VDM - A Formal Method at Work, Proceedings of the VDM-Europe Symposium 1987*, pp. 49-62, LNCS 252, Springer, 1987

[Stoy 1977]: Stoy, J.E., *Denotational Semantics: The Scott-Strachey Approach to Programming Language Theory*, MIT Press, 1977

[Thatcher/Wagner/Wright 1981]: Thatcher, J.W., Wagner, E.G., Wright, J.B., "More on advice on structuring compilers and proving them correct", *Theoretical Computer Science*, 15 (3), pp. 223-249, 1981

[Völler 1983]: Völler, R., *Entwicklung einer maschinenunabhängigen Zwischensprache und zugehöriger Übersetzeroberteile für ein Mehrsprachenübersetzersystem mit Hilfe von VDM*, Dissertation, Christian-Albrechts-Universität Kiel, 1983

Using VDM with Rely and Guarantee-Conditions
Experiences from a Real Project

J.C.P. Woodcock[*]
B. Dickinson[†]

Abstract

In his extension of *VDM*, Jones added a rely and a guarantee-condition to the usual pre and post-condition pair[1]. This extension to the technique permits the specification and development of concurrent, shared-variable systems. We describe the technique in detail by giving an example of a simple, but formal, development. A description of part of a substantial system development that has been carried out on a real project is given in the full version of this paper [Woodcock & Dickinson, 1988]. Conclusions are drawn, both about the rules for concurrent data reification, and about the efficacy of the technique and of the industrial use of formal methods in general.

1 Introduction

Over the past 10 years the Vienna Development Method *(VDM)* has been shown to be well suited to developing sequential software. Many projects have been developed using *VDM*, so that now we may rightly claim that for several software companies its use has become *routine*. Its success is due in part to its having a *development method*: there is the ability to *isolate* development steps and to tackle subproblems *separately*. Such a hierarchical development technique is vital if we are to develop anything but small systems; in particular, it is vital for industrial-scale software systems.

A challenge for computing scientists is to discover hierarchical development techniques for parallel programs (for a survey of the field, see [Barringer, 1985]). The problem here is that interference between parallel programs invalidates the assumption of isolation. By strictly partitioning the system state between processes and limiting interference to synchronisation and the passing

---

[*]Joint Atlas Rutherford-Pembroke Research Fellow, Oxford University Computing Laboratory, Programming Research Group, 8-11 Keble Road, Oxford OX1 3QD.

[†]Head of Software Methods Group, GEC Telecommunications Ltd, P.O.Box No.53, Telephone Works, Coventry CV3 1HJ.

[1]We shall call this extension of *VDM* with rely and guarantee-conditions, *VDM+*.

of messages, the problem becomes more tractable and mature bodies of theory have been developed, such as *A Calculus of Communicating Systems* [Milner, 1980] and *Communicating Sequential Processes* [Hoare 1985].

Often, however, a model of concurrency different from message passing is wanted, or is forced upon the designer by an existing system. It may be that the state is very large and must be shared between many different processes in the system. In such a case, we must look for a development technique that allows us to implement shared-variable parallel programs correctly from a system specification.

The approach taken in [Jones, 1981] is to continue to use *VDM*, but augmented in such a way that limits can be placed on the interference that can be caused by an operation on the state, and that it in turn can tolerate.

The first part of this report describes the technique by giving a small example: the development of a monitor which keeps track of the failure of components in an industrial process. The literature on *VDM*$^+$(namely [Jones, 1981, 1983a, 1983b, & Barringer 1985]) deals with operation decomposition, and in particular the decomposition of an operation into a collection of parallel operations. In this paper we deal with a more general development technique, where we would like to refine data types as well as decompose operations; sometimes we would even like to do both a data refinement and an operation decomposition in the same step.

First, a specification is given for the problem. Next, a design is produced and is proved correct against the specification in all but one respect. Although the example is a simple one, it reveals a problem with the rules for operation decomposition and data reification [2]. This leads us to examine another topic: the decomposition of atomic operations. We would like to be able to specify certain operations as atomic at an abstract level: nothing interferes with them, and either they haven't yet happened, or they have. Then we would like to decompose each abstract atomic operation into several concrete operations with the obvious property that nothing interferes with their combined effect: they really do amount to an abstract atomic event. We show that such a development is not admitted by *VDM*$^+$.

In the full version of this paper, there is a description of the specification and design of part of an operating system—a backing store interface. It comes from the development of the storage allocator for the operating system for System X telephone exchanges, being produced by GEC Telcommunications and Plessey. The intention is to show how a typical development proceeds rigorously, rather than formally.

Apart from the work by Jones [Jones, 1981, 1983a, & 1983b] and a description in [Barringer, 1985], no evaluation of *VDM*$^+$ has appeared in the literature. It is hoped that those interested in state-based concurrency will find this report of interest.

---

[2] As is revealed below, the design that we produce is intuitively right, but cannot be proved to be correct using the refinement rules. Therefore, we conclude that the rules are incomplete.

2 A Formal Development

2.1 Introduction

In this section we present the formal development of a very simple system, which in itself is of little real interest, rather it is the technique that we wish to explore. We describe the application of Jones' method for the development of interfering programs [Jones, 1981], where operations interfere through sharing parts of a common state. Although an implementor can't assume that an operation will run in isolation, limits can be imposed on the extent of any interference. This is an extension of the popular *Vienna Development Method* for program development [Jones, 1980 & 1986], in which the pair of predicates used to characterise an operation are augmented by an extra pair. In *VDM*, an operation is specified using a predicate on the initial state—the *pre-condition*—which describes those states in which it is appropriate to invoke the operation, and a predicate on the initial and final states—the *post-condition*—which describes the effect of the operation. In the development of interfering programs we must record, for each operation, the extent of the interference that can be tolerated and that may be caused. Both of these are described by predicates on pairs of states—just like the traditional post-condition—the former by a *rely-condition*, and the latter by a *guarantee-condition*. To summarise,

- **pre-condition:** What an implementation may assume about the state before an operation.

- **post-condition:** Those changes to the state that an implementation promises to make.

- **rely-condition:** What an implementation may assume about how the state changes.

- **guarantee-condition:** Those changes to the state that an implementation may make.

If we consider that progress in a system is made by the interleaving of atomic steps made by the constituent processes (as is also the case in CCS [Milner, 1980], and CSP [Hoare, 1985]) then, viewed from a particular operation, a rely-condition is merely the post-condition for any atomic step that the rest of the system may make. Similarly, the guarantee-condition is merely the post-condition for any atomic step made by the operation itself.

To return to "sequential" *VDM*, an operation in isolation has a rely-condition which states that nothing changes between its atomic steps, and a guarantee-condition that says nothing about how it changes the state before reaching its post-condition. So if the state before an atomic step is denoted by $\overleftarrow{\sigma}$ and that after by σ, we would have the following rely and guarantee conditions

$$\text{rely } \sigma = \overleftarrow{\sigma}$$
$$\textbf{guar true}$$

An important point to note is that the granularity of the concurrency in the system—the *atomicity* of the events—is not necessarily fixed by a rely and guarantee-condition description. Thus, we may claim that it may be used as a *hierarchical* development technique. As we have already described, the importance of this will be clear to all those with experience in the development of *large* systems. This claim will be further examined at the end of this paper.

The operation developed in this part of the paper is a simple one; the intention is to demonstrate the technique and the proof obligations generated by development steps. Still less than a *useful* development, it fails to be a *model* one. In practice one would proceed in larger steps and not go through the full tedium of our rather too detailed proofs. Nevertheless, it is hoped that the reader might find the development as interesting an introduction to the technique described as the authors did. As we shall see, this example raises questions about the nature of data reification[3] in the presence of interference.

2.2 A Formal Development of a Monitoring System

2.2.1 The Specification

Many systems depend for their reliability on duplication of components; in this way they can survive a limited number of faults. Consider, if you will, the monitoring of such a system where we require that we know which components have failed, and also how many—we may need to act quickly once we know that some limit has been reached. Also, failure is irreversible: we shall never repair a component. Suppose that in our system there are m components that we might want to monitor

$$m : \mathbf{N}$$

We do not need to give the precise value of m yet, and instead we leave it undefined; thus the specification is parameterised by m. We can model the components as a set; we may as well use a segment of the natural numbers for this[4]

$$Comp = \{1, \ldots, m\}$$

We shall use the following simple data type[5]

$$Flag = \{on, off\}$$

The state of the monitoring system contains the set of components whose failures have been reported, an estimate of the size of this set, and a flag to say that this estimate is accurate

$$
\begin{aligned}
St_0 \; :: \; & s \; : \; \textbf{set of } Comp \\
& n \; : \; \mathbf{N} \\
& f \; : \; Flag
\end{aligned}
$$

We shall not consider just any old collection of values from these three components' types as constituting a possible value for St_0. Rather, we shall constrain acceptable combinations of values by giving a predicate—*a data type invariant*—as part of the definition of St_0. Whenever we have a value drawn from this type we may assume that it satisfies the data type invariant. Thus, if we have a predicate such as a pre, post, rely, or guarantee-condition that mentions a value drawn from this type, we can conjoin to the predicate the invariant applied to the value. A more detailed

---

[3] *Reification*, as both Michael Jackson and Cliff Jones have pointed out, is a more fitting way of describing that which usually goes under the name of *refinement*.

[4] Here, the set $Comp$ contains all the natural numbers between 1 and m. At present, we permit m to be *any* natural number, even 0, since $\{1, \ldots, 0\}$ is the empty set by definition.

[5] In this definition in *VDM*, we understand *on* and *off* to be distinct.

discussion of data type invariants is to be found in [Jones, 1986][6], which describes a more central rôle for invariants than that in [Jones, 1980]. The new use of invariants is similar to that in Z [Hayes, 1986].

Our invariant on St_0 happens to tell us when the estimate is exact: just when the flag is off[7]

$$inv\text{-}St_0(mk\text{-}St_0(s, n, f)) \quad \triangleq \quad (f = \mathit{off} \;\Rightarrow\; n = \mathsf{card}\, s)$$

The initial value for our state is that there have been no failures, and that s and n agree

$$init\text{-}St_0 = mk\text{-}St_0(\{\,\}, 0, \mathit{off})$$

We must ensure that the initial value that we have specified *actually is* an element of the type St_0, though this is trivial in this case.

Over a period of time, standards of workmanship being what they are, components do fail. We define an operation on the monitor's state to report on a number of failed components. This operation, called Add_0, is known to be the only operation that has write access to the monitor's state. Add_0 takes as its argument a set of components and updates the state to record these failures; it doesn't matter if the monitor is told more than once about the failure of a component—a failed component is a failed component.

In the following operation definition, the names in the pre-condition refer to the variables in the state before the operation. In the post-condition, names decorated with an overhook refer to variables in the state before the operation, and undecorated names refer to variables in the state after the operation[8]. In the rely and guarantee conditions, the decorated names refer to variables in the state before a step is taken by the environment or the operation, and undecorated names refer to those after such a step.

As the operation progresses, the set s grows in size, taking new members only from the set x. The fate of n is uncertain until the operation finishes with f off; then the data type invariant says that n must be the cardinality of s. Also the fate of f is uncertain, except that upon termination it is off. Of course, if f is off at any instant during the operation of Add_0, then n must agree with the size of s.

Add_0 $(x \colon \mathsf{set\ of}\ Comp)$
ext wr s : set of $Comp$
 wr n : $\mathbb{N}$
 wr f : $Flag$
pre $f = \mathit{off}$
rely $s = \overleftarrow{s} \wedge n = \overleftarrow{n} \wedge f = \overleftarrow{f}$
guar $\overleftarrow{s} \subseteq s \wedge s \subseteq \overleftarrow{s} \cup x$

---

[6] Chapter 5, particularly p138

[7] In the definition of a new type, the component names used are really the names of projections from the type. The "make-function" is an injection into the type, which, given values whose types correspond to those of the components, constructs an element of the type.

[8] Those more familiar with the Z notation—or some of the variations on the *VDM* concrete syntax (for example [Jones, 1980])—would expect to see f and f', rather than $\overleftarrow{f}$ and f respectively.

post $s = \overleftarrow{s} \cup x \wedge f = \textit{off}$

There are proof obligations here: rely and guarantee conditions should be both reflexive and transitive. Also, it would be helpful if the operation really were *implementable*, that is, whenever the operation is applicable, a final state satisfying the postcondition can be reached. This implementability requirement can be formalised as follows. Let $\overleftarrow{\sigma}$ denote the state before the operation is invoked, and σ denote the state after the operation. Then

$$\forall \overleftarrow{\sigma} \cdot \text{pre-}Add\_0 \;\Rightarrow\; \exists \sigma \cdot (\text{rely-}Add\_0 \vee \text{guar-}Add\_0)^* \wedge \text{post-}Add\_0$$

where R^* denotes the transitive closure of the relation R. This operation is clearly implementable.

2.2.2   The First Level Design: Introducing Parallelism

In reality things are not so straightforward: the sensors that report upon component failure are actually *independent*. Therefore, we refine our operation to reflect this fact: the new operation *Add* now takes as its argument just a single component. Now we have many operations acting in parallel upon the state: an *Add* for each component. We shall consider each *Add* as being named by the component it is adding to the state. Thus we cannot get away with the trivial rely and guarantee-conditions that we had before.

Our new state is

$St \;::\; s \;:\; \text{set of } Comp$
$\qquad n \;:\; \mathbf{N}$
$\qquad p \;:\; \mathbf{N}$

Our refinement step takes us from a simple semaphore which is either *onn* or *off*, to one which either has the name of an *Add* operation (that is, a component name) or some other natural number. The invariant tells us now that the estimate is exact when the refined flag p doesn't contain the name of a component

$$\text{inv-}St(\textit{mk-}St_1(s, n, p)) \;\triangleq\; (p \notin Comp \;\Rightarrow\; n = \text{card } s)$$

We shall find the following two constants useful

$c_0 \in Comp$
$c \notin Comp$

We now require that m, the number of components in our system, which we previously left undefined, be at least 1; this ensures that $Comp$ is nonempty, and thus the existence of c_0. The fact that $Comp$ is a finite subset of $\mathbf{N}$ ensures the existence of c.

The initial value for our state is that there have been no failures, and that s and n agree

$$\text{init-}St = \textit{mk-}St_1(\{\,\}, 0, c_1)$$

Again, we must ensure that this particular value actually has type St; this once more is trivial.

It is important to document the relationship between this more concrete state and the abstract one. In the set of proof rules that we are using for this development, this relationship between concrete and abstract must be *functional* and *total*. Fortunately in this case, this documentation is a simple matter

$$retr_0 : St \rightarrow St_0$$
$$retr_0(mk\text{-}St(s, n, p)) \quad \triangleq \quad \text{if } p \in Comp$$
$$\text{then } mk\text{-}St_0(s, n, on)$$
$$\text{else } mk\text{-}St_0(s, n, o\!f\!f)$$

The totality of $retr_0$ follows from the (implicit) universal quantification of s, n, and p, and from the totality of $mk\text{-}St$. The functionality of $retr_0$ follows from the fact that the fate of each (s, n, p) triplet is uniquely determined by p's membership of $Comp$.

Notice that

$$\forall st \in St \cdot$$
$$s(retr_0(st)) = s(st)$$
$$n(retr_0(st)) = n(st)$$
$$f(retr_0(st)) = \text{if } p(st) \in Comp$$
$$\text{then } on$$
$$\text{else } o\!f\!f$$

Thus we may safely use the same names s and n for the projections from St_0 and St[9]. From this, we can prove the following lemma

$$\forall st \in St \cdot p(st) \in Comp \;\Leftrightarrow\; f(retr_0(st)) = on$$

Proof:

	from $st \in St$	
1	from $p(st) \in Comp$	
	infer $f(retr_0(st)) = on$	lemma(h1)
2	$(p(st) \in Comp) \in \mathbf{B}$	h, $Comp$-defn
3	$p(st) \in Comp \;\Rightarrow\; f(retr_0(st)) = on$	$\Rightarrow$ -I(1,2)
4	from $f(retr_0(st)) = on$	
4.1	from $p(st) \notin Comp$	
4.1.1	$f(retr_0(st)) = o\!f\!f$	lemma(h4.1)
	infer $on = o\!f\!f$	=t-subs(4.1.1,h4)
4.2	$(p(st) \notin Comp) \in \mathbf{B}$	h, $Comp$-defn
4.3	$p(st) \notin Comp \;\Rightarrow\; on = o\!f\!f$	$\Rightarrow$ -I(4.1,4.2)
4.4	$on \neq o\!f\!f$	$Flag$-defn
	infer $p(st) \in Comp$	vac $\Rightarrow$ -E(4.3,4.4)

[9] Strictly speaking, it must be an abuse of notation to use the same component name in two different state descriptions in the same specification, since it means that we have two projection functions with the same name, but with different types. However, it seems harmless and even desirable, since we would like to emphasise that the component has not been reified by this design step. It is reminiscent of the use in Z of the same names in different parts of a specification with the intention that they should be identified.

5	$(f(retr_0(st)) = on) \in \mathbf{B}$	h, St-defn, $retr_0$-defn
6	$f(retr_0(st)) = on \Rightarrow p(st) \in Comp$	$\Rightarrow$ -I(4,5)
7	$p(st) \in Comp \Rightarrow f(retr_0(st)) = on \wedge$	
	$f(retr_0(st)) = on \Rightarrow p(st) \in Comp$	$\wedge$-I(3,6)
infer	$p(st) \in Comp \Leftrightarrow f(retr_0(st)) = on$	$\Leftrightarrow$ -defn(7)

The retrieve function reflects our design decision that the values for our reified flag are partitioned into two sets; one partition corresponding to the flag being raised, and the other to the flag being lowered. We had better make sure that $Comp$ contains at least one element, otherwise we shall not be able to implement our design; this we have already done. Our new operation description takes all this into account. Each suboperation is indexed by the component that it is trying to insert into the shared set. Moreover, it promises that if the semaphore p is raised, then it will change the shared data structure only if *it* is the owner of the semaphore. If the semaphore p is down, then it has the opportunity of raising it. Each suboperation relies on the fact that no change can be made to the shared data if it is the owner of the semaphore p; if it is not, then it can tolerate an increase in size of s.

$Add \quad (y: Comp)$

ext wr s : set of $Comp$

   wr n : $\mathbf{N}$

   wr p : $\mathbf{N}$

pre $p \notin Comp$

rely $(\overleftarrow{p} = y \Rightarrow s = \overleftarrow{s} \wedge n = \overleftarrow{n} \wedge p = \overleftarrow{p}) \wedge (\overleftarrow{p} \neq y \Rightarrow \overleftarrow{s} \subseteq s)$

guar $(\overleftarrow{p} = y \Rightarrow \overleftarrow{s} \subseteq s \wedge s \subseteq \overleftarrow{s} \cup \{y\}) \wedge$

   $(\overleftarrow{p} \in Comp - \{y\} \Rightarrow s = \overleftarrow{s} \wedge n = \overleftarrow{n} \wedge p = \overleftarrow{p}) \wedge$

   $(\overleftarrow{p} \notin Comp \Rightarrow s = \overleftarrow{s} \wedge n = \overleftarrow{n})$

post $y \in s \wedge p \notin Comp$

We must now show that a parallel combination of Add processes *implements* Add_0. Given

$$x \in \text{set of } Comp$$

we must show that

$$\underset{y \in x}{\big|\big|} \ Add(y) \quad \text{sat} \quad Add_0(x)$$

To do this we must discharge the proof obligations in the following sections.

Adequacy The new data type must be *adequate* with respect to the retrieve function $retr_0$. In simple terms—well, for us at least—$retr_0$ must be a surjection. Perhaps in even simpler terms, it means that every state in the abstract level is represented in the concrete level. One might object that some of the abstract states were unreachable anyway, so this insistence upon all of them being implemented might seem strange. But in fact, tightening the abstract data type invariant adequately—good practice in any event—*finesses* this.

We can frame this proof obligation as

$$\vdash \forall st_0 \in St_0 \cdot \exists st \in St_1 \cdot retr_0(st_1) = st_0$$

The proof of this is fairly routine

	from $st_0 \in St_0$	
1	$f(st_0) = on \vee f(st_0) = off$	$flag(\text{h})$
2	from $f(st_0) = on$	
2.1	$c_0 \in Comp$	c_0-defn
2.2	$mk\text{-}St(s(st_0), n(st_0), c_0) \in St_1$	$mk\text{-}St(\text{h})$
2.3	$retr_0(mk\text{-}St(s(st_0), n(st_0), c_0)) = $ if $c_0 \in Comp$	$retr_0$-defn(2.2)
	$\qquad$ then $mk\text{-}St_0(s(st_0), n(st_0), on)$	
	$\qquad$ else $mk\text{-}St_0(s(st_0), n(st_0), off)$	
2.4	$retr_0(mk\text{-}St(s(st_0), n(st_0), c_0)) = mk\text{-}St_0(s(st_0), n(st_0), on)$	if-E(2.1,2.3)
2.5	$retr_0(mk\text{-}St(s(st_0), n(st_0), c_0)) = mk\text{-}St_0(s(st_0), n(st_0), f(st_0))$	=t-subs(h2,2.4)
2.6	$retr_0(mk\text{-}St(s(st_0), n(st_0), c_0)) = st_0$	=t-subs(h,2.4)
	infer $\exists st \in St_1 \cdot retr_0(st_1) = st_0$	$\exists$-I(2.2,2.6)
3	from $f(st_0) = off$	
3.1	$c \notin Comp$	c_1-defn
3.2	$mk\text{-}St(s(st_0), n(st_0), c_1) \in St_1$	$mk\text{-}St(\text{h})$
3.3	$retr_0(mk\text{-}St(s(st_0), n(st_0), c_1)) = $ if $c \in Comp$	$retr_0$-defn(3.2)
	$\qquad$ then $mk\text{-}St_0(s(st_0), n(st_0), on)$	
	$\qquad$ else $mk\text{-}St_0(s(st_0), n(st_0), off)$	
3.4	$retr_0(mk\text{-}St(s(st_0), n(st_0), c_1)) = mk\text{-}St_0(s(st_0), n(st_0), off)$	if-E(3.1,3.3)
3.5	$retr_0(mk\text{-}St(s(st_0), n(st_0), c_1)) = mk\text{-}St_0(s(st_0), n(st_0), f(st_0))$	=t-subs(h3,3.4)
3.6	$retr_0(mk\text{-}St(s(st_0), n(st_0), c_1)) = st_0$	=t-subs(h,3.5)
	infer $\exists st \in St_1 \cdot retr_0(st_1) = st_0$	$\exists$-I(3.2,3.6)
	infer $\exists st \in St_1 \cdot retr_0(st_1) = st_0$	$\vee$-E(1,2,3)

Initial State The retrieve function must respect our initial state. That is,

$$\vdash retr_0(init\text{-}St) = init\text{-}St_0$$

This, fortunately, has a short proof

1	$c \notin Comp$	c_1-defn
2	$init\text{-}St_0 = mk\text{-}St_0(\{\,\}, 0, off)$	$init\text{-}St_0$-defn
3	$init\text{-}St_0 = retr_0(mk\text{-}St(\{\,\}, 0, c_1))$	ifelsubs(1,2)
4	$init\text{-}St = mk\text{-}St_1(\{\,\}, 0, c_1)$	$init\text{-}St_1$-defn
5	$init\text{-}St_0 = retr_0(init\text{-}St)$	=t-subs(4,3)
6	$retr_0(init\text{-}St) = init\text{-}St_0$	=-comm(5)

Applicability Whenever Add_0 is applicable, so too must any Add; we may *weaken* the precondition in a development step. That is,

$$\vdash \forall st \in St_1, x \in \text{set of } Comp, y \in x \cdot$$
$$\text{pre-}Add_0(retr_0(st), x) \;\Rightarrow\; \text{pre-}Add_1(st_1, y)$$

	from $st \in St_1, x \in Comp, y \in x$	
1	from pre-$Add_0(retr_0(st), x)$	
1.1	$f(retr_0(st)) = \text{off}$	pre-Add_0-defn(h1)
1.2	$p(st) \notin Comp$	Lemma(1.1)
	infer pre-$Add(st_1, y)$	pre-Add_1-defn(h1)
	infer pre-$Add_0(retr_0(st), x) \;\Rightarrow\; \text{pre-}Add_1(st_1, y)$	$\Rightarrow$ -I(1,2)

Reliance We must show that none of the Add operations relies on more than Add_0 did: in any development step we may *weaken* the rely-condition

$$\forall \overleftarrow{st}, st \in St, x \in \text{set of } Comp, y \in x \cdot$$
$$\text{rely-}Add_0(retr_0(\overleftarrow{st}, retr_0(st), x) \;\Rightarrow\; \text{rely-}Add(\overleftarrow{st}, st, y)$$

Sadly, this is not a theorem; in the case that

$$p(\overleftarrow{st}) \in Comp \wedge p(\overleftarrow{st}) = y$$

at best we can rely only on the *"on-ness"* or *"off-ness"* of $p(st)$—we can't rely on the *ownership* of $p(st)$ remaining unchanged. More formally, the strongest thing that we can prove from rely-Add_0 is

$$s(st) = s(\overleftarrow{st}) \wedge n(st) = n(\overleftarrow{st}) \wedge (p(st) \in Comp \;\Leftrightarrow\; p(\overleftarrow{st}) \in Comp)$$

which is weaker than the result that we want. There is no way of strengthening the abstract rely-condition to resolve this problem. One way around this is to change the abstract data type St_0 so that it contains enough values for us to insist that the ownership of p remains unchanged. This means that we would be forced to make $retr_0$ a bijection; this would make a somewhat unadventurous development step. Moreover, the additional values have no place in the abstract type: it would be wrong to put them there.

Intuitively, there is no problem: no other operation apart from Add_0 has write access to the f component of St_0. This is a refinement step that seems right, and yet we cannot prove it correct using the proof rules. This suggests that the proof rules are incomplete. In fact, we have been devising new refinement rules that allow us to prove this particular refinement step. We intend to study these rules further to ensure their completeness.

Co-existence The new operations must be able to co-exist

$$\vdash \forall \overleftarrow{st}, st \in St, x \in \text{set of } Comp, y \in x; z \in x \cdot$$
$$y \neq z \wedge \text{guar-}Add(\overleftarrow{st}, st, y) \;\Rightarrow\; \text{rely-}Add(\overleftarrow{st}, st, z)$$

	from $\overleftarrow{st}, st \in St, y, z \in Comp$
1	from $y \neq z \wedge \text{guar-}Add(\overleftarrow{st}, st, y)$

1.1	guar-$Add(\overleftarrow{st}, st, y)$	$\wedge$-E(h1)
1.2	$(p(\overleftarrow{st}) = y \;\Rightarrow\; s(\overleftarrow{st}) \subseteq s(st) \wedge s(st) \subseteq s(\overleftarrow{st}) \cup \{y\}) \wedge$	guar-Add-defn(1.1)
	$(p(\overleftarrow{st}) \in Comp - \{y\} \;\Rightarrow\; s(st) = s(\overleftarrow{st}) \wedge n(st) = n(\overleftarrow{st}) \wedge p(st) = p(\overleftarrow{st})) \wedge$	
	$(p(\overleftarrow{st}) \notin Comp \;\Rightarrow\; s(st) = s(\overleftarrow{st}) \wedge n(st) = n(\overleftarrow{st}))$	
1.3	from $p(\overleftarrow{st}) = z$	
1.3.1	$y \neq z$	$\wedge$-E(h1)
1.3.2	$z \neq y$	=-comm(1.3.1)
1.3.3	$p(\overleftarrow{st}) \neq y$	=t-subs(h1.3,1.3.2)
1.3.4	$p(\overleftarrow{st}) \in Comp \vee p(\overleftarrow{st}) \notin Comp$	h, $Comp$-defn
1.3.5	from $p(\overleftarrow{st}) \in Comp$	
1.3.5.1	$p(\overleftarrow{st}) \notin \{y\}$	$\in$-property(1.3.3)
1.3.5.2	$p(\overleftarrow{st}) \in Comp \wedge p(\overleftarrow{st}) \notin \{y\}$	$\wedge$-I(h1.3.5,1.3.5.1)
1.3.5.3	$p(\overleftarrow{st}) \in Comp - \{y\}$	$-$-property(1.3.5.2)
1.3.5.4	$p(\overleftarrow{st}) \in Comp - \{y\} \;\Rightarrow\; s(st) = s(\overleftarrow{st}) \wedge n(st) = n(\overleftarrow{st}) \wedge p(st) = p(\overleftarrow{st})$	
		$\wedge$-E(1.3)
1.3.5.5	$s(st) = s(\overleftarrow{st}) \wedge n(st) = n(\overleftarrow{st}) \wedge p(st) = p(\overleftarrow{st})$	$\Rightarrow$-E(1.3.5.4,1.3.5.3)
	infer $s(st) = s(\overleftarrow{st})$	$\wedge$-E(1.3.5.5)
1.3.6	from $p(\overleftarrow{st}) \notin Comp$	
1.3.6.1	$p(\overleftarrow{st}) \notin Comp \;\Rightarrow\; s(st) = s(\overleftarrow{st}) \wedge n(st) = n(\overleftarrow{st})$	$\wedge$-E(1.3)
1.3.6.2	$s(st) = s(\overleftarrow{st}) \wedge n(st) = n(\overleftarrow{st})$	$\Rightarrow$-E(1.3.6.1,h1.3.6)
	infer $s(st) = s(\overleftarrow{st})$	$\wedge$-E(1.3.6.2)
1.3.7	$s(st) = s(\overleftarrow{st})$	$\vee$-E(1.3.4,1.3.5,1.3.6)
	infer $s(\overleftarrow{st}) \subseteq s(st)$	$\subseteq$-refl(1.3.7)

Guarantee Each suboperation must guarantee at least as much as the overall operation: we mustn't welch on our promises. This means that as development progresses, guarantee-conditions may be *strengthened*. First we need a simple lemma

$$\vdash \forall \overleftarrow{st}, st \in St, x \in \text{set of } Comp \cdot$$
$$s(st) = s(\overleftarrow{st}) \;\Rightarrow\; s(\overleftarrow{st}) \subseteq s(st) \wedge s(st) \subseteq s(\overleftarrow{st}) \cup x$$

The proof of this lemma is straightforward

	from $\overleftarrow{st}, st \in St, x \in$ set of $Comp, y \in x$	
1	from $s(st) = s(\overleftarrow{st})$	
1.1	$s(\overleftarrow{st}) \subseteq s(st)$	$\subseteq$-refl(h1)
1.2	$s(st) \subseteq s(\overleftarrow{st})$	$\subseteq$-refl(h1)
1.3	$s(st) \subseteq s(\overleftarrow{st}) \cup x$	sets(1.2)
	infer $s(\overleftarrow{st}) \subseteq s(st) \wedge s(st) \subseteq s(\overleftarrow{st}) \cup x$	$\wedge$-I(1.2,1.3)
	infer $s(st) = s(\overleftarrow{st}) \;\Rightarrow\; s(\overleftarrow{st}) \subseteq s(st) \wedge s(st) \subseteq s(\overleftarrow{st}) \cup x$	$\Rightarrow$-I(1)

Now for the main theorem

$$\vdash \forall \overleftarrow{st}, st \in St, x \in \text{set of } Comp, y \in x \cdot$$
$$\text{guar-}Add(\overleftarrow{st}, st, y) \Rightarrow \text{guar-}Add_0(retro_0(\overleftarrow{st}), retro_0(st), x)$$

from $\overleftarrow{st}, st \in St, x \in$ set of $Comp, y \in x$

1	from guar-$Add(\overleftarrow{st}, st, y)$	
1.1	$(p(\overleftarrow{st}) = y \Rightarrow s(\overleftarrow{st}) \subseteq s(st) \land s(st) \subseteq s(\overleftarrow{st}) \cup \{y\}) \land$	guar-Add-defn(1.1)
	$(p(\overleftarrow{st}) \in Comp - \{y\} \Rightarrow s(st) = s(\overleftarrow{st}) \land n(st) = n(\overleftarrow{st}) \land p(st) = p(\overleftarrow{st})) \land$	
	$(p(\overleftarrow{st}) \notin Comp \Rightarrow s(st) = s(\overleftarrow{st}) \land n(st) = n(\overleftarrow{st}))$	
1.2	$p(\overleftarrow{st}) = y \lor p(\overleftarrow{st}) \in Comp - \{y\} \lor p(\overleftarrow{st}) \notin Comp$	h
1.3	from $p(\overleftarrow{st}) = y$	
1.3.1	$p(\overleftarrow{st}) = y \Rightarrow s(\overleftarrow{st}) \subseteq s(st) \land s(st) \subseteq s(\overleftarrow{st}) \cup \{y\}$	$\land$-E(1.1)
1.3.2	$s(\overleftarrow{st}) \subseteq s(st) \land s(st) \subseteq s(\overleftarrow{st}) \cup \{y\})$	$\Rightarrow$-E(1.3.1,h1.3)
1.3.3	$\{y\} \subseteq x$	sets(h)
1.3.4	$s(\overleftarrow{st}) \cup \{y\} \subseteq s(\overleftarrow{st}) \cup x$	sets(h,1.3.3)
1.3.5	$s(st) \subseteq s(\overleftarrow{st}) \cup \{y\}$	$\land$-E(1.3.2)
1.3.6	$s(st) \subseteq s(\overleftarrow{st}) \cup x$	$\subseteq$-trans(1.3.5,1.3.4)
1.3.7	$s(\overleftarrow{st}) \subseteq s(st)$	$\land$-E(1.3.2)
	infer $s(\overleftarrow{st}) \subseteq s(st) \land s(st) \subseteq s(\overleftarrow{st}) \cup x$	$\land$-I(1.3.7,1.3.6)
1.4	from $p(\overleftarrow{st}) \in Comp - \{y\}$	
1.4.1	$p(\overleftarrow{st}) \in Comp - \{y\} \Rightarrow s(st) = s(\overleftarrow{st}) \land n(st) = n(\overleftarrow{st}) \land p(st) = p(\overleftarrow{st})$	
		$\land$-E(1.1)
1.4.2	$s(st) = s(\overleftarrow{st}) \land n(st) = n(\overleftarrow{st}) \land p(st) = p(\overleftarrow{st})$	$\Rightarrow$-E(1.4.1,h1.4)
1.4.3	$s(st) = s(\overleftarrow{st})$	$\land$-E(1.4.2)
	infer $s(\overleftarrow{st}) \subseteq s(st) \land s(st) \subseteq s(\overleftarrow{st}) \cup x$	Lemma(1.4.2)
1.5	from $p(\overleftarrow{st}) \notin Comp$	
1.5.1	$(p(\overleftarrow{st}) \notin Comp \Rightarrow s(st) = s(\overleftarrow{st}) \land n(st) = n(\overleftarrow{st}))$	$\land$-E(1.1)
1.5.2	$s(st) = s(\overleftarrow{st}) \land n(st) = n(\overleftarrow{st}))$	$\Rightarrow$-E(1.5.1,h1.5)
1.5.3	$s(st) = s(\overleftarrow{st})$	$\land$-E(1.5.2)
	infer $s(\overleftarrow{st}) \subseteq s(st) \land s(st) \subseteq s(\overleftarrow{st}) \cup x$	Lemma(1.5.2)
1.6	$s(\overleftarrow{st}) \subseteq s(st) \land s(st) \subseteq s(\overleftarrow{st}) \cup x$	$\lor$-E(1.2,1.3,1.4,1.5)
	infer guar-$Add_0(retro_0(\overleftarrow{st}), retro_0(st), x)$	guar-Add_0-defn(1.6)
	infer guar-$Add(\overleftarrow{st}, st, y) \Rightarrow$ guar-$Add_0(retro_0(\overleftarrow{st}), retro_0(st), x)$	$\Rightarrow$-I(1,h)

Strength In order to show that the implementation is strong enough to achieve the effect of the specification, we need to think of a *dynamic invariant*. It is actually a rather simple one, using a familiar idea: the shared set s monotonically increases in size, until it includes every element of x

$$dinv\text{-}Add(\overleftarrow{st}, st, x) \;\triangleq\; (\overleftarrow{s} \subseteq s \land s \subseteq \overleftarrow{s} \cup x)$$

invbasis We must show that our dynamic invariant is *reflexive*

$$\vdash \forall st \in St, x \in \text{set of } Comp \cdot \textit{dinv-Add}_1(st, st, x)$$

from $st \in St$

1	$s(st) \subseteq s(st)$	$\subseteq$-reflexive(h)
2	$s(st) \subseteq s(st) \cup x$	$\subseteq$-p.o.(1)
3	$s(st) \subseteq s(st) \land s(st) \subseteq s(st) \cup x$	$\land$-I(1,2)
infer	$\textit{dinv-Add}(st, st)$	$\textit{dinv-Add}_1$-defn(3)

invpresguar In order to show that each operation preserves the dynamic invariant, we must show that each atomic step does so

$$\vdash \quad \forall \overleftarrow{st}, st', st \in St, x \in \text{set of } Comp, y \in x \cdot$$
$$\textit{dinv-Add}(\overleftarrow{st}, st', x) \land \text{guar-}Add_1(st', st, y) \;\Rightarrow\; \textit{dinv-Add}(\overleftarrow{st}, st, x)$$

The proof of this involves simple set-theoretic manipulations, helped by two small lemmas. First, the dynamic invariant is the same as the abstract guarantee condition

$$\text{guar-}Add_0(retr_0(\overleftarrow{st}), retr_0(st), x) \;\Leftrightarrow\; \textit{dinv-Add}(\overleftarrow{st}, st, x)$$

Second, the dynamic invariant is transitive

$$\textit{dinv-Add}(\overleftarrow{st_1}, st'_1, x) \land \textit{dinv-Add}_1(st'_1, st_1, x) \;\Rightarrow\;$$
$$\textit{dinv-Add}(\overleftarrow{st_1}, st_1, x)$$

from $\overleftarrow{st}, st'_1, st_1 \in St_1, x \in \text{set of } Comp, y \in x$

1	from $\textit{dinv-Add}(\overleftarrow{st_1}, st'_1, x) \land \text{guar-}Add_1(st'_1, st_1, y)$	
1.1	$\text{guar-}Add_1(st'_1, st_1, y)$	$\land$-E(h1)
1.2	$\text{guar-}Add_0(retr_0(st'), retr_0(st_1), x)$	**Guarantee(1)**
1.3	$\textit{dinv-Add}(st'_1, st_1, x)$	Lemma(1.2)
1.4	$\textit{dinv-Add}(\overleftarrow{st_1}, st'_1, x)$	$\land$-E(h1)
infer	$\textit{dinv-Add}(\overleftarrow{st_1}, st_1, x)$	Lemma(1.4)
infer	$\textit{dinv-Add}(\overleftarrow{st_1}, st'_1, x) \land \textit{dinv-Add}_1(st'_1, st_1, x) \;\Rightarrow\; \textit{dinv-Add}(\overleftarrow{st_1}, st_1, x)$	$\Rightarrow$-I(1,h)

invpresenv Of course, all this would be rather useless if the steps taken by the environment lacked respect for our dynamic invariant. The proof obligation here is similar to the last one

$$\vdash$$

$$\forall \overleftarrow{st}, st', st \in St \cdot$$
$$\textit{dinv-Add}(\overleftarrow{st}, st') \land \text{rely-}Add_0(retr_0(st'), retr_0(st)) \;\Rightarrow\;$$
$$\textit{dinv-Add}(\overleftarrow{st}, st)$$

from $\overleftarrow{st}, st', st \in St$

1   from $dinv\text{-}Add(\overleftarrow{st}, st)$, $\text{rely-}Add_0(retr_0(st'), retr_0(st))$

1.1 $s(\overleftarrow{st}) \subseteq s(st') \wedge s(st') \subseteq s(\overleftarrow{st}) \cup x$ $dinv\text{-}Add\text{-defn(h1)}$

1.2 $s(st) = s(st') \wedge n(st) = n(st') \wedge f(st) = f(st')$ $\text{rely-}Add_0\text{-defn(h1)}$

1.3 $s(st) = s(st')$ $\wedge\text{-E(1.2)}$

1.4 $s(\overleftarrow{s}t) \subseteq s(st0 \wedge s(st) \subseteq s(\overleftarrow{s}t) \cup x$ $=\text{t-subs(1.3,1.1)}$

    infer $dinv\text{-}Add(\overleftarrow{st}, st)$ $dinv\text{-}Add\text{-defn(1.4)}$

infer $dinv\text{-}Add(\overleftarrow{st}, st') \wedge \text{rely-}Add_0(retr_0(st'), retr_0(st)) \Rightarrow dinv\text{-}Add(\overleftarrow{st}, st)$

Result   Finally, we come to the proof that when each suboperation has accomplished its post-condition, then the overall post-condition of the specification has indeed also been achieved. Thus

$\vdash \forall \overleftarrow{st}, st_1 \in St_1 \cdot$

    $dinv\text{-}Add(\overleftarrow{st_1}, st_1, x) \wedge$

    $\forall y \in x \cdot \text{post-}Add(\overleftarrow{st_1}, st_1, y) \Rightarrow \text{post-}Add_0(retr_0(\overleftarrow{st_1}), retr_0(st_1), x)$

from $\overleftarrow{s}, s \in$ set of $Comp, \overleftarrow{n}, n, \overleftarrow{p}, p \in \mathbb{N}$

1   from $dinv\text{-}Add(mk\text{-}St_1(\overleftarrow{s}, \overleftarrow{n}, \overleftarrow{p}), mk\text{-}St_1(s, n, p), x)$,

        $\forall y \in x \cdot \text{post-}Add(mk\text{-}St_1(\overleftarrow{s}, \overleftarrow{n}, \overleftarrow{p}), mk\text{-}St(s, n, p), y)$

1.1 $\forall y \in x \cdot y \in s$ $\text{post-}Add\text{-defn(h1)}$

1.2 $x \subseteq s$ $\subseteq\text{-defn(1.1)}$

1.3 $\overleftarrow{s} \subseteq s \wedge s \subseteq \overleftarrow{s} \cup x$ $dinv\text{-}Add\text{-defn(h1)}$

1.4 $\overleftarrow{s} \subseteq s$ $\wedge\text{-E(1.3)}$

1.5 $\overleftarrow{s} \cup x \subseteq s \cup x$ $\cup\text{-monotonic(1.4,h)}$

1.6 $s \cup x \subseteq s \cup s$ $\cup\text{-monotonic(1.5,h)}$

1.7 $s \cup s = s$ $\cup\text{-idempotent(h)}$

1.8 $s \cup x \subseteq s$ $=\text{t-subs(1.7,1.6)}$

1.9 $\overleftarrow{s} \cup x \subseteq s$ $\subseteq\text{-trans(1.5,1.8)}$

1.10 $s \subseteq \overleftarrow{s} \cup x$ $\wedge\text{-E(1.3)}$

1.11 $\overleftarrow{s} \cup x \subseteq s \wedge s \subseteq \overleftarrow{s} \cup x$ $\wedge\text{-I(1.9,1.10)}$

1.12 $s = \overleftarrow{s} \cup x$ $=\text{set-defn(1.11)}$

    infer $\text{post-}Add_0(retr_0(mk\text{-}St(\overleftarrow{s}, \overleftarrow{n}, \overleftarrow{p})), retr_0(mk\text{-}St(s, n, p)), x)$

infer $dinv\text{-}Add(mk\text{-}St_1(\overleftarrow{s}, \overleftarrow{n}, \overleftarrow{p}), mk\text{-}St_1(s, n, p), x) \wedge$

    $\forall y \in x \cdot \text{post-}Add(mk\text{-}St_1(\overleftarrow{s}, \overleftarrow{n}, \overleftarrow{p}), mk\text{-}St(s, n, p), y) \Rightarrow$

    $\text{post-}Add_0(retr_0(mk\text{-}St(\overleftarrow{s}, \overleftarrow{n}, \overleftarrow{p})), retr_0(mk\text{-}St(s, n, p)), x)$

3 On Atomic Operations

The so-called specification of the component monitor is rather a poor one: in order to describe the required behaviour we introduced a particular synchronisation technique: a semaphore. This is not very abstract and we would like a better specification. The most important requirement for the system was that updating the two state components was *abstractly atomic*. We actually said something rather different: that transient states exist, but while the state is transient, it is not consistent. In this section we describe an operation that is atomic, and we try to decompose this abstract atomicity.

3.1 Splitting the Atom

Suppose that we have a state which contains only the set of components that we want to update, and further suppose that we have an operation that adds a pair of components to the set

$AddPair\ (x, y: Comp)$
ext wr s : **set of** $Comp$
pre $x \notin s \wedge y \notin s$
rely $s = \overleftarrow{s}$
guar $s = \overleftarrow{s} \vee s = \overleftarrow{s} \cup \{x, y\}$
post $x \in s \wedge y \in s$

We can consider that the operation is *atomic*: nothing can interfere with it. Now, as it happens, we do not have an operation that can add two elements to a set in one step, but we do have an operation that can add one at a time

$AddOne\ (x: Comp)$
ext wr s : **set of** $Comp$
pre $x \notin s$
rely $s = \overleftarrow{s}$
guar $s = \overleftarrow{s} \vee s = \overleftarrow{s} \cup \{x\}$
post $x \in s$

"Obviously", adding two elements separately is the same as adding them at the same time. That is, we would like the following conjecture to be true

Conjecture 3.1 *The atomic operation AddPair can be broken up into the sequential composition of two AddOne operations*[10]. *Formally, for distinct component names a and b,*

$$AddOne(a); AddOne(b) \quad \text{sat} \quad AddPair(a, b)$$

In order to prove this correct we need to show—*inter alia*—that we have not weakened our guarantee to the rest of the system. Part of the proof obligation is to show that

$$\text{guar-}AddOne(a) \implies \text{guar-}AddPair(a, b)$$

Making the substitutions, we find that we must show that

---

[10]Or even the parallel composition of the two operations.

$$s = \overleftarrow{s} \lor s = \overleftarrow{s} \cup \{a\} \;\Rightarrow\; s = \overleftarrow{s} \lor s = \overleftarrow{s} \cup \{a, b\}$$

It is not difficult to see that this is false if

$$s \neq \overleftarrow{s} \land b \notin \overleftarrow{s}$$

So the conjecture is not a theorem, and the reason for this is simple: we guaranteed that the original operation was *atomic*, but provided an implementation that was not. We said that at the end of any arbitrary step, *AddPair* would leave the state in one of two configurations: either unchanged since the beginning of the step, or with s containing both a and b. The implementation guaranteed something different: the state might also have s containing a, but not b.

3.2 Conclusion

When we decompose an abstract operation in VDM^+, the concrete operation may leave the state in only those configurations permitted by the abstract operation. Thus, we cannot specify that some operation is atomic, and then find some implementation that enforces this, say by using a mutual exclusion algorithm. Therefore, this development strategy, known as *event refinement*, cannot be used in VDM^+ at present. We are devising new refinement rules that allow us to decompose events.

4 The VDM Experience

In this section we describe our experiences of using *VDM* on a large, real project. The project concerned the production of the Storage Allocator Process (SA), a major component of the Operating System for System X digital exchanges. The project started in late 1986, and the software is due to be ready for integration with the rest of the system by mid 1988. It will be some time before we can come to any realistic conclusions about the cost and benefits of using *VDM*.

This section contains a mixture of facts, opinions and guidelines on the use of *VDM*, and VDM^+ in particular. We hope that it will be of interest to those involved in applying formal methods.

4.1 Notation

"Standard *VDM*"[11] was not sufficient for the development because of the concurrency inherent in the use of the storage allocator and the resulting interference between operations. Since we were already committed in various ways to the use of *VDM*, it seemed natural to adopt the use of VDM^+.

Unfortunately, real understanding of the notation came only from using it, because the literature on VDM^+ is so sparse, there being no case studies of any real substance. Quite often, the project team wanted to say something about the system, but expressed it incorrectly. For example, it seemed natural to describe critical regions as atomic operations, thus *requiring* that they should not be interfered with. The next stage of the development would then involve the precise synchronisation technique. As we showed in section 3, this is not a feasible development technique.

---

[11] We use the term guardedly!

As we have demonstrated in this paper, the rules for proving refinements correct are incomplete. Other experiments that we have carried out show that there is a serious problem with carrying out hierarchical development: sometimes one needs to perform proofs of co-existence between *refined* operations. This militates against hierarchical design because we should not need to know how the refinement of another operation is proceeding. The next step of our work is to produce a new set of refinement rules that are complete, and avoid the problems with co-existence of refined operations.

Standards are needed for *VDM* syntax and layout. The project suffered from problems due to the various dialects of *VDM* that are used in the literature and on public *VDM* courses. We are aware of work proceeding on a British standard for *VDM*, but until it is finished *and* accepted *VDM* must be considered still to be evolving.

Perhaps the biggest disadvantage in using *VDM* is the absence of a structuring technique. When we write a large specification—and SA turned out to be quite large—we want to describe each part in the simplest possible context, and then show how to put these parts together, exploiting commonalities. We don't want to end up with a monolithic state and large, tedious pieces of mathematics. The difficulty in structuring *VDM* descriptions doesn't only affect the size of a *VDM* specification, but also the ease with which it may be comprehended and reused, and the feasibility of conducting proofs about the development.

VDM[+] has been found to be appropriate for the specification and design of a multi-threaded process, where the threads can interleave their execution, and where interaction between threads is controlled by shared data. The notation is more difficult to use when processes can interleave at the instruction level, simply because more cases need to be considered. Perhaps this is why we should avoid the use of shared data in system design!

4.2 Tools

Using a notation such as *VDM*, much can be done without tools. Most of the really beautiful examples of formal specifications have been produced using just pencil and paper (for example, though not exclusively, [Hayes, 1987]). However, the use of some kind of mechanical tool becomes desirable when specifications become very large, or when they have to be shared between many people. We must try to find the most *appropriate* tools to help and not to hinder formal development.

We used a WYSIWYG[12] editor with special founts on a Macintosh system for preparing specifications. This proved to be adequate, but unreliable. Ib Sørensen has likened the use of formal methods to working in a "document factory": formal specifications, designs, proofs, and the final code are all documents. Since the main activity is in producing these documents, we shouldn't be surprised if we need to invest in equipment to help us create and maintain documents of appropriate quality. As we find more powerful and useful tools—such as a proof assistant—we shall need access to a more powerful computing environment. We also have experience of using a Sun workstation; producing formal documents using a Sun is altogether far more agreeable and effective.

The editor was in fact the only *VDM* tool available to us. We would have liked to have had

---

[12]WYSIWYG: What You See Is What You Get. This is a document preparation system where a representation of the final document appears on a graphics screen, an example is the QED editor. The usual alternative is a "mark-up" language, where commands to control layout, founts, the use of special characters, &cet, are embedded in the text. Examples are LaTeX and SGML. WYSIWYG systems are generally easier to use; mark-up languages tend to be more powerful and more flexible.

the following

- A syntax checker, a type checker, and a pretty printer for VDM^+.

- A database to store VDM^+ specifications. We could use the names of types, functions, and operations as keys, and organise the database so as to make it easier to to modify a VDM^+ specification.

- A configuration control tool to manage the changing specification and designs, and the relationships between them, and to provide a history of the development.

- A library of standard VDM functions and operations that can be used by many development teams.

- A proof assistant.

4.3 Education

All of the project team members writing VDM^+ had attended a one or a two week training course in VDM[13]. This training was indispensable but to be of maximum benefit, it must be followed by work experience using VDM. Using mathematics, there are many different ways of describing a particular requirement; this is one of the strengths of using mathematics. In VDM one can also adopt different styles of specification; this too is one of its strengths, since different styles and methods are appropriate to different projects. However, within a particular project it is desirable that a common style is used, and this must be established by the project team training and working together.

It is undoubtedly true that the lack of a standard for VDM is hindering the effectiveness of the available training courses, since there is no guarantee that people will be taught the *same VDM*. No training courses are available for VDM^+, education and understanding having to come from experimentation, review, and discussion. This is obviously a costly way of learning.

4.4 Method

A first attempt at specifying SA failed because it became too detailed, obscuring the requirements with too many implementation concerns. The second attempt started with a much more abstract specification, which was then refined towards the final implementation. After the specification, three progressively more detailed designs were produced before the final transformation into code, in this case in the programming language BT Coral. The choice of the number of levels and their content is difficult to get right: some development steps turned out to be too small and some too large. In hindsight we would probably have chosen different levels.

We found it important to get the state right: it must model the objects being specified, be at an appropriate level of abstraction, and be easy to use in the operations. Time spent here by VDM and system requirement experts was well repaid later on, since it is all to easy to specify the

---

[13]Such courses are run from time to time by the Universities of Manchester and Leicester, and are also available from software houses such as IST, Logica, and Praxis.

wrong system, or to produce descriptions that are awkward to use. At the sketching stage, a lot of experimentation was done, so the project team had to be prepared to use the waste paper bin frequently. We discovered that there were always alternative representations, and that it was always worth trying out a few of them. Using different people and using *VDM* can both help to make alternative designs more obvious. We strove to make descriptions as simple as possible, because if it was complicated in *VDM*, then it was going to be even worse in the implementation. It was possible to sketch ideas quite quickly, but getting to an agreed specification took a long, long time.

So far, only a small part of the system has reached the coding stage; it was implementable without any great amount of effort.

4.5   Reviewing

Checking the relationship between different levels was only really done informally: no formal proofs were conducted. However, rigorous arguments were used to reason about interaction between operations.

Reviews are a good way of finding errors in *VDM* specifications; such errors would normally be discovered later in the development process. The precision of the formalism helps to stimulate comments and discussion in reviews, where more traditional methods might allow important issues to be fudged. At the beginning of the development of a system, the requirements are often vague; the first review often helps to make them clearer.

Our experience is that about two-thirds of the effort used in the development was spent reviewing and reworking the specification and designs. Reviews discovered the following kinds of errors

- An incorrect use of *VDM*: for example, *VDM* text containing syntax or type errors. These could be eliminated by the use of mechanical tools, however, such errors are often interesting in themselves, betraying as they often do some subtle misunderstanding about the meaning of the formalism.

- English text and a *VDM* description which did not correspond.

- English text and a *VDM* description which corresponded, but did not capture the intended requirement.

- A formal description that could usefully be simplified.

The time taken to rework a *VDM* specification once an error had been discovered proved to be significant: it can take the same amount of time as it took to produce the original specification, or even longer. It is difficult to produce a *VDM* description that is entirely satisfactory; three major reworks were not uncommon.

4.6   Management

A development using formal methods is not something to fear as far as project management is concerned: properly used, formal methods make it easier to see exactly what the current stage of development is.

The project team consisted of the following members

- A subject specialist who was also the team leader.

- One full-time *VDM* consultant[14].

- Three engineers with some experience of formal methods, but newcomers to *VDM*.

- A part-time external consultant[15].

- Six further engineers, some of whom were able to read *VDM*.

The team was rather short on subject specialists—people who really knew the rest of the operating system and the rôle of SA. This deficiency had the obvious effect of an increased number of *VDM* specifications being produced that did not meet the real requirements, thus causing some reworking, and consequent wasted time and effort.

It is impossible to have a large number of people working on a formal specification unless they are well organised. We employed two strategies.

The Scouting Strategy We allocated the subject specialist to work with a *VDM* specialist to work ahead on the next development level, whilst the others worked on the formal description of the current level. This helped to identify false development paths early on, and to lay a foundation for the formal work to come. Finding false development paths sometimes caused reworks in the current level.

The Consensus Strategy On some levels the team worked together. First the team independently defined the state, and then jointly reworked their ideas until a consensus emerged. At this point the main formal development could then be completed using the agreed state as a basis. Sometimes a chairman was needed to resolve conflicts.

As two-thirds of the development time was spent in reviewing and reworking, every effort was made to try to get the formalism *right first time*[16], thus reducing the overall effort. However, changing requirements were the largest cause of rework in our development; most of it could have been avoided. Other developers are warned not to spend large amounts of effort on specifying a system based on requirements that are not clear, ill-founded and in a state of flux. Other reworks that were perhaps unnecessary were caused because some reviewers did not like the style that was used by an author; beware of being more concerned about the *VDM* than the subject being specified.

It takes longer to produce a formal specification than it does to produce an informal one. At present we cannot produce evidence from this project that this extra effort has been worthwhile, but we hope to clarify the situation once the project has been completed.

---

[14]Brain Dickinson.
[15]Jim Woodcock.
[16]A good slogan for formal methods!

Planning the project has been difficult: the logic of the plans has been right enough, but the time estimates have been inaccurate, and the number of reworks underestimated.

Reporting to senior management has also been difficult, due to their lack of understanding of a project development using *VDM*. This problem needs to be addressed and overcome early in a project in order to increase confidence in and support for the development method[17].

4.7 Benefits and Costs

One of the most striking benefits of using *VDM* was that newcomers to the development with *VDM* training were able to contribute to the development quickly. The various levels of the *VDM* documentation provide a good reference for the functionality of the system. On future developments of SA we may be much less reliant on experts!

Lots of errors were detected at the specification and design stages. We hope that this means a reduced number of residual errors. When compared with traditional methods, it does take more time and effort before code is produced. Also, it is likely to take more time and effort to fix bugs as several levels may need to be corrected before code can be modified.

VDM helps to produce a better design because the consequences of design decisions can be seen in terms of complexity and—crudely—volume of *VDM*, and this visibility encourages design simplification.

As we said earlier, at this stage in the project we cannot be precise about the overall benefits and costs of using *VDM* as against using more traditional methods.

4.8 SA Development

The SA *VDM* development was a redevelopment of a component of an existing system. The only formal part of the existing SA is the code, so quotes like "the *VDM* is wrong because it doesn't match the existing code" are perhaps surprising, but explicable.

The *VDM*+ notation has proved to be a good way of describing the behaviour of the SA functions and their interactions. The main problems have come when considering the shared data interfaces between SA and other processes. Here interactions occur at a very fine level of granularity, with potential interference at the machine code instruction level. Descriptions at this level are very tedious and time-comsuming.

The *VDM* description has simplified the SA design, but it has not uncovered any fundamental problems in the previous designs. Interestingly, the new design is similar in structure to the previous design produced using traditional methods[18].

---

[17]However, we would like to thank the management for keeping their nerve in the face of slipping deadlines and unfamiliar deliverables.

[18]Perhaps we have failed to break free from previous work.

	Level1	Level2	Level3	Level4
Start of scouting	October 86	January 87	February 87	March 87
Start date	November 86	February 87	March 87	August 87
End date	January 87	March 87	August 87	?
Operations	14	90	96	?
Functions	20	22(3)	38(5)	?
State items	17	32(19)	36(19)	56(37)
Types	16	17(6)	22(10)	59(43)
Sheets	90	173	227	?
VDM Effort	3(est)	5(est)	14(est)	15+
Sections	8	18	19	30(est)
Section reviews	10+	39	49	24+
Reviews/section	?	2.2	2.5	?

Table 1: Facts and Figures about the *VDM* Development of SA.

Volume of Code	30 000 lines
Traditional design phase cost	25 man months
VDM design phase cost	35-40 man months
Traditional design phase duration	9 months
VDM design phase duration	12 months

Table 2: Estimates for the Development of SA Using Traditional Means.

4.9 Facts and Figures

Various statistics which may or may not be of interest are collected together in table 1. Figures is brackets in the table denote the numbers of new items; thus at level 2, there were a total of 17 types, six of which were newly introduced. Effort is described in terms of man-months.

4.10 A Crude Comparison with Traditional Methods

Using their standard model for software development, GECOMO, GEC have produced estimates for developing SA using traditional methods. They are compared with the actual ones in table 2.

5 Acknowledgments

This work has been inspired and supported by GEC Telecommunications Ltd, Coventry; thanks are due to Gerard Wedge Adams, Carl Pulley, and Steve Ward. Discussions with He Jifeng, Steve King and Carroll Morgan in Oxford helped us to understand the technique. Valuable comments were received from the audiences at seminars at the Hatfield Polytechnic, the Informatics Group at the Rutherford Appleton Laboratory, and the Programming Research Group at Oxford University. Encouragement and suggestions for improving the paper were offered by Cliff Jones and the referees. JCPW would like to dedicate his part of the work to James Christopher Woodcock, born 29 January, 1988. Finally, thanks to Jock McDoowi, without whom nothing would have been accomplished.

6 References

1. H. Barringer, *A Survey of Verification Techniques for Parallel Programs*, Lecture Notes in Computer Science **191**, Springer-Verlag, 1985.

2. I. Hayes (editor), *Specification Case Studies*, Prentice-Hall International, 1987.

3. C.A.R. Hoare, *Communicating Sequential Processes*, Prentice-Hall International, 1985.

4. C.B. Jones, *Software Development: a Rigorous Approach*, Prentice-Hall International, 1980.

5. C.B. Jones, "Development Methods for Computer Programs Including a Notion of Interference", *D. Phil. Thesis*, Technical Monograph PRG-25, Programming Research Group, Oxford University, 1981.

6. C.B. Jones, "Specification and Design of (Parallel) Programs" *Information Processing 83*, R.E.A. Mason (ed), Elsevier Science Publishers B.V. (North-Holland), 1983a.

7. C.B. Jones, "Tentative Steps Towards a Development Method for Interfering Programs" *ACM Trans on Programming Languages and Systems*, 5(4), 576-619, 1983b.

8. C.B. Jones, *Systematic Software Development Using* VDM, Prentice-Hall International, 1986.

9. R. Milner, *A Calculus of Communicating Systems*, Lecture Notes in Computer Science **92**, Springer-Verlag, 1980.

10. J.C.P. Woodcock & B. Dickinson, "Using VDM with Rely and Guarantee-Conditions: Experiences from a Real Project", *full version*, Programming Research Group, Oxford University, 1988.

7 Summary of Proof Rules

7.1 Operation Decomposition

We shall use the following notation in the description of the rules of inference for operation decomposition

$P, \overleftarrow{P}, b$	predicates of single states.
$\overleftarrow{P}$	predicte formed from P by decorating all free variables with overhooks.
R, G, Q	relational predicates, namely rely, guarantee, and post conditions.
$(\ldots)^*$	transitive closure of $(\ldots)$.
I_x	the identity relational predicate on everything, except x
Δe	single state predicate giving definedness of e.
$Q_1 \mid Q_2$	the forward relational composition of Q_1 and Q_2

Sequential Composition

$$S_1 \, \text{sat} \, (P, R, G, P' \wedge Q_1)$$
$$S_2 \, \text{sat} \, (P', R, G, Q_2)$$
$$\overline{S_1; S_2 \, \text{sat} \, (P, R, G, Q_1 \mid Q_2)}$$

Conditional

$$S_1 \, \text{sat} \, (P \wedge b, R, G, Q)$$
$$S_2 \, \text{sat} \, (P \wedge \neg b, R, G, Q)$$
$$\overline{\text{if } b \text{ then } S_1 \text{ else} S_2 \, \text{sat} \, (P, R, G, Q)}$$

Parallel

$$S_1 \, \text{sat} \, (P, R \vee G_2, G_1, Q_1)$$
$$S_2 \, \text{sat} \, (P, R \vee G_1, G_2, Q_2)$$
$$\overline{\| \ S_i \, \text{sat} \, (P, R, G_1 \vee G_2, \overleftarrow{P} \wedge Q_1 \wedge Q_2 \wedge (R \vee G_1 \vee G_2)^*)}$$
$$\scriptstyle i$$

Atomic Assignment

$$P \wedge R \Rightarrow \Delta e$$
$$(I_x \wedge x = \overleftarrow{e}) \vee I \Rightarrow G$$
$$\overline{\langle x := e \rangle \, \text{sat} \, (P, R, G, R \mid (I_x \wedge x = \overleftarrow{e}) \mid R)}$$

Consequence

$$S \, \text{sat} \, (P', R', G', Q')$$
$$P \Rightarrow P'$$
$$R \Rightarrow R'$$
$$G' \Rightarrow G$$
$$Q' \Rightarrow Q$$
$$\overline{S \, \text{sat} \, (P, R, G, Q)}$$

Precondition

$$S \, \text{sat} \, (P, R, G, Q)$$
$$\overline{S \, \text{sat} \, (P, R, G, \overleftarrow{P} \wedge Q)}$$

8 Rules of Logic

This section contains only those rules of logic that were used in the proofs; they are taken from [Jones, 1986], appendix A.

$$= \text{-tsubs} \quad \frac{s_1 = s_2; E}{E[s_2/s_1]} \qquad \vee\text{-E} \quad \frac{E_1 \vee \ldots E_n; \quad E_1 \vdash E; \ldots; E_n \vdash E}{E}$$

$$= \text{-comm} \quad \frac{s_1 = s_2}{s_2 = s_1} \qquad \wedge\text{-I} \quad \frac{E_1; E_2; \ldots; E_n}{E_1 \wedge E_2 \wedge \ldots \wedge E_n}$$

$$f(d) \cong \text{if } e \text{ then } et \text{ else} f \qquad \wedge\text{-E} \quad \frac{E_1 \wedge E_2 \wedge \ldots \wedge E_n}{E_i}$$

$$\text{ifelsubs} \quad \frac{d_0 \in D; \neg e_0; E(ef_0)}{E[f(d_0)/ef_0]} \qquad \Rightarrow\text{-I} \quad \frac{E_1 \vdash E_2; E_1 \in \mathbf{B}}{E_1 \Rightarrow E_2}$$

$$\text{if-E} \quad \frac{e_0; E(f(d_0))}{E[et_0/f(d_0)]} \qquad \text{vac} \Rightarrow\text{-E} \quad \frac{E_1 \Rightarrow E_2; E_1}{E_2}$$

$$\frac{\neg e_0; E(f(d_0))}{E[ef0/f(d_0)]} \qquad \exists\text{-I} \quad \frac{s \in X; E(s/x)}{\exists x \in X \cdot E(x)}$$

$$\Leftrightarrow \text{-defn} \quad \frac{(E_1 \Rightarrow E_2) \wedge (E_2 \Rightarrow E_1)}{E_1 \Leftrightarrow E_2}$$

9 Set Theory

This section contains some basic facts about set theory that are used in the proofs in the paper.

$$\in \text{-prop} \quad \frac{s_1 \neq s_2}{s_1 \notin \{s_2\}} \qquad -\text{-prop} \quad \frac{s \in X \wedge s \notin Y}{s \in X - Y}$$

$$\subseteq \text{-refl} \quad \frac{}{X \subseteq X} \qquad \subseteq \text{-trans} \quad \frac{X \subseteq Y \wedge Y \subseteq Z}{X \subseteq Z}$$

$$\subseteq \text{-p.o.} \quad \frac{X \subseteq Y}{X \subseteq Y \cup Z} \qquad \subseteq \text{-defn} \quad \frac{\forall s \in X \cdot s \in Y}{X \subseteq Y}$$

$$\in \text{-prop2} \quad \frac{s \in X}{\{s\} \subseteq X} \qquad \cup\text{-mono} \quad \frac{X \subseteq Y}{X \cup Z \subseteq Y \cup Z}$$

$$\cup\text{-idem} \quad \frac{}{X \cup X = X} \qquad = \text{set defn} \quad \frac{X \subseteq Y \wedge Y \subseteq X}{X = Y}$$

Software Support for the Refinement of VDM Specifications

P. Kilpatrick and P. McParland
Department of Computer Science
The Queen's University of Belfast
Belfast BT7 1NN

ABSTRACT :

A tool set is described which supports the use of VDM in software development. The tool set aids the user both in the construction of VDM specifications and in the refinement of such specifications. A proof checker is included which checks the correctness of the associated proofs. Design decisions necessary to allow automated support of the refinement process are discussed.

Introduction

It is generally felt that widespread acceptance of the use of formal methods of software development must be preceded by the availability of suitable tools to support the use of such methods. Currently a number of tool sets are being developed to support a variety of specification notations. Examples include the RAISE project [Prehn 87] and the Meta-IV Tool Support Project [Olsen 87]. To date such projects have tended to be large scale (> 10 man years) with emphasis placed upon the construction of highly sophisticated systems which support most aspects of formal software development. Typically such tool sets include a syntax-directed editor, lexical, syntactic and static semantic analysers, pretty-printers and a range of pragmatic tools such as version control software which assist in the manipulation of specification documents. Support for interactive development of specifications is considered important. The scale of these projects has meant that, although begun several years ago, even syntax checkers are not yet widely available [Woodcock 88].

In contrast, the tool set project described here is a small scale project (< 2 man years). Emphasis has been placed on developing, over a short period, a simple (non interactive) set of tools which supports both the use of the Meta-IV notation and application of the method (i.e. construction of a series of refinements of a specification). The tool set comprises syntax and semantic checkers, a lemma generator (generating the lemmas required for proof of consistency between design levels) and a proof checker to check user supplied proofs of the generated lemmas.

The dialect of Meta-IV supported is that described by Jones in [Jones 86].

Software Development using VDM

The use of a model oriented formal method as a development methodology involves the construction of an (abstract) specification and the refinement of this specification through several intermediate levels to a (concrete) specification expressed in a style which is close to the target programming language. Thus, for our purposes, a VDM *script* comprises a number of specification levels, where each level is a refinement of its predecessor. Thus, using EBNF:

```
VDMScript  =   "SPECIFICATION" SpecName
                   DesignLevel
                   { DesignLevel  }
               "END_SPECIFICATION"


DesignLevel  =   "DESIGN" "STEP" DesignNumber "FOR" SpecName
                   DesignBody
               "END_DESIGN"
```

Each DesignBody contains data, operations, functions and - beyond the first level - data retrieve functions.

The strength of a notation such as VDM lies in the fact that, by stating and proving certain lemmas, consistency between design levels is guaranteed. The essence of the tool set described here is the mechanical assistance given in ensuring this consistency.

The Tool Set

The tool set comprises the following tools :

          i) Syntax Checker (including lexical analyser)
          ii) Semantic Checker
          iii) Lemma Generator
          iv) Proof Checker

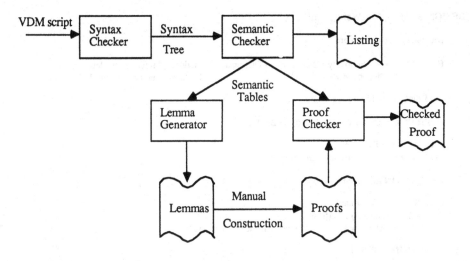

Figure 1.   The Tool Set

The user supplies a complete VDM script to the syntax checker which checks its syntactic correctness and builds a tree representation of the input. The semantic checker performs (static) semantic checks, including, for example, a check that each reified piece of data has a corresponding retrieve function. Provided no errors are found, the lemma generator produces a list of the lemmas necessary for proofs of consistency to be carried out. It is then up to the user to decide the rigour with which proofs of these lemmas are to be carried out. No theorem prover is provided in the tool set so proofs must be done manually although the proof checker may be used to verify the correctness of any (necessarily formal) proofs which have been constructed.

Figure 2 shows an example VDM script. The Meta-IV notation used in the script is the [Jones 86] dialect with minor syntactic changes; the example is taken from [Jones 86].

SPECIFICATION Word_Dictionary

    DESIGN STEP 0 FOR Word_Dictionary

        Word = undefined

        Dictionary = **set of** Word

        INIT $dict_0 = \{\ \}$

        OPERATION CheckWord (w:Word) b : Boolean

        EXT RD dict : Dictionary
        POST b $\Leftrightarrow$ w $\in$ dict

        OPERATION AddWord (w:Word)

        EXT WR dict : Dictionary
        PRE w $\notin$ dict
        POST dict = dict' $\cup$ { w } ! dict' denotes the value of dict before execution of the operation

    END_DESIGN STEP 0

DESIGN STEP 1 FOR Word_Dictionary

Dictionary = **seq of** Word

FUNCTION retr_Dictionary : Dictionary $\rightarrow$ Dictionary" ! Dictionary" refers to the definition of
    retr_Dictionary(wl) := rng(wl)   ! Dictionary at the previous design level.

INIT $dict_0$ = « » ! Empty sequence

OPERATION CheckWord (w:Word) b : Boolean

EXT RD dict : Dictionary
POST b $\Leftrightarrow$ $\exists$ i $\in$ dom(dict) . dict[i] = w

OPERATION AddWord (w:Word)

EXT RD dict : Dictionary
PRE ~ $\exists$ i $\in$ dom(dict) . dict[i] = w
POST dict = dict' $^\wedge$ « w »   ! $^\wedge$ denotes sequence concatenation

 END_DESIGN STEP 1

 END_SPECIFICATION

Figure 2.   A VDM Script.

Design Decisions

To allow automated assistance with the refinement process, a number of decisions were taken regarding the composition of a VDM script :

1) Every definition must retain the same *signature* throughout all design levels of a VDM script. The signature of a definition is defined as follows:
    . the signature of a (user specified) data type is the name of the type.
    . the signature of an (explicit) function comprises the name of the function together with the names of its associated parameters and their type names, and the names of its result parameter and its type name.
    . the signature of an operation comprises its name together with the names of its associated parameters and their type names (including external variables), and the name of the result together with its type name.

Thus in the example of Figure 2 the signature of CheckWord is

OPERATION CheckWord (w:Word) b : Boolean
EXT RD dict : Dictionary

and remains unaltered throughout the remainder of the script. Note however that the actual type of Dictionary is changed (from *set of Word* to *seq of Word*), thus indirectly affecting the types associated with Checkword.

There are two reasons for insisting that signatures remain unchanged:
1. We require that the "functionality" of each operation remain unchanged.
2. Insisting that signatures remain unchanged between successive refinement levels ensures that an implicit correspondance between definitions and their refined counterparts is maintained.

Note that keeping the signature of a definition constant during reification requires some notation to highlight references to reified definitions in the previous design level. We have chosen to decorate such definitions with a double quote character :

$\qquad$ **FUNCTION** retr_Dictionary : Dictionary $\rightarrow$ Dictionary"
$\qquad$ retr_Dictionary(wl) := rng(wl)

The retrieve function is thus a mapping from *Dictionary* (defined in Design Level 1) to *Dictionary"* (defined in Design Level 0). Other functions, such as the constructor 'mk-functions', from the preceding design level can be referenced in this way.

2) An *undefined* type is introduced to allow explicit definition of a type to be deferred to a subsequent design level, while still allowing the appropriate lemmas to be generated.

3) To allow a user to concentrate on the definitions being reified during a design step, only those definitions being changed need be presented in the design step; unchanged definitions are assumed to 'carry over' from the preceding design level. Thus, all those definitions presented in Design Step 1 of the *Word_Dictionary* specification are reified data and correspondingly refined operations and functions from Design Step 0.

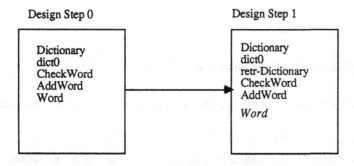

Figure 3   Refinement between design levels

The definition named in italics in Figure 3 (ie. *Word*) has not been explicitly defined in design step 1, but it is taken from design step 0. All other definitions in design step 1 have overwritten definitions in design step 0, or they are new (eg. retr_Dictionary).

A Lemma Generator

The Lemma generator generates the lemmas which must be proven to guarantee consistency between refinement levels. Lemmas are generated by using lemma templates together with information from the semantic tables constructed by the semantic checker.

The following lemmas are generated:
>   Constant Lemma
>   Operation Implementability
>   Reification Adequacy :
>>   Data Type
>>   Initial State Adequacy
>>   Domain Rule
>>   Result Rule
>   Function Result Lemma

These are essentially the same as used in [Jones 86], with the following differences:

1) The Constant Lemma.   For convenience we allow the definition of constants. For example

>   Coordinate   ==   **COMPOSE** Coordinate OF
>>   x : { -100 ... 100 }
>>   y : {-100 ... 100 }
>   **END**

>   **CONST** Origin : Coordinate = mk-Coordinate (0,0)

The constant lemma is used to ensure that any constants defined are of the correct type. Generally this lemma can be proven easily.

2) The satisfaction lemmas presented in [Jones 86] are not included in the lemma generation because these lemmas assume the existence of implementation code corresponding to the specification. To support construction of a proof that a piece of (imperative) code implements an operation (or function) a Verification Condition Generator [Gray 87] would be required to automate reasoning about the code. This has not been incorporated in the tool set.

3) No distinction is made between an operation with EXT variables and those without (implicit function specifications). All are considered to be operations and the one implementability lemma is used, *operation implementability* :

$$\forall\ \sigma' \in \Sigma\ .\ \text{pre\_OP}(\sigma') => \exists\ \sigma \in \Sigma\ .\ \text{post\_OP}(\sigma',\sigma)$$

where σ' and σ refer to states before and after execution of the operation, respectively.

Thus the implementability lemma for AddWord is :

$$\forall\ W \in \text{word},\ \text{DICT}' \in \text{dictionary}\ .$$
$$\text{pre\_ADDWORD}(W, \text{DICT}')\ \Rightarrow$$
$$\exists\ \text{Dict} \in\ \text{Dictionary}\ .$$
$$\text{post\_ADDWORD}(W, \text{DICT}', \text{DICT})$$

4) Function result lemma. For each function specified in a design level, it must be shown that the function result is of the correct type :

$$\forall\ d \in D\ .\ f(d) \in R \qquad \text{where}\ \ d\ \text{is the parameter(s) of function f and}$$
$$R\ \text{is the result type of f.}$$

For example, inclusion of a function DictSize :

FUNCTION DictSize : Dictionary --> Integer
DictSize(D) := card(D)

in the example above would result in generation of the following lemma:

$$\forall\ d \in \text{Dictionary}\ .\ \text{DictSize}(d) \in \text{Integer}$$

Such proofs are usually straightforward, even when the data types involve invariants.

A Proof Checker

Ideally a tool set of the sort described here would include a proof assistant which would aid the user in the construction of the required proofs. As a first step toward such an assistant, a proof checker has been constructed which verifies the correctness of hand constructed proofs. The proof checker has been developed using VDM with the assistance of the earlier described tools.

An abstract specification of the proof checker is given followed by some of the main data reification steps.

The proofs to be checked are in the natural deduction style of [Jones86]. To aid understanding of this section, an example from [Jones 86] is given in Figure 4, which may be referred to; the example is a proof of Data Adequacy for the data type *Dictionary* of Figure 2.

0.0	**from** d ∈ dictionary" , << >> ∈ dictionary	
1.0	retr_Dictionary(<< >>) = {}	obvious()
2.0	∃ da ∈ Dictionary . retr_Dictionary(da) = {}	∃_I(h0.0(2),1.0)
3.0	**from** d ∈ Dictionary" , w ∈ Word, w ∉ d,	
	∃ da ∈ Dictionary . retr_Dictionary(da) = d	
3.1	**from** da ∈ Dictionary, retr_Dictionary(da) = d	
3.1.1	rng(da) = d	obvious(retr_Dictionary,h3.1(2))
3.1.2	w ∉ rng(da)	obvious(h3.0, 3.1.1)
3.1.3	(da ^ <<w>>) ∈ Dictionary	obvious(Dictionary, 3.1.2)
3.1.4	rng(da ^ <<w>>) = rng(da) ∪ {w}	obvious(rng)
3.1.5	retr_Dictionary(da ^ <<w>>) = d ∪ {w}	obvious(3.1.1, 3.1.4)
	infer ∃ e1 ∈ Dictionary .retr_Dictionary(e1) = d ∪ {w}	∃_I(3.1.3 ,3.1.5)
	infer ∃ e1 ∈ Dictionary . retr_Dictionary(e1) = d ∪ {w}	∃_E(h3.0(4), 3.1)
	infer ∃ da ∈ Dictionary . retr_Dictionary(da) = d	set_ind(2.0,3.0)

Figure 4.   Proof of Data Adequacy for *Dictionary*

The proof checker validates a proof line by line. It uses pattern matching to check that the proposition at each line follows validly from preceding lines and/or hypotheses by appeal to a named axiom. Note that the proof checker cannot verify lines which appeal to properties of the data spaces underlying the specification. Such lines are justified by the dummy axiom name 'obvious'.

The proof checker was specified using the notation of VDM and two refinement steps were carried out. Here we present the abstract specification together with the data reification steps carried out.

A Proof is considered to be a mapping from a LineNumber to an Assertion.

Proof = **map** LineNumber **into** Assertion

A line number, e.g. 3.1.1 has been modelled by a sequence of natural numbers with a flag to indicate whether or not the line is an hypothesis (e.g. line 3.0 in Figure 4). The invariant states that if the line is an hypothesis, then it must have an associated *hypothesis number*. The hypothesis number is needed because there may be more than one hypothesis on a given line, e.g. line 3.0 of figure 4 has four hypotheses.

LineNumber   =   **compose** LineNumber **of**
                        IfHypothesis : Boolean
                        HypothesisNo : Natural
                        LineNo : **seq of** Natural
                end

> **where** inv_LineNumber(mk_LineNumber(IfHy, HyNo, Ln)) :=
> IfHy => HyNo > 0

A proof assertion is made up of a proposition and its justification

> Assertion   =   **compose** Assertion **of**
>   Proposition : Expression
>   Justification : AxiomCall
>   **end**

For example, line 2.0 has proposition $\exists\ da \in Dictionary\ .\ retr\_Dictionary(da) = \{\}$ and axiom call $\exists\_I(h0.0(2),1.0)$.

A justification is an appeal to an Axiom together with Parameters to be substituted for the antecedent of the axiom.

> AxiomCall   =   **compose** AxiomCall **of**
>   AxiomName : Identifier
>   Parameters : AxParameters
>   **end**

The parameters to an axiom are made up of an optional identifier (usually a function name used in a substitution rule) and a sequence of Line Numbers.

> AxParameters   =   **compose** AxParameters **of**
>   IdentName : [Identifier]
>   LNumber : **seq of** LineNumber
>   **end**

An Expression is made up of a function name and a sequence of arguments. Thus a constant/variable is just a function name without arguments.

> Expression   =   **compose** Expression **of**
>   FunctionName : Identifier
>   Arguments : **seq of** Expression
>   **end**

To allow the axioms to be stored a database is used: a mapping from the axiom name to its definition.

> AxiomDatabase   =   **map** Identifier **into** Axiom_Rule

Each Axiom consists of a number of Assumptions and its conclusion.

> Axiom_Rule =   **compose** Axiom_Rule **of**
>   Assumption : **seq of** Expression
>   Conclusion : Expression
>   **end**

Pattern matching is used to

1) match the parameters of an axiom with the assumptions of the named axiom; and

2) match the proposition (on a given line) with the consequent of the named axiom in a manner consistent with (1).

This pattern matching is represented by a mapping from identifiers to expressions. Detail of the pattern matching technique is ignored at this level.

Substitutions = **map** Identifier **into** Expression

The operation 'VDMProofChecker' accepts a proof, and indicates whether or not the proof is legal. The tables represent semantic information taken from the semantic checker. As a pre-condition, all the parameters of the axiom calls must be valid, i.e. the line numbers of an axiom call must exist and be accessible to the current proposition (this is checked by a function *LineValidation*, not presented here). The post-condition checks each assertion; if the current line is an hypothesis, no checking is required since no axiom has been used.

OPERATION VDMProofChecker (Text:Proof) r : Boolean
EXT RD AxiomRules : AxiomDatabase, **RD** Tables : SemanticInfo
PRE $\forall$ I $\in$ dom(Text) .
    rng(LNumber(Parameters(Justification(Text[I])))) subset_of dom(Text) &
    LineValidation(I, LNumber(Parameters(Justification(Text[I]))))
POST   r $\Leftrightarrow$ $\forall$ Line $\in$ dom(Text) .
    post_CheckAssertion(Text[Line], Text, AxiomRules, Tables, TRUE) $\lor$
    IfHypothesis(Line)

The operation CheckAssertion ensures that each assertion is correctly derived from previous propositions. The pre-condition states that the axiom name used must exist in axiom database. The post-condition is satisfied if the conclusion of the axiom, Ax, pattern matches with the proposition of the current assertion. Also, the assumptions of the axiom, Ax, must pattern match with the propositions, referenced by the line numbers (Params) in the axiom call.

OPERATION CheckAssertion (CurrentAssertion : Assertion, Text : Proof)
                r : Boolean
EXT RD AxiomRules : AxiomDatabase, **RD** Tables : SemanticInfo
PRE AxiomName(Justification(CurrentAssertion)) $\in$ dom(AxiomRules)
POST r $\Leftrightarrow$
  LET Ax = AxiomRules[AxiomName(Justification(CurrentAssertion))],
    Params = Parameters(Justification(CurrentAssertion))
  IN

∃ s ∈ Substitutions .

      post_IfMatch(Conclusion(Ax), Proposition(CurrentAssertion), s, TRUE)

    &

∀ Pattern ∈ rng(Assumption(Ax)),

    Target ∈ {x|x:Expression| ∃ y ∈ rng(LNumber(Params)) .

                        x = Proposition(Text[y]) }

    post_IfMatch(Pattern, Target, s, TRUE)

The post-condition post-IfMatch is satisfied if the Pattern and Target are the same, or the Function Name of Pattern is matched with Target in Matches.

        OPERATION IfMatch (Pattern : Expression, Target : Expression,

                          Matches : Substitutions) r : Boolean

POST r ⟺

    (FunctionName(Pattern) = FunctionName(Target) &

     ∀ P ∈ rng(Arguments(Pattern)), T ∈ rng(Arguments(Target)) .

       post_IfMatch(P, T, Matches, TRUE))

    ∨

       Matches[FunctionName(Pattern)] = Target

Having specified the proof checker in the above fashion, the data was reified to sequences, and an algorithmic specification of the pattern matching was incorporated. This allowed a more concrete representation of the ProofChecker to be studied.

With implementation in LISP in mind, a proof is refined to an ordered sequence of PrNode, which will be implemented as a LISP list. PrNode is composed of a line number and an assertion.

        Proof = **seq of** PrNode

        where inv_Proof(P) :=

            (∀ I,J ∈ dom(P). I ≤ J =>

                LineLessThan (LineNo(PrLine(P[I])),LineNo(PrLine(P[J])))

)

        PrNode = **compose** PrNode **of**

                  PrLine : LineNumber

                  PrEntry : Assertion

               end

The retrieve function, given a sequence of PrNode, returns a mapping from Line Number to Assertion.

FUNCTION retr_Proof : Proof --> Proof"

    retr_Proof(t) :=

        if t = << >>

        then [ ]

        else [PrLine(hd(t)) l-> PrEntry(hd(t))] ∪ retr_Proof(tl(t))

The axiom database is converted to a sequence of AxNode; again the sequence is ordered.

    AxiomDatabase = **seq of** AxNode

    where inv_AxiomDatabase(Ax) :=

      ∀ I,J ∈ dom(Ax) . I ≤ J => IdLessThan(AxName(Ax[I]), AxName(Ax[J]))

                  ! IdLessThan represents < on Identifiers.

    AxNode = **compose** AxNode **of**

        AxName : Identifier

        AxEntry : Axiom_Rule

      end

The retrieve function is similar to retr_Proof.

    FUNCTION retr_AxiomDatabase : AxiomDatabase --> AxiomDatabase"

    retr_AxiomDatabase(t) :=

        if t = << >>

        then []

        else [AxName(hd(t)) l-> AxEntry(hd(t))] ∪ retr_AxiomDatabase(tl(t))

The data was then further refined to binary trees. Appendix 1 shows the abstract specification developed above, together with the reifications performed on the data at the two succeeding design levels.

During development the lemma generator was used to generate the associated lemmas. Rigorous proofs of some of these lemmas were carried out, as a result of which some errors were detected (eg. failure to cope with empty sequences). The concrete specification was readily translated to LISP code; indeed, some of the functions translated required very minor syntactic changes.

Summary

A tool set which supports software development using VDM has been described. The tool set comprises syntax and (static) semantic checkers, a lemma generator and a proof checker. The full refinement process is supported. From the outset emphasis was placed on quickly producing a reasonably comprehensive set of tools, rather than on efficiency or sophistication of the user interface: such considerations are addressed elsewhere.

The syntax checker was developed using YACC [Johnson 78] generating C code. The remaining tools were written in Franz Lisp for ease of development; execution efficiency was not a priority. The system resides on a micro-VAX running ULTRIX 3.6.

The proof checker was developed using VDM supported by the other tools. Some (rigorous) proofs were constructed resulting in the early detection of errors. It is felt that the use of VDM led to the construction of higher quality code and was rendered more attractive by the availability of support software.

Possible future developments include incorporation of a verification condition generator to support operation decomposition and provision for the inclusion of inference rules in the axiom database of the proof checker.

Acknowledgement

The authors wish to thank Stephen Gilmore for some useful suggestions in the specification of the proof checker.

References

[Gray 87]   D.T. Gray, "A Pedagogical Verification Condition Generator", The Computer Journal, Vol. 30 No. 3, 1987.

[Johnson 78]   S.C. Johnson, "YACC: Yet Another Compiler-Compiler" , in UNIX Programmer's Manual, by B.W. Kernighan and M.D. McIlroy, Bell Laboratories, 1978, Seventh Edition.

[Jones 86]   C.B. Jones, Systematic Software Development Using VDM, Prentice-Hall International, 1986.

[Olsen 87]   A. Olsen, User Manual for TFL's META-IV tool, Telecommunication Research Laboratory, Copenhagen, Denmark.

[Prehn 87]   S. Prehn, "From VDM to RAISE," VDM - A Formal Method at Work, VDM-Europe Symposium, edited by D. Bjorner et al, LNCS vol. 252, 1987.

[Woodcock 88]   J.C.P. Woodcock and B. Dickinson, "Using VDM with Rely and Guarantee-Connditions: Experiences from a Real Project", Refinement Workshop, King's Manor, University of York, 1987.

APPENDIX 1

SPECIFICATION ProofChecker

DESIGN STEP 0 **FOR** ProofChecker

Proof = **map** LineNumber **onto** Assertion

LineNumber = **compose** LineNumber **of**
IfHypothesis : Boolean
HypothesisNo : Natural
LineNo : **seq of** Natural
end
where
inv_LineNumber(mk_LineNumber(IfHy, HyNo, Ln)) := IfHy => HyNo > 0

Assertion = **compose** Assertion **of**
Proposition : Expression
Justification : AxiomCall
end

AxiomCall = **compose** AxiomCall **of**
AxiomName : Identifier
Parameters : AxParameters
end

AxParameters = **compose** AxParameters **of**
IdentName : [Identifier]
LNumber : **seq of** LineNumber
end
where
inv_AxParameters(mk_AxParameters(IfId, Id, Lno)) := ~ IfId => Id = nil

Expression = **compose** Expression **of**
FunctionName : Identifier
Arguments : **seq of** Expression
end

AxiomDatabase = **map** Identifier **onto** Axiom_Rule

Axiom_Rule = **compose** Axiom_Rule **of**
Assumption : **seq of** Expression
Conclusion : Expression
end

Substitutions = **map** Identifier **onto** Expression

OPERATION VDMProofChecker (Text:Proof) r : Boolean

EXT RD AxiomRules : AxiomDatabase, **RD** Tables : SemanticInfo
PRE $\forall$ I $\in$ dom(Text) . rng(LNumber(Parameters(Justification(Text[I])))) subset_of dom(Text) &
LineValidation(I, LNumber(Parameters(Justification(Text[I]))))

POST r $\Leftrightarrow$ $\forall$ Line $\in$ dom(Text) .
post_CheckAssertion(Text[Line], Text, AxiomRules, Tables, TRUE) $\lor$ IfHypothesis(Line)

OPERATION CheckAssertion (CurrentAssertion : Assertion, Text : Proof) r : Boolean

    EXT RD AxiomRules : AxiomDatabase, **RD** Tables : SemanticInfo
    PRE AxiomName(Justification(CurrentAssertion)) ∈ dom(AxiomRules)

    POST r ⇔ **LET** Ax = AxiomRules[AxiomName(Justification(CurrentAssertion))],
                       Params = Parameters(Justification(CurrentAssertion))
               IN
                  ∃ s ∈ Substitutions .
                  post_IfMatch(Conclusion(Ax), Proposition(CurrentAssertion), s, TRUE) &
                  ∀ Pattern ∈ rng(Assumption(Ax)),
                                     Target ∈ {x|x:Expression| ∃ y ∈ rng(LNumber(Params)) .
                                       x = Proposition(Text[y]) } .
                  post_IfMatch(Pattern, Target, s, TRUE)

OPERATION IfMatch (Pattern : Expression, Target : Expression, Matches : Substitutions) r : Boolean

    POST   r ⇔ (FunctionName(Pattern) = FunctionName(Target) &
                ∀ P ∈ rng(Arguments(Pattern)), T ∈ rng(Arguments(Target)) .
                    post_IfMatch(P, T, Matches, TRUE)
)
         ∨
               Matches[FunctionName(Pattern)] = Target

END_DESIGN

DESIGN STEP 1 FOR ProofChecker

    Proof = **seq of** PrNode
    where inv_Proof(P) :=
    (∀ I,J ∈ dom(P). I ≤ J => LineLessThan(LineNo(PrLine(P[I])),
                                     LineNo(PrLine(P[J]))))
)

    PrNode = **compose** PrNode **of**
                   PrLine : LineNumber
                   PrEntry : Assertion
               end

    FUNCTION retr_Proof : Proof --> Proof"
                  retr_Proof(t) :=
                    if t = << >>
                    then [ ]
                    else [PrLine(hd(t)) |-> PrEntry(hd(t))] ∪ retr_Proof(tl(t))

    AxiomDatabase = **seq of** AxNode
    where inv_AxiomDatabase(Ax) :=
    ∀ I,J ∈ dom(Ax) . I ≤ J => IdLessThan(AxName(Ax[I]), AxName(Ax[J]))

    AxNode = **compose** AxNode **of**
                   AxName : Identifier
                   AxEntry : Axiom_Rule
                 end

FUNCTION retr_AxiomDatabase : AxiomDatabase --> AxiomDatabase"
        retr_AxiomDatabase(t) :=
        if t = << >>
        then []
        else [AxName(hd(t)) |-> AxEntry(hd(t))] ∪ retr_AxiomDatabase(tl(t))

END_DESIGN

DESIGN STEP 2 FOR ProofChecker

! A Proof is considered to be a binary tree accessed by LineNumber
Proof = [PrNode]

PrNode =   **compose** PrNode **of**
                PrLeft : Proof
                PrLine : LineNumber
                PrEntry : Assertion
                PrRight : Proof
             end
where
inv_PrNode(mk_PrNode(lt, line, entry, rt)) :=
             ($\forall$ lk $\in$ rng(collkeys(lt)) . LineLessThan(LineNo(lk), LineNo(line))) &
             ($\forall$ rk $\in$ rng(collkeys(rt)) . LineLessThan(LineNo(line), LineNo(rk)))

FUNCTION retr_PrNode : PrNode --> PrNode"
retr_PrNode(mk_PrNode(lt, line, entry, rt)) := mk_PrNode"(line,entry)

FUNCTION retr_Proof : Proof --> Proof"
retr_Proof(t) :=
        CASES t **OF**
          nil   --> << >>
          mk_PrNode(lt, line, entry, rt) -->
              retr_Proof(lt) ^ << mk_PrNode"(line, entry) >> ^ retr_Proof(rt)
        END

! The axiom database must also be converted to a binary tree
AxiomDatabase = [AxNode]

AxNode =   **compose** AxNode **of**
                AxLeft : AxiomDatabase
                AxName : Identifier
                AxEntry : Axiom_Rule
                AxRight : AxiomDatabase
             end
where
inv_AxNode(mk_AxNode(lt, name, entry, rt)) :=
                  ($\forall$ lk $\in$ rng(Axcollkeys(lt)) . IDLessThan(lk, name)) &
                  ($\forall$ rk $\in$ rng(Axcollkeys(rt)) . IDLessThan(name, rk))

FUNCTION retr_AxNode : AxNode --> AxNode"
retr_AxNode(mk_AxNode(lt, name, entry, rt)) := mk_AxNode"(name, entry)

```
FUNCTION retr_AxiomDatabase : AxiomDatabase --> AxiomDatabase"
retr_AxiomDatabase(t) :=
                CASES t OF
                   nil        -->   << >>
                   mk_AxNode(lt, name, entry, rt) -->
                      retr_AxiomDatabase(lt) ^ << mk_AxNode"(name, entry) >>
                      ^ retr_AxiomDatabase(rt)
                END
```

END_DESIGN

END_SPECIFICATION

The Use of VDM in the Specification of Chinese Characters

Ghee S. Teo and Mícheál Mac an Airchinnigh
Department of Computer Science
Trinity College, Dublin, Ireland

abstract

The VDM Meta–IV is an important *bridge* that joins application domain with implementation. This paper does not address the data reification aspect of the VDM. Rather the importance and centrality of the Meta–IV specification language in providing a "standard" framework for analysis and design is highlighted. In addressing the usefulness of the Meta–IV in the specification, design and implementation of graphical icons for a general purpose User Interface Management System, the authors chose to focus on the domain of Chinese characters — ideograms which have many characteristics in common with graphical icons. Two different (conceptual) models were developed. The first considered the ideogram as a stack of transparencies. The second viewed it as the modular composition of basic mathematical/graphical entities. Specifications of both models in the Meta–IV were developed and the declarative graphical programming language METAFONT was used in the implementation. To facilitate an appropriate entry level into learning and using METAFONT for the task in hand, the VDM Meta–IV was used to provide an abstract model of the language. The results reported indicate that use of the VDM Meta–IV as an expression of a common semantic base was a success.

1 Introduction

In the development of the theory and practice in User Interface Management Systems, a primary goal has been the separation of the application domain from the graphical presentation. Although there are severe problems in trying to achieve total separation, the approach when used in conjunction with an object-oriented approach has led to the acceptance of the notion of an object which has a presentation form that is distinct from the "logical" form. Smalltalk systems and the now-familiar Macintosh interface exhibit the effect.

A study of the pyschological and cognitive aspects of iconic interfaces is essential in the development of both the graphical presentation and logical content of objects and such research will undoubtedly have a major impact in the design of visual languages[2]. A first step in the design of such languages is to have tools that can generate icons effectively. Chinese characters form a set of icons, technically known as ideograms, which originated from picture signs. Hence, the design of Chinese characters provides a particular view of the set of tools that a visual language designer or a graphical interface designer may need. The Chinese character is chosen due to its well-formed structure. Some Chinese characters are so sophisticated that their design is comparable to that of any detailed icon that one might ever want to produce.

A subset of Chinese characters is defined analytically and generated using a font creation system — METAFONT — which is a declarative 2-D graphics programming language developed by Donald Knuth[4][5] for the purpose of character font design. It is beyond the scope of this paper to provide a comprehensive introduction to METAFONT itself. However, the principle METAFONT concepts used in the specification and design method employed by the authors to construct the Chinese characters is outlined in Meta-IV notation.

There have already been many attempts to use METAFONT for the design of Chinese characters [3][6][9]. In each case, the designer's perception of the Chinese character was different. Gu and Hobby[3] associated design of Chinese characters with a number of font parameters which governed the shape of strokes, radicals and characters. Li[6] perceived Chinese characters as being made up of radicals, "interim characters" and characters. Tung[9] regarded the design of the Chinese character to be a Computer-Aided Design problem, each character being made up of line segments drawn together. In the authors' design model, a Chinese character is composed of radical(s) and stroke(s) only. This model falls somewhere between those of Tung and Li and is chosen because radicals are well defined and the set of strokes is small and well-defined compared with "interim characters". However, in one of the authors' implementations the use of "extended" radicals was employed for pragmatic reasons. Such "extended" radicals are similar to the notion of "interim characters".

A knowledge of the VDM Meta-IV is assumed. For a general overview of the domain of application of the VDM Meta-IV and some tutorial material, one is referred to [1]. The notation used in this report is generally that of the Danish School. However, some notational variants are introduced here in order to cope with computer graphics specifications. Whereas the verbosity of even the Danish School might be acceptable in the context of programming language semantics, it is totally unacceptable for problem domains for which there is already an established mathematical treatment. These variants have been inspired by the notation of METAFONT[5] itself, and a variant of ML[7].

Section 2 presents the hierarchical structure of the Chinese character and demonstrates the

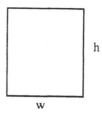

Figure 1: Dimension of a Chinese Character

fact that two competing conceptual design models of that structure are possible — the stack of transparencies model and the logical division model. Associated Meta–IV specifications accompany both. Focusing on the second of the two models, the step from specification to implementation in METAFONT is developed in Section 3. Section 4 contains the conclusions of this research work. For completeness, an implementation based on the stack of transparencies model is presented in the appendix.

2 Hierarchical Structure of the Chinese Character

The outline of a Chinese character can be perceived as a two dimensional structure (cf. Fig. 1) with a width w and a height h. Every character can be designed to have the same physical dimensions. Hence, line breaking algorithms for Chinese typesetting are trivial. This, in effect, places more of a load on font designers in the sense that they have to produce fonts of a large range of complexity to fit in the same physical dimensions. Furthermore, these fonts have to give the readers the impression that all the characters are of the same size in a passage of text.

Upon reflection on the actual writing of a character, it is clear that it is made up of a number of strokes, the simplest being one stroke and the most sophisticated being in the range of thirty strokes. A stroke is either a straight line or a curve. In the case of a "dot" stroke, it can be considered to be a very short straight line. Strokes form the basis of Chinese writing. However, users of a Chinese dictionary employ an obvious natural conceptual model of a character, based on the fact that the dictionary is indexed via a "Radical Table". A radical itself may be a Chinese character and, in general, every Chinese character contains at least one radical. There are, of course, exceptions to this rule. In the "Radical Table" lookup method one would first consider a radical which forms part of the Chinese character in question. This radical is then found in the Radical Table according to the number of strokes that make up that particular radical. A page number is given for that entry in the table. One

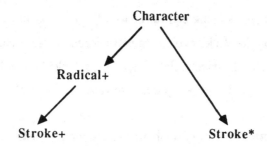

Figure 2: Composition of a Chinese Character

can then turn to this page in the dictionary to look for the character required.

This is the basic abstract model that the authors used for Chinese characters. In theory, any Chinese character can be constructed by choosing the correct radical and adding on strokes. The composition of a Chinese character is shown in Fig. 2. Given this model, a preliminary abstract specification of the Chinese character may be written in Meta–IV:

a Chinese character is composed of one or more radicals and zero or more strokes.

$$\text{CChar} :: \textit{rads}: \text{Radical}^+ \quad \textit{strs}: \text{Stroke}^* \tag{1}$$

a radical is composed of one or more strokes.

$$\text{Radical} = \text{Stroke}^+ \tag{2}$$

where

$$\text{Stroke} = \text{Mark}^+ \tag{3}$$

$$\text{Mark} = \text{Line} \mid \text{Curve} \tag{4}$$

$$\text{Line} :: p: \text{Point} \quad q: \text{Point} \tag{5}$$

$$\quad \text{for } mk\text{–Line}(p, q) \text{ use } [p, q] \tag{6}$$

$$\text{Curve} :: p_0: \text{Point} \quad p_1: \text{Point} \quad p_2: \text{Point} \quad p_3: \text{Point} \tag{7}$$

$$\quad \text{for } mk\text{–Curve}(p_0, p_1, p_2, p_3) \text{ use } p = [p_0, p_1, p_2, p_3] \tag{8}$$

$$\text{Point} :: x: \mathbf{R} \quad y: \mathbf{R} \tag{9}$$

$$\quad \text{for } mk\text{–Point}(x, y) \text{ use } z = (x, y) \tag{10}$$

Note, the special "for...use..." clause. This Meta–IV convention is used especially in the formal specification of computer graphics algorithms and was inspired by the notations of a variant of ML[7] and METAFONT[5]. Essentially, wherever there is a tree of homogeneous items, it may be regarded as being equivalent to a fixed length tuple. METAFONT curves are completely based on the Bézier cubic parametric form. A Bézier cubic curve is completely determined by four so-called control points (p_0, p_1, p_2, p_3), the first and last of which are endpoints of the curve. Thus, it seemed appropriate that the Meta–IV specification of a curve should reflect this fact.

From this very abstract model of a Chinese character two distinctly different "concrete" models were developed, again in Meta–IV — one based on the stack of transparencies concept, the other based directly on the perceived logical division of the Chinese character itself. The former model is discussed briefly in the following subsection. A more detailed discussion is to be found in [8]. The second model is presented in detail in a subsequent subsection and is the basis for the detailed discussion in the remainder of the paper.

2.1 Stack of Transparencies Model

The construction of Chinese characters or any other two dimensional structures can be viewed as a stacking of transparencies with various components drawn on each sheet. The edges of the transparencies are used as reference points. The overlapped images on the transparencies form the final picture.

In Fig. 3, a Chinese character — the "saint" — is shown to consist of separate components. At the bottom of the stack is a radical called "ear"— earrad, the next one up is a radical called "mouth" — mouthrad, and the top of the stack contains a combination of a radical and the stroke — yenrad.

Similarly, this approach can be used for other two dimensional icon constructions. In [2], a workstation icon which consists of a table, a terminal, a printer and a disk drive is given. These icons are shown in Fig. 4. The combination of these icons forms a new icon — a workstation(cf. Fig. 5) — which in the proposed model is constructed by stacking each of the icons shown in Fig. 4. Definitions for these icons are done in two stages in METAFONT. The primitives such as table, terminal, printer and disk drive are defined first. Each one of these definitions can be stored as a picture in METAFONT. These pictures are then pushed onto a stack. One can decide whether the picture formed as a result of pushing a new element constributes favourably to the desired icon. Alterations to a picture on the top of the picture stack can be made by popping it, modifying it and then pushing it again. The final desired icon is obtained by performing an *overlay* operation on the stack. A corresponding METAFONT implementation using the stack model is given in appendix A.

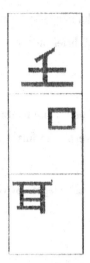

Figure 3: A Stack of Radicals and a stroke

Figure 4: Icons for Table, Terminal, Printer and Disk Drive

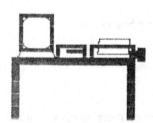

Figure 5: Composite Workstation Icon

The stack of transparencies model suggested a particular concrete specification for a Chinese character, radical and stroke. A brief outline of the specification follows.

2.1.1 Chinese Character Type

A Chinese character is composed of one or more Radicals and zero or more Strokes. There is a set of aethestic attributes that governs the final outlook of the characters.

$$\textbf{module } \text{CChar} \tag{11}$$
$$\quad \textbf{model } \text{CChar} :: rps:\ \text{Radical}^+ \quad sps:\ \text{Stroke}^* \quad atts:\ \text{A\_attribute} \tag{12}$$
$$\quad \cdots$$
$$\textbf{end module} \tag{13}$$

where

$$\text{A\_attribute} :: st:\ \text{Style} \quad sz:\ \text{Size} \tag{14}$$
$$\text{Style} = \text{Bold} \mid \text{Sung} \mid \text{Long Sung} \tag{15}$$
$$\text{Size} = \mathbf{R} \tag{16}$$

The well-formedness of a Chinese character — $is\text{-}wf$-CChar to be included in the module (cf. line 11) — is defined such that a null picture does not form a Chinese character. The size of a Chinese character to be designed has to be greater than 5 printer points (pt) and less than 25pt, the former limit seeming to be a reasonable lower bound and the latter an arbitrary upper limit. Only one of the three styles is being constructed at a time.

$$is\text{-}wf\text{-CChar: CChar} \longrightarrow \mathbf{B} \tag{17}$$
$$is\text{-}wf\text{-CChar}(mk\text{-CChar}(rps, sps, mk\text{-A\_attribute}(st, sz))) \triangleq \tag{18}$$
$$\quad rps \neq \langle\rangle \ \wedge \tag{19}$$
$$\quad st \in \{\text{Bold}, \text{Sung}, \text{Long Sung}\} \ \wedge \tag{20}$$
$$\quad 5 < sz < 25 \tag{21}$$

2.1.2 Radical Type

A radical is composed of one or more strokes. Similar to the Chinese character module (cf. line 11), the same aethestic attributes (A_attribute) are found here. The geometrical attributes consist of a reference point to the bottom left corner of the radical extent, the radical extent itself, and a scaling transformation. The geometrical attributes control the relative placement of the radical within the constructed character.

module Radical   (22)
  model Radical :: rp: Rad_picture a: A_attribute g: G_attribute   (23)
  $\cdots$
end module   (24)

where

Rad_picture = Stroke$^+$ (25)
G_attribute :: r: Ref_point e: Extent s: ScaleFactor   (26)
Ref_point :: x: **R** y: **R**   (27)
  for mk-Ref_Point(x, y) **use** (x, y) (28)
Extent :: w: **R** h: **R**   (29)
  for mk-Extent(w, h) **use** (w, h) (30)
ScaleFactor :: s_x: **R** s_y: **R**   (31)
  for mk-ScaleFactor(s_x, s_y) **use** (s_x, s_y) (32)

A well-formed radical — is-wf-Radical to be included in the module (cf. line 22) — consists of one or more strokes. The aethestic attributes are confined to those specified by the character that uses them and the transformed radical extent must lie within the design size.

is-wf-Radical: Radical $\longrightarrow$ **B**   (33)
is-wf-Radical$(mk$-Radical$(strks, a, g)) \triangleq$ (34)
  $strks \neq \langle\rangle$ $\wedge$ (35)
  let $a = mk$-A_attribute(st, sz) **in**   (36)
    $(st \in \{\text{Bold, Sung, Long Sung}\}$ $\wedge$ $5 < sz < 25)$ $\wedge$ (37)
      let $g = mk$-G_attribute$((x, y), (w, h), (s_x, s_y))$ **in**   (38)
        let $x' = ws_x, y' = hs_y$ **in**   (39)
          $(0 \leq x < sz - 5 \wedge 0 \leq y < sz - 5)$ $\wedge$ (40)
          $(1 < x' \leq sz - x \wedge 1 < y' \leq sz - y)$ (41)

2.1.3 Stroke Type

A stroke is basically a line segment with n points. It has attributes similar to those of radical and a corresponding well-formedness condition.

module Stroke   (42)
  model Stroke :: ls: Line_seg a: A_attribute g: G_attribute   (43)
  $\cdots$
end module   (44)

where

$$\textbf{module } \text{Line\_seg} \qquad (45)$$
$$\textbf{model } \text{Line\_seg} = \text{Point}^\star \qquad (46)$$

$$\textit{is-wf-}\text{Line\_seg}: \text{Line\_seg} \longrightarrow \textbf{B} \qquad (47)$$
$$\textit{is-wf-}\text{Line\_seg}(ls) \triangleq \qquad (48)$$
$$\textbf{let } n = len\ ls\ \textbf{in} \qquad (49)$$
$$n \geq 2\ \wedge \qquad (50)$$
$$\textbf{let } ls[1] = z_1, ls[n] = z_n\ \textbf{in } z_1 \neq z_n \qquad (51)$$
$$\dots$$
$$\textbf{end module} \qquad (52)$$

2.2 Logical Division Model

In the actual design of Chinese characters, the task of measuring each stroke's width, length, and other font parameters is enormous. The Chinese character may be viewed as essentially the modular composition of radicals. It is precisely this principle that is used in the Radical Table lookup method of the Chinese dictionary. Therefore, making use of the compositional property of Chinese characters one may define strokes and radicals and store them in a dictionary.

The authors propose the following four logical divisions in carrying out an analysis and synthesis of Chinese characters. All Chinese characters fall into one of these categories.

- The **Left-Right Vertical** division (cf. Fig. 6).

- The **Top-Bottom Horizontal** division (cf. Fig. 7).

- The **Exterior-Interior Rectangular** division (cf. Fig. 8).

- The final category contains non-divisible characters, i.e., any of the characters that do not fit into any of the other categories (cf. Fig. 9).

The advantage of having these logical divisions is that characters can be analysed and constructed according to these divisions. Furthermore, the first three of these divisions can be defined recursively. That is, divisions can be made within subdivisions. The illustration in Fig. 10 shows how the recursive subdivision is carried out.

To record this particular view of the Chinese character, the following specification was developed. Note, in particular, that since the aesthetic attributes of the previous model will also apply here, it has been decided to omit them for simplicity's sake. A Chinese character is now considered to be a particular logical division

$$CChar :: dt: \text{Div\_Type} \quad bx: \text{Box} \qquad (53)$$

Figure 6: Left-Right Vertical Division

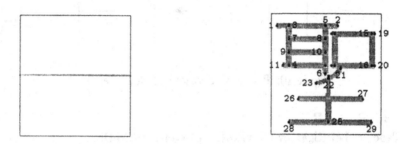

Figure 7: Top-Bottom Horizontal division

Figure 8: Exterior-Interior Rectangular division

 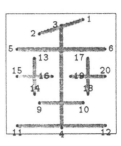

Figure 9: Category of non-divisible Characters

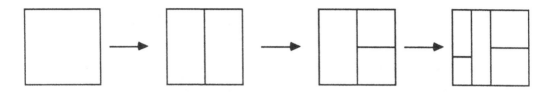

Figure 10: Recursive divisions of character box

$$\text{Box} :: w: \mathbf{R} \quad h: \mathbf{R} \tag{54}$$
$$\text{Div\_Type} = \text{LeftRightDiv} \mid \text{TopBotDiv} \mid \text{ExtIntDiv} \mid \text{NoDiv} \tag{55}$$

which has to be placed into an appropriate box. The Chinese character is subject to the following constraint:

$$\textit{is-wf-}\text{CChar: CChar} \longrightarrow \mathbf{B} \tag{56}$$
$$\textit{is-wf-}\text{CChar}(mk\text{-CChar}(dt, mk\text{-Box}(w, h)) \triangleq \tag{57}$$
$$dt \in \{\text{Div\_Type}\} \wedge \tag{58}$$
$$(5 \leq w, h \leq 25) \tag{59}$$

Each of the logical divisions, except of course for the so-called non-divisible character, is then defined recursively as a couple of PathTransformParts together with an appropriate partitioning ratio that is used for box division.

$$\text{LeftRightDiv} :: l: \text{PathTransformPart} \quad r: \text{PathTransformPart} \quad \textit{lrr}: \text{Ratio} \tag{60}$$
$$\text{TopBotDiv} :: t: \text{PathTransformPart} \quad b: \text{PathTransformPart} \quad \textit{tbr}: \text{Ratio} \tag{61}$$
$$\text{ExtIntDiv} :: e: \text{PathTransformPart} \quad i: \text{PathTransformPart} \tag{62}$$
$$\qquad\qquad \textit{rx}: \text{Ratio} \quad \textit{ry}: \text{Ratio} \quad \textit{ct}: \text{Pair} \tag{63}$$
$$\text{NoDiv} :: pn: \text{Rsp}^\star \quad \textit{trf}: \text{Transform} \tag{64}$$
$$\text{Ratio} = [0, 1] \tag{65}$$

$$\text{PathTransformPart} :: ps: \text{Rsp}^* \quad tf: \text{Transform} \quad rg: \text{Div\_Type} \tag{66}$$

$$\text{Rsp} = \text{Stroke} \mid \text{Radical} \tag{67}$$

where Radical and Stroke are specified by

$$\text{Radical} :: ss: \text{Stroke}^* \quad st: \text{Transform}^* \quad ext: \text{Extent} \tag{68}$$

$$\text{Extent} :: w: \mathbf{R} \quad h: \mathbf{R} \tag{69}$$

subject to the constraint

$$is\text{-}wf\text{-Radical}(mk\text{-Radical}(ss, st, mk\text{-Extent}(w, h))) \triangleq \tag{70}$$

$$\mathbf{len} \ ss = \mathbf{len} \ st \ \wedge \tag{71}$$

$$\mathbf{let} \ (P_i = ss[i], t_i = st[i] \mid (0 < i \le \mathbf{len} \ ss)) \ \mathbf{in} \tag{72}$$

$$\mathbf{let} \ lp = \mathbf{len} \ P_i \ \mathbf{in} \tag{73}$$

$$\mathbf{let} \ (res = \text{transformed}(P_i[j], t_i) \mid (0 < j \le lp)) \ \mathbf{in} \tag{74}$$

$$\mathbf{let} \ t_x = s\text{-}x(res) \tag{75}$$

$$t_y = s\text{-}y(res) \ \mathbf{in} \tag{76}$$

$$(0 < t_x \le w) \wedge (0 < t_y \le h) \tag{77}$$

and

$$\text{Stroke} = \text{Path} \tag{78}$$

$$\text{Path} = \text{Pair}^* \tag{79}$$

subject to the constraint

$$is\text{-}wf\text{-Stroke}: \text{Stroke} \longrightarrow \mathbf{B} \tag{80}$$

$$is\text{-}wf\text{-Stroke}(s) \triangleq \tag{81}$$

$$\mathbf{let} \ n = \mathbf{len} \ s \ \mathbf{in} \tag{82}$$

$$n \ge 2 \wedge s[1] \ne s[n] \tag{83}$$

3 From Specification to Implementation

Each letterform, line segment or picture generated by METAFONT is described mathematically. The number of graphics primitives is small. However, the ability to define macros in METAFONT expands the horizon enormously. In the plain base file of METAFONT, the number of macros that are available would require tremendous effort to master them. Therefore, it is necessary for the font designers to understand the font's structure well in order to make full use of METAFONT's features.

The authors started without knowing how METAFONT can be used to describe Chinese characters. Natural language together with computer graphics terminology and mathematics was the only means we could use to communicate with each other regarding Chinese character constructs. However, to write this down solely in English is tedious and vague. VDM Meta-IV was used to describe the structure of Chinese characters and augmented with English text.

The conceptual model of Chinese characters and the original abstract VDM Meta-IV specification enabled the first author to find a quick entry point into METAFONT. It soon became obvious that some sort of Meta-IV specification for those features of METAFONT used in the character set design would be beneficial for further work. This idea is akin to that of providing the abstract syntax and corresponding semantics for a conventional programming language. The work done in this area is still in a preliminary stage. A very brief outline of this specification is presented in the following subsection. The aspects of METAFONT which are covered include the picture — used in the stack encoding, and the two key features used in the second model — the path and the transform.

The METAFONT code presented in this section and in the appendix is given in the special typesetting style of the METAFONT book. This style is excellent for the purpose of illustration. Naturally, when coding a METAFONT program, a more ugly and obscure form is used - the ASCII character set. Moreover, the METAFONT programs can only really be understood in the context of the accompanying figures of characters or icons being designed. To assist this matching bewteen image and program, key pen positions are labelled.

3.1 VDM Meta-IV for Paths

The actual semantics of path as it occurs in METAFONT is quite elaborate. For the purposes of this paper, it suffices to present a simplified but adequate abstract model. At the most basic level, actual lines and curves may be produced by a pen which traces out a specific path — using a so-called *penstroke* command. Thus, a path, such as $z_{1e}..z_{2e}..z_{3e}$ used by the *penstroke* command is essentially a sequence of pairs of points (z_l, z_r), where (z_l, z, z_r) is the corresponding pen position.

$$\text{Path} = \text{PointPair}^* \tag{84}$$
$$\text{PointPair} :: z_l: \text{Point} \quad z_r : \text{Point} \tag{85}$$
$$\quad \textbf{for } mk\text{-PointPair}(z_l, z_r) \textbf{ use } (z_l, z_r) \tag{86}$$

A penstroke command takes a path as argument and METAFONT maps the path into a polygonal closed path which is then filled. For example, the METAFONT statement

$$\textbf{penstroke } z_{1e}..z_{2e}..z_{3e};$$

(87)

expands into

$$\textbf{fill } z_{1l}..z_{2l}..z_{3l} - z_{3r}..z_{2r}..z_{1r} - \textbf{cycle};$$

(88)

A polygonal closed path is a sequence of points:

$$\text{PolyPath} = \text{Point}^{\star}$$

(89)

subject to the constraint

$$is\text{-}wf\text{-}\text{PolyPath}: \text{PolyPath} \longrightarrow \mathbf{B}$$

(90)

$$is\text{-}wf\text{-}\text{PolyPath}(pp) \triangleq$$

(91)

$$\quad \textbf{let } n = len\ pp\ \textbf{in } n > 3 \quad \wedge \quad pp[1] = pp[n]$$

(92)

The penstroke command may be abstracted by

$$\text{Penstroke\_Cmd} :: \text{Path}$$

(93)

In the elaboration of the penstroke command, it is necessary to transform a path into a polygonal path. The algorithm is simply:

$$\text{transform\_path}: \text{Path} \longrightarrow \text{PolyPath}$$

(94)

$$\text{transform\_path}(pp) \triangleq \text{join}(\text{split}(pp))$$

(95)

$$\text{split}: \text{Path} \longrightarrow \text{Point}^{\star} \times \text{Point}^{\star}$$

(96)

$$\text{split}(\langle\ \rangle) \triangleq (\langle\ \rangle, \langle\ \rangle)$$

(97)

$$\text{split}(\langle(z_l, z_r)\rangle\ ^\wedge\ rest) \triangleq \text{split}(rest)\ \textbf{ in }$$

(98)

$$\quad (z_l\ ^\wedge\ rest_l, z_r\ ^\wedge\ rest_r)$$

(99)

$$\text{join}: \text{Point}^{\star} \times \text{Point}^{\star} \longrightarrow \text{PolyPath}$$

(100)

$$\text{join}((p_l, p_r)) \triangleq p_l\ ^\wedge\ rev\ p_r\ ^\wedge\ p_l[1]$$

(101)

Finally, the elaboration of the penstroke command may be expressed as

$$Elab\text{-}\text{Penstroke\_Cmd}: \text{Penstroke\_Cmd} \longrightarrow \text{Pixel\_Region}$$

(102)

$$Elab\text{-}\text{Penstroke\_Cmd}(mk\text{-}\text{Penstroke\_Cmd}(p)) \triangleq$$

(103)

$$\quad \textbf{let } pp = \text{transform\_path}(p)\ \textbf{in } \text{fill}(pp)$$

(104)

where **fill** is the METAFONT algorithm for flooding a closed polygon pp with pixels, and a region of pixels is specified as the map:

$$\text{Pixel\_Region} = \{0 \dots x\} \times \{0 \dots y\} \xrightarrow{\text{m}} \text{Pixel} \tag{105}$$

where

$$\text{Pixel} = \text{SmallInteger} \tag{106}$$
$$\text{SmallInteger} = \{-3 \dots +3\} \tag{107}$$

In reality a pixel value may be less than -3 or may exceed 3.

3.2 VDM Meta-IV for Pictures

A picture is a two dimensional pattern of pixels:

module Picture   (108)
  model Picture = Pixel_Region   (109)
  $\dots$
end module   (110)

Some operations on a picture are (i) initialisation, which corresponds to METAFONT's **nullpicture**, and (ii) addition and subtraction of pictures:

$$\text{init:} \longrightarrow \text{Picture} \tag{111}$$
$$\text{init} \triangleq [(i,j) \mapsto 0 \mid 0 \le i \le x, 0 \le j \le y] \tag{112}$$

$$\_ + \_ : \text{Picture} \times \text{Picture} \longrightarrow \text{Picture} \tag{113}$$
$$p_1 + p_2 \triangleq p_1 + [(i,j) \mapsto p_1(i,j) + p_2(i,j) \mid 0 \le i \le x, 0 \le j \le y] \tag{114}$$

$$\_ - \_ : \text{Picture} \times \text{Picture} \longrightarrow \text{Picture} \tag{115}$$
$$p_1 - p_2 \triangleq p_1 + [(i,j) \mapsto p_1(i,j) - p_2(i,j) \mid 0 \le i \le x, 0 \le j \le y] \tag{116}$$

A declaration, such as **picture** $p[\ ]$, gives a tuple of pictures. Plain METAFONT keeps the currently-worked-on picture in a picture variable called *currentpicture*. Thus the METAFONT code

picture $v[\ ]$ (117)
  $\dots$
  $v_1 = currentpicture;$ (118)

initialises the first picture to be that which is current.

3.3 VDM Meta-IV for Transform

An extensive range of geometric transformations, each of which is applicable to a number of basic types, is provided in METAFONT — viz., *pair, path, picture,* and *transform* itself. The *Pen* type is also subject to a geometric transformation because it is defined to be a polygonal closed path. *Picture* is subject to a restricted range of geometric transformations.

A transform is a 6-tuple of real numbers in METAFONT. For example, the declaration **transform** *t* is really

$$(t_x, t_y, t_{xx}, t_{xy}, t_{yx}, t_{yy}) \tag{119}$$

The general transformation in METAFONT, (x, y) **transformed** t is simply an abbreviation for

$$(x * t_{xx} + y * t_{xy} + t_x, x * t_{yx} + y * t_{yy} + t_y) \tag{120}$$

which is equivalent to

$$\begin{pmatrix} t_{xx} & t_{xy} & t_x \\ t_{yx} & t_{yy} & t_y \\ 0 & 0 & 1 \end{pmatrix} \begin{pmatrix} x \\ y \\ 1 \end{pmatrix} = \begin{pmatrix} x \times t_{xx} + y \times t_{xy} + t_x \\ x \times t_{yx} + y \times t_{yy} + t_y \\ 1 \end{pmatrix}$$

in matrix notation, using homogeneous coordinates. Thus the specification of transform is given in Meta–IV as

$$\text{Transform} \quad :: \quad \begin{array}{lll} t_{xx}: \mathbf{R} & t_{xy}: \mathbf{R} & t_x: \mathbf{R} \\ t_{yx}: \mathbf{R} & t_{yy}: \mathbf{R} & t_y: \mathbf{R} \end{array} \tag{121}$$

$$\text{for } mk\text{-Transform}(t_{xx}, t_{xy}, t_x, t_{yx}, t_{yy}, t_y) \text{ use } t = \begin{bmatrix} t_{xx} & t_{xy} & t_x \\ t_{yx} & t_{yy} & t_y \end{bmatrix} \tag{122}$$

Apart from transformations that are applied to types such as *pair*, METAFONT also allows geometric transformations to be applied to a *transform*. This is the equivalent of matrix multiplication. Thus, for example, rotation about the origin may be specified by

$$\text{rotated: Transform} \times \mathbf{R} \longrightarrow \text{Transform} \tag{123}$$

$$\tag{124}$$

$$\text{rotated}\left(\begin{bmatrix} t_{xx} & t_{xy} & t_x \\ t_{yx} & t_{yy} & t_y \end{bmatrix}, \theta\right) \triangleq$$

$$\begin{bmatrix} t_{xx}\cos\theta + t_{xy}\sin\theta & t_{xy}\cos\theta - t_{xx}\sin\theta & t_x \\ t_{yx}\cos\theta + t_{yy}\sin\theta & t_{yy}\cos\theta - t_{yx}\sin\theta & t_y \end{bmatrix} \tag{125}$$

3.4 The METAFONT "main" program

For completeness, a portion of the METAFONT implementation of the "Saint" shown above in Fig. 7, and based on the specification of the logical division model, is presented in the remaining subsections. For ease of exposition, the "main" program has been rearranged. The actual code for the radicals — "ear", "mouth" and "yen" (which is an extended radical) has been commented out. The radical "ear" code is presented in a separate subsection.

```
mode_setup;   % set up system parameters                                    (126)
input pt;   % call utilities routines                                       (127)
% definition of the "ear" radical                                           (128)
% definition of the"mouth" radical                                          (129)
% definition of the"yen" radical                                            (130)
% definition of the "Saint" in terms of the logical divisions              (131)


def main =                                                                  (132)
   define_size;   % prompts designer for icon size                         (133)
   initstroke;    % initialise the basic paths                             (134)
   path dw[ ];   % declare an array of path dw                             (135)
   numeric ldw;   % declare a number ldw                                   (136)

   saint(dw);   % call the routine "Saint"                                 (137)
   len(dw)(ldw);   % compute the size of the array dw                      (138)
   for i = 1 upto ldw: draw dw[i]; endfor;   % draw character              (139)
   showit;   % show picture on display                                     (140)
enddef;                                                                     (141)
```

The code for the "Saint" character, given below, invokes the "logical division" macros and passes the radicals as actual parameters.

```
def saint(text res) =                                                       (142)
   begingroup                                                               (143)
   save t;                                                                  (144)
   transform t[ ];                                                          (145)
   path erad[ ], mrad[ ], crad[ ], mmrad[ ];                               (146)
```

```
% invoke the radical macros                                    (147)
   ear(erad); mouth(mrad); yen(crad);                          (148)
% construct the appropriate transformations                    (149)
   t₁ = t₃ = identity;                                         (150)
```

$$t_1 = t_3 = identity; \tag{150}$$

$$t_2 = identity \textbf{ scaled } .8 \textbf{ shifted } (0, .1h); \tag{151}$$

$$t_4 = identity \textbf{ xscaled } .8 \textbf{ shifted } (.1w, 0); \tag{152}$$

```
% invoke the logical division macros                           (153)
   left_right(erad)(t₁)(mrad)(t₂)(.5)(mmrad);                  (154)
   top_bot(mmrad)(t₃)(crad)(t₄)(.5)(res);                      (155)
   endgroup;                                                   (156)
enddef;                                                        (157)
```

3.5 METAFONT macros for Radicals

To illustrate the encoding for radicals, that of the "ear" radical only, is included here. Note that a radical is essentially a tuple of transformed paths as per the Meta–IV specification given earlier.

```
def ear(text result) =                                         (158)
   begingroup                                                  (159)
   save p, t;   % save the previous values of p, t             (160)
   path p[ ];   % declare an array of path                     (161)
   transform t[ ];   % declare an array of transform           (162)

   % initialise p₁ ... p₆ to have values of some predefined paths  (163)
   p₁ = hst; p₂ = vst; p₃ = vst; p₄ = hst; p₅ = hst; p₆ = hst;  (164)
   % initialise a tuple of transforms                          (165)
   t₁ = identity shifted (0, .4h);                             (166)
   t₂ = identity yscaled .7 shifted (−.25w, .25h);             (167)
   t₃ = identity shifted (.3w, 0);                             (168)
   t₄ = identity xscaled .6 shifted (.2w, .2h);               (169)
   t₅ = identity xscaled .6 shifted (.2w, 0);                 (170)
   t₆ = identity xscaled .9 shifted (.1w, −.2h);              (171)
   % apply each transform to associated path                   (172)
   combinedpt(p)(t)(result);                                   (173)
   endgroup;                                                   (174)
enddef;                                                        (175)
```

$$p_1 = hst;\ p_2 = vst;\ p_3 = vst;\ p_4 = hst;\ p_5 = hst;\ p_6 = hst; \tag{164}$$

$$t_1 = identity \textbf{ shifted } (0, .4h); \tag{166}$$

$$t_2 = identity \textbf{ yscaled } .7 \textbf{ shifted } (-.25w, .25h); \tag{167}$$

$$t_3 = identity \textbf{ shifted } (.3w, 0); \tag{168}$$

$$t_4 = identity \textbf{ xscaled } .6 \textbf{ shifted } (.2w, .2h); \tag{169}$$

$$t_5 = identity \textbf{ xscaled } .6 \textbf{ shifted } (.2w, 0); \tag{170}$$

$$t_6 = identity \textbf{ xscaled } .9 \textbf{ shifted } (.1w, -.2h); \tag{171}$$

3.6 METAFONT macros for Divisions

The logical divisions for Chinese characters are also implemented as macros in METAFONT. Essentially, this interpretation is analogous to the algorithmic approach in the construction of pictures in computer graphics. The formal arguments of the macros are paths and associated transforms — the data structures that are used to implement, for example, the radicals. The actual arguments are, of course, generally radicals or extended radicals.

Although no formal equivalent between the Meta–IV specification and the actual implementation is presented in this paper, it is important to note that the specification is a recording of the design decision taken with respect to the implementation. For information, the META-FONT encoding of the Left-Right logical division is presented below. The other divisions are similarly encoded.

def left_right(**text** lp)(**expr** lt)(**text** rp)(**expr** rt)(**expr** $ratio$)	(176)
(**text** $result$) $=$	(177)
% lp is left path, lt is the left transform	(178)
% rp is right path, rt is the right transform	(179)
% $ratio$ is the partition value between left and right parts	(180)
% $result$ is the transformed paths	(181)
transform $templt, temprt$;	(182)
numeric m, n;	(183)
len(lp)(m); len(rp)(n);	(184)
% combine left transform with the partition value	(185)
$templt$ $=$ lt **xscaled** $ratio$;	(186)
% combine right transform with the partition value	(187)
$temprt$ $=$ rt **xscaled** $(1 - ratio)$ **shifted** $(ratio * w, 0)$;	(188)
for $i = 1$ **upto** m: $result[i] := lp[i]$ **transformed** $templt$; **endfor**;	(189)
for $j = m + 1$ **upto** $n + m$: $result[j] := rp[j - m]$	(190)
transformed $temprt$; **endfor**;	(191)
enddef;	(192)

4 Conclusions

In this paper, use of the VDM Meta–IV for the specification of Chinese Characters has been highlighted. Two distinctly different "concrete" models of the Chinese character based on the one underlying abstract hierarchical model were developed and implemented. At the implementation stage, the problem of learning METAFONT was facilitated by two factors. Firstly, METAFONT is a declarative graphics programming language. Secondly, by developing a preliminary VDM Meta–IV specification of those types and operations actually needed, the authors were in a better position to match up the Chinese character specification with the final METAFONT encoding.

In the development of the specification, emphasis was placed on the concept of module. Issues such as import/export clauses were ignored, not that they are unimportant, but rather that the authors are still undecided as to what exact syntatic form they ought to take, keeping in mind their preference for a terse mathematical style like that promoted by the Danish school of the VDM.

The decision to adopt the VDM Meta–IV as the common kernel language of *communication* in the task of designing and implementing Chinese characters in METAFONT was a major determining factor in the success of the work. The VDM is the most widely used formal method in European industry and a major concern has been the adoption of a specification language which has the highest probability of becoming a standard. Meta–IV is not perfect. Its notational deficiency with respect to problem domains, for which mathematical notation is already well-established, has been noted and a possible solution has been suggested. Learning a new (programming) language, in this case METAFONT, involves learning both syntax and semantics — a very time-consuming task. The use of Meta–IV to represent essential aspects of the language accelerated the learning process and is a testimony to its usefulness. Of course, much more work still needs to be done in elaborating the description of the METAFONT language in the Meta–IV format. Although a close correspondence between the Chinese character specification and the METAFONT code has been obtained, the authors intend to explore the use of the actual formal method espoused by the VDM – data reification. Another possible line of development is to replace the implementation language by PostScript and to use the Meta–IV to specify the essential parts needed.

The authors gratefully acknowledge the anonymous referees' comments on an earlier draft of this paper. Any errors or omissions that still remain are our responsibility alone.

A   The "Saint" using Stack Model

The METAFONT code for the "stack" of transparencies should be self-explanatory:

```
    numeric sz;                                                    (193)
    picture stack[ ];                                              (194)

    def new =                                                      (195)
      sz = 0;  stack[sz] = nullpicture;                            (196)
    enddef;                                                        (197)

    def push(expr p) =                                             (198)
      sz := sz + 1;  stack[sz] = p;                                (199)
    enddef;                                                        (200)

    def pop =                                                      (201)
      if sz > 0 : stack[sz] = nullpicture;  sz := sz − 1;  fi;     (202)
    enddef;                                                        (203)

    def top(expr p) =                                              (204)
      if sz > 0 : p = stack[sz];  fi;                              (205)
    enddef;                                                        (206)

    def depth(expr n) =                                            (207)
      n = sz;                                                      (208)
    enddef;                                                        (209)

    def overlay(text p) =                                          (210)
      numeric n, k;                                                (211)
      depth(n);                                                    (212)
      for k = 0 step 1 until n: addto p also stack[k]; endfor;     (213)
    enddef;                                                        (214)
```

The "Saint" (cf. Fig. 11) is then produced as a result of executing the following main META-FONT program:

```
    input para;                                                    (215)
    input bstrokes;                                                (216)
    input stack;                                                   (217)
```

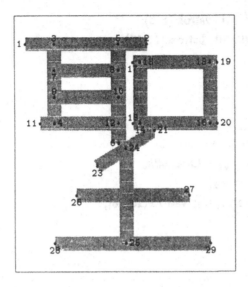

Figure 11: The Saint Version 1

def saint = $\qquad$ (218)

$\quad w^{\#} := width^{\#};\ h^{\#} := height^{\#};\ breadth^{\#} := .065w^{\#};$ $\qquad$ (219)

$\quad$ **define_pixels**$(w, h, breadth)$; $\qquad$ (220)

$\quad$ new; $\qquad$ (221)

$\quad$ earrad; push$(currentpicture)$; **clearit**; $\qquad$ (222)

$\quad$ mouthrad; push$(currentpicture)$; **clearit**; $\qquad$ (223)

$\quad$ yenrad; push$(currentpicture)$; **clearit**; $\qquad$ (224)

$\quad$ overlay$(currentpicture)$; **shipit**; $\qquad$ (225)

enddef; $\qquad$ (226)

def earrad = $\qquad$ (227)

$\quad x_1 = .05w = .65w - x_2;\ x_3 = x_1 + 2breadth;\ x_5 = x_2 - 2breadth;$ $\qquad$ (228)

$\quad x_3 = x_7 = x_9 = x_4;\ x_6 = x_8 = x_5 = x_{10} = x_{12};$ $\qquad$ (229)

$\quad x_{11} = x_4 - breadth;$ $\qquad$ (230)

$\quad y_1 = y_3 = y_5 = y_2 = h - 2breadth;$ $\qquad$ (231)

$\quad y_7 = y_8 = y_5 - \dfrac{1}{3}(y_5 - y_{12});$ $\qquad$ (232)

$\quad y_9 = y_{10} = y_5 - \dfrac{2}{3}(y_5 - y_{12});$ $\qquad$ (233)

$\quad y_{11} = y_4 = y_{12} = y_6 + 1.4breadth;$ $\qquad$ (234)

$\quad y_6 = .5h;$ $\qquad$ (235)

$$\text{hstroke}(1,2); \quad \text{vstroke}(3,4); \quad \text{vstroke}(5,6); \tag{236}$$

$$\text{hstroke}(7,8); \quad \text{hstroke}(9,10); \quad \text{hstroke}(11,12); \tag{237}$$

$$\textbf{enddef}; \tag{238}$$

$$\textbf{def } \text{mouthrad} = \tag{239}$$

$$x_{13l} = x_{14l} = x_{17} = x_{18} = x_{12r} + \textit{breadth}; \tag{240}$$

$$x_{15r} = x_{16r} = x_{20} = x_{19} = x_{12} + .45w; \tag{241}$$

$$y_{13} = y_{15} = y_{17} = y_{19} = y_2 - 1.3\textit{breadth}; \tag{242}$$

$$y_{14} = y_{16} = y_{18} = y_{20} = y_{12}; \tag{243}$$

$$\text{vstroke}(13,14); \quad \text{hstroke}(17,19); \quad \text{vstroke}(15,16); \tag{244}$$

$$\text{hstroke}(18,20); \tag{245}$$

$$\textbf{enddef}; \tag{246}$$

$$\textbf{def } \text{yenrad} = \tag{247}$$

$$y_{21r} = y_{11}; \quad y_{23} = y_{21} - 2.5\textit{breadth}; \quad y_{22} = y_{21} - \frac{2}{3}(y_{21} - y_{23}); \tag{248}$$

$$x_{21} = x_{22} + 2\textit{breadth}; \quad x_{23} = x_{22} - 2\textit{breadth}; \quad x_{22} = \frac{1}{2}(x_{18} - x_{12}) + x_{12}; \tag{249}$$

$$x_{24} = x_{22} = x_{25}; \quad x_{28} = x_4; \quad x_{29} = x_{15}; \tag{250}$$

$$x_{26} = x_{28} + 1.5\textit{breadth}; \quad x_{27} = x_{29} - 1.5\textit{breadth}; \tag{251}$$

$$y_{24} = y_{21} - \frac{1}{2}(y_{21} - y_{23}); \tag{252}$$

$$y_{26} = y_{27} = y_{24} - \frac{1}{2}(y_{24} - y_{28}); \quad y_{28} = 2\textit{breadth} = y_{29} = y_{25}; \tag{253}$$

$$\text{tristroke}(23,21); \quad \text{vstroke}(24,25); \quad \text{hstroke}(26,27); \tag{254}$$

$$\text{hstroke}(28,29); \tag{255}$$

$$\textbf{enddef}; \tag{256}$$

References

[1] Dines Bjørner, Cliff B. Jones, Mícheál Mac an Airchinnigh, and Erik J. Neuhold, editors. *VDM'87, VDM — A Formal Method at Work*. Volume 252 of *Lecture Notes in Computer Science*, Springer-Verlag, Berlin Heidelberg New York London Paris Tokyo, 1987.

[2] Shi-Kuo Chang. Visual languages: a tutorial and survey. *IEEE Software*, 4(1):29–39, January 1987.

[3] Guoan Gu and John Hobby. *A Chinese Meta-Font*. Computer Science Report STAN-CS-83-974, Department of Computer Science, Stanford University, Stanford, CA 94305, July 1983.

[4] Donald E. Knuth. *Computers & Typesetting /D, METAFONT: The Program*. Addison-Wesley Publishing Company, Reading, Massachusetts Menlo Park, California Don Mills, Ontario Wokingham, England Amsterdam Mexico City San Juan Bogotá Sydney Santiago Singapore Tokyo, 1986.

[5] Donald E. Knuth. *The METAFONTbook*. Addison-Wesley Publishing Company, Reading, Massachusetts Menlo Park, California Don Mills, Ontario Wokingham, England Amsterdam Mexico City San Juan Bogotá Sydney Santiago Singapore Tokyo, 1986.

[6] Jiarong Li. Generations of some chinese characters with metafont. In D. Lucarella, editor, *TEX for Scientific Documentation*, pages 167 –170, Addison-Wesley Publishing Company, Inc., 1985.

[7] Rod Salmon and Mel Slater. *Computer Graphics, Systems & Concepts*. Addison-Wesley Publishing Company, Wokingham, England Reading, Massachusetts Menlo Park, California New York Don Mills, Ontario Amsterdam Bonn Sydney Singapore Tokyo Madrid Bogotá Santiago San Juan, 1987.

[8] Ghee S. Teo and Mícheál Mac an Airchinnigh. *Ideograms & Icons in Meta-IV & META-FONT*. Technical Report CSC–88–04, Department of Computer Science, Trinity College, Dublin, July 1988.

[9] Yun Mei Tung. A language for chinese character design. *Software-Practice and Experience*, 11:1273–1292, 1981.

Vol. 296: R. Janßen (Ed.), Trends in Computer Algebra. Proceedings, 1987. V, 197 pages. 1988.

Vol. 297: E.N. Houstis, T.S. Papatheodorou, C.D. Polychronopoulos (Eds.), Supercomputing. Proceedings, 1987. X, 1093 pages. 1988.

Vol. 298: M. Main, A. Melton, M. Mislove, D. Schmidt (Eds.), Mathematical Foundations of Programming Language Semantics. Proceedings, 1987. VIII, 637 pages. 1988.

Vol. 299: M. Dauchet, M. Nivat (Eds.), CAAP '88. Proceedings, 1988. VI, 304 pages. 1988.

Vol. 300: H. Ganzinger (Ed.), ESOP '88. Proceedings, 1988. VI, 381 pages. 1988.

Vol. 301: J. Kittler (Ed.), Pattern Recognition. Proceedings, 1988. VII, 668 pages. 1988.

Vol. 302: D.M. Yellin, Attribute Grammar Inversion and Source-to-source Translation. VIII, 176 pages. 1988.

Vol. 303: J.W. Schmidt, S. Ceri, M. Missikoff (Eds.), Advances in Database Technology – EDBT '88. X, 620 pages. 1988.

Vol. 304: W.L. Price, D. Chaum (Eds.), Advances in Cryptology – EUROCRYPT '87. Proceedings, 1987. VII, 314 pages. 1988.

Vol. 305: J. Biskup, J. Demetrovics, J. Paredaens, B. Thalheim (Eds.), MFDBS 87. Proceedings, 1987. V, 247 pages. 1988.

Vol. 306: M. Boscarol, L. Carlucci Aiello, G. Levi (Eds.), Foundations of Logic and Functional Programming. Proceedings, 1986. V, 218 pages. 1988.

Vol. 307: Th. Beth, M. Clausen (Eds.), Applicable Algebra, Error-Correcting Codes, Combinatorics and Computer Algebra. Proceedings, 1986. VI, 215 pages. 1988.

Vol. 308: S. Kaplan, J.-P. Jouannaud (Eds.), Conditional Term Rewriting Systems. Proceedings, 1987. VI, 278 pages. 1988.

Vol. 309: J. Nehmer (Ed.), Experiences with Distributed Systems. Proceedings, 1987. VI, 292 pages. 1988.

Vol. 310: E. Lusk, R. Overbeek (Eds.), 9th International Conference on Automated Deduction. Proceedings, 1988. X, 775 pages. 1988.

Vol. 311: G. Cohen, P. Godlewski (Eds.), Coding Theory and Applications 1986. Proceedings, 1986. XIV, 196 pages. 1988.

Vol. 312: J. van Leeuwen (Ed.), Distributed Algorithms 1987. Proceedings, 1987. VII, 430 pages. 1988.

Vol. 313: B. Bouchon, L. Saitta, R.R. Yager (Eds.), Uncertainty and Intelligent Systems. IPMU '88. Proceedings, 1988. VIII, 408 pages. 1988.

Vol. 314: H. Göttler, H.J. Schneider (Eds.), Graph-Theoretic Concepts in Computer Science. Proceedings, 1987. VI, 254 pages. 1988.

Vol. 315: K. Furukawa, H. Tanaka, T. Fujisaki (Eds.), Logic Programming '87. Proceedings, 1987. VI, 327 pages. 1988.

Vol. 316: C. Choffrut (Ed.), Automata Networks. Proceedings, 1986. VII, 125 pages. 1988.

Vol. 317: T. Lepistö, A. Salomaa (Eds.), Automata, Languages and Programming. Proceedings, 1988. XI, 741 pages. 1988.

Vol. 318: R. Karlsson, A. Lingas (Eds.), SWAT 88. Proceedings, 1988. VI, 262 pages. 1988.

Vol. 319: J.H. Reif (Ed.), VLSI Algorithms and Architectures – AWOC 88. Proceedings, 1988. X, 476 pages. 1988.

Vol. 320: A. Blaser (Ed)., Natural Language at the Computer. Proceedings, 1988. III, 176 pages. 1988.

Vol. 322: S. Gjessing, K. Nygaard (Eds.), ECOOP '88. European Conference on Object-Oriented Programming. Proceedings, 1988. VI, 410 pages. 1988.

Vol. 323: P. Deransart, M. Jourdan, B. Lorho, Attribute Grammars. IX, 232 pages. 1988.

Vol. 324: M.P. Chytil, L. Janiga, V. Koubek (Eds.), Mathematical Foundations of Computer Science 1988. Proceedings. IX, 562 pages. 1988.

Vol. 325: G. Brassard, Modern Cryptology. VI, 107 pages. 1988.

Vol. 326: M. Gyssens, J. Paredaens, D. Van Gucht (Eds.), ICDT '88. 2nd International Conference on Database Theory. Proceedings, 1988. VI, 409 pages. 1988.

Vol. 327: G.A. Ford (Ed.), Software Engineering Education. Proceedings, 1988. V, 207 pages. 1988.

Vol. 328: R. Bloomfield, L. Marshall, R. Jones (Eds.), VDM '88. VDM – The Way Ahead. Proceedings, 1988. IX, 499 pages. 1988.